Popes, Councils, and Theology

Popes, Councils, and Theology

—— *From Pope Pius IX to Pope Francis* ——

Owen F. Cummings

FOREWORD BY
John Wester

PICKWICK *Publications* · Eugene, Oregon

POPES, COUNCILS, AND THEOLOGY
From Pope Pius IX to Pope Francis

Pickwick Publications
An Imprint of Wipf and Stock Publishers
199 W. 8th Ave., Suite 3
Eugene, OR 97401

www.wipfandstock.com

PAPERBACK ISBN: 978-1-7252-8892-8
HARDCOVER ISBN: 978-1-7252-8893-5
EBOOK ISBN: 978-1-7252-8894-2

Cataloguing-in-Publication data:

Names: Cummings, Owen F., author. | Wester, John, foreword.

Title: Popes, councils, and theology : from Pope Pius IX to Pope Francis / by Owen F. Cummings ; foreword by John Wester.

Description: Eugene, OR: Pickwick Publications, 2021 | Includes bibliographical references.

Identifiers: ISBN 978-1-7252-8892-8 (paperback) | ISBN 978-1-7252-8893-5 (hardcover) | ISBN 978-1-7252-8894-2 (ebook)

Subjects: LCSH: Papacy—History | Catholic Church—History | Catholic Church—History—19th century | Catholic Church—History—20th century | Catholic Church—History—21st century

Classification: BX955.2 C86 2021 (print) | BX955.2 (ebook)

06/08/21

Contents

Foreword

In reviewing the books written by Deacon Owen Cummings, it is abundantly clear that his intellectual appetite will never be sated. He has given us readers wonderful insights into the diaconate, ecclesiology, the Eucharist, the Liturgy, spirituality, mystical women, the theology of John Macquarrie, the dying of Jesus, saints, and so much more. And now, with this latest book we have yet another gem that offers new perspectives on church history even as it helps us to understand the church of today. *Popes, Councils, and Theology: From Pope Pius IX to Pope Francis* takes a fresh look at the lives of the popes and their impact on church history, theology and world affairs. Despite the upheavals and seismic shifts of the last few centuries, the Holy Spirit has gifted the church with popes who have been able to navigate a course that avoids theological extremes and political polarization, thus keeping us focused on the unity so dear to the heart of Christ. Little wonder, then, that the title "bridge builder" has come to be associated with the Bishop of Rome.

In reading the pages that follow, there is no doubt that the Holy Spirit is at work in the ministry of the popes of late, gracing them with the gifts needed to forge new paths in searching for lost sheep while remaining true to the call of the shepherd by keeping the whole flock united. This is no easy feat; and it shines a light on the genius of papal leadership, namely, the ability to find the *via media*. History demonstrates that the church moves forward in a waddle-way, more like a pendulum or a balancing act. The late Archbishop John R. Quinn captures this reality well in his book on Vatican I as he writes:

> "I hope that the reader may see the Pope and the Council in a more balanced way. The philosophers said that virtue is the middle point between extremes, between too much and too little. I offer what I have written on Vatican I as a hopefully moderate, balanced and factual account" (*Revered and Reviled: A Re-Examination of Vatican Council I.* Herder & Herder; 2017, p. viii).

Owen Cummings's book gives us a valuable look at how the Holy Spirit "balances" the church throughout history and despite landscape shifts is able to bring about greater understanding, and in the end, that virtuous mean. It is the Spirit, that bond of love of the Father and the Son, sent "among us for the forgiveness of sins" (as the prayer of ab-solution says) that in time brings unity amid diversity. The church is more like a great sailing ship that must tack in order to sail into the wind. Owen Cummings grasps this work of the Holy Spirit, breathing fresh life into the church and enabling the Barque of Peter to steer a course toward the fullness of the Kingdom with memorable popes at the helm. Deacon Cummings has once again given us a great gift. I can only imagine where this renaissance man will take us next!

Archbishop John Wester

Introduction

A "Catholic mind" is a Christian mind with
a sense of Christian history.

—OWEN CHADWICK[1]

Knowledge of history makes possible a healthy relativism, which is quite dif-
ferent from skepticism. . . . Knowledge of the past, used as a means of situat-
ing ourselves better in the present, can help us plan the future. . . . Knowledge
of the history of ecclesiology elucidates the work of Vatican II and the direc-
tion in which things are moving.

—YVES CONGAR, OP[2]

All history, that of the Church included, has taken place under the sign of
contradiction and has been full of irony, tragedy, success that breeds failure,
failure unexpectedly successful, roads not taken, and roads taken that should
not have been taken. No age has been decisively left behind, and in some
sense all earlier ages walk with us.

—GLENN W. OLSEN[3]

THE THREE CHURCH HISTORIANS cited at the beginning of this introduction—Owen
Chadwick, Yves Congar, and Glenn Olsen—together provide a necessary insight
into understanding the centrality of church history for Catholicism. From St. Peter
in first-century Rome to Pope Francis in twenty-first-century Rome there is a span
of almost two thousand years. The Pope is not the church, and the history of the papacy is not the history of the church or the history of theology. Nevertheless, popes,

1. Chadwick, *The Spirit of the Oxford Movement*, 308.
2. Congar, OP, "Church History as a Branch of Theology," 88–89.
3. Olsen, *Beginning at Jerusalem*, 13.

church history, and theology necessarily come together in a Catholic understanding as each pope makes his own particular and distinctive contribution as the tradition moves forward. In this book an attempt is made to bring together the papacy, church history, and theology from Pope Pius X in the mid-nineteenth twentieth century to Pope Francis in the twenty-first century without trying to be complete or comprehensive in treatment.

Congar's words, "a healthy relativism" invite the perception that there never was a golden age in the history of the church, free of problems and challenges, free of good things and bad, free of saints and sinners. Theologically, and church history after all is a branch of theology, every age is the golden age for the people of that age, since a fundamental Christian conviction is that the Holy Spirit never abandons the church. Yves Congar's "healthy relativism" also invites us to see with John Henry Newman that here on earth to live is to change. Newman wrote: "In another world it is otherwise, but here below to live is to change and to be perfect is to have changed often."[4] Church history helps us to acknowledge change in the past, the need for change in the present and, therefore, the hope of change in the future. Glenn Olsen's sage words invite us to avoid all triumphalism as Christians, and to confess that the history of the church is characterized by irony and tragedy as well as what may be taken to be success. Such perspective and confession liberate so that we may describe church history as a real theology of liberation. It is a real theology of liberation not in contrast to contemporary theologies of liberation, but in the very precise sense that knowing church history frees us from absolutizing events and periods in ways that are unhelpful, and so liberates us from erroneous presuppositions. Some words from the Catholic church historian Ulrich Lehner will illustrate what I mean.

> It seems that, slowly, the Catholic Church is again beginning to reconcile with modernity, having realized that to shut out modernity—which was common practice between 1850 and 1950—only prevented the updating of theology and church practice. Many proposals that are hotly debated by Catholics today—a new role for the papacy, a preferential option for the poor, married priests, divorce and remarriage—first emerged in the 1700s. Yet most Catholics are completely unaware that the question, "How can I remain Catholic and yet be part of the modern world?" is far from new. Looking at the answers of the past helps us to identify roads not taken, roads that led followers astray or into the abyss—and perhaps even roads to which the church might return.[5]

In an interview that was published in German in 1984 and in English the following year the famous theologian Karl Rahner, SJ was asked about the papacy. What follows is part of his response. "So, let's allow each pope to have his own outlook. Let's not expect

4. Newman, *An Essay on the Development of Christian Doctrine* (London: 1903), chapter 1, section 1, p. 40.

5. Lehner, *The Catholic Enlightenment*, 4.

that each pope will have the call and the ability to make each and every thing in the church better, especially when we aren't exactly certain, in this or that particular question, whether progressivism or conservatism is the better course. And if the pope does not fulfill all the promise that I or anyone else expects of him, is that really so bad? That's what happens in history and in a church that changes only very gradually over the course of history."[6] To say the least, Rahner's perspective is very balanced.

Nevertheless, inescapably there are pitfalls. Writing church history is inevitably challenging. One will feel sympathy with some persons and movements in the church, and a certain distance from others. Writing about one's favorites, as it were, will have its own particular challenges, but writing about persons and movements from which one is distanced, psychologically or conceptually, is especially difficult. This is where some words of the *doyen* of modern English-language church historians, Owen Chadwick, are really helpful. In his 1969 inaugural lecture at the University of Cambridge, Chadwick wrote:

> The man who knows that his personality enters historical study and yet seeks to keep it in control and to broaden his vision will make more contribution to our understanding than the man who believes total detachment possible. . . . You need no white paint, you need to try see things as they were. But you need to be inside the minds [of historical characters] and to forget the future which they could not know and to come towards them with the openness of mind, the readiness to listen, which a man gives to a friend.[7]

"To forget the future which they could not know," yes, but it is nonetheless imperative to make judgments about historical characters, judgments informed as much as is possible.

These ideals of Chadwick are very high indeed, but nothing less will do for the historian. Given the degree of polarization in the Catholic Church at this time in the twenty-first century, and especially in the United States, all could learn from Chadwick's principle. The historian will listen with consummate care to the past before reaching a judgment. The historian will give to listening a certain primacy, a primacy of listening to learn about the complexity of human affairs before reaching towards a conclusion, and a conclusion that will more often than not be somewhat tentative. New evidence and fresh questions never cease to arise. One of Owen Chadwick's more famous students, Eamon Duffy, takes the same line as his doctoral supervisor when he writes: "History is written backwards, hindsight is of its essence, and every attempt to characterize any great and complex historical movement is an active retrospective construction: what is left out of the story is as significant as anything included."[8] This point seems so very obvious, and yet the polarization in the contemporary Catholic Church, reflecting

---

6. Rahner, SJ, *I Remember, An Autobiographical Interview*, 95.

7. Chadwick, *Freedom and the Historian, An Inaugural Lecture*, 15.

8. Duffy, "The Staying Power of Christianity," *The New York Review of Books* (June 20, 2013), 69.

especially the last two hundred years of history, shows that its being obvious does not mean that it has been taken genuinely to heart.

Professionally, I am more of a systematic theologian than a church historian. However, when I was preparing to register for the BD (Bachelor of Divinity) of the University of Dublin, Trinity College in the very early 1970s, I was tutored in church history (and more importantly gained insight into the importance of church history) by an Irish Anglican priest and church historian, James Hartin. This was just six years or so after the close of Vatican II (1962–1965). James Hartin taught church history at Trinity College for many years and served the Church of Ireland in a number of administrative and pastoral roles also. He possessed an encyclopedic knowledge of church history, both fair and balanced, and above all marked by an ecumenical sensitivity that was all too rare in the Ireland of the early 1970s. I am so grateful for his humble and gentle insistence on the absolute centrality of church history for the understanding of theology. I am grateful also to the legion of scholars whose names and insights occur throughout these pages. Their research, their scholarly monographs, informative articles, and books have helped me to reach a bird's eye view of the time period between the nineteenth century and Pope Francis.

The first chapter, on the eighteenth century, provides us with some soundings that help us to avoid a too monochrome picture of our period in church history. We shall see that the Enlightenment and the French Revolution were powerful influences in shaping church history, arguably right up to the present day. After a brief, somewhat liberal honeymoon Pope Pius IX, the subject of chapter 2, became a fervent ultramontane and presided over the First Vatican Council (1869–1870). His years of service and for a long time afterwards, led to an excessive emphasis on the papacy and, indeed, to a certain fear of development and change. Chapter 3 describes the First Vatican Council and especially its concern with papal infallibility. Chapter 4 is given over to Pope Leo XIII. Cut from the same dogmatic cloth as Pius IX at the same time he demonstrated an awareness of socio-economic and therefore political changes in the world.

Pope Pius X, the subject of chapter 5 was a very pastorally-minded pope, especially interested in catechetics and promoting sacramental participation among the faithful. At the same time, he was very anti-intellectual in matters of philosophy and theology. So, it comes as no surprise that when elected as Pope he took the name and the ultramontane policies of Pope Pius IX as a standard. He brought about the condemnation of Modernism, the movement of thought in philosophy and theology opening up Catholicism to more contemporary ways of thinking, and entered the church into decades of suspicion concerning theological thought, and this is the subject of chapter 6. Under Pope Pius X Modernism was not only condemned but also a harsh regime of doctrinal policing came into being.

Pope Benedict XV is the subject of chapter 7. He succeeded Pius X in 1914 as the First World War began. He relaxed, at least in some measure, the worldwide persecution of suspected modernists. He was the pope of peace, an unenviable position that drew upon him the ire of the opposite warring sides of both France and Germany. He was the one who pulled out Achille Ratti, the future Pope Pius XI, from his academic ivory tower into the world of papal diplomacy, the world of the dictatorships. Pope Pius XI, the subject of chapter 8, faced the fascist leaders of Germany, Italy and Spain and the communist leaders of the Soviet Union. He was about to issue an encyclical condemning Nazism hook, line and sinker when he died in 1939.

That encyclical was never published. Pope Pius XI was succeeded by the elegant and accomplished papal diplomat, Eugenio Pacelli, who took the name Pius XII. Chapter 9 is devoted to him. He was a very complex man. Diplomacy for Pius XII was the only way to engage the enemies of the church, and so he buried the condemnatory encyclical that had been prepared by his predecessor, thinking that its publication would simply rouse the Nazis to greater persecution of the church in Germany. He was responsible for various encyclicals that seemed to open a new springtime in the liturgical and theological life of the church, but his 1950 encyclical *Humani Generis* brought at least the theological springtime to an abrupt halt. This theological springtime came to be known as "the new theology," and it is described in chapter 10.

The successor to Pius XII was, of course, the great Pope John XXIII who initiated Vatican II. Chapter 11 is devoted to him. Thought to be a transitory pope because of his age, his daring step of calling this worldwide church council, and inviting limited ecumenical participation, was for those who could see the signal that the so-called "new theology" that had made its appearance during the pontificate of Pius XII had come of age.

The next two chapters, 12 and 13, are taken up with the pontificate of Pope Paul VI and the Second Vatican Council. Paul VI continued the Council and saw it to its completion in 1965. The documents, promulgated in Latin, were quickly translated into the vernacular languages and picked up universally. It became obvious that there were two camps, so to speak, concerning the Council, its documents, and its implementation—for want of better terms "conservative" and "liberal". Those camps clustered around two new theological periodicals—*Concilium* for the liberals, and *Communio* for the conservatives, and they provide the focus for chapter 14.

The death of Pope Paul VI in 1978 was followed by the very brief papacy of Pope John Paul I (chapter 15) and then the very long papacy of Pope John Paul II (chapter 16). The evaluation of the latter's pontificate tends to take the parallel tracks of conservatism and liberalism, each side claiming something for themselves. The same is true of John Paul's successor, Pope Benedict XVI (chapter 17). The chapters devoted to these two popes are somewhat more detailed than other chapters.

This brings us in chapter 18 to the current pope, Francis, who seems to be charting quite a different course for the papacy and for the church, different in contrast to his predecessors but doctrinally, as one would expect, in continuity with them. He is at the time of writing but six years into his papal ministry, but the pastoral orientation of his pontificate would be very difficult to turn back. Finally, in chapter 19 we turn to the church of the present and the future. From where we stand now what will the church of tomorrow be like? How will it be different?

When all is said and done, the purpose of the book is to invite Catholics and interested others to a reflective consideration of what it means to be an involved and committed Catholic Christian at this time. Necessarily throughout the book the treatment has been selective—it is a series of "snapshots" and not a comprehensive video—but it is the author's hope that the treatment has been fair. Readers must judge for themselves.

1

Eighteenth-Century Soundings

The arrival of democracy almost destroyed the papacy.

—Eamon Duffy[1]

At the close of the eighteenth century the French Revolution shattered the alliance that had been the foundation of the social order in every European country, Catholic and Protestant, for centuries.

—Gerald A. McCool[2]

After the French Revolution, the church retreated to an intellectual ghetto from which it did not emerge until the twentieth century.

—Ulrich L. Lehner[3]

If Vatican II was in some sense "the end of the Constantinian era" and in another "the end of the Counter Reformation," in still another it was, or wanted to be, for Roman Catholicism "the end of the nineteenth century."

—John W. O'Malley[4]

The Eighteenth Century

The modern church and papacy is unintelligible without some grasp of the church and papacy in the nineteenth century, the century that "was not kind to the papacy."[5] That "unkindness" makes no sense unless one begins with some awareness of the

---

1. Duffy, *Ten Popes Who Shook the World*, 94.
2. McCool, *Catholic Theology in the Nineteenth Century*, 23.
3. Lehner, *The Catholic Enlightenment*, 3.
4. O'Malley, SJ, *What Happened at Vatican II*, 63.
5. O'Malley, SJ, *A History of the Popes*, 251.

phenomenon of Gallicanism and its effects on the papacy of the eighteenth century, and in turn it is necessary to have some perspective on the papacy of the seventeenth century. If we are to understand what church historian John O'Malley means in the words cited at the head of this chapter, it is impossible to understand the achievement of Vatican II, the greatest event in Roman Catholicism in the twentieth century, without first attending to the eighteenth and early nineteenth centuries. An attempt must be made briefly and therefore inadequately to sketch the background of those earlier periods, albeit, in what I am calling "soundings."

"Rome continued to attract pilgrims in great numbers and continued as the first training ground for aspiring artists. The city was resplendent with Renaissance and Baroque masterpieces. The Papal States, under control to a degree not known before and secure from foreign aggression, produced a decent revenue. . . . The popes and the institution over which they presided had settled into a comfortable mediocrity. Nonetheless, on the surface, all seemed well—at least to a superficial observer."[6] This summary offered by John O'Malley is very fair, even if not particularly detailed, but Rome and the papacy are necessarily affected, influenced, and interpreted by events elsewhere. In this introductory context, we shall simply and all too briefly point to the following: Gallicanism and the Gallican Articles, the national checking of papal authority, the Enlightenment, the Catholic Enlightenment, the French Revolution, and Napoleon. Then we shall move on to the papacy of the early part of the nineteenth century before Pope Pius IX.

Gallicanism

First, Gallicanism and the Gallican Articles. Gallicanism was the French phenomenon of valuing the national church over the pope, and it is crystallized in a serious of statements known as the Gallican Articles. Pope Innocent XI (1676–89) resisted the absolutist claims of the French King Louis XIV. These claims in respect of the church had to do especially with Louis's decrees of 1673 and 1675 expressing his right to administer the temporal and spiritual affairs of his entire kingdom. Pope Innocent XI and King Louis XIV differed on the appointment of bishops and on the revenues of vacant episcopal sees. Most of the French clergy, many of them sympathetic, submitted to the king's authority in this regard.[7] This was the immediate background to the so-called Gallican Articles.

---

6. O'Malley, SJ, *A History of the Popes*, 221–22.

7. In his *Vatican I, The Council and the Making of the Ultramontane Church*, 26–27 O'Malley writes: "Historians have refuted the long accepted view that the king (Louis XIV) dominated the meeting (the 1682 Grand Assembly) and dictated the policy, and they have conclusively shown that the articles reflected the genuine and traditional views of the French clergy (as well as the views of probably most clergy in Europe at the time)."

On March 19, 1682, there was a Grand Assembly in Paris to sort out the rights and privileges of the French clergy. The Parisian assembly produced a document, drawn up by Bishop Jacques Bénigne Bossuet (1627–1704), one of the ablest French theologians and bishops of his time, known as the "Four Gallican Articles." The first article denied that the pope had authority over temporal matters, and affirmed that kings were not subject to the authority of the church in civil matters. The second article endorsed the decrees of the Council of Constance (1414–18) that upheld the authority of a General Council of the church over the pope. This may be seen as the triumph of conciliarism, one of the traditional centers of which had been the Faculty of Theology in Paris. The third article stated that the ancient liberties of the French church were inviolable. Among these "liberties" was the idea that papal judgments on the faith had to be formally accepted by the French episcopate, usually also including the French king, before they could be published in France. The fourth article reads: "In questions of faith the leading role is that of the Supreme Pontiff, and his decrees apply to all churches in general and to each of them in particular. But his judgment is not unchangeable (Latin, *irreformabile*), unless it receives the consent of the church."[8] It is a complex statement, but it was widely maintained that the judgment of the pope is dependent upon the consent of the church, and has been described as "the most innovative and controversial."[9] Very obviously, the Gallican Articles curtailed and controlled the authority and power of the pope in the French church. The Gallican Articles were finally set aside both by Pope Alexander VIII in 1691 in the bull *Inter Multiplices*, and later by King Louis XIV in 1693, but they formed and influenced ecclesiological thought in France for generations, and indeed well beyond France, and really were checked only by the First Vatican Council in 1870.

The curtailment of papal power at this time, however, goes far beyond the Gallican Articles of the French church. Predominantly Catholic countries like Austria, various regions of Germany, and Portugal all developed policies that restricted papal power and influence in their internal affairs. The traditional Catholic governments of Europe used their veto power to ensure that no very capable popes and no very young popes ascended the throne of St. Peter.[10] The shades of papal interference in national governments, and of brokering power on the international scene made these traditional Catholic regions of Europe immensely wary of the papacy and pro-active in bringing what influence they could to bear upon it. Predominantly Protestant states, in principle, rejected the traditional function and role of the papacy in arbitrating international disputes. They wanted little or nothing to do with the papacy, and would brook no hint of papal influence on their respective territories. This, of course, was the milieu in which the United States of America was born in 1776.

---

8. Cited from Costigan, *The Consensus of the Church and Papal Infallibility*, 18.

9. By Portier, "Church Unity and National Traditions," 31.

10. Portier, "Church Unity and National Traditions," 33.

The cumulative burden of the eighteenth century, then, contributed to a very weakened papacy, finally expressed on July 21, 1773, when Pope Clement XIV, giving in to increasing pressure from various European governments—Spain, Portugal, France, and Austria—suppressed the Society of Jesus. The hatred of and opposition to the Jesuits is difficult to fathom. It certainly had to do with the institutional strength of the Society, the championing of the rights of the indigenous peoples in South America, and perhaps also, in Eamon Duffy's words, "the Society's sometimes obscure and suspect financial dealings." The net result was, again in Duffy's words, "the clearest demonstration imaginable of the powerlessness of the pope in the new world order. . . . It was the papacy's most shameful hour."[11]

A new spirit swept Europe in the eighteenth century, a spirit of free inquiry in all things, unfettered by the chains of tradition and convention, the spirit of what has come to be known as the Enlightenment. It is well captured in the cry of the German philosopher Immanuel Kant (1724–1804), "*Sapere aude!* Dare to think for yourself!"[12] The American Declaration of Independence (1776) and the Constitution flowed from this new thinking. Wonderful developments in science and technology also flowed from this enlightened spirit. These were good things. However, there was also a spirit of hostility to the church and to Christianity unleashed by the Enlightenment, and some of this hostility was in part justified.

The Catholic Enlightenment

The hostile attitude of many Catholic Church leaders to the Enlightenment is well known and documented. What is less well known is the Catholic Enlightenment, a more positive Catholic response to the Enlightenment. The concerns of the Catholic Enlightenment are described by church historian Joseph Chinnici as follows:

> Marked by an abhorrence of scholastic subtlety, these Catholics vindicated the rights of intelligence and criticism, related well with the *philosophes* and promoted ecumenism. . . . In the realm of religious practice the proponents of the Catholic Enlightenment protested against the excesses of Baroque piety. They supported the reform of the breviary, freedom from the policies of the Inquisition, the reduction of feast days, the translation of Scripture into the vernacular, a de-emphasis on indulgences, a vernacular liturgy, the elevation of the spiritual life of the clergy, the "purification" of ecclesiastical history (of ultramontane views and legendary accounts), the reception of communion under both kinds, and the active participation of the faithful in the life of the church.[13]

---

11. Duffy, *Saints and Sinners*, 245–46.

12. Kant, *Answering the Question: What is Enlightenment?* (1784).

13. Chinnici, *The English Catholic Enlightenment*, 4–5.

Chinnici's description has a very strong Vatican II resonance to it. So many of the achievements of that twentieth-century council had been anticipated by these Catholic Enlightenment thinkers. This Catholic Enlightenment took institutional form in the 1786 Italian Synod of Pistoia, and regional expression in the movements known as "Josephinism" and "Febronianism."

"Febronianism provided the theoretical justification for the Austrian model of church-state relations called Josephinism."[14] Emperor Joseph II (1765–90), influenced by the Enlightenment and known throughout Europe as an "enlightened monarch," was interested in setting up a system throughout his empire, a system that came to be known as "Josephinism," after Joseph himself. The project was to modernize the Catholic Church. Eamon Duffy says that "Joseph II was fascinated by the smallest details of church life, and he was painstaking and pious in discharging his role as the first Prince of Christendom," so much so that "Frederick the Great of Prussia sneered at 'my brother the sacristan.'"[15] At the same time, there was a movement in the Catholic Church in Germany that desired to provide the German Catholic Church with a more obvious national identity. This was to be achieved by enhancing the authority of the German episcopate over the papacy, and by seeking to reunite churches in the Reformation tradition with the Catholic Church. The name "Febronianism" comes from the pseudonym of a German bishop, Johann Nikolaus von Honntheim (1701–90), coadjutor bishop of Trier. In 1763 he published a treatise entitled *Concerning the State of the Church and the Legitimate Power of the Roman Pontiff* under the pseudonym Justinus Febronius. "Josephinism" is another version of "Febronianism." It involved religious toleration, confining papal intervention to the spiritual sphere, and the basic subjection of the church to the state.[16] Hontheim has been considered a proto-ecumenist by some because he hoped for a reconciliation between German Catholics and Protestants, a reconciliation that would be helped along by the reflections in his book. His ecumenical hope has been well described by historian Thomas Howard: "A national German Catholic Church, connected but not fettered to Rome and one that included Protestants returning to the fold, could lead the Universal Church forward into a felicitous future, away from the divisions and polemics of the Tridentine era."[17] Hontheim's hope was naïve, but was influential to the point that he was prevailed upon to recant many of his ideas. Nonetheless, his influence was to continue to shape German Catholicism, described well by Owen Chadwick as follows: "What (Hontheim) began continued as a key issue within German Catholicism until the first Vatican Council of 1870, which tried to kill the debate, and thought that

---

14. McCool, *Catholic Theology in the Nineteenth Century,* 22.

15. Duffy, *Saints and Sinners,* 248.

16. Kelly, *The Oxford Dictionary of the Popes,* 301.

17. Howard, *The Pope and the Professor,* 63.

it succeeded, but was later proved wrong" by the likes of Ignaz von Döllinger and his followers to whom we shall attend in chapter three.[18]

These enlightened ideas of Emperor Joseph proved attractive to his brother the Grand Duke Leopold II of Tuscany. He was responsible along with the bishop of Pistoia, Scipio de' Ricci, for a reforming, local, diocesan synod in 1786. Bishop de' Ricci has been described in these words by church historian Eamon Duffy: "[He was] an extremist, a man with poor judgment and no antennae for popular religious feeling. His dining room was decorated with a painting of the Emperor Joseph II ripping up a pious picture of the Sacred Heart. Ricci liked to talk of Rome as Babylon, the rule of Pope and Curia as outmoded tyranny."[19] This reforming bishop finds a complementary description in the pastoral liturgist J. D. Crichton. "Ricci wanted to cut out the Middle Ages which to him were barbarous, but more importantly, it was the time of the scholastic theology with its complications, and distinctions and the whole apparatus of its dialectic which had seriously damaged the pure and clear doctrine of the Fathers of the Church . . . ." Speaking of the liturgy Crichton continues: "Ricci found the current rite over-elaborate, pompous and remote from the people, large numbers of whom were illiterate. Ricci would go back to basics."[20] It was time to clean up the church's act, including her devotional and liturgical act.

Having adopted the four Gallican Articles of 1682, the Synod of Pistoia went on to adopt reforming religious measures including the following: denunciation of the cult of the Sacred Heart and the Stations of the Cross, the abuse of indulgences, and various aspects of devotion to the Blessed Virgin Mary. Bishop de' Ricci was in favor of the Mass being celebrated in the vernacular Italian, of the laity receiving communion at every Mass, and of the regular reading of Holy Scripture in Italian. While many of the clergy were supportive of these reforming measures, the laity were not behind them and made their protest felt. This was especially the case in the Tuscan city of Prato. St. Stephen's Cathedral had a chapel that contained the "Girdle of St. Thomas," the girdle allegedly given by the Blessed Virgin Mary to St. Thomas the apostle at the time of her assumption into heaven. When rumors got about in 1787 that the bishop of Prato, in line with the reforming spirit of the Synod of Pistoia, was going to destroy this relic, there was a riot. The bishop's *cathedra* was burned outside the cathedral and his palace was invaded by the mob and looted. Some years later Bishop de' Ricci was forced to resign by Pope Pius VI and the reforming spirit of the Synod of Pistoia came to an end.[21] The Synod of Pistoia is not the only example of liturgical reform during this period of time. Bishop Miguel da Anuciação of Coimbra in Portugal set up a liturgical academy to "retrieve ancient traditions" and "reform ritual exuberance."[22] He did not advocate state

---

18. Chadwick, *The Popes and European Revolution*, 411.

19. Duffy, *Saints and Sinners*, 249. See also Lehner, *The Catholic Enlightenment*, 18.

20. Crichton, *Lights in the Darkness*, 30.

21. See Donakowski, "The Age of Revolutions," 351–94.

22. Lehner, *The Catholic Enlightenment*, 34–35.

interference in the church in the same way that Ricci did. These attempts at liturgical renewal, however, were not widespread and came to an end until much of their positive and constructive agenda was taken up at Vatican II.

Cisalpinism in England

"Cisalpinism," meaning "this side of the mountains," was the term in England for the European Catholic Enlightenment. "It was Conciliarism seasoned with English individualism . . . ."[23] The best-known and most important members of the movement were Joseph Berington (1743–1827) and John Lingard (1786–93).[24] Since there was no seminary providing formation for Catholic priests in England at the time, many of the clergy were educated at the English College in Douai, France. In the latter half of the eighteenth century formation courses at the College tended to be "anti-Scholastic and empirical with an element of critical doubt," and "a growing attachment to critical logic and an aversion for metaphysics."[25] The European Enlightenment was having its effect in Catholic circles in England. The men educated at Douai returned to England to serve the Catholic community and naturally enough brought some Enlightenment presuppositions with them.

Joseph Berington (1743–1827), as a professor of philosophy at Douai, had absorbed important aspects of the Gallican approach to ecclesiology, and gave particular emphasis to conciliarism. In a tract of 1789, *Reflections Addressed to the Rev. John Hawkins*, Berington wrote: "[The pope] has indeed his prerogatives, but we have our privileges, and are independent of him, excepting where it has pleased the community, for the sake of unity and good order, to surrender into his hands a limited superintendence."[26] Berington accepted a primacy of jurisdiction for the pope—not unlike, for example, the understanding of St. Cyprian of Carthage in the third century—but this was not a papal-centric or ultramontane ecclesiology, but a Cisalpine ecclesiology. Cisalpine ecclesiology, anticipating something of the position of John Henry Newman in the nineteenth century, acknowledged the centrality and ultimacy of moral conscience in the individual, although this was not set in opposition to Christian doctrine and morality as such. Along with this Cisalpine ecclesiology went a severe dislike of many devotional practices that were popular on the European continent. They considered these practices as bringing Catholicism

23. Lehner, *The Catholic Enlightenment*, 19.

24. Along with the magisterial work of Joseph Chinnici, the best work to date on the English Catholic Enlightenment and Joseph Berington is by Eamon Duffy, "Joseph Berington and the English Catholic Cisalpine Movement, 1772–1803," Ph.D. diss., University of Cambridge, 1972. Substantive parts of the dissertation have been published. See Eamon Duffy, "Doctor Douglass and Mister Berington—An Eighteenth-Century Retraction," *The Downside Review* 88 (1970) 246–69; "Ecclesiastical Democracy Deleted," *Recusant History* 10 (1970) 193–209, 309–31; 13 (1973) 123–48.

25. Chinnici, *The English Catholic Enlightenment*, 7.

26. Cited in Chinnici, *The English Catholic Enlightenment*, 94.

into disrepute among their non-Catholic peers. "The earlier Cisalpines had always rejected ostentatious display as injurious to the Catholic cause and abusive of true religion. Joseph Berington railed against scapulars, medals, and beads."[27] Despite his ecclesiology, Berington's book, *Faith of Catholics* (written in concert with his friend John Kirk)[28] was one of the influences that drew the very ultramontane Henry Edward Manning into the Catholic Church, "a circumstance," in Eamon Duffy's words "which would have grieved Berington deeply."[29]

The ecclesiology of John Lingard was similar to that of Berington, reflecting Gallicanism, and especially the ecclesiology of Jacques Bénigne Bossuet. Bossuet defined the church as "a society that professes to believe the doctrine of Jesus Christ, and to govern itself by his word." Lingard would have had no trouble with this definition. "It implied the church's visibility and the offices the pope and bishops held in her. But by not mentioning the structures explicitly, it focused attention on the church as *the whole body of believers,* symbolizing the thrust of Bossuet's ecclesiology."[30] While Lingard acknowledged the primacy of the pope, he did not do so at the expense of the local episcopate. He was well aware from his studies in church history that the bishops were not simply "under Peter" but "with Peter." He was aware that throughout the tradition bishops were referred to as "brethren," "co-bishops," "fratres," "coepiscopi," and "consacerdotes."[31] In his own way and expression Lingard was anticipating the notion of episcopal collegiality that would be articulated by Vatican II.

27. Chinnici, *The English Catholic Enlightenment,* 173.

28. John Kirk (1760–1851) was a leading member of the Catholic Staffordshire clergy, strongly Cisalpine in theological orientation. He collected all manner of historical documents and it is due to his labor that we owe much of our information of Catholicism in England after 1688. Eamon Duffy points out, "Doctor Douglass and Mister Berington," 269, that "apart from one or two pamphlets, [he] did not publish much . . . and marginal annotations in his books at Oscott, reveal a violently Cisalpine and anti-papal streak which has been ignored by many of his admirers."

29. Duffy, "Doctor Douglass and Mister Berington—An Eighteenth-Century Retraction," 265. It comes as no surprise that Berington and Bishop Paul Milner often clashed. Duffy, "Doctor Douglass and Mister Berington," 247–48, offers a very balanced view especially of Berington's perspective: "To many Catholics like Milner, [Berington] was a traitor. While Milner labored to fight all the world, convinced that all the world was fighting him and, which was the same thing, the church of which he was the champion, Berington, it seemed, was busily at work tearing down the defenses from the inside. In book after book he attacked the papacy, the devotions sanctioned by the church on the continent, and that sacred cow of recusant Catholicism, the later Stuart monarchy. Milner attributed 'half the irreligion of our people' to Berington's 'uncondemned and unconfuted doctrine'. The charge most frequently leveled against him was that of being a favorer of novelty, one who led unwary Catholics into a morass of innovation. He spent his life fighting old battles—the secular/regular quarrel, the fight for bishops-in-ordinary, and the traditional English rejection of 'undue' papal interference. Even where he consciously modeled himself on the pattern of the thinkers of the enlightenment he never departed far from the traditional attitudes of the recusant church. . . . A greater part of his influence over his followers among the clergy is to be explained by the fact that they discerned in his extremely-worded writings many of the traditions and values which they shared, and which they recognized to be in danger."

30. Chinnici, *The English Catholic Enlightenment,* 88.

31. As summarized in Chinnici, *The English Catholic Enlightenment,* 89.

Like his colleague Berington, Lingard was opposed to many European Catholic devotions that were being imported into England: for example, prayers to the Sacred Heart of Jesus, May devotions honoring the Blessed Virgin Mary, the Forty Hours devotion centered on the solemn exposition of the reserved Eucharist, public processions of the Blessed Sacrament, as well as the encouragement of scapulars, relics, and medals. Lingard's language and expression went considerably further than that of Berington. Joseph P. Chinnici describes his attitude in Lingard's own words: "'They might as well have a *festum occulorum* (a feast of the eyes) or *lateris* (of the side), as *cordis* (of the heart). Besides where would they stop? They would soon have a *festum cordis Mariae*,' (a feast of the heart of Mary). When that did occur, Lingard's advice to someone in Preston was to 'insist on a direct answer to the question, in what the heart of the Blessed Virgin differed from the hearts of other women.'"[32]

It is not difficult to see how these "enlightened" points of view of the likes of Lingard and Berington would sit ill at ease with Roman trained bishops and administrators. Lingard and Berington represented the Synod of Pistoia perspective in England. Enlightened Catholics or Cisalpines and ultramontanes, those centered and focused on Rome and the papacy, did not see eye to eye.

There was something else at work too in this ecclesiology. It must be remembered that these Cisalpine priest-authors were writing before Catholic Emancipation in the United Kingdom. That would only come in 1829, when most remaining disabilities against Catholics were removed from law. Until that event and indeed even after it, representatives of the Cisalpine perception were also attempting to counter the anti-Roman and anti-papal attitudes of the English populace generally. These anti-Catholic attitudes appeared to have the ability to cross all social barriers and unite the English people against the Catholic Church. This is how historian Edward Norman describes the situation: "The anti-Catholic tradition was a striking cohesive, managing to unite the otherwise exceedingly particularist strands of English Protestantism. It was also multi-class. Leading figures of the ruling elite like Gladstone, and the stirrers of the *demos* like the numerous no-popery street orators, shared a common horror of the Roman Catholic Church—an institution which, so it seemed to them, enslaved the intellect and debased the people within its thrall."[33] Norman's description of this anti-Catholic bias reached well beyond the nineteenth century into the twentieth, but in the run-up to Catholic Emancipation and in its aftermath it was very loud and brutish. This is the context in which the Cisalpines wrote. Thus, the Cisalpines were determined "to see the English Church cleared of accusations of foreign domination." Eamon Duffy continues in this vein: "If English Catholics could be seen to be British, root and branch, neither priest-ridden or pope-ridden, emancipation would come that much sooner."[34]

32. Chinnici, *The English Catholic Enlightenment,* 172–73.
33. Norman, "When the Faith Was Set Free," 213.
34. Duffy, "Doctor Douglass and Mister Berington," 249.

During the long period of the anti-Catholic penal laws, leadership of the English Catholic Church remained largely in the hands of the gentry. Under the law there could be no Catholic bishops. As Catholics moved forward towards emancipation and legalization as church, it was inevitable that there would be some degree of tension between the traditional gentry leaders of the recusant church and the Vicars Apostolic-hoping-to-become-bishops. Bishop John Milner (1752–1826) gave expression to this tension: "After all the fine things that have been said about the liberty of [episcopal] election, the real question at present is, whether the nomination of our Pastors shall rest with *Lord Petre* or the *successors of St. Peter*."[35] The Petre family had remained staunchly Roman Catholic since the Reformation and were premier guardians of the Catholic faith and tradition in England, but with a certain measure of independence from Rome. What the Petre family stood for and represented was far removed from the horizon of Bishop Milner. Eamon Duffy offers us a pen portrait of the Bishop:

> A noted antiquarian and a leading authority on Gothic architecture he was the chief adviser of the Vicars in these disputes. He found all "Gallicanism" repugnant, and disliked the dryness of English Catholic devotion. His episcopate saw the "reform" of many features of English Catholic life, and he was responsible for the introduction of such "foreign devotions" as that to the Sacred Heart. He has been thought of as the savior of English Catholicism at a crucial period, but it may be doubted whether this assessment of the significance, based largely on a set of interpretations derived from his own voluminous polemical works and the *pietas* of an uncritical biographer, will bear much scrutiny.[36]

Essentially what the Cisalpine theologians desired and taught was not especially different from the central understanding of the long Catholic tradition. What they were opposed to was the imposition of what they considered to be alien practices and customs as central to Catholicism, and a particular understanding of the Petrine ministry and episcopacy. However, after the achievement in the United Kingdom of Catholic Emancipation in 1829 the dynamism of the Cisalpine reform movement evaporated. It was in Joseph Chinnici's words a vision of Catholicism that in 1829 "ceased to respond to social, intellectual, and religious needs."[37] It had never been uniformly attractive to the Catholic populace in England, as with the Catholic population of Tuscany, and it simply ceased to be attractive, although arguably it never quite died.

---

35. In a letter from Milner to Charles Plowden, in Farm Street Archives, cited in Duffy, "Doctor Douglass and Mister Berington," 249.

36. Duffy, "Doctor Douglass and Mister Berington," 265–66.

37. Chinnici, *The English Catholic Enlightenment*, 187.

The French Revolution

What we might call the negative social and political finale of the Enlightenment emerged in the complex of events known as the French Revolution. "The French Revolution had been a traumatic experience, in some ways more traumatic than the Reformation," maintains church historian John O'Malley.[38] Its repercussions went well beyond France, leading in many places to the virtual collapse of the organization of the church.[39] This is partly what Eamon Duffy is referring to in the words that open this chapter—"the arrival of democracy almost destroyed the papacy." As a result of the Revolution, seminaries were closed, priests, bishops, and religious were executed, and a generation grew up without the pervasive influence of the church. "There could be no doubt that after the tsunami of revolution, nothing would ever be quite the same again."[40] The terms "right" and "left" were born with the French Revolution, and in its wake the terms "conservative" and "liberal," and these terms have remained constant in both political and ecclesiastical circles, more often than not without too much mutual comprehension. The conservatives sided with the *ancien regime,* with the old and traditional ways; the liberals wanted novelty, new forms of democracy, new ways of enabling human flourishing as they saw it.

> These church-state tensions influenced the church's whole intellectual life during the nineteenth century. Fear of liberal revolution, especially in the Papal States, made the Roman curia a firm supporter of "legitimate" royal governments and an enemy of democratic popular sovereignty. . . . Rome intervened in almost every serious theological controversy during the nineteenth century and, in almost every case, the intervention was influenced by the church-state tensions.[41]

Thus was born throughout the entire Catholic world, the two dominant styles of liberalism and conservatism—sometimes called "integralism"—and the beginnings of the contemporary polarization in the church. Or, put in the fine words of Meriol Trevor "prophets and guardians."

The papacy of the nineteenth century may be seen, at least in part, as a reaction to what happened in the eighteenth century, in the Enlightenment and most especially with the French Revolution—conservative movements versus liberal movements, conservative-minded popes versus liberal-minded popes.

---

38. O'Malley, *What Happened at Vatican II,* 54. For an excellent introduction to the complexities of the French Revolution and the Catholic Church, see the chapter entitled "The Papacy, Memory, and Revolution," in Thomas Albert Howard, *The Pope and the Professor,* 16–56.

39. Norman, *The Roman Catholic Church,* 139.

40. Duffy, "The Age of Pio Nono: The Age of Paul Cullen," in Dáire Keogh and Albert McDonnell, ed., *Cardinal Paul Cullen and His World,* 50.

41. McCool, *Catholic Theology in the Nineteenth Century,* 25–26.

Pope Pius VII (1800–1823)

Luigi Barnaba Chiaramonte was a compromise candidate in the papal election of 1800, taking the name of Pius VII. In 1797 some three years before his election, as bishop of Imola he preached a Christmas sermon in which he stated that there was no necessary and inherent contradiction between a democratic regime and Christianity. This was new. Democracy was seen as a threat to monarchical Christianity. In line with this point of view Pius VII was able to reach a concordat with Napoleon Bonaparte in July 1801. This brought about a restoration of the church in France after the revolution of 1789. There were still some restrictions on Napoleon's part against the church, restrictions essentially that were the legacy of Gallicanism, and it was partly in an attempt to loosen up these restrictions that the pope traveled to France to participate in the coronation of Napoleon as Emperor in 1804. "The papacy's authority and holiness were still hard currency in the world of power politics."[42] The papal journey northwards, through Italy and France to Paris was met by lines of devout Catholics seeking the pope's blessing. Even the former bishop of Pistoia, Scipio de' Ricci, sought reconciliation with the pope as he made his way through Florence.

There is a certain comic side to the detente achieved with Napoleon, well captured by Eamon Duffy: "In 1803 five Frenchmen, including Napoleon's uncle and former quartermaster, Msgr. Fesch, were made cardinals. The Vatican even accepted the establishment of a feast of 'St. Napoleon' on 15 August, though it displaced a major Marian feast, the Assumption, and no one could come up with a convincing account of just who 'St. Napoleon' was."[43] Relations between pope and emperor deteriorated, however, and Pius became Napoleon's prisoner for a time. After the Napoleonic wars in 1814 Pius reinstated his former secretary of state, Ercole Consalvi, who had been ejected from his post at the insistence of Napoleon in 1806. Consalvi has been described as "a man of genius,"[44] and he was Pius's representative at the Congress of Vienna (1814–15). The congress put the Bourbons back on the throne of France, exiled Napoleon to St. Helena and through Consalvi's skills brought about almost the complete restitution of papal territories lost to Napoleon. That success was not to be matched, however, in the spiritual sphere. The French Revolution's program of dechristianization may have been overturned to a large extent, but negative consequences remained in place. A regular and often acerbic form of anticlericalism took root in France and the church's influence over the people greatly suffered.[45] With greater and lesser levels of intensity at different times these negative consequences of the French Revolution would play themselves out between the state and the church over the next two hundred years.

42. Duffy, *Saints and Sinners*, 267.

43. Duffy, *Saints and Sinners*, 266.

44. John N. D. Kelly, *The Oxford Dictionary of Popes*, 303.

45. Bokenkotter, *A Concise History of the Catholic Church*, 292–93.

Pius VII (1800–1823) had been the prisoner of Napoleon, and had witnessed the integration of the Papal States in Italy into the French Empire. Thus, as the French Revolution reached Italy and the papal dominions as a result of Napoleon's imperialist ambitions, church property was confiscated, as in France, and monasteries and convents were closed, as in France, and ecclesiastical dress was vetoed, as in France. Similar events occurred in the various regions of Europe temporarily conquered by Napoleon before his final defeat in 1815 at the Battle of Waterloo. Church historian Edward Norman points to two major consequences. First, Catholicism was closely associated with the politics that attempted to restore the monarchical systems of Europe prior to Napoleon. In effect, this made the papacy a prime supporter of monarchy, indeed, restored the popes in the Papal States as monarchs themselves. Second, partly as a result of the widespread collaboration of the European Catholic laity with the new Napoleonic era and its radical measures, there emerged what Edward Norman calls a "new sacerdotalism," a new and at times excessive emphasis on the priesthood and especially upon the papacy, an emphasis that has come to be known as "ultramontanism."[46] If ultramontanism was one response to the liberalism of the Enlightenment and of the French Revolution and its consequences, the teaching role of the papacy became another response.

Of course, popes have always taught. What is different in our period is that the encyclical letter becomes the major medium of teaching. Two encyclical letters were issued by Pope Pius VI at the end of the eighteenth century. Pope Pius IX in the mid-nineteenth century issued thirty-eight encyclicals, followed by Pope Leo XIII who was responsible for seventy-five. Furthermore, after Vatican I in 1870 and the definition of infallibility, what popes said and taught in their encyclicals began to assume in the eyes of many "an irreversible quality."[47] While the ultramontanes may not have won all they had wished for at Vatican I, undoubtedly at the level of the popular Catholic consciousness, ultramontanism was the order of the day. The pope was central to ordinary Catholics in ways that were historically unprecedented.

Pope Leo XII (1823–29)

Cardinal Annibale Sermattei della Genga (born 1760) spent most of his life working in the area of papal diplomacy, not with great success, due for the most part to his conservative political positions, positions which had been thrown into turmoil by the French Revolution. Nevertheless, he remained in favor with the pope. In 1816 he was named by Pope Pius VII cardinal and bishop of Senigallia and later in 1818 Spoleto. He was promoted further as Vicar General of Rome in 1820, and he was also given oversight of various curial congregations.

---

46. Norman, *The Roman Catholic Church*, 143.
47. O'Malley, *What Happened at Vatican II*, 56.

With the death of Pius VII in 1823 Cardinal della Genga, at this time according to Eamon Duffy "a sickly sixty-three year old crippled by chronic hemorrhoids," was elected pope and took the name of Leo XII.[48] Pius VII's man, Cardinal Consalvi, was noted for his more liberal political stances, and a number of conservative cardinals were desirous of a change. They were living in reaction to all that had taken place since 1789. "The modern [papal] state which Consalvi had been tentatively fostering reverted to a police regime infested with spies and intent on stamping out, with penalties ranging from petty clerical surveillance of private life to execution, any possible flicker of revolution."[49] The new Pope Leo XII (1823–29), with no real understanding of or sympathy with the new political and cultural worlds that had come into being, constantly battled what he saw as errors threatening the Catholic faith coming out of this "new" world. In this light, he basically collaborated with the now-restored, conservative monarchs of Europe.

The Jews who had experienced liberation at the time of the French Revolution were now to go back to their ghettos. Roman Jews had to attend Christian sermons every week and commercial transactions with Christians were forbidden. It was an attempt, ultimately doomed to failure, to turn the clocks back to a pre-French revolution era, convinced as Leo was that "the papacy was the God-given answer to the uncertainties and infidelities of post-revolutionary Europe."[50]

Pope Gregory XVI (1831–46)

Pope Leo XII was succeeded by a canonist, Francesco Saverio Castiglione as Pope Pius VIII, with a very short-lived pontificate from 1829–30. He was not greatly interested in politics and put his energies into pastoral and doctrinal issues. His successor Pope Gregory XVI was a convinced and single-minded conservative, totally opposed to anything that to him smacked of modernity. As Bartolomeo Alberto Cappellari he had become a Camaldolese monk and academic, publishing in 1799 a treatise entitled *The Triumph of the Holy See and the Church Against the Attacks of Innovators*. The book defended the autonomy of the Holy See from all forms of state control and upheld papal infallibility. At the time of his election as pope Cappellari was the general superior of the Camaldolese Order but not a bishop, and in fact is the last man to be elected pope before being ordained a bishop. After his election as Gregory XVI— Owen Chadwick suggests that he chose Gregory after Pope Gregory VII, the great medieval contender against European monarchs—he defended the papal office as that of a monarch. He began to use the term "infallible" well before its development and definition later in the nineteenth century.[51] He banned railways in the Papal States

---

48. Duffy, *Saints and Sinners*, 278.

49. Kelly, *The Oxford Dictionary of the Popes*, 305.

50. Duffy, "The Age of Pio Nono: The Age of Paul Cullen," 51.

51. Schelkens et al., *Aggiornamento?* 7.

and showed himself utterly opposed to the growing tide of Italian nationalism.[52] Not surprisingly, there was revolution in the Papal States, revolution that was probably more against papal administrative ineptitude than overtly for Italian nationalism. It required the intervention of Austria, and led to the major European powers demanding reforms in the papal administration.

Félicité Robert de Lammenais (1782–1854), Pope Gregory XVI and *Mirari Vos*

There are few better introductions to the figure of Félicité de Lammenais than that provided by Meriol Trevor. This is what she writes: "The tragedy of Lammenais was that when his prophetic vision was disowned by Pope Gregory XVI in 1832, he found that his belief in himself was greater than his belief in the church, and gradually moved away from it. Lammenais was a prophet of Liberty, and believed that the ideals of the French Revolution could be Christianized."[53] Born on June 19, 1782, Lammenais, or as he was known in the family and by his friends Féli, was brought up in the crucible of the French Revolution and educated in the philosophical works of Rousseau. The family were supporters of the French Revolution and so Féli endorsed and adopted what he took to be its central and positive values—democratic freedom, freedom of thought, religious freedom. Eventually he became a priest, ordained in 1815, the year of Waterloo. Having spent some time in England he was well acquainted with English culture and to some extent with Anglican theology, but he judged the climate to be too individualistic and insufficiently social. Lammenais wanted nothing to do with monarchy, promoting as much as was possible for him democracy, a key value flowing from the Revolution. "He argued that the people—not the aristocracy, or the episcopacy, or the bourgeoisie, but the common people, the peasants and artisans, the class which came to be called the proletariat . . . was emerging for the first time in history and would control the future."[54] For him Christianity was ineluctably *social*.

In 1817 he published the first of several volumes which made him famous, *Essai sur l'indifférence en matière de religion, An Essay on Indifference in Matters Religious.* The aim of the book was to underscore the importance of religious ideas for a flourishing democratic society. Many thought of him as another Pascal or Bossuet, destined to influence religious sentiment in France.[55] Turning again to Meriol Trevor we find a good summary of his thesis. "Societies, like men, *grew*. God acted through this natural tradition; Christ crowned and fulfilled it, and the Christian tradition was the way of life in which all men could find what they needed to cleanse and sustain

---

52. Chadwick, *A History of the Popes 1830–1914*, 2.

53. Trevor, *Prophets and Guardians*, 135.

54. Hales, *The Catholic Church in the Modern World*, 89.

55. Livingston, *Modern Christian Theology*, 149.

and liberate the spirit."[56] The second of Lammenais's volumes with the same theme was much less well-received. The emphasis in the second volume was on common or communal sense in contrast to autonomous reason. This he took to be the basis of certitude, as opposed to individualistic reason. This common reason provides the necessary truths for life: "the existence of God, the immortality of the soul, the prospect of eternal reward and punishment, the necessity of prayer and worship, the moral law, the fall of man, and the need for a redeemer."[57] His attack on individualistic reason, the reasoning capacity of every human person, meant that this volume was met with a great deal of opposition and at a time when the individualistic philosophy of René Descartes was still quite dominant.

What was obvious for Lammenais was the centrality of the papacy. He believed that the papacy could be a real center of political unity, preventing the despotism of government, especially secularized or anti-Christian government. What he espoused was a kind of papal theocracy. While his views were far from being uniformly and positively accepted throughout France—those who were still drinking from the wells of Gallicanism were utterly opposed to this papal centralism, and the growing number of ultramontanes were most suspicious of his emphasis on democratic freedom—he was nonetheless able to gather around him an ardent circle of disciples. They gathered at a country house, La Chesnaie, that belonged to Lammenais' grandmother. Their purpose was the renewal of both society and the church, but with each one independent of the other. Two of his best-known disciples were the layman Charles de Montalambert (1810–70) and the priest Henri Lacordaire (1802–61). They espoused together the Revolution's idea of freedom, but a freedom guaranteed by the papacy. They came to see the way forward and not only for France in the development of ultramontanism—a natural alliance between Pope and people—and so 1830 Lammenais and his associates found expression in a new periodical called *Avenir*, "The Future." It was very popular and influential. "The *Avenir* rejected the divine right of kings (to which most of the bishops still clung) and embraced the doctrine of the sovereignty of the people. It advocated liberty of conscience, the separation of church and state, the suppression of the payment of the clergy by the government, and liberty of education, of the press, and of association."[58] This is Alec Vidler's description of the paper and one can see immediately that in the wake of the French Revolution and of the Congress of Vienna it was bound to run into trouble. In December 1831 and through the spring of 1832 Lammenais, with Montalambert and Lacordaire, went to Rome to defend these ideas before the newly elected Pope Gregory XVI. His ideas were unwelcome and especially because of his espousal of freedom, the "Liberty" of the Revolution, they were

56. Trevor, *Prophets, Guardians and Saints*, 140.

57. Following Bokenkotter, *Church and Revolution*, 43.

58. Vidler, *The Church in an Age of Revolution*, 70.

condemned. "It was the first time that Lammenais was directly let down by the Pope, who was familiar with governments, not at all familiar with 'the people.'"[59]

In response to Lammenais and others, although Lammenais was never named as such, Pope Gregory published the encyclical *Mirari Vos* in 1832 in which he denounced freedom of conscience, freedom of the press, the idea of a just revolution and the separation of church and state, "a new benchmark in apocalyptic diatribe, portraying in lurid colors a hostile and depraved world as viewed from the papal bunker."[60] The encyclical condemned modern society and its trends—moral, social and political—in a way that set the church virtually in opposition to the world, creating a tone that would last until the mid-twentieth century.

Utterly disenchanted, Lammenais gave himself more and more to writing on politics. In 1834 he published *Words of a Believer*, a book that was to be condemned by Rome. In this book he passionately attacked corrupt monarchical and ecclesiastical power, and advocated a utopian vision marked by the promotion of justice and equality, so much so that it was described "as a lyrical version of the Communist Manifesto."[61] His work would be an inspiration for social and political movements later in the century. Friedrich Engels and Karl Marx considered Lamennais as something of a Communist, but the difference between them and Lamennais is pointed out by church historian Thomas Bokenkotter: "Lamennais rejected the idea of class warfare and defended the right of private property. . . .While emphatic about the rights of the people, he also spoke of their duties. 'Rights without duties is anarchy,' he said."[62] However, Féli's disenchantment was also with the church and with faith and he ended his days as a kind of pantheist.

When Pope Gregory XVI died in 1846, the world to which he was so opposed was not sorry. Owen Chadwick describes the situation: "He was not lamented, even in Rome; he died as the most unpopular of popes. The world wanted him to go."[63] The successor of Pope Gregory XVI was Pope Pius IX whose pontificate lasted thirty-one years.

59. Trevor, *Prophets, Guardians and Saints,* 145.

60. Duffy, "The Age of Pio Nono: The Age of Paul Cullen," 52.

61. Livingston, *Modern Christian Theology,* 153.

62. Bokenkotter, *Church and Revolution,* 69–70.

63. Chadwick, *A History of the Popes, 1830–1914,* 60.

2

Pope Pius IX (1846–78)

Pius was the first pope to identify himself wholeheartedly with ultramon-
tanism, i.e., the tendency to centralize authority in church government and
doctrine and the Holy See.

—JOHN N. D. KELLY[1]

The pontificate of Pius IX . . . witnessed the victory
of Ultramontanism over Gallicanism.

—CIARAN O'CARROLL[2]

HUMAN AFFAIRS ARE ALWAYS changing but the rapidity of change in the nineteenth century threw up a raft of challenges to the Catholic Church with which the church was ill prepared to cope. Europe was changing fast from being primarily a rural society to an urban one, providing rapid growth industry with workers, children as well as adults. The population of Europe virtually doubled. It is estimated that over forty million Europeans made their way to the United States of America, greatly increasing that country's ethnic mix. These demographic changes throughout Napoleonic Europe and the United States were also matched by the development of liberalism, described by Paul Collins in these words: "Derived from the thought of John Locke, liberalism says that the source of sovereignty is neither God nor kings, but the people. Liberals embraced democracy, freedom of expression and the press, separation of church and state, and the belief in progress. They saw human history as a constant ascent to a better life based on science and viewed the technical control of nature as a sign of progress. Liberalism believed that the state must be governed by constitutional principles that ensure the freedom of every individual. . . . A clash between liberalism and an absolutist church was inevitable."[3] The clash began with the Enlightenment of

1. Kelly, *The Oxford Dictionary of Popes*, 310.
2. O'Carroll, "Pius IX: Pastor and Prince," 125.
3. Collins, *Absolute Power*, 24.

the eighteenth century but came with massive force during the pontificate of Pope Pius IX, the longest-serving pope of the nineteenth century.

From Giovanni Maria Mastai-Ferreti to Pope Pius IX

The opening statements above of historians John Kelly and Ciaran O'Carroll provide a good introduction for this chapter on Pope Pius IX. Undoubtedly this Pope identified himself with ultramontanism—the point of view that centralized Catholic thought and action almost exclusively on Rome and the papacy—both consciously and unconsciously, and that identification spelled the end of Gallicanism—as we have seen in chapter one, a kind of independence movement in the French Catholic Church—not only in its French form but in any kind of thinking that might be considered critical of the papacy, for example English Cisalpinism especially of the eighteenth century. English Cisalpinism was a more moderate form of the independence movement of Gallicanism. Pope Pius IX with his ultramontane perspective shaped the excessive papal-centrism of modern times, not only in respect of church governance but also in terms of ecclesiology. His predecessor, Pope Gregory XVI, a known strict conservative in virtually everything, viewed Cardinal Giovanni Maria Mastai-Ferretti as something of an ecclesiastical liberal and said that even Mastai-Ferretti's cats were liberals. Mastai-Ferretti was elected Pope as Gregory's successor in 1846, taking the name of Pius IX, and he served the church as pope until his death in 1878. It would be fair to say that he moved from a moderate liberalism to an extreme ultramontanism.

Although concerns were raised about his suspected epileptic seizures, he was ordained to the priesthood in 1819, and was sent by Pope Pius VII to Chile and Peru, accompanying Msgr. Giovanni Muzi, the apostolic delegate to those countries from 1823 until 1825. Although he was the first pope ever to have an experience of South America, in fact this was his only prolonged trip outside Italy, and arguably his informed awareness of social and political issues was too closely identified throughout his career with Italy and Europe, particularly Catholic Europe. The South American experience, however, stimulated his interest in the missions.[4] After he returned from this extended visit to South America, he showed no particular interest in pursuing a papal diplomatic career.

He became archbishop of Spoleto in 1827, was transferred to Imola in 1832, and was made a cardinal in 1840. While in Imola, Mastai-Ferretti was very popular with the poor, and his charitable activity constantly reduced him to straitened financial circumstances. "Far from courting an easy popularity amongst the propertied classes, or the higher clergy, he continued to show, even after he had received the red hat, an independence and liberality of outlook which often cost him the friendship of the larger landholders in his diocese as well as that of the senior government officials."[5]

4. Coppa, *Pope Pius IX*, 30.

5. Hales, *Pio Nono*, 35.

With this sense of commitment to the poor it is not difficult to understand his attitude to the reformers and progressives of his day, an attitude much less suspicious than many of his peers. He sided with the progressive cohort in the church and was an advocate for political reform. His views had been influenced by the work of the priest-philosopher and politician Vincenzo Gioberti (1801–52), and he was sympathetic to Gioberti's liberalizing ideas, but E. E. Y. Hales is right to issue this caution: "It would be difficult to imagine anything more erroneous than the supposition that Pius was sailing with the wind in adopting liberal policies. He was not a great political thinker . . . but he was certainly not so foolish as to suppose that a liberal policy was going to be easy."[6] Pius was a moderate liberal, not an extremist reformer politically. And theologically? He would have had a basic awareness of theology—what Owen Chadwick calls "[theology] in outline," but also a theology "without subtleties."[7]

Pope Pius IX

In 1846 the somewhat liberalizing Mastai-Ferretti was elected pope as Pope Pius IX. "The election of Count Giuseppe Mastai Ferretti as Pope Pius IX in the spring of 1846, after the draconian years of Gregory XVI's rule, raised the sorts of hopes and expectations aroused in 1978 by the election of Karol Wojtyla after the fraught and depressing final years of Paul VI."[8] One of the first things he did as pope was to issue an amnesty for political refugees/revolutionaries from the Papal States who had been living outside of Italy. They returned in their hundreds. This generous political gesture would create a climate expectant of rapid social and political change in the direction of a unified Italy. The dream of Italian unification had begun to grow towards the end of the eighteenth century, in part stimulated by the French Revolution and the Italian conquests of Napoleon Bonaparte. Italian unification was everywhere in the air and not only in political circles, so that, for example, it had become the passion of the immensely popular dramatist and poet Vittori Alfieri (1749–1803). Allied to these Italian nationalist aspirations were the constant criticisms of political commentators in Europe. "They grumbled that the clock of Europe had stopped in Rome, which was seen to combine feudal pretensions with Renaissance extravagance and whose rigidity and isolation led to stagnation, lamenting that while the world had changed, the church and its leaders had not. The papacy, and their perspective, represented a relic of the past, finding its persistence to the present ironic and unacceptable."[9] When it comes to the social and economic circumstances of the citizens of the Papal States, it has been pointed out that they were certainly no worse off than the working classes of European

6. Hales, *Pio Nono*, 57. Schultenover, *A View from Rome*, 28 questions the common view that Pius IX was even initially a liberal.

7. Chadwick, *A History of the Popes 1830–1914*, 173.

8. Duffy, "The Age of Pio Nono: The Age of Paul Cullen," 54.

9. Coppa, *Politics and the Papacy in the Modern*, 1–2.

democracies, and in some respects were better off. There was no parallel in the Papal States, for example, to the Great Famine in Ireland (1845–52), largely mismanaged by the "enlightened" British government. Anti-papal sentiment at the time would never have acknowledged anything but what they took to be egregious mismanagement in papal government. "The Papal State was a benevolent theocracy. There may have been no longer place, in the Europe of 1860, for benevolent theocracies, and it may have been in the nature of things that the rising tide of the *Risorgimento* should sweep this State away. But that is not a reason for stigmatizing Pio Nono's government as oppressive, or corrupt, or economically backward . . . ."[10] The overly negative opinions of the Papal States were, of course, well known to Pius IX. He could not have been unaware of them. However, there never was a time when Pius considered relinquishing the Papal States. He regarded their political independence as essential, indeed willed by God, to his spiritual leadership as pope. He was never to waver on this point.

At a personal level, no one disagreed with the universally acknowledged fact that Pio Nono was a most charming man. Eamon Duffy writes: "He was genial, unpretentious, wreathed in clouds of snuff, always laughing."[11] In a more popular book on the papacy Duffy goes somewhat further but without acknowledging any detailed sources in describing Pius's affability and charm: "He was devout, kindly, unstuffy and at ease in the company of women (there were vague rumors of romantic irregularities earlier in his life, which didn't necessarily do him any harm in Italian opinion)."[12] Even his critics have to admit that he was most likable. For example, John Henry Newman, no great admirer of the pope, wrote of him: "His personal presence was of a kind that no one could withstand. . . . The main cause of his popularity was the magic of his presence, . . . his uncompromising faith, his courage, the graceful mingling in the name of the human and the divine, the humor, the wit, the playfulness with which he tempered his severity, his naturalness, and then his true eloquence."[13] Newman was to take exception to what he saw as a growing narrowness of theological and ecclesiological vision, especially in regard to the issue of papal infallibility, and so that makes his generous description of Pius significant.

Apparently, Pius's sense of fun virtually knew no bounds. On one occasion, a number of Anglican clergymen were visiting Rome and asked for his blessing. Pius pronounced over them, with humor, the prayer for the blessing of incense: "May you be blessed by him in whose honor you are to be burned."[14] Pius moved with ease in the company of women. He was an admirer of Queen Victoria, and she sent him a personal letter of sympathy in 1848 at the time of the revolution that took him into

10. Hales, *Pio Nono*, 170.

11. Duffy, *Saints and Sinners*, 293.

12. Duffy, *Ten Popes Who Shook the World*, 95.

13. Cited from Vidler, *The Church in an Age of Revolution*, rev. ed., 147.

14. Cited from Duffy, *Saints and Sinners*, 293.

exile. In some ways, he seems to have considered himself a progressive Victorian,[15] and may even have entertained the utterly unrealistic idea that Queen Victoria might one day become a Roman Catholic.[16]

As a thinker, Pius was no intellectual. Odo Russell, the British ambassador to the Holy See and a man who was genuinely fond of Pius, commented on his "amiable but weak mind."[17] In this regard, advisers became all-important, but here too Pius was not blessed with great success. "Inevitably, therefore," as Eamon Duffy writes "he was surrounded by people who endorsed and exaggerated his opinions and prejudices: as in the cabinets of Margaret Thatcher, success at the court of Pio Nono depended on being and being seen to be 'one of us.'"[18] He placed too much faith and trust, for example, in Msgr. George Talbot, a converted Anglican priest during the early years of the Oxford Movement. Talbot was unstable and reactionary. For example, he sowed suspicions in the pope's mind about the orthodoxy and fidelity of Newman. Duffy describes the man in devastating terms: "He was certainly devious, feline, wreathed in intrigue, his view of the world and the church a perpetual game of cowboys and Indians, heroes and villains."[19] Somewhat less devastating is Cardinal Manning's view of Talbot as "the most imprudent man that ever lived."[20] In 1868 Talbot was removed from the Roman Curia and placed in a mental institution near Paris, where he died in 1886.

Cardinal Giacomo Antonelli (1806–76)

While George Talbot was papal chamberlain, Cardinal Giacomo Antonelli was Secretary of State. Antonelli was born into a family that was wealthy in its own right, but his father, Domenico, realistically recognized that both securing and promoting his wealth in the Papal States would demand an ecclesiastic in his family. Giacomo was to be that ecclesiastic and so in 1823 he was enrolled in Rome's University of the Sapienza, gradually finding himself fully engaged in the faculty of jurisprudence. To make headway in a good gubernatorial position in the Papal States one had to take holy orders, and so in 1841 Giacomo was ordained a deacon. He was an ecclesiastical

15. Hales, *Pio Nono,* 129.

16. Duffy, *Ten Popes Who Shook the World,* 95.

17. O'Malley, SJ "The Beatification of Pope Pius IX," 10.

18. Duffy, "The Age of Pio Nono: The Age of Paul Cullen," 55. Church historian, John W. O'Malley in his *Catholic History for Today's Church,* 55, adds to this description of Pius: "Pius surrounded himself with mediocrities, adept principally at telling him what he wanted to hear, a fact commented on by many contemporaries otherwise favorably disposed toward him."

19. Duffy, *Saints and Sinners,* 294.

20. As reported in Leslie, *Henry Edward Manning: His Life and Labors* (London, 1921), xii, cited in Gilley, "New Light on an Old Scandal," 178. Gilley's own description of Talbot is closer to that of Duffy: "A born tittle-tattler and intriguer, whose low cunning seems the more unattractive for its sanction, an unctuous piety. His lack of mental balance eventually consigned him to a lunatic asylum at Passy, where the Pope wrote to him, charitably humoring his delusions."

careerist who never moved beyond diaconate toward priesthood. "[Domenico] was most anxious for his son to become a priest—a step which Giacomo scrupulously avoided, despite parental encouragement."[21] He received promotion upon promotion in the service of the Papal States on two counts: first, his fairly consistent conservative political positions, and second, his established and growing competence in the area of economic management.

After the election of Mastai-Ferretti as Pope Pius IX, Antonelli found himself trusted with ever more and newer responsibilities by the pope. "Antonelli analyzed and understood Pius better than the others around him, appreciating that his reformism was moderated by his obsessive concern that no measure be undertaken which might compromise his spiritual mission. . . . Pius found himself torn between the need to effect economies, and the desire to provide for the country's social ills. Confronted with this difficult choice, he sought assistance, calling upon Antonelli, who knew the finances of state inside and out."[22] Small wonder, then, that this papal reliance on Antonelli resulted in his being made a cardinal in 1847, just forty-one years of age. Reliance on Antonelli continued throughout all the troublesome years of attempts at Italian unification, even when Piedmont annexed most of the Papal States. The conservative policies of Antonelli were seen as particularly problematic by those intent upon Italian unification. He was both feared and vilified by his enemies, both privately and publicly. "[Antonelli] reportedly sought to resign but Pius would not let him do so, imploring, 'You have been with me during easy times, now that troublesome times are upon us, you must remain.' Pius appreciated that he rather than Antonelli inspired the intransigent policy, and that the removal of his minister would only expose his personal responsibility, rendering all the more difficult the course he had chartered."[23] Probably more than anyone else close to the pope, Antonelli realized the inevitability of the unification of Italy. Yet he seems never to have wavered in his support of Pius's insistence that his temporal power, the Papal States, were necessary to the exercise of his spiritual responsibilities.

Detailed and lurid accounts of Antonelli's sex life abound, making it exceedingly difficult to know what to believe. His attacks of gout were often put down to venereal disease. Church historian and historian of the papacy, Eamon Duffy, says that the cardinal "practiced celibacy only episodically."[24] One wonders, however, how fair this judgment is. Frank J. Coppa, whose area of expertise is nineteenth- and twentieth-century Italian politics and church history and who has written the most substantive and well-researched account of Antonelli in English, writes as follows:

21. Coppa, *Cardinal Giacomo Antonelli and Papal Politics in European Affairs*, 31.

22. Coppa, *Cardinal Giacomo Antonelli and Papal Politics in European Affairs*, 38–39.

23. Coppa, *Cardinal Giacomo Antonelli and Papal Politics in European Affairs*, 111.

24. Duffy, "It Takes All Sorts to Make a Saint," 1180. See also Holmes, *The Triumph of the Holy See*, 130.

Those who discounted the Cardinal's contributions and were prepared to believe the worst of him, have never adequately explained why Pio Nono, acknowledged by almost all to lead a saintly life, kept a "libertine" in his service. We know that the pope was aware of the stories which circulated about his Minister. Indeed a series of anonymous letters were sent to the pontiff, recounting the Cardinal's alleged escapades, lurid sex life, and disloyalty, calling for Antonelli's removal. Pius, distressed by these letters, discounted them.[25]

It seems most unlikely indeed, although it could never be completely falsified, that Pius would have been unaware of Antonelli's "episodic celibacy" and not have confronted him about it, or distanced himself from him.

What is not in doubt is that Antonelli used his powerful office to promote his family to such an extent that he was accused of replacing the nepotism of popes with the nepotism of the Secretary of State. Three of his brothers were given well-paying jobs in the papal civil service, and all were made papal counts. At the same time, Antonelli attended Mass daily, received communion once a week, and dispersed large amounts of money to various charities. One of the recipients of Antonelli's charity was Don Giovanni Bosco, now St. John Bosco, in his work for abandoned children. Owen Chadwick sums up Antonelli in these words: "He had not been ordained to be priestly, he was ordained because that opened a career."[26] That is not an unfair judgment, but in this world of messy human affairs perhaps one ought not to expect heroic and ideal performance.

The Unification of Italy

Italy was not the unified state that it is today with Rome as its capital. It was divided up into various kingdoms and principalities, including the Papal States. The Papal States were the constant focus of political intrigue and ambition on the part of the rulers of France, Austria as well as the various Italian monarchical parties. Mid-nineteenth-century Italian politics and history are like a chess game between these various groups. The endpoint of the game, agreed virtually but in various ways by everybody, was the unification of Italy.

A movement, ultimately to be successful, was underway in the mid-nineteenth century to unite Italy under one leader, and for a time it seemed possible that that leader might be Pius IX, a sort of president of a united Italy. The Italian philosopher-theologian Antonio Rosmini (1797–1855) dreamed and hoped of such a possibility. As has been noted, Pius was perceived by many to be something of a reformer and a liberal. Soon after his election he embarked on a series of measures designed to improve the conditions in the Papal States. As well as declaring an amnesty for former

25. Coppa, *Cardinal Giacomo Antonelli*, 185.

26. Chadwick, *A History of the Popes*, 94.

revolutionaries in his territories—something that a number of seasoned European politicians took issue with—he went on to initiate more immediately practical decisions and measures. For example, he introduced railways and gas street lighting in Rome itself and he put into place an agricultural institute to improve productivity and to help farmers make the most of their farms. He had the chains removed from the gates of the Jewish ghetto in Rome and after some time the gates were burned down. Jews had been required to attend Christian sermons weekly, but Pius abolished this absurd requirement.

Things were changing and changing fast in papal Italy. Pius ordered that insults against the Jews, fairly typical in the annual comedies of the Roman Carnival, were to cease. Frederic Ozanam, founder of the St. Vincent De Paul Society, described Pius in glowing terms as "the envoy sent by God to conclude the great business of the nineteenth century, the alliance of religion and liberty."[27] Ozanam was also an eyewitness of the torchlight processions to the pope's Quirinal Palace celebrating his popularity and his liberal policies. Putting all this in summary form one Englishman writing to another in 1848 remarked: "A pretty state we are in altogether, with a radical pope teaching all Europe rebellion."[28]

The prospect of a more liberal papal regime with whatever actual reality it had came sharply to an end in the year 1848, the year of European revolutions, and the year in which the city of Rome itself fell to Italian revolutionaries. "In spite of inevitable differences, the revolutions in Europe during 1848 were simultaneous and often inspired by a common ideology. . . . For a time it seemed that the whole of Europe was attempting to reorganize itself according to the principles of democracy and nationalism."[29] In that year Pius established an elected municipal government and agreed to a new constitution for the Papal States that included an elected chamber with the power to veto papal policy. As popular sentiment increasingly demanded the expulsion of Austria from Italy, however, Pius was called upon to give his leadership and endorsement to this move. His response was to affirm that he would not send troops against the Catholic nation of Austria and to invite Italians to return to their established princes and abandon the notion of a united and federal Italy under his proposed leadership. To say the least this was singularly naïve. Duffy describes what happened: "Overnight, from being the most popular man in Italy, he became the most hated."[30] Romans began to speak of *Pio Nono Secondo*, the second Pius IX. In November of 1848 his prime minister, Pellegrino Rossi, was murdered, and in the same month Pius had to escape from the city dressed as a simple priest, an escape orchestrated with considerable political wisdom by his loyal ally Cardinal Antonelli. Rome was in revolt. From the safe position of Gaeta, in Naples, the pope called upon the Catholic powers of Europe to

27. Aubert, *Church Between Revolution and Restoration,* 385; see also Hales, *Pio Nono,* 50–51.

28. Wilberforce to Mozley, cited in Vidler, *The Church in an Age of Revolution,* 148.

29. Holmes, *The Triumph of the Holy See,* 106.

30. Duffy, *Saints and Sinners,* 288.

restore him to Rome and the Papal States. Consequently in July 1849, French troops took Rome, and Pius returned in 1850. Duffy writes: "He never recovered from his exile of 1848, and for the rest of his life remained convinced that political concessions to democracy merely fueled the fires of revolution. The liberal honeymoon was over."[31] For the next two decades the pope depended on the presence of French and Austrian troops to maintain his position in the Papal States, and on Cardinal Antonelli's counsel and policies to maintain and to safeguard the primacy of his spiritual position. As always "[Antonelli] pledged his diplomatic expertise to implement the conservative policy flowing from the Pope's religious convictions."[32]

Reaction to European Liberalism.

Liberalism is a notoriously slippery notion, but we may add to the perspective of Paul Collins cited above a narrower definition from church historian Alec Vidler: "Broadly speaking, in the nineteenth century liberals were those people who were in favor of the new kind of state and society that had issued from the [French] Revolution."[33] "Freedom, equality, brotherhood" had been the cry of the French Revolution, and liberals were those who wanted to see that cry echoed in every aspect of society. Liberalism referred to those who espoused constitutional and representative governments, who favored religious toleration, and who advocated the separation of church and state. These ideas were commonplace in Europe and in the United States of America and were daily gaining ground also among many Catholics. Although it is dangerous to make grand and general descriptions, it is probably fair to say that political liberalism marked France and parts of Italy especially, while a more intellectual liberalism was characteristic of England and Germany. After his brief two-year flirtation with liberal ideas, Pius IX set his face firmly against liberalism in all its forms, and to further this project be encouraged the Jesuits to found the conservative newspaper *Civilta cattolica* in 1849 and he gave strong support to the establishment of another news organ, *L'Osservatore Romano*, in 1860. Negatively both organs countered liberalism and positively supported ultramontane ideas.[34]

Pius was deeply opposed to religious toleration. He came out against, for example, the modest degree of tolerance shown toward Protestant worship by the Spanish government. He took issue with the grand Duke of Tuscany, who permitted Jews to attend the university. In Italy the center of liberalism was undoubtedly the city of Turin in the Kingdom of Piedmont. Its king, Victor Emmanuel II, with his prime minister, Count Cavour, continued to promote the cause of Italian unification, especially against the

31. Duffy, *Saints and Sinners*, 288.

32. Coppa, *Cardinal Giacomo Antonelli*, 71.

33. Vidler, *The Church in an Age of Revolution,* 148.

34. James L. Heft, SM, "From the Pope to the Bishops." 59. See also Holmes, *The Triumph of the Holy See,* 135.

hated Austrian presence. "Count Cavour . . . favored a separation of Church and State. The Count explained his preference for the ecclesiastical freedom which prevailed in the United States, convinced that it would eventually take root in Italy."[35] A "liberal" policy overtly hostile to the "conservative" church was pursued in Piedmont. For example, in 1854, almost all monasteries and convents were suppressed, except for some nursing and teaching congregations. They had practical value for modern and progressive society in a way that contemplative religious foundations did not. In 1860 the Legations and the Marches of Ancona, both within the Papal States, were taken by Piedmont. This meant that a small residual strip of land on the west coast of Italy was all that remained of the Papal States. Defense forces from devout Catholics came together from all over Europe to fight on behalf of the pope. French, Spanish, Portuguese, Polish, Irish—all rallied to the papal side. The Irish Brigade was under the command of one Major O'Reilly. Eamon Duffy notes wittily that the pope was initially doubtful about the Irish contingent in these defense forces "because he feared the effects on Irishmen of the ready availability of cheap Italian wine."[36] From the perspective of Pius, the entire situation in Italy had a rather apocalyptic feel to it. On the one hand there was liberal Piedmont representing the forces of evil and, on the other, there was himself leading the legions of God. Roger Aubert comments: "To realists who tried to persuade him that sooner or later he must negotiate, Pius IX opposed a mystical confidence in divine providence, nourished by the conviction that the political convulsions in which he was implicated were only an episode in the great battle between God and Satan, in which Satan's defeat was inevitable."[37]

Pope Pius IX and Judaism

The new and liberal pope who had dismantled the Jewish Roman ghetto reinstated this ghetto after his return from exile. It was part and parcel of his struggle with liberalism. To Pius's struggle with liberalism we must add the Mortara episode.[38] Edgardo Mortara (1851–1940) was a Jewish boy whose family lived in Bologna, a city at that time within the Papal States. When he was still only one, Edgardo became seriously ill and a Christian servant in the Mortara household baptized him secretly, fearing that the child would die without the benefit of the sacrament, and so would forfeit the blessing of heaven. The story of the secret baptism broke, and the Inquisition moved in. Since

35. Coppa, *Cardinal Giacomo Antonelli*, 77, slightly adapted.

36. Duffy, *Saints and Sinners*, 289.

37. Aubert, *Church Between Revolution and Restoration*, 385.

38. See Kertzer, *The Kidnapping of Edgardo Mortara*. This is the fullest account of the Mortara affair, at least in English. Contrasting Kertzer's detailed account with other studies of Pius IX, curiously there appears to be no treatment of the Mortara incident in E. E. Y. Hales's finely documented account of Pius's papacy, *Pio Nono*. Frank J. Coppa mentions the Mortara affair very briefly in his *Pope Pius IX*, 129 and with careful attention to detail against the broader horizon of the papacy's relationship with Judaism in his *The Papacy, the Jews and the Holocaust*, 95–98.

Edgardo was now technically a Christian, and since the law forbade Christians to be brought up as Jews, the now six-year-old was taken from his parents in 1858 and put under the direct protection of the pope himself. There was, as one might expect, an uproar throughout the world, but Pius was deaf to all pleas to return the child to his parents. Owen Chadwick summarizes not only the reaction of contemporaries to the event, but what must be the sentiment of any ordinary person when he says, "Even today it is hard to read with equanimity the curial defenses of what was done: a State stealing a little boy from his mother, persecution of the Jews—the rights of the family and the rights of humanity."[39] Without intending to do so and undoubtedly from his own personal theological commitment to protecting the precious soul of the child as he saw it, the pope's involvement drew the church into the widest possible disrepute at the popular level. It confirmed the popular judgment that Papal Italy was in need of moral, social, economic, and political redemption. Duffy writes of the Mortara affair as it played out at the everyday level: "[Pius] made a pet of Edgardo, escorting him into public audiences, playing hide and seek with him under his cloak." The child was never returned to his parents, eventually became a priest, and lived into the 1930s. As a Catholic priest, Edgardo was known as Fr. Pio Maria Mortara. His autobiography was edited by the Italian religious journalist Vittorio Messori and published in English in 2017, and nowhere in it is Fr. Pio critical of what took place.[40] Not only that, but he writes of his gratitude for his vocation as a Catholic priest. All of that is very fine and well, but the issue of the kidnapping is still very problematic.

Church historian Eamon Duffy continues: "His case was both a human tragedy and a demonstration of the gulf which had opened up between the thought world of the papacy, and the secular, liberal values which were now the moral currency of Europe, even for many Catholics."[41] Duffy goes on to say that Pius himself was not particularly anti-Semitic, "except in the tragically general sense in which most Christians were anti-Semitic."[42]

The Syllabus of Errors

Pius distanced himself from every aspect of liberalism in 1864 with the publication of two documents: the encyclical letter *Quanta Cura* and the *Syllabus of Errors*. The immediate catalyst for the encyclical was a Catholic congress held at Malines, Belgium, in August 1863. Some three thousand attended. At this Congress Montalembert, a

---

39. Chadwick, *A History of the Popes*, 131.

40. Messori, *Kidnapped by the Vatican?* The book was reviewed by the American Dominican theologian Romanus Cessario in the journal *First Things*, February 2018, 55–58. In his review Cessario sides with Pope Pius IX and his associates. Cessario's review stirred up something of a controversy in the English-language Catholic press.

41. Duffy, *Saints and Sinners*, 289–90.

42. Duffy, "It Takes All Sorts to Make a Saint," 1181.

French Catholic liberal politician and friend of Félicité de Lammenais whose constant dream was the reconciliation of Catholicism and the modern world, strongly encouraged a reconciliation between the church and democracy. His speech was later published under the title "A Free Church in a Free State." In his speech Montalembert said that too many Catholics associated the church with the pre-French Revolution *ancien régime* and, while the *ancien régime* may have had its merits, it had one major demerit—it was dead. He advocated the church's universal acceptance of democracy.[43] Montalembert's democratic views were not welcomed in Rome. Another congress of Catholic scholars took place in Munich in September of the same year. The organizing figure here was the church historian and theologian Ignaz von Döllinger whose speech at the congress advocated an approach to history that was autonomous, advocating historical-critical methodologies and not subject to ecclesiastical censure. Pius's Secretary of State, Cardinal Antonelli, rebuked both Montalembert and the archbishop of Malines in 1864, and sent a papal brief to the archbishop of Munich which did not condemn Döllinger as such but insisted that all historical research should be vetted by church authority. In December of the same year, the encyclical *Quanta Cura* was published along with *The Syllabus of Errors*, a list of eighty condemned propositions based on the pope's previous statements and allocutions amounting to a comprehensive condemnation of liberalism. While the immediate context for the *Syllabus* reflected mainly the problems that Pius perceived throughout Italy, and especially in Piedmont, it was seen at large as a condemnation of modernity. This is what historian Paul Collins has to say about it: "The problem was that listing all these 'errors' gave the impression of a complete rejection of the contemporary world. It was an ill-conceived attempt to assert papal heart power by ranting at the world, and it achieved nothing but to alienate the papacy from contemporary culture."[44]

The idea of a comprehensive papal attack on modern liberal errors may have originated with one Vincenzo Pecci, bishop of Perugia, ultimately to become Pius's successor as Pope Leo XIII. The Syllabus had ten headings that dealt with a range of propositions: I, Pantheism, Naturalism and Absolute Rationalism (propositions 1–7); II, Moderate Rationalism (8–14); III, Indifferentism and Latitudinarianism (15–18); IV, Socialism, Communism, secret societies, Bible societies, and liberal-clerical societies (citing earlier texts); V, the Church and its Rights (19–38); VI, Civil Society and its relation to the church (39–55); VII, Natural and Christian Ethics (56–64); VIII, Christian Marriage (65–74); IX, the Temporal Power of the Pope (75–76); X, Modern Liberalism (77–80). Proposition 77 in *The Syllabus* denied that non-Catholics should be free to practice their religion. Proposition 80 condemned the idea that "the Roman Pontiff can and should reconcile himself with progress, liberalism, and recent civilization." To be fair, the attention of *The Syllabus of Errors* immediately stemmed from and was focused on the Italian liberals who were bent on the suppression of the temporal power

43. See Chadwick, *A History of the Popes 1830–1914*, 170–72.
44. Collins, *Absolute Power*, 38.

of the papacy and the unification of Italy. It had in mind the policies of the Piedmontese government against the church. However, it did not sound like that publicly. Taken as a whole and without contextual nuance, "it seemed that the Pope had declared war on modern society in all its aspects."[45] Virtually there was nothing good about modernity and it had to be condemned as incompatible with the church.

Alec Vidler maintains, and rightly, that it is only fair to admit that Pius near the end of his life recognized his limitations in this regard and confessed: "I hope my successor will be as much attached to the church as I have been and will have as keen a desire to do good: my system and my policies have had their day, but I am too old to change my course; that will be the task of my successor."[46]

Ultramontanism

In an excellent series of essays devoted to ultramontanism, church historian Jeffrey von Arx, SJ, provides us with a fine segue into the phenomenon in his "Introduction":

> Ultramontanism is a blind spot . . . in our understanding of the religious history of the Roman Catholic Church in the nineteenth and well into our own century. Whether inside or outside the Roman Catholic community, it is difficult for many intelligent people today to understand the depth of commitment to the ultramontane cause of so many Roman Catholics in the century and a half before Vatican II; sometimes distressing to contemplate its victory in the church; puzzling to discover how much attention and concern the progress of ultramontanism within the church drew, not only from Roman Catholics and politicians in mainly Roman Catholic countries like France, who must deal with the papacy, but also from non-Catholics and even from freethinkers in a country like Great Britain, where, saving Ireland, the Roman Catholic Church did not count for much.[47]

Literally the term "ultramontanism" means "beyond the mountains," the mountains being the Alps beyond which lay Italy and Rome, and refers to an interpretation of the Christian reality that is totally centered on the papacy. It is a point of view in which the bishops of the Catholic world "are relegated to a subordinate level while everything centers on the Pope."[48] In today's parlance, ultramontanism has probably become papal-centrism, an excessive theological and especially ecclesiological centering on the pope.

Pius IX's reign witnessed the rapid development and perhaps the climax of ultramontanism leading Alec Vidler to comment, "The mystique about the Holy Father,

45. Vidler, *The Church in an Age of Revolution*, 151.

46. Cited in Vidler, *The Church in an Age of Revolution*, 153.

47. Arx, SJ, "Introduction," 1–2.

48. Heft, SM, "From the Pope to the Bishops: Episcopal Authority from Vatican I to Vatican II." In *The Papacy and the Church in the United States*, edited by Bernard Cooke, 59.

and what often seems an unwholesome adulation of his person, dates from Pius IX."[49] In some quarters the pope was spoken of as "the vice-God of humanity." One French ultramontane bishop maintained that the pope was the continuation of the incarnate Word. The Jesuit review *Civilta Catolica* put it about that when the pope meditated, God was thinking in him. Extreme language, indeed. At the popular level and as a result of photography, Catholics all over the world had pictures of Pius in their homes, and steamships and railways enabled relatively easy frequent pilgrimage to Rome. Pilgrims streamed to Rome. Add to this the emergence of foreign correspondents for national newspapers throughout the world, and Pius became, in the words of Jesuit historian John W. O'Malley, "the first papal mega-star."[50] Needless to say, not all Catholics were ultramontane in outlook. John Henry Newman was certainly opposed to ultramontanism. Speaking of an excessive devotion to the person of the pope, the archbishop of Rheims stated that it was "an idolatry of the papacy."[51]

From the perspective of ultramontanism, anything less than a complete identification with and endorsement of the pope was less than Catholic and was immediately suspect. This is how Eamon Duffy describes ultramontanism in the church of Pius IX: "These ultramontanists saw the church as a monolithic and solitary beacon in a dark and ever-darkening world. It was an institution in which obedience was prized above all virtues and which insisted that its children—a telling epithet for adult believers—must march in step to the beat of the Vatican drum. This was a vision of the church centered above all not merely on the office but on the person of the pope."[52] Let us admit, as indeed we must, that Duffy's ecclesial description does not and cannot take into careful consideration all the differences of nuance and position in Pius IX's church. Yet, Duffy has his finger quite firmly on the ecclesial pulse here. There was little favor in Pius's church for those who did not share this ultramontane mindset.

Though the ultramontane perspective at Vatican I will be examined in more detail later in the chapter on the First Vatican Council, suffice it to say that Pius encouraged this point of view. He threatened bishops who were inclined to disagree with the definition of papal infallibility, and he raised to the episcopate men who were strongly ultramontane, in alignment with his own sympathies. One historian captures the mood in these words: "[Pius] used the apostolic nuncios as watchdogs to keep the bishops in line; recalcitrants were sometimes invited to a personal audience, which could be stormy."[53] This was also the time when national seminaries in Rome were encouraged, where young and impressionable seminarians could drink

49. Vidler, *The Church in an Age of Revolution,* 153.

50. O'Malley, "The Beatification of Pius IX," 8; see also Chadwick, *A History of the Popes 1830– 1914,* 113.

51. Vidler, *The Church in an Age of Revolution,* 154.

52. Duffy, "The Age of Pio Nono: The Age of Paul Cullen," 47.

53. Bokenkotter, *A Concise History of the Catholic Church,* 319.

in this Roman ultramontane spirit in the holy city itself and take it back to their home countries and dioceses.

In similar fashion, in April 1870 while the First Vatican Council was in session, Pius summoned the premier Vatican archivist Augustin Theiner, an Oratorian priest and a well-respected scholar, and charged him with providing documents to the anti-infallibilists, specifically the English Catholic historian Lord Acton. Pius considered anti-infallibilists his personal enemies and enemies of the church. In August of the same year Theiner was required to give up his keys to the Vatican archives. Although he was not actually dismissed and retained his title of prefect of the archives, he continued to work under the same difficult conditions as any ordinary scholar using the data of the archives for research.[54]

The Papacy and the Episcopate

Pius introduced new hierarchies into England in 1850 and into the Netherlands in 1853. During his pontificate he created two hundred new bishoprics or apostolic vicariates. Duffy notes the consequence when he says that "All this represented a massive growth of papal involvement and papal control in the local churches."[55] Bishops in the expanding church in the United States were appointed in Rome and developed a strong Rome-centeredness. Under Pius, missionary work, which he first encountered in 1823–1825 when he was in Chile and Peru, expanded throughout the world. The episcopate had been firmly integrated with the papacy theologically, but now that integration had a new, more intense and structured dimension. Bishops appointed by Pius naturally felt a personally close bond with the pope, and it can certainly be argued that while this close bond was of great value to Catholics worldwide, there was also something of a downside. If not entirely forgotten, the importance of the episcopate in its own right, so to speak, tended to fall into abeyance.

Pope Pius IX and Popular Devotion

When one looks at the latter half of the nineteenth-century Catholic Church, one recognizes that popular devotions were taking off throughout Europe. "A passion for the Middle Ages spread among romantic Catholics, who indulged in processions and pilgrimages, the veneration of relics and new devotions to Our Lady and the saints. Canonizations became more frequent during the nineteenth century and they were often carried out with impressive ceremonial. Pius IX himself took a personal interest in the rapidly expanding devotion to St. Joseph who was proclaimed patron of the universal

---

54. Chadwick, *Catholicism and History*, 63–66. Chadwick's book offers many examples of Theiner's scholarly reputation. Eamon Duffy suggests mistakenly that Theiner was actually dismissed in his article, "It Takes All Sorts to Make a Saint," 1181.

55. Duffy, *Saints and Sinners*, 304.

church in 1870."[56] Church historian Thomas Bokenkotter writes: "Pius IX's real success was with the interior renewal of the church, and he deserves credit for the magnificent leadership he gave in deepening a sense of piety and spirituality."[57]

No account of Pius would be complete if it did not turn attention to his promotion of devotion to the Sacred Heart and to the Blessed Virgin Mary. In 1856 Pius extended the feast of the Sacred Heart to the universal church. "Through these devotions, through declaring Francis de Sales a doctor of the church and through other means, Pius helped turn piety in a more heartfelt direction."[58] Some find it all too easy to pour scorn on such devotions as the Sacred Heart of Christ. Although much of the popular and widespread artwork associated with this devotion may be judged to be of a very poor quality, the very notion of the heart as a symbol of human love and commitment becomes a very powerful focus for expressing the divine love, something given particular emphasis, for example, by the twentieth-century Catholic theologian Karl Rahner.[59]

Not only piety but also the religious institutions of the church flourished during Pius's reign. During this time, the Society of Jesus almost doubled its membership, as did many other religious orders, for example, the Sulpicians, the Passionists, the Redemptorists, the Franciscans, and the Dominicans. There were new foundations too: the Blessed Sacrament Fathers, the so-called White Fathers, and the Society of the Divine Word, the latter two foundations having an especially missionary commitment, something favored by the pope.

The Dogma of the Immaculate Conception

The demands for the definition of the dogma of the Immaculate Conception of our Lady were being received in Rome long before Pius IX. The demand had been heard increasingly in France since 1830, the year of the vision of our Lady to St. Catherine Labouré in the Rue du Bac, Paris. As a result of St. Catherine's experiences the cult of the Miraculous Medal very quickly gained ground. The medal was first issued in 1832, and on one side of the medal there was an image of Mary with the inscription, "O Mary, conceived without sin, pray for us who have recourse to thee." In 1847, Giovanni Perrone, the leading theologian of the Roman schools and a Jesuit, published a thesis to show that the doctrine of the Immaculate Conception could be defined. Pius appointed a commission to study the question, including another Jesuit theologian Carlo Passaglia. From exile in Gaeta in 1849, Pius issued the encyclical *Ubi Primum*, asking the advice and prayers of the worldwide episcopate.

---

56. Holmes, *The Triumph of the Holy See*, 138–39.

57. Bokenkotter, *A Concise History of the Catholic Church*, 327.

58. John W. O'Malley, "The Beatification of Pius IX," 8. See also Collins, *Absolute Power*, 33–34.

59. Consider, for example, the retrieval of this devotion by Karl Rahner, SJ, "Devotion to the Sacred Heart Today," especially 127–28. See also Callahan, *Karl Rahner's Spirituality of the Pierced Heart*.

Of some six hundred episcopal replies, nine-tenths were entirely supportive of the dogma. The definition was drawn up by Passaglia and Perrone, creating the popular but false impression that it was an invention of the Jesuits. To offset this criticism, Pius invited a number of bishops at the last moment to modify the text of the definition. "We must accept this humiliation," he is reported to have said, "so that it won't be said that everything depended upon the Jesuits."[60]

The dogma of the Immaculate Conception was proclaimed on December 8, 1854. The proclamation of this dogma was "an innovation of the first-order, something no pope had ever done before."[61] Although the doctrine was warmly received by most Catholics and reflected popular Marian sentiment that had been growing and developing for centuries, there were those who did not accept it. One French priest, arguably mentally disturbed, who preached against the doctrine after the formal definition was suspended by the archbishop of Paris, Marie Dominique Auguste Sibour. The priest then stabbed the archbishop to death during a procession in a Paris church. Although Pius was in many ways following the movement of popular devotion in the proclamation of the Immaculate Conception, Owen Chadwick accurately states, "No previous Pope in eighteen centuries had made a definition of doctrine quite like this."[62] Needless to say, this development, allied to the growing ultramontanism, the increasing personal loyalty of so many bishops to the person of the pope, and the general and popular awareness of the pope among Catholics, contributed to a Catholic super-star view of the papacy that has not been entirely healthy.

Conclusion

Pope Pius IX died on February 7, 1878, the longest pontificate in the history of the church. With him from December 22 until his death was Henry Edward Manning, the ultramontane archbishop of Westminster, who had stalwartly supported the pope since he first met him and asked his blessing as an Anglican Dean visiting Rome so many years before. Just one month before Pius's death, King Victor Emmanuel II died in the Quirinal Palace, about a mile away from the Vatican. Strictly speaking, the king had been excommunicated for the role he had played in what was known as "the spoliation of the church." Once Pius knew that the king was dying, he "quietly allowed the King's chaplain to absolve him on his deathbed of the excommunication. . . . And Victor Emmanuel II, 'the Father of his Country,' died as a Catholic reconciled to the church."[63] Three years later when Pius's body was transferred to the Basilica of St. Lawrence-outside-the-walls in 1881, it was done at night because of

60. Hales, *Pio Nono,* 148.
61. O'Malley, *A History of the Popes,* 246.
62. Chadwick, *A History of the Popes, 1830–1914,* 121.
63. O'Malley, SJ, *A History of the Popes,* 252.

the anticlericalism raging in the city. Even so it was unpleasant and the Roman mob threw mud from the Tiber at the coffin.

The entire strategy of Pius's pontificate left its impress on the church for a century, a point well made by Eamon Duffy: "Pius IX's papacy helped lock the Catholic Church into a confrontation with the modern world from which it did not recover until the Second Vatican Council, and not entirely then."[64] While Pope Leo XIII and others attempted a friendlier and somewhat more open attitude to the modern world, according to Alec Vidler, "there was no substantial change in the authoritarian pattern which [Pius] had canonized until the dramatic reign of John XXIII."[65] The papacy became authoritarian in style, and the church at large became defensive and generally hostile to the modern world.

64. Duffy, *Ten Popes Who Shook the World*, 101. Historian O'Connell, *Critics on Trial*, 24, writes: "Pius IX's inability to differentiate among the diverse currents of thought that swirled through the nineteenth century was his greatest weakness. He never grasped, for example, the import of the profound changes European society underwent during his lifetime, when the old agricultural economy gave way to an industrialized system dominated by an aggressive middle-class and a vast urban proletariat, and when monarchies had to surrender their immemorial powers to more or less liberal and representative regimes."

65. Vidler, *The Church in an Age of Revolution*, 156.

3

Vatican I, 1869–70

Every Council is a complex and unpredictable event whose consequences run far beyond the substance of its formal decisions and decrees. No human construct is timeless, and neither an ecumenical Council of the Catholic Church, nor even that church itself, stands above the slippage, flux, and confusion of the tide of history, which carries us toward a future we cannot predict, and do not control.

—EAMON DUFFY[1]

We stand at a distance of just a hundred and twenty years from the first Vatican Council. Not so much the opening of the archives, as the healing perspective of time, has enabled students to perceive that greatest controversy of modern Christian history in more judicious and less partisan frames of mind. The infighting seems now as irrelevant and as wearisome as the infighting over the Council of Florence or the Council of Constance.

—OWEN CHADWICK[2]

Introduction

IT IS QUITE SIMPLY impossible to understand the history of the Catholic Church in the twentieth century and now into the twenty-first century without some appreciation of the First Vatican Council (1869–70). What led up to the council, what took place during its deliberations, and what happened after its premature closing in 1870 continued to have an enormous impact over the next one hundred years and more. As John W. O'Malley, the very respected Catholic Church historian, has it, "The definitions of primacy and infallibility at Vatican I provided the momentum for the making of the ultramontane church of contemporary Roman Catholicism."[3] Moving on to the quota-

1. Duffy, "The Staying Power of Christianity," 70.
2. Chadwick, *The Spirit of the Oxford Movement*, 311.
3. O'Malley, *Vatican I: The Council and the Making of the Ultramontane Church*, 242.

tions that open this chapter from church historian Eamon Duffy and Duffy's doctoral supervisor Owen Chadwick they could not be more accurate. Beginning with Duffy, the dense and detailed, messy and complex historical situation of the church must be acknowledged again and again. Fresh light is thrown on every angle of the past as historians continue their studies. Going on to Owen Chadwick, he is right about the healing perspective of time and the irrelevance of the infighting surrounding the first Vatican Council. Quite simply everything has changed with Vatican II (1962–65) and indeed the church was in the process of change before it.

There has been an enormous change of consciousness about all social and ecclesiastical structures throughout the world. Probably for the first time the peoples of the world were beginning to realize that they had certain inalienable rights about their political governance—this is part of the "liberalism" mentioned in the first chapter. The Catholic Church could not expect to be immune from this growing realization. Add to this the fact that the last reforming council of the church before Vatican I had been the Council of Trent (1545–63), and before that the Council of Constance (1414–18). "From [the Council of Constance] forward the relationship of Pope to Council became uneasy, to the point that at times the popes feared councils as if they were avenging angels."[4] Constance had deposed three claimants to the papacy and then proceeded to elect a new pope, Martin V. Conciliarism—the doctrine that supreme authority in the church lies with a council—now became an issue, and an issue that never went away entirely. Trent had met to respond to some of the issues of the Protestant Reformation in the sixteenth century. In a rapidly changing world after the French Revolution, the time was ripe for a new council.

"Vatican I was the Catholic answer to the *many* revolutions affecting the nineteenth century."[5] Among these revolutions we may count not only the revolutionary Enlightenment, French Revolution, but also the American Revolution, the Industrial Revolution, and the Scientific Revolution. Each in its own fashion created or was seen to cause problems for the church, and Vatican Council I was the Catholic answer to these problems. There are those who interpret Vatican I with such a hermeneutic of suspicion that it seems to be an expression of "stifling despotism" on the part of Pius IX and his cronies, "trying to get away with the dogma of papal infallibility."[6] While there is a grain of truth in that perception of the council in that the pope and his close allies were keen on having the dogma proclaimed, it is hardly adequate. It certainly does not take into account the many revolutions noted above, with the exception of the American Revolution all European issues and challenges. "[Vatican I's] plans, debates and documents reflected preoccupation with Europe's nineteenth-century problems: the impact of the Enlightenment and French Revolution, the influence of Kant and Hegel, nineteenth century continental liberalism. The Italian *Risorgimento*

4. O'Malley, *Vatican I: The Council and the Making of the Ultramontane Church*, 4.

5. Fitzer, *Romance and the Rock*, 5.

6. Hales, *Pio Nono*, 293.

was quite literally at the gates of Rome. A thousand years of papal sovereign rule in central Italy were in their final twelve months. Since Pius VII's time, a succession of popes had set official Catholicism's face squarely against the political, social, and intellectual temper of the times. The Vatican Council was designed by Pius IX to set the seal on that opposition."[7] As early as 1864 Pope Pius IX wished to call an ecumenical council, and finally in June 1868 this wish was announced publicly in the papal bull *Aeterni Patris*.[8] There had been no general church council since the Council of Trent in the sixteenth century and for Pius never was a council more necessary than at this time. The bull of convocation included such matters as "clerical life and its needs, providing new safeguards for Christian marriage and the Christian education of youth, taking up in this new age the ancient problems of the relations of church and state and providing appropriate guidance, so as to promote peace and prosperity in the national life everywhere."[9]

On June 29, 1868 Pope Pius IX promulgated the bull *Aeterni Patris* fixing the date for the opening of the council the next year. It seems to have been the case that the pope at least in the beginning did not have a very clear and precise program for the upcoming council. He would have been aware of the central role of councils in the history of the church, and undoubtedly "he hoped that the new Council would strengthen the church so it could better cope with the numerous attacks being made upon it."[10] The council opened on December 8, 1869, and suspended its sessions on September 1, 1870. About eight hundred cardinals, patriarchs, archbishops, bishops, abbots, and religious superiors participated, and it is estimated that about 80,000 people were tightly packed into the Basilica of St. Peter's for the opening event. Poorer bishops and vicars apostolic from missionary territories, many of whom had been created by the pope, were lodged at Pius's own expense in Rome. This gave rise to his witty remark, appreciated only in Italian, "I don't know whether the Pope will emerge from this Council fallible or infallible [*fallibile od infallibile*], but it is certain that he will be bankrupt [*fallito*]."[11]

This was the first general council of the church in which bishops assembled in Rome from every continent. It must be recalled that at the Council of Trent in the sixteenth century the world was still in the process of being opened up geographically. It is also interesting and of note that the presence and participation of English-speaking bishops in Vatican I was substantive, some one hundred and twenty taking part.[12] Historical generalizations are seldom very accurate, but in terms of an overview we may say that there were two basic groups at the council—the ultramontanist group, desirous

7. Hennessey, *American Catholics*, 168.

8. Coppa, *Cardinal Giacomo Antonelli and Papal Politics in European Affairs*, 149.

9. Hughes, *The Church in Crisis*, 299, slightly adapted.

10. Coppa, *Pope Pius IX*, 156–57.

11. Hales, *Pio Nono*, 295.

12. Hales, *Pio Nono*, 296.

of supreme authority in the church for the pope and of total Catholic allegiance to that authority, and the liberal group, who wished to promote a closer relationship between the church and modernity, "although, to be fair, the variety of positions along the ideological spectrum dispute the idea of a monolithic 'left' or 'right.'"[13]

Even a cursory awareness of the standard English language histories of Vatican I indicates some of the major problems.[14] These ranged from such practical issues as the dissemination of texts in good time for them to be read and digested by the bishops, acoustics in St. Peter's Basilica, the tedium of debate around procedural protocols, groups of bishops meeting along party lines, and so forth. Above all there was the question of papal infallibility which was always understood to be there, but did not formally surface on the council floor for several months.

Two doctrinal constitutions were promulgated, *Dei Filius* (April 24, 1870), dealing with reason and faith, and *Pastor Aeternus* (July 18, 1870), defining the primacy and infallibility of the pope. Thirty-five theologians were invited from outside Italy. Most of them were ultramontane in outlook, but Ignaz von Döllinger and John Henry Newman, both of whom were invited, were far from ultramontane. In point of fact, Döllinger was vetoed by the archbishop of Munich, Cardinal Reisach, and Newman did not accept the invitation for a number of reasons: his health, his dislike of ecclesiastical politics, and the fact that he was working on his book *An Essay in Aid of a Grammar of Assent*. While he was at work on his book, his fellow priest and former friend the very ultramontane Henry Edward Manning was hard at work promoting a conciliar definition of papal infallibility, and a very wide-ranging conciliar definition at that. Manning held an extreme view of papal infallibility.

Henry Edward Manning (1808–92)

No account of Vatican I especially for Anglophone readers could be adequate without some account of the ultramontane bishop, Henry Edward Manning. Manning is often contrasted with Newman and few have penned this contrast in such an interesting way as Owen Chadwick. "Two Oxford men, two Anglican clergymen; both converted to the Roman Catholic Church during the wave of 1843–1851; and then going their separate ways, the one to public affairs, hierarchy, power, the forefront of the Catholic fight, the purple, place, papal favor, and grandeur; the other to a monk's cell, retreating from the fight, solitary and unpretentious, a critic of hierarchy, oppressed by hierarchy, suspect to Rome, shabby in his cassock, as underground as possible;

13. Bellitto, *The General Councils*, 117.

14. For a detailed account of the council, its background, its circumstances, and its proceedings one could not do better than consult John W. O'Malley, *Vatican I: The Council and the Making of the Ultramontane Church*. See also: Cuthbert Butler, *The Vatican Council, 1869–1870*; Hennessey, *The First Council of the Vatican, the American Experience*; O'Gara, *Triumph in Defeat: Infallibility, Vatican I, and the French Minority Bishops*. Butler's and Hennessey's volumes are particularly valuable because they are laced with citations from correspondence from the participants at the council.

quiet meditator versus high ecclesiastic and politician."[15] Chadwick's contrast may be somewhat overdrawn, but it is not inaccurate. Henry Edward Manning has not been served well by his early biographers, Lytton Strachey and Edmund Sheridan Purcell. The former attacks him most unjustly in his *Eminent Victorians*, where he is presented as "a relentless power-seeker flourishing in an age of humbug."[16] Purcell's biography, while not as acid as Strachey's portrait, sets out to show Manning in a most unfavorable light. The picture painted here is hopefully more balanced and has to do largely with Manning as a propagandist for papal infallibility especially at Vatican I. But first, some details of his life are necessary.

The youngest son of William Manning, a member of Parliament, Henry Edward Manning was educated at Harrow. Thomas Bokenkotter offers a summary description of those secondary schooling years: "He spent his teenage years at Harrow, a public school noted for its brutal discipline, where little attention was given to religion and much to sports, at which he proved to be quite adept. The same talent no doubt showed up in his accuracy at stone-throwing in the pitched battles the boys fought with the local townsfolk. . . . The qualities that were later to be so prominent in his character soon became apparent: a steely determination to achieve a goal, self-confidence and self-control, and the ability to make the most of his talents and opportunities."[17] This seems a very fair representation of Manning in these early years. Following his high school years at Harrow he went up to Oxford and although not entirely expected, he gained a first in classics at Balliol College Oxford. However, his father fell into bankruptcy and Manning's circumstances changed very quickly. His hope to move into politics collapsed.

Although students of Manning sometimes debate his motives, in 1832, he decided to seek ordination in the Church of England, and he was elected to a fellowship at Merton College Oxford. Manning plunged himself into reading what he called "acres of Anglican writers," from the Caroline divines with their high church ecclesiology and sacramental theology, to more liberal Protestant authors. At this time he dined on a number of occasions with the up-and-coming John Henry Newman of Oriel College Oxford, and began to confront what one scholar has called "the doctrinal chaos in Anglicanism."[18]

The following year, 1833, he went as curate to John Sargent, rector of Lavington. He was moving more and more closely to the high church theology of the Tractarians of the Oxford Movement, and his developing high-church views are well summarized by Thomas Bokenkotter in these words: "In 1834 he was converted to belief

---

15. Chadwick, "Newman and the Historians," 158.

16. Strachey, *Eminent Victorians* (1918). The book has been reprinted many times. The quotation describing Manning is from Michael Holroyd, cited in Sheridan Gilley, "New Light on an Old Scandal: Purcell's Life of Cardinal Manning," 166.

17. Bokenkotter, *Church and Revolution*, 174–75.

18. Bokenkotter, *Church and Revolution*, 177.

in the real presence of Jesus in the consecrated bread and wine, and established daily Matins and Evensong in his parish."[19] Though he did not yet know it, Manning was becoming more and more Roman, and given his personality, upbringing and circumstances, perhaps even more Roman than the Romans themselves. In May 1833 he succeeded Sargent as rector, and later in that year he married Caroline, Sargent's daughter, but she died very suddenly in 1837. He told Newman at the time: "All I can do now is keep at work. There is a sort of rush into my mind when unoccupied I can hardly bear."[20] Although he was never at this time committed to celibacy in the way that Newman was, he never sought someone to replace his beloved Caroline. His Rome-ward tendencies continued to develop in April 1838 when he made the first of his twenty-two trips to Rome.

In 1841 Manning became Archdeacon of Chichester. Though originally Evangelical in his theological orientation, he was now firmly allied with the high-church Tractarians and authored No. 78 in the *Tracts for the Times*.[21] A recent biographer has put the case persuasively that Manning was in terms of theology an autodidact. "Theologically, the Anglican Manning was very much a self-taught man. . . . He had no teacher to direct his steps, nor did he look for one. His ideas were not shaped in the hotbed of intellectual intercourse that was Tractarian Oxford; rather, they germinated and grew up in Lavington, the fruit of study and silent contemplation."[22] Of course he was informed by the theology of the Tractarians, but due to his pastoral concerns and remoteness from the center in Oxford he was not involved in the day-to-day cut and thrust of theological exchange. He was certainly influenced by John Henry Newman's *Essay on the Development of Christian Doctrine* of 1845, but even having read it and having been largely convinced by its argument in favor of Rome he still had to make his own way, and that was gradual.[23] Newman wrote to Manning: "I think the Church of Rome the Catholic Church, and ours not part of the Catholic Church because not in communion with Rome."[24] After Newman was received into the Catholic Church, Manning wrote to him in a very warm fashion: "Only believe always that I love you. If we may never meet again in life at the same altar, may our

19. Bokenkotter, *Church and Revolution*, 179.

20. Cited in Gray, *Cardinal Manning*, 64.

21. This is what Manning wrote in a letter in 1850 to Samuel Wilberforce, bishop of Oxford who was also Manning's brother-in-law, about his theological-sacramental beliefs in 1833 when he arrived in Lavington: "When I came to Lavington in 1833 I believed, as I always did, in Baptismal Regeneration: I had no view of the Sacrament of the Body and Blood of Christ: and no idea of the Church." This letter is cited from Pereiro, *Cardinal Manning*, 10. It provides some indication of Manning's gradual movement away from evangelicalism to a more Catholic sensibility.

22. Pereiro, *Cardinal Manning*, 329.

23. Pereiro, *Cardinal Manning*, especially 67–74, highlights the contours of Manning's pilgrimage to Rome *vis-à-vis* Newman's *Essay*.

24. Gray, *Cardinal Manning*, 93.

intercessions for each other, day by day, meet in the court of Heaven."[25] He was not always to feel so warmly disposed towards Newman.

After Newman became a Catholic in 1845, a number of Anglicans looked to Manning as a leader of the Oxford Movement, but it was not to be. One of the better-known-Anglican theologians of that time, Frederick Denison Maurice, said of Manning, "His power with the clergy is very great, greater certainly than that of any man living."[26] The straw that broke the camel's back for Manning was undoubtedly the Gorham judgment, in which the Judicial Committee of the Privy Council in England found in favor of an Anglican clergyman, George Gorham, who was refused installation as a vicar because he did not accept the traditional doctrine of baptismal regeneration. Manning was received into the Catholic Church in 1851 in the Jesuit church of Farm St., London, and two months later he was ordained a priest by Archbishop Nicholas Wiseman. In 1857 he was made Provost of the Westminster Metropolitan Chapter, and he succeeded Wiseman as archbishop of Westminster in 1865. A rapid rise through the ecclesiastical ranks!

"Converts such as Newman and Manning who came barging into the church at full tilt were at odds with [the traditional Catholic] mentality in many ways, and the old Catholics resented their attitude of intellectual superiority, their enthusiasm for things Roman, and their ostentatious piety. 'Where old English priests had eschewed even black coats, convert priests gloried in sporting Roman collars and in parading in cassocks and birettas.'"[27] Manning and Newman make an interesting contrast, captured nicely by Sheridan Gilley: "Manning's private and personal influence in his way and in his own day was just as great as Newman's, but as it belonged to the realm of deeds and to the spoken rather than the written word, so it died with those who have known him, whereas heart still speaks to heart wherever Newman finds readers."[28] There is something in this careful judgment about the influence of both men. Manning was very definitely a man of action, while Newman turned the carefully crafted word. Manning was a man of the people, one who constantly thought about and protested about the social evils of his times, in the manner of Charles Dickens the novelist and Frederick Denison Maurice the Anglican theologian.[29]

Manning, however, came to distrust Newman and even to think of him as dangerous, as one who exemplified a somewhat independent English Catholicism with

25. Gray, *Cardinal Manning*, 106.

26. Cited in Gray, *Cardinal Manning*, 129.

27. Bokenkotter, *Church and Revolution*, 188.

28. Gilley, "Newman and the Convert Mind," 8.

29. See McClelland, *Cardinal Manning, His Public Life and Influence 1865–92*, 214. McClelland's book thoroughly documents Manning's concern for the poor through government action as well as charitable concern, both as an Anglican and then later as a Catholic bishop. These concerns long anticipated his participation in the settlement of the London Strike of 1889, for which he is well known, and it is alleged influenced Pope Leo XIII in his encyclical *Rerum Novarum*.

an Oxford accent. Newman's Catholicism for Manning was insufficiently certain and bold.[30] Both of them believed in papal infallibility, but while Newman thought the definition was both unnecessary and unwise and might discourage conversion to the Catholic Church, Manning was convinced that far from having an adverse reaction in England, such a definition would bring Anglicans flocking over to Rome. What Manning wanted was "downright, masculine, and decided Catholics—*more* Roman than Rome, and more Ultramontane than the Pope himself."[31] For Manning, "Ultramontanism is Catholic Christianity."[32] As a man of action, Manning set himself wholeheartedly to do all in his power to achieve the highest expression of his ultramontanism through his promotion of the definition of papal infallibility. When all is said and done, it makes a great deal of sense. Manning had left the Church of England at considerable cost to himself because of what he saw as a lack of doctrinal and traditional orthodoxy expressed in an authoritative and hierarchical structure, most obviously in evidence in the Gorham Judgment. "He was convinced that the papacy was the only bulwark against the faith-destroying forces of rationalism and atheism."[33]

Before returning to the Vatican Council, we get perhaps another insight into Manning by recalling that he shared a platform with none other than John Henry Newman's brother, Francis Newman. On October 22, 1867, at a meeting in the Manchester Free Trade Hall, Francis Newman and Archbishop Manning found themselves sharing similar views on the social problems caused by alcohol. Manning knew the problems alcohol caused, not least among his large and growing Irish immigrant flock in London, and so he allied himself with the tirade of some fervent Protestants, including Francis Newman, "against the enormous success of the trade in intoxicating drink." When Francis Newman wrote to his brother John about his enthusiasm for Manning on this issue, thinking this might be something both brothers shared in common, John replied: "As to what you tell me of Archbishop Manning, I have heard that some also of our Irish bishops think that too many drink-shops are licensed. As for me, I do not know whether we have too many or too few."[34] This was not Francis's hoped for reply. Newman knew about drink and its problems. After all, he lived in industrial Birmingham, and his first church in that sprawling industrial conurbation was in a former gin distillery.

---

30. Sheridan Gilley makes the point that Manning's biographer, Edmund Purcell, in a biographical sketch of Newman in 1881 praised Newman to the skies and denigrated his enemies, "among them by implication Manning." See Sheridan Gilley, "New Light on an Old Scandal," 170. Gilley goes on to say that this "attempt to use Newman as an instrument against Manning was one which was to recur."

31. Cited in Hastings, *A History of English Christianity 1920–1990*, 147.

32. Pereiro, *Cardinal Manning*, 255.

33. Bokenkotter, *Church and Revolution*, 191.

34. Cited in Willey, *More Nineteenth*, 47.

Ignaz von Döllinger and Lord Acton

Two opponents of the definition of papal infallibility were the Bavarian priest and church historian, Ignaz von Döllinger (1799–1890) and the English lay Catholic historian Lord Acton (1834–1902). Döllinger had been ordained priest in 1822 and from 1826 until 1873 he was professor of church history at Munich. Newman met him in the company of Ambrose St. John in the Chapel Royal at Munich *en route* back to England from Rome late in 1847. Earlier in life Döllinger leaned in an ultramontane direction, but through personal research and friendship—especially with John Henry Newman and Lord Acton—he distanced himself from ultramontanism, and was fundamentally opposed to the definition of papal infallibility which was being argued for at Vatican I in 1870. As Owen Chadwick has it, "He was a church historian who believed that history disproved the infallibility of the Pope."[35] The anonymous author of the article on Döllinger in *The Oxford Dictionary of the Christian Church* ends his contribution with these words: "His capacity for work was almost limitless and his personal life simple. He was also a great teacher."[36] It is an accurate description not only of the man himself, but also of his best-known pupil the Englishman, Lord Acton.

John Emerich Edward Dalberg Acton was born at Naples. His father died when he was only one, and his mother saw to his education first at Paris with the somewhat Gallican Abbé Dupanloup who was later to become bishop of Orleans and an important anti-infallibilist player at Vatican I, and then at Oscott College, Birmingham, where he was taught by Nicholas Wiseman who would become cardinal-archbishop of Westminster, and then at Munich as a pupil of Döllinger. While a professor of canon law and church history at the University of Munich, Döllinger enhanced his income by taking in pupil-boarders of whom Acton, arriving in 1850, was the most famous. Döllinger was to be his master-teacher. "Acton found the father he had never known, and Döllinger discovered the son whom as a celibate priest he could not beget."[37] Summarizing the relationship between the two men historian Thomas Howard writes as follows: "Polyglots both, men of serious faith and immense learning, the two kept alive their friendship—albeit not without some tensions and differences of opinion—through correspondence and visits until Döllinger's death in 1890."[38]

Döllinger became involved in German politics and for a while lost his post at the University of Munich. When he was reinstated, he gave over his time more strictly for the study of theology and church history. One fine example of his historical research was his 1853 book *Hippolytus and Kallistus*. The work came about as a result of the discovery in 1842 of a manuscript entitled "Philosophumena." Döllinger weighed carefully the claims for authorship and came down on the side of the third-century

---

35. Chadwick, *A History of the Popes 1830–1914*, 192.

36. Cross and Livingstone, ed., *The Oxford Dictionary of the Christian Church*, 416.

37. Chadwick, *Acton and History*, 4.

38. Howard, *The Pope and the Professor*, 92.

Roman presbyter Hippolytus who had found himself at odds with Pope Zephyrinus (198–217) and Pope Callistus (217–222). When the monograph came to print Döllinger found his reputation further enhanced and underscored because of his evenhanded historical methodology. Other historical and theological works flowed from his pen and his growing reputation found him in contact and in correspondence with scholars and leaders in other Christian traditions, for example, Edward B. Pusey (Regius Professor of Hebrew) of Oxford, Cardinal Nicholas Wiseman of Westminster, William Gladstone, the English prime minister, and Alfred Plummer, an Anglican theologian and historian.

Not long after Montalembert spoke at the Malines Conference in 1863, Döllinger gave a more powerful speech at a congress of Catholic theologians at Munich, "The Past and Present of Catholic Theology." In this speech he set out his understanding of historical theology, underscoring the importance of academic freedom for Catholic scholars researching the past. Döllinger argued that Catholic theology must be transformed by an essentially historical approach, especially as this was developing in German universities. Acton shared his teacher's perspective, but a position that seemingly advocated history over the timelessness of Catholic dogma was bound to provoke a negative reaction from Rome. That negative reaction came in the form of a Papal Brief, *Tuas Libenter*, to the archbishop of Munich in December 1863, but it was not published until March of the following year. The "Munich Brief," as it has come to be known, condemned any kind of scholarly research by Catholics that seemed to sit loosely to ecclesiastical authority. While Döllinger was not condemned by name, the nature of the theological-historical enterprise as he understood it clearly was. Döllinger's ongoing historical work and his developing ecclesiastical-political awareness made him an ever more steadfast opponent of ultramontanism and so also of the definition of papal infallibility at Vatican I. His opposition to papal infallibility made him reach out to others whom he took to be of a similar mind on the issue and especially John Henry Newman who thought such a declaration inopportune. Döllinger wrote to Newman in March 1870:

> In my opinion, and probably in yours too, the situation of the Catholic Church has not been more dangerous in the last four centuries than it is at present. At such a time the true sons and friends of the church ought to be communing together. . . . Every one of us, who are the theologians of the church, must cast the weight of his testimony, whatever it may be, into the scales of the balance. Your position in the church is such a high one, that silence becomes a snare for thousands. It will be said: *qui tacet, consentit* (he who is silent, consents). And yet it is impossible that you should be of one mind with [Archbishop] Manning . . . among the theologians of Germany, except a few disciples of the Jesuits, there is not one man of some note who does not abhor and deprecate this new dogma of personal infallibility, which is to be forced upon us. Of course I don't pretend to judge the reasons which you may have had to remain

silent up to this moment. But I think the crisis is so near, that those reasons must now have lost their weight. Neutrality in such a case is too near akin to lukewarmness, but if you speak out, then let "the trumpet give a clear and certain sound" and believe such a splendid opportunity to do signal service to the cause of the church will not be offered again.[39]

Newman's response was not what Döllinger had hoped for. Newman was far from naïve about the goings on of church councils in history, and yet at the same time he believed that God was working through them.

Acton too was an outright opponent of ultramontanism and all that went with it. With his formation and historical training under the tutelage of Döllinger, and as a nineteenth-century representative of the English Cisalpine tradition, a man with an enormous range of knowledge, and a defender of liberal views, Acton was strongly opposed to Pope Pius IX's *Syllabus of Errors*. He attacked ultramontanism "as a form of Catholic escapism into the teaching of the church as the sole foundation and test of all certain knowledge."[40]

Lord Acton actually attended Vatican I as a layman, attempting to influence bishops and others against the definition of papal infallibility. "Acton was at the center of the anti-infallibilist activities. Albert du Boys, a confidant of [Bishop] Dupanloup, noted in his memoirs that some fifteen or twenty North American prelates, among them Kenrick (Archbishop of St. Louis) and Connolly (Archbishop of Halifax), frequented Acton's salon and met there with their German counterparts."[41] Acton and his associates were, of course, unsuccessful. Döllinger was excommunicated in 1871 for refusing to accept the decree on infallibility but, while Acton continued to be suspect in ultramontane circles, there was never any excommunication. Suspicion of Acton, while understandable, seems undeserved in this regard. What Acton wanted was a vibrant Catholic intellectual life, a life that was marked by critical scholarship and genuine serious discernment, perhaps especially on the part of the laity. That is a good much to be desired. Newman wanted much the same thing. However, Newman's approach was much less pugnacious than Acton's. "Whereas Newman had a great deal of sympathy with Catholics like Acton, he was repelled by the autocratic and intellectually fearful positions espoused by Manning and by many members of the episcopacy."[42]

Many people regretted the excommunication of Döllinger, including the future Pope Leo XIII, and various efforts were made to effect a reconciliation between him and Rome. A strenuous effort in this regard was made by Sir Peter le Page Renouf (1822–97) and his wife during the 1880s. Both of them had been long time friends and admirers of Döllinger. Renouf was a most distinguished Egyptologist and had

---

39. *Letters and Diaries of John Henry Newman*, 84.

40. Hill, *Lord Acton*, 145.

41. Hennessey, *American Catholics*, 46.

42. Anderson, *The Great Catholic Reformers*, 178.

been engaged by Newman to teach in his Catholic University in Dublin. Their efforts came to nothing not least because Döllinger thought that he would have to renounce his basic historical and theological points of view, and not just his opposition to the papal dogma of infallibility.[43]

Dei Filius

The initial sessions of the Vatican Council were given over to the Dogmatic Constitution *Dei Filius*, which had to do with revelation and faith.[44] The initial *schema*, prepared largely by the Roman theologian Johannes Franzelin, SJ, was judged too long, too technical, and too hostile to the modern world and so it was returned for revision. The revision was undertaken by another Roman theologian, Johannes Kleutgen, SJ, and eventually this was promulgated as the Constitution *Dei Filius* on April 24, 1870.

In the accurate words of Philip Hughes, "The ten pages of text of this Constitution are so closely knit as to defy summary," but a summary must be attempted here.[45] The opening section of the Constitution reiterates Christ's presence to and in the church, guarding and assisting the church into all truth. Chapter 1 is entitled "On God the Creator of All Things." God is distinct from the world and creates not out of necessity, but freely, to manifest his perfection. Chapter 2 is "On Revelation." Its opening sentence reads: "The same holy mother church holds and teaches that God, the source and end of all things, may be known [*cognosci posse*] with certainty from the consideration of created things, by the natural power of human reason . . . ." This is a natural knowledge of God. It is important to be clear what the Constitution actually said—that it is "possible" for natural reason to know God's existence and attributes. It is important to acknowledge what the Constitution did not say. In the words of Gerald McCool, "Although the Constitution declared that natural reason had the ability to know God's existence and attributes, it did not determine whether, in point of fact, natural reason ever did so. . . . The Constitution confined itself to the declaration that natural knowledge of God was possible in principle. It did not affirm that purely natural knowledge of God had ever been achieved in fact."[46] The Constitution goes on to insist that God has made himself known also in a "supernatural way," in the Scriptures and lastly by his Son (Heb 1:1–2). Chapter 3 is "On Faith." Faith accepts what God reveals, and that acceptance is based not on "the natural light of reason" but on "the authority of God himself." Faith is a gift of God. The

43. See Howard, *The Pope and the Professor*, 215.

44. A useful summary may be found in Gerald A. McCool, *Catholic Theology in the Nineteenth Century*, 216–40.

45. Hughes, *The Church in Crisis*, 304. A very thorough account of the process that led to the promulgation of *Dei Filius* may be found in O'Malley, *Vatican I: The Council and the Making of the Ultramontane Church*, 133–79.

46. McCool, *Catholic Theology in the Nineteenth Century*, 219.

chapter also defends the reasonableness of the act of faith, insisting on this against the Fideist tradition of Protestant pietism. The Constitution maintains that "it was God's will that there should be linked to the internal assistance of the Holy Spirit outward indications of his revelation, that is to say divine acts, and first and foremost miracles and prophecies, which clearly demonstrating as they do the omnipotence and infinite knowledge of God, are the most certain signs of revelation and are suited to the understanding of all."[47] The insistence on these outward signs of revelation as well as the internal assistance of the Holy Spirit is undoubtedly responding to those theologians of the nineteenth century who emphasized the interiority of Christian experience over against all external manifestations of revelation, perhaps especially Friedrich Schleiermacher. Chapter 4, finally, is "On Faith and Reason." The conviction of the Constitution is that since God is the source of both our intelligence/reason and revelation/faith, there can be no real disagreement between reason and faith. Rather, faith and reason are mutually supportive.

Pastor Aeternus

At least at the outset, there was no pressure on the council participants to rush through important matters and to steamroll towards the definition of papal infallibility. There was full and, from the comments of the participating bishops, sometimes frustratingly repetitious debate.

The *schema* on the church could have been much finer. The scholar of nineteenth-century theology Michael Himes points out: "The Roman School's incarnational ecclesiology laid the theological groundwork and colored the actual language of *Pastor Aeternus*, but unfortunately neither its patristic richness nor its systematic vision is reflected in the document."[48] The patristic richness of the Roman School of theology owed something to the influence of Tübingen theologian Johann Adam Möhler, but it was not to make its way into the actual text of the document.[49] The document was concerned with papal primacy, and then with papal infallibility. In terms of papal primacy the canon at the end of chapter 3 reads as follows:

> If anyone says that the Roman pontiff has merely an office of supervision or guidance, and not the full and supreme power of jurisdiction over the whole church, and this not only in matters of faith and morals, but also in those which concern the discipline and government of the church dispersed throughout

47. Tanner, ed., *Decrees of the Ecumenical Councils*, 807.

48. Himes, "The Development of Ecclesiology: Modernity to the Twentieth Century," 61.

49. Himes, "The Development of Ecclesiology: Modernity to the Twentieth Century," 59, writes: "Möhler's thought played a role in the ecclesiology of the influential Roman school. The principal figures of the school—Giovanni Perrone (1794–1876) and Carlo Passaglia (1827–1887), their students Johannes Baptist Franzelin (1816–1886) and Clemens Schrader (1820–1875), and Franzelin's and Schrader's student Matthias Joseph Scheeben (1835–1888)—were all, like Möhler, influenced by patristic study and sought to place the treatment of the church within a wider systematic theology."

the world; or that he has only the principal part, but not the absolute fullness of this supreme power, or that this power of his is not ordinary and immediate both over-all and each of the churches and over-all and each of the pastors and faithful: let [them] be anathema.[50]

Few Catholic theologians and historians would have called into question papal primacy in at least broad terms, but this detailed pronouncement is somewhat extreme, in the words of commentator on the council Cuthbert Butler: "Here . . . is a summary of Catholic doctrine on the church in which there is no account taken of the hierarchy, episcopate, ministry, ecumenical councils, simply church and pope."[51]

It was not only the theology of papal primacy in the document that was lacking in nuance and richness. The atmosphere among the prelates was quickly concentrated around the acerbic issue of papal infallibility. Different groups formed around the question of papal infallibility, with the majority, in fact, being in favor of some kind of definition. Real debate took place, though it is not obvious from a cursory reading of the finished text of *Pastor Aeternus*. "The text as we have it fails to show any marks of the sweat—rather, stains of the blood—that was shed as it was being composed. It is the product of a conflict between ecclesiologies."[52]

Both in Rome and in the background were the extremist ultramontanes who advocated for the most comprehensive possible definition. William G. Ward, a convert from Anglicanism, for example, desired that all papal pronouncements be considered infallible. Some bishops came very close to sharing Ward's perspective, the most notable being Archbishop Manning of Westminster, who used excessive language of the pope such as "the incarnation of the Holy Spirit." It was not only the bishops who entered the lists on the issue of papal authority. The French Catholic layman and ultramontane Louis Veuillot, editor of the paper the *Universe*, wrote to the effect that the pope carries through the very thought of God, and, because of that, his directions must be completely followed. The Jesuit paper in Rome, *Civiltà Catolica*, said: "When the Pope thinks, it is God who is thinking in him."[53] While leaving open the element of ecclesiological truth found in these expressions, this is surely hyperbole. Those who endorsed such points of view were the "infallibilists."

A minority group was opposed to defining infallibility at the council, the "anti-infallibilists." This group included many of the French bishops, coming from a tradition of Gallicanism, sometimes perhaps unconscious and at other times quite conscious, headed by Archbishop Georges Darboy of Paris and Bishop Felix Dupanloup of Orleans. Margaret O'Gara describes Bishop Dupanloup's activities both before and at the council in these words: "Before the Council, Dupanloup had begun extensive

---

50. Tanner, ed., *Decrees of the Ecumenical Councils*, 814–15.

51. Butler, *The Vatican Council, 1869–1870*, 330.

52. Kerr, "Vatican I and the Papacy 1: A Proud Appellation," 170.

53. These citations are from O'Gara, *Triumph in Defeat*, 70.

correspondence with Rome, with other bishops, and with foreign theologians. Soon after arriving at Rome, he plunged into a series of feverish organizing activities, using his residence as a base of operation."[54] Dupanloup wrote to Pius IX late in April 1870:

> Most Holy Father, my name is not pleasing to you; I know it, and it is my sorrow. But for all that, I feel myself authorized and obliged, in the profound and inviolable devotion of which I have given so many proofs to Your Holiness, to open my heart to you at this moment . . . I would think I was betraying the Holy See and the church if, knowing what I know, and foreseeing what I foresee, I did not utter a word of warning to Your Holiness . . . while there is yet time to spare the church and the Holy See from evils that may become disasters for all Christendom during long ages . . . .

Dupanloup, as well as the other French bishops, may not simply be disregarded as marked by a false, Gallican ecclesiology that expressed itself in bitter opposition to papal infallibility. They had the good of the church at heart, and from their perspective infallibility was the wrong course to take. This was a matter of conscience. Pius replied to Dupanloup early in May:

> Venerable Brother, your name is no less pleasing to us now than in the past, nor do we love you less, or esteem less than formerly the gifts that God has bestowed upon you. . . . Return, brother, I pray you to that golden simplicity of little ones; cast away prejudiced opinions, which may obscure the holiness of your character, and which may make, if not pernicious, certainly useless for the church those great gifts of intellect, alacrity, eloquence, with which God has so liberally endowed you for the extending of his Kingdom.[55]

The tone is somewhat patronizing, to be sure, but it is not without its kindness and concern, as much for Dupanloup himself as for the church.

The reasons for the French opposition are complex, but certainly important are the Gallican tendencies of the earlier eighteenth and nineteenth centuries, when most of the French bishops at Vatican I were in seminary formation. Gallicanism, by and large, exemplifies a certain pride in French Catholicism, advocating a decentralized church, with great respect for the independence of the local diocesan community. Some of these "Gallican" French bishops not only maintained their opposition to infallibility during the council's proceedings, but left Rome before the final vote was taken on July 18, so that they would not, in conscience, have to vote against it. Some American bishops sided with the French party also, most notably Archbishop Kenrick of St. Louis. Then there were the "inopportunists," those who regarded it inopportune to promote a definition. Representative of this group was Archbishop Martin Spalding of Baltimore and many of the Austrian and German bishops.

---

54. O'Gara, *Triumph in Defeat*, 31.

55. Butler, *The Vatican Council*, 2:40–42.

Alec Vidler points out that there was ample opportunity for discussion of the matter at the council and that the inopportunists were not simply browbeaten into submission. He writes: "No doubt there was much intrigue behind the scenes, but no more than is customary, and perhaps inevitable, in ecclesiastical assemblies."[56] These are sage remarks. If we had a complete record of the proceedings of every church council, we would see in varying degrees similar intrigue, as the advocates of different theological positions made their positions clear and also tried to influence others. This is the way of conversation and debate, and there simply is no short-circuiting the process. Archbishop Manning gives us some idea of the intrigue behind the scenes. He tells us that the inopportunists "met often, and we met weekly to watch and counteract. When they went to Pius IX we went also. It was a running fight."[57] Eamon Duffy's judgment about these extreme infallibilists is surely accurate when he says: "Manning and his associates wanted history without tears, a living oracle who could short-circuit human limitation. They wanted to confront the uncertainties of their age with instant assurance, revelation on tap."[58] As things turned out, the extreme infallibilists did not get what they wanted.

In early January 1870, the infallibilists got together five hundred signatures petitioning for a definition, since the original schema on the church did not explicitly include it. The opposition managed to get only one hundred and thirty-six signatories for a counter-petition. As a result of the majority request, a chapter on infallibility was added to the schema on the church. A new constitution on the church, not including the definition of papal primacy and infallibility, was announced on April 29. Debate continued from May until the middle of July. On May 9 at the insistence of a number of bishops there was an addition made to the effect that the jurisdiction of the papacy did not in principle conflict with the jurisdiction of the episcopate. While this principle was never denied, it was found most uncomfortable by the extremist ultramontanes. The best theologian of the English episcopate, William Clifford, made a speech insisting that virtually any statement made by the council about papal authority was bound to cause some degree of misunderstanding unless it was presented within the more general framework of a statement on authority in the church as a whole. He was hissed at by some of the audience in the aula. On June 18, the Dominican theologian Cardinal Filippo Maria Guidi, archbishop of Bologna and an ardent infallibilist, made the emphatic point from the podium in the council aula that it was not the pope who was infallible but his teaching. He argued that a condition of infallibility was its prudent exercise, in consultation with the worldwide episcopate. Guidi himself was an infallibilist. However, he was keen to state the tradition that the pope was no isolated monarch, but rather was first among the bishops. When Guidi descended from the podium after his speech, he was embraced by members of the minority who appreciated

56. Vidler, *The Church in an Age of Revolution*, 156.

57. Purcell, *Life of Cardinal Manning*, 2:453.

58. Duffy, *Saints and Sinners*, 299.

his conciliatory perspective. Pius felt betrayed and summoned Guidi, and this is the famous occasion on which Pius said to him: "I am the church! I am the tradition."[59] Basing himself on the three-volume work on Pope Pius IX by the Italian church historian Giacomo Martina, SJ, the late Archbishop John Quinn adds to the normal account of Pius's outburst: "Maintaining his calm, Guidi replied that everything he had said was based on St. Thomas and on Bellarmine. With this, the Pope himself calmed down and said, 'Certainly, before deciding the Pope must take counsel,' and went on to say that he himself had in fact asked the opinion of the bishops prior to the definition of the Immaculate Conception." Quinn continues: "The unpremeditated outcry of the Pope is not a sign that he was unbalanced so much as that he was living under tremendous pressure. Furthermore, the Pope was reacting to a verbal report of his staff. He had not yet read the actual speech before seeing Guidi."[60]

The preamble to the actual text of *Pastor Aeternus* often is overlooked, and yet it is very important for an adequate interpretation of the decree, as Fergus Kerr, OP, comments: "The preamble of 'Pastor Aeternus' sets the doctrine touching the institution, perpetuity, and nature of the Petrine primacy very firmly in the context of preserving the unity of the episcopate within a church which has been founded to perpetuate the saving work of redemption."[61] Chapters one and two of *Pastor Aeternus* define "a primacy of jurisdiction over the whole Church of God," given to St. Peter and to his successors, the popes. This primacy of jurisdiction is "over all others" in matters of faith and morals, and also in matters of discipline and government. As it stands, this kind of language suggests that the bishops are nothing more than papal representatives. In chapter three of the document, however, we read: "So far is this power of the Pope from being damaging or obstructive to that ordinary and immediate power of episcopal jurisdiction by which bishops, who have been set by the Holy Spirit to succeed and hold the place of the apostles, feed and govern each his own flock, as true pastors, that their power, precisely, is asserted, strengthened and protected by the supreme and universal pastor." In other words, the bishops are not mere papal mouthpieces but succeed to the place of the apostles, and the pope's role is to assert, strengthen, and protect the pastorate of the bishops. The understanding of papal primacy is that its role is to maintain and support and never to weaken or threaten the integrity of local churches.[62]

In terms of papal infallibility, a formula on its nature and extent that came from the very ultramontane Cardinal Paul Cullen of Dublin, who had nominated Newman as rector of the Catholic University in Dublin, was finally accepted by a majority of the conciliar fathers. This formula fell short of what the more rigorous

---

59. Butler, *The Vatican Council*, 2:96–98.

60. Quinn, *Revered and Reviled*, 83. Martina's three-volume biography was published by Rome's Gregorian University Press in the 1980s, and has not been translated into English.

61. Kerr, "Vatican I and the Papacy," 169.

62. Quinn's comments on this particular issue are helpful. See his *Revered and Reviled*, 35–54.

ultramontanes wanted. Nonetheless, it won the day and was incorporated into the Constitution, *Pastor Aeternus*, which was adopted formally on July 18 by a vote of four hundred and thirty-three to two.

It is in chapter 4 of the Constitution that we find the definition of infallibility:

> We teach and define as a divinely revealed dogma that when the Roman Pontiff speaks from the chair (*ex cathedra*), that is, when, in the exercise of his office as shepherd and teacher of all Christians, in virtue of his supreme apostolic authority, he defines a doctrine concerning faith or morals to be held by the whole church, he possesses, by the divine assistance promised him in blessed Peter, that infallibility which the divine Redeemer willed his church to enjoy in defining doctrine concerning faith or morals. Therefore, such definitions of the Roman Pontiff are of themselves, and not by the consent of the church, irreformable.

The definition is complex and sounds very strong indeed, almost giving the pope free reign in matters doctrinal and moral. It demands some theological comment by way of clarification. The last sentence, "Therefore, such definitions . . . irreformable," is couched in this way to reject the position adopted by the 1682 assembly of French bishops, the Gallican Articles. These articles insist that for definitions of the pope to be binding they must have the consequent assent of the church. The concordat with Napoleon in 1801 added another strand to this Gallicanism. The clergy of France, now salaried by the government and thus to some extent controlled by the government, were caught in the tension between national interests and the international interests of the church. One historian draws the conclusion: "It was these political conditions that necessitated the dogma of papal infallibility for the same reason that the political conditions of the eleventh century necessitated the papal decree on lay investiture: The liberty of the church was at stake."[63]

Here in the text of *Pastor Aeternus* the implication seems to be that such consequent assent is unnecessary since the prior consultation with the episcopate would have taken place, thus making consequent assent redundant. It was generally assumed that no pope would proceed with an infallible definition without consulting the church, as in fact Pope Pius IX had done prior to his definition of the dogma of the Immaculate Conception of the Blessed Virgin Mary in 1854. As E. E. Y. Hales wrote: "It was, indeed unthinkable that [the pope] should do otherwise. But no wording to this effect was put into the definition."[64] That is exactly correct. If the popularly misconceived position of the pope as wrapped up in his own autonomous infallibility were in fact the correct understanding and interpretation, it would nullify the episcopate. Bishop Connolly of Nova Scotia certainly had it right when he remarked in his very un-Ciceronian Latin

---

63. Bokenkotter, *A Concise History of the Catholic Church*, 326.

64. Hales, *Pio Nono*, 309.

that "*iuxta schema, omnes episcopi ecclesiae aequivalent zero*," "according to this scheme, all the bishops of the church are equal to zero."[65]

Theological clarification from the pens of theologian and commentators is abundant, but the viewpoint of F. X. Lawlor in the former edition of the *New Catholic Encyclopedia* (and reissued in the enlarged second edition) is especially clear on this important point. Lawlor writes: "The pope's juridic autonomy does not entail discommunity or isolation; his juridic independence is never a solitary independence. He always acts as part of the Body, in the sense that he always acts within a meta-juridic community of life, based on the fact that the Spirit assumes a continuum of faith both lived and taught between the Roman Pontiff and his fellow believers in the church and his fellow bishops in the episcopate."[66] It would be difficult to better this clarification. Critics of papal infallibility point to the fact that this way of understanding is not formally explicit in the text of *Pastor Aeternus*. While that may be true, the theological datum and context explicated by Lawlor, and indeed accepted probably by the majority of Catholic ecclesiologists, give a sense of balance. Without this balancing context, papal infallibility loses its fundamental *raison d'être*, that is to say, service of the church. It is this service to the church, a service in, with and for the church that is the very hallmark of papal infallibility. The point has been grasped so well by Garrett Sweeney when he writes:

> Far from overwhelming every other authority, the papal prerogative remained obstinately dormant: to be aroused (if indeed it was then aroused) only for a brief moment in 1954 the definition of the Assumption. But this restraint can be interpreted neither as accidental nor as due to papal distrust of its own powers. It must be seen rather as the observance of built-in obligations never indeed defined, but recognized explicitly by the Conciliar Fathers as limiting the action of the papacy to rare and exceptional locations.[67]

Having acknowledged the importance of these hermeneutical principles for understanding papal infallibility, it still seems clear that this is far from the popular understanding. At the popular level, and included here is the perception of many of the clergy, there is much misunderstanding, captured accurately by one historian as follows:

> Once the council was over, misunderstanding was widespread. Most people understood it to have defined not the irreformability of papal definitions but papal infallibility, not the infallibility of the church as the basis of papal teaching authority, but papal teaching authority as the source of infallibility,

65. Cited in Sweeney, "The Forgotten Council," 163.

66. Lawlor et al., "Infallibility," in Halfmann, ed., *New Catholic Encyclopedia*, 7:450. The same basic perspective is provided by John R. Quinn, *Revered and Reviled*, 55–78.

67. Sweeney, "The Forgotten Council," 163–64. In this regard see the balanced interpretation and perspective of Patrick O'Connell, SJ, "Papal Primacy Then and Now," 103–211.

and not the right and responsibility of the bishops to govern and teach their dioceses, but the power of the Pope to teach and direct everyone, starting with the bishops.[68]

The Promulgation of *Pastor Aeternus*

The Rev. Thomas Mozley, Anglican priest, brother-in-law of John Henry Newman, and correspondent for the London *Times*—and, moreover, who knew no Italian or French and was dependent on hearsay for most of his reportage—describes the thunderstorm during which the vote was taken on *Pastor Aeternus*.

> The storm, which had been threatening all the morning, burst now with the utmost violence, and to many a superstitious mind might have conveyed the idea that it was an expression of divine wrath, as "no doubt it will be interpreted by numbers," said one officer of the Palatine Guard. And so the "placets" [positive votes] of the fathers struggled through the storm, while the thunder pealed above and the lightning flashed in at every window and down through the dome and every smaller cupola, dividing if not absorbing the attention of the crowd. "Placet," shouted his Eminence or his Grace, and a loud clap of thunder followed in response, and then the lightning darted about the baldachino and every part of the church and the conciliar hall, as if announcing the response.[69]

Critics took this as a sign of God's anger. Not Archbishop Manning, who said, "They forgot Sinai and the Ten Commandments."[70]

Sixty-one fathers submitted written protests against the definitions and left Rome on the eve of the solemn promulgation, although they accepted it once it had been passed. The two bishops who voted against it, Luigi Riccio of Caiazzo, Italy, and Edward Fitzgerald of Little Rock, Arkansas, accepted the definitions right away.

Conclusion

The day following the definition of infallibility, war was declared between Prussia and France, effectively bringing the council prematurely to an end. The French needed all their military, and so the French garrison in Rome, guaranteeing papal independence and protection, was withdrawn almost immediately. Within a month King Victor Emmanuel invaded the Papal States. Rome fell to his troops on September 20, and Pius became the self-proclaimed "prisoner of the Vatican." On October 20 Pius IX issued an apostolic letter suspending the council indefinitely.

68. Heft, "From the Pope to the Bishops," 61.
69. Cited in Butler, *The Vatican Council*, 2:123.
70. Cited Duffy, *Saints and Sinners*, 301.

No bishop left the church over the papal definitions. By the end of 1870, almost all the French bishops who had opposed infallibility had accepted it, and signified that acceptance by letter to the pope, by a pastoral letter, or by some other means of promulgating the conciliar decree in their individual dioceses.[71] Dom Cuthbert Butler says of the anti-infallibilist bishops, "It is not to be supposed that the submission of faith came automatically or easily. . . . There was a period of hesitation and interior struggle and conflict that had to be battled through, before Catholic principle came out victorious over private judgment."[72] While extreme ultramontanes like Archbishop Manning sought the most aggressive interpretation of *Pastor Aeternus*, not every bishop thought or acted in this way. The English bishops, for example, did not issue a joint pastoral letter on Vatican I until their Low Week meeting of 1875, five years later. What they came up with on that occasion was essentially an acknowledgment of the rights of local bishops. A bishop was not simply a papal vicar.

Although no bishop left the church, a number of theologians were excommunicated or left the church of their own accord. The German theologian Johann Friedrich left and with his followers formed the schismatic group known as the Old Catholics. Ignaz Döllinger, the German theologian, historian, and friend of the late Johann Adam Möhler and teacher of Lord Acton, could not accept the definition of infallibility, despite the gentle encouragement and sensitivity of his ordinary, Archbishop Gregor von Scherr of Munich, and so incurred excommunication.

It is sometimes suggested that Pope Pius IX promised preferment to those who engineered and lobbied for the definition of papal infallibility, but this seems most implausible. No one was made a cardinal for three years after the council, and then it was roughly equal between pro- and anti-infallibilist bishops. Archbishop Manning, for example, "to whom the pope was most indebted, and who had succeeded Cardinal Wiseman in 1865 as Archbishop of Westminster, was not elevated to the purple until 1875."[73]

Nonetheless, something happened at Vatican I in terms of infallibility that was not especially healthy or wholesome. A broad-based failure throughout the entire Catholic world to understand the intricacies of the issue led to an excessive focusing on the papacy, and to regarding ordinary papal teaching as bordering on infallibility, if not, indeed, latently infallible. Again, Garrett Sweeney with a sense of humor puts it right: "There may at least be a suspicion that the faithful have been trained for a hundred years to shop for nothing but Instant Infallibility from a permanently Infallible Pope, and now find that the stock has been sold out and the shelves are bare." Sweeney was writing in the wake of the encyclical *Humanae Vitae* in 1968. How might the situation be ameliorated?

71. Butler, *The Vatican Council*, 2:171.
72. Butler, *The Vatican Council*, 2:187.
73. Hales, *Pio Nono*, 312.

Can a recovery of the history of Vatican I help towards a renewal of this devotion to the Chair of Peter? Negatively: yes—in so far as it clears away misconceptions and allows it to be seen that infallible definitions are the least important role of a teaching papacy. History bears out the teaching of Vatican I but such definitions are the last desperate resort of the faithful when all other means of authentification have failed.[74]

Bishop Ullathorne, Newman's own bishop in England, desired him to go to Rome as a consultor on the commission that was preparing for the Vatican Council. Newman, of course, did not go to the council. He was working on his major work *The Grammar of Assent*, which was published in March 1870. Five years later he would bring out another publication with the title *Letter to the Duke of Norfolk*. This letter, addressed to the premier Catholic layman of England, was intended to sort out some of the confusion that surrounded infallibility. It was Newman's response to a pamphlet of Gladstone against the papacy entitled *The Vatican Decrees in Their Bearing on Civil Allegiance*. Newman is very clear that he believes in infallibility, and infallibility that touches religion only and not science, and an infallibility that safeguards theological truth. In that very precise sense, authority can never usurp the place of the individual conscience. Newman once wrote famously: "If I am obliged to bring religion into after-dinner toasts (which indeed does not seem quite the thing) I shall drink,—to the Pope if you please—still to Conscience first, and to the Pope afterwards."[75] Newman really did not have any doubts about papal infallibility, but he was concerned about its conciliar definition especially because of the misunderstandings to which it could give rise. He wrote to one who was troubled by the definition as follows, indicating the importance of historical perspective: "If you look into history, you find popes continually completing the acts of their predecessors, and councils too—sometimes only half the truth is brought out at one time—I doubt not a coming Pope, or a coming Council, will so explain and guard what has now been passed by (the) late Council, as to clear up all that troubles us now."[76] As Ian Ker points out, "This is a remarkable prophecy of the Second Vatican Council."[77]

74. Sweeney, "The Forgotten Council," 172.

75. Newman, *Difficulties of Anglicans*, 261.

76. Cited in Strange, *Newman 101*, 53.

77. Ker, *Newman on Vatican II*, 74–75.

4

Pope Leo XIII (1878–1903)

Ideologically, Leo XIII does not stand among the extremists. He was neither a reactionary, nor by any means a doctrinaire liberal. Perhaps the more neutral term "progressive" best characterizes him.

—Raymond H. Schmandt[1]

Leo was no liberal. He was a firm supporter of the Syllabus. He was no more ready to accept the loss of the Papal States as final than was Pius, and his foreign policy was dominated by wildly unrealistic hopes of persuading foreign governments to intervene in Italy for recovery of the States.

—John W. O'Malley, SJ[2]

From Gioacchino Vincenzo Pecci to Pope Leo XIII

Gioacchino Vincenzo Pecci (1810–1903), born in Carpineto in central Italy, received his doctorate in theology in 1832 from the Roman College (the Gregorian University), and went on to receive further credentials from the Roman Academy for Noble Ecclesiastics and the Sapienza University. He was ordained a priest on December 31, 1837, and his first diplomatic post under Pope Gregory XVI took him to Benevento in the Papal States, 1838 to 1841. He had a similar post in Perugia, the capital of Umbria, for one year and then, having been consecrated titular archbishop of Damietta, the thirty-three-year-old archbishop was sent to Belgium as papal nuncio in 1843. His three years there, though not free of problems with the Prime Minister, Nothomb, were to shape his outlook as pope. These years introduced him to industrial northern Europe with all its benefits and problems and also forced him to think more openly about liberal, democratic regimes. The diplomatic difficulties he encountered brought about his withdrawal from Brussels and his return to

---

1. Schmandt, "The Life and Work of Leo XIII," 35.
2. O'Malley, SJ, *A History of the Popes*, 253–54.

Perugia, but now as archbishop, and he remained until his election as Pope Leo XIII in 1878 after the death of Pius IX.

Pecci's temperament was conservative and in Perugia he promoted a small-scale version through a pastoral letter of Pius IX's "Syllabus of Errors." It was probably Pecci's example that inspired the later papal Syllabus. His brother Joseph was a Jesuit seminary professor, and it was largely through him that Pecci became interested in Thomism as the preferred way of philosophical and theological reflection of the church. He established the Academy of St. Thomas Aquinas in Perugia to promote scholasticism. At Vatican I, Pecci voted with the majority in favor of infallibility, but Cardinal Giacomo Antonelli, Pius IX's Secretary of State, was suspicious of his openness to the modern world and kept him pretty much out of Rome itself. An indication of Pecci's openness to modern civilization emerges in his Lenten pastoral of 1877, "The Church and Civilization": "Society, then, being composed of men essentially capable of improvement, cannot stand still; it advances and perfects itself. One age inherits the inventions, discoveries and improvements achieved by the preceding one, and thus the sum of physical, moral and political blessings can increase most marvelously."[3] Such sentiments would not endear him to Antonelli in the wake of the taking of the Papal States, even though Pecci took Pius IX's position on the Roman question. Despite his conservative temperament, Pecci was seen to be on the side of the progressives in the church.

The conclave of 1878 was by no means unanimous in voting for him. It was said that Pius IX, still much revered among the cardinals, most of whom he had appointed, favored Cardinal Luigi Bilio as his successor. Bilio was conservative and the primary author of Pius IX's "Syllabus of Errors." Even Cardinal Manning, archbishop of Westminster, was rumored as *papabile*. Owen Chadwick comments laconically on Manning: "There was irresponsible talk of electing Cardinal Manning of Westminster, who had made such a name as an ultramontane in the Vatican Council. Manning would have made an unsatisfactory Pope."[4] Pecci seemed a more promising candidate all round and received the required two-thirds majority. Among the factors that probably led to Leo's election was the fact that he had authored a series of pastoral letters in his diocese of Perugia, from 1874 to 1877, that seemed to overcome the alienation between the church and the world and to promote a greater harmony. As Eamon Duffy has it, "It was time for a little sweet talk."[5]

Pope Leo XIII

As Pope Leo XIII, he seemed like a breath of fresh air in the church after the pontificate of Pope Pius IX, though the contrast between them can be exaggerated. As archbishop

---

3. Cited from Schmandt, "The Life and Work of Leo XIII," 20.

4. Chadwick, *A History of the Popes 1830–1914*, 275–76.

5. Duffy, *Saints and Sinners*, rev. ed, 306.

of Perugia he had formulated his own *Syllabus of Errors*, that in part paved the way for that of Pope Pius IX. It must also be recalled, for example, that as a cardinal since 1853 he would have been close to Pope Pius IX and he would have taken full part in all the proceedings that led up to and that constituted the First Vatican Council.

Like his predecessor Leo also had a long pontificate, lasting twenty-five years. Alec Vidler sums him up in these words: "He did not mean to give the church a new look. He was a great diplomat, and by temperament an optimist. Instead of emphasizing the alienation between the church and the modern world, he wanted to convince the modern world that it needed the church and that the church was no longer sadly aspiring after the restoration of the *ancien régime*."[6]

One of the first things Leo did was to name John Henry Newman a cardinal. Suspicion had hung over Newman's head for many years. His great English rival, as it were, Cardinal Manning, thought of Newman as at least a border-line heretic. All this came to an end when Leo named him a cardinal. "My Cardinal (exclaimed the Pope to a Catholic peer, Lord Selborne)! It was not easy, it was not easy. They said he was too liberal, but I had determined to honor the church in honoring Newman. I always had a cult for him. I am proud that I was able to honor such a man."[7] Leo did away with the eunuchs, or *castrati*, who sang in the Sistine Chapel. The fact that the Vatican Council had not formally been closed in 1870 meant that the furniture for the bishops in council still existed, "just in case," but Leo gave instructions for the benches to be broken up. Whether he liked it personally or not, he recognized that there was no real hope of reconvening the council.

Leo was "a man of encyclicals."[8] The encyclical letter in its modern form began with Pope Benedict XIV 1740. Leo issued more encyclical letters than any pope before him. It was his favorite medium of communicating with the church, and indeed with the wider world. The encyclicals covered virtually everything—socialism, Scripture, the nature of philosophy, the unity of the church, Anglican orders, and so forth. Eamon Duffy writes with accuracy: "Here, for the first time, we have the pope as an inexhaustible source of guidance and instruction. No pope before or since has come anywhere near his eighty-six encyclicals. Leo talked and talked, and expected obedience."[9] Two of his encyclicals treated of Protestantism. His hope would have been that Protestants would return to the one true church. However it is really interesting that he does not refer to Protestants as heretics, but rather as "separated brethren," a term that would become common after Vatican II.[10] Relationally, Pius IX and Leo XIII make an interesting contrast, according to the reactions and sentiments of their peers. People felt that when they talked to Pius

---

6. Vidler, *Twentieth-Century Defenders of the Faith*, 34.

7. Cited in Dessain, *John Henry Newman*, 165.

8. Chadwick, *A History of the Popes, 1830–1914*, 281.

9. Duffy, *Saints and Sinners*, 317.

10. O'Malley, SJ, *A History of the Popes*, 254.

he cared for them at that moment more than for anyone else in the world. Leo, on the other hand, was "cool, formal and courteous."[11]

French Catholics and Royalism

France in the 1880s saw church and state constantly in conflict. Many Catholics dreamed of a royalist return. The French Republic saw disloyalty in such dreaming, and perhaps even treachery. Leo addressed himself to the French situation. In 1884 he published an encyclical with the title *The Most Noble Nation of the French*, and in this document, he praised the concordat of 1801 and encouraged Catholics to lay aside extreme political views for the sake of the country. The following year he put out an encyclical on the nature of the state, which insisted that the church did not privilege any particular form of government, and he encouraged Catholics to participate in the social and political life of the state.

In October 1890 he summoned the premier liberal French bishop, Cardinal Charles Lavigerie, archbishop of Algiers, to make him his ally in the promotion of his policies. Consequent upon this meeting, Lavigerie invited the officers of the French fleet to a banquet on November 12 in which the cardinal proposed a toast pledging allegiance to the French Republic. Moreover, as his guests were received, the band of the cardinal's missionary order, the White Fathers, played the Marseillaise, an anthem identified with republicanism and anathema to the Catholic right. Lavigerie's toast, with Leo's full support, opened the floodgates of controversy in France. Leo's openness on these issues did not commend him to an influential number of the hierarchy who saw hope for the church only in the return of royalism. "His efforts at reconciliation with a democracy did not succeed because his clergy and laity took their hats off to what he said but were no more reconciled to the Republic than before."[12]

Capitalism, Social Justice, and *Rerum Novarum*

The nineteenth century witnessed the development of thinking on principles of social justice and the duties of capitalists to their workers, not least through the reflection of Karl Marx and Friedrich Engels. In the churches of northern Europe there was a growing concern among some Christians about the situation of the working class. Europe in the mid-nineteenth century threw up a number of thinkers who considered pressing questions of social change such as the elimination of poverty and the introduction of universal literacy and education, and the consequent raising of economic living standards. Less well-known are the *Christian Socialist*s, a term introduced in 1848 in

---

11. Chadwick, *A History of the Popes, 1830–1914*, 284.
12. Chadwick, *A History of the Popes, 1830–1914*, 299.

England. Better known are some Catholic thinkers and leaders whose concerns and commitment crossed the divide between ultramontane and liberal.

Wilhelm von Ketteler, the liberal bishop of Mainz, had been an opponent of the conciliar definition of papal infallibility but later accepted the definition. He was constantly concerned with the relationship between workers and the church. He had read with some degree of sympathy Karl Marx's *Das Kapital* on his way to the first Vatican Council and, though he disagreed with much of it, he nevertheless realized pragmatically that to engage in a realistic way with the problems of the working class, some measure of profit-sharing had to be introduced. Though Ketteler died the year before Leo's election, his influence could still be felt. Similarly, though ultramontane rather than liberal, Cardinal Manning of Westminster became an advocate of social reform and was a leader in the settlement of the London dock strike of 1889. The ultramontane Manning, unwilling to concede what he took to be dogmatically certain in the matter of papal infallibility and the papal role in the church generally, nonetheless had a fine pastoral sense that was equally unwilling to concede on principles of social justice. A recent biographer of Manning has put it like this: "Manning, while vigorously defending the dogmatic principle in religion, was remarkably free from the dogmas of class, party, economic theory, and the like, which fettered many of his contemporaries. . . . Manning's policy was invigorated by a highly personal sense of religion, of practical Christianity."[13] Manning was a man of firm and decisive action.

Léon Harmel (1829–1915), an ultramontane French industrialist and capitalist, initiated a series of social and economic benefits for his workers and tried to promote such policies among other Catholic capitalists. He turned his textile plant near Rheims into a Christian corporation under the patronage of Our Lady of the Factory. In 1887, he went to Rome on pilgrimage with one hundred employers, fourteen hundred employees, and three hundred priests. In 1889 his pilgrimage of workers numbered ten thousand. Eamon Duffy writes: "These pilgrimages of working people, living proof that democracy and the pope might shake hands, caught Leo's imagination, and helped persuade him that industrial society need not be conflictual, that social peace under the gospel was a possibility."[14] The work and reflection of this growing body of Catholic social thinkers provided the ambience for Leo's great encyclical, *Rerum Novarum*, of 1891. It was the twenty-seventh of Leo's encyclicals and was the second longest.

Today's scholars recognize various hands behind the encyclical, but no one doubts Leo's own hand in the final redaction.[15] Both from his experience in Belgium and his general awareness of the global church Leo realized that the church was in danger of losing the working-class. Because of a failure to give due recognition to

---

13. Pereiro, *Cardinal Manning*, 336–37. The latter part of this quotation from Pereiro comes from McClelland, *Cardinal Manning*, 215.

14. Duffy, *Saints and Sinners*, 311.

15. See Massaro, "The Social Question in the Papacy of Leo XIII," 152.

the needs and the rights of working people, Leo understood that the socialists could easily gain the upper hand in winning the support of the marginalized workers. Although the encyclical condemned socialism, it tapped into the desire and the need for social and economic change. It insisted on the God-given right to private property, yes, but Leo also warned of the dangers of laissez-faire capitalism that "treats persons as atomized individuals and not as creatures of community."[16] The encyclical gave attention to the rights and the needs of workers, to their dignity, to the rights of states to promote social justice, to the right of workers to form unions, and to the right to a decent, living wage and a share of profits. Strikes should generally be avoided, maintained Leo, but some may be justified in a fashion similar to the justification of self-defense. Owen Chadwick comments on the encyclical: "In the long view this encyclical made possible the Catholic social democratic parties of the twentieth century in Italy, Germany and Belgium and at moments in France."[17] *Rerum Novarum* was not in itself a radical document; indeed, some of its language could be construed as paternalistic and perhaps even romanticist, but for the pope to say such things after the long adversarial pontificate of Pius IX was "truly revolutionary."[18] Thomas Massaro maintains that the remarkable development in this encyclical displays "a surprisingly sophisticated structural view of economic forces responsible for the exploitation of millions," and the strong encouragement given to both church and state to empower in various ways the poor of the world.[19]

The Encyclical *Aeterni Patris* on Thomism

"Theology had suffocated under Pio Nono."[20] One of the first things that Leo did was to make John Henry Newman a cardinal, lifting forever the cloud of suspicion that hung over him. It is reported that Cardinal Manning of Westminster often said that Newman was a heretic. Leo's action put an end to that kind of calumny once and for all. It needs to be remembered that, although Newman had prepared for the priesthood in Rome at the Propaganda College, he was not of the Roman schools. His theological formation had been at Oxford, a significantly different milieu from Roman scholasticism. When Leo made Newman a cardinal, implicitly he was honoring a certain limited pluralism in Catholic theology, even if he did not quite understand it in that fashion.

Writing initially in 1963 the Scottish Anglican theologian John Macquarrie states:

16. Gilley, "Pope Leo's Legacy," 10.
17. Chadwick, *A History of Christianity*, 248.
18. Duffy, *Saints and Sinners*, 312.
19. Massaro, "The Social Question in the Papacy of Leo XIII," 158.
20. Eamon Duffy, *Saints and Sinners*, 313.

The term "neo-Thomism" is commonly used for the contemporary revival of philosophical and theological ways of thinking which have their basis in the thought of St. Thomas Aquinas. This revival has taken place above all in the Roman Catholic Church, but we should notice that there are some neo-Thomists who are not Catholics, and that on the other hand there are Catholic thinkers who are not neo-Thomists. Among Catholic thinkers of recent times, Maurice Blondel would be better described as "neo-Augustinian"; and the neo-Thomist label would not be applicable to men like Baron von Hügel, Pierre Teilhard de Chardin, and Louis Lavelle, to say nothing of the Modernists.[21]

Macquarrie's 1963 book and description is a good way to begin our treatment of Pope Leo XIII and Thomism. Macquarrie acknowledges that an appreciation of St. Thomas Aquinas is much wider than Roman Catholicism, and he is thinking specifically of the Anglicans Austin Farrer and Eric Mascall.[22] The non-Thomists that Macquarrie mentions (with the exception of Louis Lavelle) will be treated later in this book, von Hügel in the chapter on modernism and Teilhard in the chapter on the "New Theology." He goes on further to acknowledge that the renewed interest in St. Thomas Aquinas owes its origin to Pope Leo XIII in his encyclical *Aeterni Patris,* and it is to this that we now turn our attention.

Despite Newman's cardinal hat and the limited realism implicit in its conferral, nonetheless, as pope, Leo privileged the thought of St. Thomas Aquinas as he had done earlier as archbishop of Perugia, and in his encyclical *Aeterni Patris* (1879), he called for a renewal of Thomistic philosophy and theology. During the pontificate of Pope Pius IX, climaxing in the First Vatican Council, and following in its wake the thought of St. Thomas Aquinas and scholasticism generally developed into "the church's official answer to the Enlightenment."[23] The strong philosophical/metaphysical thinking of the Angelic Doctor, as it was seen, provided all the defense the church needed in responding to the various revolutions—political, cultural, philosophical and theological—that had come into play since the French Revolution of 1789. "In sum: neo-Thomism was the church's philosophical and theological antidote to modernity."[24]

---

21. John Macquarrie, *Twentieth-Century Religious Thought,* 279. The first edition was published in 1963.

22. His treatment of Austin Farrer on pages 290–91 of the same book, and of Eric Mascall on pages 386–87. Much later in life Macquarrie wrote a very appreciative essay on Eric Mascall. See his "Mascall and Thomism," *Tufton Review* 2 (1998) 1–13.

23. Schelkens et al., *Aggiornamento?* 70.

24. Schelkens et al., *Aggiornamento?* 71. In his *Divided Friends: Portraits of the Roman Catholic Modernist Crisis in the United States,* 7–8, William Portier accurately describes Leo's encyclical as follows: "Aquinas *redivivus* would supply the intellectual resources necessary to restore epistemological and political order to the chaos of a post-Kantian, post-revolutionary Europe. With its massive objectivity, the neo-Thomism of Leo's *Aeterni Patris* would counter the turn to the subject in modern philosophy."

Influenced by his brother, the Jesuit Thomist philosopher Giuseppe Pecci and confirmed also by his experience in his diocesan seminary at Perugia, in 1879 encyclical *Aeterni Patris* virtually mandates the study of the thought of St. Thomas Aquinas in all Catholic institutions of higher learning.[25] The encyclical consists of thirty-four numbered paragraphs. In the very first paragraph it is noted that Christ established the teaching office in the church, "an unfailing teaching authority" echoing the teaching of the First Vatican Council's Decree on Faith, so that the church might teach the truth of the Christian faith and "teach religion and content forever against errors." Apart from the seeming echo and emphasis from the First Vatican Council the paragraph is a fair statement of Catholic teaching. Among the duties and responsibilities of the hierarchical church is the duty and responsibility of teaching authentically the Christian faith and guarding that faith from ever present errors.

Errors come from philosophy, maintains the encyclical. Errors have been found everywhere in history flowing from false philosophies. Moreover, these errors have crept perhaps unknowingly into the human mind and have been accepted by "the common consent of the masses" (paragraph 2). It would be hard to dispute this conviction because people are very easily led by ideologues and propagandists and always have been. However, the language does sound rather patronizing, as if "the masses" were incapable of any serious thought and reflection.

Philosophy is seen as a kind of preparation for revelation and for the gospel. The fathers of the church are named as exemplifying this *preparatio evangelii* perspective including Origen, the Cappadocians, Justin, Irenaeus, and especially Augustine. Thus, the encyclical continues in this vein: "Those will certainly more fully and more easily attain that knowledge and understanding who to integrity and love of faith join a mind rounded and finished by philosophic studies, as the same Vatican Council teaches that the knowledge of such sacred dogmas ought to be sought as well from analogy of the things that are naturally known as from the connection of those mysteries one with another and with the final end of man" (paragraph 6). Again, one notes the connection with the texts of Vatican I. While the apologists and great patristic authors, especially Augustine, and the medieval scholastics are all lauded in this regard, Pope Leo signals out two in particular for commendation—St. Thomas Aquinas and St. Bonaventure.

In paragraph 17 we find the highest praise for St. Thomas Aquinas. "Among the scholastic doctors, the chief and master of all towers Thomas Aquinas, who, as Cajetan observes, because 'he venerated the ancient doctors of the church, and in a certain way seems to have inherited the intellect of all.'" The pope goes on to cite his predecessors who have praised St. Thomas and his achievements, and he also notes the high esteem in which the Western councils of the church have held Aquinas—Lyons, Vienna, Florence, and the Vatican. And so, for all of these reasons Pope Leo insists on the centrality of Aquinas for all Catholic institutions of higher learning. And so, the Thomistic

25. References to the encyclical are given in parentheses in our text, and the entire text may be found at Vatican.va/content/leo-xiii/en/encyclicals/documents.

mandate began, even if it is possible that Pope Leo did not understand it quite like that. The increased authority of the pope, emergent both from ultramontanism and especially from the First Vatican Council, meant that virtually every utterance of the pope would be given a very considerable weight, and perhaps at least sometimes a weight that it did not deserve and yet could not realistically be challenged. To say the least, the encyclical *Aeterni Patris* had an enormously damaging effect on Catholic theology, a damaging effect that lasted right up through Vatican Council II and arguably into the contemporary post-conciliar situation.

In this he was influenced by his brother, now Cardinal Joseph Pecci as well as by Fr. Matteo Liberatore. "A pope who loved the Middle Ages and wished to revive their impact in the modern world tried to make the supreme exponent of a medieval philosophy the only reliable exponent of modern philosophy."[26] This is the judgment of Owen Chadwick, and it may be challenged in part, but there is no doubt of its substantial truth. In practical terms few encyclicals have enjoyed as much success as *Aeterni Patris* did. Not only did the encyclical mandate the study of Aquinas in Catholic institutions of higher education and especially seminaries, but it was also something of a catalyst for wide ranging research into the Middle Ages. The Roman Academy of St. Thomas was reorganized in 1886, and Desiré Mercier (1851–1926), later cardinal-archbishop of Malines, was nominated to a chair of Thomism at Louvain in 1882. Mercier insisted on teaching some philosophy courses in the vernacular so as "to bring the Scholastic mind within closer hailing distance of modern philosophers and their distinctive problems."[27] In 1889, with papal support, Mercier created the Institut Supérieur de Philosophie, providing a complete education in the philosophical disciplines around and in engagement with the philosophy of St. Thomas. No one would deny the importance of Aquinas or of Thomism in the history of philosophy and theology, nor their particular importance in the Catholic Church. The contemporary renaissance of interest in Aquinas evidences the constancy of his appeal and the ongoing significance of his thought. Nevertheless, it seems fair to say that Leo regarded Thomism "not as a starting point of theological reflection, but as the *end of it*."[28]

This seems to be part of the reason for the condemnation in 1887 of certain ideas and propositions of Antonio Rosmini-Serbati (1797–1855), a thinker who had considerable influence in northern Italy. Rosmini-Serbati was an encyclopedic thinker with at least initially an appreciation of Aquinas, but he sought to develop a system of thought that was organic and interlocking, that would serve as the basis of all knowledge. He went beyond Aquinas, taking account of modern philosophy. Forty propositions, taken out of context from all Rosmini's works, were condemned under Leo in 1887. Rosmini's

---

26. Chadwick, *A History of the Popes, 1830–1914*, 281.

27. Collins, "Leo XIII and the Philosophical Approach to Modernity," 200.

28. Duffy, *Saints and Sinners*, 314.

disciples insisted at the time that these propositions did not genuinely represent his thought, and the Holy See has recently confirmed their position.[29]

Holy Scripture, Marie-Joseph Lagrange, OP, and the Archives

In 1893, Leo issued his encyclical *Providentissimus Deus*, promoting the scholarly study of Scripture among Catholics, especially the study of Oriental languages and the emerging techniques of biblical criticism. In that encyclical he wrote to Catholic students of Scripture: "None of the recent discoveries which the human mind has made is foreign for the purpose of their work. On the contrary, let them make haste in any case where our times have discovered something useful in the matter of biblical exegesis to avail themselves of it forthwith and by their writings to put it at the service of all."[30] Nine years later in 1902, he set up the Pontifical Biblical Commission. The Jesuit theologian and ecumenist Gustave Weigel, wrote of this commission: "After Leo's death the commission acted more as a brake than an accelerator on biblical studies, but this was by reason of the rash temper of those times."[31] Weigel is referring to the consequent *débacle* of modernism, which will be discussed later.

In 1890 the Dominicans, under Père Marie-Joseph Lagrange, established the École Biblique et Archéologique Française de Jérusalem. This does not seem especially significant except for the fact that the Dominicans were involved at about the same time in setting up the University of Fribourg, approved by the parliament of the Swiss Canton of Fribourg in 1889. The Dominicans needed to find professors in Scripture for this new school which made it more difficult to find professors in Scripture and Oriental languages for another new school in Jerusalem. In the event his French Provincial Superior wrote in 1889 to the thirty-five-year-old Marie-Joseph Lagrange, OP, who was studying Oriental languages in Vienna. The French Dominican Provincial asked Lagrange to go to Jerusalem and initiate a school there for the study of Holy Scripture.[32] Within two years of the school's opening, the famous *Revue biblique* began to appear.[33] Thus, we see something of a leap forward both in theology and in Scripture during Leo's pontificate.

In 1879, Leo nominated Cardinal Joseph Hergenröther as prefect of the Vatican Archives. Hergenröther had been a pupil of Ignaz Döllinger (who had left the church after the definition of papal infallibility of Vatican I) and "one of the worst lecturers in

---

29. "Note on the Import of the Doctrinal Decrees Concerning the Thought and Works of the Priest Antonio Rosmini-Serbati," no. 6, Vatican City, July 1, 2001.

30. Cited from Raymond Schmandt, "The Life and Work of Leo XIII," 39. There is a useful summary of the encyclical in R. E. Brown, Fitzmyer, and Murphy, eds., *The New Jerome Biblical Commentary*, 1167–78.

31. Weigel, "Leo XIII and Contemporary Theology," 217.

32. Lagrange, *Père Lagrange, Personal Reflections and Memoirs*, 13.

33. See Barton, "The Dominican School in Jerusalem and Old Testament Studies," especially 21–22.

Germany, droning away behind a high pile of books . . . and incapable of communicating any feeling for the past as alive."[34] Yet Hergenröther was a good historian and he had a real feeling for archival research. Slowly things began to move. Two years later, in 1881, Leo opened the Vatican Archives to the historians of the world, much to the consternation of the Roman Curia, noting, "We have nothing to fear from the publication of the documents."[35] To the scholarly community, this was a real breath of fresh air in contrast to what had happened during the previous pontificate.

"Americanism"

The life and work of Isaac Hecker contributed in a major way to the phenomenon known as "Americanism." American church historian, Kevin L. Hughes, has a very succinct paragraph that introduces "Americanism." His paragraph begins with the fact of several American bishops leaving Vatican I without voting for papal infallibility, including Archbishop Peter Kenrick whom Isaac Hecker had met on board ship on the way to the First Vatican Council:

> Among those who left the Council rather than vote for infallibility were several prominent American bishops, above all Archbishop Peter Kenrick of St. Louis. Kenrick was a scholar as well as a bishop, and while in Rome he composed two pamphlets that questioned the arguments for infallibility by invoking the traditional teaching of the church. Catholicism had taken on its own character in the United States, where it lived and worked of necessity within just the sort of constitutional system that Pius IX condemned. This experience gave American Catholicism a particular sense of identity and, eventually, led some American Catholics to the brink of excommunication.[36]

It has taken the Vatican a long time to grasp something of the complexities of the church in the United States.

Immigration from Europe into the United States meant that the immigrants brought their Catholic faith with them. It is estimated that between 1790 and 1860 the numbers of Catholics had grown from some thirty-five thousand to over three million, so that in the nineteenth century Catholicism was a public presence in the country. Propaganda and animosity against Catholics grew in America, and Catholic propaganda and animosity also enjoyed a growth spurt. While "tensions were high, and violent conflict is inevitable," the time came when "this experience of hostility and persecution led American Catholics to become, if anything, 'super-patriotic,' trying to prove that Catholics could be excellent citizens."[37]

34. Chadwick, *Catholicism and History: The Opening of the Vatican Archives*, 92.
35. Cited from Schmandt, "The Life and Work of Leo XIII," 39.
36. Hughes, *Church History*, 105.
37. Hughes, *Church History*, 105–6.

The American Catholic Church during Leo's pontificate might be characterized in very general terms as both insular-conservative and open-progressive. The insular part of the church, instanced in Archbishop Michael Corrigan of New York and German-American Catholic bishops especially in the Midwest, were somewhat suspicious of American nationalism and assimilation and wished to see Catholics withdraw from the state system in education and set up on their own. The more open part of the church, characterized by Cardinal James Gibbons of Baltimore and Archbishop John Ireland of St. Paul, argued for ongoing Catholic participation in the state system and the general assimilation of Catholic immigrants to American institutions and ideals. The positions of both camps were further colored by personal animosities.[38]

In 1891, Walter Elliott wrote a biography of Fr. Isaac Hecker. Hecker gave expression as we have seen to a vibrant incarnational theology and outlook that seemed tailor-made, as it were, for the optimism of the flourishing United States of America. America was, of course, the birth child of the Enlightenment, based on liberty, equality and fraternity. Hecker's theology has been well characterized: "[His] incarnational emphasis gave his ecclesiology an anthropological orientation and his elevated appreciation of human nature a theological foundation. . . . He argued that man, heir to the accumulated wisdom of the past and equipped with new freedom, was better prepared than ever to respond to a greater outpouring of the Holy Spirit."[39] It was all rather different from recent European Catholic experience of liberty, equality and fraternity, most especially in France. In his introduction to the biography, Archbishop Ireland praised Hecker as just the kind of priest the modern world needed.

The biography was adapted and translated into French by French Catholics allied to the cause of the French Republic. Hecker as a republican, so to speak, was their man too, and it caused quite a stir in France. Those French churchmen opposed to the Republic and opposed to the Hecker biography as a seeming support for cooperation with the Republic, created "Americanism." Americanism was seen as the cumulative concessions of Catholics to modern views, to freedom and tolerance, to accommodation to the modern state and modern culture. Royalist French Catholics saw it as the very antithesis of Catholicism, that is, the countercultural Catholicism that they espoused. The ensuing controversies and debates came to the attention of Leo, who wrote the letter *Testem Benevolentiae* in 1898 to Cardinal Gibbons and the American hierarchy. Therein, having listed a number of ideas supposedly associated with Fr. Hecker (for example, undue emphasis on the inner guidance of the Holy Spirit, minimizing the need for "external" spiritual direction, emphasizing the active life over the contemplative life), Leo wrote: "We cannot approve the opinions which some comprise under the head of Americanism. If indeed by that name be designated characteristic qualities which reflect honor on the people of America, conditions of your commonwealth, or the laws and customs which prevailed in

38. See O'Brien, "Americanism," 97–99.
39. Reher, "Leo XIII and Americanism," 681.

them, there is surely no reason why we should deem it should be discarded. But, if it is to be used not only to signify but even to commend the above doctrines, there can be no doubt that our Venerable Brethren the bishops of America would be the first to repudiate and condemn it, as being especially unjust to them and to the entire nation as well. For it raises the suspicion that there are some among you who conceive of and desire a church in America different from that which is in the rest of the world."[40] No condemnation and no penalty were issued against anyone, and the pope assured his American fellow bishops in the section of the letter cited that he did not believe that the bishops held any of the positions he has listed. Cardinal Gibbons rightly said in respect of the letter that no educated American Catholic held the ideas condemned in it, but damage had been done.[41] "Americanism" was something of a phantom heresy, pointing up the bitter divisions between the insular-conservative style of Catholicism with the more open-progressive style.

It may be, in part, that Cardinal Gibbons's own participation in the Parliament of World Religions in Chicago in 1892 paved the way for this condemnation. All religions were presented in the parliament on an equal basis. That does not mean, of course, that Gibbons and other Catholics who participated understood Catholicism as on a par with other world faiths, but their very participation itself left them open to that criticism on the part of their opponents. Whatever its roots and causes, the condemnation of Americanism had a negative effect on American Catholic theology and served as a harbinger for the condemnation of modernism in the next pontificate.[42]

In a letter of 1902 to Cardinal Gibbons and the American bishops, Pope Leo XIII wrote: "Therefore, while the changes in tendencies of nearly all the nations which were Catholic for many centuries give cause for sorrow, the state of your churches, in their flourishing youthfulness, cheers our heart and fills it with delight." Archbishop John Ireland quoted Leo as saying of America, "*L'Avvenire*—'The Future.'"[43]

Relations with other Christians

Pope Leo had a considerable interest in Christian reunion. This may have been motivated by the hope that such a reunion would provide a stronger defense of the Christian faith in the face of increasing secularism. Of course, given the times, his model of ecumenism was the return of other ecclesial traditions and bodies to union with Rome and the Holy See. Leo was especially interested in reunion with the Oriental and Slavic churches, encouraged in this by Bishop Josip Strossmayer (1815–1905), the Croat bishop of Djakovo. Strossmayer, who had been a leading opponent of the definition of papal infallibility at

---

40. The entire text of the letter is printed at the end of David O'Brien's article, "Americanism." Here the citation is from page 103.

41. Avery Dulles reaches the same conclusion in his *A History of Apologetics*, 190–91.

42. Thus, Duffy, *Saints and Sinners*, 316 and Reher, "Leo XIII and Americanism," 689.

43. Cited from Schmandt, "The Life and Work of Leo XIII," 46.

Vatican I but afterwards accepted the conciliar decision, was a great advocate of church unity among the Russian and Slavic peoples.

While in Belgium as nuncio, Leo had met Fr. Ignatius Spencer, an English convert and Passionist priest, and his conversations with Spencer seem to have been his *entrée* to English affairs. *En route* from Brussels to Rome in 1846, Pecci spent about a month in England, studying its political institutions, during which time he dined with Queen Victoria and attended a session of Parliament. He knew something of English church affairs, but not a very great deal.

In 1890 two men were vacationing on the island of Madeira—the Frenchman Abbé Fernand Portal and the Englishman Lord Halifax. Halifax was a high Anglican, with a high ecclesiology and an equally high theology of the sacraments. Portal was mightily impressed with Halifax's account of Anglican belief and practice. As a consequence of their conversations, both during the vacation and afterwards, both men gave serious attention to the question of the reunion of Canterbury and Rome. Portal wrote a brief pamphlet on Anglican orders, reaching a positive conclusion, and this was endorsed by one of the greatest French scholars of the time Abbé Louis Duchesne. Duchesne's endorsement gave the question of Anglican orders high profile indeed. All was not well, however, with this incipient exercise in ecumenical relations. On the one hand, Portal did not sufficiently appreciate the complexity of the English church, and certainly not that Halifax's party of high Anglicans constituted numerically not a very large percentage of the Church of England. On the other hand, Cardinal Herbert Vaughan, archbishop of Westminster, was quite opposed to any kind of rapprochement on this matter of Anglican orders. "While [Vaughan] supported the proposed reinvestigation into the validity of Anglican orders, he suspected that it would be of very doubtful help in any way to reunion. To his mind such a reunion quite transcended any decision about orders and was, in fact, unlikely to come about in the foreseeable future."[44] Vaughan also did not like the suggestion that corporate reunion might put off individual conversions of Anglicans. Equally, Archbishop Edward White Benson of Canterbury did not take well to the speculation that Anglican orders needed any kind of recognition of their validity by Rome—or by any other body for that matter.

The entire issue was enormously complicated not only in theological terms but also in terms of personalities, past history, and ecclesiological presuppositions and loyalties. Eventually, a papal commission was appointed in 1895 to study Anglican orders. An apostolic letter, *Apostolicae Curae* was issued in 1896 condemning the orders as "null and void," both in form and in intention: "We pronounce and declare that ordinations performed according to the Anglican Rite have been and are completely null and void."[45]

---

44. Eric McDermott, "Leo XIII and England," in Edward T. Gargan, ed., *Leo XIII and the Modern World,* 145.

45. From the English text in R. W. Franklin, ed., *Anglican Orders,* 136.

Conclusion

Leo XIII was no extremist. In some ways he was very close to Pius IX, and yet in other ways he was more open to modernity and to modern ways in theology and the church. He is best understood as "progressive," his contribution to the church being "a subtle alloy of flexibility and obduracy."[46] Under him the papacy recovered something of its prestige and role of leadership in the world. In terms of the obduracy, or perhaps better "'deficit," one might point to the modernist crisis of the next pontificate. While Leo had promoted Thomism as a sure foundation for Catholic theology and philosophy, "the very ahistorical character of Thomism was unable to cope with the principal tension in Modernism: that between dogma and history."[47] This tension will be examined in the next chapters dealing with Pope Pius X and then with modernism.

46. Philippe Levillain, "Leo XIII," in *The Papacy, An Encyclopedia*, 935.

47. Heft, "From the Pope to the Bishops," 68.

5

Pope Pius X (1903–14)

The twentieth-century papacy began, as was appropriate in the age of the common man, with a peasant pope, the first for three centuries, Giuseppe Sarto.

—Eamon Duffy[1]

The only common attitudes adopted by all the Modernists seem to have been an undue confidence in contemporary developments and a rejection of that unconditional obedience which the Roman authorities had come to expect.

—J. Derek Holmes[2]

From Giuseppe Sarto to Pope Pius X

Giuseppe Sarto was born on June 2, 1835, in the village of Riese in Venetia. His father was the village postman and his mother a seamstress. After his ordination to the priesthood in 1858, Sarto spent nine years as a curate in Tombolo and then eight years as a pastor in Salzano. He had solid pastoral experience. As a successor to Pope Leo XIII, he did not share Leo's interest in the philosophical-theological-intellectual revival of Catholicism.[3] However, he continued to study as time allowed the church fathers, Scripture, and various treatises on moral theology. In fact, the better to prepare himself for his pastoral ministrations he requested permission of his bishop to read certain books that had been placed on the Index of Prohibited Books.[4] He gained quite a reputation as a preacher and was often invited to other places to preach. During his time in Salzano, he put together a catechism for his parishioners, consisting of 577 questions and answers. He wanted to be immediately intelligible so as genuinely to edify the faith of those under his pastoral care. From Salzano Sarto was appointed as spiritual director of the diocesan seminary at Treviso, a canon of the cathedral, and chancellor of

1. Duffy, *Saints and Sinners*, 320.
2. Holmes, *The Triumph of the Holy See*, 263.
3. Holmes, *The Triumph of the Holy See*, 261.
4. Chiron, *St. Pius X, Restorer of the Church*, 31.

the diocese. There he also continued his catechetical and preaching work, and he also started to read the works of the ultramontane Cardinal Pie, bishop of Poitiers. He told a priest of that diocese "I have all the Cardinal's works here and for many years now hardly a day goes by but I read a few pages of him."[5]

He was named bishop of Mantua in 1884, at the time not an easy responsibility. The diocese of Mantua bordered the diocese of Cremona, whose bishop was the open-minded Geremia Bonomelli (bishop of Cremona from 1871 to 1914). Sarto wrote to Bonomelli two days before his ordination asking for his support in view of his inexperience. The diocese was quite rundown but through the energies of Bishop Sarto was "speedily renewed."[6] Part of the rundown nature of the diocese was a consequence of Italian unification which had left the region somewhat socially and economically insecure. There was also an insecurity among the clergy. Five men left the priesthood in 1864, and in 1870 ten left. A large number for a relatively small diocese. An ecclesial scandal came about in the diocese in 1871 when Canon Roberto Ardigo (1828–1920), a well-known priest, lost his faith and became a professor of philosophy at the University of Padua. All this, of course, was before Sarto's time. During Sarto's time there was another quite public defection from the priesthood. Giovanni Grisanti, archpriest of Rovere, a principal town in the diocese, left the priesthood and became a Protestant. The morale of the local presbyterate is always affected when priests leave, especially when prominent and well-known priests leave. Sarto had his work cut out in this regard.

Bishop Sarto worked to make his diocesan seminary an attractive place, marked by appropriate discipline and serious attention to studies, including the study of St. Thomas Aquinas mandated by Pope Leo XIII. While he was trying to establish a competent faculty for his seminary, he taught moral theology himself for one year and also for a time Gregorian chant. After ordination to the priesthood, Bishop Sarto instituted a commission over which he presided to examine the newly ordained in theology. The new bishop, during his nine-year stay in this diocese, threw himself into catechetical work. In a pastoral letter of 1887 he denounced "this modern Christianity which has forgotten the ancient folly of the Cross (and where) the dogmas of faith must be adapted to the requirements of the new philosophy . . . ."[7] Such sentiments allied to his constant reading of the ultramontane Cardinal Pie may be taken as early signs of his later complete opposition to modernism. He conducted a pastoral visitation of all the parishes in his diocese, something that took him three years to complete. In 1889 he participated in the first National Catechetical Conference in Piacenza and proposed the use of a uniform catechetical text. The proposal was accepted by the conference and sent on to Rome. To counter the growing attraction of socialist groups in the area he encouraged the faithful of his diocese to organize and to develop their own

5. Cited in Chiron, *St. Pius X, Restorer of the Church*, 45.

6. Kelly, *The Oxford Dictionary of Popes*, 313.

7. Cited in Chiron, *St Pius X*, 67.

associations to meet the social and economic needs of ordinary people. When the opportunity presented itself, he made himself rector of his diocesan seminary, appointing himself also as professor of philosophy, thus ensuring that the seminarians were taught Thomism. This was a strange move for a bishop and especially for a bishop who was not especially given to intellectual matters.

Always interested in sacred music Bishop Sarto not only encouraged Gregorian chant throughout his diocese, but he also forbade bands to play secular music in his churches, a practice that was common in Italy at the time. These interests and concerns would lead after his papal election to his *motu proprio* on church music. After being made cardinal he wrote the following about Gregorian chant:

> We must promote Gregorian chant and ways of making it popular. Oh, if only I could get all the faithful to sing the *Kyrie*, the *Gloria*, the *Credo*, the *Sanctus*, the *Agnus Dei* in the same way that they sing the Litanies and the *Tantum ergo*. To me, this would be the most beautiful victory for sacred music, because it is by really taking part in the liturgy that the faithful will maintain their devotion. Sometimes I just imagine one thousand voices singing the *Missa de Angelis* on the Psalms in a country church; this thought utterly delights me.[8]

He was well ahead of his time in recognizing the importance of the assembly's active participation in the liturgy.

Patriarch of Venice

In 1893, Pope Leo XIII made Bishop Sarto a cardinal and three days later named him Patriarch of Venice. Political machinations prevented the cardinal-patriarch from entering his new see until November 1894. He remained in Mantua running the diocese until that time. Before leaving Mantua Cardinal Sarto drafted a pastoral letter to the clergy of the diocese and to the clergy of Venice. For the most part, as well as encouraging the priests to holiness of life, the pastoral letter took issue with liberalism in the church. The letter has been described by one historian and biographer as "a veritable anti-liberal manifesto in the tradition of nineteenth century anti-liberalism (from the Popes Gregory XVI and Pius IX to the great ecclesiastical and lay writers)."[9] For all practical purposes, the pastoral letter was an onslaught against modernism before the onslaught against modernism.[10] Once established in Venice Cardinal Sarto continued his prior interest in catechetics, requiring his clergy to provide instruction on the faith especially on feast days. A common catechism was published in 1896 for

8. Cited in Chiron, *St. Pius X*, 80–81.

9. Chiron, *St. Pius X*, 88.

10. Yves Chiron, *St. Pius X*, 95 writes: "Cardinal Sarto had identified the initial symptoms [of modernism], as he had in Mantua. It was during this period, moreover, that he began to take notice of the works of Alfred Loisy."

all the dioceses of Venetia. He also had published for the use of families in the region a brief history of the Old Testament, the New Testament and the major events of church history, as well as a volume on the liturgical feasts of the year. In a circular letter to the parish clergy of 1895 he emphasized the importance of substantial content in catechetical teaching, and not oratorical flourish.

> Can there be any other city like Venice for the number of Lenten sermons, octaves, novenas and panegyrics? But why, then, does all this yield personal little fruit? Give up that kind of eloquence which belongs to the stage rather than the church, and which is more profane than sacred . . . and is bereft of any supernatural effectiveness. The faithful do not profit from it; it may fill the church, but it leaves their souls empty; it may draw their applause, but it will not make them weep, and they will leave the church in the same state in which they entered: *mirabantur*, as St. Augustine said, *sed non convertebantur* (they admired, but were not converted).[11]

He also showed an interest in church music, and encouraged frequent reception of the Eucharist. He continued his vigilant interest in the local seminary just as he had done at Mantua. He called the clergy and people of the diocese to a diocesan synod which he hoped would renew the life of the diocese in all respects. In addition to the expected emphasis on serious catechetical work, he insisted that all clergy preach at the Sunday Mass and on holy days of obligation, though it was equally insisted that such sermons should not go beyond twenty minutes. In Venice too he encouraged the manual of Gregorian chant, with all the congregation participating. To this end he required all churches in his diocese to ensure the singing of the *Kyrie, Gloria, Credo, Sanctus,* and *Agnus Dei.* With respect to the Eucharist he also encouraged perpetual adoration of the Blessed Sacrament, frequent communion and the early first communion of children. Under his auspices a National Eucharistic Congress was held in Venice in 1897.

Sarto did not confine his energies to the interior and spiritual renewal of the church. Just as in Mantua, he attended to social and economic affairs also, so much so that he was described as one of Italy's major "social bishops." He associated socialism with all the evils that threatened the world. Against socialism he encouraged as much as possible Catholic endeavors in the social and economic fields, and also Catholic participation in municipal affairs.

Pope Pius X

On the very morning that he set out for Rome to attend the conclave that would elect a successor to Pope Leo XIII, Cardinal Sarto ordained twenty-seven priests and administered the Sacrament of Confirmation to a number of sick children—a

---

11. Cited in Chiron, *St. Pius X*, 94.

pastoral bishop to the last. He must have been aware that he was considered *papabile* in the popular press, but it does not seem to have been something that much engaged his attention. It is said that his neighbor-bishop asked Sarto in French in the 1903 conclave following the death of Leo XIII, whether he was an Italian bishop. Sarto replied that he was unable to speak French, to which the Frenchman replied in Latin: "It is not possible for you to be Pope; a Pope must be able to speak French." "Perfectly true, your eminence," responded Sarto, "I am not a possible Pope. Thank God."[12] The favorite seems to have been Cardinal Rampolla who had been secretary of state to Leo XIII. Rampolla was not everyone's favorite. Before the fourth ballot Cardinal Puzyna, bishop of Krakow, a diocese that was in the Austrian Empire at this time, rose to his feet to make this declaration: "Officially and in the name and by the authority of Franz-Joseph, Emperor of Austria and King of Hungary, that His Majesty, in virtue of an ancient right and privilege, pronounces the veto of exclusion against my Most Eminent Lord, Cardinal Mariano Rampolla del Tindaro."[13] This declaration was protested by the Cardinal Dean and the balloting continued freely. However, it seems that the cardinal electors wanted a different style than the Leonine and so in the seventh ballot Sarto was elected, taking the name of Pius X. "The Cardinals wanted a pastor, someone who understood how parishes work . . . and a friendly, warm-hearted man not given to cold formality."[14] The lack of fluency in French was an issue as French was the language of diplomacy at the time. Sarto was not at all fluent in French, as acknowledged in the conversation between him and the French bishop above. Nor had he held any formal diplomatic post, like some of his important successors. Eamon Duffy writes: "Not one of his nineteenth-century predecessors had been a parish priest. Sarto, even as Bishop of Mantua and Patriarch of Venice, had never really been anything else."[15]

A parish priest Sarto may have been, but taking the name of Pius was quite deliberate, as he saw himself in an adversarial position vis-à-vis the modern world, maintaining Pius IX's ultramontanism. Carlo Falconi points out that "even physically, and in his whole bearing," the similarity to Pius IX was noticeable.[16]

The new pope chose as his secretary of state Msgr. Merry del Val, apparently something of a surprise, not least because he was only thirty-eight at the time. "Merry del Val's appointment was to have serious consequences for the direction of policy in Pius X's reign. . . . [He was] intransigent, and sometimes insensitive."[17] As pope, Pius X contrasts strongly with his immediate predecessor. Undoubtedly, there is truth in seeing Pope Leo XIII as having a more open attitude to modernity, and in seeing Pius as being

---

12. Chadwick, *A History of the Popes 1830–1914*, 337.

13. Cited in Chiron, *St. Pius X*, 122.

14. Chadwick, *A History of the Popes, 1830–1914*, 341.

15. Duffy, *Saints and Sinners*, 320.

16. Falconi, *The Popes in the Twentith Century*, 15.

17. Pollard, *The Papacy in the Age of Totalitarianism 1914–1958*, 9, 18.

more intransigent and rigid. Life is not quite as clean as categories. Leo loved pomp and ceremonial and being carried around; Pius hated it. Leo let visitors remain on their knees during private, papal audiences: Pius seated them. He abolished the 260-year-old tradition of popes eating alone and discouraged the custom of clapping when he entered St. Peter's Basilica. Leo was fond of an entourage of guards, chaplains, and attendants, even on a private walk. Pius's preference was for a solitary walk, or with a secretary. Leo never wore a watch, but Pius used a cheap watch, valued because it had been at his mother's deathbed. Leo used a quill pen, especially for more important documents, but Pius used an ordinary pen, sometimes cleaning the nib on the side of his pontifical robes. In twenty-five years Leo never spoke a word to his private coachman, whereas Pius talked to and joked with everyone. Owen Chadwick continues the contrast humorously: "He hated his toe being kissed and avoided it when he could. He was a man of compassion with no time for shams."[18] One of his innovations as pope was personally to hold a catechism session for the public every Sunday afternoon, continuing the strong catechetical interest of his days as a bishop. He saw himself as a religious pope, not a political pope. He did not agree with his predecessor's policy of appeasing secular governments. He set out to insist firmly on the rights of the church. Nowhere did this become more apparent than in his dealings with France.

The French Problem

Relations between the church and France had never been easy since the French Revolution. Under the concordat with the Emperor Napoleon in 1801, the Catholic Church was acknowledged as the religion of the majority of the French, and in response to the confiscation of ecclesiastical property during the French Revolution, the state paid the salaries of bishops and parish priests. At the same time, attitudes among French Catholics were often polarized. Ardent Catholics were too often right-wing monarchists, and zealous republicans were too often left-wing anti-clericals. Leo XIII had tried to promote better relations through his not very successful encouraging of French Catholics to go some way to supporting the republican government. Perhaps because of his lack of formal diplomatic experience, Pius tended to be more confrontational. Though by no means entirely his fault alone, relations between the church and France came to a standstill in 1905.

Émile Combes (1835–1921) was prime minister of France from 1902 to 1905. There were two incidents by which Pius's actions contributed to the rift between France and the Vatican. Combes secured the law on "associations," which required many religious congregations to leave France, and forbade religious congregations of any kind to engage in teaching. In December 1903 Pius protested these laws to the president of the French Republic. President Émile Loubet responded that he was not in a position

---

18. Chadwick, *A History of the Popes, 1830–1914*, 345.

to do anything constructive. Soon after, in 1904, when President Loubet was making a courteous return visit to King Victor Emmanuel III of Italy, Pius refused the president a papal audience. Undoubtedly, of course, his refusal reflected something of the difficulty of the Roman Question—that the president was visiting a monarch who had taken over Rome and the Papal States. As Yves Chiron puts it, "coming to Rome to visit the King of Italy was equivalent to honoring the despoiler in the very place where his despoliation was most grievous."[19] But there was more to it than that. The tension continued to mount between the Vatican and France, and this came to a climax in the law of 1905, a law that abolished the concordat with Napoleon of 1801. Now church and state were to be entirely separate. The clergy would no longer receive stipends from the state. Church buildings and property passed into the hands of the state, and they were to be administered for the church by associations of the laity. The French episcopate, in a very delicate and difficult situation, sought to find a realistic compromise, or at least a *modus agendi* with the state that would be acceptable to the Vatican. Pius would have nothing to do with anything that smacked of compromise, and Merry del Val was his main support, though a number of the Roman Curia quietly thought his inexperience as secretary of state had made matters much worse than they needed to be.

Pius demanded the resignation of two French bishops accused of Freemasonry and immorality. This met with strong opposition from the French prime minister, Émile Combes, arguing that this amounted to nothing less than papal interference in the rights of the French government arguing that, according to the Napoleonic concordat, the government had the right to nominate bishops, while the Holy See had the right to institute and to ordain them. The two bishops in question were Msgr. Geay, bishop of Laval, and Msgr. L. Nordez, bishop of Dijon. Both had been in trouble with the Holy See for various reasons but Bishop Nordez was republican in his politics and was one of only three bishops who refused to sign the petition of the French bishops urging the government to let religious congregations continue to teach. After a series of communications back and forth between Paris and Rome, mostly negative, both these troublesome bishops resigned. Pope Pius X, fearing that the bishops would be left without an income by the French state, gave them both substantial pensions. In point of fact, France coughed up pensions for these prelates, but the amount was about half of what Pius had awarded them.[20]

Louis Duchesne (1843–1922)

One of the greatest French scholars of the time was Louis Duchesne. "Scholarly research and Catholicism were to remain the hallmarks of [Duchesne's] career—head and heart that he was never quite able to reconcile."[21] One suspects that the tension

---

19. Chiron, *St. Pius X,* 166.

20. Chiron, *St. Pius X,* 170–71.

21. Frend, *From Dogma to History,* 109.

noted here by William Frend concerning Louis Duchesne is far from unique to this church historian. Duchesne arrived in Rome in 1895 as director of the French school at Rome, eight years before the election of Pope Pius X. He had been professor of church history in Paris at the Institut Catholique. Another great church historian, Owen Chadwick, writes of Duchesne with high praise but absolute accuracy as follows: "He was a historian of the first rank who dedicated his work to the early history of the church and the early documents of papal history. He had a sharp wit and a brilliant sarcasm which did not endear him to his foes, and this manner led readers to think him more heretical than he was. He passed through different phases, but for most of the time he disliked the ultramontanes, and his studies in the early papacy gave him no high doctrine of papal authority."[22] That description alone would have brought Duchesne to the attention of the Holy Office, but much more did one of his most prestigious pupils, Alfred Loisy, to whom we shall turn our attention in the next chapter.

As a student of theology in Rome Duchesne tells us that he was "less interested in the lectures than in visiting the catacombs, classical ruins, and the museums."[23] He was judged as somewhat lacking in discretion by his seminary formators and there was some hesitation about ordaining him. His ordination to the priesthood took place in 1867 and at that time he was an ardent infallibilist, a position that was to change. After teaching in his local seminary for a spell, he moved to Paris, and continued with his studies in both philosophy and Greek antiquities.

By 1874 he set himself to study as scientifically as possible the *Liber Pontificalis*, a collection of information about the popes, but an admixture of both history and legend. He completed his research in 1877, published as *Études sur le Liber Pontificalis*, and almost immediately found himself in the midst of criticism. Thus, Cardinal Pitra, the librarian of the Vatican Library, thought Duchesne's work was worthwhile but he judged it to be "more German than French, insufficiently Catholic and missing the opportunity to submit a truly orthodox dogmatic thesis worthy of presentation to believers and unbelievers alike."[24] More than anything else Cardinal Pitra was alluding to Duchesne's strict scientific methodology, methodology well advanced in the Protestant faculties of Germany, and especially by the famous Adolf von Harnack in Berlin. History can be unsettling as it calls into question some cherished but relatively unexamined presuppositions.

Between the years 1877 and 1885 Duchesne taught early church history at the *Institut Catholique* in Paris. "These are among the best years of Duchesne's life. He had a secure position, teaching clergy subjects he loved, and preparing material for his great work on the early history of the church."[25] Despite these good years of teaching, however, controversy surrounded him. He questioned, for example, the early dating

22. Chadwick, *A History of the Popes, 1830–1914*, 350.

23. Duchesne, Autobiographical Note of 1909, cited in Frend, *From Dogma to History*, 109–10.

24. Frend, *From Dogma to History*, 115.

25. Frend, *From Dogma to History*, 121.

of some French sees thereby upsetting their present occupants. And so by 1885 he was ready to leave Paris for Rome as the director of the French School there, and he remained in this post until his death in 1922.

The year 1885 also witnessed the beginning of a long correspondence between Duchesne and Baron Friedrich von Hügel. Duchesne was less than optimistic about the future of theology and especially of biblical exegesis. Biblical studies with all the modern apparatus of interpretation was a passion of the Baron's. Duchesne was keen to warn him of the dangers. He wrote: "When I risk my neck for having denied the apostolic foundation of the diocese of Sens, it hardly seems a good idea to introduce novel opinions about the authenticity of the Pentateuch." And in Duchesne's opinion, again offered in correspondence to the Baron, "[Catholics] scarcely realize that there even is a Bible or that the accepted exegesis has been thoroughly discredited. They feel no need for a reformed exegesis. Such is particularly the case in France and Italy where for centuries the clergy have read the Bible with about as much attention as they have the Koran."[26]

His first years in Rome saw him continue with his historical-critical studies to great acclaim. This was to change with the advent of Pope Pius X. "Duchesne had . . . enjoyed reasonably good relations with Pope Leo XIII. Under the more limited Pius X this was to change."[27] Good relations with the church were to change for many more than Louis Duchesne, as the condemnation of modernism got under way.

Modernism

Modernism was condemned by Pope Pius X. Sometimes historians draw too clear a contrast between Pope Leo XIII and Pope Pius X, the former regarded as open-minded and the latter as closed-minded and negative. Contrasts like this can sometimes be helpful, but they can be overdrawn. The historian Émile Poulat wrote of these two popes as follows:

> One must be aware of making too much of an opposition between Leo XIII, the political, liberal Pope, open to the modern world, and Pius X, the religious Pope, retrograde and outclassed. In the case of pontiffs, it is the same model of Catholicism which is being transmitted and imposed: an "intransigent" Catholicism, . . . the product of the Counter-Reformation, but forged throughout the whole of the last century in the wake of the ordeal of the French Revolution and the other revolutions, in confrontation with modern times and the modern spirit.[28]

26. The correspondence is cited from O'Connell, *Critics on Trial*, 92.

27. O'Connell, *Critics on Trial*, 134.

28. Cited in Chiron, *St. Pius X*, 188–89.

According to Poulat, Leo's mind on these doctrinal issues was essentially the same as Pius's, and the same doctrinal challenges that had begun during Leo's pontificate were left unresolved. Modernism was as far as Pope Pius X was concerned a synthesis of all the philosophical systems that were considered wrong—idealist, subjectivist and positivist philosophies. The bulwark of defense against all such errors was the philosophy of St. Thomas Aquinas, the philosophy mandated by Pope Leo XIII, Pius X's predecessor. Was there, however, such a reality as a systematic and coherent modernism? Certainly, there were people who could be described as modernists in terms of their outlook and methodology, but arguably there was no such thing as "modernism" as such. If we may call modernism a movement, it was a movement found throughout different thinkers in Europe that included the following: in Italy, Ernesto Buonaiuti (1881–1946), and Antonio Fogazarro (1842–1911); in Germany, Joseph Schnitzer (1858–1939), and Thaddaeus Engert (1875–1945); in France, Alfred Loisy (1857–1940), Edouard Le Roy (1870 1954), and Lucien Laberthonnière (1860–1932); in England George Tyrrell (1861–1909), Friedrich von Hugel (1852–1925), and Maude Petre (1863–1942). "The assumptions made by the anti-modernists—for example, that modernism was an internally coherent system expressing itself in a carefully concerted movement—were so wide of the mark, that the understanding of modernism to be found in the Roman documents should be taken as symbolic of an attitude rather than as an accurate assessment of a factual situation."[29]

Modernism was a Catholic reform movement. Much, therefore, will depend on whether one thinks reform is necessary, or what kind of reform is judged to be appropriate. Inevitably, then, some regarded the condemnation of modernism by Pius X as an example of courageous and strong leadership, of dealing efficiently with a movement that could only threaten the well-being of the church. Others interpreted the papal action against Modernism as the "uncompromising rejection by a papacy drunk on the power of an obscurantist authoritarianism made newly possible by the definition of papal infallibility in 1870."[30]

Aidan Nichols, OP, writes carefully, albeit minimally, that "The Roman response [to modernism], despite the presence of a canonized saint on the chair of Peter [Pius X], left something to be desired."[31] The Anglican historian of modernism, Alec Vidler, is much harsher and probably more accurate when he writes: "[He] did not take the name of 'Pius' for nothing. He stood for a reversion to the conservative intransigence of Pius IX. He regarded it as his mission to stamp out all dangerous thinking in the church, and had the power to do so. . . . It is hardly an exaggeration to say that a reign of doctrinal terror was maintained until the death of Pius X in 1914, and even then was only gradually relaxed."[32]

29. Daly, *Transcendence and Immanence*, 3.
30. Lash, "Modernism, Aggiornamento and the Night Battle," 58.
31. Nichols, *Catholic Thought since the Enlightenment*, 88.
32. Vidler, *Twentieth-Century Defenders of the Faith*, 36.

Between the views of Nichols and Vidler one recognizes that there was a problem that was not well handled. It seems clear that Pius had no close awareness or understanding of all that was going on in so-called "modernist" theology and philosophy. His was essentially the response of the conservative pastor, concerned for the well-being of his people. Nevertheless, he had power and he used it, and not always well. During the process for his beatification, his private secretary, Msgr. Pescini, acknowledged under oath: "The great struggle undertaken and conducted with such energy and efficiency against Modernism was personally directed and sustained by Pius X despite considerable opposition and forces."[33] Seminary professors judged to be modernist were replaced, and a climate of fear and suspicion arose in the church.

Umberto Benigni (1862–1934)

Owen Chadwick writes that "Pius X needed a confidant who could tell him how to eradicate the treachery which he believed that he faced. He found Msgr. Umberto Benigni."[34] Umberto Benigni was born into an economically very modest family in Perugia in 1862. He was ordained as a priest at twenty-two and was sent on to Rome for further studies at the Seminario Pio, following which he returned to his diocese serving, among other things, as a professor of history.

> Benigni divided his black and white world into two forces—clericals and anti-clericals; in the latter category he lumped together liberals, socialists, masons, and Jews, the most dangerous being the socialists, the "reds," who aimed to destroy the clergy. They were the enemies of freedom and humanity. But he declared war on all the anticlericals, a war without concessions or compromise that he would wage relentlessly for the rest of his career.[35]

This anti-modern approach virtually to everything characterized his work as a priest from the beginning. He espoused right-wing projects and ideas and publications, but after a disagreement with his ordinary, the archbishop of Genoa, he moved to the Vatican Library. As he worked at the library, he also taught church history at the Roman Seminary, two of his better-known students being Ernesto Buonaiuti—who was himself condemned as a modernist—and Angelo Roncalli who went on to higher things. While he was regarded as something of an intellectual breath of fresh air, Benigni's lectures had characteristics that left something to be desired. "Ernesto Buonaiuti . . . called him extremely skeptical, hard as steel, a deep dyed pessimist. Buonaiuti was shocked one day, he said, when Benigni told him that history was nothing but a

---

33. Falconi, *The Popes in the Twentieth Century,* 53.
34. Chadwick, *A History of the Popes, 1830–1914,* 356.
35. Bokenkotter, *Church and Revolution,* 242.

continual vomiting and that one should not expect anything good from human beings; the Inquisition, Benigni declared, was the only answer."[36]

Msgr. Benigni established the *Sodalitium Pianum*/League of St. Pius V. Through this secret society of informers, he discovered modernists, or those suspected of modernism, everywhere. He created a special set of codes for his correspondence, for example, referring to Pius as "Mama." A virtual witch-hunt of Catholic intellectuals took place. "It was not only modernists who were under suspicion, it was anyone scholarly."[37]

All kinds of good, honest scholars found themselves under suspicion. One of the victims was a young professor of church history at the seminary in Bergamo, Angelo Roncalli, the future Pope John XXIII. Roncalli had been denounced to Rome for recommending that his students read Louis Duchesne's *Early History of the Church*. The story is told of Giorgio LaPiana, who later became a professor at Harvard, that he was traveling as a young priest on the train from Sicily to Rome. A traveling companion with whom he fell into conversation revealed his sympathies with modernism. LaPiana must have shown some degree of empathy in the conversation because some days later he was reprimanded and sent back to his diocese.[38] A couple of other examples will illustrate the wide-ranging reach of Benigni's spy network, as it were. A certain Canon Ulysse Chevalier (1841–1923), a French bibliographer and church historian, came under attack simply because he did not believe in the authenticity of the holy shroud of Turin, or in the transportation by angels of the Holy House at Loreto. Francis P. Duffy, a philosophy professor in the seminary for the Archdiocese of New York was the editor of a journal that tried to keep its readers abreast of contemporary developments and scholarship. The journal was forced to close down as a result of pressure from the apostolic delegate to the United States. "In the face of this situation, Duffy decided that he too would close his books and he went to work in a parish. His statue, in battle dress as chaplain of the 69th Regiment, New York National Guard, stands today just above Times Square. The *New York Review* is forgotten, but Duffy, as played by Pat O'Brien in 'The Fighting 69th,' is part of American Catholic folklore."[39]

In his Lenten letter of 1915 Cardinal Désiré Joseph Mercier, the Louvain Thomist scholar under Leo XIII and then archbishop of Malines, who had himself been suspected of modernism, wrote of this witch-hunt: "Modernism had indeed drawn some impetuous spirits, more courageous in words and deeds, into violent and insidious personal controversy. . . . Petty scribes or worthless journalists, they excommunicated all those unwilling to pass beneath the Caudine forks of their integralism. Sincere hearts were troubled by unrest: the more honest consciences suffered in silence."[40]

36. Bokenkotter, *Church and Revolution*, 245.

37. Chadwick, *A History of the Popes 1830–1914*, 357.

38. The episode, with sources, is recounted in Carlo Falconi, *The Popes in the Twentieth Century*, 41.

39. Holmes, *The Triumph of the Holy See*, 274.

40. Cited in Falconi, *The Popes in the Twentieth Century*, 38.

Pope Benedict XV, Pius's successor, got rid of Benigni, who ended his life as a fascist. It would probably be too strong to claim that this condemnation of modernism killed Catholic scholarship as such, but it did put severe restrictions on creative theological thinking. As Nicholas Lash puts it, "the condemnation of Modernism fatally delayed the flowering of the renaissance."[41] Moreover, it led to a climate in the church in which critical thinking of any kind was frowned upon. Catholics, rather, were to accept the faith of the whole church, what might be called the "integral faith," and so, "integrist" or "integralist" became a term for virtually total and complete and unthinking docility. "'Real' Catholics were 'integralists,' accepting as a package deal everything the pope taught, not picking and choosing in the 'pride and curiosity' of their intellect."[42] The situation in the church for such as theologians, philosophers and church historians was definitely one of fear, fear perhaps for one's position in the academy, or, indeed, fear for one's place within the spiritual fabric of the church. At the same time, the situation in the church was not so cut and dried as this impression may have given. One of the premier historians of modernism, Alec R. Vidler, makes this comment: "In reality, of course, the Roman Church has never been as stationary or unchanging as it liked to appear to be. The anti-modernist measures, even if they were not repealed, were gradually relaxed after the death of Pius X in 1914, so far as their application went. The reign of terror, which he had countenanced, was eased by his successor, Benedict XV."[43] When all is said and done, it remains tragically true that the Roman authorities were not well-equipped in the best sense of the word to deal with the issues and questions that the modernists were trying to respond to. As one historian has put it, "the authorities were the products of an ecclesiastical tradition that had left them incapable of dealing with Modernism."[44] On the part of Rome there was little appreciation of developments in biblical studies and of non-scholastic approaches to philosophy and theology. Indeed, they were ill-equipped. At the same time, some of those who were labeled as "modernists" were intemperate in some of their positions and judgments. Perhaps if there had been more of an agreed middle-ground between Rome and the modernists, then more balanced and better established positions would have been reached.

Pope Pius X and the Life of the Church

Pope Pius X set in motion the codification of canon law for the first time, a mere eight months after his election, and this has been described as his "greatest positive legacy."[45] The practical aspects of canon law appealed to him, and it is said that as a priest in

41. Lash, "Modernism, Aggiornamento and the Night Battle," 72.

42. Duffy, *Saints and Sinners*, 329.

43. Vidler, *A Variety of Catholic Modernists*, 188.

44. Holmes, *The Triumph of the Holy See*, 268.

45. Pollard, *The Unknown Pope: Benedict XV and the Pursuit of Peace*, 11.

Tombolo he divided his leisure reading between the *Summa Theologiae* of St. Thomas Aquinas and Gratian's *Decretals*. While patriarch of Venice, he instituted a chair of canon law with the right to confer degrees in the discipline. He wanted the ordinary priest to know his way around canon law so as to be of real assistance to his people. The task of codification was entrusted to Cardinal Pietro Gasparri, who had been a professor of canon law at the Institut Catholique of Paris for over twenty years and was the author of a number of standard Latin texts on the laws of marriage, ordination, and the Eucharist. Gasparri was assisted in this enterprise by the young priest Eugenio Pacelli, later to become Pope Pius XII. Before Pius X died, the code was almost complete and was finally promulgated by Pope Benedict XV in 1917. It made access to canon law much easier for diocesan administrators and canonists.

Owen Chadwick maintains that "[The code of canon law] was also the legal sanction of the centralization that took place during the nineteenth century."[46] The principal example Chadwick provides is the appointment of bishops in canon 329.2, "The pope nominates bishops freely." To us this seems self-evident, but it was not the universal custom in the church, even in the nineteenth century, so that Chadwick can comment: "The canon in the Codex was aspiration more than reality."[47] Perhaps, but now that aspiration was law in the church, and a law that was to be practiced and held to. In a sense, there was something of a tension between Pius's pastoral side and the juridical ecclesiology that was to be found in the new code.

In 1909 Pius established the Pontifical Biblical Institute to promote the scientific study of Scripture. In this respect he aligned himself with the "progressivism" of Leo XIII. Leadership of the new Pontifical Biblical Institute was put in the hands of a German exegete, Fr. Leopold Fonck, SJ. Again like Leo, he upheld and promoted the study of St. Thomas Aquinas in ecclesiastical schools.

His consistent interest in church music led him to publish the *motu proprio Tra le sollecitudini* of 1903. He was utterly opposed to musical theatricality in church, "in which the church became almost an extension of the opera house, with worshipers paying more attention to the choir than to the altar, waiting for the moment when their idol would appear in a cavatina or duet, for all the world as if they were on the stage."[48] Instead, Pius wanted traditional sacred music that would lift the mind and heart to God. *Tra le sollecitudini* provided norms for sacred music and powerfully encouraged Gregorian chant, and the pope used of the liturgy the phrase that would become famous in Vatican II's Constitution on the Sacred Liturgy, "full, conscious, and active participation." The first principles of the *motu proprio* are still worth reading:

> Sacred music must possess to the highest degree the qualities proper to the liturgy: *holiness,* and that excellence of form which gives birth spontaneously to

46. Chadwick, *A History of the Popes, 1830–1914,* 360.

47. Chadwick, *A History of the Popes, 1830–1914,* 360.

48. Falconi, *The Popes in the Twentieth Century,* 22.

its other character: *universality*. It must be holy, and so it must exclude all that would make it profane, not only in itself, but also in the way it is performed. It must be true art; otherwise it would not be able to have that felicitous influence on its hearers which the church intends in admitting music into her liturgy. Yet it must also be universal, in the sense that while every nation is permitted, in ecclesiastical compositions, to adopt those forms which are, in a certain way, particular to that nation, such forms must be subordinated to the general characteristics of sacred music, so that no one from another nation could be disconcerted by what he hears.[49]

These principles seem very balanced indeed and spring from a right sense of liturgy. Owen Chadwick draws a parallel between Leo XIII and Pius X: "As Pope Leo XIII made St. Thomas Aquinas the key to philosophical theology, so Pius X made the Gregorian chant the perfection of church music."[50] Chadwick is right in part, provided we recognize that the liturgy is always the backdrop for the pope's concern for sacred music. Furthermore, according to Cardinal Merry del Val, the pope "did not agree with the attitude of certain fanatics who wanted to exclude from our churches all music except Gregorian. This, he said, was an exaggeration."[51]

Up to the end of the nineteenth century, many Mass-going Catholics did not receive holy communion except a few times a year. This was largely a consequence of Jansenism. Jansenists encouraged very careful preparation for holy Communion, including sacramental confession. Leo XIII encouraged more frequent communion, but it was Pius X who seriously tried to achieve this. In a series of twelve statements issued between 1904–7, the pope encouraged people to receive the Eucharist, even on a daily basis. Through his 1910 decree *Quam Singulari* Pius brought down the age for first communion to the age of reason and ordered parish clergy to spend one hour every Sunday catechizing children. "These acts of Pius X amounted to a revolution in worshiping practices. Historians, in hindsight, if asked which act of which pope did most to affect the church since 1800, would put their finger on this change of 1905–1906, the encouragement of frequent, even daily communion, and the receiving of it by children."[52]

Conclusion

"If Leo XIII's papacy had been a cautious attempt to come to terms with the modern world, then Pius X's was a repudiation of it. . . . This papacy belongs to the nineteenth

---

49. Cited in Chiron, *St. Pius X*, 140.

50. Chadwick, *A History of the Popes 1830–1914*, 364.

51. Cited in Chiron, *St. Pius X*, 141.

52. Chadwick, *A History of the Popes, 1830–1914*, 362. Collins, *Absolute Power*, 82, writes: "A new attitude to the Eucharist emerged in the church, without doubt this Pius's most important achievement."

century rather than to the twentieth."[53] This is the judgment of the historian Paul Collins and is largely accurate. Pope Pius X was both a reformer and a reactionary, something of a prophet at times, but with a strong custodial sense. The year 1910 was the occasion for the first International Missionary Conference in Edinburgh, the first major twentieth-century step towards the establishment of ecumenism as central to the Christian enterprise. There was no encouragement under Pius for Catholics to participate in ecumenism in any sense of the word. Indeed, in that very same year Pius refused an audience to former U.S. President Theodore Roosevelt, because Roosevelt intended to speak in the Methodist church in Rome. Pusillanimity such as this may not simply be accounted for in terms of historical context and circumstances.

His approach to developing trends in theology was no less reactionary. Hence the tragedy of those such as George Tyrrell and the other modernists. Those who argue that Pius's "condemnation of Modernism did far more harm to Catholic theology than did the writings of any Modernists" are largely in the right, even if at times they do not have all the details of the picture.[54] Pius's pastoral concern was the major project of his pontificate, expressed in his liturgical and canonical innovations and, it must be admitted, even in his extremist reaction to "modernism." It is reported that Pius was deeply grieved at the outbreak of the Great War in 1914, so grieved that many said he died of a broken heart. Yves Chiron writes: "The outbreak of the World War coincided with the sudden worsening of the Pope's health, which was to prove fatal. All the testimonies agree that the outbreak of this war shattered Pius X. As Cardinal Merry del Val says: 'The horror of war tormented and obsessed him day and night. The invasion of Belgium and the news of the first battles overwhelmed him with suffering.'"[55]

Pope Pius X was canonized in 1954 by Pope Pius XII. The question remains: Does ecclesially established sanctity always correlate with consistency, and indeed, what does it mean to be consistent? Peter Hebblethwaite has written:

> It is difficult to think of any convincing ecclesial reason for canonizing St. Pius X. Once the deed was done, of course, Catholic historians had to apply lashings of whitewash. The truth is that Pius X was difficult, suspicious, neurotic and simple-minded. True, he reformed the Roman Curia, embarked on the Herculean task of codifying canon law (not completed until Pentecost 1917), introduced useful liturgical reforms, simplified church music and admitted younger children to the Eucharist. These were all positive achievements. But they hardly justify the claim made in March 1985 by Pope John Paul II at Riese, the saint's home village in the Veneto, that "in him one era of church history came to an end, and another began that would lead to Vatican II."[56]

53. Collins, *Absolute Power*, 82.

54. Thus, Daly, *Transcendence and Immanence*, 3.

55. Cited in Chiron, *St. Pius X*, 299–300.

56. Hebblethwaite, *In the Vatican*, 26. Marvin O'Connell, *Critics on Trial*, 361 writes: "Pius X's relentless pursuit, not so much of acknowledged Modernists as of the Modernists' putative allies,

6

The Modernist Crisis

Modernists wear no uniform nor are they sworn to the defense of any system: still less of that which His Holiness has fabricated for them.

—George Tyrrell[1]

The essential thing, for Catholic theologians born between 1890 and 1940, was that they should be grounded in "thomistic philosophy." This was to inoculate them against infection by the idealist, subjectivist and positivist philosophies, which were held to have created the "modernist crisis."

—Fergus Kerr, OP[2]

Introduction

As noted in the last chapter, modernism was condemned by Pope Pius X. Sometimes historians draw too clear a contrast between Pope Leo XIII and Pope Pius X, the former regarded as open-minded and the latter as closed-minded and negative. Contrasts like this can sometimes be helpful, but they can be overdrawn. The historian Émile Poulat wrote of these two popes as follows: "One must be aware of making too much of an opposition between Leo XIII, the political, liberal Pope, open to the modern world, and Pius X, the religious Pope, retrograde and outclassed. In the case of pontiffs, it is the same model of Catholicism which is being transmitted and imposed: an 'intransigent' Catholicism . . . the product of the Counter-Reformation, but forged throughout the whole of the last century in the wake of the ordeal of the French Revolution and

appears startlingly inconsistent with the ordinary and much romanticized image of the saintly Giuseppe Sarto who, as pope, brought the Eucharistic Christ to little children and who concerned himself with enhancing the beauty and significance of liturgical worship. It was indeed his antimodernist crusade—the mean-spirited witch-hunt he consciously unleashed—which stood forty years later as the single greatest barrier to Pius X's canonization. An explanation for the seeming aberration remains elusive."

1. Tyrrell, *Mediaevalism*,106.

2. Kerr, OP, *Twentieth-Century Catholic Theologians*, 1.

the other revolutions, in confrontation with modern times and the modern spirit."[3] According to Poulat, Leo's mind on these doctrinal issues was essentially the same as Pius's, and the same doctrinal challenges that had begun during Leo's pontificate were left unresolved. The words of theologian Fergus Kerr that open our chapter help our initial understanding of the phenomenon known as modernism. It was as far as Pope Pius X was concerned a synthesis of all the philosophical systems that were considered wrong—idealist, subjectivist, and positivist philosophies.

In the nineteenth century there had been various attempts to give Catholicism a liberal or more modern orientation, but they were all unsuccessful because of the ascendancy of ultramontanism in the church and especially because of the policy of the long-serving Pope Pius IX (1846–78). This anti-liberal and ultramontane attitude came back with a vengeance in the pontificate of Pope Pius X especially in his attack on modernism.

In discussing modernism, however, one of the principal difficulties is defining the term. To orient us towards an understanding of the term, the description-definition offered in the anonymous article in *The Oxford Dictionary of the Christian Church* is a good place to start: "A movement within the Roman Catholic Church which aimed at bringing the tradition of Catholic belief into closer relation with the modern outlook in philosophy, the historical and other sciences and social ideas."[4] As this definition has it, modernism is a Catholic reform movement. Much, therefore, will depend on whether one thinks reform is necessary, or what kind of reform is judged to be appropriate. Inevitably, then, some regarded the condemnation of modernism by Pius X as an example of courageous and strong leadership, of dealing efficiently with a movement that could only threaten the well-being of the church. Others interpreted the papal action against modernism as the "uncompromising rejection by a papacy drunk on the power of an obscurantist authoritarianism made newly possible by the definition of papal infallibility in 1870."[5] The most promising way to achieve a better understanding of the phenomenon is to look at some of those who were regarded as "modernists."

Alfred Loisy (1857–1940)

"[Alfred Loisy] in historical retrospect remains the most impressive, because the most learned, subtle and eloquent, of the Modernist leaders."[6] Alfred Loisy came from an agricultural family in Ambrières, France, and having showed academic promise at the local diocesan seminary, he pursued his studies at the Institut Catholique in Paris, being ordained in 1879. He spent a short time in pastoral work as a priest but

3. Cited in Chiron, *St. Pius X,* 188–89.
4. Cross and Livingstone, *The Oxford Dictionary of the Christian Church,* 926.
5. Lash, "Modernism, Aggiornamento and the Night Battle," 58.
6. Reardon, *Roman Catholic Modernism,* 16.

enthused by the historical-critical work of Louis Duchesne, whom we looked at in the last chapter, he returned to Paris for further studies, attending Ernest Renan's lectures at the Collège de France in December 1882. This was probably the beginning of his calling as a scientific student of the Scriptures.[7] As such Loisy came to the realization of the absolute need for a radical renewal of theological education. To take but one example, while in seminary he had been taught Hebrew by an upperclassman. Once this senior student's Hebraic knowledge had been exhausted, Loisy went on to a more serious study of the language on his own. "He compared Greek and Latin versions of Genesis to the Hebrew text and reveled in the insights his extraordinary gift for languages afforded him, but 'having no critical commentary to deal with, I could make no troubling discoveries.'"[8] That would soon change. Loisy came to see that historical texts without exception had to be studied by historical-critical methodologies, and this necessarily included the Bible.

In 1890 he was appointed Professor of Sacred Scripture at the Institut Catholique in Paris, but his critical biblical studies brought upon him a cloud of suspicion so that three years later in 1893 he was dismissed from this position and advised to specialize in the study of oriental languages. This advice came from the rector of the *Institut*, Msgr. Maurice d'Hulst. From 1894 until 1896 Loisy served as the chaplain to the Dominican nuns and the girls of their school at Neuilly, a fashionable Parisian suburb.

Loisy was a polyglot scholar who had published a number of books on biblical subjects but the one that achieved greatest notoriety was his *L'Évangile et l'Église*, *The Gospel and the Church*, which became known as the "little red book" because of the color of its cover. It was intended as a Catholic response to Adolf von Harnack's *What Is Christianity?* Harnack was an immensely erudite professor of theology and church history at the University of Berlin. In the winter term of 1899–1900 he presented a series of lectures to the university at large on the central meaning of Christianity. These lectures came into print as the book *The Essence of Christianity*, selling fifty thousand copies in its first year. Harnack was probably the greatest Protestant liberal theologian in Germany. His thesis was to cut away from Christianity all dogmatic and doctrinal excrescences so that the pure kernel of Jesus's teaching would emerge clearly. That teaching for Harnack was to be summed up as "the fatherhood of God and the brotherhood of men." Loisy saw his book as a straightforward refutation of Harnack. Here is a summary of Loisy's conclusions:[9]

- The gospel is not "a unique and immutable truth, but a living faith, concrete and complex" which undergoes an "evolution."

---

7. Reardon, *Roman Catholic Modernism*, 17.

8. O'Connell, *Critics on Trial*, 16.

9. Based on the summary provided by Chiron, *St. Pius X*, 191.

- The divinity of Jesus Christ and his resurrection should be understood as acts of faith: "the resurrection is not a fact that could have been directly and formally established."

- The church is nothing more than the "collective and continuous life of the gospel," and "the decisions taken by authority only sanction, so to speak, and consecrate the movement of the community's thought and piety."

- The church "does not demand belief in its formulas as if they were an adequate expression of absolute truth," and there is an "unceasing evolution of Christian doctrine."

- The church tries to regulate the external forms of devotion: they must not be seen as opposed to true piety and faith, but as forms of "the immense development which has gone on in the church," due to the necessity of adapting the gospel to the changing conditions of humankind.

"In contrast to Harnack's static image of an unsullied seed or core to which sinister barnacles of dogma and cult and institutional structures had fastened themselves, Loisy offered a picture of a vibrant organism which bloomed and blossomed, to be sure, but also shucked off dead skin and useless limbs as occasion demanded, all in accord with the evolutionary laws that determined the fate of living things."[10] The book was "the proto-event of the modernist crisis," because the real issue behind the book was whether Catholic dogma could be understood as an objective, coherent and perennially valid statement of transcendent facts, or a series of contextual responses to various situations and challenges?[11] Readers of a scholastic frame of mind rejected Loisy's book as both weak and disturbing, like the Jesuit theologian Leonce de Grandmaison (1868–1927). Other readers found the book very helpful, for example, Msgr. Mignot, the archbishop of Albi. At the beginning of 1903 the book was condemned by the Archdiocese of Paris and the people of the archdiocese were forbidden to read it, both clergy and laity. A mere seven months after this condemnation Pius X became Pope.

Loisy, after resigning from the Dominicans' school at Neuilly, found employment at the Collège de France, and an apartment at Bellevue, not far away from the college. He also coincidentally found himself accompanied on his walks in the area by Abbé Felix Klein, who had translated the *Life of Isaac Hecker* into French and contributed to the phenomenon known as "Americanism."[12] Although Loisy and Klein often walked together and must have had many conversations, they were not close friends.

When Loisy wrote *The Gospel and the Church*, it seems that he no longer believed in traditional Christological doctrine, though he still believed in God. In fact, this notion of the mystery of the transcendent God never left him. Alec Vidler, the premier

10. O'Connell, *Critics on Trial*, 246.

11. See Daly, *Transcendence and Immanence*, 49, 71.

12. For Isaac Hecker and Americanism, see Cummings, *Prophets, Guardians and Saints*, 83–99, 127–30.

English-language historian of modernism, comments: "Perhaps Loisy's agnosticism had more reverence in it, and even more faith, than the confident dogmatism of those who condemned him."[13] Vidler may well be right, but there is also in Loisy a certain bitterness toward authority. His approach to dogma, doctrine, and truth, and his inadequate Christology were bound to get him into difficulties. The final break with the church for Loisy took place in 1908. In that year he was publicly excommunicated—an act described by church historian Meriol Trevor as "an unusual severity."[14]

What of Loisy's own, personal relationship with Christianity, with Christian faith? Did that come to an end with his condemnation and exit from the church? It is notoriously difficult to grasp the interiority of another. We must be content with whatever limited facts may be available, and with particular points of view based on immediate experience. Alec Vidler, for example, who visited Loisy a number of times in the 1930s, long after his excommunication, describes him in these terms: "I can only say for my part that I do not doubt the sincerity of his faith and of his allegiance to the church up to the time when the church demanded a retraction of his modernist convictions."[15] Vidler saw Loisy as a faithful and sincere Christian, at least up to the moment of his excommunication. From two of Loisy's autobiographical writings, *Choses Passés* and *Mémoires*, it seems that he experienced a crisis of faith before 1886. This probably had to do with his idea of the failure of scholastic orthodoxy, which emerged as his biblical studies began to develop. Vidler was not close to Loisy, but Maude Petre, another "modernist," was a close friend of Loisy's, and she related to Vidler the following memory: "Ms. Petre told me that she had some years before (1941) attended a conference at Pontigny at which Loisy also was present. He could not go into the abbey church for the solemn Mass on Sunday since he was *vitandus*, but he was discovered outside with tears in his eyes."[16]

Vidler makes the interesting distinction that, though Loisy could no longer operate liturgically as a priest after his excommunication, he continued to be a priest *religiously*. By this Vidler meant that he continued to show concern with the religious aspect of human nature, and even to some extent, with pastoral ministry. The epitaph that Loisy drew up for himself contains the following words: "Alfred Loisy, a priest retired from the ministry, . . . Professor at the Collège de France, kept your will in his vows (*tuam in votis tenuit voluntatem*)." Obviously, Loisy continued to think of himself as a priest in some basic sense of the word.

Particularly difficult for Loisy was an experience he had in 1904. He had written a letter to Pope Pius X in which he had made an active submission to the condemnation of his books. The letter began: "Most Holy Father, I well know your Holiness' goodness of heart and it is to your heart that I now address myself." On March 12

---

13. Vidler, *A Variety of Catholic Modernists*, 53.

14. Trevor, *Prophets and Guardians*, 66.

15. Vidler, *Twentieth-Century Defenders of the Faith*, 46.

16. Vidler, *A Variety of Catholic Modernists*, 11.

that year, Cardinal Richard of Paris gave him the papal reply in which he read these words: "I have received a letter from the Rev. Abbé Loisy, in which he appeals to my heart, but this letter was not written from the heart." In Loisy's book, *Choses Passés*, he described the effect of the papal letter:

> Something gave way within me when I heard the opening words. The head of this church to which I have given my life, for which I have worked so hard for thirty years past, which I had loved and could not help loving still, outside of which I had no hopes nor ambitions, could find nothing else to say, when I had responded to absurd demands by a supreme sacrifice, than the harsh words: "that letter addressed to my heart was not written from the heart." All the same, it was written from the heart. Pressed into it was the last drop of feeling left in my Catholic soul.[17]

Lucien Laberthonnière (1860–1932)

Laberthonnière was a priest of the Congregation of the Oratory. Even as a young seminarian, he found himself increasingly dissatisfied with what Alec Vidler calls "the confidence and complacency of the official scholastic theology."[18] He became a professor of philosophy at the Oratorian Collège de Juilly in 1887 and remained in that position until 1903, when the French government moved against religious congregations. He thought of himself specifically as a Christian philosopher and so he spoke about a "metaphysic of charity" and sometimes of "moral dogmatism." This latter phrase points to an understanding of dogma as a practical guide for Christian living rather than as a divinely guaranteed conceptual inroad to the divine mystery. Dogma must show "what we are and what we ought to be and how we can become what we ought to be."[19] Moral dogmatism is an approach to Christian dogma that wrings out the practical, moral, and social meaning of dogma as a support and direction for living the Christian life, representing a very practical and a very personalist view of religion. If truth is to be had, it must be had from living and for living. If the objection is made that this approach to religious truth appears to push out the divine and to espouse a purely natural approach, Laberthonnière would reply that the natural is already penetrated by the divine. In a real sense, there is no such thing as a purely natural, but rather the natural is "the prolongation of the divine life into the life of man."[20]

Laberthonnière was hostile to Thomism. He saw Thomism as an instance of Greek idealism, abstract and arid and lacking vitality, in contrast to Christian realism, which was dynamic, personable, and social. He once wrote to Friedrich von

---

17. Cited in Vidler, *A Variety of Catholic Modernists*, 47.
18. Vidler, *A Variety of Catholic Modernists*, 82.
19. Cited in Vidler, *A Variety of Catholic Modernists*, 83.
20. See Macquarrie, *Twentieth-Century Religious Thought*, 183–84.

Hügel who had praised Aquinas in the preface to one of his books: "To me—I say to you in all simplicity—he appears to stand doctrinally for a radical anti-Christianity. In place of the gospel's God of love he put an egocentric God. . . . For him the church consists essentially in the ecclesiastical organization regarded as a domination that is to be exercised under the direction and to the advantage of theologians . . ."[21] Really, this is a travesty of Aquinas, understandable perhaps as a reaction to the ecclesiastically imposed scholasticism of Pope Leo XIII, but a travesty nonetheless. There can be little doubt that Laberthonnière's "persistent and violent anti-Thomism" (in Vidler's description) led to his being viewed with suspicion by Rome. Rome, after all, with Pope Leo XIII's encyclical *Aeterni Patris* had mandated the study of Aquinas and that led Laberthonnière in 1884 to write his essay, "The Cartesian Spirit and the Scholastic Spirit," in which we find these words:

> O modern scholastic philosophers, you who dream foolishly of entrapping in your formulas a human soul which has come to a consciousness of itself by genuine reflection! This soul which has felt the flame of life, which has understood, which has experienced the thirst for infinity, which loves science, a true and positive science, not an imaginary one, a science that is also poetry—you would like to force that soul to fit into your categories. Try instead to capture the passing wind and force it into a circle or a square. Your attempts will be just as vain as that.[22]

Laberthonnière's major philosophical books, *Essays on Religious Philosophy* and *Christian Realism and Greek Idealism* were placed on the Index of Prohibited Books in 1906, as were other works by him in 1913, and he was forbidden to publish. In both publications he saw Thomism as a version of "Greek idealism"—that is abstract, not having anything to do with the vital flow of life. The test of any given philosophy, as Laberthonnière understood it, is whether it can be illuminating and helpful when brought to bear on the issues and problems of life. Christian realism was much more successful in relating to life than any form of Greek idealism, including Aristotelianism and Thomism.

Laberthonnière was equally uncompromising in his negative reaction to papal authority. Rightly, he viewed the role of authority as one of service, not domination (Mark 10:45), but he saw no exercise of contemporary authority as being marked by service. Although Laberthonnière was a rebel against authority, Vidler maintains that "he stood for resistance, but not for revolt."[23] Reform had to come from within the community of faith and, above all else, Laberthonnière wanted reform. Concerning the encyclical *Pascendi* that condemned modernism, he wrote: "Silent, persevering, mortified work

---

21. Cited in Vidler, *A Variety of Catholic Modernists,* 85–86.

22. Cited in O'Connell, *Critics on Trial,* 80–81.

23. Vidler, *A Variety of Catholic Modernists,* 87.

will do more than anything else."[24] Descartes was one of Laberthonnière's philosophic icons and, while he hoped in his own work to bring greater religious sentiment to bear on the work of Descartes, the latter never ceased to be his inspiration. "There is a grandeur in Descartes. Too bad for those who do not realize this. What I admire most in Descartes, even more than his ideas, is his method of philosophizing. In following it I have staked out my own interior independence."[25]

Edouard Le Roy (1870–1954)

"Le Roy, it is true, is not so well known as his fellow modernists Alfred Loisy and George Tyrrell, but this Gallic logician . . . penetrates to the heart of the modernists' difficulties with traditional Catholicism."[26] Joseph Fitzer in this comment is pointing to Le Roy's influential essay, "What Is a Dogma?" but, before we turn to this, we should say something about the man.

Edouard Le Roy was a layman, a philosopher, a student of the influential philosopher Henri Bergson, and a very devout Catholic. He developed his teacher's evolutionary philosophy toward "a Christian 'psychistic' idealism," the notion that all reality has at least the potential for psychic life. The more concentrated an organism is in terms of growing complexity, the more "psychic" it is. In humankind, evolution continues on the plane of spirit, ever subject to the divine transcendent-creative action. If this sounds somewhat like Teilhard de Chardin, there is an obvious reason. Le Roy was very friendly with Pierre Teilhard de Chardin, SJ. Vidler writes of their friendship: "There was an obvious concordance and concurrence in their ideas about the meaning of history and the cosmos."[27] At Le Roy's death in 1954, Teilhard wrote of him:

> There are few men whom I have so deeply admired and loved as I did him.
> So serene, so completely human—and so deeply Christian, . . . I owed him a
> very great debt. It was not exactly that I owed any particular idea to him, but
> that, particularly between 1920 and 1930, he gave me confidence, enlarged
> my mind (and my feeling of loyalty to the church), and served (at the Collège
> de France) as a spokesman for my ideas, then taking shape on "hominiza-
> tion" and the "noosphere."[28]

We shall come to Teilhard later, in the chapter on the "new theology."

Le Roy's association with modernism stems from his treatment of dogma in an article of 1905, "What Is a Dogma?" and a book of 1907, *Dogma and Criticism*, which was put on the Index of Prohibited Books by the Vatican. Although Le Roy submitted

---

24. Vidler, *A Variety of Catholic Modernists*, 87.

25. Cited in O'Connell, *Critics on Trial*, 83.

26. Fitzer, *Romance and the Rock*, 9.

27. Vidler, *A Variety of Catholic Modernists*, 93.

28. Cuenot, *Teilhard de Chardin: A Biographical Study*, 58.

formally to the judgment of the church, he did not actually abandon his ideas. Dogma for him does not so much convey positive knowledge as it guards against false ideas. Dogma has a negative sense, but it also has a practical purpose. It is a rule of practical conduct. Thus, for example, to affirm that God is personal tells us less something positive about God, and more that personal relations are to be thought of as ultimately valuable. Again, the resurrection of Christ is less an affirmation of a past event than a personal commitment to live as a contemporary of Christ.

Even after his books were placed on the Index, Le Roy never broke with the church. Philosophically, he valued the church very highly as the premier institution in the West for encouraging religious attitudes and action. More pragmatically, he recognized that any realistic attempt to renew or reform the church must come from within. As Vidler puts it: "He realized that identification with the church involved being apparently identified with elements in it which one deplored, but that was not a sufficient reason for breaking away: on the contrary, reform was possible only from within."[29] Le Roy's book *Dogma and Criticism* ends with these words:

> To my opponents whom I wish to regard as my friends, I confidently address
> . . . this appeal before God: let us help one another to grow in the truth and
> let us strive for unity rather than to triumph over one another. We profess the
> same faith, we share in the same life, we are committed to the same obedi-
> ence, we have communion in the same prayer, we have at heart the same
> desire and the same love.[30]

The understanding of dogma in Laberthonnière and Le Roy is very close. Both emphasized the pragmatic meaning of dogma. Although one can hardly quarrel with that—the Christian life necessarily has to do with how to live—dogma is understood to do more. For traditional Christianity it is the least inadequate language for speaking of God and things divine. All language about God is problematic to some degree. Language, including dogmatic language, is, in Herbert McCabe, OP's wonderful term "second hand clothing" for God.[31] None of the dogmatic clothing fits God perfectly. At the same time, a Catholic approach also recognizes accuracy about God in the dogmatic language, even if accuracy may not be construed as intellectual exactitude. This seems to be the dimension missing from Laberthonnière and Le Roy. Unlike Loisy and some others, they recognized the need to work for ecclesial reform from within.

Baron Friedrich von Hügel (1852–1925)

The anonymous author of the article on George Tyrrell in *The Oxford Dictionary of the Christian Church* writes that "[Tyrrell's] friendship with Friedrich von Hügel led to

---

29. Vidler, *A Variety of Catholic Modernists*, 92.

30. Edouard Le Roy, *Dogma and Criticism*. Unfortunately, I have lost the precise reference here.

31. McCabe, "The Involvement of God," 3.

his acquaintance with the writings of H. Bergson, M. Blondel, L. Laberthonnière, and A. Loisy, which contributed to his increasing hostility to scholasticism and his stress on the anti-intellectual and experiential aspects of religion."[32] Behind this intellectual description of George Tyrrell lies a deep and lasting friendship between the two men, a friendship that certainly was intellectual in every sense of the word, but also a genuine one-to-one friendship. This was true of other scholars whom von Hügel knew and cultivated so much so that Marvin O'Connell offers this description of him: "From Rome to Paris to London: the multilingual and peripatetic Friedrich von Hügel would provide, whether by land or by sea, whatever fragile unity or coherence possessed by the movement to be labeled Catholic Modernism."[33]

Baron Friedrich von Hügel, or as he was known among his friends "the Baron," was the son of a Scottish mother, Elizabeth Farquharson, and an Austrian diplomat, Carl Alexander Anselm von Hügel, who was a Baron of the Holy Roman Empire. Friedrich's early life was spent in Tuscany and Belgium. In 1867 the family settled in England. He was educated privately by a variety of tutors. His culture was cosmopolitan, and his religious affinities were ecumenical. He additionally embraced philosophy, theology, history, biblical criticism, and geology. He combined this massive, largely self-taught scholarship—Nicholas Lash calls him an "immensely learned amateur"[34]—with a deep spiritual life and devotion to the Catholic Church. Living in London, von Hügel spent a great deal of his time studying in the British Museum reading room.

What von Hügel referred to as his "first conversion" began when he witnessed a particular incident in the Cathedral of Mainz. He watched from behind a pillar while a distraught young woman prayed in front of the high altar. Apparently, her baby had just died. She came away from the altar comforted.[35] This had a profound affect on him. In the words of Meriol Trevor, "He had watched an encounter with God and felt that his doubts on the efficacy of prayer were ended."[36] In 1870, the year of the First Vatican Council, von Hügel's turning to prayer, as it were, was aided by a Dutch Dominican in Vienna, Fr. Raymond Hocking.

In 1873, Friedrich married Lady Mary Herbert, a convert to Catholicism. John Henry Newman wrote to Lady Mary, promising to celebrate Mass for her and Friedrich on their wedding day, November 27. In the ensuing years they had three daughters: Gertrud, Hildegard, and Thekla. Friedrich was devoted to his children in every respect, and not least in their education. Although Lady Mary had a rather simple and uncomplicated Christian faith and did not share her husband's *penchant*

32. Cross and Livingstone, *The Oxford Dictionary of the Christian Church*, 1401.

33. O'Connell, *Critics on Trial*, 42. Vidler, *A Variety of Catholic Modernists*, 113, says that von Hügel was "the chief engineer of the modernist movement."

34. Lash, *Easter in Ordinary*, 175.

35. See Bedoyère, *The Life of Baron von Hügel*, 18.

36. Trevor, *Prophets, Guardians and Saints*, 49.

for theological and philosophical analysis, she entertained with Friedrich a constant stream of visitors and scholars in their home in London. Michael de la Bedoyère, von Hügel's biographer, writes that von Hügel had an "intimate acquaintance with all the leading religious figures in Britain, France, Italy, and Germany, to all of whom he could speak and write in their own tongue."[37]

During a visit to France in 1884, von Hügel was introduced to the Abbé Henri Huvelin. From this French spiritual guide, he found a sense of direction through his multiple intellectual pursuits. Huvelin was attached to a large Parisian parish and was well established as a gifted spiritual director. It was through Huvelin's ministrations that Charles de Foucauld was converted, finally going as a hermit to the Sahara and to his death. "It was this powerful influence from a true mystic which later helped the Baron to stay within the church when many of his friends were leaving it."[38]

This great theological autodidact received an honorary degree from the University of St. Andrews, Scotland, in 1914, his very first academic honor. His Scottish roots were further strengthened when the University of Edinburgh invited him to give the prestigious Gifford Lectures in the session 1924–26 and proposed to confer on him the degree of Doctor of Divinity. Ill health prevented him from delivering the Giffords, but the lectures were published posthumously as *The Reality of God*.[39] He was buried in the cemetery close to the Benedictine Downside Abbey, near Bristol in England.

Scholars evaluate von Hügel's role in the modernist movement quite differently. Meriol Trevor writes: "He made himself a kind of international communications officer, introducing people from different countries to each other and sending books and letters across the frontiers."[40] This is certainly true. When von Hügel came across a persuasive position in a new book or learned article, he introduced it to those who he considered would be particularly open. He also introduced new ideas and theology to those who he thought should be open. It is true that he held positions not especially favored by the church, not least in the area of Scripture. He was, for example, in touch with the Scripture scholar Alfred Loisy for years, benefiting from his research. Nor could he be considered an ultramontane in his ecclesiology.

Von Hügel had a profound influence on others, particularly George Tyrrell, SJ. Thus, during the decades of the modernist movement from 1890 to 1910, von Hügel found himself deeply troubled, especially when his friend George Tyrrell fell afoul of the church. Undoubtedly he must have been concerned about his role in the *débacle*. He himself did not waver in his own ecclesial faith and belonging. It may be that there was in von Hügel a certain naïveté when it came to the study of theology and the Vatican. He was guilty of naïveté very possibly, but never of any malice. His immense delight in theological and philosophical learning left him in some degree innocent of

---

37. Bedoyère, *The Life of Baron von Hügel*, 124.

38 Bedoyère, *The Life of Baron von Hügel*, 51–52.

39. von Hügel, *The Reality of God and Religion and Agnosticism*.

40. Trevor, *Prophets and Guardians*, 47. See also Daly, *Transcendence and Immanence*, 117.

ecclesiastical attitudes and politics. Graham Wilcox, English church historian, has the position of the Baron right when he comments: "Despite this activity [in spreading the theological views of continental Modernists, especially Alfred Loisy], von Hügel was a cautious and diplomatic figure who wished to avoid a direct conflict with ecclesiastical authority in the church and he had an almost naïve optimism that the church hierarchy could gradually be persuaded to accept the findings of modern scientific historiography provided that radical gestures were avoided."[41] Von Hügel's own personal piety and devotion, his mystical dimension, kept him within the church. Meriol Trevor puts it like this: "Anchored as he was in a spiritual life fed by Eucharistic devotion and by his love of historical actuality, he was able to continue to believe both in Christ and in the church."[42] Moreover, he had nothing particularly to lose in the sense of an academic or ecclesiastical position. After all, he was, in Marvin O'Connell's words, "a well-fixed, private layman, free to indulge his interests in a private manner and free also to encourage, cajole and admonish others less advantageously positioned than himself."[43] Despite the immanentist tendencies of some of those whom he knew, he never lost the sense of God's utter transcendence. Vatican Council II in many ways fulfilled a number of the dreams and aspirations von Hügel had had for the church.

George Tyrrell (1861–1909)

The doyen of Anglophone scholars of modernism in the twentieth century, Alec Vidler, spoke of George Tyrrell in a highly laudatory way: "Of all the theologians I have written about, Tyrrell has meant more to me than any of the others and I return to him most often . . . ."[44] From Vidler's description his interest in Tyrrell was not simply that of a church historian examining an exciting albeit turbulent period of Catholic church history. He also found personal inspiration and edification in Tyrrell's theology. As we shall see, Tyrrell was not an easy colleague in the Society of Jesus, and certainly not an easy subject for Pope Pius X. Nonetheless, Marvin O'Connell's overall description of George Tyrrell resonates with what Alec Vidler thinks of him: "Through the blinding headaches and nausea, through the moods of self-loathing through all the doubts that had afflicted him from Dublin to Malta to Stonyhurst, George Tyrrell never ceased striving after the blessed vision of peace, for himself and for all God's wayward children. The love he inspired stands as a permanent tribute to him as a man and a priest."[45]

George Tyrrell was born in February 1861, Dawson Street, Dublin, a stone's throw from Newman's Catholic University. His father William had been a journalist

---

41. Wilcox, *Freedom and Authority in Church and Society*, 19.

42. Wilcox, *Freedom and Authority in Church and Society*, 65.

43. O'Connell, *Critics on Trial*, 51.

44. Vidler, *Scenes from a Clerical Life, An Autobiography*, 184.

45. O'Connell, *Critics on Trial*, 189.

and sub-editor of the *Dublin Evening Mail*, as well as Irish correspondent for *The Times*. He died shortly before George was born, and his mother was left with little money and three small children: William (known as Willie, born in 1851), Louisa (known as Louy, a one-year-old) and George. The Tyrrell family was nominally Anglican as members of the Church of Ireland. The elder William Tyrrell had been widowed before meeting George's mother, and he had also lost a one-year-old daughter in death, and died himself at the end of December 1860. The younger William Tyrrell, George's brother, had an accident as a child that left his spine damaged. These biographical facts have led Tyrrell scholar Ellen Leonard to say of George that he was "In many ways . . . a tragic figure."[46] Who could dispute that? Although he had never known his father, some aver that George was very like him in that he was irritable, a compulsive writer, and yet warm-hearted.[47]

George considered himself something of an unbeliever between the ages of ten and fourteen. He says of his faith at this time that "It vanished as completely as Jack and the Beanstalk." His atheism, if indeed that is what it was, was in large measure probably due to the influence of Willie who had become a very successful student at Trinity College Dublin, taking what has been described as "an outstanding degree."[48] Later, Tyrrell wrote: "What men deny is not God, but some preposterous idol of the imagination," and so it may be that during these impressionable years he was pulling away from dysfunctional images of God to a more mature perspective.[49] When he was fifteen, Willie was surprised to find George reading Bishop Butler's *Analogy of Religion*. As the always perceptive church historian, Meriol Trevor, puts it, "[George] was trying to find his way to a real belief of his own and like many young people swung emotionally between extremes."[50] In his own autobiography, made over in later years to Maude Petre, he compares the turbulent years of his adolescence to the Augustine of *The Confessions*. To what extent he benefitted immediately from the classical education he received at school is not entirely clear, because of the self-deprecating description George gives of himself at the time. During his last two years at secondary school he was tutored in Hebrew, and he tried for a Hebrew sizarship at Trinity College Dublin (a sizar was a student who received a certain amount of scholarship assistance), but failed.

Meriol Trevor writes of Tyrrell's developing ecclesial allegiances: "Just because it was considered not quite the thing in Dublin, he was attracted by Anglo-Catholicism."[51] The Church of Ireland had traditionally been rather low church in orientation. George's attraction took him to a relatively high Anglican church in Co. Dublin, All Saints,

46. Leonard, *George Tyrrell and the Catholic Tradition*, 3.
47. Sagovsky, *"On God's Side,"* 2.
48. Sagovsky, *"On God's Side,"* 5.
49. Trevor, *Prophets and Guardians*, 38–39.
50. Trevor, *Prophets and Guardians*, 73.
51. Trevor, *Prophets and Guardians*, 40.

Grangegorman. The vicar was Dr. Maturin, "a Prayer-Book man of the early Tractarian type, with a 'high' doctrine of the Church and the Eucharist."[52] Just at the time that George was coming to a closer acquaintance with high-church Anglicanism, his brother Willie, who had been a student at Cambridge for a year, returned to Ireland in the summer of 1876 and died very suddenly in August. George now became associated with and fell under the influence of Robert Dolling, a young Christian socialist who combined his service to the poor with Catholic devotion. At a time in life when George experienced overwhelming failure, grief over Willie's death and adolescent confusion, Dolling became for him a sort of mentor.

Eventually, George made his way to England in 1879, to Catholicism through the Farm St., Jesuit Fr. Christie, and then to the Society of Jesus, whose English novitiate he entered in 1880.[53] The provincial superior of the English Jesuits at the time wisely decided to make this would-be Jesuit wait for a year before entering the Society, and so sent him to a small Jesuit school in Cyprus, and then to another school in Malta. He made his profession as a Jesuit in 1882, and then it was on to the traditional studies in philosophy and theology in preparation for priesthood. His early experience with the Jesuits was to stamp and mold his entire understanding of Catholicism, so that he saw is as marked by uniformity, centralization, and a blind obedience to authority.[54]

The times were changing in Catholic approaches to the study of philosophy as a result of the 1879 encyclical letter of Pope Leo XIII, *Aeterni Patris*. This letter mandated the study of St. Thomas Aquinas in Catholic institutions, especially seminaries. Traditionally, the Jesuits studied Aquinas not directly through his own writings but rather through a Jesuit commentator, the sixteenth-century Spanish theologian Francisco Suarez (1548–1617). Tyrrell, in line with the pope's mandate but contrary to traditional Jesuit philosophical pedagogy, preferred the text of St. Thomas. Obviously, this was bound to set up certain tensions in the classroom with his teachers and examiners.

In 1888 Tyrrell moved on to the study of theology. His theology classes took place at St. Beuno's, Wales, where the poet-mystic Gerard Manley Hopkins also had done his theology. Theology would have been in a very definite neo-scholastic vein,

---

52. Sagovsky, *"On God's Side,"* 7.

53. Farm Street was the Jesuit residence in London's fashionable Mayfair district. Christie is described as follows by Marvin R. O'Connell, *Critics on Trial*, 110: "In the person of that priest the long shadow of John Henry Newman fell, lightly to be sure, upon Tyrrell for the first time. Albany James Christie had been an undergraduate at Oriel from 1835 and a fellow of the same college from 1840. Through his time in Oxford he had been a stout Tractarian, more under Pusey's influence than Newman's, but it was Newman who had persuaded him that in his state of mind he could not honestly accept Anglican ordination. Christie had resigned his fellowship and had come to live with Newman at the latter's retreat at Littlemore during the portentous summer of 1845. He was received into the Catholic Church on October 18 of that year, nine days after Newman himself. Until 1847, when he joined the Society of Jesus, he had remained more or less in Newman's entourage. He had resided at Farm Street for many years."

54. Leonard, *George Tyrrell and the Catholic Tradition*, 11.

with an equally strong dependence on the teaching authority of the church. In due course Tyrrell was ordained a priest in 1891, two years after the death in Dublin of Gerard Manley Hopkins, who had been a (rather unhappy) professor of Greek at the Catholic University.

From 1893–94, he was working in a parish in Lancashire. His superiors recognized his intellectual ability and his interests, and he was appointed Professor of Philosophy to Jesuit students at St. Mary's Hall, Stonyhurst, Lancashire. He remained there from 1894 through 1896, but not without difficulty, especially in respect of the older Jesuit professors. The earlier tensions were resurrected. The older Jesuit professors preferred the traditional Jesuit reliance on a Suarezian interpretation of Aquinas, whereas Tyrrell advocated the text of Aquinas himself. There must have been on Tyrrell's part a sense of *déjà vu* here. The Jesuit authorities decided that his presence in the philosophate was "too disruptive," and he was removed, and this was understandably "a great blow to Tyrrell's self-esteem."[55] The Jesuits may have been eager to remove him from teaching, but they did not want to lose him. George's sister, Louy, had, like his mother, been widowed and left in poverty. Briefly and with a sense of sadness about the situation Meriol Trevor notes: "There was some talk of his leaving the Society to become a secular priest, so that he could make a home for her, but the Jesuits wanted to keep him and he wanted to stay, so they agreed to pay his sister fifty pounds a year for life. It was not for long, for she died in 1897."[56]

Now Tyrrell was assigned in 1896 to the staff of a Jesuit periodical, *The Month*. Based in London, he was also involved in preaching, giving retreats, as well as writing. "After a slow start, this became a period of great creativity as a theological writer."[57] It was through his writing in *The Month* that he came to the attention in 1898 of a French Jesuit, Henri Bremond (1865–1933), who was four years younger than him. They began a friendship that ended only with Tyrrell's death. This period witnessed Tyrrell moving away from the scholasticism he had so readily embraced. Outside the rather hothouse atmosphere of a Jesuit seminary he began to realize that the subtleties and niceties of scholastic philosophy were not immediately intelligible nor widely persuasive. He aspired after a theological way of thinking that would speak to the lived experience of people. During these London years Tyrrell experienced the influence of Baron Friedrich von Hügel, and through von Hügel he was introduced to the works of many scholars, both Catholic and Protestant. He wrote to von Hügel: "All the vast help you have given me—and surely I have grown from a boy to a man since I knew you—has been in opening my eyes to an ever fuller and deeper knowledge of the data of the great problems of life."[58] Von Hügel was like a clearing-house of ideas from continental Europe for Tyrrell and for many others.

55. Rafferty, "Tyrrell's History and Theology" in his *George Tyrrell and Catholic Modernism*, 22.

56. Trevor, *Prophets and Guardians*, 46.

57. Rafferty, "Tyrrell's History and Theology," 22–23.

58. Leonard, *George Tyrrell and the Catholic Tradition*, 17.

Tyrrell published his first book in 1897 made up from meditations he had given to the Jesuit lay brothers, *Nova et Vetera,* "New Things and Old." In 1899, he published an article on hell, entitled "A Perverted Devotion." The article showed the influence of the fifteenth century anchoress Julian of Norwich with her emphasis that God shall make well all that is not well, although we do not know how this shall happen. For Julian this was the mystery of God's love and justice, with the primacy given to God's love. Taking his cue from this primacy, Tyrrell recommended a certain reverent agnosticism about the occupancy of hell. Tyrrell was not attacking the doctrine of hell as such, but certain theologizing about it. It created quite a stir. Not that Tyrrell shrunk from creating a stir! His biographer, Nicholas Sagovsky, writes that "he had no use for self-preservation, especially when he regularly met people who, like himself, were stifled by the banality of conventional devotion."[59] The English Jesuits were very supportive of Tyrrell, but their support was unable to prevent him going through very severe bouts of depression. He stopped celebrating the Eucharist for a while, and it seems that he may even have contemplated leaving the church.[60]

In 1900, as a result of the difficulties over this article, he was sent to a quiet Jesuit mission in Richmond, Yorkshire where he spent the rest of his life as a Jesuit. Before leaving London for Yorkshire, Tyrrell preached his last Ignatian retreat. One of the retreatants in that group was Maude Domenica Petre, described as follows: "Dressed simply and severely, her dark hair piled untidily atop her head, a rather plain face, with its deep-set eyes and slightly protruding teeth, offered small testimony to the intelligence and sensitivity that burned within."[61] This thirty-seven-year-old woman entered Tyrrell's life, and stayed with him until the end. In Petre's own words, "From the hour in which George Tyrrell entered my life something happened for good."[62]

In the Jesuit house in Richmond Tyrrell spent his time studying many volumes on contemporary philosophy and biblical studies. The year 1901 saw him write his autobiography. He interpreted most of his Jesuit experience negatively. The Society was judged to be rigid and inflexible. St. Ignatius of Loyola, on the other hand, was understood to be more open, more elastic. In many ways this attitude infected the church at large for Tyrrell. He was looking for a different kind of Catholicism. He wanted to reach out in an intelligent way to the "large class of reluctant believers (again, of every grade) who are affectively and often effectively, religious-minded."[63] Tyrrell was genuinely concerned with unbelief, and he felt the church did not reach out adequately to such persons. He felt the same way about those educated Catholics who confused their inability to accept current Roman theology and practice with loss of Christian faith.

59. Sagovsky, *"On God's Side,"* 51.

60. Apparently, he confided in Wilfrid Ward to this effect. See O'Connell, *Critics on Trial,* 192.

61. O'Connell, *Critics on Trial,* 192.

62. Petre, *My Way of Faith,* 129.

63. Cited in Barman, *Baron Friedrich von Hügel and the Modernist Crisis,* 163.

Given the state of the church at the time under Pius X, and given Tyrrell's rocky relationship with his Jesuit superiors in Rome, it comes as no great surprise that in 1906 he was dismissed from the Society of Jesus. His friend, Henri Bremond, had also left the Society of Jesus in 1904, and it may be that Bremond's departure had some influence on Tyrrell's separation from the Society. In a letter that he wrote to the Jesuit General in 1905 Tyrrell expressed himself in these terms: "The Society has become an avowedly reactionary institution; I am, and always will be, impenitently progressive. As such, my position in her ranks is dishonest; unfair to her and to myself. That I believe myself true in principle to St. Ignatius is neither here nor there; for my duty is to the actual and living Society and to her interpretation of St. Ignatius."[64]

Since a priest must in terms of canon law be incardinated in a diocese, several bishops offered him a place in their dioceses, but Rome forbade him to write and publish, and so he never took up the invitations since the various diocesan censors would never have let his thinking see print. The archbishops of Westminster and of Dublin both refused to receive him. Tyrrell, realistic about his situation, wrote: "A bishop who takes me knows well enough that he is freely patronizing a known 'liberal' and that he will be responsible to Rome for my pranks."[65] Tyrrell did not think well of bishops as a rule: "Don't look, don't see, don't think; listen to us; we know *a priori* there are no difficulties; still don't look or you might see something."[66] It is hardly surprising to note that Tyrrell did not have a diocese when he left the Society of Jesus.

Tyrrell was excommunicated, at least in the sense that he was forbidden to receive the sacraments. Tyrrell himself understood this formally to be excommunication. Meriol Trevor with her customary care and sensitivity to historical detail writes:

> At Storrington [Tyrrell's place of retirement after the Jesuits and excommunication] he continued to attend Sunday Mass at the priory till he was asked not to come because he was scandalizing the other Catholics—a priest not saying Mass, not even communicating. This censorious, suspicious attitude is all too typical of the respectable flock during the height of the anti-modernist crusade. Surely it would have been more Christian to accept his presence in church as at least a sign of hope?[67]

For many years Tyrrell had suffered from severe migraine headaches, and was later diagnosed with Bright's disease. On July 15, 1909 he died at Storrington. He received conditional absolution and was anointed, but he was refused Catholic burial. He was buried in the Anglican churchyard of St. Mary's, Storrington. His friend, Abbé Henri Bremond, addressed the small gathering of mourners and blessed the grave. For this

---

64. Cited in Leonard, *George Tyrrell and the Catholic Tradition*, 22.

65. From a letter from Tyrrell to von Hügel, cited in Barman, *Baron Friedrich von Hügel and the Modernist Crisis*, 172.

66. Cited in Leonard, *George Tyrrell and the Catholic Tradition*, 25.

67. Trevor, *Prophets and Guardians*, 73.

Bremond was suspended from priestly duties until he retracted his errors. According to Tyrrel's own request, his tombstone bears the emblem of the chalice and the host and these words: "Of your charity pray for the soul of George Tyrrell, Catholic priest who died July 15 1909. Aged 48 years. Fortified by the rites of the church. RIP."

Maude Dominica Petre (1863–1942)

Ellen Leonard's major study of Maude Petre opens with these words: "Having completed a study of George Tyrrell with only a passing reference to Maude Petre, I decided to take another look at this woman."[68] Maude Domenica Petre, a modernist theological writer, spans both the nineteenth and twentieth centuries. She came of a titled family, her father being a younger son of Lord Petre and her mother Lady Catherine Howard, a daughter of the Earl of Wicklow. Both her parents died within months of each other when she was nineteen. Her family, or at least her father, belonged to the cisalpine wing of the church—like John Lingard and Joseph Barrington in the eighteenth century—that is to say, to those who were in favor of a degree of local control, of a measure of independence from Rome, much like the Gallican tradition in France. Cisalpine and Gallican stand against ultramontane.[69] She viewed her father as the last English representative of Cisalpinism, defined by her as the English version of Gallicanism, and she wrote that, "I really do not think that my father ever wholly accepted the definition of papal infallibility."[70] In the broader historiography of Catholic modernism Petre receives attention usually in conjunction with George Tyrrell and Friedrich von Hügel, but seldom in her own right.[71] Von Hügel certainly had a very high regard for her. This is what he wrote of her in 1900 to George Tyrrell: "A remarkable mind and soul . . . I think of her always as the one woman I have ever known . . . who quite naturally turns to thinking and philosophy as a necessity and as a help. It is also very refreshing, because all so utterly and entirely prompted by her own inner needs, so completely the fruit and the food of her whole personality."[72]

68. Leonard, *Unresting Transformation*, 1.

69. Maude could have found, maintains Francis Oakley, relief in conciliarism during her own period of anguish and difficulties with ecclesiastical authority. That she did not shows how marginalized conciliarist constitutionalism had become in Catholic ecclesiology and church history in the wake of Vatican I. See Oakley, *The Conciliarist Tradition*, 251.

70. Petre, cited in Wilcox, *Freedom and Authority in Church and Society*, 27.

71. This has been remedied in no small way by the excellent work of Crews, *English Catholic Modernism*, Leonard, *Unresting Transformation*, and especially in terms of Petre's later theology the unpublished doctoral dissertation of Wilcox, *Freedom and Authority in Church and Society*.

72. Cited in Leonard, *Unresting Transformation*, 29. After the death of George Tyrrell, Petre distanced herself from von Hügel. The tensions between them are well summarized by Graham Wilcox, *Freedom and Authority in Church and Society*, 61 as follows: "She later came to accuse von Hügel of excessive caution in this period and indeed of a relief that Tyrrell had died and he was now free from compromising associations. . . . In the difficult period after Tyrrell's death and burial von Hügel wrote to her in September 1909 urging caution and to refrain from upsetting the church authorities and

Maude's private tutors could hardly keep up with her developing intellect—in Nicholas Sagovsky's description she had "a kind of intellectual and moral fearlessness" and in 1885 she set off for Rome to study scholastic theology.[73] Her aunt, Lady Lindsay, said of her at the time, "Maude has gone to Rome to study for the priesthood!"[74] Of course, in Rome at this time, she was unable to enroll in any of the pontifical universities, and so she studied scholastic theology under the direction of a personal tutor. In a somewhat humorous vein Marvin O'Connell describes her studies. "Accompanied by a chaperone she settled down every evening to read 'a textbook by the terrible dry-as-dust (Matteo) Liberatore,' as well as selected parts of Aquinas's *Summa Theologiae*."[75] In 1890 she entered the Society of the Daughters of the Heart of Mary in London. This was what would be known today as a lay institute. Petre remained with them until 1907, when she was dismissed for publishing a book entitled *Catholicism and Independence* without permission. The title of the book is revealing. Throughout her own life and theological reflection there is a certain tension between personal/individual liberty and authority in the church, just like George Tyrrell.

Petre was the friend of a number of modernists, but especially of George Tyrrell, as has already been noted. Though she had met Tyrrell several times before, it was on a retreat conducted by him in July 1900 that she came to be affected by him and to love him. She later wrote in her autobiography: "It was between thirty and forty . . . that I knew, in the complete sense, of what it was to love, . . . I had that consciousness of eternity; that sense that nothing else mattered on earth or in heaven; that it was the one priceless pearl for which all else could be sold or cast away as dross; . . . that I could accept slavery or ill-treatment; that, finally, as I said to the one friend who guided me through this experience, I would 'go to hell with him' if that was where he went."[76] She was speaking, of course, of George Tyrrell. Tyrrell knew of her affection and at least at times tried to respond appropriately since they were both members of religious congregations, but there is also some evidence that he may have been homosexual, and so may not have been able to respond as she might have wished.[77] Petre always attempted to purify her love for him, so that it would never be untoward. When all is said and done, however, in relation to Petre, Tyrrell veered between affection coupled

---

spoke of the wisdom of 'saying perhaps too little rather than perhaps too much. After all it will be a very great point gained if you and I remain uncensored.' This was certainly not a conviction shared by Maude Petre . . ."

73. Sagovsky, "On God's Side," 57.

74. Petre, *Modernism: Its Failure and Its Fruits*, 56.

75. O'Connell, *Critics on Trial*, 193. An excellent summary of the dry-as-dust Liberatore may be found in McCool, *Catholic Theology in the Nineteenth Century*, 145–66.

76. Petre, *My Way of Faith*, 235.

77. In 1897 he began a correspondence with André Raffalovich in which he felt free to reveal that his most passionate feelings as a younger man had been directed to members of the same sex. See Trevor, *Prophets and Guardians*, 35–36, and Sagovsky, "On God's Side," 67.

with intellectual companionship and annoyance linked to frustration with her stifling devotion to him and her jealousy of any female competition.

Soon after this July retreat, Tyrrell went to live with the Jesuits in Richmond, Yorkshire, and he remained there until he left the Society in 1906. Petre, suffering from fatigue and depression as a result of her growing responsibilities in the Society of the Daughters of Mary, went for a rest to Engelberg, Switzerland, "where she went for long walks alone in the mountains and attended the Divine Office daily in the great Benedictine Abbey."[78] She made a perpetual vow of celibacy in 1901. When Tyrrell became seriously ill after he had been expelled from the Jesuits, she let him have a cottage on her property at Storrington, provided him with some financial assistance and it was there he died in 1909. She wrote over twelve books, mostly on Tyrrell, von Hügel, Loisy, and modernism generally. Her *Life of Tyrrell*, a two-volume work published in 1912 and the first volume of which is largely penned by Tyrrell himself, is especially important not only for George Tyrrell's own biography but also for insight into his developing theology. This book was placed on the Index of Forbidden Books in 1913.

During World War I, Petre served as a nurse in France and attended the wounded from the bloody battle of Verdun. In her diary for April 1916 she entered: "All the men are from Verdun—I saw my first two cases direct from the front—appalling ones, a real butchery, it makes me savage. I can't put it all down to the Germans; it seems to me a disgrace to all mankind, for why has science ever been directed to such evils?"[79] She went on to serve as a fire warden at the time of the London blitz during World War II, even though she was almost eighty years old. She was an ardent spokesperson for social and spiritual issues and an advocate of the League of Nations. After her death in London in 1942, there was a requiem Mass in Assumption Convent, Kensington Square, in the Archdiocese of Westminster. She was buried not far from George Tyrrell in the Anglican Cemetery of Storrington. Bishop Peter Amigo of the Diocese of Southwark did not permit a priest to attend the graveside services because Maude Petre was being laid to rest but one grave removed from her life-long friend George Tyrrell.[80]

Recent writing about Maude Petre is in agreement that she was not an academic theologian. Ellen Leonard, for example, insists that her ideas emerged from her own experience of life, much like George Tyrrell.[81] She certainly does not rank in the same scholarly way as does Friedrich von Hügel. However, serious theology is more than what may be construed as academic theology, and Maude Petre was a serious theologian. Maude Petre's theology is complex and in so many ways caught up in the turmoil of modernism. Nonetheless, it is possible to give some sense of her thinking without

78. Trevor, *Prophets and Guardians*, 30.

79. Cited in Wilcox, *Freedom and Authority in Church and Society*, 99–100.

80. Crews, *English Catholic Modernism: Maude Petre's Way of Faith*, 99. Crews's book is an excellent guide to Petre's thought.

81. Leonard, *Unresting Transformation*, 1–7.

descending to great detail. In an early essay published in the Jesuit periodical *The Month*, she sets out a theme that will permeate much of her later work: ordinary human thought and experience are the primary places for locating the things of God.[82] This was in contrast to a supernatural extrinsicism that views a transcendent reality of God *alongside* human experience. For Petre, God is immanent, and yet not to the point where God's transcendence is compromised into a form of pantheism.[83] The encyclical of Pope Pius X, *Pascendi*, would condemn "vital immanence," but Petre's theology would not fall under that condemnation. She understood the reality of divine transcendence too well for that. She was certainly under George Tyrrell's influence in respect of the universal Christ in the universal Spirit:

> It is God whom we seek in Christ; and it is in the life of Jesus of Nazareth that, for us, the primary, classic and supreme revelation has been made. . . . Our difficulties begin when Jesus Christ must not only be to us the chief manifestation of the Divinity, but must be it in such a way that those who are without him are without any such revelation. . . .The mystical Christ of the church is God, and God belongs to all men, and is revealed in a greater or lesser degree in every religion. The connection between that mystical Christ, who is God, and the Jesus of history, is the special face of Christianity; the connection between the mystical Christ, by whatever name he may be known, and Divinity itself, is a faith that reappears in many other religions.[84]

Ecclesiology was a concern of hers, especially between 1901 and 1902, focusing on the relationship of the church to the modern world. One contemporary commentator sees in Petre something of an anticipation of Vatican II: "Her ecclesiology roamed freely over questions of asceticism, discipline, mission, and reform. Such writings anticipated the call of the Second Vatican Council for a church *semper reformanda*— always in need of reform."[85] In a letter of 1923 to Lord Halifax, the English peer who enthusiastically promoted Anglican union with Rome, Petre wrote of the church: "The Church is our home—our ark on the immeasured waters. We know that we know but little, but we trust that the spiritual goods set before us are pledge of those that are to be."[86] No one could take issue with her ecclesiology thus far. However, when she was seen to be calling into question the authority of the church, that was another matter. In December 1907 both her religious superior and the archbishop of Westminster, Francis Bourne, asked Petre to withdraw from publication her book *Catholicism and Independence*.[87] She maintained that this was impossible and, as a result, her

---

82. Petre, "An Englishwoman's Love Letters," *The Month*, 120–24.

83. Crews, *English Catholic Modernism*, 17.

84. Petre, *Modernism: Its Failures and Its Fruits*, 95.

85. Crews, *English Catholic Modernism*, 21.

86. Crews, *English Catholic Modernism*, 104.

87. Petre, *Catholicism and Independence*.

connection with the lay institute was terminated. The reason may be clearly seen in the opening pages of her book: "To our own mental and moral conscience all doctrines and laws must make their last appeal."[88] Petre's approach to doctrine and morality can hardly be construed as anarchist. Rather, we may see in this statement a reflection of her Cisalpine heritage, her own independence of mind, as well as the general, though limited, influence of modernist thinking. Given the temper of the times, this was enough to draw more deeply the suspicion under which she already labored as a result of her association and friendship with George Tyrrell. *Catholicism and Independence* sounded like the entire liberal agenda of the nineteenth century in modernist dress. Petre appreciated and respected the church's role in faith and morals, but it was for her a qualified role: "The church has lighted my way. Instead of struggle through a wilderness I have had a road—a road to virtue and truth. Only a road—the road to an end, not the end itself—the road to truth, and not the fullness of truth itself."[89] Her distance from a superficial doctrinal relativism may be found in this statement: "To be undenominational and consequently tolerant is nothing; but to be denominational in the best sense, and likewise tolerant, is much."[90] Nor is there espousal here of a lazy, anti-intellectual tolerance, but rather tolerance as the recognition of intellectually convinced denominationalism that can from a position of strength engage with other points of view. Even so, these were not things the Catholic hierarchy of England wanted to hear at this time of the condemnation of modernism.

The progression of Maude Petre's theological thought over the years essentially took two forms. First, gradually she reached a more mature and balanced position on the church's handling of modernism. Thus, in 1937 she wrote: "I am quite sure I made some mistakes but I also adhered throughout to what I believed to be my call and duty. . . . I am perfectly willing to recognize the inevitability of certain disciplinary acts of authority, for the church is a church of the present and not of the future."[91] As Graham Wilcox comments, "The bitterness against ecclesiastical authority which was clear for example in her earlier work on *Modernism* (published in 1918) had now been mitigated by reflection."[92] Second, her thoughts moved out into more social and political directions, not least because of her experience of and reflection on World War I. While she continued to hold German aggression, and indeed, the support given by the German academics responsible for much that happened, she is still able to admit that "we are able to apportion the share of blame to either belligerent up to a certain point only; but there is a dark background from which all human action only partially emerges."[93] She finds war morally abhorrent for a convinced and practicing

88. Petre, *Catholicism and Independence*, x–xi.

89. Petre, *My Way of Faith*, 341.

90. Petre, *Catholicism and Independence*, 158.

91. Petre, *My Way of Faith*, 243.

92. Wilcox, *Freedom and Authority in Church and Society*, 172.

93. Petre, *Reflections of a Non-Combatant*, 22.

Christian. "We must accept it, then, as one of the contradictions of a state of war, that we cannot pray without some treason either to our monotheistic beliefs, or to our patriotic sentiment . . . we cannot uphold the universal Fatherhood of God without admitting, as its corollary, the universal brotherhood of mankind."[94] It may well be the case that the latter part of this statement was directed at the German Lutheran theologian Adolf von Harnack, who had published his very famous book, *What Is Christianity?* to which Alfred Loisy had responded. In this text with his customary liberal theological reductionist methodology von Harnack arrived at the conclusion, noted above, that the essence of Christianity consisted in the recognition of the Fatherhood of God and the brotherhood of mankind. Von Harnack was one of the public signatories endorsing Germany's participation in World War I. Petre clearly perceived *pace* those who believed that this was the war to end all wars that there would be serious ongoing international problems when the war was over: "The period of reaction will be a dangerous one. . . . During that period there may be sown the seeds of undying international hatred, to bring forth, perhaps in many years to come, a fresh outbreak of the horrors we have witnessed, unless all the best that is in mankind be brought to bear on the making of peace."[95]

Although her own Bishop, Peter Amigo of Southwark, refused her holy communion in any parish of the diocese, all Petre had to do was cross the River Thames and she was in the Archdiocese of Westminster, and there she could receive the Eucharist without difficulty or impediment. She did so almost on a daily basis.

Maurice Blondel (1861–1949)

Maurice Blondel was never a modernist, but he is often associated with them. John Macquarrie writes of him: "Although his writings undoubtedly influenced [modernism], he himself, like Baron von Hügel, remained essentially loyal to Catholic teaching. He still has his followers in Catholic circles among those who pursue a neo-Augustinian rather than a neo-Thomist tendency."[96] It is a very fair description of Blondel. Two of his writings in particular are important for understanding the development of Catholic theology. The first is his 1893 doctoral dissertation in philosophy, *L'Action: Essai d'une critique de la vie et d'une science de la pratique,* in its English translation *Action.*[97] The second is his 1896 *Letter on Apologetics* and the third his 1904 *History and Dogma.*[98]

---

94. Petre, *Reflections of a Non-Combatant,* 101.

95. Petre, *Reflections of a Non-Combatant,* 134.

96. Macquarrie, *Twentieth Century Religious Thought,* 173.

97. It was published in Paris in 1893 by Alcan. A complete English translation came out in 1984—Maurice Blondel, *Action: Essay on a Critique of Life and a Science of Practice.*

98. The English translation of both texts is available as Blondel, *The Letter on Apologetics and History and Dogma.*

In terms of his *Action* the central point is that we are always acting, and we are never not acting, as it were. Our actions, understood as the history of our personal choices in acting, never reach a point of final and complete satisfaction. There is always more, we desire to continue to act. There is no exception to this process. The book opens with his question: "Yes or no, does human life have a meaning and does man have a destiny?" He makes a distinction between what is explicitly willed and acted upon, *la volonté voulue*, "the willed will," and the ongoing "willing will," *la volonté voulante*. There is a kind of gap between the former and the latter, as the "willing will" continues to expand "the willed will." The question is whether there is any point at which "willing/ acting" comes to finality and completion and satisfaction such that no further "willing/ acting" is necessary. Blondel believes that for action to be fully intelligible there must be an *unique necessaire*, something that renders finally and fully intelligible the necessary and incessant process of action that each human being is. This *unique necessaire* is God for Blondel. "This is the genesis point of the supernatural order in the natural."[99] Every human being has, or better is a necessary orientation towards God. This necessary orientation comes to us as gift from God so that the human restless quest for God is already a graced experience of God's immanent presence.

Blondel's scholastic critics found his thesis wanting, charging that it dispensed with the gratuitousness of grace, making the supernatural absolutely dependent on the natural, God on the human person. This was to misunderstand him. Part of his goal was to avoid the notion that God, the supernatural, was simply extrinsic to the human person in his lived experience. He found this to be one of the reasons why people dispensed with the notion of God. On the other hand, Blondel wished to situate God and the supernatural intrinsically within the person, that is to say, in human willing and acting. One contemporary student of Blondel's thought puts it very clearly like this: "[*Action*] calls each person to follow the contours of their own world and action so as to establish what is in deepest accord with their most intimate needs. His philosophy could be described as a discernment of the mystery of divine presence, which penetrates concrete human existence and bestows upon the drama of human action a transcendent bearing and meaning."[100]

Developing methodologies in history, including the historical-critical approaches to Scripture, were to have an enormous impact as we have seen during the modernist crisis. Here too Blondel would make a significant contribution. He read Alfred Loisy's *The Gospel and the Church*, exchanged a series of letters with him in 1903, and went on to publish his *History and Dogma* in 1904. In that publication, Blondel sought to avoid what he regarded as unacceptable approaches in historical-scriptural-theological investigation. The first approach, which he found instanced in Alfred Loisy he called "historicism," an approach "concerned wholly with the investigation and determination of facts which it subsequently treats as if

99. Conway, "Maurice Blondel and *Ressourcement*," 68.
100. Conway, "Maurice Blondel and *Ressourcement*," 71.

they were in themselves substantial units of reality."[101] Although he did not put it this way, what Blondel objects to is really the pretense of absolute neutrality, the absence of all manner of presuppositions, in attempting to understand the past. Historicism is epistemologically flawed. Equally flawed in Blondel's opinion is what he called "extrinsicism," "which was reflective of the dogmatism of theologians who would claim to impose on facts an interpretation drawn from faith."[102] Avoiding both historicism and extrinsicism Blondel postulates an understanding of tradition as a living and vibrant reality that grounds both history and dogma. A contemporary interpreter of Blondel provides a summary of what this means for theology: "This means that, for Blondel, any historical enquiry into the person of Christ must not lose sight of the reality that this cannot, with impunity, be cut off from the living Christ who is met in the intimacy of living faith. This living reality of Christ is not to be confused with the dissected and reductive moments of either historical research or, for that matter, dogmatic statement."[103] His position on tradition would inspire the theologians of the "new theology" later in the twentieth century—one thinks especially of Yves Congar—but it put him at odds with historicist scholars like Loisy and neo-scholastic dogmaticians who thought that dogma floated uncontaminated above the flow of history. Historian of modernism in the United States, William L. Portier, writes of Blondel: "Much of the drama of twentieth-century Catholic theology is played out in the eventual vindication and even triumph of Maurice Blondel. . . . More than a century after *Pascendi*, the recent history of Catholic theology, read from a certain angle, might be faithfully described as the 'triumph of Blondel.'"[104]

The Condemnation of Modernism

On July 3, 1907, the Holy Office published the decree *Lamentabili*, containing some sixty-five extracts from various modernist writings, and especially from the work of Alfred Loisy, the French exegete and theologian. Although it is difficult to be absolutely certain, there are grounds for believing that not only did Loisy adopt newer methods of historiography and Scripture scholarship, but also that he began to lose his Catholic faith, at least as far as that is conventionally judged. Beginning in 1903 a number of his books were put on the Index and, to be fair, Loisy submitted. While Pius X, in the words of J. Derek Holmes, "cruelly questioned his sincerity," to be fair one must also recognize the words of the pope to Loisy's bishop: "Treat him kindly, and if he takes one step towards you, take two towards him."[105] Pope Pius X went further on September 8 1907 with the encyclical *Pascendi*. The modernists were seen

---

101. Conway, "Maurice Blondel and *Ressourcement*," 74.

102. Conway, "Maurice Blondel and *Ressourcement*," 74.

103. Conway, "Maurice Blondel and *Ressourcement*," 75.

104. Portier, *Divided Friends*, 11, 57.

105. Holmes, *The Triumph of the Holy See*, 265.

in extremely negative light, "feigning a love for the church," and "vaunt[ing] themselves as reformers of the church . . . assailing all that is most sacred in the work of Christ."[106] This is very strong language indeed, and, while doubtless there were men of acerbity among the modernists, this does not apply to many good people who suffered needlessly under this denunciation. Loisy was excommunicated formally on the feast of St. Thomas Aquinas in 1908. Falconi sadly comments, "The church was showing a quite new aspect of itself, devouring its own children."[107] Many twentieth-century studies of modernism, to say the least, are much less negative than Pope Pius X. Yves Chiron, on the other hand, points out that "the archives of the Secretariat of State contain hundreds of enthusiastic and grateful letters" in respect of the condemnation of modernism.[108] While this may be true, it seems that a more subtle hermeneutic would need to be applied to such letters, interpreting not only what they say but what they mean contextually.

There was some speculation about who was the author of the encyclical *Pascendi*. It now is clearly the case that the one who composed the doctrinal part of the encyclical was the procurator-general of the Oblates of Mary Immaculate, Fr. Joseph Lemius, a staunch Thomist and implacably hostile to what he took to be modernist ideas.[109] A number of theologians apparently had submitted possible drafts but none was found particularly satisfactory. Merry Del Val then approached Fr. Lemius and his version was approved by Pope Pius X, and "the Scholastic theology of Joseph Lemius came perilously close to being identified with Catholic faith."[110]

The philosophical foundation of the heresy is seen in agnosticism, a system of thought that confines human reason to empirical data and phenomena (paragraph 6). Another central principle is "immanence," the rooting of religion in "sentiment, a movement of the heart" (paragraph 7). To this is also allied a theological immanence, that is to say, the immanence of God within humankind, an immanence expressed externally in religious dogma and doctrine. This latter certainly has a Loisy-like feel to it. Perhaps we can see in immanence and in religious immanence something of the religious epistemology of Friedrich Schleiermacher, so widespread in the nineteenth century but doubtfully of overwhelming influence among Catholic theologians. For Schleiermacher the roots of religion are to be found in the feeling of absolute dependence, innate in all human beings, and religious doctrine is but a conceptual explication of that sense. *Pascendi* addresses a central tendency in nineteenth-century theology, but not particularly widespread among Catholics of the time. Modernism is "the synthesis of all heresies" (paragraph 39). In order to counteract it, the encyclical proposes a series of measures: the systematic study of scholastic philosophy; careful diligence in examining and

---

106. *Pascendi,* par. 2, cited from Claudia Carlen, ed., *The Papal Encyclicals 1903–1939,* 71.

107. Falconi, *The Popes in the Twentieth Century,* 35.

108. Chiron, *St. Pius X,* 201.

109. Jodock, *Catholicism Contends with Modernity,* 27.

110. Portier, *Divided Friends,* 28.

selecting candidates for ordination; episcopal vigilance over publications and especially publications in philosophy and theology; censorship; careful oversight over congresses and convocations; and diocesan watch committees.[111]

As one historian has put it, "the authorities were the products of an ecclesiastical tradition that had left them incapable of dealing with Modernism."[112] On the part of Rome there was little appreciation of developments in biblical studies and of non-scholastic approaches to philosophy and theology. Indeed, they were ill-equipped. At the same time, as will have emerged from the narrative, some of those who were labeled as "modernists" were intemperate in some of their positions and judgments. Perhaps if there had been more of an agreed middle-ground between Rome and the modernists, then more balanced and better established positions would have been reached. In many ways, the *debacle* surrounding modernism was to repeat itself with the emergence of the "new theology" in the mid-twentieth century. This will be the subject of a later chapter.

111. Carlen, *The Papal Encyclicals*, 92–96.
112. Holmes, *The Triumph of the Holy See*, 268.

7

Pope Benedict XV (1914–22)

The election of Giacomo Della Chiesa as Benedict XV to succeed Pius X, was as explicit a reaction against the preceding regime as it was possible to get.

—EAMON DUFFY[1]

Benedict begins the papal transition from the nineteenth to the twentieth centuries. He couldn't avoid confronting the modern world with the war raging around him. He gradually retreated from the integralism of the Sarto papacy and attempted to rein in the modernist heresy hunt.

—PAUL COLLINS[2]

From Giacomo della Chiesa to Pope Benedict XV

IT IS SAID THAT when Cardinal James Gibbons of Baltimore arrived in Naples after his Atlantic crossing and was told of the election of Giacomo Della Chiesa as Pope Benedict XV, he replied, "Who's he?" Della Chiesa had been a cardinal only four months, and was largely unknown to the Catholic world.

Giacomo Della Chiesa was born Genoa on November 21, 1854. In 1875, he graduated from the University of Genoa with a doctorate of law, but it was only then that his father agreed to his entering the seminary. Della Chiesa attended the Gregorian University. These were the years just after the First Vatican Council (1869–70), and one of his teachers was the famous Johann Baptist Franzelin, SJ, (1816–86), one of the major influences on the schema *Dei Filius* of that Council.[3] Ordained to the priesthood in 1878, he remained in Rome to complete the requirements for doctorates in theology and canon law. During these studies he moved from the *Capranica* to the Academy of Noble Ecclesiastics, to be trained as a papal diplomat.

---

1. Duffy, *Saints and Sinners*, 333.
2. Collins, *Absolute Power*, 108.
3. McCool, *Catholic Theology in the Nineteenth Century*, 218–21.

One of the key influences on the young priest's life was to be Monsignor Mariano Rampolla del Tindaro. When Rampolla was appointed nuncio to Spain in 1882, he chose Della Chiesa as his assistant. Della Chiesa returned to Rome with the now Cardinal Rampolla, appointed secretary of state by Pope Leo XIII in 1887, eventually becoming under-secretary of state in 1901. We get two interesting impressions of Della Chiesa from Americans at the time. The first comes from William O'Connell, rector of the American College in Rome from 1895 to 1901, and later to become cardinal-archbishop of Boston. O'Connell wrote:

> I had known Monsignor Della Chiesa quite well during the days of my rectorship of the American College. . . . Nearly every morning his frail figure, clothed in the simplest clerical garb, might be seen walking from his apartment along the narrow streets that led to the Vatican. . . . He might well pass unnoticed for any impressiveness of appearance, for his figure was rather angular and he walked with something of a limp. His complexion was sallow and his head, generally tilted to one side, gave no indication of the very fertile brain within it. . . . Not once, but several times . . . I joined him in the walk, but as he was a person of most extreme reticence, conversation was mainly about the weather.[4]

O'Connell's remarks offer a very favorable impression of Della Chiesa. Less favorable are some comments of Michael Corrigan, archbishop of New York. These were the years of the "Americanism" controversy, with various members of the American episcopate marked by quite different points of view on the appropriate relationship and response to the wider culture.[5] For example, on the one hand there was Archbishop John Ireland of St. Paul, advocating close integration of and participation in the United States of American Catholics, including in the state system of education. On the other hand, there was Archbishop Michael Corrigan, who was suspicious of assimilation and who wanted to see Catholics set up their own parallel system of education. The Vatican publication *L'Osservatore Romano* carried an article defending various policies of Archbishop Ireland. The anonymous article drew the ire of Archbishop Corrigan, who sought out the identity of the author, and it was Della Chiesa. This is Archbishop Corrigan's comment: "[Della Chiesa is] a gentleman without any influence whatever in theological circles, and whose name consequently if published would carry absolutely no weight with it. I have direct and reliable information that Mgr. Della Chiesa wrote the article, and the estimate of his standing is also beyond question."[6] Corrigan was no fan of Della Chiesa. He did not live to see him elected pope, but Ireland did and rejoiced in the fact.

---

4. O'Connell, *Recollections of Seventy Years*, 340.

5. See Cummings, *Prophets Guardians and Saints*, 127–30.

6. Moynihan, *The Life of Archbishop John Ireland*, 100.

In the wake of Pope Leo XIII's death Rafael Merry del Val was appointed secretary to the conclave. He moved on as the new Pope Pius X's personal secretary and eventually as his secretary of state. He certainly had the new pope's ear and his confidence, and he was not especially fond of his under-secretary, Giacomo Della Chiesa. Merry Del Val (1865–1930), the son of Don Rafael Merry Del Val, secretary to the Spanish legation in London, had been elevated to the dignity of papal chamberlain while he was still a seminarian. He had met Della Chiesa upon his return from Spain at the Roman Academy for Noble Ecclesiastics, but there was no friendship between the two men. While Della Chiesa was slight of stature and had a limp, Merry Del Val was handsome, a fine athlete and excelled in all kinds of sports. Della Chiesa was an introvert, Merry Del Val an extrovert—very different personalities. Further, the new Pope, Pius X, appointed Merry Del Val as secretary of state, and made him a cardinal.

There were differences also about how to handle matters with France and Italy, and there were differences about modernism. Merry Del Val invited Monsignor Umberto Benigni, who was to become the director of the anti-modernist campaign, to join the staff of the secretary of state in 1906. Along with Pope Pius X, Merry del Val was the chief supporter of Benigni and his tactics. Della Chiesa, still under secretary, was no modernist, although he was suspected of liberalist tendencies. However, he did not agree with the rather crude methods employed against the modernists. There can be no doubt that Merry del Val was very keen indeed to rid himself of Della Chiesa in the secretariat of state. Thus, Pope Pius X, most probably at the instigation of del Val, named Della Chiesa archbishop of Bologna in 1907. It got him out of the way.

Although from the perspective of Vatican careerism the appointment to Bologna was "a defeat, and a banishment from the Vatican," Della Chiesa threw himself energetically into the service of his diocese.[7] John Pollard provides a detailed description of his daily schedule, a schedule he maintained substantially after his election as pope:

> He rose at 5.00am, and after saying his morning prayers, Breviary, Mass, meditation and thanksgiving he would breakfast at 7.00am. Between breakfast and lunch at 1.30pm, he would deal with correspondence and appointments. This would be followed by a visit to the Exposed Sacrament in one of Bologna's churches, and by more Breviary interspersed by further business. Shortly after the recitation of the Rosary and supper at 8.30pm, followed by a period of conversation with his household, he retired to his study for yet more reading and more writing.[8]

He complained in a letter to a friend in 1909 about dealing with the odd priest who found celibacy a bit of a challenge, about the low level of theological formation among the clergy, and about the poor commitment to spirituality after ordination. He was certainly no integrist as is made clear in his first pastoral letter in the diocese:

7. Pollard, *The Unknown Pope*, 26.

8. Pollard, *The Unknown Pope*, 34.

"It is far from my intention to condemn every new form of doctrine, indeed I applaud scientific/scholarly progress wherever it is found, . . . but I believe that it is increasingly necessary to test every new theory against the 'sense of the Church', in order to have a secure criterion of acceptability."[9]

He was no friend of the severe suppression of suspected modernists in his diocese. He initiated on the feast of Corpus Christi 1908 the *Sacra Visita*, a canonical visitation of every parish in the archdiocese, a project which would take four years to complete. When he had finished, he had visited three hundred and ninety two parishes, including the chapels, convents, schools, and hospitals connected with them.[10]

Although Bologna was traditionally a cardinalatial see, Della Chiesa was made a cardinal only in May 1914, almost seven years after becoming archbishop. Undoubtedly, this was due in part to his refusal to go all the way with the anti-modernist witch hunt. Walter Peters says laconically: "That Merry Del Val and Della Chiesa disagreed sharply on integralism was no secret to their contemporaries." Peters also points out that when Pius X assembled the cardinals in order to read out the names of the new cardinals, the list had been prepared in Merry Del Val's hand, but Della Chiesa's had been inserted in the pope's own distinctive handwriting. Four months later he was elected pope, in part because with the outbreak of World War I it was felt that the church needed an experienced diplomat in the Chair of Peter. He would not have been the choice of Cardinal Merry del Val, his chief rival in the conclave. It is said that when he was elected on the tenth ballot, Cardinal del Val challenged the validity of the election, suggesting that Della Chiesa had voted for himself. Della Chiesa had to wait until every ballot had been reopened and it was finally determined that the new pope had not voted for himself. Eighteen out of the thirty-one non-Italian cardinals were from nations and countries involved in the war. The choice of the name Benedict is interesting. It is fairly clear that Della Chiesa wanted to distance himself from the policies of Pius X, his predecessor, and so would not have chosen Pius, but he might have been expected to choose Leo in whose pontificate his star had risen, as it were. But Benedict? He later claimed that he was "influenced by the example of the founder of the great monastic order and his search for peace."[11]

World War I, 1914–18

It has been pointed out that "[Benedict's] election followed that of Woodrow Wilson, professor of political science at Princeton University, as president of the United States (1913–21)," and that their paths will cross more than once.[12] World War I overshadowed Benedict's pontificate and Wilson's presidency. This war was a major catastrophe

---

9. Cited in Pollard, *The Unknown Pope*, 42.

10. Peters, *The Life of Benedict XV*, 61.

11. Pollard, *The Unknown Pope*, 66; Peters, *The Life of Benedict XV*, 80.

12. Coppa, *Politics and the Papacy in the Modern World*, 78.

for the world, and perhaps especially for the world of Christians. This is how church historian Diarmaid MacCulloch puts it: "The war which began in August 1914, triggered by complex diplomacy and a tangle of fears and aspirations, . . . involved four Christian emperors—German and Austrian Kaisers, the Russian Tsar and the British King-Emperor—but such rulers had habitually ignored their common faith to fight each other."[13] It was the war that killed Christendom. Two days after his coronation, Benedict XV published an exhortation to the Catholics of the world in which he said: "We are firmly resolved, so far as it is in our power, to leave nothing undone which can conduce to the more speedy ending of this calamity."[14] His efforts on behalf of peace remained consistent, even as they were to be frustrated. In his first encyclical of November 1, 1914, *Ad Beatissimi*, Benedict put forward some causes of the international conflict including: national and personal selfishness, a growing disregard for legitimate authority, bitterly divisive class struggles and materialism:

> Surely there are other ways and means whereby violated rights can be rectified. Let them be tried honestly and with good will, and let arms meanwhile be laid aside. . . . Peoples are more divided by jealousies than by frontiers; within one and the same nation, within the same city there rages the burning envy of class against class; and amongst individuals it is self-love which is the supreme law over-ruling everything.[15]

Some commentators on modern Catholicism note that the pope's analysis was "not so different from that offered by communists who saw war as the outgrowth of bourgeois greed."[16] Very soon after his election as Pope Benedict the somewhat unbending Cardinal Merry Del Val who had been very close to Pius X found himself in disagreement with "the skillful and more conciliatory Cardinal Pietro Gasparri."[17] Pius X Observed a fairly strict neutrality for the Holy See in concert with his friend and secretary of state Cardinal Gasparri, Benedict nevertheless condemned inhuman forms of warfare. Gasparri's policies were consistently those of conciliation and diplomacy, and they were to outlive the pontificate of Benedict XV. These policies were greatly to influence Gasparri's protégé, Eugenio Pacelli, who would later become Pope Pius XII. In line with these policies Benedict consistently refused to condemn any of the participant nations with the obvious result that he was found lacking by each side. Belligerents on all sides appealed to the Vatican to condemn the atrocities perpetrated by their enemies. The Vatican's typical reply may be evidenced in an allocution of Benedict in January 1915: "And We do proclaim it without modification, condemning openly every

---

13. MacCulloch, *A History of Christianity*, 916.

14. Cited in Holmes, *The Papacy in the Modern World*, 2–3.

15. Carlen, *The Papal Encyclicals*, ad loc., par. 4, 7.

16. Atkin and Tallett, *Priests, Prelates and People*, 196.

17. O'Malley, *A History of the Popes*, 272.

injustice by whatever side it may have been committed."[18] While one could not quarrel with the high ground of the reply, it certainly failed to satisfy all those seeking particular condemnations by Benedict. To take but one example, the English Cardinal Francis Gasquet (1846–1929) asked the pope to condemn the sinking of the British ship, the Lusitania. The ship was struck by a torpedo from a U-boat off the south coast of Ireland on May 7, 1915, and of the 1959 people on board 1198 perished. This huge loss of civilian life shocked the world. But Benedict stuck to the line of Cardinal Gasparri and no particular condemnation was issued. And so to the French he was the German pope, and to the Germans he was the French pope, while to ultra-nationalist Italians he was, contrary to the literal meaning of his name, "Blessed," *Maledetto XV*. Consequently the politicians did not listen to him.

However, it was not only the politicians who refused to listen. In France, the great scholar Père Antonin Sertillanges, OP (1863–1948), the Thomist scholar whose output came to over seven hundred books and articles, and whose appointment to the editorial board of the *Revue Biblique* was something of a corrective to the supposedly "controversial" views of the editor Marie-Joseph Lagrange, OP, said publicly in the presence of and with the agreement of Cardinal Amette of Paris: "Holy Father, for the time we are unable to listen to your words of peace. Like the apparent rebel in the gospel, we are sons who reply, 'No, no.'"[19] One historian has aptly commented that "Benedict was—like truth itself—one of the first victims of the war."[20]

The year 1916 saw the rebellion in Ireland, known as the Easter Rising. This rebellion, occurring for the most part in the city of Dublin, was the work of the Irish Republican Brotherhood. The leaders of this doomed rebellion against the might of the British Empire were deeply Catholic. They included Patrick Pearse, schoolmaster and poet who virtually identified the almost inevitable death of the Easter rebels with the death of Christ, so as to pave the way for the resurrection in freedom from British rule over the Irish people. Also included was the poet Joseph Plunkett. Plunkett's father was George Noble Plunkett, a papal count, and it so happened that the elder Plunkett had a papal audience with Benedict XV in April 1916. He warned the pope of the forthcoming Irish rebellion at Easter. When the Vatican heard about the actual rebellion, Benedict telegraphed the archbishop of Armagh, Cardinal Logue, requesting news of the situation. When Logue received the papal request, the Easter Rising was in fact over, and he responded to the Holy Father: "Happily the revolt is at an end. The insurgents surrendered unconditionally. Peace, let us hope, is restored."[21] Wishful thinking on the part of the archbishop, but the exchange between Pope Benedict and Cardinal Logue is further confirmation of the pope's desire for and work for peace.

---

18. Cited in Peters, *The Life of Benedict XV*, 121.

19. Cited in Holmes, *The Papacy in the Modern World*, 12.

20. Cited in Holmes, *The Papacy in the Modern World*, 1.

21. Moran, "Arms and the Churchman," *The Tablet*, March 11, 2006, 20.

It has been pointed out that Benedict's peace efforts had been largely ignored in the standard English-language treatments of World War I, at least until the early 1970s.[22] The summer of 1917 witnessed a number of gropings toward a negotiated peace. It is within this context that on August 1, 1917 Benedict drew up his "Peace Note," and sent it to the warring powers on August 15. It contained the following proposals:[23]

1. Substitution of "the moral force of right" for the law of the material force of arms.

2. A simultaneous and reciprocal decrease of armaments.

3. International arbitration.

4. True freedom and community of the seas (a most important consideration due to the introduction of submarine warfare).

5. Reciprocal renunciation of war indemnities.

6. Evacuation and restoration of all occupied territories.

7. A conciliatory examination of rival territorial claims and disputes.

It was a plan that was soundly based on justice and not simply on victory. Only Great Britain made a positive response to the papal appeal, but it was not strong enough to carry the day. In the words of John N. D. Kelly, "[the papal appeal] was stillborn."[24] In all likelihood the final nail in the coffin of the papal peace plan came from President Woodrow Wilson of the United States of America who had argued that it was simply impossible to trust the political leaders of Germany. John Pollard comments: "As [the emerging future leader of the world] Wilson would brook no rivals. This Calvinist idealist who was 'convinced of his own moral and intellectual superiority' was also notoriously anti-Catholic (though not at election time), and tended to see all Europeans as parochial and unenlightened, including Benedict."[25]

However, it remains to say the least interesting that President Wilson's "Fourteen Points" peace speech of January 1918 is both terminologically and substantially so close to Benedict's "Peace Note" that some argue that the presidential speech was inspired by the papal note. Whether Wilson was directly influenced by Benedict or not is something historians may continue to debate. What seems beyond dispute is the stark contrast in attitude between them. For Benedict peace rested on a multi-lateral willingness to forgive. Wilson seemed more motivated by an urge to punish Germany

22. For example, by Althann, SJ, "Papal Mediation During the First World War," 219. Althann refers particularly to E. E. Y. Hales, *The Catholic Church in the Modern World*, 167–68, and A. J. P. Taylor, *English History 1914–1945*, who ignores Benedict's peace work, though he mentions other peace initiatives.

23. Pollard, *The Unknown Pope*, 126.

24. Althann, "Papal Mediation During the First World War," 234; Kelly, *The Oxford Dictionary of the Popes*, 315.

25. Pollard, *The Unknown Pope*, 128, slightly adapted.

and its allies. Church historian John O'Malley concludes with a degree of persuasiveness that if Benedict's point of view had been heeded more widely "World War II might possibly have been avoided."[26]

The failure of the "Peace Note" was a bitter disappointment to the pope. So too was the fact that, as a result of the Allies' secret Treaty of London (1915), the Vatican was excluded from the post-war peace settlement. This was mainly due to the influence of the Italian government which did not want any European influence being brought to bear on the resolution of the Roman Question in any peace settlement, something that Benedict was keen to achieve.

Benedict's relief work for those who had been wounded and for refugees was very real indeed, amounting to some 82,000,000 lire, in Eamon Duffy's words "leaving the Vatican safes empty."[27] This does not include other moneys that he gave away for the relief of the war's victims. For example, in 1914, he asked Cardinal Mercier, the Primate of Belgium, to use the funds collected for "Peter's Pence" in Belgium to help those Belgians most in need. The Vatican had to borrow money for Benedict's funeral and the subsequent election of Pope Pius XI. Given the Vatican's complex circumstances, the success of Benedict's relief work is simply staggering. By the spring of 1915 he had set up in the Secretariat of State an organization that dealt with 600,000 items of correspondence. Within this correspondence were some 170,000 inquiries concerning missing persons, 40,000 appeals for help in the return to their homes of sick prisoners of war, and the facilitation of 50,000 letters between prisoners and their families. This Vatican project has been compared to the work of the International Red Cross.[28] We may see similar pastoral concern on Benedict's part when he protested by means of a letter to Sultan Mehmed V. about the Armenian massacre, a genocide of one million people. In the letter, but diplomatically without naming the perpetrators, Benedict asked the sultan to put an end to the slaughter and to rescue the survivors. His witness did not remain at the level of protest. He established an orphanage in Constantinople for Armenian orphans.[29] Historian, John F. Pollard, author of a fine study of Benedict and of a meticulous study of Vatican finances in the century 1850 to 1950 concludes that Benedict's support for children, all children and not only the Armenian orphans, was so constantly generous that he could well be thought of as one of the founders of the Save the Children Fund.[30]

26. O'Malley, *A History of the Popes*, 272.

27. Duffy, *Saints and Sinners*, 334.

28. Pollard, *The Unknown Pope*, 113.

29. See Jedin and Dolan, eds., *The History of the Church*, 10:38–39.

30. Pollard, *Money and the Rise of the Modern Papacy*, 115.

Treason in the Vatican

When nations are locked into competition of one sort or another, espionage abounds, and especially so during times of conflict. Ethnic ties and the shared stories that are history give rise to nationalist feelings. The Vatican is not exempt. One of Benedict's close working associates was a Bavarian, Monsignor Rudolf Gerlach (1886–1946). Working in the Curia, he came to the attention of Benedict and was appointed first chamberlain, and was in constant contact with the pope during the work day and also during private audiences. When Italy entered the war on the side of the Entente in 1915, German and Austrian nationals were required to leave Italy, but Benedict arranged for Monsignor Gerlach to stay. The provision was that he would voluntarily remain within the confines of the Vatican. However, Gerlach wandered freely around Rome and was involved with "people of questionable political activities," to use the expression of Walter Peters.[31] At the same time, his lavish personal expenditure was out of all proportion to his modest income as a papal chamberlain.

On August 2, 1916, the Italian warship the *Leonardo da Vinci* exploded in the harbor of Taranto with the loss of 248 seamen. Monsignor Gerlach apparently commented to the effect that "Well, a few hours ago, Italy paid the price of her treachery to Germany." The strange thing was that his remark had been made several hours before news of the sinking reached Rome from Taranto. It seems that Gerlach was involved in a plot to sabotage the whole Italian navy. His role was minor, probably nothing more than paymaster for the Central Powers to the Italians who carried out the sabotage. Clearly, however, he compromised Vatican neutrality, especially since he was so close to the pope. The net result was that he was handed over to the Italian authorities who escorted him to the Swiss frontier early in 1917. He married a woman from Holland, and died in England in 1946, apparently reconciled to the church.

The Post-War Situation

Benedict's peace-initiative continued in his work after the war for international reconciliation, especially in his encyclical of 1920, *Pacem Dei Munus*. In that encyclical he wrote: "The joy which has been brought to us by the conclusion of peace is mixed with numerous and very bitter inquietudes. . . . Because if the hostilities have almost ceased everywhere, if indeed certain conventions of peace have been signed, the germs of inveterate hatred still exist." Prescient words. Benedict supported in general the work of the League of Nations, although the Vatican's exclusion from the League left something of a residue of negative feelings.

With the newly drawn map of Europe, Benedict attempted to forge good and solid church-state relations, sending Achille Ratti [later Pope Pius XI] to Poland and Lithuania, and Eugenio Pacelli (later Pope Pius XII) to Germany. Relations with

31. Peters, *The Life of Benedict XV*, 132.

France, consistently difficult since the French Revolution in 1789 and formally broken in 1905, were resumed in 1921. In the previous year the pope had canonized Joan of Arc, a symbolic gesture that undoubtedly smoothed the way for the Vatican-French reconciliation. In point of fact, and doubtless due to Benedict's diplomacy, the number of countries represented at the Holy See rose from fourteen to twenty-six. This included a British representative, in fact the first time since the seventeenth century that Britain had sent a representative to the Holy See.

Benedict sent clear signals to the Italian administration that he was ready to find an honorable settlement between the Italian state and the Vatican. His secretary of state, Cardinal Pietro Gasparri, during the last year of Benedict's life was instructed to meet with the Italian government to find a harmonious and just way forward. He distanced himself from the policy of the Vatican that the pope should not meet with world leaders with whom the Italian king met. Thus, for example, Benedict met with President Woodrow Wilson. Further, he referred to the king of Italy as "his majesty," in clear contrast to his predecessors after 1870 who spoke of him only as "the Duke of Savoy." Though he did not live to see these positive overtures come to full fruition, his efforts were recognized. For the first time since 1870, the flags in government buildings in Rome flew at half-mast at his death.

He neither aided nor hindered the "Popular Party," an immensely popular centrist political party led by the Italian radical priest and former Vatican official, Don Luigi Sturzo. He did not require Sturzo to resign. This party and Benedict's at least tacit approval returned Catholics to the political life of Italy after the *débacle* of 1870. The new party was welcomed by the vast majority of the Italian episcopate. Though the Popular Party was inspired by Catholic teaching, especially Leo XIII's *Rerum Novarum*, it was not a Catholic party as such. It was non-confessional, independent of church authority, and had an impressive agenda: condemnation of imperialism, proportional representation, the vote for women, land reform, separation of church and state, respect under the law for freedom of conscience, and an increase in local autonomy. Benedict was sympathetic to a degree, personally supporting among other things the extension of the vote to women, but finding some difficulty with the complete separation of church and state and the issue of freedom of conscience, issues that had been central in nineteenth-century papal policy. In the 1919 election Catholics went to the polls with church encouragement for the first time, and the Popular Party won 20 percent of the vote and one hundred parliamentary seats. "Ominously, one loser was a 'gentleman' from Verona, Benito Mussolini, whose party didn't gain a seat."[32]

32. Bokenkotter, *Church and Revolution*, 278.

Church Activities

Benedict's first encyclical, *Ad Beatissimi*, was issued on November 1, 1914. November 1 is, of course, the Feast of All Saints, and it may be that Benedict wished to draw attention to the communion of saints and to the consequent problem of Christians killing other Christians. Certainly, the war was to the forefront of this encyclical, but it is of the greatest importance that Benedict refused simply to indict the central powers as war criminals. Each side in the conflict wanted the pope for itself. That was not Benedict's away. Almost immediately in the encyclical, his thoughts turned to the conflict, and especially to its devastating consequences, described as follows:

> Yet, while with numberless troops the furious battle is engaged, the sad co-horts of war, sorrow and distress swoop down upon every city and every home; day by day the mighty number of widows and orphans increases, and with the interruption of communications, trade is at a standstill; agriculture is abandoned; the arts are reduced to inactivity; the wealthy are in difficulties; the poor are reduced to abject misery; all are in distress.[33]

At the root of this calamitous war he saw four fundamental causes: the lack of mutual love among people; a disregard for legitimate authority; strife between the different classes of society; and a pervasive greed, "the striving for transient and perishable things." He noted the entirely different vision of civilization presented by the Gospels, and went on to comment: "Never perhaps was there more talk about the brotherhood of men than there is today. . . . But in reality never was there less brotherly activity amongst men than there is at the present moment."[34]

Some French critics saw the words as a condemnation of the *fraternité* of the French Revolution, and so of the contemporary French Republic. That seems unlikely. More credibly, it is difficult not to see behind his words about "the strife between classes" an echo of fast-growing Marxist sentiment. The Russian Revolution was but a few years away, and Marxist thought had made advances throughout Europe. At the same time, the words about "the brotherhood of man" are very reminiscent of the famous lectures, sixteen in all, delivered to over six hundred students at the Humboldt University of Berlin by the great church historian Adolf Von Harnack in 1899–1900. Although delivered extemporaneously, they were taken down in shorthand and published as *What Is Christianity?* Harnack's answer in the lectures to the question posed in the published title may be summarized, although it is broader and richer than this, as "the Fatherhood of God and the brotherhood of man." This moral consciousness was the essence of Christianity for him, and the book was very influential.[35] The popular demand for it in Germany in the year of its publication was such

---

33. Carlen, *The Papal Enclyclicals,* par. 7.

34. *Ad Beatissimi,* in Carlen, *The Papal Encyclicals,* par. 7.

35. See Vidler, *Twentieth-Century Defenders of the Faith,* 12–18, and for a wider hermeneutich perspective Sykes, *The Identity of Christianity,* 123–47.

that the main railway station in the city of Leipzig was blocked by railway cars loaded with copies to ship around Germany and around the world. The book was translated into English by November 1900, and spread rapidly throughout the English-speaking world. "More than any other book it represented the spirit of Protestant liberalism in the decades just prior to World War I."[36] And yet Harnack was firmly on the side of the war and of Germany and of the Kaiser. Church historian William Frend writes: "Amidst the collapse of the Kaiser's regime and the civil conflicts of 1918–1919, [Harnack] stuck to the ideals of 'Freedom, Equality and Brotherhood' for which he believed Germany had fought the war."[37] Was Benedict addressing this failing brotherhood vision of Harnack? It is just possible.

The encyclical also brought an end to the internecine bitterness between conservatives and liberals during the controversy over modernism. It is for this reason that *Ad Beatissimi* is described by Richard McBrien as "the most important and abidingly relevant achievement of his pontificate."[38] Like Pope John XXIII Della Chiesa probably was sympathetic in some degree to some of the ideas of the modernists, and he certainly did not approve of the extreme measures in the anti-modernist crusade undertaken by Pope Pius X. The disciplinary norms required by the oath against modernism remained in place, even as Benedict was opposed to the severe restrictiveness of the integralist perspective. He was sympathetic at least in the sense that he refused to condemn legitimate differences of viewpoint in the church on matters that had not been declared dogma:

> As regards matters in which without harm to faith or discipline—in the absence of any authoritative intervention of the Apostolic See—there is room for divergent opinions, it is clearly the right of everyone to express and defend his own opinion. But in such discussions no expressions should be used which might constitute serious breaches of charity; let each one freely defend his own opinion, but let it be done with due moderation, so that no one should consider himself entitled to affix on those who merely do not agree with his ideas the stigma of disloyalty to faith or to discipline.[39]

Interestingly, Joseph C. Fenton, a conservative theology professor from Catholic University of America, turned to Benedict's words in an article he had written in 1956 concerning "more than a suggestion of theological acerbity." While Fenton condemns any deviation from church teaching, he used these fine words of Benedict XV to guide different points of view in a spirit of charity.[40]

36. Livingston, *Modern Christian Thought*, 290.
37. Frend, *From Dogma to History*, 28.
38. McBrien, *Lives of the Popes*, 358.
39. Cited in Carlen, *The Papal Encyclicals,* par. 23.
40. Fenton, "Pope Benedict XV and the Rules for Theological Discussion," 39–53. Unfortunately, Fenton went on to single out for condemnation as one who set himself up in opposition to the magisterium Baron Friedrich von Hügel, but nowhere does he advert to the fact that von Hügel was never

There is a remark attributed to him in the hearing of the cardinals just after his election as pope in September 1914: "And we assure you that the Holy Father is not a modernist!"[41] Indeed, it may have been, at least in part suspicion of an insufficiently tough position on modernism that removed him from the Vatican and to his appointment as archbishop of Bologna.[42] Of course, it was impossible to remove all anti-modernists from high office in the church, and Benedict did not do that. The *Sapiniere* organization directed by Monsignor Benigni was not finally suppressed until November 1921.

"There they remained, exercising a more cautious but far-reaching influence and training suitable juniors to carry on the same inflexible system. 'Modernism' remained a condemned heresy and 'Veterism' ['being imprisoned in the past' as Blondel called it] continued to be the criterion of orthodoxy."[43] These are the words of church historian Meriol Trevor.

In large measure Trevor seems correct in her judgment. But is it possible that "modernism" and "veterism" are constant temptations, perhaps with roots in the human psyche and temperament, in every age of the church, and even in society? One thinks of Peter and Paul at Antioch, with Peter the "veterist" and Paul the "modernist." Or Hippolytus and Callistus in early third-century Rome, with the learned Hippolytus as "veterist" and the former slave Pope Callistus as the "modernist." These issues run through the entire tradition. People are not easily classified. Benedict, bringing an end to the modernist witch hunt, was also responsible for lending support and encouragement for the establishment of the first chair of ascetical-mystical theology in the history of the church, at the Angelicum University, and the occupant from that time until 1959 was none other than Reginald Garrigou-Lagrange, OP, who would be the scourge of "modernists" under Pope Pius XII. But more about Garrigou in the chapter 6 on the "new theology."

Socialism, of course, was much in the air. Though he issued no great encyclicals on Catholic social teaching, Giacomo Della Chiesa, long before becoming pope, showed himself clearly sympathetic to the line of Pope Leo XIII in his 1891 encyclical, *Rerum Novarum*. In a letter of 1897 to a bishop-friend, Della Chiesa wrote: "The Holy See wishes to see the bosses and the rich taken down a peg or two, and does not disapprove of the talk about the rights of the workers; at the same time, however, it is necessary not to forget to remind them of their duties." Benedict's openness towards trade unionism contrasts favorably with the negative attitude under Pope Pius X.[44]

In 1910 the World Missionary Conference had taken place in Edinburgh, Scotland. For the first time, missionaries in the Reformation tradition from all over the

actually condemned.

41. Peters, *The Life of Benedict XV*, 81.

42. Pollard, *The Unknown Pope*, 26.

43. Trevor, *Pope John*, 91.

44. Pollard, *The Unknown Pope*, 13.

world met to discuss how their being disunited yet seeking to win others to Christ was nothing short of scandalous. The Catholic Church did not participate. Yet, an Italian cleric, the liberal Bishop Geremia Bonomelli (1831–1914) of Cremona, wrote a letter of great encouragement to the Edinburgh Conference. This entire letter was read out at the conference by Bonomelli's friend, the American Episcopal layman, Silas McBee. Apparently, Bonomelli expected to be hammered by the Vatican for his letter, but it did not happen.[45] Another friend of Bishop Bonomelli's with whom he had theological and ecumenical conversations was the Italian priest, Don Angelo Roncalli, later to become Pope John XXIII. In June 1908, Roncalli spent three days visiting Bonomelli discussing theological issues in the church, and the latter proposed to Roncalli the need for an ecumenical council in these words: "Perhaps a great ecumenical council, which would discuss rapidly, freely and publicly the great problems of religious life, would draw the attention of the world to the church, stimulate faith and open new ways for the future."[46] Roncalli took up Bonomelli's idea some fifty years later.

One of the outgrowths of the Edinburgh Conference was the "Faith and Order" movement, taken up with doctrinal and ecclesiological issues, and the "Life and Work" movement, focusing on Christianity's impact on economics and politics. Representatives of "Faith and Order" made contact with the Vatican secretary of state towards the end of Pius X's pontificate, Cardinal Gasparri. This continued into the pontificate of Benedict XV through a series of encouraging letters from the pope, but with no great sense of urgency. The year after the landmark Edinburgh Conference, 1911, saw the Holy Office issuing a decree forbidding Catholics to participate in any ecumenical congresses, except with the formal permission of the Holy See. The longtime Catholic ecumenist, George Tavard writes: "It was most unfortunate that Benedict XV, despite his interest in the unity movements and the encouragements that he had lavished on them, was obliged to turn down the invitation given to the Catholic Church to participate in the great assemblies that were pending."[47]

Such formal participation in the ecumenical movement would have to wait until Vatican II. Benedict, however, worked for reunion with the separated churches of the east, and to that end he established the Congregation for the Oriental Church and the Pontifical Oriental Institute in Rome in 1917. Probably Benedict's immediate concern was to safeguard the existence and rights of the eastern branches of the Roman Catholic Church, the so-called Uniate churches, but he also had in mind the longer term goal of reunion with the world of Orthodoxy. In similar vein in 1920 he elevated the Syrian Deacon, St. Ephrem of Nisibis, as a doctor of the church. The pope compared Ephrem and Jerome: "Jerome and Ephrem were almost contemporaries, . . . both lived in Syria, and both were marked out by their knowledge and love of the Sacred Writings; so that one might say they were like 'two burning candles' destined

45. See Delaney, "From Cremona to Edinburgh," 33–49.

46. Cited in Hebblethwaite, *Pope John XXIII*, 62.

47. Tavard, *Two Centuries of Ecumenism*, 93.

to enlighten one the West and the other the East."[48] Ephrem has been considered "the greatest poet of the patristic age, and perhaps the only theologian-poet to rank beside Dante."[49] It is, therefore, appropriate to acknowledge Benedict's encyclical *In Praeclara Summorum* of 1921, a text commemorating the sixth centenary of the death of Dante. In it, Benedict extolled not only Dante's poetic genius but also his theology. "It is impossible," wrote the pope, "to express the intellectual enjoyment procured by the study of the supreme poet!"[50]

Benedict's longest encyclical, *Spiritus Paraclitus* in 1920, was given over to biblical scholarship. The occasion of the encyclical was the fifteenth centenary of the death of St. Jerome. Two aspects of the encyclical may be singled out for comment. First, there is a certain negative tone in relation to biblical scholarship, although he acknowledged its gains: "We warmly commend, of course, those who with the assistance of critical methods, seek to discover new ways of explaining the difficulties in Holy Scripture."[51] It may be that Benedict was afraid that his abandonment of the anti-modernist excesses might open the door to greater problems in interpreting the Scriptures than those occasioned by scholars like Alfred Loisy. Second, and more important, the encyclical stressed the need to make the Bible available in its entirety to Catholics, and not just the Gospels. Nonetheless, John Pollard's judgment on the whole seems accurate when he writes: "In this sense, *Spiritus Paraclitus* had positive results, but more broadly speaking its consequences were negative: it 'froze' Roman Catholic biblical scholarship until Pius XII reopened the subject with his encyclical *Divino Afflante Spiritu* of 1943."[52]

While agreeing with Pollard, more may be said of Benedict's interest in the promotion of the Scriptures. He had long been closely associated with the "Pious Society of St. Jerome for the Diffusion of the Holy Gospel," a society that published a cheap edition of the New Testament for dissemination among ordinary people. He wanted ordinary Catholics to have direct access to the Word of the Lord. At the same time, he wanted to see that access enhanced by biblical preaching. Thus, in 1917, in his encyclical *Humani Generis*, he takes to task those preachers who indulge in "frequent allusions to profane and non-Catholic literature to the exclusion of Sacred Scripture. . . . We see that not a few of our sacred preachers overlook in their sermons the Sacred Scriptures."[53]

During Benedict's pontificate the cult of the Sacred Heart of Jesus reached its highpoint. In 1915 the pope dedicated all the nations at war to the Sacred Heart. In 1919 the Basilica of the Sacred Heart was consecrated in Montmartre in Paris. At the

48. Cited in Rope, *Benedict XV, the Pope of Peace*, 251.

49. Murray, SJ, *Symbols of Church and Kingdom*, 31.

50. Cited in Peters, *The Life of Benedict XV*, 262.

51. Carlen, *The Papal Enclyclicals*, 181.

52. Pollard, *The Unknown Pope*, 192.

53. Cited in Peters, *The Life of Benedict XV*, 214.

time he wrote: "The Sacred Heart shows in a moving manner the immeasurable love of Jesus toward his children so often oblivious of it. This love, however, is destined to be exhibited to all men, even to enemies, because we are all sons of God and have all been redeemed by the blood of Christ."[54]

Courageous, evangelical words, just one year after the World War I. Also in 1919 he gave permission for the establishment in Milan of a Catholic university dedicated to the Sacred Heart. Finally, in this regard in 1920 Benedict canonized Margaret Mary Alacoque (1647–90), the saint who popularized and encouraged devotion to the Sacred Heart.

The post-war situation had created enormous problems for the missions. In his letter *Maximum Illud* of 1919 Benedict encouraged missionary bishops to liberate themselves from European imperialist interests and to establish native clergy. It would be a long time before nationalist, colonialist interests seeking to exploit missionary work would disappear from the scene. In practical matters the pope endorsed the spread of missionary associations, such as the Clergy Missionary Association, to help financially with the missions. In this regard he brought to Rome one Angelo Roncalli to take a lead in fund-raising.

His pastoral concern may be illustrated in the person of Carlo Monti, a lifelong friend of Benedict and constant go-between for the Vatican and the Italian state. According to his own testimony, Benedict found out in 1918 that Monti was "living in sin." Though undoubtedly aware of the problem of scandal in one so close to himself, Benedict persuaded the widowed Monti to remarry, and presided at the wedding himself.

Conclusion

It has been said of Pope Benedict XV that he was the most invisible and unappreciated pope of the twentieth century. The public lack of appreciation of the papacy began in modern times with the eighteenth-century Enlightenment and moved through the period of two World Wars. The papacy was largely viewed as a relic of a long gone past, occasionally noticed but not taken seriously by modern, intelligent, enlightened people. It is that attitude essentially that explains both the deafness of European politicians to Benedict's unceasing pleas for peace during the Great War and what has been called his "chilly exclusion" from the Treaty of Versailles at its end.[55] John Pollard wisely comments: "What makes a pope great is . . . very hard to say. In Benedict's case, what made him great was the way in which he rose to meet the tremendous challenges posed by the state of the secular world, and especially the horrors of the First World War."[56]

54. Cited in Peters, *The Life of Benedict XV,* 175.

55. Lawler, *Popes and Politics,* 36.

56. Pollard, *The Unknown Pope,* 215.

The veteran Catholic Church historian, Philip Hughes, spoke of Benedict's greatness in these terms: "Never did the papacy set the world a better example of all-embracing charity."[57] Benedict XV refused all nationalism, all ethnocentrism, not only in protesting this latest of humankind's follies that was World War I, but also practically doing all he could to relieve the suffering of countless victims of political blindness and ineptitude. One might add to Pollard's historical judgment that Benedict's greatness was also to be found in his work for peace in the church after the modernist witch-hunt and its consequent polarization. He was no political modernist, personally much more comfortable with the *status quo*, and he was no theological modernist, despite his limited appreciation of new ways of thinking in the church. He was truly a man of peace, without and within. Therein lies Benedict's greatness. "He is undoubtedly the first pope of the twentieth century."[58]

57. Hughes, *A Popular History of the Catholic Church*, 271.
58. Collins, *Absolute Power*, 127.

8

Pope Pius XI (1922–39)

Within seven years the paleographer had become a diplomat, the diplomat an Archbishop, the Archbishop a Cardinal: and within six more months Achille Ratti was Pope.

—ANTHONY RHODES[1]

An authoritarian himself, [Pius] saw no particular evil in strong leadership, and he valued Fascism's emphasis on the family and social discipline, . . . but he detested the racial doctrine which underlay Nazism.

—EAMON DUFFY[2]

From Achille Ratti to Pope Pius XI

THE AGE OF THE dictators from 1920 to 1939 set the agenda for international politics, and largely defined the pontificate of Pope Pius XI. In the wake of World War I and the Treaty of Versailles, country after country succumbed to dictatorial regimes, most notably Italy, Germany, and Spain. While this must be quite properly an important consideration in our treatment of Pius, it cannot be the only one.

Ambrogio Damiano Achille Ratti was born near Milan in 1857, the son of a silk-factory manager. As a schoolboy, apart from the ordinary course of studies, he had two favorite authors, Jules Verne and Mark Twain. Apparently, Ratti was so interested in the African-American figures in the Twain novels that his peers referred to him as "the African." Ordained to the priesthood in 1879, he was a student at the Gregorian University and at the Academy of St. Thomas Aquinas from 1879–82. He served as a seminary professor in Milan from 1882–88 teaching homiletics, apologetics and Hebrew, and then moved to the Ambrosian Library in Milan in 1888. In England, John Henry Newman was still alive.

---

1. Rhodes, *The Vatican in the Age of Dictators, 1922–1945*, 18.
2. Duffy, *Saints and Sinners*, 343.

The Ambrosian Library was founded in 1609 by Cardinal Federico Borromeo, the cousin of St. Charles Borromeo and his successor as archbishop of Milan. The library was really a research library and museum for scholars interested in very specialized disciplines and in antiquity. It suited the interests of Achille Ratti down to the ground. One biographer of Ratti describes him at work there. "Dr. Ratti's intellectual interests were vast and varied. Whether he is engaged in writing on art such as his monograph on an ancient mosaic in the Basilica of St. Ambrose; or in contributing important data in his biographical study of St. Charles Borromeo or in deciphering some old palimpsest, or in archaeological research as in his article on a Latin inscription of the first century, found in Milan in 1904, or in editing his *Missale Ambrosianum Duplex*, he is always original in his approach and impartial in his treatment of the facts. Never does the apologist blind the faithful historian."[3]

Ratti's interest in Hebrew continued and he was known to consult from time to time with the chief Rabbi of Milan, Alessandro da Fano, and other Jewish scholars in respect of Hebrew texts.[4] The Italian historian Emma Fattorini relates that Don Ratti, teaching Hebrew in the seminary in Milan, took the seminarians with him to hear the chief rabbi in the synagogue. His relationship with Rabbi da Fano continued when he was elected pope. As Pius XI he received the Rabbi on a number of occasions. Fattorini writes: "Those meetings would be recalled by Ratti as an example of the good relationships he enjoyed with the Jews."[5]

Ratti was an accomplished paleographer and, among other things, he edited the Ambrosian Missal, as noted above. A considerable number of his publications focused on St. Charles Borromeo, the reforming archbishop of Milan, a love he shared with another historian, the young Angelo Roncalli. Ratti was also a mountaineer, and published a book on Alpine climbing. During the summer of 1900, Ratti spent a vacation in England studying at the British Museum and the Bodleian Library and Oxford.[6] Undoubtedly because of his expertise and scholarly accomplishments in Milan, he came to serve as pro-prefect in the Vatican Library in 1911 under the prefect the German Jesuit Franz Ehrle (1845–1934), and in 1914 he became its prefect. In that capacity and as Vatican Library representative he attended the celebration of the seventh centenary of the birth of the Franciscan scholar Roger Bacon in Oxford in 1914. On that occasion Ratti was able to announce the discovery by scholars of two manuscripts of Roger Bacon in the Vatican Library.[7]

All told, Ratti had been a librarian for some thirty-one years. In 1918, therefore, it came as a surprise that Pope Benedict XV sent him to Poland as apostolic visitor without any prior experience in diplomacy. The following year he was consecrated

---

3. Browne-Olf, *Pius XI, Apostle of Peace*, 36.

4. Dalin, *The Myth of Hitler's Pope*, 37.

5. Fattorini, *Hitler, Mussolini and the Vatican*, 21.

6. Browne-Olf, *Pius XI*, 45.

7. Little, *Roger Bacon*.

archbishop and was promoted to nuncio. Two issues in particular made an indelible impression on Ratti: the experience of Judaism and of Communism in Poland. In respect of the Jews historian David Kertzer writes:

> Had Benedict XV not appointed the scholarly cleric to the diplomatic post in Warsaw in 1918, the whole twentieth-century history of the Church might have been different. . . . This was the man who, as pope, would guide the Church's response to the rise of fascism in Italy and Nazism in Germany. . . . It was in Poland, amid Europe's largest Jewish population, that he experienced firsthand the potent mix of Catholicism, nationalism, and anti-Semitism.[8]

Poland had experienced pogrom after pogrom, as well as numerous accusations on and attacks against the Jews. It may be that Ratti was influenced to some extent by the Judeophobic members of the Polish hierarchy, but what is clear is that he hesitated to condemn outright the hostility towards and persecution of the Jews.[9] Kertzer goes on to document with some precision the crude and jaundiced views that Ratti had concerning the Jews. He saw the Jews as enemies of Christianity and the church. In June 1919, for example, he wrote: "One of the most evil and strongest influences that is felt here, perhaps the strongest and the most evil, is that of the Jews."[10] Such excerpts from the reports that Ratti made for Cardinal Gasparri, the Vatican secretary of state, make chilling reading today. The excerpts provided by Kertzer come from the Vatican archives. What are we to make of this? They leave one with a profound sense of sadness and shame as the Jews are judged in the most unfavorable ways by Ratti. Emma Fattorini comments candidly: "Ratti's statements are one more sign of the fluid way in which Catholic hostility toward Judaism could translate into the fierce anti-Semitism of the interwar years, even in a figure like Ratti, who would devote the last years of his life to combating just that. In the 1920s similar sentiments were widespread among Catholics, and could be found in other important nuncios, such as Eugenio Pacelli."[11] Ratti shared the anti-Jewish prejudices of his day, and there can be no denial of that, but it is important to recognize that he moved beyond that with the rise of Nazism, when as Pope Pius XI, he came to the defense of the Jews.

When it comes to the Communists, in 1920 a Bolshevik attack was threatened on Warsaw, and Ratti refused to leave the city. Eamon Duffy writes: "The experience left him with a lasting conviction that Communism was the worst enemy Christian Europe had ever faced, a conviction which shaped much of his policy as pope."[12] Communism was to shape papal policy also during the ministry of Pope Pius XII, and it made the running for the foreign policies of American administrations during

8. Kertzer, *The Popes Against the Jews*, 244.

9. Coppa, *The Papacy, the Jews and the Holocaust*, 143.

10. Cited in Kertzer, *The Popes Against the Jews*, 251.

11. Fattorini, *Hitler, Mussolini and the Vatican*, 26–27.

12. Duffy, *Saints and Sinners*, 336; Murphy, *The Papacy Today*, 44–45.

this time frame too. At the end of his stay in Poland, Benedict XV appointed him archbishop of Milan and cardinal in 1921.

Ratti took as his episcopal motto the Benedictine *Ora et Labora*, "Pray and Work." He spent a month on retreat at the Benedictine Abbey Monte Cassino in preparation for his episcopal ministry in Milan. As things turned out, he remained in the diocese a mere five months before being elected to the papacy, but during that short period of time he threw himself into pastoral activity. "He proved himself [a] solicitous shepherd, throwing himself wholeheartedly into his new work with all his customary ardor. Not a day passed in which he did not visit hospitals, schools, clerical and lay institutions, prisons and houses of correction. Each Sunday he went to outlying districts, visiting numberless villages and parishes on his way. His sermons were known to number as many as six and eight a day."[13] Even acknowledging the quasi-hagiographical nature of the description, it points to a full and active pastoral commitment.

Pope Pius XI

Next year, 1922, Ratti was elected pope taking the name of Pius XI. Fourteen scrutinies or ballots were taken before the required two-thirds vote was reached. Cardinal O'Connell of Boston, like Cardinal Gibbons before him, arrived too late for the election. He let his chagrin be known but in a humorous fashion, but it was effective. Pius XI took steps to lengthen the time period between the death of a pope and the conclave, so that cardinals from far-flung places could exercise their rightful roles. He extended in a *motu proprio* the period for cardinals making their way to Rome from ten to fifteen, and even eighteen days if necessary. His first act as pope was to give the traditional blessing, *Urbi et Orbi*, from St. Peter's Basilica, something that had not been done since the unification of Italy and the occupation of Rome in 1870. This powerful gesture continued the positive overtures to the state of Italy begun by his predecessor Benedict XV. Eamon Duffy describes the style of the new pontificate in these words: "[Pius] accepted advice, if at all, only when he had asked for it, and he soon became famous for towering rages which left his entourage weak and trembling. Even visiting diplomats noted that the key word in the Vatican had become obedience."[14]

Peter Hebblethwaite writes of the pontificate of Pius XI:

> Achille Ratti, Pius XI, who reigned (the appropriate word for him) from 1922 to 1939, was the Pope with the mostest. He had the most canonizations, and the most Holy Years. He had the most concordats, including those with Benito Mussolini and Adolf Hitler (though the latter concordat is less sinister if one recalls that it was already being negotiated long before Hitler came to prominence or power). He wrote the most encyclicals, and it was in his pontificate

13. Browne-Olf, *Pius XI,* 110.

14. Duffy, *Saints and Sinners,* 336–37; Francis X. Murphy, *The Papacy Today,* 48–49.

that the notion of ordinary *magisterium* began to occupy a firm place in the theology manuals. It meant taking the pope seriously as a teaching authority, whatever the occasion. Of course it never meant that everything he said was strictly infallible, but all his utterances acquired, as it were, an aura of infallibility. It was a case of "creeping infallibility" as Sir Arnold Lunn, a famous convert of the 1930s, put it some years later.[15]

Sometimes Pius was intimidating beyond the boundaries of propriety. The British prime minister of Malta accused the pope of trying to hand over the island to Mussolini and of Italianizing the church there. Lord Strickland was a devout and practicing Catholic, but sometimes most intemperate in his language. He wrote, to offer but one example, in a newspaper article: "If enough money were forthcoming, the Pope would make a horse a Papal Marquis."[16] Pius had the archbishop of Malta interdict Strickland's political party, forbidding the sacraments and excommunicating those Catholics who voted for it, and relented only when the prime minister wrote public letters of apology both to him and to the archbishop. To say the least this smacks more of medieval conflicts between church and state than of modernity. Pius entertained a "sacral concept of papal prerogatives" and papal power.[17] As a result of the Maltese *débacle* and to demonstrate British disapproval of how matters had been handled, the British representative was withdrawn and no British minister was appointed to the Vatican for almost three years.

The Church

Pius was an avid promoter of Catholic Action, the collaboration of the laity with the hierarchy in the church's mission. The purpose of Catholic Action was to reanimate society at all levels and in every way with Catholic spirituality, rooted and founded in the doctrines of the faith and morals. It emerges with a sense of urgency in his first encyclical, *Ubi Arcano*, in 1922.

The Lambeth Conference of 1930 moved the Anglican Communion away from a complete condemnation of contraception. This evoked from Pius XI in December of the same year the encyclical *Casti Connubii*. The pope wrote: "Certain persons have openly withdrawn from the Christian doctrine as it has been transmitted from the beginning and always faithfully kept." The encyclical continues in this vein:

> The Catholic Church, to which God himself has committed the integrity and decency of morals, now standing in the ruin of morals, raises her voice aloud through our mouth, in sign of her divine mission, in order to keep the chastity of the nuptial bond from this foul lapse, and again promulgates: Any

15. Peter Hebblethwaite, *In the Vatican*, 28–29.

16. Cited in Rhodes, *The Vatican in the Age of Dictators*, 57.

17. Murphy, *The Papacy Today*, 52.

use whatever of marriage, in the exercise of which the act by human effort is deprived of its natural power of procreating life, violates the law of God and nature, and those who do such a thing are stained by a grave and mortal fault.

Peter Nichols comments that "The cement looked to be set hard."[18]

Pius sought to commemorate the fortieth anniversary of Pope Leo XIII's encyclical *Rerum Novarum* with an encyclical of his own, but on a wider scale. The project, along with various notes of his own, was given over by the pope to a German Jesuit economist, Oswald Nell-Breuning, and saw the light as *Quadragesimo Anno* in 1931. Nell-Breuning had completed a doctorate in economics in 1928 with a dissertation on the morality of the stock-exchange. The times were very hard indeed. Germany was crippled by its war debt. The straitened financial circumstances that came about as a result of the depression thrust left-wing parties in Europe into prominence among the working class, and right-wing parties into equal prominence among the middle class. In this encyclical Pius pointed out the importance for the Christian of avoiding egocentric individualism and its opposite extreme, socialistic collectivism. He warned about the excesses of capitalism. He affirmed the right to private property and the necessity of a stable economic and political order. To avoid the extremes of individualism and collectivism Pius advocated intermediate structures, "corporations" or unions, in some ways like the medieval guilds. These corporations or "vocational groups" would devote themselves to a number of the projects which the modern state was now handling.[19] The political and economic system entertained in the encyclical, focused on the corporations, was not well received by secular academics and politicians, but though not intended by the pope, it was used to their advantage by the dictators, including Mussolini and Hitler, as a cover for their totalitarian systems. "It was only much later, after he realized the use that has been made of it, that Nell-Breuning had doubts about the value of the document."[20] His concerns for social justice went well beyond the encyclical. He supported the Young Christian Workers, the movement founded by the Belgian priest Joseph Cardijn. When a French bishop, Achille Lienart of Lille, was attacked by right-wingers as a Marxist and reported to the Vatican because he gave money to a strike fund, Pius replied by making Lienart a cardinal.

Pius continued the missionary activity of his predecessor, Benedict XV. He encouraged an indigenous clergy in missionary territories, and renounced Eurocentrism. To that end he ordained the first six indigenous Chinese bishops in 1926 and in 1927 the first Japanese bishop of Nagasaki. From his 1926 encyclical letter *Rerum Ecclesiae* we read the following statement: "The church always opposes among its ministers any worldly influence or nationalistic spirit. But above all it opposes these things among those sent in its name to preach the gospel in foreign lands. It has

18. Nichols, *The Pope's Divisions*, 256.

19. Giblin, "Quadragesimo Anno," 802–13.

20. Murphy, *The Papacy Today*, 55.

always claimed the right to preach the gospel without political interference. It has never permitted its missions to be used as a political instrument by earthly powers." One church historian judges that these actions of Pius constitute "one of the most significant visible steps in the huge shift of leadership which happened almost everywhere in the course of the century."[21] By 1939, as a result of this combined policy of Benedict XV and Pius indigenous priests reached seven thousand in number. Missiology became under Pius an established theological discipline, a faculty of missiology being established at the Gregorian University in Rome, among other places. While an excessive nationalism was growing throughout the world and especially in Europe, this particular policy of Pius XI underscored the importance of the internationalization of the Catholic Church.[22] Perhaps this is the context in which to note his establishment of the Russicum in Rome in 1929, a college to prepare priests to be missionaries in the "Godless" Soviet Union.

France

Since the French Revolution of 1789, the Holy See had a history of difficult relations with France. Pius worked hard to establish good relations with the French government. His main objective was to give encouragement to those French Catholics who wanted to work constructively with the French republic. That was problematic for some. France was marked by a constant tension between those who favored democracy and those who supported royalism. The twentieth century witnessed an extreme anti-republican movement, *Action Française*. This movement had its own newspaper with the same name edited by Charles Maurras. Maurras was an atheist, but an atheist who admired both the gubernatorial structures of Catholicism as he understood them and the church's conservatism. He was most influential among French Catholics, including some of the bishops. Though blessed by Pope Pius X who was somewhat sympathetic to the conservative and restorationist views of Maurras and regarded him also as a support against modernism, Pius XI saw Maurras and *Action Française* as a barrier to progress in the church's relations with France. Pius's movement against Maurras was resisted even by some among his Vatican staff, but in 1926 he had Cardinal Paulin Andrieu, archbishop of Bordeaux, condemn it, placed *Action Française* on the Index, and in 1927 excommunicated the movement's supporters. Needless to say, Pius was accused of being a Freemason and a friend of the Jews. The influential French theologian, the Jesuit Cardinal Billot, who in fact had placed the papal tiara on Pius's head on the day of his consecration, wrote a letter of sympathy to *Action Française*, and subsequently had to resign his cardinalate.

21. Hastings, "The Twentieth Century," 222.
22. Duffy, *Saints and Sinners*, 338.

Mexico

Communists came to power in Mexico in 1917, just five years before Pius was elected. A constitution was arrived at in which the church was clearly subordinate to the state and in which church property was confiscated. Other actions followed such as the expulsion of foreign clergy and the destruction of religious shrines. Seven years later, in 1924, the attempt was made systematically to eradicate Catholicism. Church historian E. E. Y. Hales writes of Mexico's extreme anti-Catholicism at this time:

> The venom with which it was pursued is unique in the modern history of persecution in the New World and can only be compared with what has taken place in countries behind the Iron Curtain in Europe since the Second World War. It was a real "war to the death," which reduced the priesthood to a handful of less than two hundred hunted men, under sentence of death for the crime of being priests, whose pitiful position has been most vividly portrayed in Mr. Graham Greene's novel, *The Power and the Glory*.[23]

The pope appealed to a number of countries to protest what was occurring in Mexico, but the European powers were reluctant to do anything that might place at risk their financial and commercial assets in Mexico. Eventually pressure brought by the United States ended physical persecution—pressure not unrelated to the Mexican government's seizure and nationalization of foreign-owned oil fields in 1938—but by this time enormous damage had been done to the Mexican church, damage that could only begin to be repaired twenty years later with the empowerment of a new generation on the eve of World War II. It is very difficult to understand the situation of the church in Mexico at this time with the extraordinary hostility of the government. Where did the hostility and the venom come from? Part of the answer, but only part surely lies in the fact that the Mexican church in the late nineteenth and early twentieth centuries had vast holdings of land and property. Priests charged considerable fees of the ordinary people for the sacraments. There was too often a sense of clerical superiority over the laity. These comments are in no way intended to excuse what occurred, but rather to offer some degree of contextualization.

The Concordat with Italy

Historian David Kertzer describes the strange and strained relationship between Pope Pius XI and Benito Mussolini in these terms: "The dictator relied on the Pope to ensure Catholic support for his regime, providing much-needed moral legitimacy. The Pope counted on Mussolini to help him restore the church's power in Italy."[24] Kertzer thoroughly documents the relationship between Pius and Mussolini

23. Hales, *The Catholic Church in the Modern World*, 260.
24. Kertzer, *The Pope and Mussolini*, xxx.

throughout his book. He draws attention to the role played by the Italian and fascist Jesuit, Pietro Tacchi Venturi (1861–1956). This priest-historian helped to bring about the donation by Mussolini of the library of the Palazzo Chigi, the Italian prime minister's headquarters. The Vatican had been interested in procuring the library for some time, and it included three thousand antique manuscripts as well as thirty thousand books. Venturi was a key player in bringing about the donation, and he continued to be a very influential go-between Pius and Mussolini. He met Mussolini regularly, at least once a month, relaying messages and communications of various kinds from the pope, cementing in every way he could their relationship.

Recent historians have said of Pius: "For Pius, concordats were everything, reflecting his naive trust in the written word and the integrity of international guarantees."[25] There is truth in this judgment. Concordats were not necessarily everything for him, but they were the political and diplomatic norm at the time for the Vatican. It is difficult to imagine an alternative. His trust in the written word was naive surely, but it was a naiveté shared by many, including Neville Chamberlain in his famous Munich statement after conversation with Adolf Hitler, "Peace in our time." Words remain of supreme importance in politics, written words, even when there is a high probability that people will not remain true to their word. The alternative is a circle of suspicion that is ultimately self-defeating. At the same time, one recognizes that through this policy of concordats the church seemed to be aligning itself with conservative political regimes, and while it is difficult pragmatically to imagine an alternative, it needs to be acknowledged for the sake of fairness that "this was generally the fruit of strategic positioning rather of inherent adhesion to the political Right."[26]

In 1925 Pius published the encyclical *Quas Primas* in which he instituted the Feast of Christ the King. This is most important because it was prior to his concordats with Italy and Germany and sets the final theological horizon within which those concordats ought to be interpreted. In that letter we find these words:

"States, princes and governments are rulers in their own domains, and Christ, whose kingdom is not of this world, has no wish that his Church should interfere therein; but she must remind them of the spiritual and moral principles to which their labors should conform, and declare repeatedly that they too are bound to promote the kingdom of God." The words are clear. The secular political realm enjoys a proper degree of autonomy, but that autonomy is relative and never absolute. The political realm must be supportive of spiritual and moral principles expressive of the kingdom of God. It is within this horizon that Pius's interest in and promotion of concordats must be understood. Otherwise, the concordats will inevitably seem like the church seeking her own privilege and well-being in a politically pragmatic fashion. Historian David Kertzer draws attention to the fact that Protestants felt singularly undermined by this encyclical. "While Catholics greeted the encyclical, and the new holiday it

25. Atkin and Tallett, *Priests, Prelates and People*, 204.
26. Norman, *The Roman Catholic Church*, 168.

announced, with enthusiasm, the same could not be said of Protestants. In the United States, the National Lutheran Council blasted the encyclical as 'sectarian in the worst sense' and 'hostile to very large groups of Christians.' It called on Protestants everywhere to boycott the pope's new holy day."[27]

Pius established concordats with some twenty states in order to protect the position and the rights of the church, the three most important being with Italy, Germany and Spain. The Lateran Treaty of 1929 with Benito Mussolini, prime minister of Italy, had been prepared for by the policies of Benedict XV. The actual negotiations of the concordat were carried out by Cardinal Gasparri and Francesco Pacelli, brother of Eugenio Pacelli who was to become Pope Pius XII. Before this concordat could be entered into, Mussolini and his fascist government brought pressure to bear on the Vatican for the removal of Don Luigi Sturzo, the leader of the "Popular Party." Sturzo would not consider any form of alliance with Mussolini, and was finally persuaded to resign as president of the party in 1923, and he then went into exile first in England and then in America. This drew the teeth of the Popular Party. Now the Vatican recognized Italy as a kingdom with Rome as its capital city, and the newly recognized kingdom indemnified the Vatican for the loss of the papal states with a lump-sum of 1,750, million lire (roughly equal to $70,000,000 dollars at the time) as well as one billion lire in Italian bonds (totaling roughly one billion 2013 US dollars), and formally accepted Catholicism as the official religion of the state.[28] The money enabled Pius in the inimitable phrasing of Eamon Duffy, "to spend like a Renaissance prince."[29] New presses were purchased for *Osservatore Romano* and for the Vatican Polyglot Press. The Vatican radio station was set up under the personal supervision of Marconi. The Vatican Observatory was modernized and set up at the papal residence of Castel Gandolfo. He also modernized the Vatican library and museums. The fact that the papacy through the concordat of 1929 committed not to interfere in the government and politics of Italy, and that the Italian government committed not to interfere in the church—all of this might be said to have brought to an end a period of papal history that had lasted for 1,500 years more or less.[30]

However, the concordat with Italy did not please everyone, and in the Vatican it had its own critics, even if their criticism was careful. Actually, Pope Pius XI found

27. Kertzer, *The Pope and Mussolini*, 84. There can be little doubt that Pius harbored a certain animus against Protestants. This was witnessed not only in his encyclical letter on ecumenism, *Mortalium Animos*, but in his general attitude towards them. Pius expected Mussolini to keep Protestants in Italy in check. David Kertzer, *The Pope and Mussolini*, 185 writes as follows: "Mussolini pointed out [to Pius] that only 135,000 Protestants lived in Italy, 37,000 of them foreigners—a mere speck amid 42 million Catholics. The pope acknowledged that the Protestants were few but argued that the threat was nonetheless great. . . . Over the next years he would bombard the dictator with requests to keep the Protestants in check."

28. Kertzer, *The Pope and Mussolini*, 107.

29. Duffy, *Saints and Sinners*, 339.

30. O'Malley, *A History of the Popes*, 278.

himself in considerable tension with his secretary of state, Cardinal Gasparri, who along with Francesco Pacelli was the principal Vatican negotiator of the Lateran Accords. Gasparri, who was the mentor of Eugenio Pacelli, was a very strong advocate of neutrality and impartiality. Pius was more inclined to be confrontational, including with Mussolini. Tension between him and Gasparri was inevitable. "Pius XI would not allow his Secretary of State Gasparri to pursue a policy or course that contradicted his own. When he did, the infuriated pope fired him."[31] One of the sharpest critics of the Lateran Accords was Msgr. Giovanni Battista Montini, whose father had been prominent in the Popular Party of Don Luigi Sturzo. He thought the agreement was merely "a pseudo-reconciliation, a non-event from which Mussolini had gained a great deal of favorable publicity."[32] Two years later in 1931 Mussolini dissolved the Catholic youth movements, and this met with Vatican opposition. Pius wrote in that year a very forthright encyclical, *Non Abbiamo Bisogno*, "We do not need this," and to promote its circulation outside of Italy in case the Fascists suppressed it, he sent Msgr. Francis Spellman with it to Paris. But it was in 1938 when Fascist Italy adopted the racist policies of Nazi Germany that we see a very noticeable change of emphasis in Pius. He began to distance himself as much as possible from Mussolini.

However, the question may be raised: How complete was that distancing? The Vatican was heavily invested in Italian industry, including armaments. When Mussolini declared war on Ethiopia in 1935, this certainly presented a major challenge for Pius. Prior to the war, and in line with the thinking of *Non Abbiamo Bisogno*, the pope seemed to take a position against the Mussolini government. He refused to bless Italian troops preparing for the invasion and to make a forthright statement in support of the war. While he prayed for peace, he made a statement in which he says if the "hopes, the demands, the needs of a great and good people, who are [my] people . . . will be recognized and satisfied, . . . but with justice and peace."[33] Not exactly an endorsement of the war, but hardly a condemnation of this act of unilateral aggression. Further, there seems to be little or no evidence that Pius supported the League of Nations or other agents seeking to mediate between Italy and Ethiopia.

The Concordat with Germany

Since the declaration in 1920 of Bishop Clemens August Graf von Galen of Münster that no Catholic could accept the Nazi program without denying essential elements of his faith, there had been a series of strong anti-Nazi statements by the German episcopate.[34] However, it must be said that not all the episcopate was anti-Nazi. While not for a moment detracting from the egregious horrors of the Nazi era, it is important to recognize

---

31. Coppa, *The Life and Pontificate of Pope Pius XII*, 102.
32. Hebblethwaite, *John XXIII*, 65.
33. Cited in Coffey, *Lion by the Tail*, 127.
34. See Coppa, *The Life and Pontificate of Pope Pius XII*, 150.

that for many good people the times were marked by a deep ambiguity. Historian Emma Fattorini provides us with a paragraph that points up this ambiguity.

> All the bishops shared an attachment to the nation, patriotic loyalty, and a rootedness in their individual countryside, cities, and *Länder*. It was a loyalty that they often hoped would serve to lighten the persecution of the church in the name of national solidarity. Loyalty to the homeland was a source of great embarrassment for the episcopacy and generally for the German Catholic community; on the one hand their national loyalty was recognized while on the other their protests against Nazism raised suspicion of defeatism and betrayal. Such was the difficult spot in which the bishops found themselves, between the need to offer reassurances of their loyalty to the nation while at the same time opposing Nazism, not only to defend the German church but on behalf of all the German people. Driven by the overriding need to survive among divergent tactics . . . and uncertainty and concern about the regime's reaction, the German episcopacy wrestled with these dilemmas but failed to find a solution.[35]

Take, for example, Conrad Gröber, the priest from Messkirch who had encouraged the philosophical studies of the young philosopher from the same village, Martin Heidegger. Gröber was a friend of Monsignor Eugenio Pacelli, the nuncio of Pope Pius XI to Germany. In 1932, Gröber was appointed archbishop of Freiburg. Initially, Archbishop Gröber attempted to find common ground between the church and Nazism. The priests of his diocese were counseled to adopt a conciliatory approach to the party and its philosophy so that they might be able to bring some Christian influence upon it. The church historian of the Nazi era, Klaus Scholder, reports that Gröber donated personal monies to Nazi organizations.[36] These were difficult and ambiguous days. Heidegger's appointment as rector of the University on April 21, 1933 was something of a concession to the professors of Freiburg who had publicly opposed Hitler in 1933. Heidegger was supported for the rectorship among a significant number of his colleagues. However, two lectures in May and June of the same year by Heidegger indicate his sympathies at the time: "The Self-Assertion of the German University" and "The University in the New Reich." Theologian John Macquarrie acknowledges that these lectures "while they certainly express support for the regime, they are not extreme or fanatical and—very importantly—they do not contain any anti-Semitic utterances."[37] While Heidegger dismissed professors who were either Jewish or politically dissident, historian Robert Krieg writes: "The University's fifteen theologians and its instructors in theology taught approximately 320 seminarians in 1933. No theologian was a member of the Nazi party, and none of them joined the

---

35. Fattorini, *Hitler, Mussolini and the Vatican*, 127.

36. See Krieg, *Catholic Theologians in Nazi Germany*, 141, 201.

37. Macquarrie, *Heidegger and Christianity*, 112.

AKD, despite Archbishop Gröber's support for it."[38] The Catholic archbishop, and his protégé now University Rector were, at least in some respects, on one side, the Nazi side, while the theology faculty was on the other. Towards the end of 1933 and not yet a year in office, Heidegger began to realize that he was not being particularly effective in changing the climate of National Socialism, and so he resigned from the rectorship in February 1934. Archbishop Conrad Gröber, though something of an enthusiast of Nazism at the outset and a broker of the Vatican's concordat with Germany, later changed course and became an opponent of the system. In December 1945, Heidegger, who had become *persona non grata* with the Nazis and now enjoyed that status also with the occupying allied forces, appealed to Gröber who had some influence with the allies for assistance in attempting to recover his professorship in philosophy at Freiburg. Gröber wrote on his behalf, but to no avail.[39]

In 1933 the concordat, the initiative for which came from Adolf Hitler through the Reich vice chancellor, the Catholic Franz von Papen (whom we shall meet again in the chapter on Pope John XXIII), had been negotiated by Cardinal Eugenio Pacelli, Pius's secretary of state. Pacelli had spent most of the twenties in Germany as nuncio and knew the situation well. This concordat with National Socialist Germany "temporarily enhanced the prestige of the regime and curbed Catholic opposition to it, but for which [Pius] was heavily criticized."[40] As in Italy, there was in Germany a powerful Catholic party led by Monsignor Ludwig Kaas. Like Don Luigi Sturzo in Italy, Kaas and the party were sacrificed to pave the way for the concordat with Hitler. There is evidence to suggest that Msgr. Kaas and his centrist Catholic political party were not exactly expected to dissolve themselves by Cardinal Pacelli. It is probably more the case that they fell by the wayside because they did not receive adequate support from the highest Catholic quarters both in Germany and in the Vatican in the face of the concordat with Hitler. This is certainly the opinion of Robert Ventresca who writes:

> Abandoned by most of their erstwhile allies, with no support from the German bishops or the Vatican, the Bavarian People's Party and the Center Party willingly dissolved themselves in the first week of July 1933. While it may be technically true that the disbanding of the German Catholic parties ultimately came from within, the absence of meaningful ecclesiastical support made the outcome all the more likely. Pacelli, taking his lead from Msgr.

38. Macquarrie, *Heidegger and Christianity*, 143.

39. Safranski, *Martin Heidegger Between Good and Evil*, 351.

40. Kelly, *The Oxford Dictionary of the Popes*, 317. John Tracy Ellis, preeminent American Catholic Church historian, offers some further details but which are impossible to verify as such, even as there is no need to doubt their veracity: "For an hour or more during which [Dr. Heinrich Breuning] told me that as Chancellor he had sent to Rome numerous documents by way of warning Pope Pius XI of the Nazi peril, only to learn to his chagrin that they had never reached the pontiff. They were withheld, he said, by the Secretary of State, Eugenio Cardinal Pacelli, the future Pius XII." See Ellis, *Faith and Learning, a Church Historian's Story*, 43.

Kaas and the German bishops, was resigned to the fact that Hitler was moving towards a one-party state.[41]

Pacelli and the Vatican were trying to salvage what was possible for the Catholic Church in Germany. The treaty with the German Reich was ratified formally in September 1933.

Although Cardinal Pacelli and Pope Pius XI were both firmly of the opinion that the non-confrontational concordat course was the only way forward with Nazi Germany, overall this was in all probability more Pacelli's perspective than that of the pope. Pacelli and Pius make an interesting contrast, well summarized by Ventresca as follows: "Theirs was a unique relationship, characterized by mutual admiration, even genuine affection. Yet they were vastly different men in temperament. Ratti (Pius XI) was a colorful character, emotive, outspoken, and argumentative. Pacelli was decidedly more reserved and introspective. The two were capable of open disagreement with each other, but nothing, it seems, seriously threatened their mutual respect and common sense of purpose."[42] Doing all that was possible to protect Catholic interests with constant reference to the concordat was probably also the majority view among the German bishops. While Pius himself certainly believed that a concordat with Nazi Germany was the only way to protect the church, there can be little doubt about Hitler's view of the church. "Hitler regarded the Catholic Church as a great institution that had served its purpose and outlived its usefulness."[43]

However, the Nazi refusal to honor the terms of the concordat drew in 1936–1937 thirty-four notes of protest from the pope, even as Cardinal Pacelli counseled great caution so as not to threaten the concordat.[44] Towards the end of 1936 Cardinal Pacelli on behalf of the pope asked five prominent German bishops to come to Rome to discuss the ongoing crisis in Germany. These bishops were: Cardinal Adolph Bertram, Cardinal Michael von Faulhaber, Cardinal Josef Schulte, Bishop Konrad von Preysing (of Berlin), and Bishop von Galen (of Münster). The meeting with the pope took place in January 1937, but the bishops met with Pacelli first. He informed them of Pius's unpublicized chronic medical situation—he suffered both from diabetes and heart problems—and apparently he told them that he did not think the pope would survive two more years. As Frank J. Coppa notes, while some interpret Pacelli's meeting with the German bishops as simply preparing them for their encounter with the very ill Pope, others take a different line. "Others have perceived a more sinister motive, subtly suggesting that since the Pope would not be with them much longer they need not fear disagreeing or

41. Ventresca, *Soldier of Christ*, 84.

42. Ventresca, *Soldier of Christ*, 97. Throughout her excellent study, *Hitler, Mussolini and the Vatican* and having had access to the Vatican archives historian Emma Fattorini consistently makes the same point as Ventresca.

43. Holmes, *The Papacy in the Modern*, 101.

44. Coppa, *The Life and Pontificate of Pope Pius XII*, 158–60.

challenging his wishes."[45] Whether this negative interpretation is true or not, it does fit Pacelli's style of conciliation over confrontation, and he was well aware that Pius felt justified theologically and morally in being confrontational with the Third Reich.

With some input from these German bishops the Vatican confrontation/protest with the Third Reich reached its climax later in that year of 1937 in the encyclical letter, *Mit brennender Sorge*, "With Burning Zeal." This encyclical was smuggled into Germany by an American cleric from the Vatican, Monsignor Francis Spellman of Boston.[46] Cardinal Michael Faulhaber of Munich and Cardinal Pacelli were essentially of the same mind, that is to say, the concordat should not be brought into jeopardy by the actions of the Vatican. Printed locally, the encyclical was disseminated secretly by motorcyclists throughout the country, and was read from every Catholic pulpit on Palm Sunday 1937. It denounced the Nazi breaches of the 1933 concordat and Nazi racial doctrine: "Whoever exalts race, or the people, or the state, or a particular form of the state, or the depositories of power, or any other fundamental value of the human community . . . whoever raises these notions above their standard value and divinizes them to an idolatrous level, distorts and perverts an order of the world planned and created by God."[47]

The encyclical emphasized the importance of the Old Testament: "Whoever wishes to see banished from church and school the biblical history and the wise doctrines of the Old Testament, blasphemes the name of God."[48] "The impact of the encyclical was immense, and it dispelled at once all suspicion of a fascist pope."[49] While that judgment undoubtedly remains true, it must be noted that not all agreed with the papal action. The summary of Frank Coppa is clear and concise: "Pius XI's anti-Nazi policy failed to resonate in much of the German church and part of the Curia. Critics complained that *Mit brennender Sorge*, rather than tempering the Nazis, had enraged them, leading to a greater repression of German Catholics. These voices, including that of Pacelli and the Secretariat of State, invoked diplomacy and the use of the concordat to redress grievances."[50] Pacelli with his colleagues in the Secretariat of State had in fact contributed to the creation of the encyclical and, although Germany, Nazism or Hitler were never mentioned as such in the document, it was obviously directed against them and confrontation was not the Pacelli style.

Hard on the heels of *Mit brennender Sorge*, in fact five days later, came another encyclical, *Divini Redemptoris*, condemning Communism. There is a difference between the two encyclicals, a difference that Pius saw between Fascism and Communism, and a difference well captured by Peter Hebblethwaite in these words:

45. Coppa, *The Policies and Politics of Pope Pius XII*, 98.

46. Murphy, *The Papacy Today*, 54.

47. Carlen, *The Papal Encyclicals*, ad loc., par. 8.

48. Carlen, *The Papal Encyclicals*, ad loc., par. 16.

49. Duffy, *Saints and Sinners*, 344.

50. Coppa, *The Life and Pontificate of Pope Pius XII*, 163.

Pius XI did not quite put both dictatorships in the same bag. The emphasis in *Divini Redemptoris* fell on the "intrinsically evil" nature of atheistic Communism, with which no Catholic could collaborate. *Mit brennender Sorge* eloquently denounced those who "idolatrously divinize race or the People or the State or a particular form of State," complained that the Church's rights were being violated, but that might be remedied if the Concordat were properly applied. There was no Concordat with Communists, anywhere.[51]

Hebblethwaite is correct in that no actual concordat with any Communist state or government was ever achieved. However, efforts had been made. Frank J. Coppa points out that "efforts to conclude a concordat with the Soviet Union continued for almost a decade right up until 1927, when the attempt was abandoned."[52]

Nonetheless, there was a definite favoring of the political right on the part of the church but it had more to do with strategic positioning over against Communist states, with their overt materialist and atheistic ideology, rather than with an absolute endorsement of conservative regimes.[53] It was thought, rightly or wrongly, that there was the possibility of the church working with fascist regimes, but with regimes that were in principle atheist this was impossible, and indeed such regimes had to be constantly opposed whenever possible. This perspective has the ring of truth to it during the pontificates of both Pope Pius XI and Pope Pius XII, even as one acknowledges that the most dreadful atrocities were perpetrated by these fascist political regimes. The Jesuit sociologist, John LaFarge, however, writing hard on the heels of both encyclicals makes the point very firmly that both Nazism and Communism had much in common: "There is no essential difference between the mob that takes a human life out of contempt for a so-called inferior race . . . and the Communist who preaches violence in the name of class warfare."[54] It would be extremely difficult if not impossible to disagree with LaFarge. Perhaps one could say that in practical terms Pius XI was opposed to both fascism and Communism, but in theoretical terms, in terms of political and theological analysis Communism posed the greater threat.

Continuing to denounce Nazism blatantly and publicly, Pius came to the support of Cardinal Mundelein of Chicago. Mundelein described Hitler as "an Austrian paperhanger, and a poor one at that." The German government protested this to the pope, but far from rebuking Mundelein, Pius praised him.[55] When Hitler visited Rome in May 1938, the pope had the Vatican museums closed, having been made aware that Hitler wished to visit them. Members of the Roman Curia were warned to have nothing to do with this visit in terms of attending functions, dinners or receptions. The official Vatican newspaper *Osservatore Romano* had been instructed to say nothing about Hitler's visit.

51. Hebblethwaite, *In the Vatican*, 76.

52. Coppa, *The Policies and Politics of Pope Pius XII*, 66.

53. Norman, *The Roman Catholic Church*, 170–71.

54. LaFarge, SJ, "The Pope Deals with Nazi Persecution," 211.

55. Coppa, *The Policies and Politics of Pope Pius XII*, 165.

Finally, Pius left for his residence at Castel Gandolfo. The position of the pope with regard to Hitler's visit to Rome should have caused no surprise. After all, he had written in the encyclical *Mit brennender Sorge*, "None but superficial minds could stumble into concepts of a National God, of a national religion; or attempt to lock within the frontiers of a single people, within the narrow limits of a single race, God, the Creator of the Universe." Both Hitler and his host Mussolini, already in very strained relationships with the Vatican, were infuriated by Pius's snub of Hitler.

Pius XI's Secretary of State, Cardinal Gasparri and his successor Cardinal Pacelli were wary of the pope's outspoken and confrontational style. Theirs was a way of diplomacy and conciliation. Gasparri and Pacelli disagreed with the pope when it came to responding to the fascists' anti-Semitism. "[Pacelli] repeatedly warned the Pope of the adverse consequences that would flow from a disruption of relations with Fascist Italy and the Third Reich. These admonitions convinced Pius XI that he could not rely on his secretary of state for a strong and unequivocal condemnation of racism and anti-Semitism, and looked elsewhere."[56] In fact, he looked primarily to an American Jesuit, the sociologist John LaFarge.

The Hidden Encyclical

Pius commissioned in 1938 another encyclical to condemn anti-Semitism.[57] It was drafted by three Jesuit scholars—John LaFarge, Gustav Gundlach, and Gustave Desbuqois. LaFarge (1880–1963) was known to the pope. He had been the author of a study of racial discrimination in the United States, *Interracial Justice*, a study that Pius had read and liked. LaFarge had completed a BA in Latin and Greek classics at Harvard, continued his theological studies at the University of Innsbrück, Austria, and was ordained to the priesthood in 1905. Then he joined the Society of Jesus, serving in Jesuit colleges and in other ministries. For fifteen years he served in a variety of

56. Coppa, *The Policies and Politics of Pope Pius XII*, 71–72. In his *The Life and Pontificate of Pope Pius XII*, Coppa writes on pages 105–6: "They [Pope Pius XI and Cardinal Pacelli] disagreed on how to respond to those who violated the principles [of the concordats], and the Pope eventually realized that his Secretary of State, like most in the Curia, did not share his intransigent opposition to the fascist regimes. The differences between the two are subtly but unmistakably manifest in the reports Pacelli made of his meetings with the Pope from 1930 to 1938."

57. Frank J. Coppa makes some interesting comments on the lack of accurate information surrounding this unpublished encyclical. He approached Fr. Robert Graham, one of four Jesuit scholars who was given access to the papers of Pope Pius XII. Here are Coppa's comments: "While personally cordial, indeed friendly, he repeated he knew nothing about the projected encyclical supposedly commissioned by Pope Pius XI. I later learned that the Benedictine monk of Maredsous in Belgium Georges Passelecq, found Graham equally evasive. Perhaps Father Graham was under a vow of secrecy. If so, he adhered to it. I was not much surprised that the text was not in the Vatican archive—but wondered why there was no record of its creation and eventual fate. Graham later acknowledged that there was a dossier on this unreleased encyclical in the Vatican archive—but reported that it remained closed and inaccessible. I was not alone in questioning the reason for such secrecy and could not help wondering who was responsible for its closure." See Frank J. Coppa, *The Policies and Politics of Pope Pius XII*, 9.

situations in racially mixed Jesuit parishes and missions in rural Maryland. This became the foundational context for his book, *Interracial Justice*. In 1926, his provincial appointed him to the staff of the Jesuit weekly, *America*.

In his capacity as a priest-reporter-writer for *America*, LaFarge was sent in April, 1938 to the Eucharistic Congress in Budapest.[58] The pope's representative at the Budapest Congress was Cardinal Eugenio Pacelli. LaFarge heard Pacelli speak at the Congress and he must have taken note of the fact that the cardinal avoided any criticism of Nazi anti-Semitism, a reality about which everyone would have been aware. LaFarge would also have witnessed the devotional events of the Congress, perhaps including this event described by Peter Eisner: "Pacelli knelt at the bow of a steamer on the Danube before a three-foot-tall Eucharistic altar inset with jewels and silver. An army of Catholic clergy, monsignors, priests, and nuns surrounded him, all holding candles. The candlelight shimmered all along the river as the procession started at dusk."[59]

The Eucharistic Congress was undoubtedly a very successful devotional event for the Catholics of Hungary. At the same time, what might be described as the ethical consequences of authentic Eucharistic piety did not translate into a loving concern for the Jews of Hungary. There was at the time considerable anti-Jewish sentiment among Catholics of Central and Eastern Europe especially, but one year only after the Eucharistic Congress anti-Jewish measures were passed by the Hungarian authorities.

Probably not participants in the Eucharistic Congress but certainly aware of it because they had become Catholics in the early 1930s were the parents of Geza Vermes (1924–2013) later to become a leading authority on the Dead Sea Scrolls and preparing to enter the seminary in Budapest. Vermes's mother certainly seems to have embraced her Catholicism more fully than her husband, as Vermes himself writes: "How did conversion affect my parents? My mother became a devout Catholic; she prayed daily, attended mass in church every Sunday, ate no meat on Friday, and moved almost exclusively in Christian circles." He continues with a very difficult sentence: "What happened to her piety in the hell of Auschwitz or whichever hell she had to pass through, God alone knows. I only hope it helped her."[60]

LaFarge was to do more than attend and report about the Eucharistic Congress in Budapest. At the same time, he was to inform himself about the political situation

58. The Nazi regime had made the determination that any Germans or Austrians who wished to attend this Eucharistic Congress would need to get a travel visa. As a result, maintains Peter Eisner, "none of the 25,000 Germans and 30,000 Austrians who had planned to attend did so." See Eisner, *The Pope's Last Crusade*, 47.

59. Eisner, *The Pope's Last Crusade*, 48.

60. Vermes, *Providential Accidents, An Autobiography*, 15. On page 11 Vermes provides a very moving account of the last occasion on which he saw his mother when she visited him in the seminary in Budapest. "In late May 1944, watching my mother walking away in the afternoon sun ready to set, I was watching her from the basement window of my hiding-place. Tall, holding herself straight, but bearing the burden of the world, she walked slowly. She wore a yellow blouse to conceal the compulsory distinguishing mark of the yellow Star of David. . . . I watched the yellow figure of my beloved mother until it reached the corner of the street and disappeared. I never saw her again."

in Europe, and to acquaint himself more closely with other Jesuit publications such as *The Month* (England), Études (France), and *Stimmen der Zeit* (Germany). LaFarge had no idea how his trip to Europe would develop, but develop it did through a commission given to him by Pope Pius XI. Pius had read LaFarge's book, *Interracial Justice*, describing the situation of African Americans and proclaiming the importance of the church as a moral force in combating racism. Pius saw strong similarities between the situation described by LaFarge in America and the anti-Semitism in Europe. He had no idea that LaFarge was actually in Europe attending the Eucharistic Congress in Budapest and subsequently was on his way to Rome.

Pope Pius XI received LaFarge privately at Castel Gandolfo on June 25. The pope asked him on that occasion, and in the strictest confidence, to write an encyclical letter on the Nazi treatment of the Jews, and to write it as if he were the pope. He was under instructions to keep the assignment secret so that not even the Secretary of State Cardinal Eugenio Pacelli was informed about it. LaFarge worked on the encyclical with the collaboration of two other Jesuits, Gustave Gundlach and Gustave Desbuqois, in Paris during the very hot summer of 1938. Gundlach had authored the article "Anti-Semitism" for the German theological encyclopedia. *Lexikon für Theologie und Kirche.* Gundlach had also been responsible for a broadcast on German-language Vatican Radio on April 1, 1938, condemning the *Anschluss,* the annexation of Austria by the Third Reich. The *Anschluss* had taken place on March 12, and during that month, statements had come from the archbishop of Vienna, Cardinal Theodor Innitzer, and the Austrian episcopate, supportive of National Socialism, both in what it had done for building up the German nation and in its utter opposition to atheistic Communism.[61] Gundlach was informed that he would be arrested if he returned to Germany, and did not do so until after the war was over. There is no doubt about where he stood concerning Nazism.

The final draft edition of the encyclical was completed by LaFarge and his collaborators on September 18, 1938 with the title *"Humani Generis Unitas/The Unity of the Human Race."* The finished text was presented to the Jesuit superior-general, Wlodimir Ledochowski, who was known to be very anti-Semitic, towards the end of September, and he said that he would pass it onto the pope immediately. One of LaFarge's brothers had died while he was in Europe and another was now seriously ill. Understandably he wanted to return to America as soon as possible and equally understandably, although according to some critics naïvely, he trusted Ledochowski to give the completed document to the pope. So, LaFarge sailed back to the United States from Boulogne on October 1. The encyclical affirmed the unity of all humankind and denounced in very forthright terms racialism, especially anti-Semitism, and demonstrated an absolute opposition to Nazism.[62] However, while LaFarge's encyclical was delivered to the superior-general of the Jesuits, Wlodimir Ledochowski, by the end of September 1938,

61. See Passelecq and Suchecky, *The Hidden Encyclical of Pius XI*, 50ff.

62. For both text and context of the encyclical see Passelecq and Suchecky, *The Hidden Encyclical.*

it was not actually given to Pius XI. Ledochowski seems to have had his own personal reservations, and he was certainly aware of Pacelli's non-confrontational point of view, and, of course, rumors were rife in the Vatican about the pope's impending death.[63] "Only when an angry Pope demanded that it be delivered to him at once did the encyclical belatedly materialize."[64] It seems that the pope received the encyclical on January 21, 1939, but it remains unclear whether he actually read it before his death three weeks later. Ledochowski had held onto the document for four months.

Pope Pius XI died on February 10, 1939. In some quarters there was a suspicion of foul play. "Cardinal Eugene Tisserant, prefect of the Vatican Library, even launched the charge that the Duce, aroused by the Pope's opposition, had him murdered. Although Mussolini looked forward to the election of a 'less contentious pope,' as did the conciliatory contingent in the Vatican, there is no evidence to suggest that the seriously ill pope did not die from natural causes."[65] The encyclical was found on his desk after his death among other papers dealing with similar matters but, as Frank Coppa wryly but accurately puts it, "we do not know when they were put there."[66]

Because war was imminent, his successor Pope Pius XII did not see the encyclical through to publication, but put his energies into the prevention of war. Frank J. Coppa reports that "in a memorandum of February 15, 1939, Secretary of State, Eugenio Pacelli, ordered the Vatican printing house to destroy all evidence of the papal speech which he feared would widen the rift with Mussolini's Italy and his Nazi allies. The draft of the 'secret' encyclical against Nazi racism was returned to its authors."[67] Nonetheless, when Pacelli became Pius XII, he included various sections of the draft in his own first encyclical, *Summi Pontificatus*, in 1939.

Spain

From 1931 the new socialist republican regime in Spain was hostile to the church. Church and state were to be separated, church property confiscated, education secularized, divorce introduced, and at least formally Spain was de-catholicized. The new government was unable to maintain control over extremists who set about destroying

---

63. Frank J. Coppa writes in his *The Life and Pontificate of Pope Pius XII*, 119, as follows: "Father Heinrich Bacht, who translated the draft [of the encyclical] into Latin, reported that Ledochowski found LaFarge's draft 'too strong and provoking' and like Pacelli deemed it unwise to stumble into a head-on confrontation with Rome and Berlin. He therefore sought to tone down the draft, which reflected the sentiments and convictions of the pope. We do not know if Pacelli or the Secretariat of State played any part in keeping the projected encyclical from the pope and called for its 'moderation.' We do know that both were determined to avoid antagonizing Fascist Italy and Nazi Germany, which would have undoubtedly have occurred if *Humani Generis Unitas* had been released."

64. Coppa, *The Policies and Politics of Pope Pius XII*, 177.

65. Coppa, *The Life and Pontificate of Pope Pius XII*, 122.

66. Coppa, *The Policies and Politics of Pope Pius XII*, 107.

67. Coppa, *The Policies and Politics of Pope Pius XII*, 72.

churches, monasteries, and convents throughout the country. Consequently, in 1933 Pius protested the policy of separation of church and state in Spain, demanded religious freedom for the church and protested the violence. But, and this is key, he did not attack the new Spanish Republic as such.[68] Despite some positive political developments, the Spanish situation did not substantially improve, and civil war became virtually inevitable, breaking out in 1936. Churches and religious buildings were destroyed ruthlessly or, alternatively, turned to secular use such as cinemas, markets, and even arms dumps. The number of people killed included twelve bishops, 5,255 priests, 2,492 monks, 283 nuns, and 249 novices. Often clergy were publicly humiliated before being executed, for example, being paraded naked, or being forced through a form of marriage. Of course, the Nationalists were also guilty of murdering their opponents and their victims are said to have numbered about 40,000. While there can be little doubt that Pius's general sympathies in the civil war lay with General Francisco Franco, there was, despite Franco's seeking it, no formal Vatican approval for his regime until the end of August 1937. Not only was no endorsement forthcoming, but Pius criticized Franco's attacks on Spanish civilians. Just two weeks before he met with LaFarge in Rome, *Osservatore Romano* condemned Franco's bombing of the Basque country insisting that these areas "have no military interest nor are they mere military centers or public buildings which affect the war."[69] It has been pointed out by one prominent historian of the period that "on three occasions Pacelli urged the Pope to endorse Franco's national Catholicism and the request was discarded on three occasions."[70] Needless to say and given his critical position *vis-à-vis* Hitler and Mussolini, Pius did not approve of Franco's close association with these Fascist leaders. With Franco's Spain also the pope was inclined to be confrontational, but his secretary of state, consistent as always, was in favor of diplomacy and conciliation. This diplomacy of Pacelli's was at work during the period of the Spanish Civil War. He respected as best he could the duly constituted Spanish government, even as he waited until the Spanish political situation brought about recognition of a new government on the part of the Vatican. When this new government emerged Pacelli had become Pope Pius XII, and from his new position he welcomed the victory of General Francisco Franco and thanked Franco's forces in these terms—"for the gift of peace and of victory, with which God has seen fit to crown the Christian heroism of your faith and love, demonstrated in so much selfless suffering."[71]

68. Holmes, *The Papacy in the Modern World*, 97.

69. Cited in Eisner, *The Pope's Last Crusade*, 106.

70. Coppa, *The Policies and Politics of Pope Pius XII*, 86.

71. Cited in Ventresca, *Soldier of Christ*, 107.

Ecumenism

The Anglican-Roman Catholic Malines Conversations, initiated by the Anglicans, had begun in 1921 not long before Benedict XV died. It was, however, during the pontificate of Pius XI that most of the conversations occurred. The Lambeth Conference of 1920—this is the meeting every ten years of the bishops of the Anglican Communion—had shown a real interest in Christian unity. They launched an appeal for Christian unity, "The Lambeth Appeal to All Christian People." A copy of this ecumenical appeal had been sent by the archbishop of Canterbury, Randall Davidson, to a number of Catholic bishops, including, of course, the pope. Cardinal Mercier, archbishop of Malines, Belgium, was one of these bishops, and, furthermore one who had shown an interest in promoting ecumenical dialogue.[72] He agreed to host ecumenical conversations with the Anglicans at his residence. Hence, they have become known as the Malines Conversations. This met with Pius XI's approval. His secretary of state, Cardinal Gasparri, wrote to Mercier: "The Holy Father authorizes Your Eminence to tell the Anglicans that he approves and encourages your conversations, and prays with all his heart that the good God will bless them."[73] There were five meetings in six years.

The first occurred in December 6–8, 1921, with three Catholics and three Anglicans. The Catholics were Cardinal Mercier himself, his vicar-general Bishop Van Roey, and the famous Abbé Fernand Portal, who was well known for his ecumenical interest with the Anglican Communion. The Anglicans, all "high church," were Lord Halifax, Walter Frere, the bishop of Truro and a liturgist, and Armitage Robinson, the dean of Wells. Participation expanded to include Bishop Charles Gore and Beresford Kidd the church historian, and on the Catholic side most notably Msgr. Pierre Batiffol, also a church historian. Papers were read and discussed on episcopacy and papacy. The fifth conversation was held in 1926, largely reviewing what had been achieved, but earlier that year both Cardinal Mercier and Abbé Portal had died, and without their presence and commitment, it became practically impossible to move further. Mercier and Portal were "the heart and soul of the venture."[74] In 1925 Cardinal Mercier read a paper at the conversation, a paper written by Dom Lambert Beauduin, entitled "The Church of England, United, Not Absorbed." Along with the self-evident value of actually meeting and conversing on ecumenical matters, it was probably this paper of Beauduin's that was the most important fruit of the Malines Conversations. The paper studied the pre-Reformation relations between the See of Canterbury and the Holy See, and reached the conclusion that unity without absorption was a real possibility, that the Anglican Communion could enjoy a certain independence of Rome while united with Rome. One historian of Anglican-Catholic relations has described it in these words: "It was a plan for a Uniat Church of England in communion with the

72. Pawley and Pawley, *Rome and Canterbury Through Four Centuries*, 281–82.
73. Cited in Tavard, *Two Centuries of Ecumenism*, 101.
74. Quitslund, *Beauduin, A Prophetic Witness*, 72.

Holy See."[75] Beauduin's paper and thesis began to broaden for Catholics the model of church unity. In some small degree, perhaps, Catholics were now aware of the ecumenical challenge and the ecumenical movement. In a pastoral letter to his diocese on ecumenism in 1924 Mercier had written these fine words: "For nothing in the world would I have one of our separated brethren say that he confidently knocked at the door of a Roman Catholic bishop and that this Roman Catholic bishop refused to receive him."[76] Christians in the Reformation tradition were for Mercier "separated brethren"—a term coined by Pope Leo XIII—in 1924, but it would take another forty years for that expression to become common Catholic currency. While the Malines Conversations now form part of the history of the ecumenical movement in the twentieth century, and, indeed, have been surpassed by the ecumenical gains of the Anglican-Roman Catholic International Commissions, the spirit of those conversations still speaks powerfully. It has been well expressed by an historian of the Conversations in these words: "The Malines Conversations—with their atmosphere of openness and Christian brotherhood—inspired by Cardinal Mercier's conviction that they were all 'brothers in the Christian faith' provided a model for dialogue, captured the spirit of ecumenism, and set the stage for an ecumenical project which is far from complete."[77] When Mercier lay dying in a Brussels hospital, Lord Halifax came to see him for the last time. This was the occasion on which Mercier gave to Halifax his pastoral ring as a sign of ecumenical hope. This was also the occasion of what Cardinal Suenens was to call "the final Malines Conversation." It is interesting to note that one of Mercier's seminarians in the early 1920s was Léon-Joseph Suenens. Suenens, as we shall see later, was to play a major role at Vatican II, and was a firm promoter of Christian unity. He had an excellent relationship with the Anglican Communion, and especially with the archbishop of Canterbury, Michael Ramsey. Much later, a journalist asked the now Cardinal Suenens whether the Malines Conversations had been a failure. This was his response: "Not at all. They caused a spring to surge, and for some years it continued to flow—underground. Then, one day. It welled up and formed a stream, then a river. At the council, the river headed out to sea."[78] But this is to jump ahead!

Unfortunately, Catholic participation in the ecumenical movement also suffered a huge setback under Pope Pius XI. In 1928, Pius published an encyclical on ecumenism, *Mortalium Animos*. Of this encyclical Eamon Duffy writes with wit but accuracy: "His least attractive encyclical . . . he rubbished the infant Ecumenical Movement. . . . The encyclical made it clear that the ecumenical message of the Vatican for the other churches was simple and uncompromising: 'Come in slowly with your hands above your head.'"[79] Duffy has it right. Pius condemned what he called the "pan-Christians"

75. Pawley and Pawley, *Rome and Canterbury Through the Ages*, 295.

76. Cited in Tavard, *Two Centuries of Ecumenism*, 107.

77. John A. Dick, "The Malines Conversations, The Unfinished Agenda," 75.

78. Suenens, *Memories and Hopes*, 20–21, 161.

79. Duffy, *Saints and Sinners*, 346. See also Hebblethwaite, *In the Vatican*, 29.

of the ecumenical movement. He assumed the movement to be a lowest common denominator form of Christianity. His reaction to ecumenism with the Reformation traditions was not particularly different from that of his predecessor, Pope Benedict XV. It was largely a "return to Rome" approach. Pius forbade "any intercourse with those who professed a mutilated and corrupt version of Christ's teaching."[80]

Yet, like Benedict XV, he did actively promote ecumenical concerns with the East. He reorganized the Oriental Institute and encouraged the study of Oriental theology. In 1929 he issued an encyclical letter, *Rerum orientalium*, requiring courses in Oriental theology in all major seminaries. His most significant ecumenical endeavor in this regard, however, has to do with his request to the abbot primate of the Benedictines, Fidelius von Stotzingen, asking him to initiate Oriental studies among the Benedictines. This request was made in 1924. "The Pope's idea was to have some monks specialize in the study of Eastern theology and liturgy, and to get them together in monasteries that would become centers of action in the unity apostolate. In a word, he wanted to establish Benedictine monasteries of the Byzantine Rite."[81] The request saw fruition in the establishment of the monastery at Amay, Belgium, in 1925, transferred to Chevetogne in 1929.

Conclusion

It has been hypothesized by Nino Lo Bello in a book entitled *The Vatican Papers* that Pius XI may have been murdered. It is said that just a mere twenty-four hours before he was due to make a strong anti-Fascist address to a group of bishops, that he was given an injection by a physician, Francesco Petacci. This physician was in fact the father of Mussolini's mistress, Clara Petacci. Conspiracy theorists think that the doctor injected the pope with some poisonous material before he made this anti-Fascist speech because he died the very next morning. The evidence is very slight, and not particularly convincing, although Lo Bello maintains that the source of his hypothesis was a private diary of Cardinal Eugene Tisserant.[82]

A balanced, judicious summary of Pius XI's pontificate is offered by church historian John O'Malley: "There was a soft side to Pius XI. His subordinates never saw it. He was as authoritarian in his manner as any of his predecessors. He brooked no opposition and exploded into angry tirades. He got advice only when he asked for it, and brave were the souls who dared to volunteer it. His church was the church militant, and he was commander-in-chief."[83]

Very little changed theologically, ecumenically, or liturgically under Pope Pius XI. He followed the received wisdom of the day in these areas, with perhaps the

80. Carlen, *The Papal Encyclicals,* 3:313–19.

81. Tavard, *Two Centuries of Ecumenism,* 94.

82. Cornwell, *A Thief in the Night,* 47–48.

83. O'Malley, *A History of the Popes,* 276–77.

exception of the missions. When it comes to the political issues and crises of his pontificate, however, it is another matter. "The death of Pius XI at the age of eighty-one ended a pontificate memorable not only for his vigorous, unbending personality, but for the violent attacks on his Church in the aftermath of the Great War, a period of spiritual, intellectual and political upheaval unknown since the French Revolution."[84] These evaluative comments by Anthony Rhodes seem very fair, at least on the political front. Karl Rahner, the German Jesuit who lived through this Fascist era and, indeed, knew the Nazi scourge at first hand made the point in an interview that one would have to have lived through this historical period to appreciate its sheer complexity. He said: "Times of collective madness like this are basically unexplainable. . . . One doesn't even know what one did right or wrong during that period."[85] In terms of the political dictators one has to concede that Pius in his concordats did what he could. In the longer run, history may prove that he would have been better to back the various Christian democratic parties and especially those sacrificed to Mussolini and Hitler, but what Rahner terms "collective madness" must not only be taken seriously but literally.

84. Rhodes, *The Vatican in the Age of Dictators*, 211.
85. Rahner, *I Remember, An Autobiographical Interview with Meinold Krauss*, 51.

9

Pope Pius XII (1939–58)

He seemed born to be pope. Austere, intensely devout, looking like a character from an El Greco painting, Pacelli was everyone's idea of a Catholic saint.

—EAMON DUFFY[1]

Pacelli was a man of deep traditional piety and diplomatic experience, rather than of pastoral or administrative experience.

—J. DEREK HOLMES[2]

Only calm and balanced historical research can hope to transcend the temptation to fall either into the apologetic trap of those who would see Pius XII as the greatest saint of the twentieth century or into the opposite one depicting him as Hitler's pope.

—EMMA FATTORINI[3]

From Eugenio Pacelli to Pope Pius XII

"EUGENIO PACELLI REMAINS ONE of the most studied but least known figures of the modern era."[4] This is how Frank Coppa, an important commentator on papal history in the nineteenth and twentieth centuries, begins an important study of Pope Pius XII. He is referring, of course, to the controversies and misunderstandings and exaggerations that have surrounded Pacelli, especially in the latter half of the twentieth century. In his 2013 *The Life and Pontificate of Pope Pius XII* Coppa states: "[He is] the most controversial pope of the twentieth century. Although long studied, his

---

1. Duffy, *Saints and Sinners*, 346.
2. Holmes, *The Papacy in the Modern World 1914–1978*, 119.
3. Fattorini, *Hitler, Mussolini, and the Vatican*, xv.
4. Coppa, *The Policies and Politics of Pope Pius XII*, 1.

turbulent pontificate remains one of the least understood in recent times."[5] Who is this long studied yet least understood pope? The point is made time and again by Frank J. Coppa that it is impossible to develop an adequate perspective on Pope Pius XII simply by attending to his years on the chair of St. Peter, and yet so many studies of this pope ignore his earlier life, education, and career. Historical investigation into Pope Pius XII is hampered by the fact that he was an intensely private person and he did not keep a personal diary as an adult. Nonetheless, Coppa's point is well taken and this chapter on the pope, though in a much abbreviated fashion, will begin with an account of his earlier life, education and career.

Eugenio Pacelli, born in Rome 1876 during the last two years of the reign of Pope Pius IX, was the son of a lawyer, and came from a family of jurists, a family that had served the church in important positions since the mid-nineteenth century under Pope Pius IX. His paternal grandfather, for example, Marcantonio Pacelli, served Pius IX in various capacities including as a founder of the Vatican newspaper *L'Osservatore Romano*, and his uncle Ernesto Pacelli was an advisor to Leo XIII, and his father Filippo (1837–1916) was an important Vatican lawyer. Throughout the nineteenth century the Pacelli family had remained steadfastly loyal to the papacy and "initially rejected all offers to the to the national cause championed by the Risorgimento, which called for the unification of the peninsula and a united Italy's absorption of the Papal State."[6] Eugenio's father Filippo and his brother Francesco were very closely allied to the policies of Pope Pius IX against the usurpation of the papal territories in Italy, although in the long run Francesco Pacelli was a key player in Pope Pius XI's Lateran Accords of 1929 with Mussolini. Ultimately, as the course of history has established, these policies were to fail lamentably. In this regard, Coppa interestingly notes of Eugenio: "It appears that the failure of the papal policy of intransigence was one of the factors that played a part in moving the young, impressionable, and sensitive boy to shun intransigence for accommodation, which he found useful in childhood and beyond. It was a trait he acquired in his family long before he entered the religious life or the diplomatic service of the Vatican."[7]

His schooling gave him a very solid grounding in the traditional curriculum of the day, but the young Eugenio had "a particular affinity for the study of the classical languages and history, but above all for poetry and literature," so much so that "he was barely a teenager when he began to compose his own poetry."[8] As one might expect he had a particular fondness for Italian literature and poetry. In an essay that he wrote on history during his teen years he provides us with an insight into his understanding of the complexities of history: "I would define the life of men and peoples as a struggle, more or less miserable, more or less disgraceful, but a struggle; continuous

5. Coppa, *The Life and Pontificate of Pope Pius XII*, xi.

6. Coppa, *The Life and Pontificate of Pope Pius XII*, 6.

7. Coppa, *The Life and Pontificate of Pope Pius XII*, 9.

8. Ventresca, *Soldier of Christ*, 23. Ventresca's study is the best contemporary study of Pius XII.

and non-stop struggle, which is directed towards the achievement of certain ideals." Even with this rather negative outlook, Robert A. Ventresca recognizes in these words and in Pacelli's attitude generally the genesis of his concern—perhaps we could say his struggle—to protect the church from hostile world rulers.[9] The Pacelli family was religiously very devout and the centerpiece of that religious devotion was undoubtedly the blessed Virgin Mary. This familial Marian devotion made and continue to have a strong impression on Eugenio, and is described by Robert Ventresca thus: "Whether it was reverent veneration or obsession, or both, Pacelli's Marian devotion was one of the great constants of his spiritual life."[10] During his high school years he became a close friend of a Jewish schoolmate, Guido Mendes. The friendship was to last. Much later, when Italian Jews were under fascist threat, Cardinal Eugenio Pacelli as secretary of state to Pope Pius XI, assisted the Mendes family to make their way safely out of Italy, Switzerland, and finally to Jerusalem.

He did not follow the family tradition of law, but entered upon studies for the priesthood. A brilliant student but with poor health, Pacelli was given permission to study towards the priesthood as a day student—having already tried most unhappily college living as a boarder like the other seminarians—at the Capranica College, the residence for seminarians of the diocese of Rome. For theology he attended the Gregorian University. Living with his own family made a huge difference to his life, both physically and psychologically. There may have been other consequences as well. Frank Coppa comments:

> Not surprisingly, the seminarian who was content to remain within the bosom of his family while a student, as Pope would later adopt his housekeeper, private secretary, and confessor—all of whom he brought from Germany—to serve as a sort of surrogate family to whose company he could withdraw. It was habit rather than vanity or a superiority complex that led Pacelli, when he became Pope, to take his meals alone. For Pacelli solitude was a need that with the passage of time became a virtual necessity.[11]

The young seminarian and pope-to-be was a loner, an introvert, and a deeply private person. Robert A. Ventresca goes further when he describes Pacelli as projecting "the aura of a mystic, one who was detached from worldly concerns."[12] His introversion and his desire for solitude are fully intelligible given his background and upbringing,

---

9. Ventresca, *Soldier of Christ*, 24–25.

10. Ventresca, *Soldier of Christ*, 39. Coppa writes in his *The Life and Pontificate of Pope Pius XII*, 11: "Eugenio also totally absorbed his family's Marian convictions and was especially influenced by his mother's devotion to Mary. This explains some of his actions when he assumed the tiara, and his placing his pontificate under the special patronage of the Virgin. In the years that followed he would become the most Marian pope in church history."

11. Coppa, *The Life and Pontificate of Pope Pius XII*, 38. See also the comments of Ventresca, *Soldier of Christ*, 25.

12. Ventresca, *Soldier of Christ*, 26.

but describing him as having "the aura of a mystic" seems excessive, or, at least, it may betray a particular a-worldly model of mysticism.

During the period of his theological studies prior to ordination Pacelli was exposed to various currents of modern theological thought. These included what would later be described as "modernism." One of his professors to whom he was especially devoted, Msgr. Francesco Faberj, was later accused of modernist tendencies. During the mid to late 1890s this teacher introduced some of his seminarians including Pacelli to Friedrich von Hügel, the great friend and confidant of the (to be) condemned modernist George Tyrrell. Pacelli and von Hügel first met in January 1896 and regularly for at least some months afterwards, discussing matters in theological and biblical studies. Some scholars are of the opinion that von Hügel was thinking of Eugenio Pacelli when he wrote to his friend Alfred Loisy concerning changes in attitude among his Roman acquaintances: "A young priest whom I found quite open in the spring, I find quite closed in the autumn." The young priest is considered to be Pacelli.[13] Two von Hügel specialists take different positions on the length of the Pacelli-von Hügel relationship. On the one hand, Lawrence Barmann believes that they lost touch after 1897.[14] On the other hand, Michael de la Bédoyère, author of a detailed biography and study of Baron von Hügel, considers that the two men remained in touch for some years afterwards.[15]

About this time he also attended church history lectures by Louis Duchesne, so much so that Ventresca concludes in this fashion: "It is clear, at the very least, that Eugenio Pacelli's clerical training included exposure to cutting-edge research and liberal minded professors who skirted and sometimes crossed the limits of orthodoxy."[16] Having been ordained a priest on Easter Sunday, 1899, he entered the papal service in 1901. He moved on up through the secretary of state's various positions until he was appointed nuncio in Munich. The year 1901 also saw him as emissary of Pope Leo XIII to London after the death of Queen Victoria, delivering the pope's condolences to King Edward VII. He would return again to the United Kingdom in 1908 for the Eucharistic Congress in London, and during his stay at that time he met Winston Churchill among other politicians. Pacelli returned to London once again in 1910 for the coronation of King George V. He was well received.

13. Ventresca, *Soldier of Christ*, 35.

14. See Barmann, *Baron Friedrich von Hügel and the Modernist Crisis in England*, 62–64.

15. Describing the anti-modernist spirit in Rome on a personal note for von Hügel, de la Bédoyère writes as follows: "A more personal, and therefore more painful, example of the prevailing spirit of repression was given to von Hügel when he heard from Rome that his son-in-law was suspended from the Papal Noble Guard for a technical fault, but in circumstances which forced him to send in his resignation. This unfortunate incident, which was followed up by the Baron for two years, and in which he sought to enlist the help of Msgr. Pacelli, was believed to be aimed at von Hügel himself, though one can have no proof of this." See Bédoyère, *The Life of Baron von Hügel*, 250.

16. Ventresca, *Soldier of Christ*, 34–36. Of course, what Ventresca means by "orthodoxy" here is open to further analysis and debate.

Pacelli certainly belonged to the Roman "black aristocracy," the rather exclusive group of Roman families who over the years had provided the Vatican with administrative, legal and ceremonial officials after the unification of Italy. Even as he entered the diplomatic service, however, Pacelli worked at St. Philip Neri's Chiesa Nuova teaching catechism, hearing confessions and preaching. While his pastoral experience may not have been broad and extensive, it was real and appeared to give him joy, even as his intellectual leanings and personal inclinations led him in other directions.[17] Further studies led him to a doctorate in both civil and canon law in 1902. His doctoral dissertation was on the nature and importance of concordats, clearly a topic that would serve him well in later life as a papal diplomat. He also lectured in canon law and was Cardinal Gasparri's assistant in the preparation of the code of canon law set in motion by Pope Pius X.[18] In fact, as a result of his reputation in canon law, he was invited in 1911 to accept a chair in that discipline at the Catholic University of America in Washington. One historian writes, "Eugenio was torn between the law and the religious life—and some believe he eventually and ingeniously managed to blend the two."[19]

At the same time, Pacelli also took part quietly in the anti-modernist campaign conducted by Umberto Benigni (1862–1934) on behalf of Pope Pius X.[20] Given the fact that Pacelli had been introduced to modernist theological and biblical ideas by Faberj and von Hügel, one can only surmise both that he found some of these ideas wanting—as perhaps indicated in the comment of Baron von Hügel above—and also that he did not wish to fall foul of his ecclesiastical superiors. Benigni was well known for his anti-Semitism and, while Pacelli worked with him from 1906 to 1911, there is no evidence either that he shared or that he was influenced by this anti-Semitism.[21]

During World War I, and because of his proven administrative skills, Pacelli was Pope Benedict XV's primary agent in providing relief for refugees and prisoners of war. He worked closely with the International Red Cross, using all the resources the Vatican committed to such relief efforts. This war-time experience demanded considerable diplomatic awareness also, and so Pope Benedict ordained him as archbishop on May 13, 1917, the very same day that the Virgin Mary was said to have appeared to three

17. Hatch and Walshe, *Crown of Glory*, 63.

18. Coppa makes the point that "It is difficult, if not impossible, to understand the relationship between Pope Pius XI and his successor Pope Pius XII, without exploring the profound influence and impact that Cardinal Pietro Gasparri had upon both." See Coppa, *The Policies and Politics of Pope Pius XII*, 21.

19. Coppa, *The Life and Pontificate of Pope Pius XII*, 17.

20. Coppa, *The Policies and Politics of Pope Pius XII*, 17. See also Wolf, *Pope and Devil, The Vatican's Archives and the Third Reich*, 36.

21. Coppa, *The Life and Pontificate of Pope Pius XII*, 44–49. Coppa concludes on page 49: "The fact that [Pacelli] preserved a cordial relationship with an anti-Semite . . . should not lead to the conclusion that he espoused the biases. . . . Pacelli simply transposed the conciliatory and cautious approach he had developed over the years in his private life and interpersonal relations to his official duties and his diplomatic assignments."

children at Fatima in Portugal, asking for prayers for the conversion of Russia. This co-incidence meant a great deal to Pacelli. Pope Benedict sent the new bishop to war-torn Germany, as nuncio to Bavaria in 1917. "It is highly unlikely that Pacelli would have entered the diplomatic service had he not found it congenial and eminently suited for his personality, education, and training. The law and diplomacy have long been major interests whose study and experience he continued to pursue."[22]

From 1920–29 Pacelli was not only nuncio in Munich under Pope Benedict XV, but also nuncio in Berlin, moving back and forth between the two cities, finally taking up residence in Berlin in 1925. En route by train to Bavaria Pacelli stopped at the Benedictine Abbey of Einsiedeln. Here he met the Bavarian Msgr. Rudolf Gerlach, banished by Pope Benedict XV for espionage. Probably not too much should be read into this meeting. Pacelli would have known Gerlach when he worked in the Vatican, and since he was representing the pope in Bavaria, he took the opportunity to consult this Bavarian about Bavaria.

His political savvy was very considerable. At a meeting in Munich in 1922, he listened enthusiastically to and applauded a speech by Konrad Adenauer, future chancellor of West Germany, expounding the ideals of republicanism from a Germany reeling from World War I and, one might say, from monarchy. It was during his stay in Munich that he came across the Franciscan sister from Altötting, Sister Pasqualina Lehnert, who was to remain an important part of his household for the rest of his life. "Although his junior by almost two decades, the twenty-three-year-old sister served as a sort of mother substitute and confidant as well as his cook, housekeeper, and secretary, first in Munich, then in Berlin, and finally in Rome."[23] He was to remain in Munich from 1917 until 1925, and then in Berlin from 1925 until 1929.

The nuncio was equally and somewhat earlier a fierce opponent of Communism. His correspondence with the Vatican secretary of state, Cardinal Gasparri, indicates that he grasped very clearly that if Germany did not receive reasonable and just treatment at the end of World War I, matters very easily would play into the hands of Bolshevik inspired Germans. He had immediate, first-hand experience of socialist rioting in Munich in 1919. In the disastrous period consequent upon not only Germany's defeat but also humiliation through the Treaty of Versailles, social and political unrest was rife throughout Germany. Communists marched and went on the rampage. In April 1919 Communists took over the Bavarian government, declaring Bavaria a discrete Communist state. Most of the diplomats representing their governments in Munich, abandoned the city. Pacelli remained. He faced down the Communist rioters when they forcibly made their way with pistols into the nunciature. The leader of the group threw his automatic pistol at the nuncio, striking and denting his pectoral cross. Pacelli dreamt of this event for the rest of his life, and it left him with a deep fear of socialism in all its forms. He gave the dented cross many years later to Cardinal

22. Coppa, *The Life and Pontificate of Pope Pius XII*, 41.
23. Coppa, *The Life and Pontificate of Pope Pius XII*, 72.

Spellman of New York, for whom he had a great affection.[24] His awareness of the meaning of Communism was to continue to develop at this time. A series of Catholic church historians summarize it in this way: "Throughout the 1920s, Pacelli was involved in secret conversations with the Soviet Ministry of Foreign Affairs, attempting to safeguard the freedom of Catholics in the Soviet Union. This failed, however, and in 1927 the conversations were ended, resulting in the loss of control from the side of the Vatican over religious affairs and Soviet Russia."[25]

This period in Germany was also the beginning of the Nazi ascendancy. Pacelli loathed Nazi racial theory, but he developed and maintained a deep love for German music and culture. Frank J. Coppa in a balanced judgment states that there was a degree of anti-Judaism as well as anti-Communism in the reports that Pacelli sent back to the Vatican. "In his reports on the revolutionary events in Bavaria, Pacelli almost always mentioned the Jewish background of the revolutionaries cataloging their personal and political excesses. Whether the anti-Judaism expressed in this correspondence was reflective of his own sentiments, or was presented to placate the anti-Judaism of Gasparri, and others in the Curia, remains questionable."[26] To be fair, Coppa also points out that this anti-Judaism was widespread in the church, including also in the American church. He draws attention to Fr. Frederick Zwierlein, a professor of church history for over thirty years at St. Bernard's Seminary in Rochester New York, who "daily spewed out derision and hatred of the Jews," and to Fr. Charles E. Coughlin whose "anti-Semitic radio broadcasts attracted a wide audience."[27] Such acknowledgments do not entirely exonerate Pacelli but, given the context and the time, render his prejudices somewhat more intelligible.

Pacelli was still in Munich working on the details of the Vatican's concordat with Bavaria when there took place in Munich Adolf Hitler's so-called "Beer Hall Pütsch" on November 8–9, 1923. This attempt to overthrow the Bavarian government and to thrust Hitler and his newly established Nazi party on the national stage failed. After his trial Hitler served nine months in prison during which time he along with Rudolf Hess wrote *Mein Kampf*. The whole event did not seem to make a huge impression on Pacelli. Frank Coppa explains why.

> Immersed in these delicate operations [concerning the Bavarian concordat] and determined to impress the new Pope [Pius XI], Pacelli paid little attention to the Hitler Putsch, . . . which did not arouse in him the same antagonism provoked by the earlier "red revolution." This has led some to conclude that the nuncio was more opposed to Bolshevism than Nazism because the first opposed Christians while the Nazis' principal target was the Jews. Actually Pacelli's relatively muted response to the Hitler putsch was due to his

24. Coppa, *The Life and Pontificate of Pope Pius XII*, 84.

25. Schelkens et al., *Aggiornamento? Catholicism from Gregory XVI to Benedict XVI*, 103.

26. Coppa, *The Life and Pontificate of Pope Pius XII*, 39.

27. Coppa, *The Policies and Politics of Pope Pius XII*, 42.

preoccupation in negotiating the concordat with Bavaria as well as the fact
that the attempted Nazi revolution did not succeed, and therefore it had little,
if any, impact on most in Bavaria.[28]

Coppa's account is somewhat persuasive, but perhaps he underestimates Pacelli's
firm and constant opposition to Communism, rooted in his awareness not only of its
ideological atheism but also in his personal experience of the attack on the Munich
nunciature.

In Berlin from 1925 until 1929, one wonders if Pacelli ever met the young Dietrich
Bonhoeffer (1906–45). Bonhoeffer was a student of theology at the Humboldt University of Berlin at the time which had some very famous professors including, for example,
Adolf von Harnack, Adolf Deissman, Karl Holl, and Rudolf Seeberg. Bonhoeffer's father
Karl was a professor of neurology and psychiatry at the university. Given Pacelli's love
of German literature and culture there must have been occasions when he was thrown
into the company of these academics. It is perhaps just possible that he came across the
young Lutheran theologian Dietrich Bonhoeffer, who was to be executed by the Nazis
in 1945, just weeks before the end of World War II. Jumping ahead a little, Bonhoeffer's brother-in-law Hans von Dohnanyi (1902–45) who was well placed in the Nazi
bureaucracy and had access to secret documentation although he was entirely anti-Nazi
himself, funneled certain information in 1939 through the first part of 1942 to Pope Pius
XII through Fr. Robert Leiber, a close associate and private secretary of the pope-to-be.[29]
This information was made available to the allies through various channels, showing
that Eugenio Pacelli/Pius XII "was capable of bold decisive leadership, and of subter-
fuge—more than even those close to him knew."[30]

In 1929 Pacelli was made a cardinal, succeeding Cardinal Gasparri as secretary of
state. He left Germany forever, but always maintained a love for the language, the culture and most especially the people. He returned to Rome with a cohort of Germans in
his circle: Sr. Pasqualina, Fr. Robert Leiber, his private secretary, and his confessor, Fr.
Augustine Bea, SJ (1881–1968) who was a distinguished biblical scholar and professor
at the Pontifical Biblical Institute in Rome, and who was made a cardinal by Pope John
XXIII and the first president of the Secretariat for Promoting Christian Unity (later to
become the Pontifical Council for Promoting Christian Unity).

Pope Pius XII

Eugenio Pacelli was elected pope as Pius XII in 1939. His election was no great surprise. While a pope cannot choose his successor, there is no doubt at all that Pius XI
had been preparing and grooming Pacelli, and "at this time of international tension

---

28. Coppa, *The Life and Pontificate of Pope Pius XII*, 89.

29. See Ventresca, *Soldier of Christ*, 163.

30. See Ventresca, *Soldier of Christ*, 164.

his wishes would undoubtedly have influenced the Curia."[31] Pacelli had been sent as papal representative all over the world. He was Pius's representative at the coronation of King George VI in London in 1937. Desirous of visiting the United States, in a specially chartered plane he had flown all over the country and had met President Roosevelt in Washington, and had lunched with the Roosevelts in their Hyde Park home in New York. There was mutual admiration between both men, although it was clearly quite deliberate that their lunch meeting did not take place until after Roosevelt had been reelected as president. "When reporters tried to pry something more out of the Vatican's Secretary of State, they were cut off abruptly by Bishop Spellman. The American prelate and longtime Pacelli confidant evidently knew well enough to deal with persistent American media, more so than the cardinal, who, in the words of one newspaper, seemed 'bewildered' by intense media questioning as he left Hyde Park."[32] Although this 1936 visit to America was billed as a personal vacation rather than as in any way political, astute political commentators recognized that there could be no such thing as a purely personal and individual visit to the country from Pope Pius XI's secretary of state, in fact the first time ever that a Vatican representative of his rank had ever visited the country. His skills and his experience were such that Anthony Rhodes concludes: "It is not surprising that such a man should believe that all international problems can be solved by negotiation; and he was to remain all his life essentially a diplomat."[33]

Pacelli was Pius's man. Robert Ventresca maintains that "Pacelli was the favorite even of leading German and Italian diplomats, notably German Ambassador to the Holy See Diego von Bergen and Italian Foreign Minister Galeazzo Ciano." Ventresca concludes that "Pacelli, it seems was a *papabile* for all seasons."[34] He was seen by the Axis powers as one who would lend his support to democracy, and not, as they saw it, to the "new world" of the dictators. The British favored him. He had made a good impression at George VI's coronation, and the *Manchester Guardian* could write of him in politically glowing terms: "Pacelli is a man big enough and strong enough to refuse to be dragged at the tail of any party . . . he will remain above them all." And the *New York Times* had the same line: "Pius XII—not the pope the totalitarians desired. This ally of Western democracy will uphold the claims of human personality and brotherhood against a sea of enemies."[35] Given the urgency of the times, it seems appropriate that this was the shortest conclave since 1623. Not only was it the shortest, but it was also the first time in the history of the papacy that all the cardinals had entered a conclave.[36] "[The cardinals] quickly decided that Pacelli was the figure best able to

31. Rhodes, *The Vatican in the Age of the Dictators (1922–1945)*, 219.

32. Ventresca, *Soldier of Christ*, 113.

33. Rhodes, *The Vatican in the Age of the Dictators (1922–1945)*, 222.

34. Ventresca, *Soldier of Christ*, 134–35.

35. Cited in Rhodes, *The Vatican in the Age of the Dictators (1922–1945)*, 223.

36. Chadwick, *Britain and the Vatican During the Second World War*, 46.

calm the dictators and spare the church their revenge. Thus, it appears that Pacelli was not elected to continue the confrontational policies of his predecessor, but elected to reverse the confrontational course of his predecessor."[37] Pacelli was crowned as Pope Pius XII on March 12, 1939. President Roosevelt sent his ambassador to the United Kingdom, Joseph Kennedy, as his representative at the coronation of the new pope, "an unprecedented gesture and a measure of just how seriously Roosevelt intended to cultivate his administration's working relationship with the Vatican."[38] Three days later Adolf Hitler occupied Czechoslovakia. April 7, in fact Good Friday, witnessed Mussolini's annexation of Albania. Europe stood on the brink of war.

World War II

"A number of factors determined Pius XII's diplomacy toward Nazi Germany including a deep affection for that nation and its people; an unwillingness to place German Catholics in a position where they would be constrained to choose between their religion and their state; a strong commitment to the preservation of the Reich Concordat of 1933; and overriding opposition to Communism; and above all fear of the wrath of an enraged Hitler assisted by Fascist Italy, which surrounded the Vatican."[39] This summary of Frank Coppa's is comprehensive, and it also points up the complexity of the situation as experienced by Eugenio Pacelli, now Pope Pius XII. Anything less than this comprehensive description will fail to do justice to the papal attitude towards Nazi Germany, especially after war had been declared. If the Allies found Pius wanting because he refused to condemn the Nazis outright, so also the Axis Powers, the German and Italian Fascists, tended to find him much less supportive than they would have desired, even if they judged him much less confrontational than Pope Pius XI.

Something of the ordinary complexity of the Nazi regime for German Catholics is afforded by an anecdote from the memoirs of the English Jesuit philosopher Frederick Copleston. Copleston, in order to improve his knowledge of German, was in Germany from the fall of 1938 through the spring of 1939, completing his Jesuit tertianship. This is what he has to say about the young German Jesuit tertians with whom he was living: "They doubtless loved their country, and some of them at any rate found it difficult not to feel pride in the expansion of the German Reich and the recovery of the nation's power and self-respect. But they saw it dominated by a, in prominent respects, detestable regime, clearly headed for developments which might bring Germany either to a leading position in Europe or to utter destruction."[40] Copleston's observation of his German Jesuit colleagues doubtless could be applied to many in the population as a whole.

37. Coppa, *The Life and Pontificate of Pope Pius XII*, 127.
38. Ventresca, *Soldier of Christ*, 139.
39. Coppa, *The Life and Pontificate of Pope Pius XII*, 138.
40. Copleston, SJ, *Memoirs*, 82–83.

Cardinal Gasparri and his protégé Eugenio Pacelli had espoused for decades that the Vatican should always reach for diplomatic solutions to international crises, and never issue political condemnations. There were times when Pope Pius XI most strenuously resisted this established policy but essentially it remained in force. It is impossible to understand the mindset of Pope Pius XII without some deep appreciation of this principle. Indeed, Ventresca speaks of "a typically Pacellian amalgam of principle and pragmatism, . . . a delicate balancing act, one that was sure to alienate and disappoint many people," a description that fits the pope's mindset, how he was trained diplomatically, the influence of Gasparri, his approach to the global political situation during World War II, and how he was interpreted by others.[41] Equally, it is impossible to understand World War II without acknowledging that "there was no such thing as a common Catholic experience of the war."[42] There were Catholics on all sides—both the Axis Powers (Germany and Italy) and the Allies (USA, UK, and USSR). Pius XII was concerned for them all, and immediately set himself to the promotion of peace. His desire for peace among warring nations, his commitment to the policies and methods of conciliation and diplomacy, his concern to avoid doing anything that might make the daily lives of Catholics in Germany and Italy more difficult—all contribute to making historical judgments about this part of his pontificate very difficult. As Frank Coppa succinctly puts it, "[Pope Pius XII] was thus both pope of peace and apostle of appeasement, hoping to attain the first through the latter."[43]

A popular and probably false etymology suggests that the name Pacelli derives from the Latin *pax coeli*, "peace of heaven." Whatever its value it is clear that Pius XII saw himself as the Pope of Peace, trying to avert war until September 1, 1939. As late as August of that year he said, "Nothing is lost by peace; everything may be lost by war." His Christmas allocution for 1939 reiterated the principles for a just and lasting peace including: general disarmament, recognition of minority rights, and the right of every nation to independence. His approach to peace, however, was always that of the diplomat. It was what he knew. The French ambassador to the Vatican, Charles-Roux, made this comment: "To a robust Milanese mountaineer succeeded a Roman bourgeois, more passive in temperament. A diplomat took the place of a student."[44] Born to diplomacy, as it were, diplomacy dictated his attitudes throughout the period of World War II. The diplomacy often found expression in a rhetoric that seemed to throw up barriers to progress in communication and understanding. Owen Chadwick does not mince his words in this respect: "[Pius's] thought was subtle, but he clothed it in an envelope of old-fashioned if not obsolete rhetoric, which had the effect of making every point that he made sound weaker. He grew up in a nineteenth-century

41. Ventresca, *Soldier of Christ*, 156–57.

42. Conway, *Catholic Politics in Europe 1918–1945*, 79.

43. Coppa, *The Life and Pontificate of Pope Pius XII*, 150.

44. Cited in Atkin and Tallett, *Priests, Prelates and People*, 245.

tradition of Vatican circumlocution, fitted it naturally, and carried it to the ultimate."[45] Needless to point out, however, this does not impugn Pius's personal moral integrity. No one has the right, based on certain knowledge, to question that. However, Chadwick does put his finger firmly on this very real problem, and a problem fraught with huge socio-political consequences—Vatican diplomacy and obfuscating rhetoric, even if and perhaps especially if well-intentioned, lacked a degree of realism. His lack of realism finds expression, for example, in his 1939 message to Hitler, "expressing his 'deep satisfaction' that the Führer had escaped an assassination attempt"—and Frank J. Coppa is surely correct in describing this as "a questionable decision at best."[46] Questionable also was Pius's congratulations in April 1939 offered to General Francisco Franco, the victor in the Spanish Civil War.

> Here, too, Pius XII departed from the stance of his predecessor. While Pius XI had opposed Franco's actions and was suspicious of his exploitation of Catholicism to achieve his political ends, his successor acclaimed Franco's victory as a defense of the faith and Christian civilization against those who championed atheism. Subsequently, he hailed the veterans of Franco's "crusade" as "defenders of the faith." In applauding Franco's victory he abandoned the impartiality he cited in dealing with Nazi Germany.[47]

This judgment of Frank Coppa's is accurate, but there is more to it. Atrocities were committed on both sides during the Spanish Civil War, but in lauding Franco over the Communists in the way in which he did, Pius XII was yet again expressing his utter abhorrence of and indeed fear of Communism and all it stood for.

Pius tried to keep Italy out of the war until June 10, 1940, when Mussolini declared war on Britain and France. The war was supported by a number of nationalistic Italian bishops. The rector of the Catholic University of Milan Fr. Agustino Gemelli, who was known to be both anti-Jewish and pro-Fascist, declared: "Let us obey the Duce. In God's eyes nothing is nobler in time of war than sacrifice." The Vatican attempted to remain neutral. The Vatican's neutrality, expressed in never condemning particular nations by name in war-time, was for Pius XII especially anxious. As the war advanced, Pius moved from thinking in the beginning that Germany might win as Hitler simply occupied much of Europe to being really worried about the participation of the Soviet Union in victory over the Axis Powers and the creation of a new Europe. Because of his attitude towards Communism Pius appears, at least for a while, to have approved of Germany's invasion of Russia, even as he refused German and Italian requests to support the invasion of Russia as a crusade against Communism. Not all Italian bishops were as nuanced. Archbishop Constantini, head of the Congregation for the Propagation of the Faith, made a public statement lauding Italian

---

45. Chadwick, *Britain and the Vatican During the Second World War*, 50.

46. Coppa, *The Policies and Politics of Pope Pius XII*, 119.

47. Coppa, *The Policies and Politics of Pope Pius XII*, 135–36.

soldiers who participated in the invasion of Russia for their fight against the great Satan of Communism. Behind this kind of rhetoric lies the understanding that while Nazism was militarily dangerous and no great friend of the church, it was less dangerous than Communism which was in principle utterly opposed to religion.

The Pope and the Jews

Before entering upon a consideration of Pope Pius XII and the Jews, a historian must simply lament the treatment of the Jews on the part of the church, especially in the centuries after the Emperor Constantine's Edict of Milan. Many historians and scholars of religion have commented on this tragic history, not least, for example, Arthur Roy Eckardt (1918–98) in his influential 1967 book *Elder and Younger Brothers: The Encounter of the Jews and Christians*.[48] This has been followed by a spate of popular publications, including James Carroll's *Constantine's Sword: The Church and the Jews*, and David I. Kertzer's *The Popes against the Jews*. Eckardt and many other authors judge that the church's long history of anti-Judaism prepared the way, not necessarily deliberately and intentionally but nonetheless really, for the anti-Semitism of the twentieth century, especially with the rise of Nazism.[49] At the same time, it has been pointed out by many other scholars that the historical record is complicated, and that it is important to get "beyond the assumption that the entire scope of Christian-Jewish relations must be viewed through the lens of a one-sided intolerance and persecution."[50] This is an area of historical study in which it is morally impossible to be entirely objective and impartial, but it is no less important to be even-handed in one's account. It would be difficult to find a more even-handed and excellent account than that offered by Robert A. Ventresca who writes:

> In his response to the Nazi persecution of Jews, from the 1930s onward, Pius XII revealed himself to be a man of his time, which is to say a man of limited vision with a correspondingly limited ability to perceive the precise nature of the Nazi war against the Jews. In this respect, he bore the unmistakable signs of a generation of clerics who had received their training in the late nineteenth and early twentieth century, when the church was reacting against the modern world, including the secular state.[51]

Jews were often associated in the minds of conservative Catholic leaders with political and philosophical liberalism and secularism, and ineluctably this association made

---

48. Eckardt, *Elder and Younger Brothers*.

49. Carroll, *Constantine's Sword: The Church and the Jews*; Kertzer, *The Popes against the Jews*.

50. Coppa, *The Papacy, the Jews and the Holocaust*, 303. See also Schelkens et al., *Aggiornamento?* 102, where we read: "In many studies on Pius XII, the authors tend to limit all attention to the 'Jewish Problem' and read the entire pontificate—and occasionally his entire life—through this single perspective."

51. Ventresca, *Soldier of Christ*, 176.

its way into seminary training at all levels. In that sense Ventresca is quite right. Pope Pius XII would have been affected necessarily by this rather uninformed and aggressive presupposition. But there is more to be said.

"The suffering of the Jews, so well documented by historians and others, resulting in the deaths of some 6 million, remains almost as difficult to grasp for contemporaries today as it was for people at the time. Genocide on this scale was wholly unprecedented. In this respect the Pope was as much at a disadvantage as anyone else."[52] These words express the carefully formed judgment of two contemporary historians, Nicholas Atkin and Frank Tallett. Nonetheless, as they go on to point out and this is the central issue, the pope was not just another human being. His moral prominence throughout the world, allied to the Catholic conviction that he was the vicar of Christ on earth, placed him in a unique leadership role. It is this leadership role that is problematic for Pius XII *vis-à-vis* the Holocaust. If it is true that Pius believed that Hitler was possessed by Satan and that the pope attempted what has been described as "long-distance exorcisms," this exacerbates the difficulties of interpreting the papal leadership role.[53] The traditional understanding of exorcism has been that the exorcist and the alleged demon-possessed subject are in close proximity. To speak of "long-distance exorcisms" is to invite incredulity.

Frank Coppa is of the opinion that in respect of Pius's diplomatic relationships with Nazi Germany three "basic continuities" shaped his approach: his love for the German people and culture, the fruit of many years spent in Germany on behalf of the Vatican; an overwhelming fear of Communism, so that Communism was regarded as a greater evil than fascism; his inflexible commitment to the ways of diplomacy in general, and to the 1933 concordat with Germany in particular.[54] Coppa's judgment provides an eminently balanced hermeneutic context for interpreting the papal actions during this period.

While the controversy concerning Pius XII began almost immediately in 1939 with his accession to the chair of St. Peter, the popular catalyst for its intense continuation is undoubtedly the play, *The Representative*, published by the German playwright, Rolf Hochhuth, in 1963.[55] One contemporary historian has written: "The subject of Pius XII and the Holocaust has become one of the most contentious arguments in recent history. Many of the journalists and historians who have written on the subject are no closer to agreement today than they were after Hochhuth's drama was

---

52. Atkin and Tallett, *Priests, Prelates and People*, 255.

53. See Wolf, *Pope and Devil, The Vatican's Archives and the Third Reich*, 10.

54. Coppa, *The Papacy, the Jews and the Holocaust*, 185. In the midst of a vast and growing literature on the topic of the church's attitude to the Jews in the twentieth century Coppa's book remains one of the best.

55. There is some evidence, though difficult to verify, that the Soviet Union may have had, a hand in Hochhuth's attempt to discredit Pius XII. See Frank J. Coppa, *The Policies and Politics of Pope Pius XII*, 3–4.

produced in 1963."[56] This judgment is accurate. The play, which was translated into more than twenty languages, makes Pius XII out to be avaricious and anti-Semitic. In the wake of this play, for example, the distinguished man of letters George Steiner wrote a letter to the London *Sunday Times* for May 5, 1963 in which he says: "The Nazis feared the possibility of Papal and Catholic Action. . . . The King of Denmark put on a yellow star. The Vicar of Christ did not . . . ." The German philosopher and former pupil of Martin Heidegger, Hannah Arendt, made a similar statement to the effect that more was expected of the "Vicar of Christ" than of politicians and national leaders.[57] The trouble with statements like this is that they insinuate so much more than they actually say. What if the Vicar of Christ did not actually put on a yellow star on his clothing, but in fact did much to save the lives of Jews? Would his efforts then count for nothing *vis-à-vis* the symbolic gesture? What is to be made of the fierce and sometimes abrasive criticism of Pius for not speaking out firmly enough against the Nazi atrocities, and especially those perpetrated against the Jews? It is certainly the case that since this 1963 play authors writing about Pius XII may often be characterized either as canonizing or demonizing him. Getting out an even-handed and balanced understanding of the truth is far from easy.

Even when we concede the bias, acerbity, and sheer inaccuracy of Hochhuth's play and perspective, we are still left with some areas of discomfort around the issue of Pius XII and the Jews. For example, a close adviser of the pope was the French Thomist, Reginald Garrigou-Lagrange, OP—one of the most influential theologians in Rome for over fifty years and the supervisor of the future Pope John Paul II's doctoral dissertation—who allegedly reassured the Vichy ambassador to the Vatican that "His Holiness was comfortable with the anti-Jewish measures adopted by the Marshal's [Pétain] regime."[58] Of course, the pope cannot be held responsible for everything said by everyone around him, but Garrigou-Lagrange was hardly some lowly official. At the same time as one finds Garrigou-Lagrange's position anti-Semitic, one must also recognize that the attitude was widespread.[59] Widespread yes, but not total. Many ordinary people, anonymous in the history books, did all manner of wonderful things in their own contexts and circumstances to help the Jews. One of Garrigou's great theological opponents was the French Jesuit and inspirer of *la nouvelle théologie*, Henri de Lubac. De Lubac has written about his efforts on behalf of the French Jews, efforts that were in his own words inspired by Pope Pius XII.[60]

56. Sanchez, *Pius XII and the Holocaust*, 173.

57. Coppa, *The Life and Pontificate of Pope Pius XII*, xvi.

58. Cited in Atkin and Tallett, *Priests, Prelates and People*, 256; see also Kerr, OP, "French Theology: Yves Congar and Henri de Lubac," 112.

59. Peddicord, O.P. attempts to place Garrigou's politics within a broad framework, even while showing clearly his differences with someone like Jacques Maritain, in his book *The Sacred Monster of Thomism*, 80–113.

60. Lubac, SJ, *Christian Resistance to Anti-Semitism*.

At the same time, it must be said that the record of world leaders is far from clean. The Jewish Holocaust historian, Eva Fleischner, has written:

> Whatever the controversy or criticism that swirls around Franklin Delano Roosevelt or Winston Churchill, for example, it scarcely contains the harsh judgments heaped on Pius XII. Yet, it can be argued, given the power and resources available to them, their record is no better than his. Indeed, theirs is in some ways worse. Roosevelt, for instance, can ultimately be held responsible for sending the *St Louis's* ill-fated Jewish refugees back to Europe, where the Nazis eventually murdered many of them.[61]

The reference to the *St Louis* is particularly poignant. It was a ship in May 1939 carrying 930 German Jewish refugees seeking asylum. They sought to enter Florida, but they were turned back by the refusal of President Roosevelt. In point of fact, the first concrete step Roosevelt took on behalf of European Jews would not be until the establishment of the War Refugee Board in January 1944, a full seventeen months after he had learned of the Nazi extermination policies.[62] Again, although it is clear that the Vatican had information about the massacre of the Jews in 1942, Frank Coppa questions the extent to which this was really comprehended by the world community. He points out, for example, that "As late as August 1943 the American administration contested the reports of Jewish groups on the exterminations, asserting that these claims could not be confirmed and insisting that the Jews in the camps were working!"[63]

However, our concern is with the pope. Pius's defenders point to a range of measures: his unmistakable denunciations of extermination on the grounds of race, albeit in general terms; his Christmas address of 1942 in which he spoke of "Statolatry" or worship of the state and "the hundreds of thousands of innocent people put to death or doomed to slow extinction, sometimes merely because of their race or their descent."[64] The 1942 Christmas message angered Hitler, but the Allies thought it much too weak. Behind the wording and shape of the message lay Pius's conviction that further protest would result in greater and more egregious barbarism. His defenders point to the assistance he personally gave, or connived at for the Jews. This is amply documented in the study of the historian, Rabbi David G. Dalin, *The Myth of Hitler's Pope.*[65] To take just one small example, he offered to supply 15 of the 50 kilos of gold demanded by the German head of police in 1943 as a ransom for the safety of Roman Jews. The chief rabbi of Rome, Rabbi Israel Zolli, sought out Pius's help when this demand for gold was made. A biographer of Pius has written: "Pius did not hesitate. Within twenty-four hours the

---

61. Fleischner, "The Spirituality of Pius XII," 123.
62. Lewis, *The Catholic Church in History*, 157.
63. Coppa, *The Papacy, the Jews and the Holocaust*, 200.
64. Cited in Duffy, *Saints and Sinners*, 349.
65. Dalin, *The Myth of Hitler's Pope*, especially chapters 1–4.

ransom was paid. Though he has never told how the gold was obtained, it is known that he ordered holy vessels melted down to provide the funds."[66] Interestingly, Rabbi Zolli (1881–1956) converted to Catholicism at the end of World War II and he took as his Christian name Eugenio after Pope Pius XII.

A few examples of what other Catholics were doing on behalf of the Jews, often with Pius's encouragement, help to broaden the horizon of his defense. Some 80,000 baptismal certificates were issued to Jews in Hungary. Archbishop Angelo Roncalli, the papal representative in Bulgaria rescued several hundred Jews. When the Jewish writer Pinchas Lapide congratulated Roncalli as Pope John XXIII for his work for the Jews during war-time, John told him that on each occasion he was acting on the orders of Pope Pius XII.[67] Msgr. Hugh O'Flaherty in the Vatican itself hid hundreds of Jews and British soldiers, arranging when possible for their escape. At Castel Gandolfo, the papal residence outside of Rome, thousands of Jewish refugees were housed. About Castel Gandolfo Rabbi Dalin makes the following statement: "Amazingly, Castel Gandolfo has never once been mentioned in the anti-Pius volumes of Cornwell and Zuccotti (two historians with a particular *animus* against Pope Pius XII). Yet at no other site in Nazi occupied Europe were as many Jews saved and sheltered for as long a period as at Castel Gandolfo during the Nazi occupation of Rome."[68]

One could continue to multiply such examples. When everything that Pius XII had done on behalf of the Jews has been laid out clearly, the questions still remain, "Was it enough? Could he have done more? Should he have excommunicated Hitler?" When a street bomb in Rome killed some German soldiers in 1944, Hitler responded by having all the houses in the vicinity reduced to rubble and some 350 men, women, and children executed. This leads historian Anthony Rhodes to comment: "What effect would excommunication have had on such a man in 1943? The lessons learnt from other upstart modern dictators indicate that Hitler would not have behaved as Henry IV did at Canossa."[69] Above all else, Pius had this deeply ingrained belief in the value of diplomacy. Papal diplomacy had been his entire life and professional career in the church. In many ways, this seems to be the root of the problem. Diplomacy dictated that matters might be worsened for German Catholics if Pius uttered any outright and total condemnation. Diplomacy, however, was out of its depth with Hitler.

Anxious neutrality had given way to tortuous diplomacy, and, while subsequent investigation through the publication of Vatican documents has shown the falsity of Roch Hochhuth's caricature of Pius, this tortuous diplomacy of the pope will continue to raise unanswerable questions. It remains a singularly sobering thought that six million Jews alone perished in what had been traditionally Christian Europe. How much more the Vatican could have done is impossible to calculate, but that more could

---

66. Hatch and Walshe, *Crown of Glory*, 168.

67. Rhodes, *The Vatican in the Age of the Dictators (1922–1945)*, 340.

68. Dalin, *The Myth of Hitler's Pope*, 92.

69. Rhodes, *The Vatican in the Age of the Dictators (1922–1945)*, 344.

have been done seems beyond doubt. It seems to have been the case that in private Pius expressed questions, perhaps even doubts about his "silence," for example, to the Italian ambassador Alfieri, from notes taken of a meeting by Monsignor Montini, and to the archbishop of Cologne in 1944. Also, Angelo Roncalli recorded as much in his journal after a meeting with the pope on October 11 1941.[70]

The famous French philosopher, Jacques Maritain, was appointed French ambassador to the Holy See after the war. He was convinced that elements of church teaching and theology had contributed to the hatred that took the lives of so many Jews, and so on July 12 1946, he wrote to his friend Monsignor Montini about this, asking Pope Pius XII formally to address the issue. Maritain appreciated the papal motives for silence during the war, but now he felt the pope needed "to make his voice heard." Maritain received an audience with the pope four days later, but it was unsatisfactory, and while he did not make public his reasons, he resigned as ambassador. Frank Coppa comments on this episode as follows: "The Frenchman deemed Pius's postwar attitude much more damning than his silence during the war. Most of Pius's defenders have failed to address this issue."[71] The controversy continues.

There seems little doubt that Pius XII feared Communism far more than Nazism. Indeed, it has been said by historian Michael Phayer "Pius XII's obsession with communism is the key to understanding his papacy."[72] Phayer is speaking primarily about Pius's attitude to politics, the complex politics of his pontificate from 1939 until his death in 1958 rather than his contribution to the internal growth of the church. Phayer revised his opinion about Pius in an earlier book in which he had judged that the pope had not spoken out about the Holocaust.[73] Phayer now argues that Pius did in fact speak out in his 1942 Christmas broadcast. It is unmistakably clear from everything that Pius said and wrote that he had a massive concern about the spread of Communism. That is simply a statement of fact and of record. However, to maintain that it is the key to understanding his pontificate is simply too un-nuanced.

Nonetheless, Phayer has marshaled a goodly amount of evidence both from the Vatican archives and from the US National Archives and Records Administration that

70. Coppa, *The Papacy, the Jews and the Holocaust*, 203–8.

71. Coppa, *The Papacy, the Jews and the Holocaust*, 215. See also Coppa, *The Life and Pontificate of Pope Pius XII*, 172–73. Ventresca, *Soldier of Christ*, 229 writes as follows: "Just a few weeks earlier the Polish town of Kielce had witnessed what the *New York Times* called the 'worst anti-Semitic outbreak' since the end of the war. In scenes that were eerily similar to episodes from the past, fictitious tales of Jewish ritual murder of Gentile children sparked mob violence against local Jews; some forty Jews were killed in the violence. Word of a renewal of anti-Semitic violence, in Europe and beyond, is what had prompted Maritain to approach the Vatican in the first place. A flabbergasted Maritain noted in his diary that the Vatican newspaper was dismissing the Kielce violence as 'non-racial.' It was clear, he wrote, that 'Catholic conscience is poisoned' by anti-Semitism and that 'something has to be done.' In his letter to Montini, Maritain had singled out as especially disconcerting the role that Catholics continued to play in the 'development' of anti-Semitism in Europe and also in South America."

72. Phayer, *Pius XII, the Holocaust and the Cold War*, 259.

73. Phayer, *The Catholic Church and the Holocaust, 1930–1965*.

suggests that after World War II Pius was involved knowingly in projects to enable war criminals to evade the bar of justice by providing "ratlines" to South America. How and to what degree the pope was involved remains a question, but what is not in question is the Vatican-backed schemes that enabled war criminals to escape trial and punishment.[74] The Vatican, for example, asked the British Foreign Service to set free various Catholic Croat war criminals who had been responsible for the deaths of hundreds of thousands of Orthodox and Muslims in what was to become Yugoslavia. The Vatican was met with outrage and indignation. This is how Phayer sums up his position:

> Beginning with Ante Pavelić [the pro-Nazi Croatian dictator], the Vatican knew the identity of many of the individuals it harbored and assisted and knew that they had committed multiple murders. Others were not known by name to the Holy See but were known by name to [Bishop Alois] Hudal and [Fr. Krunoslav] Dragonović, whom the Vatican had engaged to operate its emigration programs. . . . As we have seen, the Holy See kept a list of Croatian clerics believed to have engaged in atrocities. But since the war had ended as it had with the Soviet Union on the doorstep of the West, Pius made a purely political decision to shelter the guilty from the courts of justice.[75]

Phayer surmises that part of Pius's motive was to provide a bulwark in South America against any further Communist infiltration and influence. The memory of Communist aggression in Mexico was still all too fresh. There can be no denial that Pius was obsessed with Communism, nor can there be any denial that the threats posed by Communism to world-order were all too real. But, to say the least, in Michael Phayer's work there is a very strong case to be answered by specialist historians in reaching towards a balanced judgment on the pontificate of Pope Pius XII. The time surely has come to let all the evidence, in complete transparency and in a desire for complete accountability, stand in the open for access to reputable historians and their judgment. If historians such as Michael Phayer are right, they will be seen to be right, and if not, the self-correcting process of learning will take place. This self-correcting process of learning is absolutely necessary if a balanced judgment is to be reached about Pope Pius XII and the Holocaust. Frank J. Coppa insists as follows:

> Many of the problems in the "historiography" flow not from a lack of sources but from the dismissive attitude and unwillingness of some partisan writers to consider any evidence that contradicts their preconceived notions. The divisive debate has rendered difficult reaching an objective assessment so there is more partisanship than detachment in the "studies" of Pius XII's response to the Holocaust and the other policies of his pontificate.[76]

74. See Ventresca, *Soldier of Christ*, 253–74, a very balanced account of the data available.

75. Phayer, *Pius XII, the Holocaust and the Cold War*, 267. See also Coppa, *The Life and Pontificate of Pope Pius XII*, 202–3.

76. Coppa, *The Life and Pontificate of Pope Pius XII*, xxvi.

Clemens August Graf von Galen (1878–1946)

For a moment or two, let us move back from Pius and the Vatican to Germany itself, and look at the situation of the church and the Jews from the perspective of a German Catholic bishop and leader, Clemens August von Galen, bishop of Münster from 1933–46. The point is to see another context and set of circumstances in which a Catholic bishop has come under considerable scrutiny in respect of the Jews. Von Galen became bishop in the year of the Nazi ascendancy 1933. In fact, he was the first Catholic bishop to take the oath of loyalty to the Third Reich. He died one year after the war, just weeks after being made a cardinal by Pius XII for his outspokenness during the Nazi era.

He was a central member of the German Catholic hierarchy, and was renowned for his opposition to Nazism. This is especially true of famous sermons he preached in 1941 against the Reich's policy of selective euthanasia and the appropriation of church property. The sermons were widely circulated both among clergy and laity. He became known as the "Lion of Münster." These sermons of 1941 brought the bishop very quickly to the attention of the Nazi authorities. Some thought that his influence was so insidious, undermining patriotic spirit both at home and at the front that he should be charged with high treason and executed as an example. Hitler told some of his friends that "Bishop von Galen had irritated him . . . [and] assured his entourage that he would 'take care of him' at the end of the war, and in the settlement not a thing would be forgotten."[77] The bishop was a hero.

However, the "Lion of Münster" did not take the part of the Jews, at least not obviously, not explicitly. There are those who speak of historical actions in terms of "the art of the possible." For them, the question is: In reality, what could Bishop von Galen have done? What good would a protest against the anti-Jewish project of the Nazis have actually accomplished? Would such intervention have exacerbated the already atrocious situation? There are those who claim that the Jews of Münster approached Bishop Galen and asked him not to intervene on their behalf because it would have made their dire situation even worse. While this claim is not easily documented, it remains entirely credible given Galen's moral stature.[78] However, there are also those who see von Galen differently, and these too must be heard. Historian, Beth Griech-Polelle, who has written a revisionist study of von Galen, states: "It would be more useful to portray von Galen as a person who practiced selective opposition and who revealed the fluid nature of the boundaries between conflict and consensus in Nazi Germany. Above all, he missed bringing Catholicism's universal moral concerns to the aid of other beleaguered subjects of the regime."[79] The "beleaguered subjects" to whom she refers are, of course, the Jews. Griech-Polelle shows time and time again in her

---

77. Cited in Griech-Polelle, *Bishop von Galen*, 88.

78. Thus, for example, Dalin, *The Myth of Hitler's Pope*, 79.

79. Griech-Polelle, *Bishop von Galen*, 166.

study that despite his criticisms of the Reich, Bishop von Galen, like so many others, chose not to speak on behalf of the atrocities perpetrated against the Jews, at least in the most explicit terms. In Griech-Polelle's judgment, "He lost sight of the larger, more humane questions involved in the brutality of the Nazi regime." His interests followed the concordat with Germany, and so were for the most part the interests of the church. He was intensely patriotic, as his aristocratic family always had been. Indeed, Griech-Polelle suggests that the intensity of his patriotism and that of many other German Catholics was something of a reaction to the *Kulturkampf* of the late nineteenth century under Bismarck. Catholics were out to show themselves as good as their fellow German Protestants. They were loyal to the fatherland. One might point out that the Catholic Münster philosopher Josef Pieper, for example, remarked of von Galen in his autobiography: "It is just not true that, in the summer of 1933, when the name 'Galen' was announced as the new Bishop, the whole diocese broke out in rejoicing. . . . Nor is it the case that Galen was immediately recognized as being a great opponent of the despotic regime. On the contrary, the pugnacious pastor of St Lambert's [the Bishop's church] was regarded, to put it bluntly, as a Nazi."

When Pieper visited the bishop to say farewell after being drafted into the army in 1943, he reports that when Galen saw him to the door, he said, "And now go and serve your fatherland." Pieper comments: "I was somewhat baffled; it was a long time since I had heard such words, but on his lips they were by no means a mere pathetic cliché; he meant them in all seriousness; they were to be taken literally."[80] There is no good reason to call Pieper's testimony and memory into doubt. However, alongside Griech-Polelle and Pieper, one must not lose sight of the fact that von Galen constantly protested the euthanasia program of the Nazis, the racial ideologies of the regime, Gestapo tactics and disappearances without trial, and he continued to call forth for social justice when the war ended and the Allies were occupying Germany. He was undoubtedly a prophetic figure in the best sense of the word.

Perhaps like the pope, von Galen, because of his patriotism and his love for his country, his love for and dedication to the church, and his determination to stand by the concordat, was unable—politically and perhaps also psychologically—to take his part in firm protest against the anti-Jewish genocidal policies of the regime. Perhaps. He was the product of his environment, and the political circumstances were enormously complex and no less challenging. While one might hope for better from the bishops of the church, it seems to me absolutely necessary for the historian to acknowledge the universal reality of human weakness and lack of moral consistency, and to confess that "the better" is always easier to define after the fact. The reality of the matter is the witness unto death of people like Alfred Delp and Franz Jägerstätter and countless anonymous others, alongside of and in the midst of the witness of Bishop von Galen. Since no one can know with absolute certitude the interiority of another, it seems to me that the historian must exercise appropriate caution and

80. Pieper, *No One Could Have Known*, 93, 190.

restraint in reaching judgment. Finally, and from an ecclesiological point of view, the fact that von Galen was beatified, that is to say declared "Blessed" by Pope Benedict XVI in 2005 after the required thoroughgoing process of examination of all the relevant data, is not insignificant, unless, of course, one espouses a thoroughgoing skepticism about all these matters.

The Church in Eastern Europe

The Communist Iron Curtain came down upon Eastern Europe after the war.

> During the thirteen years of his pontificate following the close of the World War (1945–1958), Pius generally pursued an anti-Communist, though not necessarily conservative, course. During this time, Pius found his voice, as he called for the banishment of atheism and the indestructibility of spiritual values in the struggle against Communism. . . . In the postwar period the formerly cautious pontiff who avoided confrontation during the war years, minced no words in his condemnation of Communism.[81]

The pope sent an American, Bishop Joseph P. Hurley, to the newly-formed Communist state of Yugoslavia in the hope of establishing normal diplomatic relations. Relations did not improve. Archbishop Aloysius Stepinac, the primate of Yugoslavia, was put on trial in 1946 for treasonable collaboration with the Nazis. The charge was untrue. Stepinac, in point of fact, had intervened in saving Jews and Muslims as well as Christians from Nazi concentration camps. He was sentenced to sixteen years hard labor and Bishop Hurley was expelled. It is estimated that four hundred Yugoslavian priests had been executed, three hundred put in prison, and over ninety were unaccounted.[82] Stepinac as archbishop of Zagreb was outspoken in his condemnation of not only Nazi atrocities but also of the Croatian Pavelić's atrocities, according to Michael Phayer.[83] Condemned at the bar of incontrovertible evidence was his episcopal colleague the archbishop of Sarajevo, Ivan Sarić, a collaborator with and supporter of the Pavelić regime.[84]

In 1946 the primate of Hungary, Joseph Mindszenty, was made a cardinal. He had suffered imprisonment under the Nazis. His constant protests over the treatment of the church by the Communist regime in Hungary, however, led to his trial and imprisonment on trumped up charges in December 1948. Mindszenty had been appointed by Pius XII, and continued to be supported by him in his anti-Communist policy. Thus, in mid-February 1949 Pius convened a special meeting of the College of Cardinals to

81. Coppa, *The Policies and Politics of Pope Pius XII*, 154.

82. Hatch and Walshe, *Crown of Glory*, 195.

83. See Phayer, *The Catholic Church and the Holocaust*, 48 and *Pius XII, the Holocaust and the Cold War*, 9–16.

84. Phayer, *Pius XII, the Holocaust and the Cold War*, 9–16 and Kent, *The Lonely Cold War of Pius XII*, 48–49.

review the case of Cardinal Mindszenty. Later on in February the pope addressed the people of Rome in these words, reported by Robert A. Ventresca: "'Can the Pope be silent when a state, exceeding the limits of its competence, arrogates to itself the power to suppress dioceses, to depose bishops, to upset the organization of the church, and to reduce it below the minimum requirements for the effective cure of souls?'" Ventresca comments: "Gone was any trace of that circumspection that the world had come to expect of Pius XII's speeches during the war. Here, finally, was the kind of address so many people had been hoping for when the full brunt of Nazi occupation was bearing down on helpless civilian populations, especially the Jews."[85]

The Leonard Feeney Episode

The American Jesuit priest Leonard Feeney, who was both a poet and a somewhat charismatic speaker, had been assigned to St. Benedict's Center, Cambridge, Massachusetts, to look after the Catholic students attending both Harvard University and Radcliffe College. Among his spiritual charges was the young Harvard student Avery Dulles. By the late 1940s Feeney, along with some like-minded friends and associates, developed the perspective that outside the Roman Catholic Church there was no salvation, a very hard line and an inflexible attitude. He got into difficulties with both his Jesuit superiors and with Cardinal Richard Cushing, the archbishop of Boston. Matters came to a head on July 27, 1949, when the Holy Office (as the Congregation for the Doctrine of the Faith was known at the time) issued a decree with the approval of Pius XII that formal membership in the Catholic Church was not necessary for salvation. Despite various efforts, Feeney refused to accept the decree and was excommunicated, although he and some of his followers were reconciled with the church in 1972.[86] The importance of the Feeney episode is, at least, to show that, despite the insularity of Pius's *Humani Generis*, there was a wider awareness of the broad Catholic tradition of ecclesiological thinking.

Some Important Encyclicals

"Pius's encyclicals," maintained Peter Hebblethwaite, "were a judicious combination of liberalism and conservatism; while opening some doors they shut others; essentially they let Catholic theologians know 'how far they could go.'"[87] This is especially true of his 1950 encyclical *Humani Generis* which condemned all kinds of false opinions that were judged to be detrimental to Catholic faith. "The most recurring complaint of *Humani Generis* was that theologians were not giving due respect to the official teaching of the church, especially as expressed in encyclicals. Pius decried again and again criticisms

85. Ventresca, *Soldier of Christ*, 243.

86. Fogarty, SJ, "The Vatican and the American Church Since World War II," 126–27.

87. Hebblethwaite, *Paul VI*, 181.

of Thomistic/scholastic theology and programs designed to replace or modify it."[88] The so-called "new theology" and the papal condemnation of it in this encyclical deserve separate treatment and that will be provided in the next chapter.

The encyclical of Pius XII on the Mystical Body, *Mystici Corporis* of 1943, paved the way, at least in part, for the Constitution on the Church/*Lumen Gentium* of the Second Vatican Council. The encyclical was a partial endorsement of the ecclesiological developments of the nineteenth-century Tübingen theologian Johann Adam Möhler and later, with the church understood as the mystical Body of Christ. The theology is unfolded in stages: the church is a Body; the church is the Body of Christ; Christ is the Head of that Body; and the church is the mystical Body of Christ. When the letter goes on to outline the union of the faithful in Christ, however, it tends to do so along lines that are more institutional than anything else. "The true meaning of the word 'mystical' therefore reminds us that the Church, which must be held to be a perfect society in its own order, does not consist merely of social and juridical elements nor rest solely on such grounds. . . . That which raises the Christian society to a level utterly surpassing any order of nature is the Spirit of our Redeemer, the source of all graces."[89] There is a certain distance from institutionalism here, but its presence is still strong. Vatican II moves further away from institutionalism, and also from Pius's almost exclusive description of the mystical Body's members as Roman Catholics. The major author of *Mystici Corporis* was the Dutch Jesuit, Sebastian Tromp (1899–1975), who along with Emile Mersch, had been the great mid-twentieth century retriever of the mystical Body in Catholic ecclesiology. In 1946 Tromp published his Latin treatise, *Corpus Christi quod Est Ecclesia*, "the Body of Christ which is the church," a book that has been described as "the richest anthology of patristic texts on the notion of the Church as the Body of Christ."[90] Tromp was one of the principal architects of the document on the church at Vatican II, but his institutionalist and triumphalist notes were to be rejected by the council fathers. Even at the time, the limited but gradually growing experience of ecumenical contact among Catholic theologians was already calling into question this virtually exclusive identification of the Roman Catholic Church with the Body of Christ. Peter Hebblethwaite puts it succinctly: "At a time when Catholics and Protestants were meeting each other and dying together in concentration camps, *Mystici Corporis* contradicted their ecumenical experience. Hitler did not distinguish between Dietrich Bonhoeffer and Alfred Delp SJ, hanging them both on meat hooks. Why should anyone else?"[91] The encyclical also left very little room to make sense of a church of sinners, a reality all too easily verifiable.

In 1943, Pius published his *Divino Afflante Spiritu*. The encyclical was issued to commemorate the fiftieth anniversary of Leo XIII's *Providentissimus Deus*, and was

88. O'Malley, *A History of the Popes*, 287.

89. *Mystici Corporis*, in Carlen, *The Papal Encyclicals*, 54.

90. By Bouyer, *The Church of God*, 304.

91. Hebblethwaite, *Paul VI*, 183.

authored by the Jesuit Augustine Bea and the Dominican Jacques-Marie Vosté.[92] It encouraged attention to the original languages in which the Scriptures were written, and ordered fresh translations from those languages. In terms of the Vulgate, for so long the western privileged translation, *Divino Afflante Spiritu* "makes specific that the 'authenticity' of the Vulgate is primarily juridical (free from error in faith and morals) rather than critical (always an accurate translation)."[93] The exegete is to be concerned principally with the literal sense of Scripture, but simultaneously careful attention is also to be given to the spiritual sense. There is no either-or in the approach of the encyclical. The study of literary forms was encouraged, a study that was arguably "the greatest single contribution" of the letter. In summary, *Divino Afflante Spiritu* was a *magna carta* for Catholic biblical studies, and fed into Vatican II's Constitution on Divine Revelation, *Dei Verbum*.

One of Pius's last encyclicals was the 1957 *Miranda Prorsus*. It dealt with the new media of radio, cinema and television. It shows him interested in all aspects of the media. And it resonates with a little-known fact about Pius, that is that he was something of "a passionate film fan," always with a ready welcome for Hollywood film stars.[94]

Liturgy

One historian has written: "When the Second Vatican Council's Constitution on the Sacred Liturgy was promulgated in December 1963, it was not difficult to see in it the climax of a century and more of scholarship and apostolic effort in which from the outset of the present century, the papacy had increasingly taken the lead."[95] The lead was most notably taken during the pontificate of Pope Pius XII. The year 1947 saw the publication of Pius's great encyclical on the church's liturgy, *Mediator Dei*. He comes across as a staunch supporter of the liturgical movement that finds, of course, its conciliar expression in Vatican II's *Constitution on the Sacred Liturgy* some fifteen years later. We are surely justified in thinking that the conciliar constitution brings to fulfillment the vision of *Mediator Dei*, since in its wake has come the renewed sacramental rites and their overwhelmingly positive reception on the part of the church.

---

92. In Schelkens et al., *Aggiornamento?* 108 we read: "In 1930 Augustine Bea, a German Jesuit, became the new director of the Biblical Institute and under his guidance the Institute began changing course. It finally adopted the historical-critical method developed by Marie-Joseph Lagrange in 1903. In 1945, when Cardinal Pacelli had been active as Pope Pius XII for several years already, Bea became his personal confessor until his final years. This would have tremendous consequences for the development of Catholic biblical scholarship. During the modernist crisis the neo-scholastic and anti-modernist currents had been identified with the magisterium's positions and had openly attacked Lagrange's views. Now, in 1943, this identification of the anti-modernist integrist positions with the Catholic magisterium had begun to fade."

93. Brown, SS and Collins, OP, "Church Pronouncements," 1170.

94. Johnson, *Pope John XXIII*, 98.

95. Purdy, *The Church on the Move*, 307.

On the other hand, theologian Aidan Nichols points to various aspects of *Mediator Dei* which he finds more substantial than the conciliar Constitution. Most especially, he thinks, for example, that the theology of devotion behind Pius's encyclical, what the pope called "internal worship," is much better developed than in the *Constitution on the Sacred Liturgy*. The second chapter of the encyclical is given over to a consideration of the false antithesis between what Pius called "objective" and "personal" devotion, and "his insistence that subjective devotion is not only helpful but necessary if the liturgy (including the sacraments, and above all the Mass) is to be full of effect in worshippers' lives."[96] Nichols argues that this insistence on Pius's part had to do with the "hyper-liturgism," an excessive concentration on the liturgy to the detriment of personal devotion, that had become associated with the Benedictine Odo Casel's liturgical theology. One can argue whether Nichols has it right here about Casel, but there can be no argument about his clear insistence on the importance of personal devotion in *Mediator Dei*. It takes up far more room than in Vatican II's liturgical constitution. Yet, Pius's concern is to be found in the *Constitution on the Sacred Liturgy*. There we read that personal devotion and piety should relate to the liturgy as the public worship of the church. Paragraphs 12–13 of the conciliar constitution may be shorter than the corresponding paragraphs 23–37 of *Mediator Dei*, but are no less insistent on the importance of personal devotion. The Constitution insists that: popular devotions should be warmly commended; should harmonize with the liturgical seasons; and should lead people to a more fruitful participant in the liturgy. There is an obvious congruence between the two documents in this respect.

Another point of real congruence has to do with the eucharistic presence of Christ. A number of Catholics found Vatican II's notion of the manifold eucharistic presence of Christ somewhat challenging—that Christ is present in the assembled church, in the person of the minister, in the proclaimed word, and especially in the eucharistic gifts.[97] For some, this seemed to detract from the received doctrine of transubstantiation. If, however, careful attention had been paid to Pius's *Mediator Dei*, they would have found in that encyclical a clear articulation of this very traditional understanding of the manifold presence of Christ: "Along with the Church, therefore, her Divine Founder is present at every liturgical function: Christ is present at the august Sacrifice of the altar both in the person of His minister and above all under the Eucharistic species. He is present in the Sacraments, infusing into them the power which makes them ready instruments of sanctification. He is present finally in the prayer of praise and petition we direct to God . . . ."[98] Pius was no innovator in this regard, but rather was simply handing on the tradition.

In 1951 Pius reformed the Liturgy of Holy Week so that the liturgy of the Easter Vigil which had nonsensically been transferred to the morning of Holy Saturday,

---

96. Nichols, "A Tale of Two Documents," 26.

97. Vatican II, *Sacrosanctum Concilium*, 7.

98. *Mediator Dei*, 20.

could be celebrated in the evening. He introduced relaxations of eucharistic fast and in 1953 evening masses. These had become necessary during wartime, and had become popular among Catholics.

We have then in Pius XII a liturgically minded pope. However, from the very beginning, he refused to see the liturgy disconnected from the broader panorama of life and global concerns. In a letter he wrote to Bishop Preysing of Berlin in 1943, the pope had this to say:

> You know that the Holy See has considered the liturgical questions which have been raised among you to be important enough to merit its attention. But we must admit that we attach far more importance to protecting Christian consciences against all the poisons that threaten them. What use would it be to make the liturgy of the church more beautiful if, outside the church, the thoughts and actions of the faithful in their daily lives became alien to the law and love of Christ?[99]

The Blessed Virgin Mary

Stemming ultimately from his family Pius XII had a strong personal Marian piety and he "would become the most Marian Pope in church history."[100] He saw the Marian cult as a defense against Communism and atheism. In 1942 he consecrated the human race to the Immaculate Heart of Mary. He promoted the cult of Our Lady of Fatima. It had a sort of mystical meaning for him. Indeed, the historian Paul Johnson says that Pius "was obsessed by the prophecies of the Fatima-miracle children."[101] As already noted, he had been ordained a bishop on the very same day in 1917 as the first apparition.

In 1950 he promulgated the dogma of Mary's assumption into heaven in the apostolic constitution, *Munificentissmus Deus*. Four years before the actual definition, Pius sent a questionnaire to all the bishops of the church inquiring about the proposed dogma of the assumption of Our Lady. "The reply was almost unanimously favorable to the definition."[102] Almost unanimously, because the definition had its critics. Among them was the archbishop of Milan, the Benedictine Cardinal Ildefonso Schuster and the theology faculty of the Catholic University of Milan. They considered the definition inopportune for ecumenical reasons.

Although Pius spoke of Mary's mediation and her role in redemption in his 1954 encyclical, *Ad Coeli Reginam*/"To the Queen of Heaven," he is very clear that she is "Mediatrix not so much *with* the Mediator as *in* him and *through* him," and it is certainly of note that he never used the title of Co-Redemptrix of Mary. There was to be

---

99. Cited in Purdy, *The Church on the Move*, 312.

100. Coppa, *The Life and Pontificate of Pope Pius XII*, 11.

101. Johnson, *Pope John XXIII*, 106.

102. Cardinale, "Pope Pius XII and the Blessed Virgin Mary," 253.

no misunderstanding, especially in the post World War II years when the ecumenical movement was getting up a full head of steam, concerning the absolute oneness of Jesus Christ's redemptive action.[103] The Anglican priest-theologian, John Macquarrie, who was a young Presbyterian chaplain in the British Army when the dogma of Mary's assumption had not yet been defined, tells us that even in 1946 he "sensed that the Assumption is an authentic part of that whole fabric that we call the catholic faith" and he "hoped that some day [he] might come to understand it better." Macquarrie offers us half a century later an insight into the assumption that is profoundly Catholic: "It is not just a personal dogma about Mary (though it is that) but a dogma about the Church, the whole body of the faithful of whom Mary is the type. Mary's glorious Assumption, we may say, is the first moment in the glorious assumption of the Church."[104] Macquarrie's interpretation, not only of the assumption of Mary but of all Marian doctrine, anticipates substantially what is said of the blessed Virgin Mary in the final chapter of Vatican II's Constitution on the Church, *Lumen Gentium*.

Pius as Teacher

One of the strongest images of Pius that has perdured is as a teacher. This notion of the pope as teacher acknowledges not only his important contributions to the church and its mission. There was another side to Pius the teacher. He had, for example, a very strong linguistic competence, to the delight of pilgrims to the holy city. In fact, just before his death, it was rumored that he had begun the study of Arabic!

To accomplish so much in the area of teaching demands massive preparation. It is said that Pius slept only four hours per night. In a wonderfully descriptive passage Eamon Duffy writes this of Pius the teacher:

> He cultivated his role as Vatican oracle. Teaching gushed from him, unstoppable, a speech a day. Since the pope was the church's hotline to God, everything he had to say must be of interest. Pius himself came to believe that he had something valuable to contribute on every subject, no matter how specialized. He lived surrounded by encyclopedias and monographs, swotting up for the next utterance. Midwives would get an update on the latest gynaecological techniques, astronomers were lectured on sunspots.... The notion of the pope as universal teacher was getting out of hand.[105]

Duffy seems to me correct in his judgment here. It is one thing for the pope to show a sympathetic awareness of his different audiences as he meets them. It is something entirely different to feel the compulsion to swat up on the details of a given group's profession so as to say something significant to them. At the same time, the very fact that

103. Cardinale, "Pope Pius XII and the Blessed Virgin Mary," 255–56.
104. Macquarrie, *Mary for All Christians*, 91.
105. Duffy, *Saints and Sinners*, 354–55.

he went to such trouble with jurists, midwives, scientists, and so forth indicates on Pius's part an opening out, a real opening out of the church and the papacy to the world.[106]

Pope Pius XII: The Bitter End

Piecing together Pius's encyclicals and his teaching, recognizing the dynamism of the *nouvelle théologie* whose flames may have been dimmed but not put out by the action of *Humani Generis*, it would be true to say that Vatican II was truly in gestation. It was almost ready to come to birth. Pope Pius XII was not to witness these events. He died early in the morning of October 9, 1958. The papal doctor, Galeazzi Lisi, in reality an optometrist, sold to the world's press some very candid photographs he had taken of the pope at the end. One church historian describes Dr. Lisi's preparation of the pope's body in these terms: "[He] prepared the remains for display and burial in the manner (he blandly explained at a press conference) used for Jesus Christ after his crucifixion. The result was a mortician's nightmare."[107]

The pope's housekeeper in Rome, the famous Sister Pasqualina who had come with him many years ago from Germany and enjoyed a less than happy reputation, was told by the *camerlengo*, the orientalist Cardinal Eugene Tisserant, that she had twenty-four hours to leave the Vatican. Church historian John Hughes offers this description of her departure: "Before the Pope's funeral, newspapers round the world published pictures of her climbing into a taxi in St. Peter's Square clutching a brace of bird cages containing the late pontiff's canaries." Quite a comedown for such a powerful woman! Hughes goes on to add the following: "The resourceful Sister landed on her feet, however. Through the good offices of Cardinal Spellman, who owed her more favors than we may ever know, she found a berth in the kitchen of Rome's North American College."[108]

Conclusion

How is one to summarize the pontificate of Pope Pius XII? "The last, unassailed representative of the medieval Counter-Reformation anti-Modernist paradigm," concludes Hans Kung.[109] This hardly seems fair. A pope of diplomacy, with all the implied multiple layers of meaning, yes. A pope whose diplomacy cautioned him to a degree of silence about the Holocaust when the world might have benefited from a more forthright style of leadership, yes. A pope who, while encouraging the study of Scripture and the renewal of liturgy, put the brakes on the development of theology, yes.

---

106. O'Donnell, *Ecclesia: A Theological Encyclopedia of the Church*, 365.

107. Hughes, *Pontiffs: Popes Who Shaped History*, 257.

108. Hughes, *Pontiffs: Popes Who Shaped History*, 258.

109. Küng, *The Catholic Church, A Short History*, 177.

Yet, while Pius XII would undoubtedly have associated himself personally closer with the ecclesiology of Vatican I than that of Vatican II, it is a fact that he is frequently cited in its documents. The frequency of citation, of course, requires interpretation. Perhaps the Irish theologian, Christopher O'Donnell has it about right when he makes this comment: "Though [Vatican II] did not always follow the precise line of this pope, he can be said to have opened the way for many of its initiatives, or helped the minority at the council to accept them. Notwithstanding the fact that in recent years his reputation has suffered some eclipse, his influence on the council was significant and generally very positive."[110] This can be immediately and amply verified by looking at how often Pope Pius XII is quoted in the footnotes to the council's documents. With Pius XII's ante-natal care the council was coming, but it was the midwifery of his successor Pope John XXIII who brought it to birth.

---

110. O'Donnell, *Ecclesia*, 366.

10

The New Theology

*The years ranging from 1935 to 1959 constitute the period that immediately pre-
ceded the Second Vatican Council. Many of the issues raised and developed during
that council can only be fully understood against the background of this period.*

—Karim Schelkens, John A. Dick, and Jürgen Mettepenningen[1]

*Modernists and nouveaux théologiens looked to the tradition of Christian
mysticism that found the transcendent in the material and the immanent;
the quotidian transformed. But in challenging the reigning theology of their
day, they attracted the hostility of others, whose careers were invested in the
certainties now being questioned.*

—Gerard Loughlin[2]

The Liturgical Movement

Nouvelle Théologie, "new theology," was a movement in Catholic European theology in the mid-twentieth century. The term, in all probability coined by the Roman
theologian in the Holy Office Pietro Parente (1891–1986), is not actually accurate
because the movement was marked not so much by innovation as it was by a return to
the oldest sources and traditions of Catholic faith and theology—the Scriptures, the
fathers of the church, and the liturgy.

Mention of the liturgy as a contributory factor to the "new theology" is a powerful
reminder of the liturgical movement in the early twentieth century. Other movements
were afoot in the church, for example, the biblical movement and to a lesser extent
the ecumenical movement, beginning with the 1910 World Missionary Conference
in Edinburgh. The ecumenical movement lacked serious Catholic participation until
the Second Vatican Council, and while the biblical movement was growing slowly in

1. Schelkens et al., *Aggiornamento?* 101.
2. Loughlin, *"Nouvelle Théologie,* A Return to Modernism?" 36.

confidence, it really had to wait until Pope Pius XII's encyclical *Divino Afflante Spiritu* of 1943. Leading up to the condemnation of the new theology by Pope Pius XII in his encyclical of 1950, *Humani Generis* was his interest in the liturgical movement climaxing in his 1947 encyclical, *Mediator Dei*. While the ferment of the new theology was going on, and while the interest in biblical studies was slowly gathering steam, they were both preceded by and accompanied by a renewed interest in the liturgy.

The twentieth-century liturgical movement is usually traced to Dom Prosper Guéranger, O.S.B. (1805–75), the restorer of the French Benedictine Congregation at Solesmes, as Louis Bouyer remarks: "There is no achievement whatever in the contemporary liturgical movement which did not originate in some way with Dom Guéranger. The very least that we can say in his praise is that he brought the liturgy back to life as something to be lived and loved for its own sake."[3] This re-established Benedictine community of Solesmes under the inspiration and guidance of Guéranger became "a nursery of liturgical scholars"[4] Thus, the two Wolter brothers, at first diocesan priests, then monks at St. Paul's-Outside-the-Walls in Rome, came to Solesmes, and from there returned to Germany and founded the Benedictine monastery of Beuron, a center of liturgical renewal in 1862. From this monastery in 1872 a group of monks founded the monastery of Maredsous in Belgium, and then from this monastic house was founded the abbey of Mont-César in Leuven, another powerhouse of liturgical renewal. The central player in the Benedictine house of Maredsous was the Benedictine monk born in Ireland Dom Columba Marmion (1859–1923). He helped to found the Abbey of Mont-César in 1899 becoming its first prior, and then Abbot of Maredsous in 1909.[5] Marmion was not strictly speaking a liturgical scholar but he became very influential through his writings and from a liturgical point of view especially his *Christ in His Mysteries* (1924).[6] His spiritual vision was rooted in the Scriptures and the tradition of the church, and perhaps particularly in the letters of St. Paul, and the latter's understanding of the church as the Body of Christ. Marmion's appreciation of the liturgy has been actually summed up by a contemporary liturgical scholar in these words: "The liturgy, like the word of God in the Bible, is not in the first instance a relic of the past or an object for study. Surely the liturgy and the word of God are also this, but first and foremost they are a reality to live in and to live from. This, at least, is something Marmion himself lived to the full."[7] One of Marmion's monks at Mont-César was Lambert Beauduin (1873–1960) who was to become a great liturgical leader, and

---

3. Bouyer, *Liturgical Piety*, 57.

4. Crichton, *Lights in the Darkness: Forerunners of the Liturgical Movement*, 151.

5. Among his many spiritual retreats and various monastic responsibilities, it should be noted for the historical record that Marmion was also the confessor of Cardinal Mercier.

6. This book has been in print fairly consistently but was reissued by Zaccheus Press of Bethesda, MD, in 2008, with an introduction by Aidan Nichols, OP.

7. Geldhof, "Retrieving the Liturgical Movement," 101.

Marmion's influence on him was immense.[8] "Thus, Marmion would massively influence the future generation of Benedictine monks who would be so closely connected to the liturgical movement and give actual shape to it."[9]

A word about Lambert Beauduin (1873–1960), whose "theological contribution will probably never be studied, for unlike such contemporaries as Rahner, Barth or Tillich, he has not left us a systematic presentation of his thought in neatly bound and easily accessible volumes."[10] After eight years as a diocesan priest in Liége, he entered the Abbey of Mont-César in 1906, and committed himself among other things to liturgical renewal. In his various writings he called for the full engagement of the people in the liturgy, leading Louis Bouyer to say that "In my opinion, the decisive turning point for the Liturgical Movement came in 1909, with Dom Lambert Beauduin.[11] This was the year in which Beauduin gave a famous talk on liturgy at the National Congress of Catholic Works in Malines, Belgium. In 1914 Beauduin published his *La Piété de l'Église*. In this book and following in many ways Marmion's thought, Beauduin gives emphasis to the priesthood of Christ, in which all the baptized participate, and to the church as the mystical Body of Christ. One passage from his text gives a flavor of his liturgical theology: "As a true member, the Catholic ought to adapt himself, unite himself as intimately as possible, to the mystical body of Christ. The state of his soul, his activity, his mentality, his whole moral being, should be modeled on the intimate nature of the church, should vibrate with the very pulse-beat of the church. He must be not only in the church, but of the church, live from the fullness of her life, be cast in the same mould."[12] These key ideas were the foundations for him of a renewed liturgical practice. His project may be considered as having four parts: translating the Roman Missal into the vernacular so as to make available to people the complete text of Sunday Mass and Vespers; making the effort to have all piety and devotion grow from the liturgy and lead to the liturgy; fostering Gregorian chant for the singing of the liturgy; and encouraging choir members in each parish to make annual retreats in some center of liturgical life such as a Benedictine Abbey for their own personal as well as corporate renewal. In his own words: "What a shame that the liturgy remains the endowment of an elite; we are aristocrats of the liturgy; everyone should be able to

8. Geldhof, "Retrieving the Liturgical Movement," 98. Geldhof goes on to point out that "Columba Marmion had been a parish priest and professor at the seminary in the archdiocese of Dublin before he entered the monastery at Maredsous in 1886. This is a striking biographical parallel with Beauduin's own life and cannot but have been a matter of conversation between these two striking personalities" (102).

9. Geldhof, "Retrieving the Liturgical Movement," 98.

10. Quitslund, *Beauduin: A Prophet Vindicated*, 239. Quitslund demonstrates in detail Beauduin's commitment to ecumenism, showing that commitment in one area of the life of the church flows into others, but consideration of this aspect of his work is not our focus here.

11. Bouyer, *Liturgical Piety*, 58.

12. Beauduin, *Liturgy the Life of the Church*, 32.

nourish himself from it, even the simplest people: we must democratize the liturgy."[13] As an intrinsic element of his desire to revitalize the liturgy Beauduin was equally keen to emphasize that from the celebration of the liturgy especially the Eucharist there flowed a range of social and moral mandates, so that the work of social justice was an intrinsic consequence of the celebration. This project of Beauduin's leads Louis Bouyer to comment: "Here, then, is the clue to the great importance of the Belgian movement—that it never got lost in archaeologism and antiquarianism, and it was never tempted to wander off into innovations of doubtful value. This movement consisted in the pure and strong rediscovery of living tradition as it is: not a thing of the past, but the actual reality of the church of today to be lived by the people of today, a reality so continually overflowing with riches as yet unknown as to render foolish any wish to look for something different until this reality as it is has been once more fully explored and put to use."[14] Beauduin benefitted from the scholarship of his time including, for example Fernand Prat's theology of St. Paul, the contributions of Maurice de la Taille and Emile Mersch, but especially Henri de Lubac's 1938 *Catholicism*, "a book, he used to say, that he would have liked to have written himself."[15]

Maria-Laach was another Benedictine abbey founded from Beuron, and it was to produce the great Odo Casel (1886–1948), described by one contemporary scholar as "the great father of the twentieth-century liturgical movement" who "set out to provide . . . an evangelical ontology of the liturgy."[16] In 1932 Casel published his *The Mystery of Christian Worship*.[17] In the mystery of worship there takes place the integration of the Church in the mystery of Christ. There were three levels of the mystery for Casel: the mystery in God, that is to say, the work of redemption as existing eternally in the mind of God; the mystery of Christ, the execution of that salvific divine will of the Father in history—the incarnation-paschal mystery-ascension; and the mystery of worship = the liturgy, through which the redemptive work of Christ is reactualized in the church. The Eucharist is the mystery *par excellence*, re-actualizing the sacrifice of Christ on the altar. In it alone Christ exists by a permanent presence of his body and blood. At the same time, Christ and his redemptive work are also present in the other sacraments and rites of the church. The sacraments, with the Eucharist at the center, perpetuate the work of Christ for all ages.[18] One could go on to mention other liturgical pioneers like Romano

13. Cited in Quitslund, *Beauduin: A Prophet Vindicated*, 16.

14. Bouyer, *Liturgical Piety*, 63.

15. Quitslund, *Beauduin: A Prophet Vindicated*, 243.

16. Nichols, "Odo Casel Revisited," 18.

17. Casel, O.S.B., *The Mystery of Christian Worship*. The original publication came from Westminster, MD: The Newman Press, in 1962.

18. To get a sense of the widespread influence of Casel one might consult some of the following contributions: Bouyer, "Liturgy and Mystery: Dom Casel's Theory Explained and Discussed"; Davis, "Dom Odo Casel and the Theology of Mysteries"; Kilmartin, S.J., *The Eucharist in the West*, 268–82; Neunheuser, O.S.B., "Dom Odo Casel and Latest Research," and Kilmartin, S.J., "Masters in Israel: 5. Odo Casel"; O'Callaghan, "The Theory of the 'Mysteriengegenwart' of Dom Odo Casel."

Guardini (1885–1968), who was enormously influential in Germany and a particular influence on the theologian Joseph Ratzinger who was to become Pope Benedict XVI, but the intention is not to provide a comprehensive treatment of the liturgical movement as such and more to offer a taste of the liturgical renewal that was ongoing and to some extent contemporary with the "new theology."[19] The liturgical movement was the most significant and important element behind Pope Pius XII, *Mediator Dei*, November 20, 1947, in which we read: "The holy liturgy, therefore, is the public worship which is offered to the Father by our Redeemer as Head of the Church; it is also the worship offered by the society of the faithful to its Head, and through Him to the Eternal Father; in a word, it is the whole worship of the Mystical Body of Jesus Christ, that is, all the Head and of its members." Of this encyclical Louis Bouyer comments that "We may well say that this document is in itself an index to the truths of lasting value which have been proposed by the contemporary liturgical movement, and that it is also a climactic product of that movement itself."[20] It would have been impossible for the leaders of the "new theology" not to have known about the liturgical movement and these authors and to have been influenced not only by their texts but also by the rejuvenated awareness of the liturgy that they created. This is especially the case given the fact that in 1943 two Dominican theologians, Pie Duployé and Aimon-Marie Roguet, Dominican colleagues of Congar and Chenu, founded in Paris the Centre de Pastoral Liturgique, and two years later the liturgical journal *La Maison Dieu*.

The Biblical Movement

If we begin our consideration of biblical studies with Pope Leo XIII's 1893 encyclical, *Providentissimus Deus*, then, despite the fact that he underlines the importance of scientific linguistic and exegetical studies, there is clearly a certain hostility to biblical criticism, and the hostility that would continue in the pontificate of Pope Pius X in his condemnation of modernism. Although the same Pope Leo established the Pontifical Biblical Commission in 1902, extreme caution still prevailed with regard to the study of Scripture. The Pontifical Biblical Commission issued a number of decrees on biblical interpretation between 1905 and 1915, and are best described as follows: "These decrees . . . were precautionary and, while conservative in tone, were often phrased with perception and nuance. But since they bound Catholic scholars to assent, they gave to the non-Catholic world the unfortunate image of a monolithically conservative Catholic attitude that did not discuss questions on the basis of an exchange of scientific opinion but solved all by mandate from centralized authority."[21] The precautionary and conservative tone and the perceived monolithically conservative Catholic attitudes to

19. See Krieg, *Romano Guardini, A Precursor of Vatican II*, especially 70–90 and Cummings, "Eucharistic Teachings of the Church I: Pope Pius X to Vatican Council II," 52–63

20. Bouyer, *Liturgical Piety*, 36.

21. Brown and Collins, "Church Pronouncements," 1167.

Scripture would remain largely in place until the pontificate of Pope Pius XII. In a somewhat paradoxical fashion, this pope while largely hostile to the "new theology" was remarkably open to fresher approaches to the study of Scripture as evinced in his 1943 encyclical *Divino Afflante Spiritu*. This document opened fresh horizons for Catholic scholars and "inaugurated the greatest renewal of interest in the Bible that the Roman Catholic Church has ever seen."[22] In 1955, the secretary of the Pontifical Biblical Commission stated that now Catholic biblical scholars had complete freedom (*plena libertate*) in respect of the earlier Commission's decrees of 1905–15, except where they touched on faith and morals, and, of course, they did not. Although not entirely plain sailing for Catholic Scripture scholars, the way ahead was certainly much freer and full of promise than it had been before.

The Ecumenical Movement

Writing in the mid-1960s the Presbyterian theologian Robert McAfee Brown made the following remark, "So much has happened that even if ecumenism were slowed down, it would be impossible to stop it."[23] Brown had been an observer at all the sessions of Vatican II, and was absolutely committed to furthering the cause of Christian unity. In its twentieth-century iteration the ecumenical movement may be regarded as having its origin in the 1910 World Missionary Conference at Edinburgh, Scotland, in which the question of church unity was central. "Mere cooperation among the sending agencies and the practice of comity in the overseas fields were not sufficient to the task of 'the evangelization of the world in this generation': both at home and abroad, leaders with a deeper vision saw that the existence of confessional and institutional division constituted a counter-testimony to the gospel of reconciliation."[24] At Edinburgh some 1,200 delegates were present from around the Christian world. No Catholic was present, but a letter of encouragement was sent to the Edinburgh Conference by Bishop Geremia Bonomelli of Cremona, Italy. Significance? Bonomelli was a friend of the young man who was to become Pope John XXIII. It is surely interesting that the bishop in the small Italian diocese *knew* about the Edinburgh conference. Bonomelli had said to the young Roncalli/Pope John XXIII that the church really needed a new ecumenical council to renew herself and speak persuasively in the modern world. Roncalli gave Bishop Bonomelli his wish when he convened Vatican II, and this was the point at which the Catholic Church entered the modern ecumenical movement with its Constitution on the Church and its Decree on Ecumenism.

Prior to the council Catholics did not participate formally in the ecumenical movement. Indeed, as we have seen, Pope Pius XI in his encyclical letter *Mortalium Animos* vetoed Catholic participation. This did not stop individual Catholic scholars, however,

22. Brown and Collins, "Church Pronouncements," 1167.

23. Cited in Granfield, *Theologians at Work*, 8.

24. Wainwright, *Is the Reformation Over?* 4.

from learning about the movement and from broadening Catholic theological horizons with regard to Christian unity. Foremost among them was the "new" theologian treated below in this chapter, the Dominican Yves Congar.[25]

The "New Theology"

Leaders of the movement were French Dominicans and Jesuits, Dominicans at their theology school Le Saulchoir (first in Belgium, then in Paris) and Jesuits at theirs in Lyons-Fourvière. These priest-theologians did not constitute a uniform school of theology, indeed it was "less a school of thought than a common sensibility."[26] While there was obvious definite common ground between these Dominicans and Jesuits, there were also differences. Perhaps not always conscious and explicit and intentional, the Jesuits of Fourvière inclined towards the Greek fathers with their Neoplatonic implications, while the Dominicans of Le Saulchoir were much more Aristotelian given their grounding in the thinking of St. Thomas Aquinas.[27] Historian of theology, Jürgen Mettepenningen, has documented this movement in a detailed and very even-handed way and he proposes four consecutive phases of the movement.[28] In this chapter plotting the "new theology" we shall follow the outlines of his proposal, from its beginnings in the 1930s until Vatican II, recognizing, of course, that these four phases require much nuance and refinement.

The First Phase, 1935–42

The leaders in this first phase were undoubtedly the Dominicans and especially Yves Congar, Marie-Dominique Chenu (1895–1990), and Henri-Marie Feret, the latter less well-known than Congar and Chenu. Articles were written by these theologians challenging various aspects of the regnant neo-scholasticism, stemming from Pope Leo XIII, which they regarded as arid, lacking vitality, and unrelated to Catholic life and faith. For them theology "ha[d] to be centered around the living faith, not around a 'dry' system based on Thomistic commentaries from the sixteenth and seventeenth centuries."[29] They wanted to reach behind these neo-scholastic commentaries towards a strong historical sense in the development of theology.

---

25. For further insight here, see Goodall, *The Ecumenical Movement*, Tavard, *Two Centuries of Ecumenism*, and many of the entries in Lossky et al., eds., *Dictionary of the Ecumenical Movement*.

26. Boersma, *Nouvelle Théologie and Sacramental Ontology, Return to Mystery*, 9.

27. Boersma, *Nouvelle Théologie and Sacramental Ontology, Return to Mystery*, 11.

28. See his, "*Nouvelle Théologie*: Four Historical Stages of Theological Reform Towards *Ressourcement* (1935–1965)," 172–84. This essay abbreviates Mettepenningen's much fuller presentation of the movement in *Nouvelle Théologie/New Theology*.

29. Mettepenningen, "*Nouvelle Théologie*, Four Historical Stages," 175.

The young Dominican student Chenu was sent to Rome in 1914 and completed the statutory seven years of neo-scholastic studies there. Later he was to become regent of studies at Le Saulchoir, the Dominican school, from 1928 to 1942. As a Dominican Chenu was schooled in the thought of St. Thomas Aquinas and he went on to complete a doctorate in theology in 1920, *De Contemplatione/On Contemplation*, at the Angelicum University in Rome under the supervision of Reginald Garrigou-Lagrange, OP. Chenu differed from his supervisor in approaching both St. Thomas and Thomism from a historical-critical point of view. "The younger man wanted to develop a radically different way of reading Thomas Aquinas from the one inculcated at the Angelicum. The conflict of interpretations which divided them so bitterly soon emerged."[30] As regent of studies Chenu introduced this historical-critical perspective and methodology throughout the school. His historical work showed certain similarities between St. Bonaventure's *Itinerarium mentis in Deum Journey of the Soul to God* and St. Thomas's *Summa Theologiae*, and so pointed up the Platonic element in Aquinas's thought. In 1937 he published his *Une école de théologie: le Saulchoir*, "A School of Theology: the Saulchoir," which "enjoyed enormous success within the [Dominican] order."[31] His approach had broken with the style of his teacher Garrigou-Lagrange and many other Dominicans. Despite its very considerable success there was opposition to the book and to the historical methodology adopted by Chenu. He was summoned to Rome in 1938 to be investigated—Fergus Kerr says "bullied"—by his Dominican colleagues. Chenu writes of the experience: "I gave in to a sort of psychological pressure, I let myself be intimidated. One of them—no doubt to pacify Roman irritations—asked me to sign a series of ten propositions. I signed."[32] The book was placed on the Index of Prohibited Books in 1942. Kerr's comment about the experience and the event is to the point: "It may seem incredible that grown men would come up with the proposition that 'It is glorious for the Church to have the system of St. Thomas as truly orthodox', and suchlike and, badger Chenu into putting his signature to such poppycock—but that is symptomatic of the theological pathology of those days."[33] Chenu's approach to St. Thomas was thoroughly holistic, refusing the separation of theology from spirituality and of faith from reason. His understanding of and approach to St. Thomas was seen by his opponents as not only a theoretical issue but an immensely practical one with implications for the seminary curriculum. "As standard seminary pedagogy required, should philosophical studies precede entry into theology? Neo-scholastic apologetics, the crown of the philosophy course, mistakenly regarded as 'traditional', completely misrepresents the relationship between reason and faith, 'as if it was a matter of two worlds outside one another, for which happy concordances had to be

---

30. Kerr, *Twentieth-Century Catholic Theologians*, 17.
31. Mettepenningen, *Nouvelle Théologie/New Theology*, 48.
32. Cited in Kerr, *Twentieth Century Catholic Theologians*, 19.
33. Cited in Kerr, *Twentieth Century Catholic Theologians*, 19–20.

found."[34] Well-established certitudes in the Catholic approach to philosophy, theology and by implication seminary formation were under fire.[35]

Allied to Chenu's methodology was his friend and colleague Yves Congar (1904–95), born in the French Ardennes close to the Belgian border. Prior to joining the Dominicans Congar studied philosophy with Jacques Maritain at the Institut Catholique in Paris. "There he found a new approach to St. Thomas, one which relied more on the actual text of the author than on the use of his text for apologetic purposes and for support of narrow positions of the magisterium."[36] With the Dominicans he was greatly influenced by the broad horizons of Chenu. In a 1935 article, "The Deficit of Theology," Congar compared neo-scholastic theology to "an expressionless face, lacking any genuine connection with reality."[37] Unlike his friend and his mentor Chenu Congar did not remain in this retrieval of a more historical approach to Aquinas but developed strong ecclesiological interests, not least in ecumenism, and not only out of his theological research but also through personal contact with Lutheran pastors in Germany and with Anglicans, and especially the great Arthur Michael Ramsey who was to become archbishop of Canterbury.[38] In 1938 he published his *Divided Christendom: A Catholic Study of the Problem of Reunion*.[39] In this ecumenical study Congar viewed the divisions between East and West in the eleventh century as stemming as much from cultural and political factors as theological, and threw himself into a more realistic and historically informed understanding of the Reformation of the sixteenth century as well as the more recent ecumenical movement. World War II, however, was on the horizon. Congar served in the French military during World War II, was captured by the Germans in 1940 and spent the next five years as a prisoner of war. In Fergus Kerr's words, "In 1945 the Christian faith, and especially the Catholic Church, was rising

34. Kerr, *Twentieth Century Catholic Theologians*, 25.

35. Kerr, *Twentieth Century Catholic Theologians*, 24–29 aptly summarizes Chenu's perspective: "The message of Chenu's manifesto lies, most provocatively, in the layout: the chapter on philosophy comes after the one on theology. In effect, Thomas Aquinas is to be read as a theologian from the outset. There is no need to be able to defend the Twenty-Four Theses before one is allowed to pass into theological studies. It is far more important to reconstruct Aquinas's historical context than to master the metaphysical theorems that supposedly lie at the basis of his theology. . . . In short, in a list of examples, Chenu opens up a quite different approach to reading the *Summa Theologiae* from the one inculcated by the lecture courses and textbooks supposedly composed according to the mind of St. Thomas. Failure to allow for the context which he took for granted—the Christian mystery, liturgically performed, lived in disciplined contemplation—leaves the *Summa Theologiae* as arid an exercise as most seminarians found it. Far from reducing the rigorously intellectual achievement of the *Summa*, Chenu was out to demonstrate that we miss the achievement altogether unless we get to know the mind the fruits of whose contemplation are set down—incarnated, so to speak—in the texts which we have inherited."

36. O'Donnell, *Ecclesia*, 102.

37. Mettepenningen, "*Nouvelle Théologie*, Four Historical Stages," 175.

38. Congar visited Ramsey in 1937, became a great admirer of Anglican liturgy, and of Ramsey's own ecclesiological study, *The Gospel and the Catholic Church* of 1936.

39. The French edition appeared in 1938 and the English edition the following year.

from the dead, returning from hell to new life."[40] Congar's return to academic life saw fruit in his 1950 ecclesiological study, *True and False Reform in the Church*, a work of some 650 pages,[41] and three years later his *Lay People in the Church: A Study for the Theology of the Laity*.[42] These publications demonstrate Congar at his best, "one could keep in tension two poles· tradition and the actual situation of the church. He sought to serve the church and its faith by a contemporary exposition rooted in the riches of the past."[43] Just as Chenu's studies on a more appropriate, historically informed understanding of Aquinas brought him into trouble with the church, so Congar's ecclesiological works brought suspicion upon him as well. These Dominican theologians wanted a fresh face for theology, a face that was living and dynamic and persuasive to their contemporaries. Their opponents viewed their efforts as another dose of modernism, condemned at the beginning of the century.

The Second Phase, 1942–50

Now "the Dominicans withdrew into the background and the Jesuits took the lead."[44] Mettepenningen points to three publications by Jesuits. The first is the 1944 publication of Henri Bouillard's doctoral dissertation entitled *Conversion and Grace in St. Thomas Aquinas*.[45] Not only did Bouillard advocate a more appreciative historical approach to St. Thomas but he also concluded that "a theology which is not related to contemporary life, is a false theology."[46] The false theology was in his judgment neo-scholasticism. The second publication was the 1946 article of Jean Daniélou, "Present Orientations of Religious Thought," which came out in the French Jesuit journal *Études*.[47] Here Daniélou insisted that a return to the Scriptures, liturgy and patristic theology/sources was to be preferred "to a theology that owed its existence

---

40. Kerr, *Twentieth Century Catholic Theologians*, 35.

41. The second edition of this book was translated into English by the American Dominican Paul Philibert and published in 2010 as *True and False Reform in the Church* (Collegeville: Liturgical, 2010). Fergus Kerr notes of this book: "The very idea of reform, whether true or false, in the Catholic Church, was a provocation. The papal nuncio in Paris, Archbishop Angelo Roncalli, inscribed in his own copy the question 'A reform of the church—is it possible?' Less than ten years later, when he had become Pope John XXIII, the idea that the Catholic Church could be reformed—renewed, anyway— was firmly on the agenda." See Kerr, *Twentieth Century Catholic Theologians*, 36.

42. The 1953 French edition came into English in 1965 with the Newman Press, Westminster, MD.

43. O'Donnell, *Ecclesia*, 103.

44. O'Donnell, *Ecclesia*, 177.

45. Paris: Aubier, 1944. In his helpful account of the "new theology," Francis Fiorenza mistakenly describes Henri Bouillard as a Dominican. See his "The New Theology and Transcendental Thomism," in Livingston et al., *Modern Christian Thought, vol. II, The Twentieth Century*, 202.

46. Cited in Mettepenningen, "*Nouvelle Théologie*: Four Historical Stages," 177.

47. *Études* 79 (1946) 5–21.

to a single medieval theologian."[48] Understandably, a commotion followed and he was removed as the editor of the journal.[49]

The third publication came from the pen of Henri de Lubac. Through his engagement with patristic theology—he was a co-founder of the patristic series *Sources Chrétiennes*—he entered upon a careful critique of the dominant neo-scholasticism. The result was his *Surnaturel* in 1946 rethinking the distinction between nature and grace with a permeative critique of neo-scholasticism. Francis Fiorenza offers a very clear summary of the book in these words:

> It argues that much of the malaise of contemporary Christianity is due to the neo-scholastic separation of the supernatural from the natural. Neo-scholasticism affirmed the gratuity of supernatural grace and abstractly contrasted the supernatural with the concept of "pure nature," that is, with an idea of nature independent of any historical dimension. De Lubac charges that such abstract separations lead to a theology of grace that separates grace from life. . . . By separating nature and grace, religious doctrine is "elevated" to a distant province about human nature. Such a theology seeks to affirm the transcendence of the Divine, yet its effect is to cut the Divine off from the human, as if God were not the creator of both nature and grace or did not create nature with a view toward grace.[50]

Many contemporary theologians would have no hesitation in endorsing de Lubac's critique, but in the mid-twentieth century it was a dangerous ecclesiastical position, so much so that Fergus Kerr describes *Surnaturel* as follows: "The most bitter controversy within twentieth-century Thomism, and in Catholic theology at large, was set off in 1946 with the publication of Henri de Lubac's *Surnaturel*."[51]

Despite the intentions of these authors their published work was misunderstood to be simply an attack on neo-scholasticism and Thomism more generally, and the fundamental reason behind this misunderstanding was the failure on the part of Rome to appropriate a historical consciousness in theology. This was the crucial issue at the time of modernism at the beginning of the twentieth century, and was certainly the crucial issue in the *débacle* over the "new theology." Mettepenningen sums it up crisply: "Via the integration of the historical perspective, theology was called upon to cross the boundaries of a closed meta-historical Thomism, a meta-historical

---

48. Cited in Mettepenningen, "*Nouvelle théologie*: Four Historical Stages," 177.

49. Jean Daniélou (1905–74), a French Jesuit, was a highly celebrated patristic scholar—his doctoral thesis was on the theology of St. Gregory of Nyssa—and one of the founders of the patristic series *Sources Chrétiennes*. As well as his contributions to patristic theology he was the author of a number of books opening a wide understanding of Christian theology not addicted to neo-scholastic or Thomist ideas and terminology. A good account of his theology may be found in Marc Nicholas, *Jean Daniélou's Doxological Humanism*. Jean's brother was Alain Daniélou (1907–94), the noted Indologist, and convert to Hinduism.

50. Fiorenza, "New Theology and Transcendental Thomism," 203.

51. Kerr, *After Aquinas: Versions of Thomism*, 134.

'magisteriumism', and a meta-historical orthodoxy to a historically oriented, open Thomism, and a source theology."[52]

Pope Pius XII, *Humani Generis,* and Reginald Garrigou-Lagrange, OP

In the vanguard of the opposition to this way of doing theology historically and contextually was the most celebrated Thomist in the Roman schools, Reginald Garrigou-Lagrange, OP (1877–1964), who published an article in 1947 with the title "La nouvelle théologie où va-t-elle?"—"The new theology, where is it going?"[53] His answer to the question, which is the title of his essay, is "the new theology is returning to Modernism."[54] As one who had an influential role both with Pope Pius XII and with the Curia he was bound to make his voice heard in the forthcoming encyclical. "When *Humani Generis* appeared, it was hard to miss his influence," though there is no clear and unambiguous evidence that he had a hand in its actual writing.[55] It is so easy to characterize one's favorite theologians positively and those less favored negatively, perhaps especially at this time of *ressourcement* and the *nouvelle théologie.* It has been pointed out by scholars well-versed in the neo-Thomism of the Garrigou-Lagrange variety that he made a substantive contribution to ascetical and mystical theology, and also "the encouragement he offered to the view that a call (at least 'remote' if not 'immediate') to contemplation was the baptismal birth-right of all Christians."[56] Yes, for Garrigou the "new theology" was a reincarnation of modernism, and this had already been condemned by the church under Pope Pius X. The encyclical letter of Pope Pius XII, *Humani Generis,* of 1950 was a kind of parallel to Pope Pius X's *Pascendi*, and in the judgment of Mettepenningen "this encyclical (*Humani Generis*) can be understood as Rome's final serious defense of neo-scholasticism as a normative framework determining the orthodoxy of theology."[57]

While Reginald Garrigou-Lagrange may not have been the author of Pope Pius XII's encyclical *Humani Generis,* there can be no doubt that his thinking lay behind it. For most of his academic life he taught at the Pontifical University of St. Thomas Aquinas in the City, known simply as "the Angelicum." He exemplifies what has come to be known as Thomism of the Strict Observance, that is to say, the Thomism that largely dominated Roman Catholic theology from about World War I to the opening of the Second Vatican Council in 1962. This kind of Thomism does not restrict itself to the actual texts of St. Thomas himself, but takes very seriously Thomist scholars

---

52. Mettepenningen, *"Nouvelle théologie,"* 178.

53. In *Angelicum* 23 (1946) 126–45.

54. Nichols, *Reason with Piety*, 130.

55. Kerlin, "Reginald Garrigou-Lagrange," 110. For an attempt to recognize the positive side of Garrigou's disputation, see Peddicord, *The Sacred Monster of Thomism,* 50–53.

56. Nichols, *Engaging Theologians,* 113.

57. Mettepenningen, *"Nouvelle théologie,"* 179.

who have interpreted the master's thought down through the ages. Aidan Nichols, OP describes it like this:

> It is a Thomism which, for the sake of the conceptual merits furnished by the Thomist tradition at its most intellectually powerful, was willing to sacrifice, if need be, the historical St. Thomas to the independent claims of the later commentators. Not of course that Thomists of the Strict Observance would want to admit that a gulf separated the master from the commentaries, but it would not worry them if told that this or that formulation, preferred for coherence, precision, or the clarity of its connection with fundamental principles, could not be found in Thomas's corpus in just this form.[58]

Aidan Nichols rightly sees this Thomism as coming powerfully into play over against modernism in the late nineteenth and early twentieth centuries, and Garrigou saw that modernism re-emerge in the *nouvelle théologie*. He was utterly opposed to it.

The pope was displeased with those who were critical of Thomism and who desired "to bring about a return in the explanation of Catholic doctrine to the way of speaking used in Holy Scripture and the Fathers of the Church."[59] In reality *la nouvelle théologie* was a reaction against the a-historical mentality of the many scholastic textbooks used in seminaries and universities, and is nicely described by John O'Malley in a way that goes beyond simply an anti-Thomist point of view: "The recovery of the patristic mode, *along with a recovery of a more genuine Thomism*, was a return to the life-giving wellsprings. It would show forth the richness of the Catholic tradition and at the same time suggest that the tradition was bigger than any system. It would thus suggest that mystery was the first quality of the tradition."[60] Notice O'Malley's words—a recovery not only of patristic theology and its insights but also "of a more genuine Thomism." This more genuine Thomism is more historically conscious and more aware of the problematic of what had hitherto been understood as the natural/supernatural orders. While this more genuine Thomism helps one to recognize that "the coherence of Thomas' *Summa* is, in fact, stunning, intellectually beautiful—a cathedral of the mind," what might be termed the severe analytical methodology that lies behind the enterprise is not the only way to do theology.[61]

Some of the "New Theologians"

Aidan Nichols considers Jean Daniélou (1905–74), perhaps the least commented on of the "new theologians," as "the epitome of *ressourcement* theology, the purest example

58. Nichols, *Engaging Theologians*, 2–3.
59. Pope Pius XII, "Human Generis," in Carlen, *The Papal Encyclicals*, 177.
60. O'Malley, "Vatican II: Did Anything Happen?" 66.
61. See O'Malley, *Four Cultures of the West*, 98. This book of O'Malley's is a wonderful engagement with the various ways of doing theology that have characterized the West.

of its type."[62] Daniélou taught at the *Institut Catholique* in Paris for twenty-five years, participated as a *peritus* at Vatican II, and was made a cardinal by Pope Paul VI in 1969. He published widely, including highly regarded studies of Philo of Alexandria, Origen of Alexandria, Gregory of Nyssa, and on patristic biblical exegesis.[63] While he had little time for neo-scholasticism, Daniélou admired the neo-Thomist philosopher Jacques Maritain, although "he could not stomach the systematic quality of Maritain's Thomism."[64] This does not mean that he had no appreciation of the value of philosophy. He was not a fideist. "While recognizing that the Bible and tradition are regulative for theology, he sees that contemporary philosophical terms are needed to interpret the realities of revelation."[65] There had been a rupture between theology and life, according to Daniélou, and that rupture was a major contribution to the massive spread of secularism and alienation from Christianity. Daniélou believed that the currents of thought that marked the so-called "new theology" could help to heal and bridge the rupture and alienation between Christian faith and the modern world.

In 1956 Daniélou published *Dieu et Nous—God and Us*—which in so many ways expresses his synthesis of Christianity based and rooted in his studies of Scripture and the fathers of the church.[66] In this book he argues against some biblical scholars who seem to wish to restrict revelation to the Semitic categories of the Scriptures. Daniélou advocates a much broader perspective, in-line, of course, with the patristic tradition. Thus, he argues that there is a knowledge of God to be found in philosophy and the pagan religions, albeit in his terms an imperfect knowledge of God. He writes about "a revelation of God that speaks to every human soul through the cosmos, the conscience, and the spirit."[67] "[The climax of this revelation] is given in the Bible and in the life of the church. The Old Testament depicts God in terms of truth, justice, love and holiness. The New Testament unfolds the mystery of the Trinity. And the knowledge of God is developed in the sacramental life of the church, and in mystical experience."[68] *God and Us* communicates a dynamic sense of God's relationship with humankind. Daniélou is concerned especially with promoting an understanding of theology that goes beyond the intellectual level. "Theology is inadequate if it does

---

62. Nichols, *Engaging Theologians*, 53.

63. Kerr, judges that Daniélou's work on Origen inaugurated the revival of interest in this father of the church, especially among Catholic theologians. See his *Twentieth Century Catholic Theologians*, 80. For a more comprehensive awareness of Daniélou's patristic contribution see Pottier, "Daniélou and the Twentieth-Century Patristic Renewal."

64. Nichols, *Engaging Theologians*, 56.

65. Macquarrie, *Twentieth-Century Religious Thought*, 295.

66. *Dieu et Nous* (Paris: Grassett, 1956). The English translation was made by Walter Roberts, the United Kingdom edition as *God and Us* (London: Mowbray, 1957) and the American edition as *God and the Ways of Knowing* (New York: Meridian, 1957). References here are to the United Kingdom edition.

67. Daniélou, *God and Us*, 41.

68. Thus, Macquarrie summarizing Daniélou in his *Twentieth-Century Religious Thought*, 296.

not end in mysticism," he maintains, and he understands mysticism as "a living encounter with the living God."[69] So central is this perspective to the entire *oeuvre* of Daniélou that one contemporary student of his theology describes it as "doxological humanism": "The human person *qua* human is only able to find true happiness when he realizes that he has a vocation—an essential human quality—which is realized in worship, adoration, and contemplation."[70] Unless this doxological dimension to the human person is acknowledged, human life is reduced individually and socially. Writing just after Vatican II began in 1961, Daniélou states:

> This relationship with God does not represent some kind of accessory truth, fitted onto a humanism which could exist substantially apart from it, but is constitutive of man as such. Hence a man who refuses to consider it, a man without adoration, is mutilated in his person. When we raise our voice today against every sort of atheistic humanism, whether this be Marxist humanism or liberal humanism, it is not simply God that we are defending, but man himself. A man without God is not fully human.[71]

Daniélou's teaching was interrupted during World War II when he worked with the French Resistance during the years of the Nazi occupation of France, something that he has in common with two of his peers, Yves Congar, OP and Henri de Lubac, SJ. None of these men gave any support to the Vichy regime, as allegedly Garrigou-Lagrange had done. In fact, Congar as a military chaplain was taken prisoner and spent most of the war years at Colditz. De Lubac constantly denounced Nazism, and was on the run from the Gestapo for six months in 1943. The "new theology" emphasized the spiritual nature of the church, and signaled a move away from a severe institutionalism.

De Lubac, arguably "the greatest of all this generation of French theologians . . . who illuminated everything he touched," became associated with a retrieval of the Greek fathers and the corporate nature of Catholicism.[72] In 1944, De Lubac published a magnificent book *Corpus Mysticum*, a book translated into English some fifty years later. The book essentially completed by about 1939 had to wait for publication until 1944 because of the complexities of the war years. In it, de Lubac took issue with an excessive fixation on the eucharistic presence of Christ, something he traced back to the controversy with Berengarius (ca. 999–1088), and ultimately to the tensions between Paschasius Radbertus (785–865) and Ratramnus (died ca. 868).[73] De Lubac worked to restore in his book something of a balance between

---

69. Daniélou, *God and Us*, 162.

70. Nicholas, *Jean Daniélou's Doxological Humanism*, 146.

71. Daniélou, *The Scandal of Truth*, 160–61.

72. Kerr, "French Theology: Yves Congar and Henri de Lubac," 108–11.

73. See Macy, *The Theologies of the Eucharist in the Early Scholastic Period*.

the eucharistic Body of Christ and the ecclesial Body of Christ without in any way downplaying the eucharistic presence of Christ.

De Lubac published in 1946 his large work on grace, *Surnaturel*. In this outstanding work he struggled to sort out the relationship between nature and grace, between the natural and the supernatural. Like Daniélou's desire to overcome the rupture between theology and life de Lubac sought to overcome what he saw as the rupture between nature and grace, a rupture that he believed with his "new theology" colleagues had contributed to the contemporary alienation from the church and Christian doctrine. "De Lubac argued, in uncompromising fashion, that nature and the supernatural were not two parallel orders, running alongside one another, each with its own, distinct end. Instead, he argued that God had created nature in such a way that from the beginning it had a supernatural goal for its purpose. The natural desire for the beatific vision that this implied seemed, to the neo-Thomists at least, to endanger the gratuity of divine grace: if human beings contributed a natural desire, the process of salvation did not seem to be originating only with God."[74] In other words, nature is "first grace." Creation does not have to be. Creation is, therefore, gift, and, therefore, grace. Grace does not enter creation extrinsically but is already there, developmentally, from the first moment of its existence.

De Lubac also went on to produce studies on exegesis, Origen, atheism, and even Buddhism. His studies of Holy Scripture helped to bring about a more traditional and sacramental understanding of the Word of God. While appreciative of the enormous gains of the historical-critical approaches to Scripture, he recognized the fundamental spiritual understanding of the text, an understanding that contributed to Vatican II's Constitution on Divine Revelation. Arguably, the kind of sacramental appreciation of Scripture that emerged in Catholic theology especially from de Lubac's work was already anticipated in part in the work of Edward Bouverie Pusey, the nineteenth-century Anglican theologian, Hebraist, and friend of John Henry Newman.[75] Pusey's high theology of the sacraments was matched by an equally high theology of Scripture. The Old and New Testaments were not to be understood as a set of texts waiting to be analyzed and taken apart by Semitic and Greek philologists— the "dead repository of barren technicalities." "The more he studied the Fathers, the more strongly he became convinced that they were truer interpreters of Scripture than modern writers; ancient Catholic truth better represented the meaning of the Bible than did modern private opinions."[76] From the church fathers and their understanding of allegory and typology Pusey understood Scripture as the living word of

---

74. Boersma, *Nouvelle Théologie and Sacramental Ontology, Return to Mystery*, 26.

75. Edward Bouverie Pusey, "Lectures on Types and Prophecies of the Old Testament," a series of unpublished lectures delivered in Oxford in 1836, now housed in Pusey House, Oxford. See the excellent 2012 Durham doctoral dissertation, supervised by Andrew Louth, of George Westhaver, "The Living Body of the Lord: E. B. Pusey's 'Types and Prophecies of the Old Testament.'"

76. Prestige, *Pusey*, 46.

God to humankind. In some respects, Pusey anticipated de Lubac. Like Pusey, de Lubac does not wish simply to comment negatively on the various historical-critical approaches to Scripture. He wishes to emphasize that those modes of interpretation do not exhaust the meaning of the biblical text. "Just as the supernatural is not extraneous to the natural, neither are the typological and Christological interpretations of the Hebrew Scriptures extraneous to its meaning."[77]

One name de Lubac's pen touched and, indeed, illuminated is that of his brother Jesuit Pierre Teilhard de Chardin. He wrote several lucid books on Teilhard, dispelling something of the suspicion that had hung over him, and he certainly regarded Teilhard as a mystic. De Lubac's outstanding book *Catholicism* retrieves a social view of the person, eschewing any form of individualism, and underscores the social and cosmic dimensions of Catholic doctrine, not least in the doctrine of the church itself. "The cosmic dimension of Catholicism within de Lubac's work becomes evident in the Christian dimension of the cosmos in de Chardin's evolutionary work."[78] In the words of de Lubac's most famous "pupil" and friend, Hans Urs von Balthasar—while de Lubac was in the theologate at Lyons Balthasar was there as a Jesuit student, but de Lubac did not actually teach him—the time after *Humani Generis* was a crucifixion: "The next ten years became a *via crucis* for him. He was deprived of permission to teach, expelled from Lyons and driven from place to place. His books were banned, removed from the libraries of the Society of Jesus and impounded from the market."[79]

De Lubac was made a cardinal by Pope John Paul II in 1983, bringing to an end (if that were necessary) the cloud of suspicion that had hung over him. He was appointed a member of the International Theological Commission. Yet, in various parts of the French church, including among some of his fellow Jesuits, he was considered "as yesterday's man."[80] Like de Lubac Yves Congar also picked up on the corporate dimension of the church, but added the active role of the laity and ecumenism. As a result of Congar's published research in these areas, Fergus Kerr comments, "The contribution of his research to the massive shift in Roman Catholic ecclesiological self-understanding at Vatican II cannot be overestimated."[81]

Garrigou was not, of course, alone in his interest in Thomism. Thomism received its own injection of new life from the "new theology" as hinted at above by John W. O'Malley. In 1950, Marie Dominique Chenu, OP, published his *Introduction to the Study of St. Thomas Aquinas*. He insisted that Aquinas had to be grasped and interpreted within his historical milieu, the Paris of seven centuries earlier. Chenu's method was a serious challenge to the still dominant a-historical approach to Thomism, Garrigou's approach, regarded as a system belonging to all ages, and thus intelligible outside of its

77. Fiorenza, "The New Theology and Transcendental Thomism," 204.

78. Fiorenza, "The New Theology and Transcendental Thomism," 204.

79. Balthasar, *The Theology of Henri de Lubac*, 17.

80. Nichols, *Engaging Theologians*, 105.

81. Kerr, "French Theology: Yves Congar and Henri de Lubac," 107.

historical setting. If you like, Chenu advocated thinking *with* Aquinas over thinking *as* Aquinas. It was inevitable that some of Chenu's interpretations of Aquinas would clash with those whose appreciation was somewhat a-historical. Chenu had been one of Garrigou-Lagrange's best students at the Angelicum University in Rome during World War I, but Chenu's attempt as Regent of Studies at the Dominican house near Paris, Le Saulchoir, to develop this historical context for understanding not only Aquinas but the whole tradition of theology was bound to create some distance between him and his former teacher. One commentator writes: "Although Garrigou-Lagrange never wrote about Chenu or le Saulchoir and denied any direct role in their official censure, he did participate actively in the effort to reign in what he and others saw as tendencies denigrating speculative theology and moving toward Modernism and especially toward philosophical and theological relativism."[82]

This theological renewal, this "new theology" was (largely, albeit not entirely) in Eamon Duffy's words "a false dawn."[83] While it must be acknowledged that a certain opening up of the church took place under Pius, an opening up expressed in the encyclical letters *Mystici Corporis* for ecclesiology, *Divino Afflante Spiritu* for biblical studies and *Mediator Dei* for liturgical reform, *Humani Generis* gave voice to the a-historical and juridical approach to theology that had been in place since at least the modernist controversy. Pius XII published his encyclical letter *Humani Generis* in 1950 in which he warned against the accommodation of Catholic theology to modern intellectual trends. He gave support to the regnant Thomism after the manner of Garrigou-Lagrange, but he ignored the growing reaction against scholasticism prompted by a greater appreciation of patristic theology, and the appreciation of medieval Augustinian theology, as well as of Orthodox and Reformation theologians. The pope warned also against the historical contextualizing of dogma, a method that could only lead to a self-defeating relativism. In a similar fashion, he warned against a "false irenicism" in respect of other Christian traditions. As for evolution, it was judged as not completely certain or proved, and polygenism seemed to be in conflict with the received doctrine of original sin, though Pius did not outright condemn it.

While no theologians were actually named, Peter Hebblethwaite remarks that to know against whom the encyclical was intended, "the only course was to consider which theologians lost their jobs."[84] The three Henris of the Jesuit school of theology at Fourvière, Lyons, were forbidden to teach: Henri de Lubac, Henri Bouillard, and Henri Rondet. Also the Dominicans at Le Saulchoir in Paris, Yves Congar and Marie Dominique Chenu were both silenced and forbidden to teach or publish.

Congar went into a kind of exile. Part of this was spent in Cambridge, England, with the Dominican community there. Living under the cloud of *Humani Generis* was enormously difficult for Congar. He had sought to do nothing but build up the church

82. Kerlin, "Reginald Garrigou-Lagrange: Defending the Faith," 108.

83. Duffy, *Saints and Sinners*, 350.

84. Hebblethwaite, *John XXIII, Pope of the Century*, 112.

through his theological researches, and now to be held in suspicion was the lowest of blows. Fergus Kerr, the Scottish Dominican, describes Congar's state of mind, based on his letters and journal of the time:

> In 1956, Congar spent six profoundly unhappy months in Cambridge; worse by far than his experience as a prisoner of war in Colditz and Lubeck. [He] seems to have been in such a deep depression that he really needed psychiatric help. [A letter to his mother] offers small insight into the appalling cost of the years when he was suspected and sanctioned by church authorities. It seems that he was unable to recover from the deleterious effects of that tenebrous period in his life.[85]

Bishops and religious superiors were encouraged to be vigilant in such a way that *Humani Generis* invited explicit comparison in some quarters with Pius X's *Pascendi* and its condemnation of modernism. This is not entirely fair. Admittedly, the theological renewal in France was something of a "false dawn" in Eamon Duffy's words but in reality *Humani Generis* and Pius XII were far more balanced than *Pascendi* and Pius X. Suspicion followed inevitably after the publication of the encyclical, but there was nothing like the *Sodalitium Pianum*, the international spy-ring that followed the condemnation of modernism. The theological dawn may have been hailed somewhat prematurely, but a dawn there was nevertheless.

Church historian Adrian Hastings describes this time as one of enormous theological creativity in the church. The great theological revival catalyzed by Vatican II was already largely in place before the council as a result of *la nouvelle théologie* and associated movements in Scripture, liturgy and ecumenism.[86] Hastings's positive evaluation would have been in some measure endorsed by Giovanni Battista Montini, Pius XII's under secretary in the Secretariat of State, and later to be Pope Paul VI. Montini wrote a letter in December of 1944 to the French philosopher Maurice Blondel. Blondel departing from the ecclesiastically backed scholasticism as we have noted earlier to a more dynamic, a more Augustinian, a more "immanent" approach to reality had been suspect in the modernist era and certainly had contributed in the background as it were to the development of the *nouvelle théologie*. Montini's letter was commendatory of Blondel and gained for Montini credibility among the silenced theologians in the wake of the forthcoming *débacle* around *Humani Generis*.

The Third Phase, ca. 1950—the Eve of Vatican II

As a result of *Humani Generis* a number of theologians like de Lubac lost their jobs, but the encyclical did not bring an end to the new theology. This new, historically conscious

---

85. Kerr, "Yves Congar: From Suspicion to Acclamation," 276–77. See also William Henn, "Yves Congar and *Lumen Gentium*," 591–92.

86. Hastings, "The Twentieth Century," 168.

way of doing theology, marked by an intense study of patristic and medieval texts and sources in alliance with more recent philosophical methodologies such as phenomenology and existentialist personalism, spread throughout Europe especially. It gave rise to in different ways and in different degrees such increasingly influential voices as Edward Schillebeeckx, OP and Piet Schoonenberg, SJ (The Netherlands) and Karl Rahner, SJ and Hans Urs von Balthasar in the German-speaking world. As the works of these theologians gradually made their way into English, so the impact of the new theology in the English-speaking world grew quite rapidly throughout the 1950s.

The Fourth Phase, Vatican II (1962–65)

The fourth phase of the new theology is quite simply the Second Vatican Council itself. Although many if not most of the bishop participants in that council would have been trained in neo-scholastic theology, some of the European bishops brought as their consultant theologians representatives of the new theology, for example, Yves Congar, Henri de Lubac, Jean Daniélou, Edward Schillebeeckx, Karl Rahner. Their very presence at the council and the impact they had in the development and promulgation of the council documents once and for all put an end to the cloud of suspicion that had hung over the new theology and, at least in some respects, over some of the representatives of modernism at the beginning of the twentieth century. "Thus *la nouvelle théologie* passed from the status of a cast out minority to that of a legitimate partner in the conversation."[87]

Pierre Teilhard de Chardin, SJ (1881–1955)

"In light of the contributions of Bouillard, Daniélou and de Lubac, one should also reflect on the position and work of Pierre Teilhard de Chardin."[88] Many who have never read a page of the "new theology" will know about, even if they have never seriously read or studied, the French Jesuit palaeontologist/geologist Pierre Teilhard de Chardin. His hopeful perspectives and his non-adversarial stance *vis-à-vis* the world and particularly the world of science helped to pave the way for the new awakening that theologically was the "new theology" and that ecclesially was to be Vatican II (1962–65).

As already noted, Henri de Lubac wrote two books outlining the theological vision of Teilhard and at the same time demonstrating his orthodoxy which had been called into question by the Holy Office. The Australian novelist Morris West published a best-selling novel in 1963, *The Shoes of the Fisherman*, in which a French

87. These are the words of Etienne Fouilloux as cited in Portier, *Divided Friends*, 40.
88. Schelkens et al, *Aggiornamento?* 125.

priest-scientist, Jean Telemond, becomes an intimate friend and lasting influence on the pope. Teilhard was the reality behind Telemond.

Teilhard's spiritual and theological passion might be summarized in this fashion: "I would like to be able to have a great love for Christ in the *very act* of loving the universe. Is that a dream or a blasphemy? Besides union with God and union with the world, isn't there a union with God through the world?"[89] Teilhard recognized that for many educated people of his time—and, indeed, of our own time—Christianity seems too small, too insular, disconnected from contemporary, especially scientific experience. "The ecclesiastical directives and the preoccupations of the faithful are slowly sealing the Church in an artificial world of rituals, of routines, of pious practices, a world completely separated from the mainstream of life."[90] The French Jesuit priest-scientist wanted to counter this disconnect.

Teilhard was born in 1881 near Clermont in central France, into a pious and devout French family, and his real passion as a young man was, like his father, natural history, collecting mineral and wildlife specimens. His secondary schooling took place at a Jesuit boarding school at Mongré, where one of his teachers was Henri Bremond, the friend of George Tyrrell. Bremond wrote of Teilhard: this "pupil from Auvergne, very intelligent, first in every subject, but disconcertingly sophisticated. Even the most restive or dull-witted boys sometimes took a real interest in their work. . . . Not so this boy and it was only long afterwards that I learned the secret of his seeming indifference. Transporting his mind far away from us was a jealous and absorbing passion—rocks."[91] In 1899 Teilhard entered the Jesuit novitiate. In 1901 the French Republic took up an anti-clerical policy in which the Jesuits were expelled from France along with many other religious orders. So, in 1902 the French Jesuits set up their house of studies on the English Channel Island of Jersey, where Teilhard studied science and philosophy for three years. After a spell from 1905–8 in Cairo teaching science and physics at the Jesuit College, he returned to England for his theological studies at Ore Place, Hastings, in East Sussex. It was at this time that he read Henri Bergson's *Creative Evolution* in which "he found, or thought he found, a rationale for his new feeling of union with the vegetable and animal world. . . . For him 'Matter' and 'Spirit' were becoming two faces of the same coin."[92] Reading Bergson helped to develop Teilhard's growing sense of the immanence of God in nature. He was ordained to the priesthood in 1911 by Bishop Peter Amigo (1864–1949) of Southwark. This was the same Bishop Amigo who, two years earlier, had suspended *a divinis* Abbé Henri Bremond, Teilhard's high school teacher, for attending the funeral and blessing the grave of his friend the modernist George Tyrrell.

---

89. Cited in Faricy, SJ, *Teilhard de Chardin's Theology of the Christian in the World*, 4.

90. Cited in Faricy, *Teilhard de Chardin's Theology of the Christian in the World*, 19.

91. Cited in Smulders, SJ, *The Design of Teilhard de Chardin*, 2.

92. Lukas and Lukas, *Teilhard, A Biography*, 33–34.

The years 1912–14 saw Teilhard undergoing further studies in science at the *Institut Catholique* and the Paris Museum of Natural History. With World War I Teilhard was called up and his regiment saw action at the Marne and at Ypres. His devoted friend Henri de Lubac, also drafted into the French Army in 1914, wrote of Teilhard's experience at the front: "At the front, in the shadow of death, far from the conventions of ordinary life, in the solitude of night-watches, or, during intervals of rest a little behind the lines, he thought, and prayed, and looking ahead into the future he made the offering of himself. The presence of God possessed him."[93] Those last words of de Lubac that "the presence of God possessed Teilhard," especially in tandem with his own profound eucharistic reflections, demonstrate Teilhard's growing mystical awareness.

For many years Teilhard worked in China and gained an international reputation as a paleontologist. The years of World War II were spent in China. Among the European exiles there at the time were naturally enough German and French, and given the conditions in Europe hostilities existed among them. "To the despair of certain friends, [Teilhard] always found something kind to say about the most unpleasant people. One day, after someone mentioned a thoroughly despicable local gunrunner, he mumbled something like, 'Oh, he has his good points, too.' To which Leroy replied exasperated, 'I honestly believe that if you met the devil in the street, you'd think of something nice to say.' 'Why not?' Teilhard said, shrugging."[94] During his first period of his paleological fieldwork in China, in 1923 through 1924, he wrote one of his earliest spiritual-mystical texts, *The Mass on the World*. He returned to France in 1924 to find that his teachings had drawn suspicions upon his orthodoxy. The reasons for the suspicions are twofold: first, "the zeal with which Teilhard preached evolutionism on every possible occasion"; second, his close friendship with the "modernist" philosopher, Edouard Le Roy.[95]

As a result of the growing controversy surrounding him and his thinking, Teilhard returned to fieldwork in China in 1925, and he was to remain there until the end of World War II. During this long extended period in China he composed two of his most famous works—during the winter of 1926–27 *The Divine Milieu*, a strongly experiential treatise on the spiritual life, and from 1938 to 1940 *The Phenomenon of Man*. Both of these important works fell foul of his Jesuit censors. Partly this had to do with his strongly evolutionist vision, the symbiosis of matter and spirit, but it also had to do with the emergence of the "new theology," being espoused by his friend Henri de Lubac. He returned to France in 1946 after the end of the war. His reputation needless to say had preceded him and he was extremely popular among French Catholic intellectuals so much so that someone once quipped, "If you want to fill an auditorium, all

93. Lubac, SJ, *Teilhard de Chardin, the Man and His Meaning*, 19. To explore further the impact of World War I on Teilhard see Mel Thompson, *Through Mud and Barbed Wire: Paul Tillich, Teilhard de Chardin and God after the First World War*.

94. Lukas and Lukas, *Teilhard, A Biography*, 165.

95. Smulders, *The Design of Teilhard de Chardin*, 4.

you have to do is advertise that you have Teilhard or Jean-Paul Sartre."[96] Although he was offered a professorial chair in the prestigious Collège de France, his Jesuit superiors refused him permission to accept the invitation, and he spent his remaining years largely in New York. In 1954, the year before he died he wrote to a friend: "Less and less do I see any difference now between research and adoration."[97] In a similar vein he wrote on Good Friday 1955 to a friend, "Evil is not 'catastrophic' (the fruit of some cosmic accident), but the inevitable side effect of the process of the cosmos unifying into God."[98] On March 15, 1955, Teilhard told some of his friends that he hoped he would die on Easter Sunday, the thirty-first anniversary of his *Mass on the World*. That in fact is what happened. He went to confession on Holy Saturday, and died of a heart attack on Easter Sunday. An American fellow Jesuit, John LaFarge, who had known Teilhard since 1948 wrote of him: "He was a man of unalloyed holiness, manly personal integrity and deep human sympathy, and of an astonishing degree of childlike conscientiousness and humility. . . . He kept the rules of the Society, not with ordinary correctness but with intense delicacy of childlike exactitude."[99]

A brief conspectus of some of his ideas will establish some of the reasons for his ever-growing popularity. Matter is all-important for Teilhard. "By means of all created things, without exception, the divine assails us, penetrates us, and moulds us."[100] This is no espousal of pantheism for Teilhard. It emerges, rather, from his profoundly Christocentric cosmology, two of his favorite New Testament passages being the prologue to St. John's Gospel and Colossians 1:15–20. In both of these passages creation comes to be through the Word, and in the Johannine passage the Word becomes flesh. Matter, then, for Teilhard is never just matter, but is Trinitarian and Christocentric. It is the Divine Milieu. One commentator writes that "Teilhard is not far from Aquinas's notion that God is in all things by power, presence, and essence (ST 1a.8 ad.3), or . . . from the Eastern Fathers with their sense of the cosmos as the theater of divine energy."[101] Evolution for Teilhard has a direction towards higher degrees of material complexity, higher degrees of organization, and towards higher degrees of consciousness. In other words, the universe is evolving towards greater spiritualization according to a law of what he called "complexity-consciousness." This is explicitly linked with Christian faith because as he understood it the universe is evolving towards a point/center that somehow is already present and that somehow is personal, and he identifies this personal center with Christ. Henri de Lubac describes his thoughts as

---

96. Smulders, *The Design of Teilhard de Chardin*, 4.

97. Lukas and Lukas, *Teilhard, A Biography*, 328.

98. Lukas and Lukas, *Teilhard, A Biography*, 342.

99. John LaFarge, cited in Smulders, *The Design of Teilhard de Chardin*, 10. LaFarge was one of the scholars invited by Pope Pius XI to write the encyclical, never actually published, condemning Nazism.

100. Teilhard de Chardin, *The Divine Milieu*, 112.

101. Williams, "The Traditionalist *malgré lui*: de Chardin and *Ressourcement*," 114.

follows: "The concrete Presence at the heart of the Universe, dominating it, animating it, and drawing it to him—the presence of a personal God—super-personal, i.e., ultra-personal—of a loving and provident God, of a God who can reveal himself, and has in fact revealed himself—of a God who is all Love—this was for Teilhard the supreme truth." At the same time, he was entirely opposed to the limitations of anthropomorphism: "To nine-tenths of those who see him from outside, the Christian God appears as a great landowner administering his estates."[102]

The Omega of reason, of Teilhard's physics of evolution and the Christ of revelation are one and the same reality. He grounds this way of thinking in the New Testament, especially in the cosmic-Christological affirmations of St. John and St. Paul. Thus, he combines the evolutionary concept of cosmogenesis with his Christian tradition so as to rethink cosmogenesis in terms of Christogenesis. In the wake of modernism and of all the suspicions attendant upon the "new theology," it is not especially surprising that Teilhard was constantly running into difficulties with his Jesuit superiors. Equally, they wanted him to desist from both publishing and teaching. According to Mary and Ellen Lukas, by June 1925 he was asked to sign a set of propositions including "a statement of belief in the literal truth of the book of Genesis—Adam, Eve, forbidden fruit, and all."[103]

One of his most influential and popular books written in 1927, "as prayerfully and uncontentiously as possible," was titled *The Divine Milieu*. The book was dedicated "to those who love the world" and espoused the notion that material reality was the necessary medium through which the human person reached God. The human spirit was not to be understood as an "insubstantial specter" but as the sum and essence of all the vitality and consistency of the body—as "Matter at its most incendiary stage."[104] This explicitly devotional book was to draw suspicion upon him yet again. In 1939, his Jesuit censors took him to task for "The Spiritual Phenomenon," the paper in which he challenged the Aristotelian distinction between spirit and matter. The paper implied that "germs of consciousness" necessarily existed in even the smallest particles of matter. This viewpoint was to make its way into the most systematic articulation of his vision, *The Phenomenon of Man*.

Under a cloud during his lifetime, he was constantly forbidden to publish many of those works that posthumously have been regarded as seminal. Just as Vatican II was getting underway in 1962 a *monitum*/warning was issued against his thought by the Holy Office, but this did little or nothing to delimit his immense and growing popularity. On the centenary of his birth in 1981, in a letter issued under the name of Pope John Paul II, the Vatican acknowledged him as "a man seized by Christ in the very depths of his being, and who struggled to honor at once faith and reason."[105]

102. Lubac, *Teilhard de Chardin*, 23–25.

103. Lukas and Lukas, *Teilhard, A Biography*, 93.

104. Lukas and Lukas, *Teilhard, A Biography*, 104.

105. Cited in Modras, *Ignatian Humanism*, 197.

Conclusion

The ferment of the new theology then did not disappear with Pope Pius XII's encyclical, *Humani Generis*. The works of the theologians mentioned in this chapter began to be published in other languages than their own, and most especially English, leading Anglican theologian John Macquarrie to affirm that "although there is naturally a family likeness among Catholic theologians, there is no dreary uniformity, and the magisterium of the church does not rule out a rich diversity of theological thought."[106] The English-speaking bishops at Vatican II constituted a very large cohort, taking into account not only the United Kingdom and the United States, but also Canada, large areas of Africa, Australia and New Zealand, India, etc. The advent of the new and richly diverse theology in English created a small vanguard of bishop-thinkers who may not all have been ready for the council, but for a number of whom important theological seeds were sown. In that sense, the final phase of the "new theology" was developing well before 1962.

Not only did the "new theology" become a major contribution to the renewal of Vatican II, but in more recent years since the council it has become a focus of interest also for Protestant theologians and so for ecumenism. Yves Congar did groundbreaking work in his 1937 book *Divided Christendom*, translated into English in 1939, one of the first serious Catholic attempts to engage with the twentieth-century ecumenical movement. Beyond such individual contributions, however, the "new theology" has itself become a factor in ecumenism. One of its premier advocates, Hans Boersma, writes as follows: "Protestant sensitivity towards the authority of Tradition is further evidence that a project of *ressourcement* may echo across ecclesial boundaries. A number of evangelical Christians have embarked on explicit attempts at evangelical *ressourcement* of the great Tradition, taking their cue directly from the Catholic movement of *nouvelle théologie*."[107] This was something that the leaders of the "new theology" could never have contemplated in their time. This kind of ecumenically rich exploration of the Christian tradition, allied to the multilateral and bilateral ecumenical conversations and agreements, opens up exciting new horizons for Christian unity.

---

106. Macquarrie, *Twentieth Century Religious Thought*, 298.

107. Boersma, *Nouvelle Théologie and Sacramental Ontology*, 14–15. Throughout his book Boersma is constantly alert to the ecumenical implications and consequences, especially for Protestantism, of the various theological themes that characterize the "new theology."

11

Pope John XXIII (1958–63)

Not only did Angelo Roncalli not choose or even actively seek the steps that de-
fined his journey to the papacy, he was not remarkably successful in most of
them, at least not in the judgment of most of his superiors. He went where he
was told and did what he was commanded. . . . Pope John had by the force of his
personality and by the charm of his manner demystified the papacy.

—Joseph Komonchak[1]

When Cardinal Roncalli was elected pope in 1958, there may have been general
relief that he did not take the name "Pius," but no one could have guessed what
were to be the effects of his five years' pontificate.

—Alec R. Vidler[2]

Angelo Roncalli: From Peasant Priest to Papal Diplomat

Angelo Giuseppe Roncalli was born on November 25, 1881, in the village of Sotto
il Monte, near Bergamo, N. Italy. John Henry Newman was still alive in England and
would remain so until 1890. As Roncalli was to become, "Newman was a prophet with
a mission to the Church in the modern age; he was one of the first to perceive history
as a process of development and apply this to Christianity."[3] Roncalli was born just
four years into the pontificate of Leo XIII, and some see in that pope the pivotal precursor to John XXIII. He was still pope when the young twenty-one year-old Angelo
Roncalli was in the major seminary preparing for priesthood. It is probably true to say
that Leo's "moderation and sense of sympathy succeeded in softening the militancy

---

1. Komonchak, "Remembering Good Pope John," 11.
2. Vidler, *The Church in an Age of Revolution*, 270.
3. Trevor, *Pope John*, 84.

of modern Catholicism, and gave hope to liberal Catholics everywhere, particularly those engaged in ministries of social regeneration."[4]

Roncalli's initial seminary studies took place locally in the Bergamo seminary, but since he showed some scholarly promise in 1901 he went on to complete his studies in Rome. He had kept a diary from his teen years, and, during the seminary period, one priest-historian provides this description of his diary entries: "[They] contain many self-reproofs about his tendencies to gossip, to overeat, to pride, and ambition (in a celibate priesthood the clerical form of lust)."[5] In many ways, these reproofs are typical for a young man in the ecclesiastical context of a seminary at the time. His seminary spiritual regime would, of course, have involved daily Mass, but the reception of Holy Communion would have been only once a week, due to the residual influence of Jansenism. Undoubtedly, his studies also created something of a gap between himself and the rest of his large family in Bergamo. He was being educated far beyond the rest of the family circle, and this ineluctably creates its own challenges.

Among his fellow students in Rome was Ernesto Buonaiuti (1881–1946). Buonaiuti was probably the most prominent Italian condemned and excommunicated for modernism.[6] Since personal friendships were discouraged in seminary formation, students going out for a walk were assigned a companion, and so Roncalli and Buonaiuti often walked together around Rome. Buonaiuti was ordained one year before Roncalli, and was Roncalli's assistant at his own ordination. There must have been a strong bond between them. A brilliant young scholar, Buonaiuti was dismissed from his teaching post in 1915 for holding modernist views, and eventually in 1926 he was excommunicated. As Pope John XXIII, Roncalli found in his own file at the Holy Office a postcard addressed to him by his friend Buonaiuti.

Curiously, among Roncalli's professors was church historian Umberto Benigni, who was to become the mastermind behind the anti-modernist spy campaign under Pope Pius X. "He contributed to Angelo's choice of history as his special field."[7] Benigni wrote in 1907 a *Social History of the Church*. Another of his professors was Don Eugenio Pacelli, the future Pius XII, who taught canon law. Roncalli loved his studies. In 1903 the young seminarian was to write in his journal: "Tomorrow the lectures begin again: I feel a need and a passionate desire to study, . . . I feel a restless longing to know everything, to study all the great authors, to familiarize myself with the scientific movement in all it manifestations."[8] This is experientially what the Canadian Jesuit Bernard Lonergan would call "the unrestricted desire to understand." This unrestricted desire won for the young seminarian a prize for Hebrew. His passion for study shows

4. Cahill, *Pope John XXIII, A Life*, 73–79.

5. Hughes, *Pontiffs: Popes Who Shaped History*, 227.

6. For a helpful recent account of Ernesto Buonaiuti, see Giacomo Losito, "Ernesto Buonaiuti and *Il programa dei modernisti*," 71–96.

7. Hebblethwaite, *John XXIII, Pope of the Century*, 18.

8. Pope John XXIII, *Journal of a Soul*, 110–11.

him breaking out of the narrow confines of the traditional seminary curriculum of the time, and moving into a richer and broader way of thinking. His ordination retreat took place at the house of the Passionist Fathers in Rome, Sts. John and Paul. He seems to have had an affection for this eighteenth-century religious community founded by Paul Daneo, later St. Paul of the Cross. During the retreat, he practiced saying Mass in the room where St. Paul of the Cross died. From time to time he made his retreat with the Passionists, even in a Passionist house in Bulgaria.[9] After his retreat, Roncalli was ordained on August 10, 1904. The Roncalli family did not attend, unable to afford the travel expenses. He said his first Mass at one of the altars in the crypt above St. Peter's tomb the following day, close to where he would one day be buried. On that same day he received a personal blessing from Pope Pius X.

For nine years he was secretary to the bishop of Bergamo, Giacomo Radini-Tedeschi, a progressive bishop who was wholly committed to the cause of "Catholic Action" and social justice in the organization known as *Opera dei Congressi*. This was the only church body able to interact with the Italian government on national moral and political issues, given the unreconciled relationship between the Vatican and Italy at the time. *Opera dei Congressi* was judged "irreverent and unacceptable" by Cardinal Merry del Val in 1903, the new secretary of state under the new pope, Pius X, and Pius X dissolved the organization. In the wake of its dissolution Radini-Tedeschi was appointed bishop of Bergamo in 1904.[10]

While Roncalli was the episcopal secretary, during this time he also taught apologetics, church history and patristics in the Bergamo seminary. New ways of studying history were emerging on the scene, typified by the work of the great Monsignor Louis Duchesne.[11] Professor Roncalli was using Duchesne's *History of the Early Church* for his lectures. Historical consciousness was making its impact felt in the field of theology, and this appealed to the young Roncalli. As one author puts it, "Angelo belongs instinctively to this camp, though to its most considered and Catholic branch. Never willing to throw out the baby with the bathwater, he prefers to save whatever he can from the past, especially . . . from those historic churchmen whom he takes as his models and whom he can admire for their intellectual and affective amplitude."[12]

Nevertheless, Roncalli's use of Duchesne made him suspect in the new anti-modernist regime. Duchesne's three-volume history of the early church was placed on the *Index of Forbidden Books* in 1912. In December 1907, the year in which Pope Pius X condemned modernism, Roncalli gave a lecture at the seminary entitled "Faith and Scientific Research." The lecture was to commemorate the third centenary of the death of Cardinal Cesare Baronius (1538–1607), the Oratorian and church historian. He spoke of Baronius as the founder of historical criticism. Undoubtedly because of his

---

9. Trevor, *Pope John*, 62, 147.

10. Elliott, *I Will Be Called John*, 46–48.

11. See the admirable account of Louis Duchesne in Frend, *From Dogma to History*, 100–143.

12. Cahill, *Pope John XXIII, A Life*, 88.

interest in church history, and the liberating perspectives that follow from such study, Roncalli was unjustly accused of modernism. He was relatively open to new ideas, new movements of thought that might serve the mission of the church. Not long before his ordination he had written these words in his journal:

> I do not despise criticism, and I shall be most careful not to think badly of critics or treat them with disrespect. On the contrary, I shall love it. I shall study new systems of thought, their continual evolution, and their trends; criticism for me is light, is truth, and there is only one truth (i.e., the supreme truth of Christ cannot ultimately be in conflict with other truths). But I shall always try to introduce into these discussions, in which too often ill-considered enthusiasms and deceptive appearances have a part to play, a great moderation, harmony, balance, and serenity of judgment, allied to a prudent and cautious broadmindedness.[13]

Quite a liberating and yet balanced perspective for a young churchman at that time!

One striking instance of his openness lies in a visit he undertook in June 1908. From June 1–3, Roncalli spent time with Bishop Geremia Bonomelli of Cremona. In 1908 Bonomelli wrote, as already noted in chapter 2 above: "Perhaps a great ecumenical council, which would discuss rapidly, freely and publicly the great problems of religious life, would draw the attention of the world to the church, stimulate faith, and open up new ways for the future." Peter Hebblethwaite comments: "Almost exactly fifty years later, Roncalli took up Bonomelli's idea in almost identical terms."[14] In 1911 Roncalli published an article in the diocesan newspaper in which he criticized a series of lectures that had been given at the seminary by an extreme anti-modernist, lectures that were abusive and violent in tone. Roncalli deplored the tone and commented: "If the truth and the whole truth had to be told, I do not see why it had to be accompanied by the thunders and lightnings of Sinai rather than the calm and serenity of Jesus on the lake and on the mount."[15] His association with Buonaiuti and Bonomelli and the publication of this article probably had the effect of his delation to the Holy Office as a suspected modernist. As Pope John XXIII in 1958 he asked to see his file at the Holy Office. It had been marked "Suspected of Modernism." John wrote on the file: "I was never a Modernist." He was preeminently a churchman, never undermining the church's mission or message, but he was far from closed to the exciting and new ideas that were in the air. He saw fear behind the anti-modernist witch-hunt and he was not a man of fear. His appreciation of church history demonstrated for him time and again that history is the teacher of life, and a truly informed historical perspective diminishes if not banishes fearfulness.

---

13. Cited in Cahill, *Pope John XXIII, A Life*, 96.

14. Hebblethwaite, *John XXIII*, 33.

15. Johnson, *Pope John XXIII*, 37.

Roncalli served as a chaplain in the Italian army during World War I. When the war was over, he was appointed the spiritual director in the Bergamo seminary. Effectively this meant an end to any concern about his alleged modernism. Roncalli also began about this time his chief scholarly work in the field of church history, a multi-volumed study of St. Charles Borromeo. Decades later, he would choose for his papal coronation the feast day of St. Charles. Borromeo, the premier diocesan bishop of the Tridentine reform. "This [multi-volume] work meant that Roncalli saw the Council of Trent not as an anti-Protestant polemic, but as a reforming council in a world he knew well."[16] Interestingly, Achille Ratti, the librarian of the Ambrosian Library in Milan and the future Pope Pius XI, secured some photocopied documents on Borromeo for Roncalli, but they had no close relationship. This work on Borromeo was to be a lifetime's project. The fifth and final volume was completed in 1958, the year in which Roncalli was elected to the papacy and some fifty years after the project had been begun. Meriol Trevor makes an interesting comment both about Roncalli and about church historians: "Roncalli always modestly disclaimed the title of scholar, but had he remained all his life teaching in the Bergamo seminary this is the sort of scholarly historical work he would have done, and earned for himself an honorable position in that useful but unspectacular field." Church history may be an unspectacular field, but it is indeed useful. In 1962 as he opened the second Vatican Council Roncalli was to say, "History is the teacher of life."[17]

Called to Rome and Sent to the East

In 1921 Roncalli was called to Rome to work for the missions in the curia department of *Propaganda Fide*. This had been expanded as a result of Pope Benedict XV's 1919 encyclical on the missions, *Maximum Illud*. Peter Hebblethwaite amusingly describes Roncalli at this time as "the itinerant pedlar of the importance of the missions."[18] He was a most successful pedlar. He more than doubled the money collected for *Propaganda*, from 400,000 lire in 1920 to over a million in 1922. In 1924 he was also appointed Professor of Patrology at the Lateran College, a part-time appointment. The Pontifical Lateran Athenaeum was the upgraded version of his old Roman seminary, and is now the Lateran University. The appointment was brought to an end after only

16. Hebblethwaite, *John XXIII*, 30.

17. Trevor, *Pope John*, 101. Church historian, John W. O'Malley, *A History of the Popes*, 293–94 writes: "[Roncalli] continued to work on this scholarly edition [of St. Charles Borromeo's pastoral visit to the diocese of Bergamo in 1575] in his spare time for the next twenty-two years, until the final volume was published the year before he became pope. Roncalli was, therefore, a scholar in his own right, a fact often overlooked in assessments of him. . . . It is plausible that Roncalli's fascination with Borromeo, who saw the bishop as the primary interpreter and implementer of the Council of Trent and who therefore convoked a number of diocesan and provincial councils to do so, played a role in John's 'inspiration' to call a council. At any rate, John had through his almost lifelong study of Borromeo a perspective on the history of the church that was not explicitly Rome-centric."

18. Hebblethwaite, *John XXIII*, 49.

one term. Dom Lambert Beauduin, to whom we shall turn momentarily, has stated that Roncalli's lectures were suspected of modernist tendencies. Perhaps. But his ordination as a bishop and his inclusion, however lowly in the papal diplomatic corps, suggests that the real reason lies elsewhere.

Quite suddenly, however, in 1925 he was ordained an archbishop, and dispatched to Bulgaria as apostolic visitor. Historians speculate about the strangeness of this move, given the fact that Roncalli had not spent time in the Roman nursery for papal diplomats. One reason that seems credible is his support of the *Partito Populare*, the PPI. Along with other democratic-liberal groups, the Popular Party faced the growing power of the Fascists, and seldom with the support of the highest authorities in the church.[19] Roncalli was a fervent supporter of the PPI, as were many young Italian priests including Giovanni Battista Montini (later Pope Paul VI), and his move to Bulgaria may have been motivated in part by a Vatican desire to remove him from the scene, especially as the groundwork was being prepared for the concordat with Mussolini.

As Roncalli attempted to equip himself for the Bulgarian posting, he came into contact with the great Belgian ecumenist, Dom Lambert Beauduin, OSB, who was to be a significant influence for him.[20] Beauduin had entered the Benedictines at Mont-César, Louvain, in 1906. Responding to Pius XI's call to the Benedictines to interest themselves in the Christian East, Beauduin founded in 1925 at Amay, later moved to Chevetogne, a monastery for both Western and Eastern monks. This Benedictine ecumenist had also attended Cardinal Mercier during the Malines Conversations, and was responsible for the famous sound-bite with regard to the Anglican Communion, "united to Rome, not absorbed." The Beauduin connection contributed to Roncalli's growing appreciation for the cause of Christian unity. A basic friendliness in Christ was his primary orientation to ecumenism. Dialogue with other Christians was impossible from a starting-point of condemnations.[21] During the years 1922–24, Beauduin was also shaping another enthusiastic ecumenist and later friend of Roncalli, Léon-Joseph Suenens, who was a seminarian in Rome at the time. This is Suenens's memory of those years: "After Sunday vespers, at St. Anselm on the Aventine, [Dom Lambert Beauduin] . . . would often speak to me, with contagious enthusiasm, about the Greek fathers, about Trinitarian theology, and about the Holy Spirit. I was a young seminarian and I drank in his words eagerly."[22] Vatican II was under way!

Roncalli's mission—diplomatic, ecumenical and pastoral—was very successful. He was known among the 62,000 Catholic Bulgarians as *Diado*, "the good father." "He brought concern to a forgotten people."[23] He visited Catholics throughout the

19. Bokenkotter, *The Church and Revolution*, 286, my emphasis.

20. Hebblethwaite, *John XXIII*, 57.

21. Hebblethwaite, *John XXIII*, 60.

22. Suenens, *Memories and Hopes*, 28.

23. Suenens, *Memories and Hopes*, 59.

entirety of the country, despite extremely difficult traveling conditions. He found himself also embroiled in a controversy. In 1930, King Boris of Bulgaria of the Orthodox faith was to marry Princess Giovanna of Italy, a Roman Catholic. The marriage was encouraged by Mussolini, hoping thereby to expand his influence in the Balkans. Roncalli as the Vatican representative had to inform the King that the marriage should be in accordance with Roman canon law, thus involving a canonical dispensation. This was no easy feat for Roncalli. So, the wedding took place in Assisi in October of that year. When the newly-weds returned to Bulgaria, Boris insisted on an Orthodox ceremony in the Cathedral of St. Alexander Nevsky in Sofia. Roncalli was publicly in a difficult position. He was summoned to Rome, went at once to the papal apartments, and found himself on his knees angrily rebuked by a furious Pius XI.[24] When a daughter was born to the couple in January 1933, despite Boris's acceptance of the Roman position, the child was baptized as Orthodox. This too created problems for Roncalli. It is difficult to see what more he could have done, and, indeed, it is just as difficult to see what else King Boris could have done, given the political and ecclesiastical situation of the time. It says much for Roncalli's pastoral care and concern that he remained on friendly terms with the King and Queen, and continued to minister to her as occasion demanded.

Roncalli was constantly in financially straitened circumstances during his Bulgarian mission. He continued to lend his support to the expanding Roncalli family back home, as well as to deal with his own responsibilities as the papal representative. During his Bulgarian years he met an American priest working at the Vatican, Francis Spellman, and Spellman arranged to have regular Mass stipends sent to Roncalli from the United States to ease his situation.[25] His concern and love for the Bulgarians emerged with real beauty in his Christmas homily in Sofia before he left: "Wherever I may go, if a Bulgarian passes my door, whether it's night-time or whether he's poor, he will find that candle lighted at my window. Knock, knock. You won't be asked whether you're a Catholic or not; the title of Bulgarian brother is enough. Come in. Two fraternal arms will welcome you, and the warm heart of a friend will make it a feast-day."[26]

In 1934 he was sent as apostolic delegate to Turkey and Greece. This was a very difficult appointment for Roncalli, but the episcopal motto he had chosen was "Obedience and peace," and "Your will, our peace." Speaking of these sayings, Roncalli was later to say: "This is the mystery of my life; don't look for other explanations." It was a profound sense of divine providence guiding every human life, and most especially his own. It gave him real serenity, even in the midst of great difficulty and challenge. Living in Turkey, the modern name for Asia Minor, also gave Roncalli a sense of Christian origins that appealed to his historian's instincts, as well as an increasing knowledge of the Oriental tradition. In Peter Hebblethwaite's words, "He was delivered from the

24. Elliott, *I Will Be Called John*, 110–11.

25. Elliott, *I Will Be Called John*, 119.

26. Cited in Hebblethwaite, *John XXIII*, 68–69

narrowness of Roman theology."[27] It is a very fair comment. His travels in Greece and Turkey took him, as one might expect from a church historian, to many ancient Christian sites. Meriol Trevor says that, "Few popes can have visited the sites of so many councils as Pope John."[28] Nicaea, Ephesus, Constantinople, Chalcedon—all of these places fell under his pastoral jurisdiction in so far as they contained Roman Catholics. Did these visits contribute to a growing conciliar awareness? Perhaps.

Roncalli's deliverance from theological insularity, however, was not just towards the Oriental tradition. He began to learn something of the Anglican Communion also. One of his first visitors in Istanbul was the Reverend Austin Oakley, chaplain to the British Embassy and the archbishop of Canterbury's personal representative to the patriarch of Constantinople. Through Oakley he came to develop an appreciation of Anglicanism, as Meriol Trevor writes: "Roncalli soon returned his visit and they became friends. Austin Oakley was the first Anglican Roncalli came to know well." Roncalli and Oakley prayed together, and visited one another's chapels, a rather rare experience between a papal delegate and an Anglican priest at this time.[29] Oakley visited Roncalli later in 1961 as Pope John XXIII, and was received with great personal warmth so much so that some Vatican officials asked Oakley, "You're not an archbishop are you?"

His years in Turkey saw the rise of Nazism and the beginning of World War II. He helped Jewish refugees en route to the Holy Land in Istanbul in September 1940, providing them with clothes, money and documents. He was in contact with Isaac Herzog, grand rabbi of Jerusalem, over the liberation of some 55,000 Jews stranded in Rumania, after Soviet seizure of that country. With the apparent connivance of Franz von Papen, Berlin's man in Istanbul, Roncalli was able to save the lives of some 24, 000 Jews. He later testified at the Nuremberg trials on von Papen's behalf, and von Papen offered the same testimony on Roncalli's behalf to the postulator of his beatification.[30]

Sent to France and Called to Venice

The years 1944–53 saw Roncalli promoted as nuncio to the France of General Charles de Gaulle. This was a somewhat unusual posting from the relatively obscure responsibilities in Bulgaria, Turkey, and Greece. The move invites speculation. A fair number of French bishops had felt it their duty to obey the *de facto* government of Marshall Petain, the Nazi-cooperating Vichy government. The new de Gaulle government after the liberation of France wanted Msgr. Valerio Valeri, Pius XII's representative to the Vichy government and some thirty-three bishops removed. It was a very difficult time in France. Some priests who had been judged cooperators with the Vichy regime had been

---

27. Hebblethwaite, *John XXIII*, 85.
28. Trevor, *Pope John*, 171.
29. Trevor, *Pope John*, 171.
30. Cahill, *Pope John XXIII, A Life*, 135–37.

shot. Some historians suggest that "by moving a little-regarded diplomat from one of the lowest posts in the Vatican service to one of its most important, Pius XII had found the best way to express his irritation with de Gaulle."[31] En route to Paris through Rome, Roncalli met the ousted Valeri who gave him the speech he would need to deliver as the senior diplomat in France in the New Year's Day, 1945. It had long been the tradition in France that the papal representative was understood to be the dean of the diplomatic corps, and that he would deliver the expected New Year's greeting to the president of France. Roncalli had no time to prepare such a greeting, and he never forgot this kindness on Valeri's part, and when both were cardinals at the 1958 conclave, Roncalli's vote went to Valeri. In the end, as a result of Roncalli's diplomacy, only seven bishops had to be removed. One historian notes: "Roncalli asked one of the ousted bishops, an auxiliary of Paris, to be his confessor—a typical gesture of kindness."[32] That was the manner of the man. He endeared himself to the French by his sheer ordinariness and sense of fair-play. One of his pastimes was visiting Parisian bookshops, a pastime not approved of by Pope Pius XII. Pius did not think his personal representative should walk informally around Paris.[33] In Paris Roncalli kept up his affection for the Passionist Fathers. They had responsibility for the English-speaking church in Paris, St. Joseph's on the Avenue Hoche. Roncalli was an occasional visitor.

One of Roncalli's earliest projects in France was his personal support for a seminary for German prisoners-of-war near Chartres. The rector of the seminary was a German priest, Franz Stock, who had been ministering to German-speaking Catholics in France since 1934. This makeshift seminary had 947 seminarians, of whom it is estimated 600 were ordained to the priesthood.[34] Roncalli did all he could to help. He eased Vatican recognition of the seminary and ordained two of its candidates as priests in the prison chapel at Easter 1947.

The Worker-Priest Movement began in France during Roncalli's time. It began in the outskirts of Paris in 1946 when some six priests went to work in factories and to live with ordinary people. Their objective was clear: to bring the living witness of the joy of the gospel into people's lives. It was a form of what might be called "incarnational ministry." The priests did not work out of territorial parishes, and were immediately responsible to the archbishop of Paris, Cardinal Suhard, one of whose major concerns was the evangelization of the alienated working-class. The movement spread to other places including Lyons, Limoges, Nice and Le Havre so that by 1949 about fifty priests were involved. Roncalli watched with interest. From the beginning, however, the movement was beset with problems. It received excessive publicity, and the consequent attention perceived it as an oddity rather than as a legitimate expression of the church in mission. Some of the priests joined workers' unions that were Communist-dominated. Their

31. Komonchak, "Remembering Good Pope John," 13.
32. Hughes, *Pontiffs: Popes Who Shaped History*, 247.
33. Trevor, *Pope John*, 207.
34. Hughes, *Pontiffs: Popes Who Shaped History*, 248.

superior educational background compared to their fellow workers was such that they were asked to serve in positions of leadership in the unions. This made them especially vulnerable to the charge of compliance with Marxism, particularly by politically and religiously conservative elements in France. The movement was viewed with considerable suspicion in Rome, especially when some priests left to get married. The upshot was its condemnation and the movement came to a bitter end in 1953. While some blame Roncalli for not giving it greater support, the evidence suggests that his advice to the Vatican was to let the movement alone for the time being so that it might either show itself to be a successful form of mission and evangelization or not. By the time the fallout came he had been transferred to Venice.

During his time in France, Roncalli interested himself in the work of Simone Weil (1909–43), the Jewish-Christian writer and mystic. Weil was not particularly well known at the time. In 1952 Roncalli wrote to her father, Dr. Bernard Weil, with a view to visiting her room, noted for its austerity, having a sleeping bag but no bed. He cherished the text from Weil: "I believe in God, the Trinity, the Incarnation, the Redemption, the Eucharist and the Gospel" but then explains why she must remain "on the threshold of the church." As Pope John he gave a copy of this text to Cardinal Augustin Bea in 1962.[35]

In 1950 one of Roncalli's visitors at the nunciature in Paris was the German theologian Romano Guardini. They had a three-hour conversation that made a deep impression on Guardini, who reported to a priest friend that Roncalli had a cultured mind and was full of "a goodness and human warmth of such a quality rare enough in our world."[36] During his tenure in Paris there was much discussion of the theology of Pierre Teilhard de Chardin, SJ. Teilhard was not allowed to publish, but many of his works were being circulated through private copies. It seems that Roncalli, although probably quite distant personally from Teilhard's theology, made himself informed and aware of it.

In 1953 Roncalli accepted the papal invitation to return home to Italy as cardinal and patriarch of Venice. In Venice he was most fortunate in finding a non-Roman trained priest as his secretary, Loris Capovilla. Capovilla was to become much more than a secretary to him: "A spiritual son, a literary executor, a *confidant* and a Boswell."[37] Every two years in Venice there took place a great exhibition of modern art known as the Biennale. Since the patriarchate of Cardinal Sarto, later to become Pope Pius X, this exhibition had been judged by the church as unacceptable and the clergy had been forbidden to visit it. This was not in the Roncalli style. He was interested in art, knew a fair amount about it, and so he not only lifted the ban on clergy attendance but he also hosted a reception for the artists at his residence.[38]

---

35. Hebblethwaite, *John XXIII*, 57.
36. Trevor, *Pope John*, 218.
37. Hebblethwaite, *John XXIII*, 117.
38. Cahill, *Pope John XXIII, A Life*, 162.

In 1956 the patriarch of Venice found himself back in Paris for an ecumenical conference honoring the Eastern churches. In 1957 he was in Sicily giving a talk during the annual week of prayer and study run by the Association for the Christian East. Ecumenical interests generated during his time in Bulgaria, Turkey, and Greece continued to develop. In the course of his talk in Sicily he asked the question, "Does the whole responsibility [for the eleventh-century schism] really lie with our separated brethren?"[39] Within a few short years this ecumenical sentiment would flourish into the perspectives of Vatican II's Decree on Ecumenism.

The new patriarch of Venice loved being back in his own neck of the woods, but it was not to be for long. Pope Pius XII died in 1958, and Angelo Roncalli was elected at seventy-seven as a caretaker pope. Pius XII had not created any new cardinals for some time, and it had been a long pontificate. The cardinals needed time to get to know one another, and it seemed to them that Roncalli would provide them with the time, not too much time, as the new pope. While the cardinals were reaching a compromise, as it were, over Roncalli, it seems that the French Oratorian and professor at the *Institut Catholique*, Louis Bouyer, was already thinking of him as *papabile*. Louis Bouyer's best known doctoral student, Hans Küng, reminisces in this fashion: "I am one of the few who aren't completely surprised by this choice [of Roncalli]. *A long time previously* my doctoral supervisor Louis Bouyer had predicted to me on a visit to our family in Sursee that the next pope would be Roncalli. Why? Because he was 'jovial, pious and not all that intelligent.'"[40] Obviously, as the nuncio in France Bouyer would have known of Roncalli, but perhaps did not know him all that well!

In all likelihood the most obvious and in many ways the most capable candidate was the archbishop of Milan, Giovanni Battista Montini, but he was not yet a cardinal. And so, Roncalli was elected, took the name of John XXIII, and fixed the date of his coronation as November 4, the feast of St. Charles Borromeo. On that occasion, "He would have the full ceremonial, complete with the Franciscans burning smoking flax to remind him of mortality, . . . the fans of ostrich plumes, the *sedia gestatoria* or portable chair, and the tiara. . . . He enjoyed pomp."[41] But why the name John? Why not Pius, as probably many expected? The name was a little problematic because Pope John XXIII had been the anti-pope associated with the reforming Council of Constance in 1414. Roncalli in choosing the name John appears to have settled this problematic issue. He wrote at the time:

> The name John is dear to me because it is the name of my father. It is dear because it is the title of the humble parish church where we received baptism. It is the solemn name of innumerable cathedrals throughout the world, and first of all the blessed and holy Lateran Basilica, our Cathedral. It is the name which, in the long series of Roman Pontiffs, has been most used. Indeed there

39. Trevor, *Pope John*, 235.
40. Küng, *My Struggle for Freedom, Memoirs*, 171.
41. Hebblethwaite, *John XXIII*, 149.

have been twenty-two unquestionably legitimate supreme pontiffs named John. Nearly all had a brief pontificate.[42]

Prescient words.

The Johannine Style

Historian Paul Johnson has a fine phrase that captures the Johannine style of papacy. "Almost from his first day in office, he broke through this *carapace of anonymity*, and emerged as a vivid human being."[43] Vivid human beings are seldom entirely consistent and conventional. Pope John liked to smoke cigarettes. He enjoyed the pomp and circumstance that attends papal ceremonial, but his papal style was to stand in real contrast with that of Pope Pius XII. John did not like the traditional white skullcap for the very practical reason that it kept slipping from his bald pate. So, he reintroduced the red and ermine cap of Renaissance popes. Ceremonial was still very traditional, but not his personal style. This is how one recent commentator describes the Johannine style: "Roncalli found gentleness and humility—and patience—too often lacking in churchmen. 'A caress is better than a sting,' he once wrote; he preferred the style of St. Francis de Sales to that of St. Jerome."[44] Or, as the cardinal-archbishop of Westminster, John Carmel Heenan, put it in a letter of July 1964 to his archdiocese after John's death: "His great achievement was to teach the world of the twentieth century how small is hatred and how great is love." It is in this context of the greatness of love that his restoring and placing of the third century statue of Hippolytus of Rome should be understood. As noted earlier in the book, Hippolytus was implacably opposed to the bishop of Rome, the former slave Callistus, and set himself up as the first anti-pope. By placing the statue in a prominent place, the entrance to the Vatican Library, perhaps John was saying not only that history is the best of teachers but also that love wins out. Hippolytus was amicably reconciled to the church before his death.

The Johannine style created something of both a security and a financial nightmare. On the security front, John left the Vatican to visit his Roman flock in hospitals and prisons. This was a first. Often he would get out of his car, walk the streets and just talk to people. On the same level he would develop his approach to Communists. While he disapproved of Marxism, he welcomed Communists as brothers and sisters. Khrushchev's Russia had in the newspaper *Pravda* described Pius XII as "the Pope of the Atlantic Alliance," but it was much more positive about John XXIII. He had been visited in the Vatican by Nikita Khrushchev's daughter and son-in-law. On the financial front, in 1959 John raised Vatican salaries by about 50 percent. However, he had not consulted anyone, and, while the raise was by any

---

42. Cited in Trevor, *Pope John*, 248.
43. Johnson, *Pope John XXIII*, 117.
44. Komonchak, "Remebering Good Pope John," 14.

standards very overdue, it left the financial department of the Vatican in a bind as to how to provide the extra money.

"In a period of less than five years he almost single-handedly transformed the Catholic Church from a clericalistic, monarchical, unecumenical, and theologically rigid body to a community of radical equality in Christ—laity, religious and clergy alike—open to dialogue and collaboration with other Christian and non-Christian communities, with nonbelievers, and with the world at large"—the words of Richard McBrien.[45] A mere three months after his election the caretaker pope announced the calling of a general council of the church. This was to be a pastoral council to open up the church, not to barricade it in. For John "there were to be no condemnations or excommunications."[46] The proposal met with curial resistance. To be fair, John had no detailed blueprint for what he wanted the council to achieve. Nonetheless, as Eamon Duffy writes: "The Council he had called, with no very clear notion of what it might do, proved to be the most revolutionary Christian event since the Reformation."[47] But more about that when we come to Vatican II.

Central to this general council of the church was an ecumenical openness. We have seen this growing for Archbishop Roncalli over the years, and now it was to bear ecclesial fruit. Thus, Giuseppe Alberigo, the Bologna church historian, notes in his brief history of Vatican II: "Since his mission in Bulgaria, which began in 1925, Roncalli's contact with the ecumenical movement had never diminished, and it had fostered such an internalization and mastery of the issue of Christian unity that this became one of the essential and characteristic elements of the 'dowry' that he brought to the office of the papacy."[48] On December 2 1960, Pope John received Dr. Geoffrey Fisher, the archbishop of Canterbury at the Vatican. This was the first time an Anglican archbishop of a Canterbury and a pope had met since the Reformation. John had some sense of Anglican theology and Anglican ways, stemming back to the influence of Dom Lambert Beauduin and his Istanbul friendship with Austin Oakley. They were the conduits of ecumenical openness and grace for him. This is well expressed by Peter Hebblethwaite: "He thought theological dialogue alone was insufficient. He needed this personal contact with Church leaders to begin to understand the historical context in which they had emerged and their present positions. History held the key to understanding. From his previous experience, Pope John knew a great deal about the Orthodox Churches; but now he was learning fast about Canterbury, Geneva, Moscow, Cairo, and so many other places."[49]

John would never see the council's Decree on Ecumenism, but in a very real way, he anticipated the substance of that decree experientially. He anticipated

45. McBrien, *Lives of the Popes*, 367.

46. Duffy, *Saints and Sinners*, 358.

47. Duffy, *Saints and Sinners*, 360.

48. Alberigo, *A Brief History of Vatican II*, 23.

49. Hebblethwaite, *John XXIII*, 211.

experientially also Vatican II's Declaration on the Relationship of the Church to Non-Christian Religions. On his first Good Friday as Pope in 1959, Pope John went to the Church of the Holy Cross (Santa Croce) to celebrate the liturgy. In the general intercessions he took out from the prayer for the Jews the adjective *perfidies/faithless*. Later in 1959 he redrafted a text published by Pope Leo XIII, an act of consecration of humankind to the Sacred Heart of Jesus. The redrafted text omitted references that were offensive to Jews and Muslims.

Pope John XXIII died on June 3, 1963. He was anointed by Bishop Peter Canisius van Lierde, OSA, the papal sacristan on his five senses. The bishop was very attached to John, and, "overcome by emotion, he forgets the right order. John helped him out."[50] Typically non-materialistic throughout his long life, at his death Angelo Roncalli left his family about ten thousand lire, roughly ten dollars apiece.

Pope John XXIII's Encyclicals

"What we may call the admonitory tone of Pius XII has been the characteristic note struck by the papal encyclicals in the modern age.... What place have the encyclicals of John XXIII in this tradition? Clearly they do not belong to it. The note of alarm and admonition is scarcely audible."[51] His encyclicals radiate a fundamental joy, hope and confidence, and a definite openness to the world. He is not so much the world's schoolmaster as a loving parent, oozing common sense and wisdom, inviting to collaboration for the benefit of all.

Just a word or two from solid commentators to get a flavor of his approach. First, *Mater et Magistra*.

> With *Mater et Magistra* we are, in fact, brought right into the world of the Welfare State. Gone is not only the semi-feudal world in which Leo saw the simple workman, surrounded by his family, settling down to his frugal but sufficient meal, the just reward of his labor. But gone too is the world of Pius XII, who referred, with evident alarm, to communal kitchens, free health services, and free education. Now it is not only free education that is being claimed; it is further education for all those suited by their ability to benefit from it. The pope is not merely accepting, he is embracing what many would call socialism, and he is acknowledging that a new concept of the duties of the State is involved.[52]

In *Pacem in Terris* John asserts that every person has the right "to worship God in accordance with the right dictates of his own conscience, and to profess his religion both in private and in public." This is new.

---

50. Hebblethwaite, *John XXIII*, 257.
51. Hales, *Pope John and His Revolution*, 36–37.
52. Hales, *Pope John and His Revolution*, 45.

What Roncalli said about religious liberty probably did more than anything else to persuade mankind that he had the well-being of the whole world at heart, as well as the flock that acknowledged him as its shepherd. And the same impression was strengthened by his pragmatism. He was seldom doctrinaire either about communism or about anybody else. He never pretended that he regarded Communist philosophy as other than false; but he did not see why this should prevent Catholics and Communists from collaborating fruitfully where they had the same objectives.[53]

Vatican II

The first official notice of the ecumenical council came in *Osservatore Romano* for January 26–27 1959. To meet the errors of the time and its excessive materialism, the pope proposed to take three steps: to hold a diocesan synod of the clergy of Rome; to summon an ecumenical council of the universal church; to bring the code of canon law up to date. In a further paragraph, the coming council's purpose was briefly indicated: "The enlightenment, the edification and the joy of the Christian people, and a *friendly and renewed invitation to our brothers of the separated Christian Churches to share with us in this banquet of grace and brotherhood*, to which so many souls in every corner of the world aspire." In the authorized version of his speech, however, "Churches" gets changed to "communities."[54] John's favorite word for the council was *aggiornamento*, bringing up to date the church's message, but also reawakening the awareness of spirituality. In her fine account of Pope John XXIII, church historian Meriol Trevor writes: "As Pope, Roncalli took the extraordinary step of calling a Council to modernize the Church—what else does his much quoted word *aggiornamento* mean? The immediate explanations issued to modify its impact show how dangerous a word it appeared to officialdom."[55] The word "modernize" sound very close to "modernist"!

However, John made the curial cardinals presidents of the preparatory commissions. Why? Because he wanted the curia to think it was their council, so that they would not try to thwart it? Perhaps this is too subtle. A simpler explanation might be that he hoped for a friendlier curia having raised the number of curial cardinals to thirty-three. After all, "Nothing is more difficult for any government than to carry out a policy of which the heads of its own civil service disapprove."[56] Between January 1959 and the opening of the council in October 1962, there took place a concerted effort by conservative forces in the curia to ensure that the council would be conducted along what had been understood as traditional lines. The council opened on October 11 1962 with what Peter Hebblethwaite describes as "a

53. Hales, *Pope John and His Revolution*, 69.
54. Hebblethwaite, *John XXIII*, 163.
55. Trevor, *Pope John*, 79.
56. Hales, *Pope John and His Revolution*, 106.

baroque endurance test. . . . The bishops neither participated nor communicated at the Mass; liturgy as spectacle."[57] The resistant curia and the Baroque liturgy did not initially hold out great hopes for this council. But the Curia was not to have its way, and a participatory liturgy would be one of the major successes. "Only when the proceedings actually began did it become clear that a large majority of the bishops was no longer willing to be dictated to by the Curia."[58]

The special quality of the pope's opening address to the council was optimism. This contrasts with a certain negativism or even pessimism toward the world since the time of Pio Nono. Some would say much more, for example, church historian Edward Hales: "The general temper of the church, since the seventeenth century, has inclined toward pessimism. She has evidently been more concerned to raise the barriers, to stave off further losses, than to risk collaborating with others."[59] Doom and gloom were not the Johannine style, as John himself stated: "It seems to us necessary to express our complete disagreement with these prophets of doom, who give news only of catastrophes, as though the world were nearing its end."[60]

Conclusion

Church historian Meriol Trevor, in her biography of Pope John XXIII, recognizes the difficulties and the challenges that he faced throughout his life, not only throughout his own personal life but also his life in the church and in the very turbulent world of the first half of the twentieth century. She writes: "The human psyche is remarkably tough and most of that generation, like Pope John himself, seem to have taken in their stride all the taboos and inhibitions and to have survived some sixty years of chaotic change with sanity and humor."[61] It is a fine comment and, indeed, a fine message for us all. Pope John XXIII was canonized by Pope Francis on April 27, 2014.

57. Hebblethwaite, *John XXIII*, 221.

58. Vidler, *The Church in an Age of Revolution*, 271.

59. Hales, *Pope John and His Revolution*, 138–39.

60. Cited in Hales, *Pope John and His Revolution*, 139.

61. Trevor, *Pope John*, 28.

12

Pope Paul VI (1963–78)

When Cardinal Montini became Paul VI, this meant that one of the most thought-ful and determined of the moderately progressive conservatives was now pope.

—ADRIAN HASTINGS[1]

Paul VI was a good and holy man who in 1975 proclaimed the need for a "Civili-zation of Love" which prefigured the "New World Order" so desperately needed in the 1990s. He was, in short, a modern man and the "first modern pope."

—PETER HEBBLETHWAITE[2]

From Giovanni Battista Montini to Pope Paul VI

GIOVANNI BATTISTA MONTINI BORN at Concesio, near Brescia, September 26, 1897. His father, Giorgio Montini, was a friend and collaborator of Don Luigi Sturzo, the founder of the "Popular Party," and he represented the party in three legislatures from 1919–26. When Mussolini suppressed the Popular Party in 1926, Montini retired to Brescia, con-tinuing to support freedom in the face of Fascism. The young Giovanni Battista's health was poor, and he studied much of the time at home. He was shy, but possessed of a great appetite for books and learning, something that never left him.

Ordained in 1920, he went on to graduate studies in Rome, staying at the Lom-bardy College. His bishop, Giacinto Gaggia had been an historian and he advised the young priest to avoid scholastic manuals and throw himself into church history, an interest that would have been solidified by seeing each day the church historian, Louis Duchesne, walking slowly to the *Ecole Française*.[3] Coming to the attention of Monsignor Giuseppe Pizzardo in the Secretariat of State, the young priest entered the Pontifical Academy of Noble Ecclesiastics as well as continuing studies at the

1. Hastings, "Catholic History from Vatican I to John Paul II," 5.
2. Hebblethwaite, *Paul VI, The First Modern Pope*, 1.
3. Hebblethwaite, *Paul VI, The First Modern Pope*, 54.

Gregorian in canon law, a subject that he did not especially like and in which he did not excel. From 1922–54, Montini worked in the Secretariat of State, except for a brief spell in 1923 when he was in Warsaw. He rose through the ranks in the Secretariat of State until he left for Milan in 1954.

From 1924–33 Montini was deeply involved in the Catholic Student Movement. Constantly involved in mediating contemporary European thought to his students, he made quite an impression on them, able as he was to converse about such contrasting philosophers as Jacques Maritain, Henri Bergson, Oswald Spengler, and Thomas Mann. These philosophical authors informed his talks to the students. Montini translated into Italian and wrote an introduction to Jacques Maritain's *Three Reformers*. Maritain and Montini became friends. The book dealt with Martin Luther, Rene Descartes, and Jean-Jacques Rousseau. Each was seen as promoting a subjectivity that moved away from objective truth and authority and as preparing the way for the "modern world." Attracted to Maritain's *Art and Scholasticism*, he began to develop a genuine interest in art, reading all he could on the subject, again to write an article for his students in 1931. Maritain's influence on Montini was to last a very long time. As Paul VI he quoted the French philosopher in his encyclical *Populorum Progressio*. At the end of Vatican Council II, the pope placed in Maritain's hands the church's message to the intellectuals of the world.[4] If Pius XII could be characterized as pro-German in many respects, Montini could be described as pro-French.[5]

Montini did not abandon the reading of theology. In 1925 he read and absorbed the Tübingen theologian Karl Adam's *The Spirit of Catholicism*. Crafted as a reply to Adolf von Harnack's *The Essence of Christianity*, this ecclesiological work had a profound impact on Montini, not least Adam's notion that the church was constantly in need of reform. When the book was censured by the Vatican and consequently withdrawn from Roman bookshops, it is said that Montini bought up the remaindered copies and distributed them to his friends.[6] Montini was also influenced by the theology, and especially the ecclesiology of the French Jesuit, Henri de Lubac. He had a copy of de Lubac's *Méditation sur l'Église*, in English *The Splendor of the Church*, which had been pondered so much its pages were dog-eared.

In the years running up to the Lateran Treaty in 1929, Montini observed at first hand the inevitable clashes between the Catholic Student Movement and the rising Fascists. There were clashes at the intellectual level between Catholic and Fascist students, but more seriously there were violent encounters resulting in injury. He has been described as "the covert leader of the intellectual opposition to the Fascists."[7]

4. Doering, "Jacques Maritain," 307.

5. In his *The Year of Three Popes*, 2, Peter Hebblethwaite writes: "He was theologically formed by reading Maritain, Congar and de Lubac, and intellectually formed by Pascal, Bernanos and Simone Weil."

6. Hebblethwaite, *Paul VI*, 95.

7. Hebblethwaite, *Paul VI*, 93.

Despite the agreement of 1929, Mussolini suppressed all Catholic youth movements in 1931. Despite his strong denunciation of the Fascist action in the encyclical *Non Abbiamo Bisogno*, Pius XI still entertained some small hope of accommodation with the Mussolini regime. Not so Montini, and his criticisms led to his dismissal as national chaplain to the students in 1933

In 1937 Montini became assistant to Cardinal Eugenio Pacelli, the secretary of state. He was to remain in the Vatican for seventeen years. When Pacelli became Pope Pius XII, Montini was named in 1952 pro-secretary of state. While increasingly buried in mountains of diplomatic paper in his Vatican office, Montini found time for teaching church history at the Pontifical Academy for Noble Ecclesiastics. Peter Hebblethwaite comments with insight: "Montini turned to the past as a refuge from an uncongenial present, but also as a pointer to the future."[8]

In 1953 it is said that he declined a cardinal's hat. The following year 1954 he was appointed archbishop of Milan, and ordained by Cardinal Eugene Tisserant—since Pius XII was ill at the time—in St. Peter's. Montini's Vatican apartment was lined with books of all kinds. One of his biographers rightly says "His only passion of acquisition centered in books."[9] When he left for Milan, ninety crates of his books went with him, a collection that came to some six thousand volumes. When the new archbishop reached Lombardy, the region of his archdiocese, he got out of the car, prayed, and kissed the ground of his new archdiocese. Montini knew the importance of symbolic gesture.

Rome to Milan

Why the move to Milan? Various answers are proposed, but the most suasive account is as follows. Five influential Roman curial cardinals—Ottaviani, Pizzardo, Piazza, Canali, and Micara—affectionately known as the Pentagon, were suspicious of what they took to be Montini's liberalism. He was too favorable to "the left." He had tried, for example, to get the somewhat notorious Catholic novelist Graham Greene to write in *L'Osservatore Romano*. He had even recommended Greene to Pope Pius XII. There seems to be truth in this but, when all is said and done, it probably was Montini's desire to remain in touch with the Catholic youth movement that brought Vatican suspicion upon him. With so many others, including his father Giorgio, Montini had seen the Youth Movement, with its inspiration and training of future Catholic lay leaders, as a means of discrediting and countering lingering neo-Fascist elements in Italy, well after the downfall of Mussolini. One of these neo-Fascists was Luigi Gedda, a Turin educated doctor who was very active politically. Gedda was totally opposed to the Communists who were fast gaining ground in post-war Italy. Gedda was also a favorite of Pope Pius XII. Both were prepared to do whatever it took to keep the

8. Hebblethwaite, *Paul VI*, 120.

9. Clancy, *Apostle for Our Time, Pope Paul VI*, 79.

Communists out of power, even if that meant appealing to the right and the far-right, including the post-war neo-Fascists. Montini's history of opposition to the Fascists, including his unease with the resurgence of Fascism to oppose Communism, meant that he was a rather difficult member of the curial team. In some respects, then, his appointment to Milan was effectively being "kicked upstairs."[10] Montini himself must have had some thoughts along these lines.

Archbishop Montini did not wait for the people of Milan to find him. He went out to find and meet with them. He threw himself into pastoral work. Visiting the northern Italian steel city of Sesto San Giovanni, sometimes known as "little Stalingrad" because of Communist presence and influence, he let the workers know that he identified with them, and he became known as "the workers' bishop." His pastoral objective was to persuade his people that "Christianity will have the power to raise the people up anew, to bring about the return of justice, to elevate the working class."[11] Montini refused to see the world in which his working-class people lived as one that had to be opposed and avoided and corrected. He set out to persuade the industrial masses of Milan that the gospel and the church was on their side, not locked into self-serving opposition. He took this message to the factories. He celebrated Mass in factories for workers who were not liturgically hungry. Not all appreciated his efforts. He was vilified in some quarters, but he was making an impact, an impact that led to the Communists bombing his residence at 2:00am on January 5, 1956.

Naturally enough, Archbishop Montini showed an interest in the liturgy in his diocese. He had been interested in the liturgy and liturgical renewal for some years. In the summer of 1928, for example, he had visited various Belgian Benedictine monasteries that were engaged in the promotion of liturgical renewal in various ways: Maredsous, Mont-César and the Abbey of Saint André near Bruges. He probably at this time viewed parish liturgy as an adaptation of monastic liturgy, since so much liturgical renewal had come from monastic quarters. He probably also hoped for a vernacular liturgy, at least in part. Thus, in 1947 he wrote in a letter to the liturgical theologian Aimé-Georges Martimort, the editor of *Maison Dieu*, the Catholic liturgical journal, that he thought a significant part of the Mass would be one day in the vernacular. In the correspondence Martimort judged that such a development would take a century. Montini replied: "No, a development that would once have taken a century can now be realized in twenty years."[12] Montini, through the liturgical reforms of Vatican II, was to be proved right. Recalling that this is well before Vatican II, Montini wrote to his diocese: "There are still those who consider the liturgical renewal as an optional matter, or as one of the numerous devotional currents to which a person may adhere or not as he chooses. . . . [There are still those] who think that the liturgical movement is a troublesome attempt at reformation, of doubtful orthodoxy; or a petrified, external

10. Hebblethwaite, *Paul VI*, 255.

11. Cited in Clancy, *Apostle for Our Time*, 96.

12. Clancy, *Apostle for Our Time*, 218.

ritualism which has to do merely with rubrics; or an archeological fad, formalistic and 'arty'; or else a product of the cloister ill adapted to the people of our world; or finally, a preconceived opposition to piety and popular devotions."[13]

Here was a bishop who had absorbed the spirit of Pius XII's encyclical on the liturgy, *Mediator Dei*, and who had in his own way anticipated the thrust not only of Vatican II's *Sacrosanctum Concilium*, the Constitution on the Sacred Liturgy, but also *Gaudium et Spes*, the Pastoral Constitution on the Modern World. He was a conciliar bishop before the council.

The Anglican Connection

During his time in Milan, in 1956, he was also involved with ecumenical discussions with Anglicans in whom he always seems to have been interested. As early as February 1948, Herbert Waddams, the archbishop of Canterbury's secretary for foreign/ ecumenical relations, paid a visit to Montini in the Vatican. Among other things Montini was keen to talk about the upcoming inaugural meeting of the World Council of Churches in Amsterdam and the Lambeth Conference also in that year, a meeting of the Anglican bishops throughout the world. Montini showed himself interested in the Church of South India. This was an ecumenical union that came into being in 1948 too, a union of Anglican and Free Churchmen.

In 1949 the archbishop of Canterbury, Geoffrey Fisher, had sent the Anglican patristic scholar and theologian George Leonard Prestige to Rome to sound out the ecumenical climate. Prestige had been advised by his close friend, the Anglican Benedictine Dom Gregory Dix, to seek out Monsignor Montini in the Vatican. Among the reasons given by Dix was the fact that "he knew him to have a real understanding of the Church of England."[14] On December 29 1949, the English Dominican, Gervase Matthew, wrote to Prestige: "I am happy that everything went so well and particularly that you liked Msgr. Montini. He (and in a sense he alone) is the key to the situation. It is difficult to overestimate his significance as he may so easily be Pius XIV."[15] Matthew certainly got the papal succession right, and was equally correct in hinting at Montini's positive ecumenical attitude. Later, in 1955, during Montini's time in Milan, the famous Anglican bishop-ecumenist George Bell visited him. Bell wrote of the occasion: "I was never more impressed, even by my friends among Catholic bishops in the north of Europe, than by that man's desire to learn."[16] Other visits by Anglicans took place in 1956. As Paul VI he maintained some of these friendships, especially with the Anglican church historian John Dickinson and the New Testament scholar Colin

---

13. Cited in Clancy, *Apostle for Our Time*, 106–7.
14. Chadwick, "The Church of England and the Church of Rome," 95.
15. Hebblethwaite, *Paul VI*, 219.
16. Pawley and Pawley, *Rome and Canterbury Through Four Centuries*, 327.

Hickling. These ecumenical encounters between Archbishop Montini and Anglicans led Sir Owen Chadwick in 1966 to make the following statement:

> Pope Paul VI, during the years when he was Monsignor Montini, had taken a close interest in the Anglicans. In 1956 . . . he asked Bishop George Bell to send him some Anglicans, . . . [they] accompanied him on his daily work. When he visited or confirmed, he would ask, how do Anglican bishops do this? What is the custom in the Church of England? It is an understatement to say that this Pope knew more than any other Pope about the Church of England. He was the only Pope who had given the necessary time and trouble to understanding the Church of England.[17]

Years later, on the occasion of the canonization of the English and Welsh Martyrs in 1970 and, indeed, on an occasion that could be seen as contrary to the new growing spirit of ecumenism after Vatican II, Montini as Pope Paul VI made the following statement, a statement that had been crafted in his own hand:

> May the blood of these martyrs be able to heal the great wound inflicted on God's church by reason of the separation of the Anglican Church from the Catholic Church. . . . Their devotion to their country gives us the assurance that on the day when—God willing—the unity of faith and life is restored, no offense will be inflicted on the honor and sovereignty of a great country such as England. There will be no seeking to lessen the legitimate prestige and usage proper to the Anglican Church when the Roman Catholic Church . . . is able to embrace firmly her ever-beloved sister in the one authentic communion of the family of Christ.[18]

He refers to the Anglican Church as "ever-beloved sister," a clear indication not only of his affection for Anglicans but also of his understanding of the ecclesiological relationship. To Montini's outreach to the modern world, and to his liturgical commitment must be added his ecumenical concern, well before Vatican II.

Pope Paul VI and Vatican Council II

Very soon after his election, Pope John XXIII made Montini a cardinal in 1958. He had known Montini for decades in the Secretariat of State. They had been friends. After John made the announcement of an ecumenical council, news that was not universally well received, Cardinal Montini wrote to the people of his diocese: "This Council will be the greatest that the Church has ever celebrated in the twenty centuries of its history, the greatest in numbers and in spiritual impact, called in complete and peaceful unity with the hierarchy. It will be the most 'catholic' in its dimensions,

---

17. Chadwick, "Anglican Initiatives and Christian Unity," 104.
18. Cited in Hebblethwaite, *The Year of Three Popes*, 22.

truly reaching out towards the whole world and all civil societies."[19] Montini went on to submit a plan for the council, a plan that would put a degree of coherence and order on Pope John's grand but unstructured vision. The Montini plan along with Cardinal Suenens's reordering of the first drafts of the circulated schemata shaped the agenda of the council's sessions to a remarkable degree. In fact, the seventeen projected documents provided by Montini-Suenens turn out to be "astonishingly close, in form and content, to the final tally of the sixteen Council documents."[20]

Of course, Montini followed his friend in 1963 when he was elected pope as Paul VI. He had been one of the very few who stayed with John XXIII in the Vatican during the earliest sessions of the Second Vatican Council. Apparently John had written in his private diary that it was Montini whom he would like to succeed him as pope. Reactions in the Vatican and the Curia must have been quite varied, but the following judgment of Michael Collins seems balanced and fair: "For the conservatives who had been polarized by John, Montini offered a track record of faithful and unobtrusive service. For the liberal wing, Montini was a cultured man with an open and generous attitude to a rapidly changing world."[21] Balanced and fair as Michael Collins is, the fact remains that some twenty-two to twenty-five cardinals did not vote for Montini, and they "were mostly Italian and mostly in the Curia."[22] This did not augur well for collaborative ministry from the halls of the Vatican, and it may explain something of Paul VI's subsequent behavior.

Seeing a council through is far more challenging and difficult than opening one. In respect of the council Pope Paul VI was performing a constantly balancing act. While working with the progressives, he made interventions to accommodate conservative worries, including perhaps his own. He felt the need deeply to bring the conservatives, and even perhaps the intransigents along with him. Yet he steadily pushed the council's changes ahead. Fergus Kerr says that "he did his best to prevent disputes over the implementation of the Council's decisions from issuing in secessions and schisms," and Kerr concludes that "his policy succeeded: there was no secession comparable with that of the 'Old Catholics,' after 1870, refusing to accept the dogma of papal supremacy."[23] To say the least, this is no mean accomplishment.

After Vatican II

Paul VI was the first pope to travel by plane and helicopter, visiting all five continents. As Peter Hebblethwaite once it, "If Pius XII could be called . . . 'the Pope of

---

19. Cited in Hebblethwaite, *Paul VI*, 284.

20. Hebblethwaite, *Paul VI*, 314–15.

21. Collins, *The Fisherman's Net*, 242.

22. Hebblethwaite, *Paul VI*, 331.

23. Kerr, OP, *Twentieth-Century Catholic Theologians*, 204. See also Hebblethwaite, *The Year of Three Popes*, 15, and Nichols, *The Pope's Divisions*, 88.

the Atlantic Alliance' and John XXIII 'the Pope of the opening to the East', Pope Paul VI merited the title of 'Pope of the Third World.'"[24] He was the first pope since Pius VII's forced exile by Napoleon to travel outside Italy. Especially memorable was his 1965 visit to the United Nations when he spoke those outstanding words *Jamais plus la guerre/* "No more war."

Paul instituted the International Synod of Bishops. This was an attempt to establish episcopal collegiality, something advocated by the ecclesiology of Vatican II, in action. The Synod, however, was to be merely a consultative body, an instrument of assistance to the pope. Paul was being careful not to collapse the papal office into the college of bishops. "However much he believed in the church of the Second Vatican Council, however sincerely he fostered episcopal collegiality, he had been formed in the church of Vatican I and never abandoned the lofty and lonely vision of papal authority which underlay the earlier Council's teaching."[25]

In 1970 Paul made Saints Catherine of Siena and Teresa of Avila the first women doctors of the church. Admittedly, in 1976 his *Inter Insigniores* took up a negative position on the vexed question of the ordination of women, but, as Peter Hebblethwaite points out, "it was not presented as a definitive statement for all time and was wholly devoid of the male chauvinist vehemence found in some clerics."[26]

Ecumenism

At the beginning of the second session of the council, Paul VI committed himself to the ecumenical cause with these words: "If among the causes of division any fault could be imputed to us, we humbly beg God's forgiveness and ask pardon too of our brethren who feel offended by us. And we willingly forgive, for our part, the injuries the Catholic Church has suffered and forget the grief endured through the long chain of dissensions and separations."[27] Some took issue with the minimalism or the parsimony of Paul's word "if" in this statement—one thinks of Gregory Baum, OSA who was a consultor for the Secretariat for Christian Unity—but more subtle ecumenical observers saw in this word very considerable courage, given that Paul was offending very deeply powerful curial presences.[28] His ecumenical outreach took practical form in December 1963 when he announced his intention to visit the Holy Land as a pilgrim. Almost immediately, the patriarch of Constantinople expressed his wish to join the pope on pilgrimage. Thus pope and patriarch, Paul VI and Athenagoras I met in Jerusalem in 1964. They prayed together the great prayer of Jesus for unity in John 17. It was prayed verse by verse, Paul praying in Latin and Athenagoras responding in Greek. On December

24. Hebblethwaite, *The Year of Three Popes*, 29.

25. Duffy, *Saints and Sinners*, 368.

26. Hebblethwaite, *Paul VI*, 6.

27. Cited in Holmes, *The Papacy in the Modern World 1914–1978*, 225.

28. Hebblethwaite, *Paul VI*, 350–51.

7 1965, before the celebration of Mass a joint declaration by himself and Athenagoras was read out, deploring and lifting the mutual anathemas of 1054. The same day witnessed the abolition of the Holy Office with its Inquisition and the Index of Forbidden Books. The Holy Office was replaced by the Congregation for the Doctrine of the Faith. The next day Paul confirmed all the decrees of the council. He signed them not as supreme pastor of the church or the Roman pontiff, but simply as *Ego Paulus, Catholicae Ecclesiae* Episcopus/"I, Paul, Bishop of the Catholic Church," an action of considerable ecumenical significance, an expression of collegiality.

Needless to say, these important events did not dispel the suspicions of many Orthodox about the pope and Roman Catholicism. Such suspicion made it impossible for Athenagoras to visit Paul in Rome lest he be seen as subordinating and submitting himself to the pope. And so Paul made the decision to visit the patriarch of Constantinople in his own city Istanbul. One historian says that the pope's letter to the patriarch concerning this visit "seemed so incredible that Athenagoras had to read it three times before he could believe it," and when the actual visit occurred in July 1967, the patriarch described the pope as "the Bishop of Rome, the first in honor amongst us, he who presides in love."[29] In October of that same year the patriarch of Constantinople, for the first time since 1451, visited the pope of Rome. In 1975, when receiving in the Vatican Metropolitan Meliton, the representative of the patriarch of Constantinople, Paul got down on his knees and kissed his feet. His gesture before the people of Lombardy when he went to Milan as its bishop was repeated before the Orthodox.

In 1966 Paul received the archbishop of Canterbury, Michael Ramsey, in the Sistine Chapel as his "dear brother," and referred to the Anglican Communion as a "sister church": "By your coming you rebuild a bridge which for centuries has lain fallen between the Church of Rome and Canterbury." Pope Paul VI had been interested in rebuilding this bridge with Canterbury for some time. Montini had an informed feel for the Anglican Communion long before his election as pope, as has been noted. In his own words he had "a great affection for [the] Book of Common Prayer."[30] The path was not difficult, then, for Archbishop Ramsey and Pope Paul VI to set up the Anglican-Roman Catholic International Commission to promote dialogue. This particular ecumenical dialogue has been enormously successful. When the English and Welsh martyrs were canonized in 1970, Paul added to his address on the occasion some comments about the Anglican Communion:

> May the blood of these martyrs be able to heal the great wound inflicted on God's Church by reason of the separation of the Anglican Church from the Catholic Church. . . . There will be no seeking to lessen the legitimate prestige and usage proper to the Anglican Church when the Roman Catholic Church—this

---

29. Holmes, *The Papacy in the Modern World*, 227.
30. Cited in Chadwick, *Michael Ramsey, a Life*, 317.

humble "servant of the servants of God"—is able to embrace firmly her ever-beloved sister in the one authentic communion of the family of Christ.[31]

At the level of sheer, ordinary practicality—though replete with theological and ecumenical presuppositions—Paul VI issued a *Motu Proprio* on the controverted subject of inter-church marriage. This permitted what had been called "mixed marriages" to take place without a Catholic priest as witness, and, for good reasons Catholics to marry before non-Catholic ministers. The non-Catholic party was no longer required to put in writing a promise to bring up the children as Catholics. An inter-church marriage, that is a marriage between a Catholic and a validly baptized non-Catholic, could be celebrated within the context of the Eucharist. This amounted to a huge step forward in inter-church relations. At a very personal level, but still reflecting ecumenical concern, Paul ordered the *Acta Apostolicae Sedis/*"Acts of the Holy See" and the Vatican newspaper *Osservatore Romano* to drop the monarchical titles and to refer to the pope simply as the "Holy Father."

Encyclicals

When he felt the need to be, Paul could be firm, but he was not an authoritarian. No one was excommunicated while he was pope, and while some theologians were investigated, none was condemned. This too was the tone of his encyclicals.

In 1965 Paul published *Mysterium Fidei/*"The Mystery of Faith." Essentially, this was a reaffirmation of traditional eucharistic doctrine, especially in respect of the real presence of Christ. Underlining the value of the commitment of celibacy was the message of the 1967 letter, *Sacerdotalis Caelibatus/*"Priestly Celibacy." This had become a very fractious issue since the council, the intensity of which may be gauged from the fact that "The number of priests and religious who left the active ministry in the ten years from 1960 to 1970 has had no parallel since the sixteenth century."[32] That same year, 1967, saw the publication of *Populorum Progressio/* "The Development of Peoples," an encyclical given over to the pressing questions of the development of social justice. The letter denounced in unmistakable terms the unequal distribution of wealth and power throughout the world. Surplus wealth ought to be given to the poor.

1968 witnessed probably the most well known of Paul's encyclicals, the famous *Humanae Vitae/*"Of Human Life." This letter, though speaking in considerable depth of the theology of sexuality, also expressed the condemnation of artificial birth control. It is this particular condemnation for which it is most remembered. "The long-drawn-out battle over contraception cast a permanent shadow over Paul VI's pontificate through the 1970s. There was so much that was positive in this humane

---

31. Holmes, *The Papacy in the Modern World*, 227.
32. Holmes, *The Papacy in the Modern World*, 241.

and private man's exercise of his leadership."[33] So much of the positive contribution of Paul was eroded by the waves of negative criticism and indeed ire provoked by this condemnation of artificial means of contraception.

Paul had earlier withdrawn the issue from debate on the council floor. A majority of an advisory Commission on Population and Family Life, set up by John XXIII but enlarged by Paul, reported in favor of a change with regard to contraception in certain circumstances. A minority of that commission, but a minority headed by Cardinal Alfredo Ottaviani, voted for no change. The encyclical had a very hostile reception, and the pope was profoundly shaken by the critical international reaction. In an interview with a Milanese journalist in 1966, Paul VI admitted that he was thoroughly confused on the birth-control issue, not knowing which way to turn. One historian comments that, while the pope was undoubtedly disturbed by the extremely negative reaction to *Humanae Vitae*, it did have one desirable consequence: "In the longer term, the unintended effect of *Humanae Vitae* has been to put the emphasis where it truly belongs—upon the consciences of individual Catholics."[34] In the judgment of some, the crisis consequent upon the encyclical threw into high relief the conflict between authority and freedom in the Catholic Church. While there is truth in this position, it neglects to acknowledge that this conflict in more recent tradition had been a decided feature since the nineteenth century as exemplified in Gallicanism, the position that questioned the authority of the papacy on a number of issues, but especially concerning the appointment of bishops. For the next ten years Paul agonized over divisions within the church and over his own unpopularity. He never wrote another encyclical. Henry Chadwick is on to something important when he says apropos of this encyclical, "More 'collegiality' could have discouraged Paul VI from making too lonely a decision and from leaving many bishops qualifying their support."[35]

Humanae Vitae, 1968

Hans Küng makes an interesting and helpful comment on Paul VI's encyclical letter, *Humanae Vitae*, comparing the reaction to it with the reaction to Rolf Hochhuth's anti-Pius XII play, *The Representative*: "Ten years earlier, in the debate over Rolf Hochhuth's *The Representative* (1963), the whole Catholic milieu—press, organization, clergy and politicians—felt that they had to protect Pius XII. . . . But especially after Paul VI's 1968 encyclical letter *Humanae Vitae*, the mood had changed and there had been a change in mentality—from an uncritical veneration of the Pope to critical loyalty or even repudiation."[36] From "papal defense" to "papal rejection" is some distance. What was it about *Humanae Vitae* that had this effect?

33. McCulloch, *A History of Christianity*, 973.

34. Holmes, *The Papacy in the Modern World*, 236.

35. Chadwick, *Tradition and Exploration: Collected Papers on Theology and the Church*, 201.

36. Küng, *Disputed Truth, Memoirs II*, 276.

The question of birth control had been raised at Vatican II, but, as noted, Pope Paul VI withdrew the question from consideration and referred it to a special commission that had been set up by Pope John XXIII. Paul VI genuinely attempted to make this commission broadly representative of bishops, theologians, media experts, and married Catholic laity. After a number of years, the commission voted by a large majority to relax the traditional ban on contraception, and leaks to this effect occurred throughout 1967. As a result, a certain expectation of change in Catholic official moral thinking had been anticipated in many quarters. Add to this the broader context of thinking about contraception, and the expectation of change becomes greatly accentuated: positive global thinking on contraception above and beyond the Roman Catholic tradition; growing alarm over world population; concerns about the economics of supporting large families; the value of sexual intimacy for the nurturance of married people; the ready availability of cheap and efficient contraceptive devices virtually everywhere at least in the West. The world, and the Catholic world expected a change in the church's moral teaching with regard to contraception, but that change did not come with *Humanae Vitae*. Why did Pope Paul VI go against the majority advice of his own commission? The strongest reason seems to be that it would have deviated from what the church had taught for a very long time, especially from what his more immediate predecessors had taught.[37]

A brief précis of *Humanae Vitae* would highlight the following elements in the encyclical. "The most serious duty of transmitting human life, for which married persons are the free and responsible collaborators of God the Creator, has always been a source of great joy to them, even if sometimes accompanied by not a few difficulties and by distress" (par. 1). The holiness of marriage is clearly stated: "Marriage is not the effect of chance or the product of evolution of unconscious natural forces; it is the wise institution of the Creator to realize in mankind his design of love" (par. 8). The holiness of the vocation to marriage is set out as a process of self-emptying self-gift: "This love is total . . . it is a very special form of personal friendship, in which husband and wife generously share everything, without undue reservations or selfish calculations. Whoever truly loves his marriage partner loves not only what he receives, but for the partner's self, rejoicing that he can enrich his partner with the gift of himself" (par. 9). Husband and wife become co-creators with God of new life, and Pope John XXIII is cited in this respect: "Human life is sacred; from its very inception it reveals the creating hand of God" (par. 13). This high, sacramental view of marriage is opposed to all that threatens human life, "directly willed and procured abortions, even if for therapeutic reasons, are to be absolutely excluded as licit means of regulating birth. . . . Direct sterilization, whether perpetual or temporary, whether of the man or of the woman . . . and every action to render procreation impossible" (14). This, then, leads to the statement that became utterly central in the ensuing controversy: "Artificial contraception is intrinsically disordered" (14). Nonetheless, the encyclical goes on to

37. See Curran, "Dangers of Certitude," 23–24.

say that "For serious reasons births may be regulated through natural methods," but also that "artificial forms of birth control will lead to conjugal infidelity and the general lowering of morality, loss of respect especially for women" (par. 16–17). Following on from this line of thought we read: "It is to be feared that the man, growing used to the employment of anticonceptive practices, may finally lose respect for the woman and, no longer caring for her physical and psychological equilibrium, may come to the point of considering her as a mere instrument of selfish enjoyment, and no longer as his respected and beloved companion" (par. 17). Finally, the importance of self-discipline for individual persons and families is emphasized (par. 21).

After the publication of the encyclical, in the widespread expectation of a change in papal teaching, episcopal conferences throughout the world gave varied responses/ interpretations, with some conferences coming close to defending the legitimacy of conscientious dissent.[38] The variety of response on the part of episcopal conferences was matched by perhaps an even greater variety from individual theologians and ethicists. On the positive side, here are some words of the Catholic moral theologian, Janet Smith: "No one would be sadder than [Pope Paul VI] to learn how true his predictions were. . . . That there has been a widespread decline in morality, especially sexual morality, in the last twenty-five years, is very difficult to deny. . . . It would be wrong to say that contraception is the single cause of this decline, but it would also be unthinkable not to count contraception among the contributing factors."[39] More critical than Smith, and yet still very positive in appreciation, is the Jesuit moral theologian, Richard A. McCormick, who writes:

> The encyclical had many beautiful things to say about marriage and marital love. In this sense it was a gift. But its most controversial and "irritating" aspect was its rejection of every contraceptive act as intrinsically disordered. . . . Absent that teaching, *Humanae Vitae* would be bannered as a beautiful contemporary statement on conjugal love and responsible parenthood. . . . I view the matter of the Church's teaching on birth regulation as dominantly an authority problem.[40]

It is extremely difficult to analyze the consequences of *Humanae Vitae*, both its reception and its non-reception in the Catholic community at large, but Avery R. Dulles in an article published in 1993 seems to me to illustrate with considerable clarity both the negative consequences of the condemnation of artificial contraception, and also a more positive way forward for the church.[41] For Dulles, the negative consequences are as follows:

---

38. See some brief, judicious comments of church historian Collins, *Pope Benedict XVI: The First Five Years*, 47.

39. Smith, "Pope Paul as Prophet," 52.

40. McCormick, S.J., "*Humanae Vitae* 25 Years Later," 6–12.

41. Dulles, S.J., "*Humanae Vitae* and the Crisis of Dissent," 774–77.

1. The church, according to Vatican II, is a sacrament of unity, something affirmed in the very first paragraph of the Constitution on the Church. This, however, was much less the case after the publication of *Humanae Vitae*. The same conciliar text sought to acknowledge for the laity a more active role in the life of the church and in the development of doctrine, something found in Newman's theology. But, notes Dulles, with many people at odds with the magisterium on this issue, unity is impaired and the reality and the process of consultation is gravely inhibited. It may be true, as Dulles avers, that ecclesial unity is impaired as a result of the encyclical. At the same time, however, it seems to me that something has been gained, that the conscience of the adult has in a sense come of age. In a very famous interview with Cardinal John Carmel Heenan, archbishop of Westminster, the British journalist David Frost asked some very pointed questions about the encyclical in the role of personal conscience.[42] After a number of preliminary but probing questions, Frost came to this issue of conscience: "Or, in other words, if the Catholic couple take the decision on serious grounds of conscience to use a contraceptive, then the church will not interfere with that." Here is Heenan's response: "The teaching of the church is very clear. A man is bound to follow his conscience even if his conscience is in error; this is a basic teaching of the church, that every man, the Pope, you, I, everyone, must follow conscience. Now it's the duty of a Catholic to inform his conscience. But it could happen easily, particularly after this long period of dispute and doubt, it could happen that a couple might say conscientiously: I'm quite sure that this is the right thing for me to do. And if that can be said conscientiously, then, of course, they must follow their conscience. There is no dispute about this." Frost followed up: "And if they go to their priest and say that they're doing precisely that, what should the priest say?" Heenan's response: "'God bless you.' If they're really following their conscience in the sight of God, which is all that matters—the priest, the bishop, the pope doesn't matter compared with God." Cardinal Heenan could never have been regarded as a liberal theological thinker. Yet on this issue he reiterates traditional Catholic teaching concerning the ultimacy of conscience.

2. Priests are placed in difficult positions as teachers, preachers, confessors. On the one hand, they do not wish to antagonize their people by constantly drawing attention to the teaching of the encyclical, and yet, on the other, priests who support the encyclical often find themselves outnumbered by their colleagues. There is widespread confusion and hurt in local presbyterates as a result.

3. The dissent over *Humanae Vitae* has led to massive confusion about the authority of the magisterium, a point already noted by Richard McCormick. The role of ecclesiastical authority and the responsible obedience on the part of the laity was

---

42. This interview, originally published on December 14, 1968, the year of the encyclical's promulgation, has been republished as David Frost and Cardinal Heenan, "Conscience and the Pill," 9–10, 15.

changing and changing fast. The French theologian Marie-Dominique Chenu illustrates this in a confidential letter that he wrote to the French episcopate: "It could be that Rome has lost, in a stroke, the authority that it took sixteen centuries to construct."[43]

4. Relations between bishops and theologians, which had been very cordial during Vatican II, have become strained over their respective attitudes to the encyclical. Dulles puts it accurately: "Bishops are tempted to regard theologians as sowers of dissent. . . . Scholars who continue to work cordially with the hierarchy are sometimes portrayed as sycophantic court theologians."

5. The appointment of bishops now becomes very controversial. There is a growing suspicion that suitable episcopal candidates are rendered ineligible if they do not accept *tout court* the teaching of the encyclical. Dulles concludes that, if this is an over-riding concern, inevitably it leads to a very restricted pool of episcopal candidates.

6. Episcopal conferences, which began so well after Vatican II as an expression of collegiality, are now "stunted by the controversy about birth control."

7. Finally, and from an ecclesiological perspective as well as a deep love for the church, Dulles writes: "Enough has been said to make it clear that dissent is a deep wound in the body of Christ."

Dulles also points to a way forward out of the seeming *impasse*:

1. "The dissenters must recognize that public dissent by its very nature impairs the authority of the magisterium and weakens the church as a community of faith and witness."

2. "Those who are strongly convinced by the arguments for or against contraception should recognize the extreme difficulty of the question and should therefore respect the intelligence and sincerity of those with whom they differ."

3. "In making appointments to sensitive positions such as seminary professorships, the hierarchy must take account of the candidates' general fidelity to Catholic doctrine. *Humanae Vitae* should not be made the sole litmus test."

4. "No amount of insistence by church authorities will bring about unanimity." "The issue of contraception should be addressed in the context of more general questions about family life and procreation."

The analysis offered by Avery Dulles seems balanced, fair, and pastorally sensitive. However, he does not capture the actual situation of many Catholics both before and after *Humanae Vitae* with the *finesse* of the Catholic novelist, David Lodge. In 1980 Lodge published a novel entitled *How Far Can You Go?* in which he describes with

43. Cited in Chappel, *Catholic Modern*, 236.

great accuracy the life-circumstances of a representative group of middle-class educated Catholics: "For all of them the promulgation of *Humanae Vitae* in 1968, and the controversy that followed, was a watershed . . . and it occupies a pivotal position in the narrative." The Catholic characters of his 1980 novel had attained, or were in the process of attaining a degree of moral autonomy, or perhaps moral maturity with respect to the entire apparatus of authority and obedience in which they had been brought up. Writing in 2008 and attempting to say how things are now for the children of his fictional characters, Lodge seems to me to be right on the mark: "The married ones would have observed that for their grown-up children contraception was not and never had been a moral issue. Even if these children continued to be practicing Catholics most of them would have lived with a partner before getting married, if they married at all, and such a lifestyle depends on reliable contraception."[44] Time goes on, and so do people, and this may in the long run simply be part of the ongoing process of reception of church teaching. Pope Paul VI never wrote another encyclical.

Conclusion

Eamon Duffy writes of Pope Paul VI: "No pope since the time of Gregory the Great has had so daunting a task."[45] Paul had to steer the church through the turbulent years following the Second Vatican Council. This turbulence was exacerbated by the fact that Western societies were passing through a time of rapid and multi-faceted change, and this broader societal change had an enormous impact on the council and its reforms. In 1975 Paul at 78 wrote of himself: "What is my state of mind? Am I Hamlet or Don Quixote? On the left? On the right? I don't feel I have been properly understood. I have had two dominant feelings: *Superabundo Gaudio*. I am filled with comfort. With all our affliction, I am overjoyed. (2 Cor. 7:4)."[46]

It may be sentiments such as these that led papal historian Philippe Levillain to say of Pope Paul VI, "He responded to the political and theological or reception of the work of Vatican II by retiring into little-noticed years of mysticism."[47] It may be that this mystical milieu in which he spent his last years served him well on the day of his death. On Sunday, August 6, 1978 at Castel Gandolfo he was anointed by the Cardinal Secretary of State, Jean Villot, and he continued to pray to the very end. "His last words were an unfinished *Our Father*."[48]

44. Lodge, "How Far Have We Come?" 16.
45. Duffy, *Saints and Sinners*, 364.
46. Hebblethwaite, *Paul VI*, 7.
47. Levillain, "Paul VI," in Philippe Levillain, 1146.
48. Hebblethwaite, *The Year of Three Popes*, 3.

13

Vatican Council II (1962–65)

*The Council proved to be the most revolutionary Christian event
since the Reformation.*

—EAMON DUFFY[1]

*Vatican II was, indeed, unlike any Council that preceded it. In fact, by adopting
the style of discourse that it did, the Council in effect redefined what a Council is.
Vatican II did not take the Roman Senate as its implicit model. I find it difficult
to pinpoint just what the implicit model was, but it was much closer to guide,
partner, and friend than it was to lawmaker and judge.*

—JOHN W. O'MALLEY, SJ[2]

There has seldom been a council without great confusion after it.

—JOHN HENRY NEWMAN[3]

Vatican II Was Coming!

EARLIER CHAPTERS HAVE ESTABLISHED that Vatican II was decades in the making,
gradually and slowly but decidedly, perhaps especially with the kind of theological
thinking associated with the *nouvelle théologie*. However, the point has been excep-
tionally well made by historian Stephen Schloesser that in the post-1945 world the
Second Vatican Council was a necessary response "to cataclysmic shifts in the mid-
twentieth century." He points to shifts such as World War II, the Holocaust, the Cold
War between the USSR and its empire and the West, the atomic bomb exemplified
at Hiroshima and Nagasaki, and the slow but ongoing process of decolonization
with the consequent ending of Western hegemony, heralded by the independence

1. Duffy, *Saints and Sinners*, 359.
2. O'Malley, SJ, "Trent and Vatican II: Two Styles of Church," 318.
3. Dessain and Gornall, *The Letters and Diaries of John Henry Newman*, 175.

of India from Britain in 1947. These shifts pushed the church to think about its own identity in this very fast-changing world. In this world marked by the increasing fragmentation of humankind as a result of these shifts, Vatican II emphasized the unity of humankind, a unity found sacramentalized in the church. By the time the council had ended in December 1965, maintains Schloesser, a broad and expanded ecclesial horizon had emerged:

"While not neglecting the details of the church's internal life, it had stepped back from perspectives specific to Catholicism, Christianity, and even religion in general. It had stepped back to see the world—humanity, history, existence—from the perspective of the broadest possible horizons. It asked anew what its purpose was—and what the purpose of Christian believers was—in a world populated by nations and cultures whose difference and diversity were finally being acknowledged in a postcolonialist world."[4] This was a church emerging and, as Schloesser has it "forced" to emerge from the parameters of the anti-modern, fortress-like mentality that had characterized it in the nineteenth century and into the mid-twentieth century.

If world-changing events had made the council virtually a moral necessity, its closest parallel in the conciliar tradition would probably be the Fourth Lateran Council in 1215. This is the judgment of the church historian, Christopher Bellitto, who maintains that Lateran IV had been "the culmination of a century's theological and reform developments—and that is precisely what Vatican II eventually became."[5] If Vatican II was the climax of theology and reform developed over a period of one hundred years, it was so in a pastoral way. That is to say, it was not specifically concerned with a particular threat or a particular challenge, unless one wants to say that a certain opening up to the modern world constituted the challenge. This opening up to the modern world is best expressed in Vatican II's text, "The Pastoral Constitution on the Church in the Modern World." There we see the church letting go of an adversarial style *vis-à-vis* the world since at least the time of the French Revolution. On a much smaller scale we may see this opening up to the modern world expressed in the fact that journalists were in Rome for the council. That is true of Vatican I also, but not to the same extent. Hundreds of journalists were present so that in the words of Diarmaid MacCulloch, "Now the Vatican was forced to employ a press officer, although, with a disdainful symbolism, he was not actually given anywhere to sit during his attendance at the Council's proceedings."[6]

This opening up of the Roman Catholic Church to the world seems to have been at least implicit in the two aims that Pope John XXIII had for the council

---

4. Schloesser, SJ, "Against Forgetting: Memory, History, Vatican II," 138. Schloesser is, of course, not the only scholar to make this important point. For example, the church historian Giuseppe Alberigo indicates, suggest and hints as much in his *A Brief History of Vatican II*, but, as the very title points out, Alberigo's treatment is "brief," that is to say, contextually underdeveloped.

5. Bellitto, *The General Councils*, 128–29.

6. MacCulloch, *A History of Christianity*, 969.

when he announced it on January 25, 1959: first, "the enlightenment, edification, and joy of the entire Christian people"; second, "a renewed cordial invitation to the faithful of the separated churches to participate with us in this feast of grace and brotherhood."[7] Many point out that these aims are not especially clear and specific. While that is true, it seems to me that they indicate a "certain opening up" to the modern world. The aims are positively expressed, and the second aim was not an invitation to return to Rome but rather to participate. Admittedly, these invitees could not vote in the deliberations and debates of the council, but the matter of fact is they were there, and their very presence was "a symbol that the church was going to reach out beyond its traditional fortifications."[8]

During the years of World War II, theological work went on, formally and informally. One thinks of the "new theologians" discussed earlier in chapter 9, but theological fermentation was going on elsewhere as well. For example, Léon-Joseph Suenens of the University of Louvain, describes what went on in his residence: "Outside the turmoil of public events, a small group met regularly in my home during the war, to exchange ideas on theological matters. The group, which was originally my idea, included Canons Cerfaux, Gerard Phillips, Dondeyne, as well as Fathers Malevez, SJ, and Levie, SJ. . . . Later, Fr. Dhanis, SJ, future rector of the Gregorian University, and Mgr. Thils, joined our group."[9] The list is a veritable roll-call of the theologians who were to influence or to be present at Vatican II. Without knowing it scholars such as these and many others, including especially those involved in the *nouvelle théologie*, were creating the theological climate of the Second Vatican Council. Theologians and leaders in the biblical movement, the liturgical movement and the ecumenical movement almost by their very existence and reflection were shaping the church for Vatican II. This perception leads one of the premier historians of the council, Giuseppe Alberigo, to say, "Something new had been happening in Catholicism, something that had been underway for a long while."[10]

The directing principle of Vatican II was provided by Pope John XXIII in the Italian term *aggiornamento*, "encompassing not only an 'adaptation' to the outward life of contemporary society but also the presupposition of a complete inward change of thought,"[11] and the French term *ressourcement*, a return to the sources. In reality, *ressourcement* was the primary engine of *aggiornamento*. The 2,540 voting council

---

7. Cited in O'Malley, "Introduction," in Schultenover, *A View from Rome*, 3.

8. MacCulloch, *A History of Christianity*, 969.

9. Suenens, *Memories and Hopes*, 38–39.

10. Alberigo, *A Brief History of Vatican II*, 3. Consider also the following comments from church historians Schelkens et al. in their *Aggiornamento?* 107: "A nuanced reappraisal, keeping in mind the complex and simultaneous presence and intersection of continuities (in plural) and discontinuities (again in plural) in the development of Catholicism is needed to evaluate the pontificate of Pope Pius XII and its relationship with what came next in the history of the Catholic Church. . . . What happened at Vatican II did not fall out of the sky."

11. This is the definition, slightly adapted, from Franzen and Dolan, *A History of the Church*, 432.

fathers met in St. Peter's Basilica itself, remodeled for this purpose into an auditorium. The council consisted of four chronologically distinct meetings: the first session, from October 11 to December 8, 1962; the second session, from September 29 to December 4, 1963; the third session from September 14 to November 21, 1964; the fourth and final session, from September 14 to December 8 1965.

An ante-preparatory commission was set up under the presidency of Cardinal Tardini. This commission sent out questionnaires to curial officials, bishops, male religious superiors, university faculties, and individual theologians. However, as the commission received its responses from around the world, it classified these responses along the lines of canon law and neo-scholastic theology. The last task of the anti-preparatory commission was to propose members for the actual preparatory commissions that would draw up the draft documents for the bishops to discuss and to debate. The net result was that these preparatory commissions were largely in the hands of the curial officials, and they were known not to be wildly enthusiastic about the forthcoming council. Anglican church historian and theologian Henry Chadwick, with a degree of sympathy for the Roman Curia, sums up the situation accurately when he says, "The overworked Curia found itself inevitably responsible for preparing the agenda, the procedure and the schemata of a Council for which it felt little or no enthusiasm."[12] Seventy draft documents were drawn up, but without any particular plan for their deliberation. The situation was a recipe for conciliar disaster.

This led Cardinal Suenens to speak to Pope John in March 1962. This is Suenens's recollection of the event: Suenens to Pope John: "'Who is working on an overall plan for the Council?' 'Nobody,' said Pope John. 'But there will be total chaos. How do you imagine we can discuss seventy-two schemata . . . ? 'Yes,' John agreed, 'We need a plan. . . . Would you like to do one?'"[13] With consultation and collaboration with other European cardinals, Suenens drew up a plan for the council, which was sent to Rome, to Cardinal Cicognani, but did not go anywhere. In September 1962, Cardinal Frings of Cologne had a memorandum also for Cardinal Cicognani drawn up by the theologian he was taking to the council to the effect that the language of the texts to be debated and ultimately promulgated should not be the scholastic and manualist language of the traditional Roman textbooks, but rather "the vital language of Scripture and the Church Fathers." Frings's theologian who drafted this memorandum was the young Joseph Ratzinger.[14] Many were utterly dissatisfied with the scholastic register of discourse in which the draft documents had been written.

During the very first week of the council, October 1962, two things happened that were to change the course of events. First, the assembled bishops made the decision to elect from among them who would be appointed to the various commissions, effectively displacing the curial control. Second, Cardinal Montini wrote to Cardinal

---

12. Chadwick, *Tradition and Exploration*, 195.

13. Suenens, "A Plan for the Whole Council," 88–91.

14. See Wicks, "Six Texts by Professor Joseph Ratzinger," 233–311.

Cicognani asking whether there was any plan for the deliberation of the council documents. With the approval of Pope John, Montini edited Suenens's plan, and so the council got underway.

Pope John XXIII, *Gaudet Mater Ecclesia*

On October 11 1962, the very first day of the council, Pope John delivered an address, *Gaudet Mater Ecclesia*/"Mother Church Rejoices."[15] He had prepared this text with great care, a care well described by Giuseppe Alberigo: "The manuscript pages were carefully revised; they contain corrections, rearrangements, and additions, all in the Pope's own handwriting. The same is true of the typewritten copy, which contains more personal modifications in Roncalli's own hand, testifying to an exacting attention to the revision and perfection of the text."[16]

Almost immediately the Second Vatican Council was polarized. The various draft documents that had been produced by the Roman Curia were rejected by a majority of the bishops. They were after something quite different, an ecclesial perspective that was more open and sensitive to the actual pastoral realities they faced in their dioceses throughout the world. At the same time, many of them were trapped, if that is not too strong a word, in the neo-scholasticism of their own seminary days, without too much awareness of developments in the study of the Bible and of the move from classical to historical consciousness.[17] In a very real sense, the bishops of the world were going back to school! Apart altogether from being in St Peter's Basilica for episcopal debate and discussion, many of the bishops spent time in the evening attending lectures by various theologians who were at the council in the capacity of "experts" or *periti*. One fine example of a bishop back at school is provided by Bishop Albino Luciani, later to become Pope John Paul I, but more of that in the chapter on his pontificate.

It was inevitable from an historical perspective that the polarization would continue. Conservatives felt that Pope John XXIII had introduced liberal reforms in the church that led to clamors for greater change. Liberals felt that the changes were a good beginning, but there was a need to press ahead. While describing the pre-history of *Lumen Gentium*, Cardinal Suenens provides an accurate glimpse of the two different and fundamental approaches to theological reflection at the council:

> There was here a confrontation between two different conceptions of the church. The Holy Office had prepared a draft text inscribed by an ecclesiology that was deeply marked by the canonical and institutional aspects of the church, rather than emphasizing and giving priority to the spiritual and

15. The entire text may be found as an appendix in Abbott, SJ and Gallagher, *The Documents of Vatican II*, 710–19.

16. Alberigo, *A Brief History of Vatican II*, 21.

17. Fagan, SM, "Theology in the Making," 69. Fagan is echoing, of course, language made possible by Bernard J. F. Lonergan, SJ.

evangelistic aspects. In our eyes, it was a matter of stepping out of a legalistic ecclesiology and into an ecclesiology of communion, centered on the mystery of the church in its most profound Trinitarian dimensions.[18]

The English church historian Edward Norman describes the Second Vatican Council in these terms: "The Council [took] place in a decade of crisis in western cultural values; a time of escalating expectations, when the past often seemed burdensome and the future seemed to beckon humanity to new hopes." Norman's statement is balanced. There was a burdensome element about the church in the experience of many Catholics—rules and regulations, ways of expressing doctrine that were not especially intelligible and persuasive, and so forth. Very definite new hopes emerged among the faithful, perhaps especially among the priests, and at times some of these hopes were in some degree unrealistic, perhaps even utopian. That leads Edward Norman to conclude: "The remarkable thing about the Council was that it was able to produce more or less exactly what it set out to do: a statement of the Catholic faith in modules of understanding intelligible to modern culture yet completely conformable to past tradition."[19] Norman desires to underscore the element of continuity between the church as it was and the church as it was becoming at the council. This is a laudable position. At the same time, it seems to overlook dialogue and discussion, conversation and debate and the desire for responsible change on the council floor among the bishops, and also when they gathered in various language groups outside the council.

Conservatives and Progressives

The detailed histories of Vatican Council II provide insight into some of these conversations during the council, and so we can see, for want of better terminology, conservatives and progressives, right-wing and left-wing. This leads the German Catholic theologian, Hermann J. Pottmeyer, to open an essay on the reception of Vatican II with these words: "Whereas the two preceding councils, Trent and Vatican I, had aimed at restoring internal stability and establishing a dogmatic front, Vatican II sought to relax rigid fronts and achieve an opening. As experience has shown, however, such an attempt leads to instability. For this reason, Vatican II has a place apart among the councils. Given this situation, the Catholic Church in the post-Vatican II period has proved surprisingly stable."[20] Locating the council as "transitional," Pottmeyer notes its lack of precise dogmatic statements and definitions, and, at times, a certain ambiguity in expression. As a result, he argues, both "conservative" and "progressive" interpreters of the council can find their positions amply verified in its statements. He concludes that it has been impossible to agree upon "a proper

18. Suenens, *Memories and Hopes*, 132.
19. Norman, *The Roman Catholic Church*, 178.
20. Pottmeyer, "A New Phase," 27.

hermeneutic for the Council."[21] There is real truth in that statement. It does not especially matter what terms are used—conservative and liberal, majority and minority, closed and open—but what is clear is that there were different points of view, and points of view held by people in good faith. A recent commentator puts it like this: "Regardless of which 'camp' a particular council father represented, two things are clear about all of them: they loved their church and they tried to be attuned to the Holy Spirit in their midst."[22] Edward Norman's understanding of continuity noted above is nothing but the truth, but not the whole truth. There were differences of emphasis at the council from more recently held positions, and there were differences in both understanding and reception among the conciliar fathers. How could there not be? The Scottish Dominican, Fergus Kerr writes: "In each case, the final texts were the product of hard-won compromise: what the minority feared should not be ignored if we are to have a balanced interpretation."[23] In effect, this would demand a redaction-history of each and every conciliar text. That is not my concern in this book, and, indeed, such is now available in the magisterial series *History of Vatican II*, edited by Giuseppe Alberigo and Joseph Komonchak.[24]

Another word needs to be said about the distinction between self-styled "conservative" and self-styled "liberal" or "progressive." These positions have become quite hardened in the years since the council. But the positions themselves and the mindsets that they instantiate need a broader description than simply for or against the theological horizon of Vatican II. I believe that broader description may be accessed in the thinking of the Jesuit philosopher-theologian Bernard Lonergan. In an essay which has become quite famous in its own right, "The Transition from a Classicist World View to Historical Mindedness," Lonergan contrasts two ways of thinking, two worldviews, two mentalities: "One may be named classicist, conservative, traditional; the other may be named modern, liberal, perhaps historicist (though that word unfortunately is ambiguous). The differences between the two are enormous, for they differ in their apprehension of man, in their account of the good, and in the role they ascribe to the church in the world. But these differences are not immediately theological. They are differences in horizon, in total mentality. For either side to understand the other is a major achievement, and when such understanding is lacking, the interpretation of Scripture or of other theological sources is most likely to be at cross-purposes."[25] This contrast between what Lonergan called

21. Pottmeyer, "A New Phase," 29.

22. Sullivan, OP, *The Road to Vatican II*, 41.

23. Kerr, *Twentieth-Century Catholic Theologians*, 204.

24. Alberigo and Komonchak, *History of Vatican II*; and O'Malley, "Vatican II: Did Anything Happen?" 55, writes of these volumes: "Yes, between the lines and sometimes in the lines, one can detect sympathy for 'the progressives.' But I am generally impressed with the authors' efforts to be fair to the so-called conservatives or minority and especially to be fair to Pope Paul VI, whom they recognized as being in an extraordinarily difficult and delicate situation."

25. Lonergan, "The Transition from a Classicist World View to Historical Mindedness," 127.

a classicist mentality and a historically minded mentality—what the contemporary church historian Mark Massa has described as "Lonergan's brilliantly succinct identification of the real issue behind the heated exchanges between American Catholics"—is constantly being played out in the contemporary Roman Catholic Church.[26] Some of these tensions may be found in two theologians who were influential both before and after Vatican II, Karl Rahner and Hans Urs von Balthasar, and so to these scholars we turn our attention in the next chapter.

The Documents of Vatican II

The council produced and agreed the following texts:

- The Dogmatic Constitution on the Church
- The Dogmatic Constitution on Divine Revelation
- The Constitution on the Sacred Liturgy
- The Pastoral Constitution on the Church in the Modern World
- The Decree on the Instruments of Social Communication
- The Decree on Ecumenism
- The Decree on Eastern Catholic Churches
- The Decree on the Bishops' Pastoral Office in the Church
- The Decree on Priestly Formation
- The Decree on the Appropriate Renewal of Religious Life
- The Decree on the Apostolate of the Laity
- The Decree on the Ministry and Life of Priests
- The Decree on the Church's Missionary Activity
- The Declaration on Christian Education
- The Decree on the Instruments of Social Communication
- The Declaration on the Relationship of the Church to Non-Christian Religions
- The Declaration on Religious Freedom

"Sixteen decrees, but not a single dogma!" This is how the distinguished church historian August Franzen describes the council's output.[27] Needless to point out, not all these documents are of equal value, nor were they all received in quite the same way in the years consequent upon the council. Perhaps the real and compelling question is, "How are these sixteen texts to be read?"

26. Massa, *The American Catholic Revolution*, 13.
27. Franzen and Dolan, *A History of the Church*, 439.

How Are These Documents to Be Read?

"The lived experience of Vatican II was in part a dramatic struggle over varying ideas about what the council ought to be, do, and say. This struggle did not end with the council. It continues today."[28] These words of theologian and ecclesiologist Joseph Komonchak are extremely perceptive. He draws attention not only to the struggle at the council, but also to the struggle in the church today about its meaning, a struggle exacerbated now by internet websites and blog spots, in which people are free to say what they wish without the need for informed verification and evaluation. For the sake of argument, there are two basic lenses through which the conciliar texts may be read. Through the first lens, the council is judged to be in all important regards continuous with the Catholic past, what has been called the Ruini-Marchetto line of interpretation.[29] Through the second lens, the council was entirely novel, different from previous councils, and is marked by an underlying "reformist" ideology, the so-called Alberigo-Bologna line of interpretation.[30] The latter lens makes of the council an "event," that is to say, "novelty, discontinuity, a 'rupture,' a break from routine, causing surprise, disturbance, even trauma . . . ."[31] In respect of these two ways of looking at Vatican II, church historian John O'Malley made the following statement in a lecture commemorating the council at Yale University in the fall of 2005: "As a practicing historian I have come to realize that in any social entity the continuities run deeper and tend to be stronger than the discontinuities."[32] The church is by essential definition a conservative society, conserving the tradition flowing from Christ and the apostles. Continuity there must be. At the same time, Alberigo, with the Bologna School, has a point. The council did say things that, if not *entirely* new in the longer and fuller tradition of the church, certainly sounded new to many of the conciliar bishops. Or, in a word, there was change. If that is not true, maintains O'Malley, then the church is reduced to "a collection of more or less interesting stories, as the church sails through the sea of history unaffected by it."[33]

28. Komonchak, "Vatican II as 'Event,'" 24.

29. According to O'Malley this is the position of Cardinal Camillo Ruini & Archbishop Agostino Marchetto, in Marchetto's book, *The Ecumenical Council Vatican II: A Counterpoint for Its History* (Vatican City, 2005).

30. This is the position, according to O'Malley of Giuseppe Alberigo and the "Bologna School."

31. Komonchak, "Vatican II as 'Event,'" 27. Komonchak is exploring the historiographical notion of "event."

32. O'Malley, SJ, "Vatican II: Did Anything Happen?" 57. (Lecture at Yale Divinity School, September 26, 2005.)

33. O'Malley, "Vatican II: Did Anything Happen?" 58. Similar comments have been made by many different commentators. Crisp and brief is the comment of Francis Fiorenza in his essay "Vatican II and the Aggiornamento of Roman Catholic Theology," 264: "The progressives have stressed the contrast between the pre-conciliar and post-conciliar church and have seen the resistance to change in Rome as responsible for curtailing their creativity and influence. On the other hand, traditionalists see the Council, especially in its statements on religious freedom and on the church and the world, as surrendering to Modernism, liberalism, and secularism."

A few examples will help clarify the point. In *Lumen Gentium,* a sacramental understanding of the church is given priority over a juridical view of the church, and yet the latter is not simply jettisoned. In that same document the chapter entitled "The People of God" comes before that concerned with the hierarchical constitution of the church, and yet, in Catholic ecclesiology one may not be had without the other. Finally, as an example, the infallibility of the whole church comes textually before the infallibility of the magisterium. None of these issues is new, but their placement, and how they were heard had a new sound among the council participants and in the church in general. Hermann J. Pottmeyer, refers to this as the method of juxtaposition. In his judgment this method is not to be thought of simply as pragmatic compromise between opposed groups. That would be entirely too superficial. Rather, it is to be thought of along the lines of ecclesial communion, that is to say, the method is driven by "the will to compromise [as] simply the will to remain united as long as the truth of the faith itself is not an issue, and to preserve *communion* with one another and in continuity with doctrine."[34] To get beyond what might be described as "mere juxtaposition," and more, to get beyond ecclesial alienation and polarization, Vatican II employed, in O'Malley's phrase, a "rhetoric of invitation": language and meaning such as brothers and sisters, people of God, cooperation and partnership, collaboration, dialogue, collegiality, development, progress, evolution are constantly in use. By entering into this rhetoric of invitation, and by according a certain priority to positions with which one is not in complete agreement for whatever reasons, in other words by deliberately eschewing an overly selective reading and interpretation of the conciliar texts, progress will be made towards a new ecclesial synthesis. This, however, is a long process.

A Suggested Reading of the Documents

The best way to appreciate the documents of Vatican II is to read them thoroughly and carefully, preferably accompanied by a standard commentary such as that edited by the German theologian and pupil of Karl Rahner, Herbert Vorgrimler. That is an individual task, and commentary on the documents is beyond the scope of this book. The objective here is to look beyond the immediacy of the texts and consider what happened. In the light of all the changes that occurred, the Anglican church historian Alec Vidler asks the question, "Has a great church ever acquired a new look so swiftly?"[35] What were the highlights of the "new look"? John O'Malley has described the new look as a definite change of style from previous ecumenical councils. That change of style was towards an apodeictic rhetorical style, inviting and persuading, not condemning or anathematizing.[36] This style worked its way through the final

34. Pottmeyer, "A New Phase," 38.

35. Vidler, *The Church in an Age of Revolution*, 272.

36. It is described in detail by O'Malley in his essay, "Vatican II: Did Anything Happen?" 52–91.

redaction of the conciliar texts and has been crisply summarized by O'Malley in the following way[37]:

1. The process of Roman centralization was reversed by balancing the emphasis on the papacy at Vatican I with a renewed emphasis on episcopal collegiality.

2. "There was a moderation of the influence of Greek metaphysics on the formulation of beliefs which had been operative since the patristic era and sanctioned by the Scholastic enterprise of the High Middle Ages." New ways of studying philosophy and theology exploded throughout the church.

3. "There was a concomitant attempt to insert into doctrinal formulations some considerations of a more biblical and historical character." Historical consciousness emerged on the Catholic scene with a vengeance. Conciliar and doctrinal texts were to be understood within the flow of developing tradition, within the flow of history, and this led to a greater degree of intelligibility.

4. "A more appreciative attitude developed towards other religious communities." Catholics opened up to other Christians, especially to Christians of the Reformation traditions, in ways that they had never done before. Inevitably, this opening up led to both enrichment and challenge. When it comes to the Decree on Ecumenism, Aidan Nichols has it right when he makes the following comment: "The conciliar decree had distinguished between 'churches'—bodies isomorphic with the local churches of the Catholic Church itself save for the feature of communion with the Roman see—and 'ecclesial communities', where other crucial elements of a Christian commonwealth were lacking—above all, continuance in the apostolic succession to which a plenary sacramental life and corporate instinct for the apostolic preaching are linked."[38] Of course, not all brought to their reading of the Decree on Ecumenism the subtlety and sophistication found here in Aidan Nichols, and undoubtedly, in practical terms this lack of theological subtlety and sophistication led often both to utopian expectations concerning Christian unity and despairing frustration that they were not realized. At the same time, at a slower pace but with increasing ecumenical realism, the Christian world was transformed as a result of the Decree on Ecumenism. Conversations began at all levels—locally, nationally, and globally—that enabled Christians better to know each other and to become more informed about their differing theologies, as well as to take practical action where that was possible.

5. "Catholics became more deeply engaged in problems of justice and peace in the world at large." The world was not seen any longer as a hostile jungle, but God's good creation in which grace was at work, inviting a positive cooperation on the part of Catholics. This is the perspective of the Pastoral Constitution on

37. O'Malley, SJ, *Tradition and Transition*, 17–18.
38. Nichols, *Catholic Thought Since the Enlightenment*, 161.

the Church in the Modern World. This document, "an innovation in a genre," represents a sort of digest of the church's policies towards the world.[39] Some have interpreted the document as much too optimistic, perhaps even somewhat pelagian in character. This, however, seems wide of the mark. The document has been aptly characterized by Nicholas Boyle, a Catholic Germanist at England's University of Cambridge as follows: "A profoundly courageous and missionary document, it knows that the Church's founding commission is to go out and teach all nations, and that a Church that has grown timorous and fearful for its future serves no purpose at all."[40] Boyle has nicely captured the flavor of the entire text. There is no gloom, no lamenting the state of the world, no judging the world—though the councils fathers had no need to be appraised of the world's problems and challenges—but rather the note is "joy and hope," the literal English translation of the Latin title, *Gaudium et Spes*. To anticipate some words of Eamon Duffy in the chapter on Pope Benedict XVI, there is a scandal of pessimism every bit as much as there is a scandal of optimism.

The interpretation of *Gaudium et Spes* remains contested. In a somewhat tendentious analysis Australian theologian Tracey Rowland believes that there are at least five different positions taken by Catholic theologians on the meaning of this text and on the general spirit of Vatican II. Alongside that of Nicholas Boyle noted above, there is the position of the traditionalist that wants no accommodation whatsoever with the culture of modernity. Third is the position of Johann Baptist Metz (1928–) and Juan Luis Segundo (1925–96), described by Rowland in these terms: "*Gaudium et Spes* was the manifesto of a bourgeois revolution in modern Catholicism, which was a movement forward from Pius IX's aristocratic stance of unmitigated opposition to modernity, but it did not go far enough. What is now required is a proletarian revolution." Fourth is the position of scholars like Lieven Boeve of Leuven University, a position that juxtaposes modernity with postmodernity in this way: "The idea of hooking Catholicism up to the modern project just a few short years before leading European intellectuals were declaring the project a failure was not very farsighted and, as a project itself, a failure, but the more basic orientation which underpinned it, of keeping the church in a constant dialogue with the best of contemporary thought, is still worth pursuing." The fifth position is that of Joseph Ratzinger. In Rowland's analysis Ratzinger has points of contact with all four positions but in the last analysis he sees "the whole point of *Gaudium et Spes* correctly interpreted, as that a 'daring new' Christocentric theological anthropology is the medicine that the world needs, and that it is the responsibility of the church to administer it."[41] While the sympathies of the author tend to lie with Nicholas Boyle, it needs to

39. Nichols, *Catholic Thought Since the Enlightenment*, 157.
40. Boyle, "On Earth, as in Heaven," 12.
41. Rowland, *Ratzinger's Faith*, 42–47.

be acknowledged that there is truth in Rowland's analysis, and it could be argued that Ratzinger's hermeneutic of *Gaudium et Spes* offers genuine hope of a new synthesis based on what is valuable in the other interpretations.

6. "A style of piety was fostered based more directly on biblical sources and on the public liturgy of the church, to replace the so called 'devotionalism' and the paraliturgical practices that had characterized the late Middle Ages and had showed great vitality in the nineteenth and early twentieth centuries." This is a very complex issue, but whatever one makes of it, a plethora of devotional practices in most Catholic parishes vanished virtually overnight.

Much else vanished virtually overnight in the wake of the liturgical reforms. This is how some of the vanishing is described by church historian Diarmaid MacCulloch:

> Overnight, the Tridentine rite of the Mass was virtually banned (with carefully hedged-around exceptions), and its Latin replacement was used almost universally in vernacular translations. The service of Benediction of the Blessed Sacrament, which had sustained and comforted so many for so long . . . was widely discountenanced by the clergy in an effort to concentrate the minds of the laity on the Mass, and in large sections of the Catholic world it disappeared. The altar furniture that had grown with such exuberance in churches in the wake of the Council of Trent was rendered redundant by the decision to reposition the celebrant at Mass facing the people: the priest therefore stood behind the altar, which had previously been affixed to a wall of sculpture and painting and thus had been designed for celebration in the other direction. A multitude of tables often cheap in appearance if not in cost camped out in historic church buildings, while the emphasis on celebrating congregational Masses at a single main altar left the greater galaxy of side altars dusty and neglected.[42]

As an Anglican MacCulloch has no particular axe to grind here. While progressive or liberal Catholics might not warm to what he is saying, his comments may assist them in understanding how more conservative Catholics are hurting. If the church is truly to be a communion such hurt may not be simply dismissed.

7. "There was a de-emphasis of the distinction between clergy and laity." This too is complex, and local collaboration between clergy and laity at parish level has not yet furnished a nomenclature and a uniform understanding of roles that refuses to diminish either, or to insist upon the superiority of one over the other. The universal call to holiness, however, accompanied by a retrieved understanding of lay participation as church has had one very significant gain: it has pointed to the fact, the traditional fact that it is the entire structured community of the church

42. MacCulloch, *A History of Christianity*, 974.

that celebrates the liturgy and especially the Eucharist, and not just the person presiding over the celebration. It has pointed to the fundamental importance of Baptism. The priest is not "saying Mass" for the laity. *All* are celebrating the Eucharist, but appropriately, in accordance with the structured communion that is the church. This is how theologian Nicholas Lash has captured this de-emphasis: "There are many weaknesses in liturgy today: the banality of so much that we sing, the uneven quality of translations, the poverty of so much preaching and our failure to make the liturgy what Paul VI called a 'school of prayer', among others. But to dwell on these would risk distracting our attention from what is the Council's single most profound and significant achievement."[43]

8. "There emerged a greater sensitivity to local needs and customs, especially in missionary lands, and an effort to abandon the presupposition of European cultural superiority and dominance in missionary efforts." This is the phenomenon known as enculturation and has become somewhat controversial.

One might debate the pros and cons of this summary of John O'Malley, adding both nuance and subtlety in the process. If, however, O'Malley's summary of what happened at and after Vatican II may be taken as reasonably accurate, then a certain pluralism of ecclesial positions and interpretations was inevitable. There was both loss and gain. "Catholicism became again a community of internal dialogue rather than monolithic accord," in the words of Adrian Hastings.[44]

Polarization in the Church

Part of that internal dialogue had to do with ecumenism, the promotion of unity between Catholicism and other Christian traditions. Ecumenism was not welcomed by everyone. The Irish Jesuit and ecumenist Michael Hurley wrote in 1969: "A pessimistic attitude to ecumenism is so widespread among Christians that it might well be considered the greatest obstacle to the cause of reconciling the Churches and the clearest sign of the evil and sinfulness of our disunity. In various ways this pessimism provides an excuse for the indifferent, a difficulty for the interested and a temptation for the committed."[45] *Mutatis mutandis*, these words apply to the years after Vatican II and the changes in the church more generally. The changes that occurred after the council were welcomed by some as they were resisted by others. The differences in viewpoint may be understood in terms of Bernard Lonergan's two total mentalities,

---

43. Lash, *Theology for Pilgrims*, 228. See also the useful comments of the church historians Schelkens et al., *Aggiornamento?* 127–61, and more particularly here 148–52.

44. Hastings, "Vatican II, Council of," 739.

45. Hurley, SJ, *Theology of Ecumenism*, 86. See Cummings, *One Body in Christ*, 40–52 for a sympathetic summary of Michael Hurley's ecumenical witness and commitment.

the classicist worldview and the historical mindedness worldview.[46] The classicist perspective is focused on the horizon that does not change—no development of doctrine, liturgy, moral practice, and understanding. Historical mindedness, on the other hand, recognizes that the church is organic and, to use John Henry Newman's words from his 1845 *Essay on the Development of Doctrine*, "In heaven it may be different, but here on earth to live is to change and to be perfect is to have changed often."[47] Change can be very difficult for people, and so acceptance and resistance have always been found in the wake of an ecumenical council. However, disagreement in itself is not a bad thing. Indeed, as Nicholas Lash points out, "A Church in which there were no serious disagreements would be dead." While respectful disagreement is a sign of vitality, the dramatized simplification of disagreement that is polarization is most destructive, and this unfortunately is much in evidence.[48] Arguably, the internal dialogue in the church has given rise to an unnecessary degree of acerbity between Catholics of different perspectives with regard to Vatican II and its implementation. This has led at times to a lack of charity, well put by the late Canadian Dominican ecumenical theologian, Jean Tillard: "It is easy for me to declare my love for the Scythian or the barbarian who is at a distance; it is difficult for me to love the Scythian or the barbarian who is my neighbor. Our membership in the same local church is what constrains me. Is it not the place of Christ's visitation?"[49]

If the local church is the place of Christ's visitation, it becomes a challenge of the greatest importance to overcome the hideously destructive polarization among Catholics. Polarization, needless to say, is not unique to Catholics. At the point of any great change in any society, it is almost sadly inevitable. I cannot think of a better way to confront this insidious and destructive polarization than by drawing attention to the wise words of two Christian leaders, Fr. Timothy Radcliffe, OP, former Master General of the Dominicans, and the former archbishop of Canterbury, Rowan D. Williams. Both men have written sanely and sagely about the issue of polarization in their communities.

In Radcliffe, we read:

> Opposition between right and left, between "conservative" and "progressive" is largely incompatible with the deepest institutions of Catholicism. . . . Truth also opens up communion between people who are divided. When I disagree with someone, we can overcome our differences by looking for the larger truth that embraces my little truth and that of the other. The search for the truth means that we need not be stuck forever in our failure to agree, our mutual incomprehension. Belief that it is possible to arrive at the truth, the objective truth, implies the promise of reconciliation, arriving at a clarity of perception

46. Lonergan, "The Transition from a Classicist World View," *passim*.

47. Newman, *An Essay on the Development of Doctrine*, 39.

48. Lash, *Theology for Pilgrims*, 231.

49. Tillard, *I Believe Despite Everything*, 15.

in which we recognize and understand what is true for the other. . . . If I find myself in disagreement with others, rather than just tolerating their opinion, I should try to find out how far I might be in the wrong.[50]

In Williams we read:

When we call on others to repent, can we hear God calling us to recognize our own rebellion, whatever it is? If not, have we understood faith? We are always in danger of the easiest religious technique of all, the search for the scapegoat. . . . I am "grieved" by the failings of others. I too have to accept that I am part of this failing or "catastrophic" church. . . . We can look at and listen to the language we use of each other and watch how easily we are ready to let it slip from proper and honest disagreement towards contempt and mutual exclusion. Yet, as baptized believers, we still have something to offer each other; and the friendship of the baptized should remain, whatever else divides.[51]

Both of these theologians, with a genuine love and concern for their own churches, recognize the degree of polarization, of misunderstanding and ambiguity and hurt that has taken place over recent years. Both offer a hermeneutic of ecclesial misunderstanding and difference, and invite conversion, an invitation to repentance of any contribution made to this ecclesial polarization either on the right or the left, either by self-styled conservative or self-styled liberal. This is no recipe for an easy and lazy tolerance that is nothing short of intellectual and ecclesial complacency. Rather, it is to recognize that truth which matters most to human beings is not-already-out-there-now, but must be agonized towards in a communion of receptive difference and enormous patience. Or as Radcliffe puts it pithily, "We can resist the compulsion to evict those who disagree with us,"[52] and the Irish Augustinian ecumenical theologian, Gabriel Daly, "The truly Christian task is to enable [conservatives and progressives] to live charitably together while disagreeing with each other's convictions."[53]

Concluding his book *The Theology of Vatican II* Bishop Christopher Butler, who had participated in all sessions of the council, wisely has this to say: "The Council has to be digested and assimilated by the universal church, and the process will take not years

---

50. Radcliffe, *I Call You Friends*, 37–81.

51. Williams, "Archbishop's Presidential Address," 18–25.

52. Radcliffe, *What Is the Point of Being a Christian?* 212.

53. Daly, *The Church: Always in Need of Reform*, 137. Daly continues in this vein: "There are two conflicting mindsets in the church, which can loosely be described as conservative and liberal; and there is no possibility of consensus between them. To pretend that there can be substantive intellectual accord between them could involve mental dishonesty and lack of transparency. Every Christian is bound to seek peace and loving care; but that peace must not offend against truth and logic. To seek agreement between two opposing mindsets may seem a laudable venture; but it must be an agreement to accept the differences rather than pretend that there is intellectual compatibility between them. Consensus on mutually contradictory intellectual and moral convictions is not possible without self-deception."

but many decades."[54] Very obviously, we remain in this decades-long process of digestion and assimilation and the reception of the spirit of the council is, to say the least, not uniform across the church. What seems very clear, however, is that there is no going back, no returning to some imaginary golden age prior to Vatican II.

54. Butler, *The Theology of Vatican II*, 211.

14

Concilium and Communio: Karl Rahner, SJ (1904–84), and Hans Urs von Balthasar (1905–88)

In recent years, at least within Catholicism, there has been an unfortunate tendency to ideologize and polarize these stances. It is strange to run into those who will read and follow only von Balthasar or only Rahner . . . and see the positions of others as almost heretical.

—Michael Paul Gallagher, SJ[1]

Karl Rahner and Hans Urs von Balthasar are the two most significant figures of twentieth-century Roman Catholic theology. . . . Each had periods in the ascendancy and periods when they were, one might say, in the doghouse, and it is probably still too soon to say which will be taken as the more important thinker in the long run.

—Karen Kilby[2]

Introduction

VATICAN II ENDED IN 1965, so that post-conciliar theology extends from 1965 to the present. Both pre-conciliar and conciliar theologians have made their contribution and impressions, and have influenced the ways in which theology is done from 1965 until the present. It is out with the scope of this book to identify all the significant players in the period after Vatican II. Nonetheless, it is probably true to say that two theologians in particular have dominated the post-conciliar period, the German Jesuit Karl Rahner and the Swiss former Jesuit Hans Urs von Balthasar, not only in terms of their actual theological reflection, but also just as much in terms of their theological methodology. Rahner and Balthasar represent two contrasting ways of doing Catholic theology both before and especially after Vatican II. Their own immediate theological output was

1. Gallagher, *Clashing Symbols*, 141.
2. Kilby, "Balthasar and Karl Rahner," 256.

enormous, the amount of secondary commentary and interpretation continues to grow, and they represent, obviously with significant qualification stemming from contemporary insights and perspectives, the dominant approaches today.

Introducing Rahner and Balthasar, Concilium, and Communio

The English Dominican Cornelius Ernst noted in an essay on the 1970 congress to do with the theological journal, *Concilium*: "Gossip; a new periodical said to be coming out soon to challenge *Concilium*, under the names of H. U. von Balthasar, Ratzinger and Le Guillou."[3] This new journal coming to birth was *Communio. Concilium*, Latin for "council," suggested a continuation of the achievement of Vatican II in the liberating mode of the council, and *Communio* the inner reality of the church and of the Trinity and of ongoing re-creation from the doctrinal heart of the tradition. If *Concilium* was largely associated with Rahner, *Communio* became identified with von Balthasar and his circle.

Many of the criticisms of Rahner need to be seen against the background of Vatican II. There are those who feel that the council went much too far in surrendering tradition to modernity, and find Rahner a type, perhaps *the* type of this surrender.[4] Others are of the view that the implications of Vatican II are insufficiently implemented, and so view the current interest in Balthasar as expressive of a restorationist perspective. Though it is a caricature, Karl Barth is seen to Friedrich Schleiermacher as Balthasar is to Rahner. Both Schleiermacher and Rahner in their different ways sought to modernize Christian faith by rooting it anthropologically. Barth and Balthasar maintained the integrity of Christian faith by keeping the focus on God where it ought to be, and not on the human subject. Yet, it is utterly simplistic to associate Rahner with the progressive wing of Catholicism and Balthasar with its conservative wing without qualification. The Rahner scholar, Philip Endean, says of Rahner devotees: "His fans often present him as a figure who adapted Catholic tradition to the modern world. But friends like these only make his critics' case appear more plausible."[5] Could we adapt for Balthasar? "His fans often present him as a figure who saved Catholic tradition from the acids of the modern world. But friends like these only make his critics' case appear more plausible."

Rahner and Balthasar had been close friends. Their friendship continued until the early 1960s. Rahner's student, Herbert Vorgrimler, tells of a visit that he and Rahner made to the house of Balthasar and Adrienne von Speyr in the Münsterplatz in Basel in 1961. This was to be the last visit between the two theologians, and it was both open and friendly. However, alienation set in between them to which personal factors made a contribution. Balthasar was not invited to participate in Vatican II as

---

3. Ernst, *Multiple Echo*, 42.

4. Marmion, "Christian Identity in a Postmodern Age," 170–71.

5. Endean, "Spirituality and Religious Experience," 201.

Rahner had been, and Rahner was Balthasar's rival for the chair of Romano Guardini at the University of Munich in 1963. The differences between them were more than personal, however, having to do with quite contrasting approaches to theology.[6]

Karl Rahner, SJ (1904–84)

"Karl Rahner was fond of describing himself as an 'amateur theologian.' This piece of self-effacing modesty on the part of the most influential and widely-read Catholic theologian of the twentieth century affords an illuminating perspective on his work. . . . Rahner referred to himself as an amateur theologian in part to signal the unsystematic nature of his work."[7] Rahner much preferred the genre of the essay over large volumes of systematics. Many of his collected essays find their origin in practical issues that he was addressing in the life of the church. Interviewed for his seventieth birthday, Rahner said: "Behind everything I did stood a very immediate, pastoral and spiritual interest."[8] His academic work, however, did not begin in theology but in philosophy.

Initially, his graduate work in philosophy was at the University of Freiburg. He failed his doctorate, but out of it *Spirit in the World* was published. The book breathes not only the spirit of Aquinas, albeit an Aquinas mediated by his Belgian confrère Joseph Marechal, SJ, but also shows the influence of Hegel and Heidegger. After this his superiors invited him to turn his hand to theology, and he received a doctorate in theology from the University of Innsbrück. The dissertation was entitled *E Latere Christi*, "The Church Born from the Side of Christ." The first dissertation was an interpretation of Aquinas through the lens of modern philosophy, while the second was an interpretation of Scripture through the lens of the Fathers of the Church.[9] Unlike Balthasar, Rahner spent most of his life teaching in universities. Apart from brief spells at the Universities of Münster and Munich, he spent most of his academic life at the University of Innsbrück. The theological output of Karl Rahner may be grouped under five headings:

1. **His early philosophical works:** *Spirit in the World* [1939] and *Hearers of the Word* [1941]. While *Spirit in the World* is firmly within the tradition of Thomism, Rahner makes it clear that he relies "more on the inner driving dynamism of Thomism than on specific texts."[10] "Spirit is the desire (dynamic openness) for absolute being. . . . The human spirit as such is desire, striving, action. Every operation of the spirit can therefore be understood only as a moment in the movement

---

6. Vorgrimler, *Understanding Karl Rahner*, 124.

7. DiNoia, "Karl Rahner," 118–20.

8. Cited in O'Donovan, "Karl Rahner, SJ (1904–1984)," 357.

9. Kress, "Karl Rahner: A New Father of the Church?" 254.

10. Rahner, SJ, *Spirit in the World*, 286.

toward absolute being as toward the one end and goal of the desire of the spirit."[11] Orientation of spirit to Spirit as absolute Mystery is orientation to God.

2. **His essays in theology,** gathered into twenty-three volumes in English as *Theological Investigations*. Rahner preferred the essay as his theological genre. The German title of the collected essays is simply *Schriften zür Theologie*, literally "Writings on Theology." The English title, *Theological Investigations*, has led some to think of a deliberate nod in the direction of Ludwig Wittgenstein's *Philosophical Investigations*.[12] These "writings" or "investigations" have been accurately described as "a series of brilliant experiments, intended to advance the state of discussion of particular Christian doctrines."[13]

3. **His editing of theological dictionaries,** and first, the great German theological encyclopedia, *Lexicon für Theologie und Kirche*, consisting of ten volumes, published between 1957 and 1967. In 1961, Rahner's own edited dictionary *Sacramentum Mundi* (1967–69), following in the main Rahnerian lines of thought was published. Finally, there came out in 1961 the *Theological Dictionary*, edited by Rahner and Herbert Vorgrimler.

4. **The series of books known as *Quaestiones Disputatae*,** published by Herder from 1958 onwards. Rahner wrote sixteen of these monographs either himself or co-authored with others, including Joseph Ratzinger. His final contribution was *The Unity of the Churches*, written along with Heinrich Fries.[14]

5. **Rahner's own summary version,** within his philosophical tradition, of the Christian faith, *The Foundations of Christian Faith* was published in 1976. It sums up his entire theological system, but really it should be read in tandem with the appropriate articles from the *Theological Investigations*. "Foundations" may give the wrong impression since it carries a lot of philosophical freight. In fact, the German word is *Grundkürs*, giving as a more accurate if less exciting title, *A Fundamental Course in the Faith*.

Throughout all his work, Rahner is concerned with a foundational aspect of human consciousness, that is, that our knowing and willing and the act of loving in self-gift are, *ipso facto*, a being drawn towards the transcendental horizon of absolute Mystery, the Mystery we call "God." As Anglican theologian and Rahner expert, John Macquarrie, puts it "There is a humanistic philosophy underlying much of his theology, a view of man as destined for God and seeking God."[15] This is worth spelling out at some length.

11. Rahner, SJ, *Spirit in the World*, 280–83.

12. Nichols, *Catholic Thought Since the Enlightenment*, 143.

13. DiNoia, "Karl Rahner," 120.

14. Fries and Rahner, SJ, *Unity of the Churches* (1985).

15. Macquarrie, *Twentieth Century Religious Thought*, 382.

Whether we are consciously aware of it or not, we are always already related to God. Rahner puts it like this:

> We shall call *transcendental experience* the subjective, unthematic, necessary and unfailing consciousness of the knowing subject that is co-present in every spiritual act of knowledge, and the subject's openness to the unlimited expanse of all possible reality. It is an *experience* because this knowledge, unthematic but ever-present, is a moment within and a condition of possibility for every concrete experience of any and every object. This experience is called *transcendental* experience because it belongs to the necessary and inalienable structures of the knowing subject itself, and because it consists precisely in the transcendence beyond any particular group of possible objects or categories. . . . There is present in this transcendental experience an unthematic and anonymous, as it were, knowledge of God.[16]

An example may help—the experience of driving a car: Driving a car is a concrete experience, better, a concrete series of experiences: putting the key in the ignition, looking in the mirror, accelerating, braking, and so forth. At the same time, and indeed necessarily, the driver is aware of a horizon through which he is passing. The experience of driving necessitates a horizon. The awareness of the horizon through which one is passing does not necessarily have an intensity to it, but that does not make it unreal. It is real, but without absolute lucidity, without absolutely focused awareness. The routine of driving the car is *categorical* awareness in relation to the horizon, which is *transcendental* awareness.[17] Transcendental and categorical experience are not two different experiences, but rather two dimensions of every and all human experience. In other words, in all our knowing and willing and loving we *are* a transcendent drive towards Mystery, even if Mystery is not formally and consciously named as such. It is necessarily known, if not necessarily named. Rahner's theology in this respect is like a long extended comment on the famous axiom of St. Augustine: "Thou hast made us for thyself, O Lord, and our hearts are restless until they find their rest in thee."[18]

While it may sound as if Rahner's position is that the human person is autonomously finding God unthematically in the inner reachings and dynamics of knowing and willing, that is not actually the case. The human person's experience of transcendent drive is already a being drawn by God, to God, who desires communion with everyone. Each person is a *graced* orientation towards Mystery. Thus, Rahner writes:

> Whenever man in his transcendence experiences himself as questioning, as disquieted by the appearance of being, as open to something ineffable, he

---

16. Rahner, *Foundations of Christian Faith*, 20–21.

17. I owe discussion of this car-driving analogy to many fine conversations with the Rahner scholar, the late Fr. Eamon P. Clarke, of the Archdiocese of Birmingham, England.

18. McCabe, "The Mystery of the Human," 47.

cannot understand himself as subject in the sense of an *absolute* subject, but only in the sense of one who receives being, ultimately only in the sense of grace. In this context "grace" means the freedom of the ground of being (God) which gives being to man, a freedom which man experiences in his finiteness and contingency.[19]

Thus, for Rahner, in our restless knowing and willing it is less the situation that we are reaching towards God than that God is reaching towards us, and so enabling our reaching towards God. In a word, grace is at work from beginning to end. The Anglican theologian Mark McIntosh has captured the nature of our reaching towards God nicely when he describes it as a "momentum" that God "sets loose" in us.[20] This "momentum," this gracious outreach of God to every human person is what Rahner called the "supernatural existential." All are offered this grace of Christ—there is no other grace—and all who respond to it without necessarily realizing it are in Rahner's famous phrase "anonymous Christians."

Throughout his work Rahner emphasized the sheer incomprehensibility of God. "The incomprehensible, inexhaustible, limitless reality of the presence we call God' is not a term we have not yet succeeded in understanding entirely, but rather an ultimate of intelligibility inviting us to accept and embrace it unconditionally."[21] Everything that is said and thought about God is the categorical expression of this real, primal, albeit unthematic consciousness of God, and is, therefore, always inadequate, necessarily falling short of the Mystery. The categorical expression is always secondary to transcendental consciousness. The prior, originating and transcendent experience is always primary. This has implications for all theological expression, for all theological categories without exception, even for the category "God." "God" is often considered as an object in the world of objects, even if the Supreme Object, "a member of the larger household of all reality."[22] In reality, however, God is Holy Mystery: "Whether he is consciously aware of it or not, whether he is open to this truth or suppresses it, man's whole spiritual and intellectual existence is oriented towards a holy mystery which is the basis of his being. This mystery is the inexplicit and unexpressed horizon which always encircles and upholds the small area of our everyday experience of knowing and acting, our knowledge of reality and our free action. . . . We call this God."[23] Not inevitably, and more than likely due to his studies of Ignatius of Loyola with his vision of all things in relation to God, Rahner's theological method leads in the direction of mysticism. John Macquarrie writes: "Since Rahner had a strongly mystical element in his make-up, he often speaks of God as the Nameless."[24]

19. Rahner, *Foundations of Christian Faith*, 34.

20. McIntosh, *Mystical Theology*, 98.

21. O'Donovan, "Karl Rahner, SJ," 353.

22. McCabe, "The Mystery of the Human," 52.

23. Rahner, "The Need for a Short Formula of Christian Faith," 122.

24. Macquarrie, "Ebb and Flow of Hope," 208.

What does Rahner's approach then say about the particularity of Jesus Christ, the categorical expression that *is* Jesus Christ? Is Christ but one example, even the unsurpassably unique example, of this universal orientation to the divine? One could choose to interpret Rahner along such lines. Arguably, however, there is another way of reading Rahner on Christ, that is, as the Savior, "as the decisive moment internal to the unfolding of God's universal saving will within the history of the world."[25] He is simultaneously the absolute fullness of God's self-communication to humankind and the fullness of humankind's response to the divine gift. In the particular human being, Jesus of Nazareth, God and God's creation become one, without ceasing to be what they each are. In this way of understanding, the divinity of Christ does not stand in polar opposition to the humanity of Christ. "To be human is to transcend all things, to 'go beyond' all things towards God: when this transcendence, this 'going beyond,' is carried to its single, highest and most radical instance, then in that case to be human is to be God: 'The incarnation of God is . . . the unique, *supreme* case of the total actualization of human reality.'"[26]

This approach to Christology is very interesting. Jesus is, therefore, simultaneously the coincidence of God's gracious outreach to creation and especially his human creatures, and the 'upward' striving of creation and especially human creatures towards absolute transcendence, that is, God. Rahner's language and thought patterns suggest that the difference between Jesus and us is a matter of degree. If Jesus is the supreme case of total transcendent actualization, then we are minor examples of it. This is not a reductionist interpretation. Karen Kilby has it right when she says: "It is quite possible . . . to talk about a difference of degree which is nevertheless a radical difference, and one can talk about the fulfillment of a possibility built into human nature without automatically suggesting that any of us could achieve this fulfillment if only we tried a little harder."[27] A difference of degree may be such that for all practical differences it is a difference in kind.

Rahner on Balthasar

For Rahner, Balthasar is too much under the influence of the early German idealists like Schelling. In his theology of the descent of Christ into hell, expressed in his *Mysterium Paschale*,[28] and the way in which the Trinity is engaged in that mystery, for Rahner Balthasar too radically divides the persons of the Trinity. Rahner wonders how Balthasar knows so much about God! "He asked from where von Balthasar had obtained his knowledge of the inner life of the deity."[29] Rahner writes:

25. Lane, "Karl Rahner's Contribution to Interreligious Dialogue," 95.
26. Rahner, cited in Kilby, *Karl Rahner: A Brief Introduction*, 20.
27. Rahner, cited in Kilby, *Karl Rahner: A Brief Introduction*, 21.
28. Balthasar, *Mysterium Paschale*.
29. Vorgrimler, *Understanding Karl Rahner*, 125.

It is to me a source of consolation to realize that God, when and insofar as he entered into this history as his own, did it in a different way than I did. From the beginning I am locked into this horror while God—if this word is to continue to have any meaning at all—is in a true and authentic sense the God who does not suffer, the immutable God, and so on. [In Balthasar, Moltmann, and others] I sense a theology of absolute paradox, of Patripassianism, perhaps even of a Schelling-esque projection into God of division, conflict, godlessness and death.[30]

This is in many respects the influence of Adrienne von Speyr. Not all theologians were fully appreciative of von Speyr's influence on Balthasar, including, in at least the early days, Joseph Ratzinger. In 1963, Ratzinger moved briefly to the University of Münster, and then in 1966 to the University of Tübingen where he remained until 1969. There he was a colleague of Hans Küng, who had worked to bring about his appointment. They worked together and on a friendly basis. Küng in his memoirs says that he could make nothing of Balthasar's friend, the mystic Adrienne von Speyr, and he says that this was also true of Ratzinger. He notes that Ratzinger remarked to him in regard to von Speyr that now "all is up with Balthasar," even though Ratzinger's own friendship with Balthasar was to develop.[31] This would be a fair reading of Rahner's position too.

Hans Urs von Balthasar (1905–88)

Hans Urs von Balthasar never taught in a university or a seminary as such. His doctoral work was in philosophy and literature—it has been described as "a huge and unmanageable thesis about the religious implications of German literature and philosophy"—and it was published in a three-volume work entitled *The Apocalypse of the German Soul* (1937–39).[32] He entered the Society of Jesus in 1929, and studied philosophy in Pullach with Erich Przywara (1889–1972), and it was Przywara who introduced Balthasar to a way of appreciating Aquinas that was not dominated by the arid manuals of neo-scholasticism, the latter described as something Balthasar bitterly hated.[33] Balthasar went on to study theology for the customary four years at the Jesuit house of studies at Fourvière, Lyons. There he came into contact with the likes of Henri De Lubac (though never actually taught by him), Jean Daniélou, and Gaston Fessard, and he developed a powerful and enduring love of patristic theology.

30. Imhoff and Biallowons, *Karl Rahner in Dialogue*, 126–27.

31. Küng, *My Struggle for Freedom, Memoirs*, 119. This seems at least implicitly confirmed by Ratzinger in a response to a question about Adrienne von Speyr put to him by Peter Seewald: "Was her work not so appealing to you?" Ratzinger: "Not to me, no. That differentiated us [Ratzinger and Balthasar]. One has to say he was someone defined by mysticism." See Benedict XVI with Peter Seewald, *Last Testament*, 148.

32. Nichols, *Figuring Out the Church*, 133.

33. Kerr, *Twentieth Century Catholic Theologians*, 121.

Fourvière was a center of the *nouvelle théologie*. Many years later, Balthasar describes the influence of de Lubac: "He showed us the way beyond the scholastic stuff to the Fathers of the Church. . . . And so when all the others went off to play football . . . [we] got down to Origen, Gregory of Nyssa, and Maximus."[34] After priestly ordination, he worked as a chaplain to the University of Basel. Basel was to introduce him to the two central influences on his theology, the Protestant theologian Karl Barth and the mystic Adrienne von Speyr. He attended a number of Barth's lectures, and went on to publish a book on Barth's theology that received high praise from Barth himself.[35] In 1940 Balthasar received into the Catholic Church Adrienne Kaegi-von Speyr (1902–67), a Swiss physician. From 1940 through 1944 allegedly von Speyr was the recipient of visions and mystical experiences, including bilocation and the stigmata.[36] Balthasar then headed up his own publishing company, *Johannesverlag*, in the first instance "to publish the dictations he was by now taking down from Speyr during her mystical trances,"[37] and he also developed a secular institute, the *Johannes-Gemeinschaft*, with von Speyr as "the spiritual mother and [Balthasar] the fatherly theologian and guide."[38] He left the Jesuits in 1950 to develop his work with this secular institute. Leaving the Jesuits put a certain cloud on Balthasar and was undoubtedly the reason why he was not invited to attend Vatican II. The rest of his life was taken up with theological research and writing. He was named a cardinal by Pope John Paul II in 1988 but died three days before the ceremony of conferral.

Balthasar's multi-faceted work is difficult to describe, not least because it is largely but not exclusively a densely written trilogy of fifteen volumes: *The Aesthetics*—a study of the beauty or glory of God, *The Theo-Drama*—a study of God's saving action in the world and *The Theo-Logic*—a study of the truth of God. The excellent Balthasarian scholar, Edward T. Oakes, provides at least an opening description that suggests its richness: "neither conventionally liberal nor captiously conservative, neither neo-Thomist nor modernist, critical both of Karl Rahner's transcendental Thomism and even more so of the manualist Thomism that was standard in Catholic seminaries in the wake of Pope Pius X's campaign against Modernism."[39]

34. Balthasar, *My Work in Retrospect*, 11.

35. Balthasar, *The Theology of Karl Barth*. The translator is Edward T. Oakes, SJ, one of the finest Balthasar commentators. For a very concise summary account of Barth's influence on Balthasar, one could not do better than begin with Fergus Kerr, *Twentieth Century Catholic Theologians*, 126–31. Kerr had been a student at Aberdeen University of Donald M. Mackinnon, a great admirer of Karl Barth and with whom he had a conversation in which he had praised Balthasar's book, and Mackinnon in turn was one of the earliest British theologians to show an interest in the theology of Balthasar.

36. Kerr, *Twentieth Century Catholic Theologians*, 123.

37. Kerr, *Twentieth Century Catholic Theologians*, 123. See also Riches and Quash, "Hans Urs von Balthasar," 134, and Schumacher, "Ecclesial Existence: Person and Community in the Trinitarian Theology of Adrienne von Speyr."

38. Nichols, *Figuring Out the Church*, 134.

39. Oakes, "Hans Urs von Balthasar (1905–1988)," 137: Balthasar's objective was "to salvage enough of the best divinity, spirituality, and literature of past and present to ensure that at least among

Oakes provides us with a rich description of Balthasar as a thinker not easily pigeon-holed, as a thinker whose wide range marks him as primarily dialogical. In this regard it is surely interesting that on the eve of Vatican II Balthasar published a book with the title *Martin Buber and Christianity*, in which he describes Buber as "one of the most creative minds of our age" and "the originator of the 'dialogical principle.'"[40]

If Rahner's theology is grounded in this universal, unthematic human orientation to the Mystery of God, Balthasar's theology is grounded in the Christ-event as rendered canonically in the Gospels as proclaimed by the church. Balthasar's scope is no less universal than Rahner's even as it is entirely christocentric. Mark McIntosh sums it up: "Von Balthasar liked to speak of the life, death and resurrection of Jesus as a kind of dramatic stage (*Spielraum*) upon which all human beings are able to discover their truest and most authentic calling in life; here all people may each discover the 'role' whose enactment will mean the fulfillment of their existence."[41] For Balthasar all creation comes to be through the Divine Word who is the eternal expression of the Father in self-giving love. There is and can be nothing outside the Word. Thus, the impress of the Word is to be found in everything. The historical event of Jesus Christ is: "the real meaning and enactment of the very patterns of existence by which every creature is given life and unfolds life. . . . Jesus, as the incarnation of the very same pattern of self-giving love by which all things came to be, is himself predisposed to a kind of existential openness to everyone. His life is eminently 'participable' or shareable; indeed, he seems to live by giving himself away."[42] The saints and the mystics are those who have most fully let themselves be drawn into participation in Jesus's existence. The saints and mystics are: "quite inexplicable except as participations in Christ's states." Because Christ's passion-unto-death is the ultimate expression of his life as self-donation in love—and, therefore, of that eternal Trinitarian self-donation—the saints and mystics find themselves drawn into the Passion of Christ—"something of the passion is, through the grace of the Head, constantly being made present in the body."[43]

Balthasar on Rahner

Karen Kilby writes: "Balthasar can be a subtle and sympathetic reader of the texts of others, but at times (especially perhaps in polemical moments) he paints with very broad brush strokes, and, whatever the benefits of this, fairness to individuals may be

---

his readers (and readers of other works put out by his publishing house), there would be passed on to posterity a Catholic culture, wide enough and rich enough to serve as a basis for Christian life and mission as it ought to be rather than as it often is."

40. Balthasar, *Martin Buber and Christianity*, 9.

41. McIntosh, *Mystical Theology*, 101–2.

42. McIntosh, *Mystical Theology*, 102.

43. Balthasar, "Theology and Sanctity," 199–200.

one of the costs."[44] This seems to me to be true, and perhaps especially when it comes to his reaction to Karl Rahner. In the 1960s, Balthasar's criticism of Rahner became more significant, but it was not entirely new. For example, there was a definite critical element in his 1939 review of Rahner's failed but published doctoral dissertation *Spirit in the World*. Although overall he was appreciative, he judged that Rahner was too much in the thrall of German idealism, the idealism that glorifies human autonomy to the detriment of God.

Karen Kilby points out that for a long time Balthasar showed his support of Rahner, not least when Rahner found himself in difficulty *vis-à-vis* the Vatican, but it did not remain so: "When Rahner was not yet established, or under threat of censure, Balthasar was largely supportive and appreciative; but when at the Second Vatican Council and in the years that followed Rahner's influence was 'flavor of the day,' and furthermore was associated in Balthasar's mind with disturbing developments in the Catholic Church, then the element of disagreement and criticism that had always been present came to the fore, and fiercely."[45] The premier expression of this fierce critique is undoubtedly Balthasar's 1966 book, *Cordula oder der Ernstfall*, in English, *The Moment of Christian Truth* (1994). Balthasar's criticisms amount essentially to this, that Rahner in trying to make Christianity credible to humankind today is endangering the Christian substance in the following ways: he considers Rahner to be reductive in identifying love of neighbor with love of God, reducing, as it were, religion to ethics; and Rahner does not take sin seriously enough, nor does he consider the cross of Christ in a sufficiently important way. Balthasar's judgment is debatable on both points. In respect of the unity of love of God and of neighbor, while Rahner notes a theoretical distinction, he affirms equally an indissoluble ontological connection, ultimately rooted in Matthew 25:40: "Truly, I tell you, just as you did it to one of the least of these my brothers, you did it to me." But perhaps the real and substantive difference between the two men is the way that they come at these issues. Thus, Rowan Williams makes the following comment about Balthasar's criticism of Rahner on the theology of the cross of Christ: "[Rahner] is by no means insensitive to the need for a theology of the Cross. . . . The heart of the difference here seems to be that Rahner thinks of human frustration in terms of incompletion, Balthasar in terms of tragedy."[46] We could put it differently: Rahner from a philosophical angle comes at the cross in and through an anthropological lens, while Balthasar's viewing is through great literature and especially the genre of tragedy. Balthasar allows much more for the realities of self-deceit, self-destruction and refusal. Balthasar views the anthropological approach, the approach "from below" as fraught with problems. Dialogue with the world, for Balthasar, is "so much more complex a matter than it sometimes seems to be for Rahner; because

44. Kilby, "Balthasar and Karl Rahner," 260.
45. Kilby, "Balthasar and Karl Rahner," 257.
46. Williams, "Balthasar and Rahner," 32.

the world is *not* a world of well-meaning agnostics but of totalitarian nightmares, of nuclear arsenals, labor camps and torture chambers."[47]

Balthasar also feels that Rahner's notion of the anonymous Christian leads the church in a dangerous direction. Why bother with professing Christian faith if one is already an anonymous Christian? No pain, no gain! This, however, seems to me not to come close to what Rahner is talking about. Rahner maintained firmly that no one is without grace, and that grace is the grace of Jesus Christ since there is no other, even if it is unknown. The anonymity in the first instance is not a soteriological anonymity that dispenses with Christ. It is a totally christocentric vision in which the grace of Christ is utterly prior and efficacious. Nor does it dispense the subject from receiving (or rejecting) this un-named grace which he experiences. The immediate criteria of receptivity for Rahner have to do with the qualities, the virtues, the practices that make for human flourishing in whatever one's circumstances. But that is never enough for Rahner. There is always more. There is always the invitation, provided by life itself (and necessarily under grace!) to penetrate deeper into the nature of this human flourishing, and, therefore, this receptivity to the grace of Christ. That "more" reaches its "most" in the church, in articulate and owned Christian faith. There simply is no reductionism here. Rather, Rahner maintained that if one came to a real appreciation of Christian faith, one would have to become a Christian. Actually, Balthasar reached a similar point of view to Rahner in respect of an optimism about universal salvation. But unlike Rahner he felt no need to articulate an explanation of how it worked. "The Christian may have the new and confusing experience of discovering that most of what he brings with him to the world has in some way or another already reached the world, not in its entirety of course, but in fragments."[48] For Balthasar, the aesthetic tragedian, "The beauty of God incarnate can never be determined in advance by a theological *a priori*."[49] For Rahner the philosophical theologian, in terms of knowing anything there must be some *Vorgriff*, some pre-understanding. It is this philosophical starting-point that Balthasar calls into question. Rahner for him has capitulated to the post-Enlightenment preoccupation with the turn to the subject. "Spirit swallows up nature, and the non-human world is wholly subordinated to human self-fulfillment."[50] But in fact for Rahner this beginning from the subject, this turn to the subject, is *never* an autonomous position, but is always and already a work of grace.

Maybe Balthasar has grasped Rahner aright in this summary statement: "Today, Rahner seems to stand undecided at a crossroads: his thoroughly Catholic heart wants him to be faithful to the visible, official and sacramental Church, but his speculative bent demands the relativisation of everything ecclesiastical in the name of an

---

47. Williams, "Balthasar and Rahner," 33.

48. Balthasar, *Engagement with God*, 97–98.

49. Williams, "Balthasar and Rahner," 13–14.

50. Williams, "Balthasar and Rahner," 24.

all-pervading grace."[51] Two quite different ways of theological thinking, two different ways of looking at the very heart of Christianity. In a very real way, both Rahner and Balthasar are experientially grounded. Rahner offers us a narrative of the self, grounded in knowing, willing and loving, that finds not only its term but also its origin in God. Balthasar offers us a narrative of the self, grounded in the cosmic Christ, whose identity becomes in grace our identity. Both recognize our native orientation to the Mystery of God, Rahner from the universal dynamic of human consciousness understood as God's gracious self-communication, and Balthasar from the concrete particularity of Jesus Christ in whom all things find both their origin and their *telos*. The Irish Balthasar commentator, Gerald O'Hanlon puts the difference, and we may say "tension" between the two theologians well when he says:

> Running right through [Balthasar's] thought is an unease with the attempt to build the bridge between humans and God starting from the side of the human. . . . Balthasar is afraid that this "turn to the subject" . . . in modern theology, in whatever form, ends up measuring God in terms of humanity so that there ensues that neat synthesis which is untrue to the awkwardness of life and the conflict and surprise which are intrinsic to the Christian revelation. . . . Instead of the *a priori* of human natural desire for God, he prefers to stress the *a posteriori* of the loving call of God.[52]

At the same time, both theologians, precisely as Catholic theologians, take the incarnation with the greatest seriousness, albeit from different angles. There is no abolition of the incarnation, but rather its affirmation. Paul Murray draws attention to this joint appreciation of the incarnation, while acknowledging the differences between the two theologians:

> Rahner, for example, does, in a sense, view the Incarnation itself as the achievement of God being met with absolute responsive openness in a way that recapitulates, fulfills, and redeems the story of creation, grace, and sin. He does not, however, take this as a merely static fact, but as a dynamic reality characterizing Jesus' entire life, climactically so in his death, and a movement, moreover, into which others are in turn drawn. Equally, for all Balthasar's concern to depict the contrast between the disorder of sin and the order of grace in starker terms than he finds in Rahner and, with this, to view God's judgment on sin in Jesus' crucifixion as an event of inner-Trinitarian alienation, he also views the total event of the Incarnation as the crowning and fulfillment of creation.[53]

51. Balthasar, "Current Trends," 80.

52. O'Hanlon, SJ, "The Legacy of Hans Urs von Balthasar," 401–2.

53. Murray, "Roman Catholic Theology After Vatican II," 279.

Conclusion

There is indeed a tension between Rahner and Balthasar. Tensions may be understood as signs of life, and, indeed, as signs of genuine respect for the thought of another. If such respect were lacking, one would not bother so to engage the other's thought in such a way as to engender such tension. There is enough in life with which to be concerned! Both Rahner and Balthasar have been accused of heresy.[54] Often, however, when people accuse others of heresy, their real complaint is that the theological understanding and expression of the other is not entirely isomorphic with their own, and, therefore, must be suspect! In reality, however, genuine heresy as a serious threat to the integrity of the faith is relatively rare. As John Macquarrie has pointed out, "in the long run, the only effective answer to heresy, near heresy, and errors of other kinds is for the Church to show that she has a better theology than the person suspected of error."[55]

Neither Rahner nor Balthasar was heretical, but they both demonstrate quite different ways of doing theology. Perhaps we could say that Balthasar represents a high-descending theological methodology, whereas Rahner offers a low-ascending one. Perhaps we could also say that Balthasar is a mystagogue for those captivated primarily by beauty, and Rahner is a mystagogue for those marked with a penchant for philosophical analysis. Even as I write these comments, however, I recognize how inadequate they really are. At best, both theologians offer the community of the faith different styles of theology that reflect different styles of living, and different styles of theological thinking and living that mark the post-conciliar era.

While Rahner and Balthasar are often these days played off against one another, with Rahner as the "progressive" and Balthasar as the "conservative," they both as young men had been rooted in Ignatian spirituality. Acknowledging this common root leads the Scottish Dominican philosophical-theologian Fergus Kerr to conclude that "they were never as far apart as they seem" and "each was far more complicated than the standard story allows."[56] Add to this the comment of the priest-psychologist and Franciscan author, Benedict Groeschel, who is of the opinion that many people demonstrate a strong attraction to one or another of the transcendentals. Thus, for example, the primary transcendental for Aquinas was truth, but for Francis of Assisi it was goodness. Perhaps it might be possible to say, but without the necessary and obvious qualifications, that for Balthasar the primary transcendental is beauty and for Rahner the primary transcendental is truth. They are best understood as complementary not contradictory.[57]

---

54. One thinks of Pitstick, *Hans Urs von Balthasar and the Catholic Doctrine of Christ's Descent into Hell*.

55. Macquarrie, *Thinking about God*, 50–51.

56. Kerr, *Twentieth Century Catholic Theologians*, 104.

57. I owe this reference to Benedict Groeschel to Rowland, *Ratzinger's Faith*, 8. Rowland does not acknowledge her source for Groeschel.

15

Pope John Paul I (August 26–September 28, 1978)

The first pope of demonstrably working-class origins, a man of practical common sense who captivated people with his friendly smile, it is impossible to guess what kind of policies he would have pursued had he lived.

—JOHN N. D. KELLY[1]

John Paul's September was a revolution. He swept away the throne, the crowning, the majestic "we," the word "pontificate," the formal and aloof monarchical style of the papacy.

—ANDREW M. GREELEY[2]

From Albino Luciani to Pope John Paul I

ALBINO LUCIANI WAS BORN in 1912 of poor working-class parents in Forno di Canali, near Belluno in the Dolomite Mountains of northern Italy. His father, Giovanni Luciani, a brick layer, had gone several times to work abroad. Finally, he settled in his own town as a glass-blower, marrying Bartolomea Tancon, who was to become Albino's mother. He was baptized Albino in memory of one of his father's workmates who had been killed in an industrial accident in Germany. As a migrant worker he was known for his interest in socialism, and belonged to a political party known for its anticlericalism. Giovanni Luciani did not object, however, to his son moving towards the priesthood. One of his professors in the major seminary was Alfredo Ottaviani, later Cardinal Ottaviani who, as Peter Hebblethwaite has it," could be counted on to provide manual-theology in all its intransigent rigor."[3] After the usual course of seminary studies and military service Luciani was ordained in 1935.

---

1. Kelly, *The Oxford Dictionary of Popes*, 326.
2. Greeley, *The Making of the Popes 1978*, 162.
3. Hebblethwaite, *The Year of Three Popes*, 91.

From December 1935 to 1937 he was both chaplain and a teacher at the Technical Mining Institute at Agordo. He was appointed vice rector of the seminary at Belluno in 1937. He taught general subjects in the seminary for about a decade, including the difficult years of World War II: dogmatics, philosophy, canon law, sacred art, history of art, history, patristics, sacred eloquence, and catechetics. During this time, like any good teacher, he was much given to note taking from the books that he read, and after his election as pope he sent for his many boxes of notes from his residence in Venice.[4]

After the war, in 1947, Luciani received a doctorate in theology from the Gregorian University in Rome. His doctoral dissertation, supervised by Charles Boyer, SJ, focused on the nineteenth-century Italian priest-philosopher Antonio Rosmini (1797–1855), "The Origin of the Human Soul According to Antonio Rosmini." Rosmini's philosophical publications led to severe criticism, and he was suspect of pantheistic tendencies. In 1849 Rosmini found his book *Five Wounds of the Church* on the Index of Prohibited Books, though later he was rehabilitated. This book was a fairly radical critique of the church's failure to hold on to the allegiance of the people. The five wounds to which Rosmini drew attention were: the separation of the congregation from the priest in worship, the inadequate education of the clergy, disunity in the episcopate, the nomination of bishops by the secular power, and the church's excessive concern with wealth. "The fact that he chose to write on so controversial a character indicated that Luciani had little desire for conventional advancement in the church's hierarchy."[5] Rosmini had not been rehabilitated at the time of Luciani's research and inevitably a certain and moderate pale of suspicion would have been cast over him.

In 1949 Luciani was given responsibility for catechetics for his diocese's Eucharistic Congress. This gave rise to a book entitled *Crumbs from the Catechism*. In 1958 Pope John XXIII appointed him bishop of Vittorio Veneto, a small diocese at the foot of the Italian Alps—in fact, Luciani was the first bishop appointed by Pope John XXIII—and under his direction the diocese adopted a parish in Burundi, an expression of his concern for the developing world. Later, in 1969 he was transferred to Venice as its patriarch. As a personal gift when he was leaving, the people of the diocese made him a gift of 1 million lire. Bishop Luciani returned the gift suggesting that it should be devoted to their own charities. He said to his people: "I came to you owning nothing, and I want to leave you owning nothing."[6] In between Venice-1969 and Vittorio Veneto-1958, of course, occurred Vatican II, which Bishop Luciani attended. Theologically he had been informed in the older manualist approach. The theological perspectives emerging on the floor of the council as well as in the discussions of Council theologians and bishops were inevitably a challenge to him and, indeed, to so many of the bishops. He made the effort to spend the afternoons studying in his room. Bishop Luciani wrote of his experience: "Everything I learned at the Gregorian

4. Seabeck and Seabeck, *The Smiling Pope: The Life and Teaching of John Paul I*, 23.
5. Murphy, *The Papacy Today*, 165.
6. Hebblethwaite, *The Year of Three Popes*, 100.

is useless now. I have to become a student again. Fortunately I have an African bishop as a neighbor in the bleachers in the Council Hall, who gives the texts of the experts of the German bishops. That way I can better prepare myself."[7]

He was in Venice for nine years, and during that period he was host to various ecumenical conferences including the meeting of the Anglican Roman Catholic International Commission which produced in 1976 the Venice Agreed Statement on Authority. He was also a member of the birth control commission appointed by Pope Paul VI, and he voted with the majority to change the teaching on contraception but, of course, the pope chose otherwise.

Luciani was made a cardinal in 1973 by Pope Paul VI. He published a volume entitled *Illustrissimi*, consisting of a series of letters to famous authors and characters in history or fiction, e.g., Pinocchio, Figaro, Charles Dickens, Mark Twain, and Sir Walter Scott.[8] The origin of the volume is provided by Peter Hebblethwaite. According to him Patriarch Luciani said: "When I preach in St. Mark's, I have a hundred, a hundred and fifty, at most two hundred listeners. Half of them are tourists who don't understand Italian, and the other half are wonderful people but they are . . . well, getting on in age. Then the editor of the *Messagero di San Antonio* said to me: 'Write for us, and your audience will increase a thousandfold.' He convinced me."[9] Hebblethwaite makes an interesting contrast between Luciani and Karl Rahner. "Karl Rahner, who is mentioned in *Illustrissimi* had theorized abundantly about 'everyday things'. But book for book, Luciani was better at showing how grace penetrates, if we are prepared to let it, into the remotest corners of human existence."[10] His interests were not exhausted by his work in catechetics or his literary essays. Coming from a working-class background he was keen to reach out to his own class who were not always close to the church. Thus, Patriarch Luciani was involved in an attempt to establish some sort of dialogue between the church and the Italian Communist Party in 1977. At the time a Polish bishop cautioned Luciani about involvement with the Communists, since the Polish experience of the Communists *vis-à-vis* the episcopate was the old maneuver of divide and conquer, the Polish bishop visiting Italy at the time was Karol Wojtyla, who was to become Pope John Paul II.[11] In many ways, the caution was unnecessary. Luciani was not a political nor a theological liberal. As his episcopal experience developed, so did a much more cautious style.

Historian John N. D. Kelly describes Luciani's style: "He had no use for ecclesiastical display, encouraged parish priests to sell precious vessels and other church valuables for the benefit of the poor, and in 1971 proposed that the wealthy churches

---

7. Cited in Gaillardetz, "What Can We Learn from Vatican II?" 91–92.

8. Luciani, *Illustrissimi*.

9. Cited in Hebblethwaite, *The Year of Three Popes*, 107.

10. Hebblethwaite, *The Year of Three Popes*, 108.

11. Seabeck and Seabeck, *The Smiling Pope*, 44–45.

POPE JOHN PAUL I (AUGUST 26–SEPTEMBER 28, 1978)

of the West should give one per cent of their income to the impoverished churches of the Third World."[12]

This is liberation theology at work, and it is not difficult to see here the influential perspective of Antonio Rosmini. There is some evidence to suggest that Luciani advised Pope Paul VI that there should be more study and wide ranging discussion before the publication of *Humanae Vitae*. Whether this is the case or not, it is clear that the patriarch of Venice gave his complete allegiance to the encyclical once it was published.

That same degree of critical openness (on the matter of contraception) may be found also in the letter of congratulations he wrote to Hans Küng when he published his best-selling book *On Being a Christian*.[13] Patriarch Luciani wrote to Küng: "I have read parts of it (my knowledge of German is imperfect) and have found some very fine passages. You have the gift of writing and you could do much good. I confess that I remain doubtful about some points (I am no specialist), and on others in the end I have a different opinion." The letter impressed Küng, a letter marked by "modesty, judgment and serenity" in stark contrast to a number of acerbic letters he received about the book.[14] Luciani even sent Küng a copy of his own book, *Illustrissimi*.[15]

When the patriarch of Venice was asked for a comment on the birth of Louise Brown, the test tube baby born in England, Luciani said: "I send the most heartfelt congratulations to the English baby girl whose conception took place artificially. As far as her parents are concerned, I have no right to condemn them, if they acted with honest intentions and in good faith, they could even be deserving of merit before God for what they wanted and asked the doctors to carry out."[16] One has the strong impression of a man who is devoted to the teaching of the church, and yet is thoroughly marked by a courteous but critical openness to the world.

Pope John Paul I

In the run-up to the conclave on intransigent right-wing Italian group known as *Civilta Cristiana* handed out leaflets and put up posters all over Rome to "Elect a Catholic Pope." To illustrate the left-wing approach to the conclave one might fix upon some comments of Jean-Claude Besret, formerly prior of the Benedictine house at Boquen in Normandy, who opined: "We are abundantly informed about the past life and the funeral of the dead Pope, but we are rigorously excluded from the choice of his successor.

12. Kelly, *The Oxford Dictionary of the Popes*, 325.

13. Holmes, *The Papacy in the Modern World*, 258.

14. Küng, *Disputed Truth, Memoirs II*, 392–93.

15. Greeley, *The Making of the Popes*, 138.

16. Greeley, *The Making of the Popes*, 138.

By what right is the Pope chosen in so archaic a fashion and with such complete disregard for the people whom he is supposed to serve?"[17]

Luciani's election to the papacy after the death of Pope Paul VI in 1978 was something of a surprise. However, there is some persuasive evidence that his election was being promoted by Cardinal Giovanni Benelli, archbishop of Florence, behind the scenes. His opposition to Communism in Italy and his defense of the church's position on divorce and abortion commended him to the right, while his own working-class background and care for the poor commended him to the left.[18] Luciani was not well known outside of Italy, but it seems that the cardinals wanted "a completely new style of Pope, without connections with the curial establishment."[19] Eamon Duffy suggests that his election had to do with lifting "the gloom that had descended during Paul's last years,"[20] a sentiment echoed by the Redemptorist historian, Francis X. Murphy: "It was Pope John all over again—just what the church needed."[21] Luciani was elected on the first day of the conclave and took the name of John Paul I, a token of respect for Pope John XXIII who had ordained him a bishop, and for Pope Paul VI who had made him a cardinal. He was the first pope ever to take a double name. He made clear his intention to the cardinals of continuing to implement the Second Vatican Council. He held a press conference in which, in the words of John Kelly, "he held the thousand journalists present spellbound."[22] His dislike of ostentation and display led to him to dispense with the traditional papal coronation. He was the first pope in at least one thousand years to dispense with the traditional coronation ceremony.[23] In its place he was simply invested with the pallium in St. Peter's Square on September 3.

It seems that Pope John Paul I very quickly got wind of financial irregularities at the Vatican. The editor of the financial journal, *Il Mondo*, Paolo Panarai, wrote an open letter to the pope about these irregularities. What he would have done about these financial challenges remains conjecture, but it is inconceivable, given his concern for the poor and for social justice, that he would not have risen to the occasion.

Pope John Paul I died on Thursday, September 28, about 11:00 p.m. The cause of death was a heart attack. He was found dead about 5:30 a.m. the following day by his secretary, the Irish priest Fr. John Magee. There was no autopsy, and that fact gave rise to various conspiracy theories that were popular in the press, but, as John Kelly laconically concludes, "the evidence produced was a tissue of improbabilities."[24] A number of people who knew Luciani prior to his becoming pope has noted various concerns about

17. Cited in Hebblethwaite, *The Year of Three Popes*, 47.

18. See Hebblethwaite, *The Year of Three Popes*, 70–87.

19. Kelly, *The Oxford Dictionary of the Popes*, 325.

20. Duffy, *Saints and Sinners*, 368.

21. Murphy, *The Papacy Today*, 163.

22. Kelly, *The Oxford Dictionary of the Popes*, 326.

23. McBrien, *Lives of the Popes*, 368.

24. Kelly, *The Oxford Dictionary of the Popes*, 326.

his health. These are expressed in an anecdotal but persuasive way by John Cornwell in his book dealing with the death of Pope John Paul I.[25] But in terms of the final outcome John Kelly's judgment is correct: the evidence is a tissue of improbabilities, though "the rumors made a lot of money for authors of scurrilous articles and books."[26] There is a poignancy to Peter Hebblethwaite's words about the pope's end: "The man who had loved people and conversation died alone, without the sacraments of the church, unable to communicate with anyone except God."[27]

Given a pontificate of just one month, it is impossible to say very much about the achievement of Pope John Paul I, to make judicious historical comments about his contribution and his legacy. Some remarks of Fr. Andrew Greeley, however, seem to me very much to the point. Greeley notes John Paul's success with and appeal to the ordinary people of the world and looks for an explanation. This is his explanation: "The secret of John Paul's success with the ordinary folk of the world is that the ordinary folk of the world are not concerned about ideology, liberation theology, or collegiality. Differences of the right and left don't mean very much to them. But personal holiness of the kind which says that hope and even joy are still possibilities in human life remains extraordinarily attractive."[28] This is by no means to marginalize issues concerning ideology, liberation theology, collegiality or what ever, but it is to insist, and rightly, that magnanimous hope and joy will always command respect and issue in love.

25. Cornwell, *A Thief in the Night* (2001), the original text was published by Simon & Schuster in 1989.

26. O'Malley, SJ, *A History of the Popes*, 315.

27. Hebblethwaite, *The Year of Three Popes*, 128.

28. Greeley, *The Making of the Popes*, 165.

16

Pope John Paul II (1978–2005)

*Wojtyla was by any standards a star, with a remarkable career behind him.
. . . An ultramontane, filled with a profound sense of the immensity of his
own office and of his centrality in the providence of God. . . . I think the most
striking thing about him is his personalism. . . . He's the first pope ever to
write encyclicals using the singular.*

—Eamon Duffy[1]

*There has been no hidden corner of the Church where he was not present, heard,
read, and where he was not absolute.*

—John Cornwell[2]

*Certainly the judgments about the man and his accomplishment have been, to
put it gently, contradictory.*

—George Weigel[3]

From Karol Wojtyla to Pope John Paul II

WHEN IT COMES TO Pope John Paul II, the historian is much too close to the subject
matter to reach a comprehensive and accurate assessment. This is partly what lies

1. Duffy, "Interview," www.pbs.org/wgbh/pages/frontline/shows/pope/interviews/duffy.html.
Similar sentiments come from the pen of journalist Peter Nichols, writing in 1981. "John Paul II . . .
comes so completely from the central European tradition of prince-bishops. His methods are imperial, too: the harangues to the crowds; the insistence on keeping the centralized government in his
own hands; the constant traveling to show himself to those vast throngs unable to make the journey
to Rome" See Nichols, *The Pope's Divisions*, 38.

2. Cornwell, *The Pontiff in Winter*, xii.

3. Weigel, *Witness to Hope: The Biography of Pope John Paul II*, 4. Weigel tells us that his massive
biography of the pope is the fruit of twenty years' study and research (14). Cornwell, *The Pontiff in
Winter*, xiii, in contrast to Weigel, attempts "to be selective in order to emphasize connections that
bring his character and *contradictions* to narrative life" (my emphasis).

behind Frank J. Coppa's statement that "Some have commented that most of the millions who cheered this Pope during his lifetime, and mourned him after his death, did not follow his rigid directives!"[4] Even though it is difficult to tie down accurately, there is something to Coppa's judgment. After Pope Pius IX, John Paul II was the longest reigning pope in recorded history. Further, the documentation, the sheer weight of textual and visual data is such as to be virtually beyond the scope of any individual scholar. So, to attempt a descriptive summary of the pope, we shall take our bearings principally from three commentators: George Weigel, author of a massive biography of John Paul II that included regular access to the Holy Father himself, the professor of the history of Christianity of the University of Cambridge, Eamon Duffy, who has written a widely read history of the papacy, *Saints and Sinners*, and remains a regular commentator on the papacy, and the religious journalist John Cornwell in his *The Pontiff in Winter*. Weigel tends to be uncritical of the pope while Duffy and Cornwell are more critical. In point of fact, Duffy locates the discomfort felt by an historian in reading some of the uncritical accounts of Pope John Paul II: "If they are to be believed, Karol Wojtyla is the best bishop, the best theologian, the best philosopher, the best sexologist, the best animator of talent, the most perceptive discerner of charisms, the best interpreter of women's roles and women's rights, and the best ethicist of the twentieth century—or indeed of any other."[5]

Contrast that perspective with the opinion of a former Irish politician and commentator on historical and cultural matters, Conor Cruise O'Brien, who once commented: "I frankly abhor Pope John Paul II."[6] Less acerbically, John Cornwell describes John Paul as "Superman" and then he goes on to comment that "a Superman has no place in a Church of communities that require to be fully themselves in their smallest groups; that flourish and gather strength from their own local resources as well as from the Roman center."[7] Church historian John O'Malley comments: "A more striking contrast with Paul VI is hardly imaginable. Paul, shy, frail, sensitive, introspective, given to self-doubt. John Paul II, athletic, assertive, robustly self-confident, was born for the spotlight. More is known about him and more has been written about him than any other pope. Everything about his long pontificate of nearly twenty-seven years, the second longest in history, seems oversized."[8] Who was this charismatic and gifted person who could attract such adulation and opposition?

4. Coppa, *Politics and the Papacy in the Modern World*, 200.

5. Duffy, "A Great Pope Ill Served by his Fans," 15. Duffy was reviewing William Oddie, ed., *John Paul the Great: Maker of the Post-conciliar Church* (London: Catholic Truth Society, 2003).

6. O'Brien, *On the Eve of the Millennium*, 16.

7. Cornwell, *The Pontiff in Winter*, xvi.

8. O'Malley, *A History of the Popes*, 314.

Karol Wojtyla

Karol Wojtyla was born on May 18, 1920 in Wadowice, about thirty miles southwest of Krakow, Poland, and not very far from the Czech border. In 1938 with his father he moved into Krakow to begin studies in Polish language and literature at the Jagiellonian University. The Jagiellonian dates from 1374 and is the oldest university in east-central Europe after Prague. The sixteenth-century astronomer Nicholas Copernicus had been a student here. The university was officially closed in 1939 with the German occupation of Poland and some 183 members of the faculty were arrested and dispatched to concentration camps. But by the beginning of 1942 the Jagiellonian was operating underground with five faculties and some eight hundred students.

Before the age of twenty-one Wojtyla had lost his entire family in death: his mother, Emilia Kakorowska, died when he was but seven, his sister whom he never knew died as an infant, an older brother, and finally his father when he was twenty. His brother, Edmund, a physician, died at twenty-six after contracting scarlet fever from a patient. In 1984, speaking of his father's death he said: "I never felt so alone."[9] Suffering and constant reflection on suffering are to be found throughout his work so much so that Eamon Duffy can say, "Suffering, one may feel, offers the key to his character."[10] He attended elementary school in Wadowice and then the state-run gymnasium. As a young man he wrote poetry, studied philosophy, was an actor in a theater, and gained a military exemption in the Nazi occupation by working in a quarry and in a water purification plant. His exposure to acting and the theater was more than an outlet for a young extrovert's thespian gifts. It could be described as "first philosophy": "In a certain sense his first initiation to phenomenology came about indirectly and outside of orthodox philosophy, through the theory of theater and, above all, the existential experience of being an actor."[11] His experience as an industrial worker afforded him experience that few priests have had, let alone a bishop of Rome. He worked at the Solvay chemical plant, mind-numbing labor.

In 1942 Wojtyla enrolled in theology at the underground Jagiellonian University and entered the clandestine seminary. It is said that he carried in his bag to the Solvay plant a manual of Thomist metaphysics.[12] In 1940 Wojtyla had met Jan Tyranowski, a "gentle tailor-mystic" and autodidact, who introduced him to Carmelite mysticism and especially to the work of St. John of the Cross, whose theology and spirituality remained central for him throughout his life.[13] Tyranowski also gave him access to the seventeenth-century French St. Louis de Montfort's *True Devotion to Mary* and *The*

9. Weigel, *Witness to Hope*, 68.

10. Duffy, in the interview noted above.

11. Buttiglione, *Karol Wojtyla*, 20. See also Johnson, *Pope John Paul II and the Catholic Restoration*, 6–7 for some interesting and pertinent remarks on the inter-connections of religion and theater.

12. This information comes from a fellow seminarian, Mieczyslaw Malinski, as cited in Cornwell, *The Pontiff in Winter*, 21.

13. Weigel, *Witness to Hope*, 61.

Secret of Mary. This was to prove a very important source of Wojtyla's spirituality, and it is from de Montfort that much later on he would derive his papal motto, *Totus tuus,* "Entirely yours." Many priests were being murdered or incarcerated by the Germans and this young layman Tyranowski was assisting his pastor in the Krakow parish of St. Stanislas Kostka as a kind of lay evangelist. As a consequence of the Warsaw rising against the German occupation, on August 6 1944 the Nazis rounded up and executed as reprisals a number of young men in Krakow. Wojtyla escaped the round-up, and with some other seminarians found refuge of a sort in the residence of the bishop, Adam Sapieha.[14] Peter Hebblethwaite remarks that these seminarians in the clandestine seminary "must have felt rather nervous when the notorious Hans Frank, head of the German administration in occupied Poland, visited the Cardinal."[15]

The year 1946 saw Wojtyla ordained by Cardinal Adam Sapieha. In that same year he published a volume of poetry, and proceeded to the Dominican Angelicum University in Rome for graduate study in theology. The focus of his research for the doctorate was: "The Doctrine of Faith according to St. John of the Cross," the topic undoubtedly reflecting the Carmelite influence of Tyranowski during the early 1940s.[16] The most influential theologian at the Angelicum was the famed French Thomist, the Dominican Reginald Garrigou-Lagrange, who was also developing a competence in the thought of St. John of the Cross.[17] Garrigou-Lagrange's Thomism has been described as "unrelenting" and as seeing in St. John of the Cross "a confirmation of the main theses of Aquinas."[18] This is the anti-Semitic Garrigou-Lagrange and also the Garrigou-Lagrange who was influential in the condemnation of the *nouvelle théologie* in Pius XII's 1950 encyclical, *Humani Generis.* In respect of Wojtyla's philosophical development the influence of Garrigou-Lagrange remained dominant, paramount, and yet his approach to the Carmelite mystic is more along the lines of a phenomenology of mystical experience.[19] Sapieha provided the funds for the young priest to travel widely in Western Europe to gain both pastoral experience and some

---

14. Weigel, *Witness to Hope,* 71–72. Historian Paul Johnson says of this round-up: "On 6 August 1944, following the Warsaw rising, the Nazis rounded up all males in Cracow between the ages of fifteen and fifty, and shot them without trial" (*Pope John Paul II and the Catholic Restoration,* 10). The numbers seem impossible, and the historian Norman Davies whose massively documented *Rising '44: The Battle for Warsaw,* 253, acknowledges both the round-up and Wojtyla's narrow escape, but never makes mention of "all males between the ages of fifteen and fifty." I owe the Norman Davies reference to the Polish scholar, Dr. Anna Lesiuk.

15. Hebblethwaite, *The Year of Three Popes,* 161.

16. This was translated into English by the Dominican Jordan Aumann as Karol Wojtyla, *Faith According to St. John of the Cross.*

17. Buttiglione, *Karol Wojtyla,* 45.

18. Hebblethwaite, *The Year of Three Popes,* 162.

19. Buttiglione, *Karol Wojtyla,* 35, 47. My own teacher of moral theology, the Irish Marist Sean Fagan, overlapped with Wojtyla at the Angelicum, and his PhD on "The Eternal Objects in the Philosophy of St. Thomas Aquinas and Alfred North Whitehead" witnesses to a certain breadth of perspective in the school. See Sean Fagan, "Theology in the Making," 67.

appreciation of the new currents of thought and action that were taking place. In June 1948 Wojtyla successfully defended his dissertation at the Angelicum, but the regulations required the publication of the dissertation before the doctorate could be conferred. Wojtyla could not afford this and returned to Poland, presented the dissertation to the Jagiellonian University in Krakow which conferred the doctorate in theology on him in December of that year.[20]

After eight months in a rural parish, Wojtyla was transferred to an urban parish in Krakow and to chaplaincy work with university students. Like Montini but in very different circumstances he reached out to the young, mediating to them an adult theological appreciation of Catholicism. He even had a study group that made its way through Aquinas's *Summa Theologiae* in Latin. He encouraged "dialogue" Masses, and initiated marriage-preparation courses. His long-standing interest in the theology of sexuality and marriage never remained a cerebral concern for him, but was always connected to the practicalities of marriage preparation and ongoing married life. During these years he would hike and ski with his young friends, forming bonds with them that were intellectual and theological, ecclesial and social. During his first twelve years or so as a priest his literary work flourished in both plays and poetry. Ongoing pastoral work seems to have afforded him the necessary context for creative and imaginative expression. Once when asked by a visiting bishop during a working lunch at the Vatican when he was pope whether he still wrote poetry, he replied "No, there is no context."[21]

Wojtyla's ordinary, Archbishop Baziak of Krakow, asked the young priest to undertake a "habilitation" thesis, essentially for him a second doctorate from the Jagiellonian University, that would enable him to teach at university level. This catalyzed his interest in the phenomenologist Max Scheler (1874–1928). Phenomenology has been described as the philosophical method to "bring back into philosophy everyday things, concrete wholes, the basic experiences of life as they come to us."[22] Wojtyla's interest in and work on Max Scheler, including translation from German into Polish, demonstrates some distance between him and the neo-scholasticism of Garrigou-Lagrange.[23] However much he appreciated the work of his mentor, Wojtyla had a passion for philosophy as philosophy and became conversant with personalist phenomenology. The habilitation dissertation was entitled "An Evaluation of the Possibility of Constructing a Christian Ethics on the Basis of the System of Max Scheler," and represents Wojtyla's creative synthesis between the objectivity of Thomism and the subjectivity

---

20. Cornwell, *The Pontiff in Winter*, 27, maintains that there was a difference of interpretation of the Carmelite mystic between Wojtyla and Garrigou-Lagrange.

21. See the reference in Duffy's interview noted above.

22. Novak, "John Paul II: Christian Philosopher," 12.

23. After Scheler's death in 1928, Martin Heidegger said of him that he was "the strongest philosophical force in modern Germany, nay, in contemporary Europe and in contemporary philosophy as such." See Heidegger, *The Metaphysical Foundations of Logic*, 50–52.

and personalism of modern philosophy. The most prominent member of his doctoral committee was the phenomenologist Roman Ingarden, the father of Polish phenomenology. It is not entirely clear how Wojtyla developed his phenomenological interests, but Ingarden's influence solidified it.[24] Thus equipped he made his way to the Catholic University of Lublin, the only Catholic academic institution at the time in the whole of Eastern Europe, to teach ethics in 1954. Until he became a bishop, he commuted by train from Krakow to Lublin, a journey of some three to four hours. He enjoyed and encouraged the cut and thrust of serious intellectual debate and difference in the classroom. The late Irish philosopher, James McEvoy, comments on how Wojtyla's interest in phenomenology led him to a deeper appreciation of the moral life: "Phenomenology was to teach him sensitivity to human experience, especially moral experience, the experience, that is to say, of attractions and love, of moral reflection, conscientious evaluation and judgment, the exercise of freedom, and growth as a person—topics that have been at the center of his interests during all his later life."[25]

Some of his lectures saw the light of day in 1960 as *Love and Responsibility*, an interpersonal analysis of sexual ethics published by Lublin University Press. The key to his understanding of the person and of ethics was the "Law of the Gift," that is, "Responsible self-giving, not self-assertion, [is] the road to human fulfillment."[26] One commentator has described discreetly but with accuracy an important aspect of this book as "an up-to-date discussion of sexual pleasure with an analysis of the female psyche in relation to the physiological aspects of marital relations. It proposed an idealistic solution to the problem of birth control via natural methods, based on a realistic description of the elements involved in marital love."[27] *Love and Responsibility* was translated into French, Italian, and Spanish. It seems that Pope Paul VI read it, and was won over by Wojtyla's arguments concerning contraception during the period leading up to the publication of the encyclical *Humanae Vitae* in 1968

Bishop to Archbishop to Cardinal Karol Wojtyla

In 1958 Pope Pius XII named Wojtyla auxiliary bishop of Krakow. At thirty-eight he was the youngest of the Polish bishops. The motto on his episcopal coat of arms was adapted from St. Louis de Montfort, *Totus Tuus*, "entirely yours," his dedication to the Virgin Mary. His lecturing at Lublin was necessarily cut back now, but not given up. When Archbishop Baziak died in June 1962, his young auxiliary was elected administrator of the diocese and ultimately was appointed archbishop of Krakow in 1964.

---

24. Buttiglione, *Karol Wojtyla*, 54.

25. McEvoy, "The Singular Shape of Karol Wojtyla's Studies," 127–28.

26. Weigel, *Witness to Hope*, 136–37.

27. Murphy, *The Papacy Today*, 181. For a fine account of *Love and Responsibility* within the context of traditional sexual ethics as well as phenomenology, see Rocco Buttiglione, *Karol Wojtyla*, 83–116.

Initially as bishop and then as archbishop, Wojtyla participated in every session of the Second Vatican Council, making in all eight formal council speeches. He was from beginning to end a man of the council. Later he was to describe his experience of the council as "the seminary of the Holy Spirit."[28] It was a time of creativity and of full engagement for him. He spoke and also made written interventions at all four sessions of the council. In the debate that was to give rise to the Constitution on Divine Revelation he argued that revelation ought to be understood as God's self-revelation in Scripture and Tradition rather than propositionally. This is entirely in line with his developing personalist philosophy. In the collegial reasoning that would shape up as the Constitution on the Church, he emphasized that the purpose of the church was holiness, a sharing in the Trinitarian life, and that the laity should be recognized through their baptism as fully church, and not as secondary. Thus, in the debate on the Constitution on the Church in 1963, he insisted that the church should be seen as "the People of God" before any treatment of the hierarchy. "The implications of this for the theology of the laity were considerable; and this speech . . . showed that Wojtyla was on the side of those who favored a more biblical and less clerical approach to the church. Those who misguidedly supposed that all Polish theology was a defense of sturdy peasant piety or that all Polish bishops were as traditionalist as Cardinal Wyszinski, were pleasantly surprised."[29] He insisted in the arguments around religious freedom that would issue in the Declaration on Religious Freedom that freedom *for* and not freedom *against* was implicit in the dignity of every human person. However, his primary contribution to the council was taken up with the Pastoral Constitution on the Church in the Modern World.[30] *A propos* of this document Wojtyla said: "Let us avoid all suggestion that the Church has a monopoly of truth."[31] Working on the various drafts of this document, Archbishop Wojtyla came into close contact with Henri de Lubac, SJ and Yves Congar, OP. De Lubac and Wojtyla became friends. Congar wrote in his journal in February 2 1965 of Wojtyla: "Wojtyla made a remarkable impression. His personality dominates. Some kind of animation is present in this person, a magnetic power, prophetic strength, full of peace, and impossible to resist."[32] Quite an accolade. Two paragraphs in particular of the Pastoral Constitution are the most cited passages from the council in his subsequent teaching as pope, paragraphs 22 and 24. In 22 we read: "It is only in the mystery of the Word made flesh that the mystery of man becomes truly clear, . . . all this holds true, not for Christians only, but for all men of good will in whose hearts grace is actively present." This is the radical christocentrism that will mark

28. Pope John Paul II, *Crossing the Threshold of Hope*, 159.

29. Hebblethwaite, *The Year of Three Popes*, 166–67.

30. Weigel, *Witness to Hope*, 166; Rocco Buttiglione, *Karol Wojtyla*, 193–99.

31. Cited in Johnson, *Pope John Paul II and the Catholic Restoration*, 28. See also Hebblethwaite, *The Year of Three Popes*, 167.

32. Cited in Weigel, *Witness to Hope*, 168.

Wojtyla's theology. In paragraph 24 we read: "Man cannot fully find himself except through a sincere gift of himself." This reflects Wojtyla's "Law of Gift."

During the conciliar years, Wojtyla began work on his systematic philosophical anthropology, *Person and Act*.[33] Weigel describes this complex book in these words: "a coherent, intellectually sophisticated, *public account* of the philosophical basis of Vatican II's teaching on freedom and its relationship to truth."[34] It is Wojtyla's reading of what it means to be human, inviting readers to see if it matches their own experience. The book is intended to function as a mutually corrective correlation with the engaged and critical reader. Buttiglione offers a fine description of it: "It proposes a hermeneutic of human existence which requires confirmation through the experience of each reader. Each reader is, in fact, asked to compare the results at which the book arrives with those which emerge from his or her own being in the world as well as his or her own personal reflection. In this way philosophy gains its proper status as reflection upon an experience."[35] Freedom is not personal autonomy to do what one wants, but rather self-mastery through careful decision-making. Though the book is philosophy, it is philosophy inspired by the Christian vision of God as Trinity. It is in the Triune God, the eternal divine communion of self-gift, that the Law of the Gift finds its foundation.

In 1967 Pope Paul VI named Wojtyla a cardinal so that there were now two Polish cardinals, Wyszinski and Wojtyla, but the latter always deferred to the former out of a sense of respect. Wojtyla was unprepared for this honor. "When . . . he went to Rome to receive the cardinalate . . . he was virtually penniless. To buy his cardinal's outfit, his secretary, Father Pieronek, had to borrow 200 dollars from the Polish College, where they stayed."[36]

The intellectual cardinal-archbishop of Krakow made the visitation of his diocese a priority. Parish visitations were not flying visits for the purpose of the Sacrament of Confirmation, but took several days. During these days Wojtyla would, of course, celebrate Confirmation, but he also made it a point to be in touch with married couples—continuing his already established interest in the practical application of the theology of sexuality and marriage—visiting the parish cemetery, meeting with lay groups for discussion, as well as meeting with parish catechists and religious. He had a sense of a bishop fully engaged in his diocese in the spirit of Vatican II, like the great St. Charles Borromeo, his patron, after the reforming Council of Trent. At the same time, Cardinal Wojtyla used the reluctant permissions from the Polish government to travel widely throughout the world, establishing a sense of Polish participation in international Catholicism. At the same time, he continued valiantly with his teaching at

---

33. I side with George Weigel in preferring this translation of the Polish title to what actually came out in English as *The Acting Person*. For the persuasive details, see Weigel, *Witness to Hope*, 174–75.

34. Weigel, *Witness to Hope*, 173.

35. Buttiglione, *Karol Wojtyla*, 118.

36. Johnson, *Pope John Paul II and the Catholic Restoration*, 24.

Lublin, only this time the research assistants and advanced students traveled by train from Lublin to Krakow, with money provided from Wojtyla's earnings He finished lecturing only when he left Poland to become Pope John Paul II.

Weigel gives an indication of Wojtyla's regular schedule:

> The archbishop rose at 5 or 5:30 every morning, and spent the first hour of his day in private prayer. After Mass in the chapel with his secretary and personal staff (and, sometimes, invited guests), he had breakfast in the kitchen, and then retired to the chapel, where he spent two hours every morning, between 9 and 11, writing. The period between 11am and 1pm was reserved for visitors, and the rule was that anyone who wanted to see the cardinal could come. Afternoons and evenings were devoted to more meetings, to visitations around the city or the region, and to reading and study. . . . He always insisted on vacations which he believed were essential to recharging his stores of energy. But according to everyone who knew and worked with him, the mainspring of his daily energy was his constant prayer.[37]

His devotion to prayer is clear and often commented upon, but his devotion to study as a bishop is remarkable, given all the demands made on his office. Cardinal Wojtyla remained in touch with scientists, philosophers, and literary scholars. There was a necessary connection, it seems, between his ardent prayer life and his commitment to study and to be informed.

He did not micromanage his diocese, but genuinely exercised a spirit of collegiality. To revitalize the diocese along the lines of Vatican II, he initiated in 1970 a Synod of Krakow whose purpose was to read the documents of the council guided by Wojtyla's commentary, *Sources of Renewal*, and build a genuine Christian community energized for evangelization and mission. The synod took eight years, completing its work on June 8 1979 when its bishop, now Pope John Paul II, brought it to a close.

Cardinal Wojtyla was a member of Pope Paul VI's Commission on Birth Control. In the judgment of Eamon Duffy, "Wojtyla provided a good deal of the rationale behind *Humanae Vitae*, he identifies very strongly with it. It's not just Paul VI's encyclical, it's his."[38] There is truth in this, but George Weigel persuasively argues that had the encyclical *Humanae Vitae* adopted something of Wojtyla's personalist anthropology centering on his Law of the Gift, conceivably the furore after its publication would have been less. Perhaps.

Cardinal Wojtyla was also a very active participant in the Synod of Bishops as well as in the curial dicasteries he served as a cardinal. He made a positive and strong impression on the bishops who worked with him and who got to know him. In 1976 he preached the Lenten Retreat to the Pope and the Roman Curia. In some twenty-two conferences his repertoire included the following: Holy Scripture, Christian classics

---

37. Weigel, *Witness to Hope*, 201.

38. Duffy, "Interview."

(Irenaeus, Augustine, and Aquinas), modern philosophy and theology (Martin Heidegger, Paul Ricoeur, Henri de Lubac, and Karl Rahner, Walter Kasper, and Hans Küng) as well as literature (John Milton and Antoine de Saint-Exupéry). Clearly, a well-read man with an informed repertoire of both classical and contemporary thinkers. However, it may be that the real value behind this 1976 retreat was that the curial cardinals got a close-up picture of him in action, and that they liked what they saw.[39]

Pope John Paul II

Karol Wojtyla was elected pope as John Paul II, after the ministry of one month of Pope John Paul I on October 16, 1978. It would seem that one of the king-makers at the conclave was Cardinal Franz König of Vienna who favored Wojtyla from the outset of the conclave. In Wojtyla's own favor was the fact of his pastoral experience as a pastoral bishop. It was a remarkable election involving a number of "firsts": "the first non-Italian since 1523, the first pope from the Slavic east and the first pope with direct experience of the greatest challenge Christianity has ever faced, totalitarian atheism."[40] There was no coronation, as with Pope John Paul I. "He became Pope in a time of uncertainty. In the last years of Paul VI many felt themselves adrift."[41] There was no uncertainty in Pope John Paul II. His Polish background and his Polish Catholic experience in very difficult circumstances created an enormously confident and, indeed conservative mindset.

His first visit to Poland after his election occurred in 1979. The world watched astonished at the charisma of this man. "The Communist regime watched impotently as an evangelizing Pope preached and prayed before ecstatic crowds holding aloft a forest of forbidden crucifixes."[42] There can be little doubt that the collapse of Communism owed not a little to the confrontational style of Pope John Paul II, a style significantly in contrast with the approach to Communism of Pope Paul VI and *Ostpolitik*. The way of diplomatic negotiation had a history of success, but John Paul's consistent proclamation of the human rights and religious freedom was different. This proclamation, ever on his lips in speeches and homilies, reached its most international expression in his 1979 speech to the United Nations in New York. Religious freedom, the freedom of the person to search for the truth and to adhere to it is essential for world peace was his message, but without mentioning Marxism or Communism. Senator Daniel Patrick Moynihan, a previous American ambassador to the United Nations, was present on this occasion and remarked: "I can attest from having watched that the Eastern European and Soviet delegates knew exactly what he was talking about, and for once in that

---

39. Hebblethwaite, *Pope John Paul II and the Catholic Church*, 4.

40. Johnson, *Pope John Paul II and the Catholic Restoration*, 47.

41. Duffy, "A Giant Among Popes," 4.

42. O'Malley, *A History of the Popes*, 314.

chamber, looked fearful rather than bored."[43] The pope considered Communism or any form of totalitarianism that "pulverized" the human person as entirely wrong, and proposed throughout everything he said and did his vision of a christocentric humanism. The fear that Moynihan saw in the faces of the Communist delegates was realized when John Paul first visited Poland in 1979. While sometimes very bold claims are made for the papal defeat of European Communism, what seems abundantly clear is that this first visit created "the cultural, moral and psychological conditions for the possibility of a nonviolent overthrow of communist power."[44] Political commentators were well aware of the fact that the Communist systems of Eastern Europe were "disintegrating from the inside."[45] Undoubtedly, however, the pope's visit provided a great shot in the arm for the anti-Communist resistance.

John Paul used the regular general papal audience as a medium for catechesis. This too was different from what had happened before. In effect, what began as 129 catecheses over four years came to fruition as his *Theology of the Body*.[46] Absolutely fundamental to his perspective was his anthropology, an anthropology utterly opposed to what he called "the pulverization of the fundamental uniqueness of each human person," a phrase he first used in correspondence with Henri de Lubac in 1968.[47] He challenged throughout his pontificate whatever pulverized the uniqueness of each person. The *Theology of the Body* catecheses cover four main areas: "Original Unity of Man and Woman," "Blessed Are the Pure of Heart," "The Theology of Marriage and Celibacy," and finally "Reflections on *Humanae Vitae*." The refusal to "pulverize" another, living towards and with the other/Other in terms of self-donation in contrast with self-assertion, is the absolute fundament of John Paul II's *Theology of the Body*, a theology that is entirely free of the Manichaean thread that tends to run through many Catholic treatments of sexuality. So free of this stain is John Paul's thinking that he can describe sexual love in terms of worship: "Conjugal life becomes . . . liturgical" when the "language of the body" becomes the means to encounter, through an experience of the sacred, what God had willed for the world and for humanity "from the beginning."[48]

As his theology of the body is free from any stain of Manichaeism, so his approach to Judaism is free of the blot of anti-Semitism. Eamon Duffy writes: "This Polish pope has done more than any single individual in the whole history of Christianity to reconcile Jews and Christians and to remove the ancient stain of anti-Semitism from the Christian imagination."[49] John Paul II is the first pope since

43. Cited in Weigel, *Witness to Hope*, 349.

44. Weigel, *God's Choice*, 35.

45. O'Malley, SJ, *A History of the Popes*, 318.

46. Pope John Paul II, *Theology of the Body*.

47. Lubac, *At the Service of the Church*, 172.

48. Cited in Weigel, *Witness to Hope*, 341.

49. Duffy, *Saints and Sinners*, 384. See also Coppa, *The Papacy, the Jews and the Holocaust*, 255–95.

St. Peter to visit a synagogue for prayer. In the jubilee year, in a magnificent and unforgettable gesture, the now fragile pilgrim pope placed "a prayer of penitence for Christian atrocity and a pledge of friendship with 'the people of the Covenant', into a crevice in the Wailing Wall."[50]

In 1981, the would-be Turkish assassin Mehmet Ali Agca shot the pope in St. Peter's Square, and was subsequently pinned down by the outraged crowd until the security forces arrived. His assassin was arrested, tried, and imprisoned. John Paul went to see him. "The picture of him sitting quietly in conversation with his unsuccessful assassin, Mehmet Ali Agca, has become an icon of forgiveness."[51] The pope sent one of the bullets that wounded him to the shrine of the Virgin Mary at Fatima to be placed in a crown on her statue. Later, in the jubilee year 2000, he beatified two of the three visionaries of Fatima, and published the "Third Secret of Fatima," about which there had been so much popular interest and speculation. Duffy comments that Cardinal Ratzinger's commentary on the Third Secret was in reality an exercise in damage control, suggesting that it was "an unexceptionable meditation on the difficulties of the Christian life in the modern world."[52]

Even as pope, Wojtyla's interest in philosophy continued. For a number of years, he gathered important philosophers during the summer for a week of shared reflection and exchange at the papal summer residence of Castel Gandolfo. These were not only Catholic philosophers, but were drawn from a wide variety of backgrounds. James McEvoy describes John Paul's participation in these philosophical assemblies: "The Pope himself, on holiday from Rome, attended the daily sessions, listening to the views expressed while no doubt considering the points of view underlying the expressed opinions. . . . John Paul II is a skilled listener. He did not intervene in the discussions; he was there to observe, to inform himself, to learn and discern, to evaluate silently—and also perhaps to prepare *Fides et Ratio*," his encyclical on faith and reason.[53]

The Question of the Ordination of Women

On May 22, 1994, Pope John Paul II issued an apostolic letter, *Ordinatio Sacerdotalis*, reaffirming the restriction of priestly ordination to men. "The church has no authority whatsoever to confirm priestly ordination on women and this judgment is to be definitively held by all the church's faithful" (no. 4). Obviously, there was no change here in the church's teaching on the matter. There was, however, a difficulty in interpreting the term "to be definitively held". Argument abounded on the nature of this statement. Was it an infallible statement? One year later, on October 28, 1995,

---

50. Duffy, "A Giant Among Popes," 5.

51. Rausch, *Pope Benedict XVI: An Introduction to his Theological Vision*, 2.

52. Duffy, *Saints and Sinners*, 378.

53. McEvoy, "The Singular Shape of Karol Wojtyla's Studies," 130.

the Congregation for the Doctrine of the Faith issued a clarification, *Responsum ad Dubium*. The response insisted that, while the papal apostolic letter was not in itself an infallible statement, nonetheless it "has been set forth infallibly by the ordinary and universal Magisterium." This did not settle the debate, since "it was not clear to many theologians that the church's criteria for judging that a teaching of the ordinary and universal magisterium as infallibly taught had been fulfilled."[54] This lingering debate continued and was exacerbated by another papal apostolic letter of May 18, 1998, *Ad Tuendam Fidem*. This apostolic letter added further penalties for public dissent from doctrinal truths that had been proposed in the definitive way by the magisterium. It reiterated the prior position by implication on the ordination of women. That became clear especially in the theological commentary that accompanied the apostolic letter. In that commentary Cardinal Ratzinger listed a series of truths that were to be definitively held. Among those truths were the following: the exclusion of women from ordination to the priesthood; the immorality of euthanasia, prostitution, and fornication; the legitimacy of the papal election or ecumenical council; the canonization of the saints; and the invalidity of Anglican orders. Scrolling through this list there is no great surprise, but including the invalidity of Anglican orders seemed to say the least a little odd. This goes back to Pope Leo XIII and his *Apostolicae Curae*, but much water had flowed under the ecumenical bridge since then. A series of outstanding theological agreements had been reached by the Anglican Communion and the Catholic Church. Given this background, including *Apostolicae Curae* in this list of positions to be definitively held was very disconcerting to ecumenically minded theologians. Such was the position, for example, of the impeccably orthodox theologian Avery Dulles, SJ.[55]

Some Encyclicals

A propos of John Paul's encyclicals and addresses of different kinds, George Weigel has commented: "Choosing the highlights in such a staggering mass of material is, inevitably, an exercise in idiosyncrasy."[56] The few comments offered here are meant to give a feel for the man and his message rather than a comprehensive account, and will necessarily be somewhat self-revealing of the author's theological interests.

---

54. Rausch, SJ, *Pope Benedict XVI*, 27. Rausch points to the critical commentary provided by long-time Gregorian University ecclesiologist Francis A. Sullivan, SJ. See his "Guideposts from the Catholic Tradition" and his "Recent Theological Observations on Magisterial Documents and Public Dissent."

55. Dulles, "Commentary on Profession of Faith's Concluding Paragraphs," 117.

56. Weigel, *God's Choice*, 27.

Redemptor Hominis

Five months after his election, in March 1979, John Paul published the encyclical, *Redemptor Hominis*/"The Redeemer of Man," described as "the first encyclical ever devoted to Christian anthropology,"[57] and as "a stream of consciousness meditation on Christian anthropology unlike any papal document within living memory."[58] It offers a thoroughly christocentric anthropology, really an ordering of Christian doctrine around a concern for the whole human person. Thus, "Through the Incarnation God gave human life the dimension he had intended man to have from his first beginning."[59] The human person, marked by freedom is invited by God into communion with himself. The incarnation is the great sacrament of this communion. Christology and anthropology are interlinked. At the same time, the encyclical contained what Eamon Duffy has called "a stern call" to the theological community to work closely with the magisterium of the church. Duffy goes on to say that this presaged "tighter papal control over theological freedom within the Church."[60]

Ut Unum Sint

The year 1995 saw the publication of John Paul's encyclical on ecumenism, *Ut Unum Sint*/"That They May Be One." In this encyclical he invited all Christians and, of course, especially Catholics, to recover a sense of urgency concerning Christian unity. *Ut Unum Sint*, according to Cardinal Edward Cassidy, formerly of the Pontifical Council for Christian Unity, is John Paul's own text, initially written in Polish, translated into Italian, and then submitted to the Pontifical Council for comment. It was not a curial draft to which the pope then added comments of his own. Weigel also helps provide something of a context for this encyclical when he contrasts a speech given by the secretary-general of the World Council of Churches, Konrad Raiser, in Rome's *Centro Pro Unione* just about one month before its publication. Raiser proposed a paradigm shift in ecumenism away from the doctrinal issues of past division and towards a real acknowledgment of the "de facto apartheid between rich and poor," and a "progressive degradation of the whole ecosphere." Real acknowledgment of such critical issues demanded an "urgent reordering of the ecumenical agenda."[61] Without wishing to criticize the acknowledgment Raiser was calling for, and the consequent commitment of all Christian traditions to change in this respect, "closing the books on our past struggles" is neither realistic nor possible. Such a view not only relativizes doctrinal truth and the common search for doctrinal understanding, but also fails to see how

57. Weigel, *Witness to Hope*, 288.

58. Murphy, *The Papacy Today*, 194.

59. *Redemptor Hominis*, 1.

60. Duffy, *Saints and Sinners*, 372.

61. Weigel, *Witness to Hope*, 763.

human persons are shaped in understanding and choosing by the particularity of their traditions. Choosing to ignore particular differences is like the proverbial ostrich sticking its head in the sand. This is where the encyclical on ecumenism stands in contrast with Raiser. The pope clearly is most concerned with the Orthodox Churches. They are "Sister Churches" with whom the Catholic Church seeks "full unity in legitimate diversity."[62] Unlike Pope Paul VI, who had referred to the Anglican Communion as a "sister church," Pope John Paul II used the term only of the Orthodox Churches. The model comes from the first millennium: "The development of different experiences of ecclesial life did not prevent Christians . . . from continuing to feel certain that they were at home in any Church, because praise of the one Father, through Christ in the Holy Spirit, rose from them all, in a marvelous variety of languages and melodies. . . . The first Councils are an eloquent witness to this enduring unity in diversity" (par. 61). For John Paul, there were no church-dividing doctrinal issues remaining between Rome and the East. So, why not return to the status quo ante 1054? Despite his outreach to the Orthodox world and his many personal overtures, the degree of ecumenical healing he sought eluded him. The boldest initiative in *Ut Unum Sint* had to do with the Petrine ministry itself. History, human error, and sin had made the Petrine ministry a sign of division: "I join my predecessor Pope Paul VI in asking forgiveness" (par. 88); "to find a way of exercising the primacy which, while in no way renouncing what is essential to its mission, is nonetheless open to a new situation" (par. 95). "The Bishop of Rome, 941 years after the decisive split between Rome and the East, and 478 years after the division of western Christianity in the Lutheran Reformation, was asking his separated brothers and sisters to help him redesign the papacy for the third millennium as an office of unity for the whole Church of Christ."[63]

Fides et Ratio

This encyclical was published in 1998 and obviously reflects the Holy Father's long-standing interest in philosophy and its relation to Christian faith. Indeed, we may be able to say more. Not only does this encyclical reflect John Paul's interest in philosophy *vis-à-vis* theology, but it may be understood in a more personal way: "Although he never talks about himself in it, it is actually the distillation, worked out over some eight to ten years, of his own personal experience of what it means to be a fully alive Catholic intellectual, reflecting at the same time the authentic Catholic tradition or what it means to be a fully developed Christian mind, with its two complementary dimensions, faith and reason."[64] As one would expect, he holds up St. Thomas Aquinas as exemplifying "the harmony which exists between faith and reason" (par. 43). But he also mentions by name an interesting range of more recent philosophical thinkers:

62. *Ut Unum Sint*, par. 56.

63. Weigel, *Witness to Hope*, 762.

64. Clarke, "John Paul II," 557.

John Henry Newman, Antonio Rosmini, Jacques Maritain, Etienne Gilson, and Edith Stein—to mention only the Western scholars (par. 74). Edith Stein makes an interesting comparison and contrast with Wojtyla. Stein was a phenomenologist, and had been one of Edmund Husserl's most promising students. In her spiritual pilgrimage she moved from phenomenology to an appreciation of Aquinas, while the pope moved from Aquinas to an appreciation of phenomenology, and, as the Irish Cardinal Cahal Daly, also a professional philosopher, points out, "Both were devotees of St. John of the Cross and of Carmelite spirituality."[65]

A Restorationist Pope?

Writing in 2011 about nineteenth-century ultramontanism and Pope Pius IX, Eamon Duffy makes the following remark: "That legacy has proved enduring, indeed, ultramontanism appears to be on the march once more. Temporarily eclipsed by the upheavals of the 1960s and the ferment which followed the second Vatican Council, it has recovered self-confidence and vigor during the last two pontificates, in a resurgence symbolized appropriately by the beatification of Pio Nono by Pope John Paul II in 2000."[66] As has been alluded to several times throughout this chapter, there are different interpretations of the pontificate of John Paul II, sometimes widely different interpretations. The position taken by the author in this chapter on Pope John Paul II is identical with that of Eamon Duffy. Duffy, of course, writes as an immensely informed church historian with a very broad background in the history of the church in the last five hundred years. Other church historians—one thinks of Diarmaid MacCulloch—would be in substantial agreement. But this interpretation does not remain exclusively in the realm of church historians. Theologians also take this point of view. One theological commentator, the Jesuit theologian Thomas Rausch, writes about John Paul in this vein: "His legacy for the internal life of his own church is less impressive. Many feel that the promise of the Second Vatican Council was compromised, if not diminished, under his tenure."[67]

So, was John Paul II a restorationist pope, a pope who wished to restrict the gains and benefits of Vatican II? Or, if Vatican II is seen in a largely negative light, was John Paul the one to re-direct the church after the directionless years of Paul VI? The latter is the line taken by Paul Johnson who titled his book *Pope John Paul II and the Catholic Restoration*. Johnson writes:

> The policy of the sixties and seventies was fundamentally misconceived. The great majority of Roman Catholics did not want constant change and adjustment. They had been harried into accepting it by a self-appointed militant

65. Daly, "Faith and Reason: Diatribe or Dialogue?" 220.

66. Duffy, "The Age of Pio Nono: The Age of Paul Cullen," 47.

67. Rausch, *Pope Benedict XVI*, 3.

elite. What most Catholics wanted was for the church to reaffirm its traditional teaching, offer them not doubts but certitudes, not debates and arguments but dogmatism, not responses but leadership, not politics but apologetics, not the prosaic but the supernatural, not democracy and social justice but grace abundant, not Utopia on earth—let alone Subtopia on earth—but life eternal.[68]

This is a staggering misunderstanding of ecclesial experience in the sixties and the seventies, marked by an undialectical analysis. There is truth in the judgment that in the years consequent upon Vatican II there was an experience of loss, perhaps especially in some aspects of liturgical reform. In this regard, one thinks of the liturgical theologian Francis Mannion's call for a "re-catholicization" of the liturgy, a re-discovery through faithful liturgical performance of the mysterious outreach of the Trinity towards humankind in the rites of the church. Mannion also acknowledges, for example, the high success of the liturgical changes flowing from the council. The success is measured by the acceptance of the faithful, lay and clerical, for example, of the Rite for the Christian Initiation of Adults, the revised Rite of Infant Baptism, of the Sacrament of the Anointing of the Sick.[69] When Johnson talks about Catholics "not wanting doubts but certitudes, not debates and arguments but dogmatism," one wonders whether he has taken into account what often bordered on moral infantilism with regard to the moral teaching and confessional practice of the church, what the Irish moral theologian Sean Fagan, SM, has termed "the spiritual abuse of the faithful."[70] But this is not an analysis of Paul Johnson's take on Vatican II, but rather of his interpretation of John Paul II as a restorationist pope.

Pope John Paul was not a restorationist, even acknowledging the difficulty of defining the term adequately. Yet, there were aspects of his practice that were less than desirable. For example, he made it much more difficult for priests to leave the ministry. He referred to the priests who left as "Judases."[71] Between 1962, the first year of the council and 1978 the first year of John Paul's papacy, approximately forty-six thousand priests left the active ministry, the largest number since the sixteenth-century Reformation. It is simply impossible to know the consequences of the papal action. Did some reconsider their priestly commitment? Undoubtedly. Did some feel abandoned by the church at a time of real moral discernment in their lives? Certainly. Since no one really knows the interiority of another, the consequences of not getting a dispensation can only be guessed at, but certainly damage was done to people's lives.

One of the things we discovered in Vatican II's "Constitution on the Church" was episcopal collegiality. This is fundamentally the notion that the bishops of the world govern the church along with the pope and only in communion with the pope. It is fundamental acknowledgment that the bishops are not only *sub Petro/under Peter* but

68. Johnson, *Pope John Paul II and the Catholic Restoration*, 60.

69. See M. Francis Mannion's essay in Stratford Caldecott, ed., *Beyond the Prosaic*.

70. Hanley and Smith, MSC, *Quench Not the Spirit*, 73–88.

71. Murphy, *The Papacy Today*, 195.

also *cum Petro/with Peter*. Episcopal collegiality is an aspect of Vatican II that Pope John Paul II seemed to discount. "National episcopal conferences gradually lost what little margin they had for independent decision-making. This was the dark side of his self-assurance." Church historian John W. O'Malley, SJ says "He in that regard sometimes displayed a willfulness that startled even his most fervent admirers," and he uses the example of Wolfgang Haas, bishop of the Swiss diocese of Chur. This is how O'Malley describes the situation: "[He was] radically reactionary in his theological views and in-your-face confrontational in his administrative style, almost immediately upon his appointment in 1988 alienated his whole diocese, clergy and laity alike. Public demonstrations erupted against him. Only two years later the other Swiss bishops went to see the Pope to get Haas removed." Seven years later, the Swiss diocese was divided and Bishop Haas was transferred to the new and small diocese of Vaduz, but only after John Paul II had made him an archbishop. O'Malley comments, "Such petty obstinacy was unworthy of John Paul II but indicative of his determination to demand unquestioned acceptance of papal decisions, cost what it may."[72]

When John Paul went to Latin America in 1979, to be with CELAM (the Conference of Latin American Bishops) at its Puebla meeting and with the people of Mexico, he went with an *agendum*. According to George Weigel, "What was at stake at Puebla was nothing less than the legacy of Vatican II in Latin America."[73] His opening speech at the conference provided clues about this *agendum*. He emphasized with Pope Paul VI the church's involvement with the genuine liberation of human beings, but he studiously avoided the term "Liberation Theology." Liberation theology, with an appeal to such texts as Vatican II's *Gaudium et Spes* and Pope Paul VI's *Populorum Progressio*, had sought in various ways to emphasize the liberating effect of the gospel in terms of economic and political oppression. It gets represented in starkly contrasting ways. Take, for example, the position of the church historian, Edward Norman: "The most widely read leader of Liberation Theology was the Peruvian priest Gustavo Gutierrez: his linear message, expressed in Marxist language, was a call to identify the Christian Gospel with the political aspirations of the oppressed classes of Latin America. . . . [Liberation Theology] was a systematic portrayal of Marxism as the authentic application of the Gospel, and as a political alliance between Catholicism and the forces of revolution."[74] This is excessive, to say the least. Over against some aspects of some liberation theologians, the pope wished to proclaim a Christ who "unequivocally rejects recourse to violence. He opens his message of conversion to everybody."[75] Christ was not to be understood as a revolutionary intent upon the overthrow of a Roman imperial and colonial power in first century Galilee, nor was Christ to be understood

72. O'Malley, SJ, *A History of the Popes*, 320.

73. Weigel, *Witness to Hope*, 287.

74. Norman, *The Roman Catholic Church*, 174–75.

75. John Paul II, Address to the Third General Assembly of CELAM, cited in Weigel, *Witness to Hope*, 285.

in similar terms for today. Consequently, this demands that ecclesiology *cannot* be class-based, because no one is excluded from the invitation to conversion. Nor can this mean turning one's back on the evident injustice suffered by so many. "The issue . . . was not whether the Church would be engaged with the injustices faced by the Latin American poor, but how."[76] For John Paul there can be no subordination of the gospel to Marxist values and ideology. Even the use of Marxist methodology as a tool for sociological analysis is unacceptable because process and content are really inseparable. The reductionist anthropology of Marxism is a systemic flaw, permeating all aspects of Marxist thought—anthropology, social theory, politics, and economics. John Paul had dealt with Marxism not only as a political theory but also in Poland as a political reality. At the same time, the pope was totally opposed to explicit participation of clergy in the arena of politics. Even Hans Küng points to Marxist flaws that are fundamentally problematic for liberation theology. In his memoirs, while Küng admits to a certain openness—"a selective application"—to Marxist analysis, yet he maintains that even in the 1950s in Roman study circles it was being affirmed that Marxist arguments did not convince economists. Küng also says that criticism of this kind was not well received by his liberation theology colleagues and friends: "I have to note that my Latin American friends don't like such criticism and their own criticism of economics often doesn't seem to me to be competent."[77]

There had been an unraveling of discipline in the church since Vatican II. There can be little doubt that throughout his pontificate, John Paul saw his charge as strengthening his brother bishops worldwide so as to strengthen the discipline of the church. Eamon Duffy seems to have it right when he says: "For this pope, opposition is almost a sign of authenticity. . . . For him, choice is not about letting yourself avoid hard things. It's about opting for the hard thing. That's true freedom."[78] "Freedom is the freedom to do right: what right is, is revealed for all to see in the face of Jesus Christ, and in the heart of human nature as made known in Christ. The Church's teaching is thus for him never a constraint, but the criterion of authentic freedom, the 'splendour of truth'. It is not to be questioned, but joyfully explored, the limits to that exploration to be determined by the pastors and especially the pope."[79]

In attempting to assess John Paul's pontificate there is one further factor that needs to be taken into account. The adult Catholic generations that received Vatican II are aging, and younger Catholics are coming along. They did not experience the church before Vatican II, and they have different, sometimes sharply contrasting presuppositions from their immediate forebears. This contrast certainly represents a major pastoral challenge for careful listening, true collaboration, and the recognition that genuine orthodoxy does not require absolute uniformity in theological thinking.

---

76. Weigel, *Witness to Hope*, 283.

77. Küng, *Disputed Truth, Memoirs II*, 405.

78. Duffy, "Interview."

79. Duffy, "A Giant among Popes," 4.

Pope John Paul II: Dying and Death

The dying and death of Pope John Paul II were almost entirely public. He showed us how to die, with ongoing commitment and with dignity. The debates over the meaning of St. Paul's text in Colossians 1:24 will continue among exegetes, but through John Paul II, "millions around the world caught a glimpse of what it meant to fill up what is lacking in the suffering of Christ, for the good of the Church and the world."[80] Having been diagnosed with a form of Parkinson's disease in 1994, and despite all the rumors of his immediate demise, John Paul consistently pushed on with his ministry for over ten years, towards the millennium and beyond. He demonstrated in his person how to live with serious illness, and how to die with integrity, dignity, and hope. He had a powerful sense of solidarity with the sick and the sick with him. In August 2004, during one of his last trips, he went to the Marian shrine at Lourdes, France, and described himself as "a sick man among the sick." His deeply held sense of paternity for the church was something that, despite the short-lived thought now and again, did not permit abdication. The end came on April 2, 2005. Around three-thirty that afternoon, John Paul reportedly said in Polish, "Let me go to the house of the Father," lapsed into a coma and died some time later.

His long illness, however, raises very difficult issues, issues well put by Eamon Duffy: "No one with a heart could withhold admiration for the indomitable courage and sense of vocation which drives him to such endurance. No one with a head can fail to ask whether the Church is best served by the long infirmity of its chief pastor, or to wonder what weeds flourish round him as his energies and focus fail."[81] Pope John Paul II's funeral Mass was presided over by Cardinal Joseph Ratzinger, who preached what can only be called a superb homily, and who also gave Holy Communion to Frère Roger Schutz, the retired Protestant prior of the ecumenical monastery of Taizé, France, "making it clear that he considered Schutz a fellow member of the mystical body of Christ, which is the church."[82] Many eyes turned to Ratzinger as a possible successor.

Conclusion

Eamon Duffy writes of John Paul II:

> One would have to be blind not to see the greatness of the present Pope, who will surely feature significantly in any history of the twentieth century, let alone of the Church or the papacy. But he is a man, an inspiration to many, yet also a figure of contradiction, whose vigorous but partial implementation of the complex legacy of the Second Vatican Council troubles many faithful Catholics, fellow bishops among them, and will certainly be addressed—and redressed—in

80. Duffy, "A Giant Among Popes," 4.
81. Duffy, "A Giant Among Popes," 4.
82. Kaiser, *A Church in Search of Itself: Benedict XVI and the Battle for the Future*, 222.

future pontificates. The treasure of the Gospel is carried in earthen vessels, and popes, especially great popes, are better off without fan clubs.[83]

The Vatican observer Marco Politi in his 2015 book on Pope Francis points to what he calls the "darker sides" of John Paul II's papacy.

> There was the attempt to file and forget the accusations against the founder of the Legionaries of Christ, Marcial Maciel, who was guilty of grave sexual offenses; the repression of liberation theology and innovative theological research; the nomination of bishops whose distinguishing feature was their loyalty; the refusal to allow communion for the divorced and remarried; the refusal to consider a fresh approach to matters of sexuality; the absence of any critical thinking about the crisis of vocations; the continued confinement of women to ancillary roles in the church, notwithstanding fine words in public about the "female genius."[84]

Even from the relatively short distance looking back at John Paul's pontificate Politi has it right. The list of darker sides is not, I believe, intended to be an exhaustive analysis. Nonetheless, it needs to be said that none of these issues and critical challenges for the well-being of the church has gone away. Two popes later, the papacy of Francis, demonstrates just how neuralgic each one of these issues has become.

In his more recent and very popular book, *Ten Popes Who Shook the World*, originally a series on BBC television, Eamon Duffy offers what I believe is a balanced summary of this pontificate. "John Paul's papacy represented an attempt to steady the north of the Catholic Church by regrouping it round a strong papacy, and to evangelize a directionless world by the reassertion of strong Christian values. The policy proved divisive, increasingly alienating liberal opinion in Europe and North America, but delighting those who considered that the Second Vatican Council had inaugurated a 'silly season' whose aberrations would now be rolled back."[85] Perhaps these words of Eamon Duffy are good words with which to conclude. The papal insistence on obedience and what were considered to be unambiguous choices and decisions divided Catholics. "Real Catholics," or sometimes even "John Paul II Catholics" accused other Catholics with whom they were in disagreement of disloyalty and sometimes even of heresy. In doing so they felt they had the support of the pope. The ecclesial fallout from this kind of divisiveness continues to be felt. The historical evaluation of his pontificate will go on. As a new generation of church historians comes along, with little or no immediate experience of John Paul II, they will be in a much better position to assess and to evaluate, to discuss and to discriminate, to reach towards a more comprehensive evaluation of this greatly gifted man and of his service to the church. Pope John Paul II was canonized by Pope Francis on April 27, 2014.

---

83. Duffy, "A Great Pope Ill Served by his Fans," 15.
84. Politi, *Pope Francis Among the Wolves*, 25.
85. Duffy, *Ten Popes Who Shook the World*, 132.

17

Pope Benedict XVI (2005–13)

No German since Martin Luther [has] made such a powerful impression on the
form and substance of the Catholic Church as Joseph Ratzinger.

—HEINZ-JOACHIM FISCHER[1]

I want to be true to what I have recognized as essential and also to remain open
to seeing what should change. . . . I don't deny that there has been development
and change in my life . . . [but I] have tried to remain faithful to what I have
always had at heart. Here I agree with Cardinal Newman who says that to live is
to change and that the one who was capable of changing has lived much.

—JOSEPH RATZINGER[2]

MARCO POLITI MAKES THE following observation about Pope Benedict XVI:

> After John Paul II, there was stagnation. Joseph Ratzinger adopted a defen-
> sive stance vis-à-vis Christian identity, summoning up the image of a church
> besieged by a swarm of specters: relativism, materialism, libertinism, syncre-
> tism, nihilism, consumerism, atheism, individualism, agnosticism, laicism,
> secularism. The faith, he endlessly proclaimed, is threatened by a context that
> "tends to delete God from the horizon of life and does not . . . help one to
> discern good from evil." In his thinking, Western society (with which she was
> principally concerned) is conspiring to reduce religion to the private sphere.[3]

Each one of these "specters" demands careful analytical treatment in its own right. At
the same time, Politi's summary has the ring of truth about it. There was a very definite
sense in which these specters contributed to a view of the church as in a cultural war

---

1. Fischer, *Pope Benedict XVI*, 39.
2. Ratzinger, *Salt of the Earth*, 116.
3. Politi, *Pope Francis Among the Wolves*, 26.

against the world, and especially the Western world. How did this happen? How did the forces of life of Joseph Ratzinger shaped this perspective of Pope Benedict XVI?

From Joseph Ratzinger to Pope Benedict XVI[4]

Long before becoming pope, Joseph Aloysius Ratzinger played a powerful role in Vatican II and the post-conciliar church—as conciliar peritus, as professor of theology, as bishop, and finally as prefect of the Congregation for the Doctrine of the Faith. All four aspects of his role must be considered if one is to arrive at a balanced perspective, and so avoid a truncated view of this controversial and complex man.

"The election of Joseph Ratzinger as Benedict XVI in April 2005 put a professional theologian at the helm of the Catholic Church for the first time in centuries."[5] Thus church historian Eamon Duffy, but it would be fair to say that when Joseph Cardinal Ratzinger was elected as Pope Benedict XVI in April 2005, not everyone received this as good news. A significant number saw this as the further establishment of Roman Catholic conservatism, offering little hope of change and development in the near future. Is this a reasonable picture of Benedict XVI? One non-Catholic commentator, Mark Ellingsen, has written: "Benedict XVI is theologically conservative, but no more so than a number of cutting-edge theological alternatives in the academy, particularly several that are committed to doing theology in and for the church."[6] In other words, the pope's so-called theological conservatism shares a certain kind of academic respectability. In similar fashion, Timothy George, an American Evangelical theologian suggests that Pope Benedict's pontificate might be the "harbinger of a new reformation" because Benedict XVI "takes truth seriously." For George, the new pope's theology especially speaks to the following Evangelical concerns: "his theology is Bible-focused," "his message is christocentric," "he is Augustinian in perspective," and "he champions the culture of life."[7] To appreciate what Ellingsen and George are saying it is necessary to know something of the new pope's background, education, and theological interests.

Joseph Ratzinger (1927–)

Joseph Ratzinger has provided us with much biographical information in his memoir *Milestones*. It is interesting, however, that, when he makes reference to himself, he infrequently speaks of himself from his mid-twenties to his mid-forties, the period that

---

4. The number of publications given over to the study of Joseph Ratzinger—biographical, theological, ecclesiological, liturgical, etc. continues to grow rapidly. This chapter highlights some aspects of the Ratzinger corpus, but makes no attempt to be entirely comprehensive.

5. Duffy, "Benedict XVI and the Spirit of the Liturgy," 30.

6. Ellingsen, "Joseph Ratzinger (1927–) How Conservative Is Benedict XVI?" 388.

7. George, "The Promise of Benedict XVI," 13.

established his theological reputation. Rather, his self-revelation tends to look back to his early years in Bavaria when he was nurtured into a solidly and profoundly Catholic experience of the world.[8] He was born in Marktl-am-Inn, Bavaria on April 16, 1927, the last of three children, the others being Georg and Maria. That day was Holy Saturday, and so Joseph was the first to be baptized in the newly blessed Easter water. His father was a police officer, and after the rise of Hitler, a police officer whose opposition to Nazism made his job especially difficult. He witnessed the same opposition to Nazism in his parish priest whose beating at Nazi hands he once saw at first hand. One of his fondest memories of his mother was of her taking the children often to Salzburg, the home of Mozart, to concerts and orchestral Masses. Ratzinger's love of Mozart has perdured, and as Benedict XVI he continues to play Mozart's music on his piano. He loved music and books and thought of physical education at school as torture.[9] His love of liturgy also began at this time. He became an altar-server in his parish, and he was also given a missal which had the texts of the Mass and illustrations.

His father retired from the police force in 1937, grateful to do so given increasing awareness of Nazi policies. In 1939 Joseph entered the minor seminary in Traunstein, the family having settled there after moving several times in the region. His studies were interrupted by World War II. He had to join the Hitler Youth. Resistance to joining the Hitler Youth would have been utterly futile for a sixteen year old, but "inner resistance" was something else, and the young Ratzinger was innerly resistant.[10] A friendly schoolteacher obtained for him a certificate of attendance at the compulsory rallies. At sixteen in 1943, however, he found himself in brief compulsory service in the German defense forces, along with the other Traunstein seminarians, in the telecommunications section of the anti-aircraft division in Munich. That was not to last. In September 1944, now of actual military age, he was conscripted into the infantry preparing anti-tank defenses on the Austrian-Hungarian border. He was later reassigned to a posting near his home, and he became a deserter. When the American military finally arrived in Traunstein, Ratzinger was identified as a soldier, and was taken as a prisoner-of-war. He was held prisoner for some six months until the end of the war. One Ratzinger biographer writes as follows: "For the young [Ratzingers], they were deeply troubled by the fact that the war had been fought in the heartland of Christian Europe. This was strongly to influence the development of Joseph's thought in the years to come."[11] Rupert Shortt, commenting on one of Ratzinger's autobiographical memoirs, finds his recollections wanting in at least one very important respect. *Milestones*, appearing in the year 2000, Shortt criticizes Ratzinger in these words:

8. Allen, *Pope Benedict XVI*, 2.

9. Seewald, *Pope Benedict XVI, Servant of the Truth*, 42.

10. Fischer, *Pope Benedict XVI*, 20.

11. Collins, *Pope Benedict XVI*, 19.

This book leaves a sour taste in the mouth all the same, because it fails to mention either the Jews or the Holocaust a single time. Given an ideal chance to deplore a catastrophe in which he had been a blameless bystander, the then Cardinal chose instead to emphasize Hitler's persecution of Catholics.... [H]is discussion ignored the largely supine response to the Nazis of both clergy and laity. Secondly, he drew the highly contentious lesson that the church can only resist dictatorships effectively when run as a very tight ship. Alert reviewers of *Milestones* pointed out that on the contrary, German Catholics were hamstrung by a tradition of docile obedience to authority during the 1930s, and that only Protestant Denmark provided a largely unsullied record of anti-Nazi resistance.[12]

One understands how a memoir written much later in life has to be selective, may blur certain events deliberately or indeliberately, and omit things. Nonetheless, talking about the Nazi era in Germany without some mention of the Jews and the Holocaust, a period during which one was actually living, seems very strange.[13]

In 1946 he entered the seminary, beginning his studies at the Philosophical and Theological Academy in Freising near Munich. There were about 120 seminarians under the guidance of a rector who had spent five years in the concentration camp at Dachau. Seminary conditions were very poor as a result of the post-war situation, but Ratzinger was a keen student with a real passion for study. After completing his philosophical studies, he proceeded to theology in the seminary at the University of Munich. During the seminary years he found himself attracted to the philosopher Josef Pieper and the theologian Romano Guardini. He discovered Henri de Lubac's *Catholicism* in 1949, "perhaps Henri de Lubac's most significant work, in the masterful translation of Hans Urs von Balthasar."[14] From there he moved on to de Lubac's book, *Corpus Mysticum*, in which the thesis is advanced that the Eucharist makes the church. He did not find himself attracted to the philosophy and theology of St. Thomas Aquinas, a style of thinking that was "simply too far afield from my own questions,"[15] and he preferred St. Augustine's thought "as a counter-weight to Thomas Aquinas."[16] George Weigel comments on this as follows: "His seminary experience with neo-scholasticism would also mark him permanently, and would later make him the first non-Thomist in centuries to head the Catholic Church's principal doctrinal office."[17] This is an interesting statement. The renaissance of Thomist studies in the wake of Pope Leo XIII's endorsement and encouragement was such that the world of Catholic philosophy and theology was virtually

12. Shortt, "A Layman's Guide to the Pope."

13. See the comments of Fox, *The Pope's War*, 4–12.

14. Ratzinger, *Milestones*, 98.

15. Ratzinger, *Milestones*, 44.

16. Ratzinger, *Salt of the Earth*, 60. For a close examination of Ratzinger's interest in Augustine and of the latter's influence on Ratzinger see O'Regan, "Benedict the Augustinian," 21–60.

17. Weigel, *God's Choice*, 164.

identified with the thought of Aquinas.[18] Even Pope John Paul II in his doctoral work at the Angelicum University in Rome chose the theology of that mystic who approximates most closely to scholasticism, St. John of the Cross, though later his Thomism was tempered by his studies in personalist philosophy. Joseph Ratzinger, by way of contrast, has drunk deeply at three wells: Scripture, St. Augustine, and the history of theology. In Benedict's own words interviewed by Peter Seewald and published in 2016: "I came across Augustine early in 1946 and read a few of his works. The personal struggle which Augustine expresses really spoke to me. Thomas's writings were textbooks, by and large, and impersonal somehow. That said, there is of course a personal struggle standing behind them, which you only discover later. Augustine battles with himself, and indeed continues to do so after his conversion. And that is what makes the subject compelling and beautiful."[19] Ratzinger's basic philosophical presuppositions are more Platonic than Aristotelian, reflecting the Platonism of St. Augustine and St. Bonaventure. Without going into particular nuances, one might say that for this Platonic point of view the ordinary material world, the world of our everyday experience, is but a poor reflection of the ultimate and really real. In the Aristotelian tradition, however, we find a more empirical or experiential approach to understanding and truth. Without constantly referring to Platonic philosophy and Aristotelian philosophy the distinction appears to lie behind a great deal of Joseph Ratzinger's theological thought, a privileging of ideas over concrete experience.[20] This Platonic horizon is accompanied by a certain Augustinian pessimism about the human condition, both epistemological and moral. So much is this the case that some judge him "to be much more like Jean Calvin and the Reformers than like Thomas Aquinas and his modern commentators."[21]

Ratzinger does not share the same passion for philosophy as his predecessor in the Petrine ministry, or for thinkers who, in the judicious words of Rupert Shortt, he thought of "as untutored by the heart."[22] It was during his seminary years in theology that he also encountered for the first time the writings of John Henry Newman, who was certainly tutored by the heart. In all probability his introduction to Newman was due to the seminary prefect, Alfred Läpple, who was doing doctoral research on Newman's understanding of conscience.[23]

18. The point is well made by Fergus Kerr, OP, that Ratzinger's rejection of Aquinas was more the rejection of the "textbooks that set out the Thomist 'system' . . . the version of Thomism that Ratzinger rejects here is some kind of rationalism," rather than the thought of Aquinas himself. See Kerr, "Comment: Ratzinger's Thomism," 367–68.

19. Benedict XVI with Seewald, *Last Testament*, 79. Benedict goes on to add about his Munich study days: "[The Munich school] was defined by the fact that it was completely biblical orientated, working from holy Scripture, the Fathers and the liturgy, and it was very ecumenical. The Thomistic-philosophical dimension was missing; maybe that was its real benefit" (ibid., 83).

20. See Rausch, *Pope Benedict xvi*, 42–43; for greater detail on this theme see Corkery, *Joseph Ratzinger's Theological Ideas*, 28–51.

21. Rausch, *Pope Benedict XVI*, 49.

22. Shortt, *Benedict XVI*, 21.

23. Twomey, *Pope Benedict XVI*, 22. In his comprehensive theological biography, *Benedict XVI, His*

The seminary faculty in Ratzinger's time included Michael Schmaus, the systematic and historical theologian. Ratzinger also developed a love for the liturgy, but a love that, as has been noted, had been nurtured from childhood. In this respect, he was influenced by the growing liturgical movement. Two scholars in particular were to influence him: the Benedictine Odo Casel of the Abbey of Maria Laach, and especially the liturgical thinking of his hero, Romano Guardini. After his final exams in the summer of 1950, he entered a theological competition with the hope that it might open his way to undertaking a doctorate in theology. He was very interested in and familiar with the thought of St. Augustine. He had read in Latin *The Confessions*, and in his last year of theological training in the seminary he worked his way through Augustine's sermons in order to develop his thesis. The expectation was that this project would open up the way for him to complete a doctorate in theology. Many years later as pope he was to express his love for St. Augustine in these words: "I express my personal devotion and gratitude to the one who played such an important part in my life as a theologian and a pastor, but, I would say, even more as a man and a priest."[24] He was ordained a priest by Cardinal Faulhaber for the Diocese of Munich-Freising on June 29, 1951, the Solemnity of St. Peter and St. Paul. His brother Georg was also ordained with him on that day. On August 1, 1951, he became the assistant in the parish of the Precious Blood, Munich, but this parochial experience was not to last.

In October 1952, he was lecturing to the final year students in the seminary at Freising, while completing the requirements for a doctorate in theology. This was not a doctorate in theology from one of the Roman universities. This marks him out from all of his predecessors in the twentieth century. Each one of them had received higher education in theology at one or other of the Roman universities. Inevitably, the popes up to Ratzinger thought largely in scholastic terms. His theological training was so very different, rooted in Scripture and in the patristic tradition, with a strong appreciation for the history of theology. In 1953, Ratzinger received his doctorate on St. Augustine from the University of Munich: *Volk und Haus Gottes in Augustins Lehre von der Kirche/*"People and House of God in Augustine's Theology of the Church," and it was published in 1954. In 1955, he received the *Habilitationschrift* on "The Theology of History in St. Bonaventure." This, however, was far from smooth sailing. His supervisor was Gottfried Söhngen, and the reader Michael Schmaus. While Söhngen accepted the dissertation, Schmaus rejected it, but it was finally revised and accepted in 1957. Apparently, according to Peter Seewald,

---

Life and Thought, Elio Guerriero writes: "Having quickly become friends—so much so that at his own priestly ordination in 1947, Läpple invited young Joseph to serve as master of ceremonies—the prefect and the seminarian discussed (topics related to Newman and conscience) often. And, naturally, Newman and the subject of the doctoral thesis became another tile in the mosaic of the philosophical and theological personalism that would be at the foundation of the future pontiff's thought" (ibid., 67).

24. Cited in Collins, *Pope Benedict XVI: The First Five Years*, 122.

Schmaus was aware that the young Ratzinger had made certain criticisms of him and so he suspected that he was something of a "modernizer."[25]

Professor of Theology

Early in January 1958 the young Dr. Ratzinger was appointed to teach theology at the College of Philosophy and Theology at Freising. One of his students describes his methodology as follows: "The special novelty in his discourse was (and is) the fascinating use of images, signs and symbols, which allowed him to lead us far more deeply into the mystery of God than if he had employed rational definitions."[26] Another of his former students points out the strong interrelationship between his systematic theology and preaching:

> Ratzinger's theology has always been closely related to preaching; indeed one of the volumes of his collected essays was entitled *Dogma and Preaching*. Ratzinger once remarked that when Abelard transferred the teaching of theology from monastery or church to the lecture hall and a neutral university setting this was a mixed blessing. This made it possible especially in our own day to do theology apart from spiritual practice and to create the impression that it might be taught as any purely academic topic which one might learn as a means of livelihood.[27]

A range of theologians from all the Christian traditions and not just Catholicism would concur with this judgment about theology, preaching, and spirituality. One thinks, for example, of Hans Urs von Balthasar. Not all of them have integrated their theology into preaching, but Ratzinger has. His published sermons and homilies show in a dynamic way the integration between theology and preaching.

However, in the 1950s his academic career was just beginning to take off. In 1959 he received an appointment to the University of Bonn, to the chair of fundamental theology. Among the faculty was Theodor Klauser, the church historian and historian of the liturgy, and Hubert Jedin, the church historian and an acknowledged expert on the Council of Trent. These colleagues added to his growing sense of the history of the theological tradition and his love of liturgy. His theological horizons were expanding, an expansion caught by Michael Collins in these words: "The climate of theology was a great deal more open than that taught in Bavaria, which was somewhat insular. The young Ratzinger was fascinated to meet his colleagues who debated issues which he had never heard addressed seriously during his training. In particular he enjoyed speaking with colleagues from the Lutheran traditions and

---

25. Seewald, *Pope Benedict XVI, Servant of the Truth*, 58.

26. Gruber in Seewald, *Pope Benedict XVI, Servant of Truth*, 64.

27. Fahey, "Joseph Ratzinger as Ecclesiologist and as Pastor," 82; see also O'Grady, "The Ratzinger Round," 410.

those who had studied world religions."[28] As a result of these broadening horizons Ratzinger included among his lecture topics "Church, Sacrament and Faith in the Augsburg Confession" and "Melanchthon's *Treatise on the Power of the Pope*," unusual topics for a Catholic theologian at the time.[29]

Bonn is also near Cologne and soon he found himself as a theological adviser to Cardinal Joseph Frings, archbishop of Cologne, who took him to the Second Vatican Council as his adviser in September 1962. It is thought that Ratzinger, described by Henry Chadwick as "a theologian of remarkably independent sympathies," was responsible for the speech Cardinal Frings made on November 8, 1963, attacking the procedures of the Holy Office.[30] This speech was, among other things, one of the factors that led Pope Paul VI to re-shape and to re-name the Holy Office as the Congregation for the Doctrine of the Faith. Ratzinger was probably most influential at the council when it came to the constitution *Dei Verbum* "The Dogmatic Constitution on Divine Revelation." The scholastically shaped preliminary schema on Divine Revelation was rejected, and in concert with Karl Rahner, Ratzinger helped to provide an alternative text, judged by historian Gerald Fogarty as "a barely mitigated synthesis of Rahner's systematic theology."[31]

He also helped, again alongside Karl Rahner, with the shaping of *Lumen Gentium*'s paragraphs 22 and 23 to do with bishops and collegiality. Finally, he worked closely with the Dominican ecclesiologist, Yves Congar, in the conciliar texts on the church's missionary activity. During discussions pertinent to *Gaudium et Spes/The Pastoral Constitution on the Church in the Modern World* in September 1965, he gave expression to certain negative criticisms that were later to surface in articles, books and speeches. In Dulles's words: "The schema was too naturalistic and unhistorical, took insufficient notice of sin and its consequences, and was too optimistic about human progress." Dulles also suggests that Ratzinger's views reflect his preference for Augustine over Aquinas, and perhaps it may be added that had he more of a Thomist perspective with its implicit trust in human reason, he may have been less suspicious of the so-called "optimism" of *Gaudium et Spes*.

At the same time, it needs to be pointed out that Ratzinger wrote a substantial contribution to the understanding of *Gaudium et Spes* in Herbert Vorgrimler's magisterial commentary on the documents of Vatican II. Ratzinger's commentary covers the first chapter, "The Dignity of the Human Person," including an introductory section. Paragraph 16 is entitled "The Dignity of the Moral Conscience," and evokes from Ratzinger an extraordinarily fine perspective. Given his later profile in the Congregation for the Doctrine of the Faith, the commentary is most refreshing and follows the line of John Henry Newman on conscience:

28. Collins, *Pope Benedict XVI: The First Five Years*, 33.

29. Rausch, *Pope Benedict XVI*, 17.

30. Chadwick, *Tradition and Exploration*, 196.

31. Cited in Dulles, "From Ratzinger to Benedict," 24, but with no bibliographical reference.

Since Newman and Kierkegaard, conscience has occupied with new urgency the center of Christian anthropology. The work of both also represented in an unprecedented way the discovery of the individual who is called directly by God and who, in a world which scarcely makes God known anymore, is able to become directly certain of God through the voice of conscience. At the same time, for Newman, conscience represents the inner complement and limit of the church principle. Over the pope as the expression of the binding claim of ecclesiastical authority there still stands one's own conscience, which must be obeyed before all else, if necessary even against the requirement of ecclesiastical authority. This emphasis on the individual, whose conscience confronts him with a supreme and ultimate tribunal, and one which in the last resort is beyond the claim of external social groups, even of the official church, also establishes a principle in opposition to increasing totalitarianism. Genuine ecclesiastical obedience is distinguished from any totalitarianism which cannot accept any ultimate obligation of this kind beyond the reach of its dominating will.[32]

Those who have been commenting upon the continuities and discontinuities in the thought of Joseph Ratzinger seldom seem to be sufficiently aware of this passage. One exception is the Dulles essay, "From Ratzinger to Benedict." While Dulles draws attention to "provocative comments" in Ratzinger's commentary, he never actually adverts to this passage in explicit terms. On the very next page, Ratzinger is careful to indicate that this understanding in no wise reduces to a moral relativism, and does not make conscience arbitrary. Yet, in its strength, it is balanced, liberating and reflective of the broad Catholic tradition. Dulles concludes with a contrast between John Paul II and Benedict on *Gaudium et Spes*: "Among the documents of Vatican II, John Paul's favorite was surely the pastoral constitution *Gaudium et Spes*. Benedict XVI, who looks upon *Gaudium et Spes* as the weakest of the [council's] four constitutions, shows a clear preference for the other three."[33] Prior to its promulgation Ratzinger led a certain resistance to *Gaudium et Spes*. In his judgment the document was much too hopeful and even positive in tone and did not take sufficient cognizance of human sin.

During the council he began to work closely with Karl Rahner, SJ, whom he had first met in 1956. While they clearly shared commonalities in theology, nevertheless the later Ratzinger would contrast Rahner and himself in these terms: Rahner's "was a speculative and philosophical theology in which Scripture and the Fathers in the end did not play an important role and in which the historical dimension was really of little significance. For my part, my whole intellectual formation had been shaped by Scripture and the Fathers and profoundly historical thinking."[34] Rahner's philosophical skills enabled him to do dazzling things with scholasticism and the

32. Ratzinger, in Herbert Vorgrimler, *Commentary on the Documents of Vatican II*, 134.

33. See Dulles, "From Ratzinger to Benedict," especially 28–29; Twomey, *Pope Benedict XVI*, 28.

34. Ratzinger, *Milestones*, 128–29.

tradition of the church. While Rahner had a necessary appreciation of Scripture and the history of theology—consider, for example, volume fifteen of his *Theological Investigations* dealing with the sacrament of Penance and Reconciliation, in which essay after essay unpacks aspects of the history of the sacrament—it is at least defensible that Ratzinger has a better historical sense. Prior to Vatican II Ratzinger expressed impatience with the lack of vitality in Catholic theology and wrote critically about procedures in the Roman Curia. Shortly after the council he grew more and more convinced that its real goals had been misunderstood or distorted by certain theologians.[35] The *aggiornamento* advocated by the council had been in some ways divorced from the *ressourcement*, the renewal of the church through its intellectual and spiritual sources and traditions.

In 1963 Ratzinger moved briefly to the University of Münster. Michael Collins offers an enlightening comment on this move from Bonn to Münster: "In Bonn, Joseph Ratzinger had encountered jealousy among other faculty members. Although they did not attack him openly, he learned that his doctoral candidates were being victimized by his colleagues. Rankled by their petty-mindedness and prompted by memories of his own habilitation anxieties some years earlier, he decided that Münster offered the best of both worlds."[36] However, he was not to stay there very long. In 1966 he moved to the University of Tübingen where he remained until 1969. There he was a colleague of Hans Küng, who had worked to bring about his appointment. They worked together and on a friendly basis. Küng tells us that he was responsible for finding for his new colleague and his sister an attractive house and garden in Tübingen.[37]

Küng in his memoirs says that he could make nothing of Balthasar's friend, the mystic Adrienne von Speyr, and he says that this was also true of Ratzinger. He notes that Ratzinger remarked to him in regard to von Speyr that now "all is up with Balthasar," even though Ratzinger's own friendship with Balthasar was to develop.[38] It was in Tübingen that Ratzinger presented to students the lectures on the Creed that would be published as *An Introduction to Christianity*, arguably one of his finest theological contributions. His study habits appear to have included retiring at 9 p.m. so as to rise the following morning between 3.30 and 4 a.m. for solid study hours before breakfast.[39] These study habits bore fruit in his lectures and seminars.

35. Fahey, "Joseph Ratzinger as Ecclesiologist and Pastor," 76.

36. Collins, *Pope Benedict XVI*, 40.

37. Küng, *Disputed Truth, Memoirs II*, 12.

38. Küng, *My Struggle for Freedom, Memoirs*, 119. Guerriero, *Benedict XVI*, 347–48, comments laconically as follows: "For his part, Ratzinger was rather reserved about von Speyr's numerous mystical phenomena but was enthusiastic about the powerful Catholic vision of his friend von Balthasar, about his ability to access and to render fruitful in a new way the patristic heritage, about his staunch defense of the sanctity but also of the visible aspect of the church, of the Petrine ministry, and of the symphony of truth that is capable of grasping and holding together the many aspects of the mystery and of Christian life."

39. Shortt, *Benedict XVI*, 46.

One of his students, Helmut Moll who was later to work at the Congregation for the Doctrine of the Faith, describes the seminars in these terms: "To join a seminar on Mariology you had to take a pre-examination on Greek and Latin Marian texts from the early centuries. But there was no comparison between Ratzinger and the others. The lectures that I had heard in Bonn from professors of neo-scholastic bent appeared arid and cold, a list of precise doctrinal definitions and that was it. When I listened in Tübingen to Ratzinger speaking about Jesus or of the Holy Spirit, it seemed at times that his words had the accent of prayer."[40]

His final academic move was to the recently established and more conservative University of Regensburg in 1969. The year 1968 had seen a great deal of student unrest throughout Europe, and Tübingen was no exception. Ratzinger was very perturbed by this, with its wide questioning of authority and doctrine and especially with its too frequent Marxist presuppositions. This period of radical unrest, perhaps more intense in the German (and French) academic world than anywhere else in Europe, allied to the earlier Nazi fanaticism and all that went with it, seems to have given Joseph Ratzinger a somewhat pessimistic view of the world.[41] This leads to Timothy George's understanding of Ratzinger's Augustinianism. There are indeed things about our culture, our world, with which a Christian would want to take serious issue. One thinks, for example, of economic relations, defense policies and war, familial violence and abuse, the de-stabilization of families, the sexual enslavement of women—the list would be very long indeed. Realism demands a lengthy list. Realism surely demands the refusal of "scandalous optimism," but, as Eamon Duffy points out, there is

---

40. Cited in Rausch, *Pope Benedict XVI*, 19.

41. Collins, *God's New Man*, 45–46 also alludes to the growing friction and tensions within the faculty of theology as reasons for Ratzinger's departure. Some comments from Thomas P. Rausch, *Pope Benedict XVI*, 6 flesh this out a little: "With Ernst Bloch, a Marxist philosopher teaching (at Tübingen), the reigning paradigm based on Bultmann's theology and Heidegger's philosophy gave way to new ones based on Marxist thought. According to Ratzinger, Bloch dismissed Heidegger for being 'petit bourgeois.' Two other Tübingen faculty members contributed to its increasingly engaged and, in his view, politicized theology. Jürgen Moltmann's 'theology of hope' was influenced by Bloch's Marxist analysis, and the famous Ernst Käsemann, Tübingen's professor of New Testament exegesis, argued that theology had been used to support oppressive systems and that the church itself was often complicit in the exploitation of the poor. Ratzinger was horrified by this atmosphere. He felt that the integrity of both the academy and the faith was at stake." In his autobiography, Moltmann also alludes to these experiences: "At that time, Ratzinger joined together with Wickert and Beyerhaus in Tübingen in order to resist the 'cruel face of this atheistic religiousness,' in the face of which the denominational controversies seemed to him slight. But in the disputes with the students he then abandoned us and moved to Regensburg in order 'to pursue his theology in a less over-heated milieu.' I later mentioned to him how quickly the specter whose terrible face he thought he could see at that time had disappeared. He was also a little embarrassed at having left his colleagues in Tübingen in the lurch; but for him the apocalyptic vision of the future of Christianity's 'little flock' in the great dangers of the world apparently remained. Ratzinger did not understand that for Bloch and me at that time it was not the Marxist idea but the messianic hope which became the real anti-existentialist alternative." See Moltmann, *A Broad Place, An Autobiography*, 162.

also such a thing as "scandalous pessimism."[42] A certain pessimism appears to have infected the thinking of Joseph Ratzinger, the first public sign of this pessimism being his criticism of Vatican II's *Gaudium et Spes*. One commentator has captured this "pessimism" particularly well: "His will be a theology less inclined to seek for 'seeds of the Word' or for grace hidden in the human mess of things and more inclined to identify the pollutants that distort and seduce a humanity that is constantly in need of healing and conversion." His theology seems in this way to be more prophetic than correlationist, more detective of sin than of grace.[43]

As he was moving to the University of Regensburg in 1969, he was also invited by Pope Paul VI to become a member of the International Theological Commission, an indication of the high esteem in which he was held. The yearly meetings of this body opened him to a "broader stage of scholarship," as well as making him somewhat better known in the Vatican.[44] About the same time, Ratzinger helped in the founding of the theological journal, *Communio*, along with Henri de Lubac, Walter Kasper, Karl Lehmann, and Hans Urs von Balthasar. With these men he shared the conviction that the *Concilium* based theology had moved too far in the direction of *aggiornamento*/ecclesial renewal although he himself had been on the editorial board of the journal—without the necessary rooting in *ressourcement*/returning to the sources of the tradition. Add to this updating at the expense of *ressourcement* the factor of over-expectation of Vatican II, and one can see, maintains Ratzinger, that the results of the council have not uniformly been good.[45] There has been too much talk about a *new* church, and insufficient talk about a *renewed* church, or as he puts it somewhat humorously: "Even now we sometimes hear the faithful complain that they are fed up with hearing sermons which follow the stereotyped pattern: 'Of old it was said to you ... But I say to you ...'"[46] This emphasis on the continuity between Vatican II and the pre-conciliar church is entirely right. The integral meaning of catholicity is simply lost when any period in the church is regarded as written off. Ecclesiologically it is axiomatic for Catholics that the Spirit is at work now and always. This is how theologian, Hermann J. Pottmeyer, puts this same point made by Ratzinger: "The Catholic Church believes that in every phase of its development it is effectively led by the Spirit of God, even if in different degrees and even if it must make critical distinctions between what is binding, what is conditioned by the age, and what is perhaps even sinful."[47] Any other position would be fundamentally flawed ecclesiologically.

What was Ratzinger like in the classroom? One of his doctoral students at Regensburg, the Irish theologian Vincent Twomey, provides us with a most interesting

42. Duffy, "Urbi, but not Orbi ... the Cardinal, the Church, and the World," 274.
43. Corkery, "Joseph Ratzinger's Theological Ideas: 1. Origins" 13–14.
44. Collins, *Pope Benedict XVI: The First Five Years*, 48.
45. Ratzinger, *Salt of the Earth*, 74–75.
46. Ratzinger, *Theological Highlights of Vatican II*, 184.
47. Pottmeyer, "A New Phase in the Reception of Vatican II," 34.

description: "He had an ability to promote debate and encourage nervous beginners that has remained a model for my own teaching. He listened—carefully and shrewdly, indeed, but above all patiently—and remembered all the salient points raised in the discussion, which he allowed to run its course with the least possible interruption on his part." His patient listening ability, accompanied by his capacity for accurate synthesis, are characteristics of Ratzinger to which many others also point. Twomey goes on to note Ratzinger's lightness of touch and sense of humor: "Perhaps one could say: *Ubi Ratzinger, ibi hilaritas* (in Ratzinger's company cheerfulness prevailed): anecdotes abounded."[48] Another student of Ratzinger's, from his time at Münster, Francis Schüssler Fiorenza, witnesses to both his popularity and his excellence as a theology teacher: "He was clearly the most popular lecturer around. Moreover, he had a knowledge of Scripture and the history of theology that far excelled that of the other members of the faculty. . . . His lectures were so well-crafted that, years later, as a beginning assistant professor at the University of Notre Dame, I found myself using Ratzinger's lectures as the basis for my own, even though I was theologically closer to Rahner and Metz."[49]

Archbishop of Munich

A few months before Ratzinger's appointment to Munich, the American Jesuit theologian Thomas P. Rausch interviewed him in Regensburg. Rausch was impressed by the fact that Ratzinger told him his time was limited because he was going to a May Marian devotion that evening, and yet Professor Ratzinger walked him to the street indicating where he could catch his bus. Rausch comments, "That kind of graciousness is typical of him."[50]

Julius Döpfner, Cardinal-archbishop of Munich, died suddenly and unexpectedly in 1976. Who was to succeed him? "The names of possible successors began to circulate in the diocese. Ratzinger's name, too, was on the list. The professor had no special pastoral experience or administrative abilities, but in Rome he enjoyed great confidence. He had not studied in the capital of Catholicism, but he had become well known there both through his effective participation in Vatican II and also through his work on the International Theological Commission."[51] In 1977, just forty-nine years old, Ratzinger was appointed archbishop of Munich, and then cardinal. His episcopal motto was "Co-Workers of the Truth." In later years he was to say that he finds a bishop "whose only aim is to avoid trouble a terrifying vision."[52] Archbishop Ratzinger did not seek trouble, but neither did he avoid it. The leading newspaper in Munich,

48. Twomey, *Pope Benedict XVI*, 23, 27.

49. Fiorenza, "From Theologian to Pope, A Personal View Back, Past the Public Portrayals," 57.

50. Rausch, *Pope Benedict XVI*, 8.

51. Guerriero, *Benedict XVI*, 252.

52. Cited in Seewald, *Pope Benedict XVI, Servant of the Truth*, 68.

the *Süddeutsche Zeitung*, said of him: "Of all the conservatives in the Church he is the one with the strongest capacity for dialogue."[53] Dialogue, yes, but no avoidance of making difficult decisions when he judged that they were required. For example, in 1978, he vetoed the appointment of Johannes Baptist Metz to the chair of theology at the University of Munich, the supposed reason being Metz's political/liberation theology. While Metz could not easily be accused of Marxist tendencies, there is a certain pragmatic-political aspect to his theology, and it may be this that made Ratzinger oppose the appointment. The veto of Metz angered Metz's teacher, Karl Rahner, and Rahner wrote a somewhat acerbic rebuke to Ratzinger. This is how the Ratzinger biographer Elio Guerriero comments on the episode:

> In a letter that was made public by the press, [Rahner] accused Ratzinger of not distinguishing adequately between his hierarchical responsibility and his theological views, and he challenged him to a public debate in defense of freedom of theological research. . . . [Ratzinger] responded to Rahner, saying that he had refused to debate publicly precisely out of respect for him. He did not deny his involvement in the appointment that bypassed Metz; indeed, he declared that he had followed the matter very attentively from the beginning. He then added that all three nominees were qualified for the job and that he had not intended to do Metz any harm.[54]

While Ratzinger's breach with Rahner was never to be healed within Rahner's lifetime, he did reestablish cordial relationships with Metz in the 1990s.[55]

That same year, 1978, saw the death of Pope Paul VI, and found Cardinal Ratzinger in Rome for the conclave that elected Pope John Paul I. At the first conclave of that year, he engaged in conversation the archbishop of Krakow, Karol Wojtyla, though the latter's name was already known to him. Apparently the German philosopher Josef Pieper had written to Ratzinger about this impressive Polish philosopher, Karol Wojtyla, whom he had met at a philosophical congress in Italy. At the second conclave of that year, undoubtedly Ratzinger voted for Wojtyla as Pope John Paul II.

Prefect of the Congregation for the Doctrine of the Faith

In 1982 Ratzinger was appointed prefect of the Congregation for the Doctrine of the Faith in Rome. Pope John Paul II had approached him before, but met with hesitation on Ratzinger's part. One of the reasons for this hesitation had to do with the fact that Ratzinger wished to continue writing his own books of theology, and was unsure to what extent this was genuinely compatible with being prefect of the

53. Seewald, *Pope Benedict XVI, Servant of the Truth*, 72.
54. Guerriero, *Benedict XVI*, 282.
55. Shortt, *Benedict XVI*, 57.

Congregation for the Doctrine of the Faith. On this point he received from John Paul the re-assurance he needed and wanted.

Peter Seewald describes the container taking Ratzinger's things from Munich to Rome: ". . . a walnut desk he had inherited from his parents, a piano, and two thousand books."[56] The office of prefect is both important and difficult. Established by Pope Paul III in 1542 as the "Sacred Congregation of the Universal Inquisition" with the explicit purpose of defending the church against heresy, it became popularly known as the "Holy Office." In 1600 the philosopher Giordano Bruno was burned in Rome after condemnation by this Inquisition, and, of course, the Grand Inquisitor became immortalized in Dostoevsky's *Brothers Karamazov*. Bishop Hans-Jochen Jaschke captures the mood of the inquisitors, as well as the changed perspective that Pope John Paul II and Cardinal Ratzinger brought to the office: "Their (the 'inquisitors') desire was to preserve the purity of the faith, but many official and unofficial little inquisitors rushed to help them in such a way that the light of faith no longer shone in human hearts. Pope John Paul II and Cardinal Ratzinger have publicly confessed the terrible guilt incurred by those who were intolerant and violent in God's name."[57] Ratzinger's immediate predecessor was Cardinal Franjo Seper, a Croatian who was competent but in no sense a brilliant or creative theologian. How would Joseph Ratzinger, a brilliant and creative theologian, act in this new role?

Well, he would certainly be opposed to "letting things drift" and to the avoidance of conflict where he felt that the faith of the church was at stake. Needless to say, it would be very strange if Ratzinger the prefect were to conduct himself in a way singularly different from Ratzinger the archbishop. As archbishop he had vetoed Johann Baptist Metz for a chair in theology at the University of Munich. He considered the political turn in Metz's thought particularly problematic. In a similar way, he had been severely critical of the writings of Hans Küng, his former Tübingen colleague. Viewed from the outside, from the standpoint of professional theologians, Ratzinger had displayed a very conservative style. That style was to continue as prefect.

Does this legitimate concern for the church and the integrity of its doctrine entail a view of the Congregation for the Doctrine of the Faith that is inflexible and misanthropic? Ratzinger does not think so:

> Anyone who really has to deal with us also sees that we're not inhuman but always try to find a reasonable solution. Ultimately, as in any society, the church has to find the right balance between individual rights and the good of the community as a whole. The point here is that the good in virtue of which the church exists and which keeps her together is the faith. On the one hand, those who, as it were, can't fight back intellectually have to be defended—against intellectual assault on what sustains their life. On the other hand, our work demands respect for the rights of the person concerned. The juridical procedures

56. Seewald, *Pope Benedict XVI*, 73.
57. Jaschke in Seewald, *Pope Benedict XVI*, 102.

that we have, and that we also try to keep improving, consist in correctly balancing these two things.[58]

That was the prefect's personal point of view. Undoubtedly, he believed it to be true. It is when one gets into the details of individual cases and situations that have come before the Congregation for the Doctrine of the Faith that the matter becomes exceedingly complex. One may agree or disagree with what the prefect and the Congregation have said and done, and it is almost impossible not to take sides. The complexity of the challenge resides in the fact that it is so very difficult to be in command of all the relevant data. The media often make understanding even more difficult both by caricaturing Ratzinger rather unfairly and also by using "sound-bytes." This is how it is put by Michael Collins: "In the age of sound-byte, the media reporting of his documents cropped the message to a few sentences. By the nature of the complex themes at issue, the message was often truncated and distorted."[59]

In September 1984 Ratzinger oversaw the "Instruction on Some Aspects of the Theology of Liberation." To be fair to him the CDF had already initiated investigations against the liberation theologians. It opened a file on Leonardo Boff in 1975 and one on Jon Sobrino in 1980. He was, however, already sympathetic to the Congregation's critique. In this document he upset both Communist countries and the practitioners of liberation theology. He called Communism a "shame of our times" and a "perfidious illusion." That drew protests from diplomats and leaders of various Communist countries. Liberation theologians took exception to his remark in the document that "certain forms of the theology of liberation" were unacceptable because "they drew from various tendencies of Marxist thought."[60] There is a consistency to Ratzinger's thinking here. It needs to be said, however, that a careful reading of the text suggests no withdrawal on the part of the Congregation for the Doctrine of the Faith from the struggle for justice and freedom especially in Latin America. There was, however, a very definite concern about violence, about irresponsible political partisanship, and a concern about "the political innocence of liberation theologians."[61] It must also be pointed out that Ratzinger was a contributor to the composition of Pope John Paul II's encyclical, *Sollicitudo Rei Socialis*, an encyclical with a deep biblical base and which shared a significant number of the concerns of liberation theology. Ratzinger's discomfort with liberation theology goes back earlier to his study of St. Bonaventure and his struggle with the Spiritual Franciscans. "Ratzinger has never been comfortable with a theology that looked for eschatological fulfillment within history."[62]

58. Ratzinger, *Salt of the Earth*, 89.

59. Collins, *Pope Benedict XVI: The First Five Years*, 80.

60. Fischer, *Pope Benedict XVI*, 12.

61. Ratzinger, *Salt of the Earth*, 94; Fischer, *Pope Benedict XVI*, 18.

62. Rausch, *Pope Benedict XVI*, 23.

There was an investigation of the Brazilian Franciscan theologian, Leonardo Boff. Boff met with the prefect for a conversation about his theology in Rome. However, it seems that it was the authoritarian Cardinal Josef Hamer, prefect of the Congregation for the Religious Orders, and not immediately Ratzinger, who insisted that Boff undergo a time of penitential silence. In the end, Ratzinger agreed.[63] There was a massive, negative reaction to this move that served to promote the image of Ratzinger as a "restorationist." The same image tended to be re-enforced by the lengthy interview with an Italian journalist Vittorio Messori that was published as *The Ratzinger Report*, and in which we find the prefect's views on a range of ecclesial matters. It seems that the original intention behind the interview was as a contribution to ongoing theological discussion among academics, but it became somewhat notorious at a much wider level. The *Report* seems accurately described as a "gloomy assessment of contemporary Catholicism."[64] Throughout the *Report* Ratzinger lamented what he took to be misinterpretations of Vatican II, misinterpretations represented as a rupture in tradition. His judgment was consistently that there was no rupture but an almost perfect continuity with tradition. "When [this way of thinking is] applied to Vatican II, it implies that the Council did little more than ratify the status quo and was far from being the landmark event in Christian history that most historians and other interpreters saw it to be."[65]

This restorationist interpretation leads the Catholic journalist, John Allen, to draw a certain parallel between Ratzinger's reaction to political totalitarianism and his advocacy of ecclesial totalitarianism: "Having seen fascism in action, Ratzinger today believes that the best antidote to political totalitarianism is ecclesial totalitarianism. In other words, he believes the Catholic Church serves the cause of human freedom by restricting freedom in its internal life, thereby remaining clear about what it teaches and believes."[66] This seems unduly harsh. Firmness and decisiveness with regard to matters of doctrine and morality cannot reasonably be construed as totalitarianism. Ratzinger the prefect believed firmly and decisively and acted accordingly, but that is not totalitarianism. Nor does this unfair criticism sit well alongside the almost unanimous affirmation of Ratzinger's ability to listen and to respond fairly. I believe it would be fair to say that many of the popular critics of Joseph Ratzinger have not read widely in his theological writings. Have some of his theological views changed over the years? He himself insists that such changes as have occurred are more changes of emphasis than anything else, and his former student and now commentator, D. Vincent Twomey maintains, in a very balanced statement, that "there is also a basic continuity in his theology, a continuity that is not inconsistent with significant changes in perspective, even at times contradicting isolated claims

---

63. Fischer, *Pope Benedict XVI*, 37.

64. Rausch, *Pope Benedict XVI*, 31.

65. O'Malley, "Two Popes: Benedict and Francis," 64.

66. Allen, *Pope Benedict XVI*, 3.

he made in his theological youth."[67] Is there anyone, especially any theologian who would be exempt from this kind of description?

Even as we attempt to discover something of Prefect Ratzinger, it seems to me important not to neglect other aspects of the man, aspects recently highlighted by the German religious journalist, Heinz-Joachim Fischer. During the time when Fischer was in Rome to interview Ratzinger, he had the prefect to lunch in his apartment, and Ratzinger never came without some carefully chosen gift. He shared with his hosts the fact that his sister, Maria, who had come to Rome as his housekeeper never quite felt at home in the city, and his sadness at the fact. Maria Ratzinger had been her brother's housekeeper for thirty years. When she died in 1991, he felt her loss very deeply. Surprisingly, her place was taken by Ingrid Stampa, a former professor of music at the Academy of Music in Hamburg, but now virtually a monastic living in Rome since the later 1980s. This accomplished woman, a fluent Polish-speaker and translator of Pope John Paul II's Polish writings, now devoted her life to looking after Joseph Ratzinger, and continued to care for Pope Benedict XVI. It is quite interesting that the Australian author Paul Collins, a former priest and a critic of the contemporary papacy, makes the following comment: "Keeping Stampa on his staff sends a message to the church: laypeople and women have an important role to play, even right at the very top of the ecclesiastical structure."[68]

Rupert Shortt, the English journalist, offers a nice description of Cardinal Ratzinger during the time of his prefecture:

> Ratzinger's existence over his twenty-three years as Prefect was outwardly undramatic. He did not travel much. . . . He walked most mornings from his flat, opposite the Vatican, to his office in the Sant' Uffizio, a quadrangle just south of St. Peter's Square. . . . Most of his evenings were spent in his own household, run by Maria Ratzinger, and, after her death, by Dr. Ingrid Stampa, a German musicologist. . . . The Cardinal would relax with his beloved cats, with a post-prandial cigarette, or at the piano. He reveres Bach, and loves Mozart, above all other composers.[69]

Pope Benedict XVI

Pope John Paul II died on April 2, 2005. Cardinal Ratzinger preached a very fine homily at the Mass for the Election of the Roman Pontiff. Here are some of his words:

> How many winds of doctrine have we known in recent decades, how many ideological currents, how many ways of thinking? The small boat of the thought of many Christians has often been tossed about by these waves—flung

67. Twomey, *Pope Benedict XVI*, 169.

68. Collins, *God's New Man*, 194.

69. Shortt, *Pope Benedict XVI*, 61.

from one extreme to another: from Marxism to liberalism, even to libertinism; from collectivism to radical individualism; from atheism to a vague religious mysticism; from agnosticism to syncretism and so forth. . . . Today, having a clear faith based on the Creed of the church is often labeled as fundamentalism. Whereas relativism, that is, letting oneself be "tossed here and there, carried about by every wind of doctrine," seems the only attitude that can cope with modern times. We are building a dictatorship of relativism that does not recognize anything as definitive and whose ultimate goal consists solely of one's ego and desires . . . .[70]

No matter where one stands on the epistemological, philosophical, or theological spectrum, it would be difficult to disagree with this description of the human situation. Ratzinger's description of the human situation seems very accurate indeed and, as Collins puts it, "The clarity of his thought struck many."[71] The clarity of Ratzinger's thought is self-evident. What may be lacking, however, is a thought out process of how one arrives at truth. The "dictatorship of relativism" may very easily be short-circuited to a positivist acceptance of what a person, an institution, even the magisterial church may say. Such a passive docility is no response to relativism. Rather, an agonizing towards the truth, premised on the raising of further relevant questions, so that the truth, as it were, does not seem to be entirely and totally and already in one's possession seems to be the only realistic and persuasive way forward. It may be that Pope Benedict recognizes this, but those who use his soundbite "the dictatorship of relativism" may not always be aware of this epistemological agonizing.[72]

Some were surprised, others were not that Joseph Ratziner was elected pope, having exceeded the required seventy-seven votes in the conclave, that is to say, a two-thirds majority of the 115 cardinals. Two prominent Vatican-watchers, Thomas Reese, SJ and John Allen, were convinced that there was no hope that Joseph Ratzinger would be elected pope. "He was too controversial, too identified with Pope John Paul."[73] They and so many others were wrong. Ratzinger chose the name Benedict, in honor both of Pope Benedict XV (1914–22) and also in honor of St. Benedict, founder of western monasticism and patron of the West. It was inevitable that Ratzinger's election would invite strong reactions, both positive and negative.

Benedict's address to diplomats on May 11 displayed a very keen sensitivity given the fact that he was the first German to be elected pope since the eleventh century. These are some of the words he spoke on that occasion:

> For my part, I come from a country in which peace and fraternity have a
> great place in the heart of its inhabitants, in particular, of those who, like

70. Cited from Collins, *Pope Benedict XVI: The First Five Years*, 86.

71. Collins, *Pope Benedict XVI: The First Five Years*, 87.

72. See the similar comments of Rausch, *Pope Benedict XVI*, 151.

73. Rausch, *Pope Benedict XVI*, 4.

me, knew war and the separation of brothers belonging to the same nation, because of devastating and inhuman ideologies that, cloaked in dreams and illusion, imposed on human beings the yoke of oppression. You will understand therefore that I am particularly sensitive to dialogue among all people, to overcome all forms of conflict and tension, and to make our world a world of peace and fraternity.[74]

Benedict pointed as his successor in the Congregation for the Doctrine of the Faith William Levada (1936–2019), archbishop of San Francisco. Levada had worked at the congregation during Ratzinger's tenure and was well known to him. His appointment, however, could be seen as much more than personal trust. It can be seen as a vote of confidence in the American Catholic Church, struggling at the time with the fallout from the sexual abuse scandals.

Benedict became seventy-eight just three days before his election as pope. It was necessary for him to prioritize and to conserve his energies, not least because it was confirmed that he had suffered a mild stroke somewhere between 2003 and 2005. The decision was taken, therefore, that a cardinal delegated by the pope would preside over beatification ceremonies. The one exception Benedict made was in respect of John Henry Newman. Joseph Ratzinger had been in great admiration of Newman's theology, and so during his visit to the United Kingdom in 2010 he presided over the beatification ceremony of Newman himself.

The Regensburg Address

On his visit to Germany in 2006, Pope Benedict delivered an address at the University of Regensburg. During the lecture he quoted from a fourteenth-century Byzantine Emperor Manuel Paleologus II. The pope introduced the quotation from this Byzantine Emperor with these words: "He addresses his interlocutor with a startling brusqueness, a brusqueness that we find unacceptable, on the central question about the relationship between religion and violence in general." The Emperor said: "Show me just what Mohammed brought that was new, and there you will find things only evil and inhuman, such as his command to spread by the sword the faith he preached." Following this quotation the pope went on to say: "The Emperor, after having expressed himself so forcefully, goes on to explain in detail the reasons why spreading the faith through violence is something unreasonable."[75] In an academic context, a comment like this is one that invites critical analysis and response. The trouble was that the pope was no longer simply an academic delivering an academic lecture. He was on the world stage, and the global audience—not just Catholics or Christians—was listening with interest, if not with critical acumen. Inevitably,

74. Cited in Collins, *God's New Man*, 93.
75. Cited in Collins, *God's New Man*, 129–30.

there was an extremely negative reaction from much of the Muslim world. "Even the Pope's most ardent supporters agree that the quotation at Regensburg was both inopportune and unwise."[76] On October 12 an open letter was released that had been signed by the Grant Mufti of Egypt and thirty-seven Muslim scholars and clerics clearly recognizing that the opinion of the Byzantine Emperor was not the personal opinion of Pope Benedict. Nonetheless, damage had been done and it was clear that either the pope did not share the text of this lecture with his advisers, or his advisers overlooked the potentially explosive nature of this comment on the world stage. When Benedict visited the kingdom of Jordan in 2009, King Abdullah II's religious advisor said to him, "I would like to thank you for expressing regret over the lecture in 2006, which hurt the feelings of Muslims."[77]

Before he was elected pope, Cardinal Ratzinger expressed his opinion publicly that he was opposed to the membership of Turkey in the European Union. Essentially, his claim had to do with the fact that Turkey was a predominantly Muslim country, and he could not see how that would fit with the continent that was traditionally Christian and that had been formed in and through Christian culture for almost two millennia. The cardinal's opinion could, of course, be contested on a number of counts, but it was seen in Muslim circles especially as an anti-Muslim comment. When he visited Turkey in 2006 as Pope Benedict XVI, he publicly voiced his support for Turkey's membership in the European Union, and that public support found favor as one would expect not only in Turkey but in Muslim countries generally. At the same time, some informed commentators while recognizing that the pope has made good on this issue, are not convinced that he has learned and developed adequately the skills of diplomacy. Thus, for example, Frank J. Coppa writes: "To be sure he had learned some lessons in diplomacy, but still lacked the diplomatic agility and universal image of John Paul II. An acknowledged expert in the theological realm of certainty, he remained a relative novice in the shifting sands of politics and diplomacy."[78] Coppa's judgment has the ring of accuracy. Pope Benedict XV wanted to be an academic theologian, spent a lot of time in the theological academy, continued to write theological books—that is his forte. Diplomacy is not a major personal concern, although clearly he recognizes its importance.

Theology of Scripture

Ever since his seminary days Joseph Ratzinger has been an assiduous student of Scripture and, moreover, Scripture understood as the word of God. This is quite different from what would be understood as Biblical Studies in the modern academy. With Scripture as the word of God it is impossible for Ratzinger "to get lost in a

---

76. Collins, *God's New Man*, 130.

77. Collins, *God's New Man*, 197.

78. Coppa, *Politics and the Papacy in the Modern World*, 218.

tangle of efforts to isolate the earliest form of a saying or in problematic reconstructions that are often ideologically driven."[79]

His emphasis, therefore, is on ecclesial authority in the interpretation of holy Scripture. That is the basis for his critique of the dominance of the historical critical methods. That is also the basis for his appeal to patristic sources in understanding the Scriptures. Francis Schüssler Fiorenza illustrates this approach with a personal reminiscence. His future wife, Elisabeth Schüssler, was completing a doctorate in New Testament at Münster, and he describes the theological relationship between her and Ratzinger as follows: "She and Ratzinger argued rather vigorously and at length. Whenever Elisabeth made a point, Ratzinger graciously smiled, as he often did and does, and conceded that her exegesis of the biblical texts was correct, but he maintained that the Roman Catholic position could not orient itself so primarily on Scripture without taking account of the teaching authority of the church."[80] Therein lies the heart of Joseph Ratzinger/Pope Benedict XVI's approach to Holy Scripture.

Theology of the Liturgy

It is not my concern here to provide a systematic account of Pope Benedict's liturgical theology, but to introduce his liturgical perspective. Consider these two comments on Benedict and his theology. "In fifty years of writing, there is hardly a theological subject on which Joseph Ratzinger has not expounded."[81] "If we understand what Papa Ratzinger thinks on this subject (of the liturgy), we will be close to understanding what makes him tick theologically."[82] The first citation from James Corkery, an Irish Jesuit systematic theologian, and the other from Eamon Duffy, Professor (now emeritus) of the History of Christianity at the University of Cambridge in England, help to situate the pope's understanding of the liturgy. Corkery reminds us of the enormous theological output of Joseph Ratzinger over fifty years of writing, and Duffy indicates that his thinking about the liturgy may well be the clue to his theological thinking generally. Given all the attention that accrued to the papacy during the ministry of his predecessor, Pope John Paul II, and all the recent controversy that has swirled around himself, it is not easy to get a balanced perspective on Pope Benedict XVI, and perhaps especially on his liturgical and eucharistic theology. A good beginning may be made, however, by turning to some gracious but accurate words of the liturgical theologian, John F. Baldovin, SJ:

79. Rausch, *Pope Benedict XVI*, 143. A very full account of the pope's approach to Scripture across the years of his theological study may be had on pages 65–84 of this book.

80. Fiorenza, "From Theologian to Pope," 58.

81. Corkery, "Joseph Ratzinger's Theological Ideas: 2," 2. The entire essay runs from 6–14. See also by the same author "Joseph Ratzinger's Theological Ideas: 1. Origins: A Theologian Emerges," 6–14, and "Joseph Ratzinger's Theological Ideas: 3. On Being Human," 7–24. This series of articles by Corkery is now available in book form as *Joseph Ratzinger's Theological Ideas* (Mahwah: Paulist, 2009).

82. Duffy, "Benedict XVI and the Spirit of the Liturgy," 34.

"Ratzinger's writings are characterized by great clarity combined with a lively imagination and obvious love for God and divine revelation."[83]

What is abundantly clear is that Ratzinger's interest in the liturgy is of longstanding, something already noted. This interest in the liturgy has been with him since he was a small child, learning to use the bilingual Latin-German missal.[84] During his seminary years, the young Ratzinger was attracted to the theologian Romano Guardini, who played a significant role in the history of the liturgical movement in Germany. "Joseph Ratzinger revered and reveres Guardini."[85] Romano Guardini's book, *Spirit of the Liturgy*, published in 1918, was first read by Ratzinger when he began his theological training after the Second World War, and its continued influence is reflected in his own book with the same title, *The Spirit of the Liturgy*. Guardini's book became, in the words of Eamon Duffy, "almost at once one of the foundational texts behind the twentieth century liturgical movement."[86] The book had an enormous impact. Perhaps we could say that Guardini's fundamental liturgical perspective was that, despite all the data and evidence both historical and contemporary of the church's failings, God-in-Christ-through-the-Spirit is really at work in the church's liturgy, shaping us and inviting into communion with God's Triune self. This is permeative in Ratzinger's liturgical thinking.

The real theological issue at stake for Joseph Ratzinger is this: while philosophical theology—in its Thomist form, or in any other suitable metaphysical form—is necessary to the theological task, and so to any adequate theological understanding of the liturgy, so that liturgical axioms and philosophical analysis are logically simultaneous, nevertheless, there is a primacy to revelation, and therefore, to the liturgy, a primacy that is marked by an openness to receptivity, the receiving of the gift of divinization. This seems to me to be Ratzinger's position. Going with Cardinal Frings to the Second Vatican Council, he demonstrated the growth in his love of the liturgy: "Just as I learned to understand the New Testament as being the soul of all theology, so too I came to see the Liturgy as being its living element. This is why, at the beginning of the Council, I saw that the draft of the Constitution on the Liturgy, which incorporated all the essential principles of the Liturgical Movement, was a marvelous point of departure for this assembly of the whole Church, and I advised Cardinal Frings in this sense."[87] For the very young Ratzinger, and *a fortiori* for the mature theologian, the liturgy is absolutely central to the theological enterprise, but more importantly, simply to being a Catholic Christian.

Almost as a natural consequence to his interest in the liturgy, Ratzinger's theology has always been closely related to preaching, particularly evident in his early book

83. Baldovin, "Cardinal Ratzinger as Liturgical Critic," 211–27.

84. Ratzinger, *Milestones*, 19–20.

85. Duffy, "Benedict XVI and the Spirit of the Liturgy," 39.

86. Duffy, "Benedict XVI and the Spirit of the Liturgy," 39.

87. Ratzinger, *Milestones*, 57.

Dogma and Preaching, but continuing into one of his most recent offerings, *Images of Hope: Meditations on Major Feasts*.[88] Ratzinger's viewpoint involves no depreciation of human reason, including human reason in the enterprise of theology, but he believes that rationality finds its appropriate *telos* in doxology, in the praise and worship of God. Thus, he writes: "Only if man, every man, stands before the face of God and is answerable to him, can man be secure in his dignity as a human being. Concern for the proper forms of worship, therefore, is not peripheral but central to our concern for man himself."[89] Standing before the face of God entails the recognition of the face of God, which may begin in reason but ends in worship.

He views the liturgy as something living and growing in the church. It cannot, therefore, be treated in a machine-like fashion, reducing it to something that whimsically can be "taken apart and set up differently," something that ought not to be tinkered with.[90] A proper sensitivity to liturgy and its own inner laws demands a twofold approach: respect "for what is carrying the riches of the centuries within it"; a prudential judgment about "where it is necessary and possible to supplement or to prune back in a way that is meaningful.[91] Ratzinger is neither a liturgical antiquarian nor a modernist. But he is critical of some of the aspects of the liturgical reform of recent times, especially as flowing from Vatican II. Cardinal Avery Dulles, SJ contrasts Pope Benedict XVI in this respect with Pope John Paul II: "In his many publications Ratzinger continued to debate questions that arose during the council and in some cases expressed dissatisfaction with the council's documents. In this respect he differs from Pope John Paul, who consistently praised the council and never (to my knowledge) criticized it."[92] Needless to say, Ratzinger's liturgical criticisms are by no means exclusive to him. The point is well and wittily made by John Baldovin: "In common with many of the critics of the liturgical reform of the past forty years, he perceives the liberal or progressive attitude toward liturgy as an unwarranted accommodation to the spirit of our age—going in their door and failing to come out ours."[93]

Fr. Baldovin is on target, but his comment needs more nuance. When it comes to the revised liturgy in the wake of Vatican II, Ratzinger is very clear that he is supportive. However, he expresses a concern, and a concern that would be shared by many centrist liturgical theologians: "In our form of the liturgy there is a tendency that, in my opinion, is false, namely, the complete 'inculturation' of the liturgy into the contemporary world. The liturgy is thus supposed to be shortened; and everything that is supposedly unintelligible should be removed from it; it should, basically, be transposed down to an

---

88. Ratzinger, *Dogma and Preaching*; and *Images of Hope: Meditations on Major Feasts*.

89. Ratzinger, *Feast of Faith*, 7.

90. Ratzinger, *God and the World*, 414, 416.

91. Ratzinger, *God and the World*, 414–15.

92. Dulles, "From Ratzinger to Benedict," 24.

93. Baldovin, SJ, "Cardinal Ratzinger as Liturgical Critic," 212.

even 'flatter' language."[94] An abbreviated liturgy, a liturgy expressed in pedestrian and banal language, a liturgy that seems to lack a sense of transcendent mystery is what he is opposed to. His overriding concern is that God must be at the center of the liturgy. The absolute centrality of God in the liturgy was finally expressed by the pope in 2007 when he visited the Cistercian Abbey of Heiligenkreuz during a trip to Austria: "Whenever in our thinking we are concerned about making the liturgy attractive, interesting and beautiful, the battle is already lost. Either it is *Opus Dei*, with God as its specific subject, or it is not." And so he exhorted the monks, "In the light of this, I ask you to celebrate the sacred liturgy with your gaze fixed on God within the communion of saints, the living Church of every time and place, so that it will be truly an expression of the sublime beauty of the God who has called men and women to be his friends."[95] At all costs for Pope Benedict both a personal and a congregational narcissism must be avoided, and "revision must always happen as a process of refinement and purification of what went before, never as a fresh start."[96]

It is surely interesting in this regard to recognize the sentiments of two prominent English writers, the philosopher Roger Scruton and the novelist P. D. James. Both seem to me to come very close in their own ways to Ratzinger's position on liturgy. Scruton writes: "Changes in the liturgy take on a momentous significance for the believer, for they are changes in his experience of God—changes, if you wish to be Feuerbachian, in God himself. The question whether to make the sign of the cross with two fingers or with three split a Church. So can the question whether or not to use the Book of Common Prayer or the Tridentine Mass."[97] There is a clear perception in Scruton that tinkering with the liturgy is a very serious issue because it has to do with people's experience of God, and is never simply a matter of individual taste. In a similar way speaking of some of her friends, P. D. James says that "They love the beauty of the liturgy, though now, alas, it's being increasingly lost, the order and dignity of it." James reveals something of her own churchgoing and liturgical practices in an interview with theologian of literature, Ralph C. Wood: "The church I often go to, All Saints Margaret Street, is a very fine church in which the Creed and the Gloria are often sung in Latin. They have the Angelus, and they have a professional choir. . . . Of course, I think the Eucharist has to be the heart of the action . . . that Holy Communion is the heart of the worship." In her own life James has come out of and she participates in a Christian ecclesial tradition that is centrally shaped and formed by liturgy. In terms of the contemporary situation in England James comments: "People have a belief in God and a great need for God and the need for prayer and the need for God's power, but I don't think they believe the theology of

---

94. Ratzinger, *Salt of the Earth*, 175.

95. Cited in Collins, *God's New Man*, 152–53.

96. Duffy, "Benedict XVI and the Spirit of the Liturgy," 42–43.

97. Scruton, *The Philosopher on Dover Beach*, 115, cited in Rowland, *Ratzinger's Faith*, 128.

Christianity anymore. I honestly think they don't. They don't really accept the theology of the redemption."[98] One might debate some of the things that Baroness James is saying, but my hunch is that James and Scruton are describing very real liturgical challenges that make a real impact on how people believe and how people experience God. Joseph Ratzinger would be in complete agreement.

In the light of this reasoning, Ratzinger believes that the "old rite" of the Mass should be more generously made available to those who wish it. It is not the case that he advocates its universal restoration. Where people have genuinely experienced a felt loss of transcendent mystery, this felt need, he judges, ought to be met, and if it can be met with and through the "old rite," so be it. Perhaps we hear an echo here of the dominical adage about the Sabbath being made for man. It is access to transcendent mystery that is central to Ratzinger's liturgical theology. What is necessary is a solemn celebration of the rites "to introduce us into feast and celebration, to make man capable of the mystery."[99] This is what he refers to as "a reform of the reform." It is fundamentally about receiving the new rites that flowed from Vatican II, and making the effort to appropriate them in a deep and personal way, letting communion with the Divine Communion emerge. This is why Ratzinger urges all to get beyond an attitude of suspicion with regard to liturgical suggestions and even norms coming from the Vatican. It has nothing to do with a dictatorial approach to the liturgy, but about communion with the Divine Communion in a way that is truly Catholic.

He has an affection for Latin and for liturgical Latin. Eamon Duffy does not have it quite right, it seems to me, when he says: "From a bastion of daunting antiquarianism inaccessible to ordinary Catholics, the Latin liturgy came to seem to him a precious protection against a rootless *aggiornamento*, reform understood as the adoption merely of modern intellectual and cultural fads and fashions."[100] Duffy is a first-rate church historian and theological commentator, and he is surely saying something important here. But is he *entirely* right? It seems to me that Latin is not endorsed by Benedict for antiquarian or for purely personal reasons. Rather, he views Latin as not only a protection against careless presidential liturgical spontaneity, but also and perhaps more importantly as a defense of catholicity. Latin has traditionally been the language of Western Catholicism. While the Liturgy of the Word ought to be celebrated in the vernacular, so as to enable a real intelligibility and personal response, there is room for having some of the common parts of the Mass—the *Gloria*, the *Sanctus*, for example—sung or prayed in Latin, not at every celebration of the Eucharist but surely on some occasions as a reminder that the local church is one with the universal church. This would, he is convinced, provide "a basic stock of Latin elements that would bind us

---

98. James was interviewed by Ralph C. Wood in an interview published on his website as "The Mystery of Iniquity: An Interview with P. D. James," cited in Cummings, *Thinking About Prayer*, 101–12.

99. Ratzinger, *Salt of the Earth*, 177.

100. Duffy, "Benedict XVI and the Spirit of the Liturgy," 40.

together."[101] Benedict sees the total abandonment of Latin as a real loss, but he does not appear to be rigid about it. On the occasion of his visit to St. Paul—Outside-the-Walls on April 25 2005, for example, the booklet for the liturgy which he was to lead had been prepared in Latin. In point of fact, however, Benedict led the liturgy in Italian. Michael Collins nicely comments on this event that "he wished to speak to the people in their own language, not in that of their ancestors."[102]

Unfortunately, there is another side to the concern over the Latin language. It has to do with the *motu proprio, Summorum Pontificum*, issued on July 7, 2007 by Pope Benedict XVI, permitting all priests to celebrate the Mass according to the Missal of Pope Pius V. The Missal of Pope Paul VI is to remain the ordinary expression, but alongside it now is the extraordinary expression of the Missal of Pope Pius V. The language is, of course, Latin. Judged by many as an act of generosity, albeit somewhat controversial, on the part of Benedict, reaching out to those who genuinely felt deprived by the liturgical reforms consequent upon Vatican II, and especially the *novus ordo* (the Missal of Pope Paul VI), it has come to be even more controverted. Some priests and people without an adequate facility in Latin seek out the Latin Mass as somehow more mysterious/mystical (in the best sense) than the *novus ordo*. Others who seem to prefer the Missal of Pius V make outlandish comments. In May 2008, for example, Cardinal Dario Castrillon Hoyos, president of the Ecclesia Dei Commission in Rome and prefect emeritus of the Congregation for the Clergy, arrived in Westminster Cathedral, London, in *cappa magna*, to celebrate Mass in the extraordinary form. Hoyos is reported to have said on this occasion that it was the wish of Pope Benedict XVI to see the extraordinary form of the Mass celebrated in every parish alongside the *novus ordo*. If this were true, it would call into question in the eyes of many the value of the reformed rite, and perhaps even of the other liturgical reforms coming from the council.

From the vantage point of church history, making this "extraordinary form" so readily and immediately accessible is, though perhaps unintentionally, undermining the liturgical reforms consequent upon Vatican II. Often and for seriously uninformed reasons the old Latin Mass, as it is called, may appear to be more solemn, more dignified, even holier than the Missal of Pope Paul VI. Add to those considerations the oft-heard view that Latin is a sacral language. Fundamentally, every language spoken by people everywhere is a sacral language, unless one adopts an absolute and never-to-be-questioned Eurocentrism. The Eurocentric heyday is over in Catholicism. Demographically, there is a massive shift to the Southern Hemisphere, fleshing out what some have called the emergence of the "world-church." This is, for example, the insight of Karl Rahner, SJ, who saw this "world church" coming, even as he had little or no real experience of it himself. Rahner wrote in a famous essay: "The Second Vatican Council is the beginning of a tentative approach by the church to the

101. Ratzinger, *God and the World*, 418.

102. Collins, *Pope Benedict XVI, The First Five Years*, 49.

discovery and official realization of itself as world-church."[103] This transition from a European Christianity to a genuine worldwide church, for Rahner, had happened only once before when the church made the transition from Jewish Christianity to Gentile Christianity. It is not entirely clear what liturgy in a world-church rather than a Eurocentric church might be like. While recognizing the usefulness of occasional Latin as a badge of catholicity Rahner, writing in 1981, is careful with his language. Vatican II was the *beginning* of a *tentative* approach by the church. It is far from clear what the future might hold in this regard.

Ad Orientem or *Versus Populum*?

Sometimes allied in the minds of many to the question of the extraordinary form of the Mass in Latin, and yet quite distinct from it theologically, is the location of the altar and the position of the priest at the altar during the celebration of the Eucharist. Should the priest stand facing the people, *versus populum,* or facing East, *ad orientem*?

In 1993 Ratzinger contributed a preface to the German liturgist Klaus Gamber's book, *Reform of the Roman Liturgy*.[104] Ratzinger advocates a caution in respect of the altar being turned towards the people, eventing in what he takes to be a more horizontal experience of the liturgy rather than a more transcendent-mysterious experience. In later writings he has continued to reflect on this question.[105] This is an area where one could argue forever. Whatever good reasons may be found for such a reversal—historical, architectural and theological—pastorally, it would be very problematic. It may be the case that in some situations the transcendent-mysterious dimension of the Eucharist has been reduced to the horizontal level, but many pastors who celebrate the Eucharist according to the mind of the church, facing the people, would witness to the contrary. Many ordinary people find their faith in the Eucharist deepened and strengthened by the present arrangement. Could this be a case of the *sensus fidelium,* worldwide and across many cultures, indicating the way forward? Ratzinger makes a distinction between participation in the Liturgy of the Word, which involves "external" reading and singing, and participation in the Liturgy of the Eucharist, where such actions are secondary: "*Doing* really must stop when we come to the heart of the matter: the *oratio*. It must be plainly evident that the *oratio* is the heart of the matter, but that it is important precisely because it provides a space for the *actio* of God. Anyone who grasps this will easily see that it is not now a matter of looking at or toward the priest, but of looking together toward the Lord and going out to meet him."[106] It may be the case that some presiders cultivate a style that draws excessive attention to themselves

103. Rahner, "A Basic Theological Interpretation of the Second Vatican Council," 78.
104. Gamber, *Reform of the Roman Liturgy*.
105. For example, in Ratzinger, *The Spirit of the Liturgy*, 62–84.
106. Ratzinger, *The Spirit of the Liturgy*, 174.

as liturgical entrepreneurs, instead of "exercising enormous self-discipline."[107] It may also be the case that *physically* the congregation is looking at or toward the priest, but *spiritually* it is toward the priest as *in persona Christi*, and through him to the Christ who is sacramentally present for them, for their further transformation into the Divine Communion. The question of facing East or facing the people is not straightforward by any means. Although the pope makes some excellent points, "many would argue that the pastor or the priest facing the people better accords with a deeper sense of the communal dimension of the liturgy and its origin in the meal Jesus shared with his disciples the night before he died." But, as Thomas Rausch goes on to add, "Ratzinger has difficulties with these views as well."[108]

Some professional liturgical theologians, such as Pierre-Marie Gy, OP [1922–2004], have taken Ratzinger's liturgical theology to task.[109] Gy asks the question in an article with the same title: "Is Cardinal Ratzinger's *L'Esprit de la Liturgie* (Spirit of the Liturgy) faithful to the Council?"[110] Gy finds fault with Ratzinger's understanding and Ratzinger finds fault with Gy's understanding! This author tends to find Ratzinger's liturgical theology more nuanced than his critics would allow. Having different liturgical views is a good thing. Condemning others' liturgical views as though we had the fullness of liturgical truth is quite another. As Timothy Radcliffe, OP, has superbly put the challenge noted earlier, "We can resist the compulsion to evict those who disagree with us."[111] Those who disagree with Benedict on the liturgy with informed and good argumentation may yet learn from him, and those who agree with Benedict with informed and good argumentation may yet learn from those who disagree. Radically attentive listening is so important and eviction, in any sense of the word, is both unnecessary and scandalous. In his wide-ranging essay "Benedict the Augustinian," theologian Cyril O'Regan makes the following point about Benedict's understanding of liturgy: "Much more could be said of Benedict's attempt to articulate an adequate understanding of the liturgy and to revive the adorative matrix, threatened as they are by modern conceptions, and in much the same way that the historical-critical method has threatened, in fact if not necessarily in principle, the very notion of Scripture."[112] O'Regan is suggesting that there is a kind of parallel between Benedict's theology of liturgy and his theology of Scripture, that many modern approaches coincide in

107. Baldovin, SJ, "Cardinal Ratzinger as Liturgical Critic," 222.

108. Rausch, *Pope Benedict XVI*, 130.

109. Gy was Director of the Institut Supérieure de Liturgie at the Institut Catholique in Paris from 1964–86, and a most accomplished liturgist. His mature views of the conciliar reforms may be read in his 2003 Père Marquette Lecture, *The Reception of Vatican II Liturgy Reforms in the Life of the Church*.

110. Originally in the liturgical journal, *La Maison-Dieu* 229 (2002) 494, and in English in Pierre-Marie Gy, OP, "Is Cardinal Ratzinger's 'Spirit of the Liturgy' Faithful to the Council?" 426–32. Ratzinger's gracious response in the latter publication is Ratzinger, "The Spirit of the Liturgy, or Fidelity to the Council: A Reply to Pierre-Marie Gy, OP," 550–55.

111. Radcliffe, *What Is the Point of Being a Christian?* 212.

112. Cyril O'Regan, "Benedict the Augustinian," 48.

reducing both liturgy and Scripture to a humanistic level that not only betrays the tradition but also erodes the theological basis of both. Undoubtedly this is a real danger and a danger to which Benedict has been consistently and particularly alert. At the same time, it may be argued that at times he neglects the humanistic levels of liturgy and Scripture in ways that leave his position unbalanced.

Ecclesiology

"Pope Benedict's liturgical interests come together in his Eucharistic ecclesiology. The Eucharist constitutes the church as a real communion in the body of Christ. 'The Church is Eucharist.'"[113] Dominican theologian Aidan Nichols, a longtime commentator on the theology of Joseph Ratzinger, makes the point that Ratzinger's ecclesiology represents "a full-scale, systematically elaborated, 'Eucharistic ecclesiology.'"[114] In other words, the Eucharist makes the church, as the church makes the Eucharist, or, quite simply, "The Church is Eucharist."[115]

At first blush this Eucharistic ecclesiology seems to rule out in advance any possibility of real connection with the ecclesial communities of the Reformation tradition. However, although it is true to say that Ratzinger's position on the validity of the Eucharist in these Reformation traditions is somewhat unclear, he does seem to acknowledge that Christ is truly present in some fashion. For example, in 1993 he wrote to the Lutheran Bishop Johannes Hanselmann: "I count among the most important results of the ecumenical dialogues the insight that the issue of the Eucharist cannot be narrowed to the problem of 'validity.' Even a theology oriented to the concept of succession, such as that which holds in the Catholic and in the Orthodox Church, need not in any way deny the salvation-granting presence of the Lord in a Lutheran Lord's Supper."[116] So his position on Eucharistic presence in the Reformation traditions is more nuanced and subtle than one might be led to think. The Lutheran (now Roman Catholic) ecumenical theologian Michael Root provides theological reflections that are particularly helpful in this regard. Root argues that Catholic theology needs a "more or less" approach that is different from an absolutely valid/invalid approach both to ordination and by implication to Eucharist. He argues for "a flexible, scalar category to apply to the episcopacy and ministries of the ecclesial communities, especially to the churches of the Lutheran and Anglican Communions that affirm and practice episcopal succession."[117] Arguably, if this theological line of Root's, and Ratzinger's, were to be developed, the cause of Christian unity would be considerably advanced.

113. Rausch, *Pope Benedict XVI,* 136. Rausch is citing Ratzinger, *Called to Communion,* 75.

114. Nichols, *The Thought of Pope Benedict XVI,* 31.

115. Ratzinger, *Called to Communion,* 75.

116. Cited in Rausch, *Pope Benedict XVI,* 117.

117. Root, as cited in Rausch, *Pope Benedict XVI,* 117.

Deus Caritas Est, 2006

Benedict published three encyclicals in his own name and published one in conjunction with his successor Pope Francis. Here we shall comment only on his first encyclical, "God Is Love." "As Pope, he has surprised many people, even professional theologians who had dismissed him without ever reading his writings or assumed that his theology was limited to the (sometimes poorly written) documents he signed as prefect of the Congregation for the Doctrine of the Faith."[118] For many people his first encyclical came as something of a very pleasant surprise. The central theological emphasis on God as Love and the way it is expressed reminded Thomas P. Rausch, SJ of Andrew Greeley's emphasis on God's passionate love for humankind![119]

It is an inspiring theological reflection on the nature of love. It has an introduction and two parts. Part I is sub-titled "The Unity of Love in Creation and in Salvation History, Part II "The Practice of Love by the Church as a 'Community of Love.'" The document is refreshing in its attention to Holy Scripture, and perhaps especially the Old Testament. This is also true of its careful and nuanced historical perspective. In the introduction the pope takes his point of departure from the beautiful words of 1 John 4:16, "God is love, and he who abides in love abides in God, and God abides in him." At the same time, he acknowledges that the notion of God's love is also to be found in Israel's faith, in Deuteronomy 6:4–5 loving the Lord God with one's whole person, the Shema, and in Leviticus 19:18, loving neighbor as self.

Part I is, in Benedict's own words, "more speculative." "Love" is a much-misused word, and so it is helpful to distinguish *Eros* and *Agape. Eros* is worldly sexual love, and *Agape* is oblative, sacrificial love. In pagan antiquity, both Greek and Ancient Near Eastern, the erotic love between a man and a woman was divinized in the various cults involving sacred prostitution. The Old Testament, however, not only demythologizes this divinization of love, but also shows its ascent towards God. This becomes particularly evident in the Song of Songs. There two Hebrew words are used for love: *dodim,* described as a love that is "insecure, indeterminate and searching"; *ahabah,* translated in the Greek Septuagint as *agape,* "love now become[s] concern and care for the other" (par. 6). Though *Eros* and *Agape* can never be completely separated, Benedict notes that there may be an ascending movement from a somewhat selfish *Eros* to an oblative *Agape,* and it finds in the New Testament its supreme manifestation in the person of Jesus whose entire life was a movement of self-giving: "Starting from the depths of his own sacrifice and of the love that reaches fulfillment therein, he . . . portrays . . . the essence of love and indeed of human life itself" (par. 6). In Benedict's phenomenology of love there is no sheer dissociation of natural love from its biblical understanding. "Biblical faith does not set up a parallel universe" (par. 8). What Scriptures achieves is a purification and revelation of further dimensions of natural love.

---

118. Twomey, *Pope Benedict XVI,* 38.

119. Rausch, *Pope Benedict XVI,* 33.

"God's way of loving becomes the measure of human love" (par. 11). This abstract expression finds its concreteness in Jesus' teaching and action, his death on the cross as the *telos* of his loving. Further, in the Eucharist the oblative and literally crucial love of Jesus finds its "enduring presence" (par. 12). As we receive the Eucharist, "we enter into the very dynamic of his self-giving" (par. 13). This generates what the pope calls a "sacramental mysticism," but a sacramental mysticism that is "social in character," placing the communicant in communion with all other communicants (par. 12-13). In the Eucharist "God's own *agape* comes to us bodily, in order to continue his work in us and through us," and the encyclical notes that the very word *agape* came to be a term for the Eucharist.

Part II considers the church as the practice of charity. Charity belongs to the very essence of the church. The Pauline hymn to love in 1 Corinthians 13 "must be the *Magna Carta* of all ecclesial service" (par. 34). The church's nature is expressed in *kerygma*/proclamation, *leitourgia*/sacramental worship, and *diakonia*/works of charity. The pope charts briefly various chapters in the history of charity, even down to considering the Emperor Julian the Apostate who set up a parallel pagan hierarchy charged with charitable activity. While the modern political state is obligated to seek the promotion of social justice, even in states where this justice seems to prevail, "there is no ordering of the state so just that it can eliminate the need for a service of love" [par. 28]. Finally, the encyclical ends with a recognition of the saints whose lives express paradigmatically this ecclesial charity, and, as one might expect, among them are the Blessed Virgin Mary and Blessed Teresa of Calcutta.

The editorial in *The Tablet*, a British based weekly Catholic newspaper, noted for its sometimes quite critical positions, said of *Deus Caritas Est*: "This is a remarkable, enjoyable and even endearing product of Pope Benedict's first few months. If first encyclicals set the tone for a new papacy, then this one has begun quite brilliantly."[120]

The Apostolic Constitution, *Anglicanorum Coetibus*, 2009

On November 4, 2009, Pope Benedict set out a new canonical structure, an Ordinariate, to facilitate Anglicans who wish to enter into full communion with the Roman Catholic Church, while maintaining "the liturgical, spiritual and pastoral traditions of the Anglican Communion within the Catholic Church, as a precious gift nourishing the faith of its members of the Ordinariate and as a treasure to be shared."[121]

The new structure had been anticipated in an announcement on October 20 by Archbishop Vincent Nichols of Westminster and Archbishop Rowan Williams of Canterbury. Archbishop Williams was irritated by the fact that he was informed about this almost at the last minute. It was not surprising, then, that when Archbishop Williams met Pope Benedict about one month later there was, in the words of Michael Collins,

120. Editorial, "The True Face of Catholicism," *The Tablet* (January 28) 2006.

121. Collins, *God's New Man*, 210.

"smiles and handshakes for the cameras," but "during the discussion both men found little common ground."[122] Small wonder! As church historian Kevin Madigan puts it, "One would be hard-pressed to imagine a moment in the past century when Archbishop of Canterbury, however graciously he may have spoken of the Vatican in his public utterances, felt more shock, incredulity, and perhaps even mistrust than this past October."[123] Shock, incredulity, mistrust—all very understandable on the part of Archbishop Williams, even if the initiative taken by Pope Benedict was intended to be generous. Madigan goes on to comment by way of elucidation that it was the pope who was approached by Anglican clergymen, and not the other way around.

Hans Küng and Benedict

On September 24, 2005, Pope Benedict met Hans Küng his former colleague at the University of Tübingen for over four hours, including dinner, at the papal residence of Castel Gandolfo. The meeting had been requested by Küng who told *The Tablet* that he had wished to speak with Pope John Paul II from the time of his election but "he never gave me the opportunity in twenty-seven years." Benedict XVI, on the other hand, "was immediately prepared to meet. He answered my letter in a very gentle way and it was extraordinary."[124] Küng has been a very sharp critic of the Congregation for the Doctrine of the Faith and of Joseph Ratzinger, especially since his license to teach as a Catholic theologian was withdrawn in 1979. The meeting established that both scholars differ on a number of important doctrinal issues, but Küng made this comment: "But the things we have in common are more fundamental. We are both Christians, both priests in the service of the church, and we have great personal respect for one another."[125] It was a meeting, said Küng, that was "very joyful, with no reproaches, no polemics." Not only that, but they prayed together. "We said an Ave Maria together in the gardens," said Küng.[126] Prior to the meeting, Küng had sent the pope a copy of his new book, *The Beginning of All Things: Science and Religion.* Benedict expressed appreciation for the work Küng has been doing in promoting moral values among the great religions of the world and in inter-faith dialogue. Küng summarized his meeting in these words: "For me, at times it has been like walking a tightrope and now it has ended in such a good way. It was for both of us, well, like going up a small mountain when there have been mis-steps along the way and on both sides."[127]

---

122. Collins, *God's New Man*, 211.

123. Madigan, "Pope Benedict, Disaffected Anglicans, and Holocaust-Denying Bishops," no pagination provided in the online edition.

124. Mickens, "New-found Harmony?" 5. See also Neuhaus, *Catholic Matters*, 100.

125. A telephone interview with the *National Catholic Reporter*, posted on their web-site on September 26, 2005.

126. Mickens, "New-found Harmony?" 5.

127. Mickens, "New-found Harmony?" 5.

In 2010 Küng wrote an open letter to the bishops of the world listing the mis-steps that continued to be made by Benedict XVI. The mis-steps included the following: various missed opportunities for *rapprochement* with Protestants, reconciliation with Jews, dialogue with Islam, reconciliation with the European colonized peoples of Latin America, the fight against HIV/AIDS, the refusal to accept stem cell research and to promote reforms within the church. Küng pointed out the particular failures of *Summorum Pontificum* and *Anglicanorum Coetibus*. Küng called for a new council of the church to take up these and other issues. Michael Collins comments in the wake of the Küng letter: "Evaluating the Benedictine papacy in Germany, the media were notably cool. The initial pride which most German Catholics had felt had largely dissipated. Many criticized him for opportunities lost. Hans Küng was by no means on his own in the negative view of the first five years."[128]

Benedict in the United States and Australia, 2008

When visiting the United States, the pope was met at Andrews Air Force Base by President George W. Bush and members of his family. All the stops were pulled out for Benedict's visit, including the singing of happy birthday on the lawn at the White House on the day of his eighty-first birthday. When it comes to his various speeches in the United States, one heard the usual and expected and important messages: "the dictatorship of relativism," "the subtle influence of materialism," "the sharp decline of the family," etc. Perhaps however his most important words and encounter had to do with the sexual abuse crisis that has done so much damage in the US church. At a Mass in Washington DC he said, "No words of mine could describe the pain and harm inflicted by such [sexual] abuse." In point of fact, it was the first time the pope had mentioned this particular issue at a papal Mass, and also the first time in public.[129] Perhaps at the urging of Cardinal Sean O'Malley of Boston, the epicenter of the sexual abuse scandal, Pope Benedict took the initiative on April 17 of interrupting his schedule to meet privately with five victims of sexual abuse from the Archdiocese of Boston. The meeting took place at the nunciature in Washington, since Boston was not on the papal itinerary. On public radio two of the victims spoke of how moving this meeting was and of its healing potential. Prior to the meeting, Benedict, en route to the United States, said of the scandal, "We are deeply ashamed, and we will do all that is possible that this cannot happen in the future." The pope also noted that the crisis was "sometimes very badly handled." Responding to the same issue of sexual abuse in Malta in 2010, Benedict listened to the stories of eight young men who claim to have been abused by clergy. "The Pope was visibly moved and his eyes filled with tears. 'I don't know what to say,' he repeated several times. 'I don't know how such horrible things happened.

128. Collins, *God's New Man*, 218–19.

129. Collins, *God's New Man*, 165.

It is too much for us, perhaps too much for God."[130] This extremely sensitive issue of the sexual abuse of children by clergy, allied to the cover-up of such abuse by bishops, continued to develop during Benedict's pontificate. It was not just that the witness of the Catholic Church had been seriously tarnished by the scandals, though that remains self-evidently true. The fact is that many Catholics have left the church as a result. Calculating the number is virtually impossible given the complexity of the issue, but there is simply no denying that it has been and continues to be the case. During this American trip he visited Ground Zero, where the Twin Towers had been attacked on September 11, 2001. He lit a large candle in memory of the victims, and then met briefly twenty-five survivors and family members of the terrorist attack.

In July 2008, Pope Benedict made his way to Australia for World Youth Day, under the auspices of Cardinal George Pell of Sydney (1941–). By all accounts the event was a great success. Young pilgrims came from all over the world, and as he had in Cologne in the year of his election, Benedict showed himself gracious in his outreach to them. In Australia too he reached out to the victims of clergy sexual abuse. To say the least, the Catholic youth of the world respond to Benedict with nothing less than the enthusiasm with which they responded to his predecessor John Paul II.

The Society of St. Pius X

Over the years a number of attempts had been made to effect reconciliation with the Society of St. Pius X. On January 24, 2009, Pope Benedict lifted the excommunications of the four bishops who had been consecrated illicitly by Archbishop Marcel Lefebvre in 1988. Unfortunately, this gesture of reconciliation ran into difficulties. One of these bishops, Richard Williamson, had been interviewed on Swedish television some days before, and in the course of the interview Williamson had denied that the Holocaust had been as dreadful as historians believe. He insisted that a few hundred thousand Jews had been murdered by the Nazis, and not the some six million alleged by historians. Naturally this caused an uproar. It was obvious that the pope knew nothing of Williamson's interview when the excommunication was lifted. As with the Regensburg address, it would seem that the pope was not adequately informed and prepared by his advisors. Williamson continued to be the *enfant terrible* of the Society of St. Pius X, with his anti-Jewish positions, his very pre-modern understanding of the role of women in society, and a variety of bizarre conspiracy theories. His vocal and public opposition to Bishop Bernard Fellay who is the leader of the Society of St. Pius X led to his expulsion from the society in 2012.

130. Collins, *God's New Man*, 223–24.

Pope Benedict's Resignation

On Monday, February 11, 2013 Pope Benedict stunned the world by announcing his resignation, to take effect at the end of February. The resignation has been described as "the best-kept secret in a pontificate marked by leaks."[131] The last time a pope resigned the chair of Peter was in 1415 when Pope Gregory XII resigned to help bring an end to the Great Western Schism. He gave as his reasons his health concerns, including the basic energy to fulfill the requirements that his position demanded. Apart from his brother and his personal assistant, Archbishop Georg Gänswein, very few seem to have known about the resignation ahead of time. Certainly, Benedict had thought about this before. In 2010 in a lengthy interview that he gave to Peter Seewald, the journalist asked Benedict: "Is it possible then to imagine a situation in which you would consider a resignation by the Pope appropriate?" Benedict answered: "Yes. If a pope clearly recognizes that he is no longer physically, psychologically, and spiritually capable of handling the duties of his office, then he has a right and, under some circumstances, also an obligation to resign."[132] Eamon Duffy offers a most helpful theological comment on the resignation: "His resignation is more than the escape of a frail old man from an unbearable burden. It is a major step to reintegrating the papacy into a working ecclesiology, in which a pope's competence is something which even loyal Catholics are entitled to discuss."[133]

Conclusion

Paul Elie writes: "In many ways the central fact of the papacy in the modern age is the gap between the pope's growing power in the Church and his diminishing influence on the religious lives of individual believers. This gap is one that John Paul and his predecessors sought to close. Under Benedict the gap is open—wide open. He will govern more but matter less than John Paul—and will probably matter less to the lives of individual Catholics than any other pope of the past half century."[134] These remarks are somewhat cryptic. Elie, a senior editor at the New York publishing house of Farrar, Straus and Giroux, is a careful, judicious, and balanced commentator.[135] "He will govern more but matter less"—that seems to me not necessarily a bad thing. I take it that Elie means that in the ordinary daily lives of most Catholics the pope will

---

131. O'Connell, *The Election of Pope Francis*, 9.

132. Seewald, *Light of the World*, 29–30.

133. Duffy, "Pope Benedict's Resignation," *The Irish Times*, February, 2013. I have not been able to find the precise date in February of Duffy's piece.

134. Elie, "The Year of the Two Popes," 68.

135. Elie, "The Year of the Two Popes," 92. See also Johnson, "After the Big Chill: Intellectual Freedom and Catholic Theologians," 10. For a sense of Elie's balanced judgment see his *The Life You Save May Be Your Own* for a fine treatment of Flannery O'Connor, Thomas Merton, Walker Percy, and Dorothy Day.

not be a major presence. This is not by any means to say that the pope is unimportant or irrelevant to the lives of Catholics, but it is to say that in the daily run of events he does not matter in a major way. That is not the role of the Petrine Ministry in Catholic understanding. The papal office in the church is to preside over the communion of the church in love. It is God finally who matters, and communion between the person and God matters, and all church structures serve that end. Perhaps that is why at the end of his fine essay Elie suggests: "We ought to turn away from the question of what the pope believes and consider just what it is that we believe—turning our attention away from Rome at long last and back to the world in which the real religious dramas of our time are taking place."[136] There is no necessary tension or antithesis between what the pope believes and what the individual Catholic believes, but certainly the accent ought to be on the actual life situation of the ordinary believer with God rather than on an excessive preoccupation with the pope.

136. Elie, "The Year of the Two Popes," 92.

18

Pope Francis (2013–)

It was clear that Papa Francesco was by instinct and pastoral conviction a reformer, a priest of the streets not, like his scholar-predecessor, a man of the study and the sacristy.

—EAMON DUFFY[1]

Meeting Catholics where they are is what post-secular relevance requires. Francis shows himself to be remarkably open to this encounter. He recognizes that Catholics' lived realities are secular realities and simultaneously are infused with God's presence and the meanings and beliefs endowed by Catholicism.

—MICHELLE DILLON[2]

"NO ONE EXPECTED BENEDICT XVI to resign. No one expected Jorge Mario Bergoglio to be elected his successor." Thus, Church historian John O'Malley.[3] On March 13, 2013, Jorge Mario Bergoglio, cardinal archbishop of Buenos Aires, Argentina, was elected pope, taking the name of Francis, a name not chosen by any pope before him. Bergoglio was a member of the Society of Jesus, the first Jesuit to be elected to the chair of St. Peter. He became archbishop of Buenos Aires in 1998, and was made a cardinal in 2001. Electing the first pope from South America and one who chose the entirely novel name of Francis seems to augur a new era in papal history. Francis has enjoyed immense popularity around the world and he appeared in 2013 as *Time* magazine's "Man of the Year." And yet he is something of a paradox, described by Paul Vallely in these terms: "Jorge Mario Bergoglio is a doctrinal traditionalist but an ecclesiastical reformer. He is a radical but not a liberal. He seeks to empower others and yet retains a streak of authoritarianism."[4]

---

1. Duffy, *Saints and Sinners*, 432.
2. Dillon, *Postsecular Catholicism, Relevance and Renewal*, 157.
3. O'Malley, "Two Popes: Benedict and Francis," 66.
4. Vallely, *Pope Francis, Untying the Knots*, xi.

Jorge Mario Bergoglio

Jorge Mario Bergoglio was born in Buenos Aires, Argentina, on December 17, 1936. His paternal grandparents were Italian immigrants to Argentina and his father, Mario José Bergoglio met his mother, Regina Maria Sivori, in the family's newfound home in Buenos Aires. He was a devout child but not excessively so, a keen soccer player, and a good dancer, especially the tango and the milonga. He graduated from college with a diploma in technical chemistry, but a growing interest in theology fueled a vocation to the priesthood. At twenty-one, he joined the Jesuits. Bergoglio was ordained a priest in 1969, thus making him the first pope to be ordained a priest after Vatican II. A mere fifteen years after joining the Jesuits, at thirty-six, he found himself appointed the provincial superior of the Society of Jesus in Argentina.

His time as provincial superior was marked by serious difficulties and challenges. "Politics in Argentina is dominated by Peronism, a curious amalgam of forces not normally associated with one another: the military, the trade unions and the church."[5] In this complex Peronism the extreme, anticlerical left-wing was influenced by Chairman Mao, Fidel Castro, and Che Guevara, while the right-wing regarded themselves as defenders of the Catholic Church against atheistic Communism. Bergoglio was associated with the right-wing. This was a difficult period in Latin America as liberation theology began to develop rapidly. Catholics were divided over this new theological movement, some seeing it as Marxist inspired and ideologically driven, while others recognized in it hope for the poor and the marginal. People took sides, including the Jesuits. The provincial superior of the Jesuits in Argentina prior to Bergoglio had been very supportive of liberation theology, encouraging his priests to work with the poor. At the same time, people were leaving the Society of Jesus in significant numbers, leaving the Society fractured and polarized over liberation theology and its consequences. It was at this point that Bergoglio was made provincial superior in place of his predecessor. He insisted on clerical dress, something that had fallen by the wayside, appointed more conservative teachers for Jesuit students and yet, while he "wanted to erase any trace of liberation theology inside the Argentinian Jesuits, he was keen for them to maintain their contact with the poor."[6] Like many other religious orders in the years following Vatican II, there was a prolonged period of struggle between left and right, between conservative and progressive. These were not easy years for Bergoglio and others in positions of authority. Decisions and actions were misconstrued on both sides of the spectrum. However, the Jesuit province of Argentina found itself out of step with the rest of the Jesuits in Latin America, many of whom were in the forefront of developing liberation theology.

The superior general of the Society of Jesus, Pedro Arrupe, sent one of his assistants, the English Jesuit, Michael Campbell-Johnston, to Argentina to help deal with

---

5. Vallely, *Pope Francis, Untying the Knots*, 40.

6. Vallely, *Pope Francis, Untying the Knots*, 49.

the complex situation. Paul Vallely interviewed Campbell-Johnston who had this to say about his visit to Argentina and Bergoglio:

> At the time there were an estimated 6,000 political prisoners in Argentina and another 20,000 people who had been "disappeared," and there was widespread evidence of torture and assassination. Yet in Argentina the Jesuit Social Institute was silent on all that. I discussed this at length with Fr. Bergoglio. He defended his position, between the Catholic military and the very secularist anti-church Left. I tried to show him how it was out of step with our other social institutes on the continent. Our discussion was lengthy but in the end we could not agree.[7]

Bergoglio's conservative style continued throughout his duration as provincial superior. When his term of office was finished, Bergoglio was sent to Germany to the Jesuit school of philosophy and theology in Frankfurt to explore various possibilities for a PhD. He returned several months later with many photocopied articles and books and an interest in the work of Romano Guardini, but without any particular commitment to a given theme or topic. It has been suggested that his premature return to Argentina before finishing his research had to do with his "concerns regarding the situation in the Jesuit province, fearing that the new leadership was dismantling many of the reforms he had put in place."[8] He began to teach at the Jesuit school of theology in Buenos Aires. Bergoglio's successor as provincial superior decided that this was not working well and so he was sent to the city of Córdoba, about 400 miles away, with the purpose of doing pastoral work as well as working on his doctorate. This period of exile came to an end in 1992 when he was made auxiliary bishop of Buenos Aires, and later archbishop of Buenos Aires.

Fr. Francisco Yalics and Fr. Orlando Yorio

Frs. Francisco Yalics and Orlando Yorio were both Jesuit priests working with the poor in Buenos Aires. They had been sent there by their Jesuit superior, Fr. Ricardo O'Farrell, the idea being that they would continue their work as academics and writers but also minister in the slum communities at the weekend. "Among those with whom they worked in the slum where activists from the *Peronismo de Base* movement, a group with Marxist leanings working among the underprivileged."[9] After the military overthrew the democratically elected government in 1976, there was a deliberate attempt to squelch any opposition, or any activity that could be regarded as opposed to the policies of the new military government, especially what has come to be known as liberation theology, regarded in right-wing circles as Marxism.

---

7. Cited in Vallely, *Pope Francis*, 57.

8. O'Connell, *The Election of Pope Francis*, 35.

9. Vallely, *Pope Francis*, 73.

Bergoglio at this time, and with increasing pressure from the Vatican concerning "Marxist" liberation theology and liberation movements, told the priests to end their activity in the slum. In point of fact, both Jalics and Yorio had been teachers of Bergoglio. They knew him well. A difficult discussion over a protracted period took place between the Jesuit superior and his priest subjects.

Finally, both priests were arrested on May 23, 1976 and taken to a prison in the city, a prison from which many people never emerged. Both men were consistently tortured, and they believed that they had been betrayed by their Jesuit superior, Jorge Mario Bergoglio. This was not the case. In fact, Bergoglio did all he could to have the two Jesuits released. A friend from those years who remains his friend, the lawyer Alicia Oliveira comments as follows: "[Bergoglio] did a lot to try to release them. He visited the head of the junta, General Videla, and Videla told him it had been done by the Navy. So he went to see the head of the Navy, Massera. He talked to the Jesuits in Rome. He talked to the Vatican." Finally, both priests were released some five months later, Yorio going off to Rome to study canon law, and Jalics ending up in a retreat house in Germany. Although some still contest this, it seems very probable that Bergoglio was deeply involved in effecting their release. Paul Vallely in a balanced way sums up this very difficult situation.

> In the end, diligent examination of Bergoglio's conduct leaves unanswered questions. But if there is, finally, a shortage of definitive facts, there is no lack of opinion among those most intimately involved. Yorio died convinced Bergoglio was a duplicitous traitor. . . . Yet Jalics, who once thought the same, has resiled from that view. He announced in March 2013 that years after his grim ordeal he and Bergoglio had met and concelebrated Mass together and shared what Jalics called "a solemn embrace," after which he was reconciled with Bergoglio.

Speaking many years later as pope about those troubled times when he was the Jesuit provincial superior he acknowledges, "I had to learn from my errors along the way, because, to tell you the truth, I made hundreds of errors, errors and sins."[10]

Archbishop of Buenos Aires

The metropolitan area of Buenos Aires has an estimated population of about 13 million, the city itself being about three million, and it is estimated that about 700,000 poor people live in 110,000 makeshift houses in the slums of Buenos Aires. "Jorge has experienced both faces of the urban periphery: uncurbed violence and great humanity."[11] In Bergoglio's time, the number of priests working in the slums increased fourfold. He himself would wander in the alleyways of the slums, talking to people, mixing with

10. Cited in Duffy, *Saints and Sinners*, 422.

11. Politi, *Pope Francis Among the Wolves*, 8.

them, drinking tea with them. One of his priests captured Bergoglio's mode of action in these words, "Liberation has to start, not with an ideology nor with charity, but with people" and Paul Vallely comments as follows: "Yorio and Jalics and the other Jesuits whom Bergoglio once ordered out of the slums for saying such things would have been astonished to hear that, almost forty years on, the same man would not just be tolerating such sentiments but endorsing and blessing them."[12]

His style as archbishop of Buenos Aires differed significantly from his predecessors. He turned his palatial residence into a hospital for priests and nuns. He provided other work in the diocese for his chauffeur. He traveled by public transport. He cooked his own meals in his apartment, wore ordinary clerical dress, and eschewed the archiepiscopal purple. He continued many aspects of the same style when he moved to the Vatican as pope. As Eamon Duffy has it, somewhat tongue-in-cheek, "It was clear that this pope would have no interest in styles of head-gear or hand-made red slippers."[13] The Vatican observer Marco Politi draws comparisons of Bergoglio with his papal predecessors:

> Karol Wojtyla was tempered in a clandestine theater movement in defiance of the Nazi occupation and by hard labor in a quarry and at the Solvay factory. Benedict XVI was formed in university lecture halls. Pius XII and Paul VI were schooled in the offices of the Vatican Secretariat of State. John XXIII came to maturity among the Orthodox Christians of Bulgaria and the Muslims of Turkey. Jorge Mario Bergoglio is reborn in his trips on the subway, observing the innards of the city, measuring the distance from one tumbledown slum dwelling to the next with his steady tread.[14]

He developed very good relationships with the Anglican community in Argentina and with other Christians. Paul Vallely writes:

> He was "a friend to Anglicans," who made clear that he thought Benedict XVI's Anglican Ordinariate—set up to attract disaffected members of that Communion into the Catholic Church—was unnecessary because the wider world needed the diversity of the Anglican witness. Similarly, he reached out to Evangelical Protestants, whom many in the Catholic Church treated suspiciously as the rivals who were enticing away the faithful to more colorful and charismatic styles of worship. Bergoglio took the opposite view and went to pray with them.[15]

His ecumenical openness did not endear him to Catholic traditionalists in Argentina. This ecumenical openness reached out also to the Jewish community. A book of conversations that he had on a variety of religious and moral topics with Rabbi Abraham Skorka

12. Vallely, *Pope Francis*, 100.

13. Duffy, *Saints and Sinners*, 417.

14. Politi, *Pope Francis Among the Wolves*, 10.

15. Vallely, *Pope Francis*, 107.

was published.[16] John O'Malley says persuasively of this book: "For an archbishop to sit down with a rabbi for such an exchange would have been utterly unthinkable before Vatican II. Even in the half-century since the Council, no other high-ranking prelate has ever dared go so far. No pope in history has ever had such an experience or had an experience even remotely equivalent to it."[17]

That style of openness embraced Catholics who experienced alienation from the church. One such was the progressive former Bishop Jeronimo José Podesta. Podesta established in 1967 a relationship with his secretary Clelia Luro, a single parent with six children. She concelebrated Mass with him. Podesta fled after the military junta took over the country and returned in 1983 when they were overthrown. He died in 2000. Bergoglio visited him on his deathbed. Podesta was not someone to be despised or ostracized, as so many clergy thought. Bergoglio has continued to be supportive to Podesta's widow.

Paul Vallely asks the obvious question: What changed Bergoglio? His response is that various factors effected the change. Especially important was his growing familiarity with the poorest of the poor in the slums of Buenos Aires. No less significant was his developing understanding of the theology of liberation. Behind these changes, however, there seems to have been a determination to move away from his fairly authoritarian style as Jesuit provincial to a more relaxed, flexible pastoral style when he became an auxiliary bishop of Buenos Aires. This could not have been easy for Bergoglio, but it became very real, and it appears to remain very real in his papacy.

Pope Francis[18]

"Bergoglio was elected on a reform ticket, and the rhetoric of renewal is central to his appeal."[19] He himself reflects on his choice of name, Francis.

> Some thought of Francis Xavier, Francis De Sales, and also Francis of Assisi. I will tell you the story. During the election, I was seated next to the Archbishop emeritus of São Paulo of the Congregation for the Clergy, Cardinal Claudio Hummes: a good friend, a good friend! When things were looking dangerous, he encouraged me. And when the votes reached two-thirds, there was the usual applause, because the Pope had been elected. And he gave me a hug and a kiss, and said: "Don't forget the poor!" And those words came to me: the poor, the poor. Then, right away, thinking of the poor, I thought of Francis of Assisi. Then I thought of all the wars, as the votes were still being counted, till

16. Bergoglio and Skorka, *On Heaven and Earth: Pope Francis on Faith, Family and the Church in the Twenty-First Century.*

17. O'Malley, *Catholic History for Today's Church*, 71.

18. For an excellent account of the conclaves that elected Pope Francis see Gerard O'Connell, *The Election of Pope Francis.*

19. Duffy, "Style Is Not Enough," 6.

the end. Francis is also the man of peace. That is how the name came into my heart: Francis of Assisi.[20]

His style since being elected pope is Franciscan—simple, unostentatious, without pomp, relational. The former Master-General of the Dominicans, Timothy Radcliffe, has described the style of Pope Francis in these words: "He is undermining one thousand years of papal monarchy. He is adopting a more Trinitarian church—a mutuality of listening. It is not just about the reform of the Curia; it's about a shift in our understanding of church. The community which presides in love: that is putting the Pope back in the college. It is ecclesiastically radical. He has thought through what he is doing. It is the product of the many years of practical theology."[21] Closely related to these sentiments is "mercy" or "compassion" for Francis. "On the first day of the conclave, the German Cardinal Walter Kasper, who had recently published a little book entitled *Barmherzigkeit*, made him a gift of the Spanish translation, *La misericordia*. 'This is the name of our God. Without mercy we are lost!' Bergoglio exclaimed."[22]

Soon after being elected pope, Bergoglio contacted one of the premier liberation theologians in Brazil, Leonardo Boff. Boff had been a Franciscan priest, got into trouble with the Congregation for the Doctrine of the Faith for his theological writings, and eventually left the priesthood and got married. Pope Francis asked him to send him his more recent theological writings on ecology, and this is one of the influences that has resulted in the pope's justly acclaimed encyclical on the environment *Laudato Si*.

Francis set up a committee of eight cardinals to advise him on the government of the church. The coordinator of this committee is Cardinal Oscar Rodriguez Maradiaga, the archbishop of Tegucigalpa in Honduras, and the other members are: Reinhart Marx, archbishop of Munich; Laurent Monswengo Pasinya, archbishop of Kinshasa; Oswald Gracias, archbishop of Bombay; Francisco Javier Errazuriz Ossa of Chile; Sean Patrick O'Malley, archbishop of Boston; George Pell, archbishop of Sydney; Giuseppe Bertello, of Vatican City. The distinguished professor of church history at the University of Modena, Alberto Melloni, describes the establishment of this committee as the "most important step in the history of the church for the past ten centuries."[23]

This ecclesiological development emerges very clearly in his fall 2013 apostolic exhortation, "The Joy of the Gospel," an exhortation that has been described as "ecclesiological dynamite." These are the words of the late theologian Gerard Mannion, who goes on to say, "It is difficult for anyone working in fields such as ecclesiology to reach any conclusion other than the simple fact that on so many of the most important issues, there is very, very little substantive continuity with the ecclesial agenda

---

20. Cited in Vallely, *Pope Francis*, 160–61.
21. Cited in Vallely, *Pope Francis*, 166.
22. Politi, *Pope Francis Among the Wolves*, 18.
23. Cited in Vallely, *Pope Francis*, 184.

of Pope Francis' predecessors."[24] In some ways, this language is overblown. There must be substantive continuity—sheerly from a historical point of view—from one pontificate to the next, and yet there definitely has been a shift of emphasis. Eamon Duffy asks the question: "Might Francis be the Pope who at last returns responsibility to the local churches, converting the papacy into an instrument of service rather than a steel-fisted center of government?"[25]

It is not, however, Francis's creation of an inner cardinalatial consultative council alone that expresses the conversion of the papacy into an instrument of service. It also has to do with what has come to be called his emphasis on synodality. "Synodality" refers to a much more consultative and dialogical style of ecclesial government. Vatican observer and journalist Michael Sean Winters writes: "Unlike his concern for the poor and a more simple papal style that were immediately apparent, something not discernible that first night (after his election) turned out to be foundational: Pope Francis has retrieved a sense of synodality that had been obscured, but never eliminated, after almost two centuries of Ultramontanist ecclesiology."[26] The centralization on the papacy and the monarchical style of the papacy that emerged fully during the pontificate of Pope Pius IX and lasted through until at least the pontificate of Pope John XXIII is being laid to rest by Pope Francis, and, while all is far from clear at this point, consultation at every level, dialogue and debate about even the most neuralgic issues, is being encouraged. This is part of what is meant by synodality. In the words of Winters, "Synodality is about more than structures. It is about listening to each other. Synodality requires that we do not seek to 'win' an argument about what the church should do, so much as we, together, seek the Spirit's promptings and move forward together, always together."[27]

Later generations of church historians and commentators will have a much fuller picture, but it is necessary for the sake of completeness to attempt a summary or a synthesis of what Francis has achieved so far. Let us begin with the positives.[28] Francis eschews clericalism in any kind of way. The clergy are to be servants of the people of God and in no way to dominate them, or lord it over them or, in another mode infantilize the laity. The laity are to be treated as the adult Christians that they are, with all the dignity that accrues to them through their baptism. Allied to this

24. By Gerard Mannion, cited in the *National Catholic Reporter*, April 1, 2014, in an article by Joshua J. McElwee, "Francis a complete break from predecessors, conference says." No pagination for the online edition.

25. Duffy, "Style is not enough," 7.

26. Michael Sean Winters, "Sixth year may go down as the most decisive in Francis' papacy," *National Catholic Reporter*, March 13, 2019. No pagination for the online edition.

27. Michael Sean Winters, "Sixth year may go down as the most decisive in Francis' papacy," *National Catholic Reporter*, March 13, 2019.

28. For an exemplary summary of Pope Francis's achievements thus far one could not do better than consult the essay by Thomas Reese, SJ, "The good, the bad and the merciful: Pope Francis after six years," *National Catholic Reporter*, March 13, 2019. No pagination for the online edition.

is his constant emphasis, from the very beginning of his pontificate, on compassion and mercy. The church in his understanding is a field hospital for sinners to be welcomed and received, to be made well so that they may become saints; it is not a rest-home for the perfect. Furthermore, it is to be a church for the poor.[29] When it comes to the matter of theology, the understanding of the Christian faith, his preference is to articulate this in simple (albeit not simplistic) language and concepts, rather than reach for the sometimes-arcane complexities of academic theologians. His approach has been described by theologian Richard Gaillardetz as an emphasis on "the pastorality of doctrine," that is to say, that doctrine is intended to serve, guide and direct the people of the church. It is not meant to be dictatorial or tyrannical or beyond normal human intelligence. Jesuit theologian and Vatican observer Thomas Reese puts it quite sharply:

> Francis' focus on the simple message of the gospel is quite threatening to those Catholics who confuse theology with the faith. Theology is how we explain the faith to ourselves and others. St. Augustine used Neoplatonism to explain the faith to a generation whose intellectuals were all Neoplatonists. St. Thomas Aquinas used Aristotelianism, the avant-garde thinking of the thirteenth century, to explain the faith in his day. The mistake today's conservatives make is to simply quote these great thinkers, rather than imitate them in developing new ways to explain Christianity to people of the twenty-first century. With few Neoplatonists or Aristotelians around today, theologians must have the freedom to discover new ways of explaining Christianity, even if this leads to new ways of understanding of human rights, justice, sexuality, marriage and the role of women.[30]

Richard Gaillardetz's notion of the "pastorality of doctrine" coincides, albeit in slightly different terms, with the understanding of theologian Clemens Sedmak. Sedmak raises the question with regard to Pope Francis's emphasis on the church of the poor, "What does a church of the poor mean for an understanding of orthodoxy?"[31] Being poor in Francis's understanding is much broader, although it clearly includes financial, socio-economic poverty. The term, maintains Sedmak, reaches out to include all on the peripheries, that is to say, all who are disempowered, or who feel disempowered, who live in situations of deep vulnerability. A church of the poor does not construe orthodoxy simply in terms of propositional orthodoxy—"Do you believe X or Y?" Orthodoxy in a church of the poor insists on a radical and receptive listening to those on the peripheries. Listening to the complexities of their experience and insights into life leads to a broader understanding of orthodoxy in which propositional beliefs help to serve and to enable the flourishing of all human beings under God. This

29. See Sedmak, *A Church of the Poor*.

30. I am unable to find the exact location of Fr. Reese's commentary, but its substance remains consistent with his columns in the *National Catholic Reporter*.

31. Sedmak, *A Church of the Poor*, xv.

is what Gaillardetz means by the "pastorality of doctrine." Doctrine within the framework of orthodoxy is about "the acceptance of certain propositions as true; these are propositions that have been declared true by the authority of the church."[32] However, it is more than that. It is about an orthodoxy that serves pilgrims in this world who are on their way to the final and eschatological possession of truth, and not simply in possession of that truth in its totality here and now. This leads Sedmak to what Gaillardetz calls the "pastorality of doctrine." Sedmak writes: "Living the truth as a pilgrim will always have a tentative aspect to it; there may even be a paradox here: the more I am rooted in my faith, the deeper my insights into my sinfulness, the firmer my trust in God, the clearer my view of my (spiritual, moral, and epistemic) fragility." He then goes on to cite Pope Francis and to comment further: "Pope Francis has underlined the image of the pilgrim: 'We must never forget that we are pilgrims journeying alongside one another. This means that we must have sincere trust in our fellow pilgrims, putting aside all suspicion or mistrust, and turn our gaze to what we are all seeking: the radiant peace of God's face' (*The Joy of the Gospel*, 244). We are pilgrims, and as pilgrims we are seekers, and as seekers we embrace orthodoxy in a particular way."[33] This way of thinking will necessarily clash with the overly propositional approach to orthodoxy that often characterizes traditionalist Catholics.

The polarization between traditionalists and conservatives over against liberals and progressives has become very sharp during this pontificate. In his 2017 novel *Origin* Dan Brown (author of the *Da Vinci* Code) portrays in a somewhat histrionic fictional mode the conflict between the "liberal" Pope Francis—although he is never actually named—and a Spanish, schismatic, traditionalist opposition.[34] *Origin* is, of course, a piece of fiction, but the opposition to Pope Francis is not. There are some who publicly accuse Pope Francis of confusing the faithful with doubtful teaching, and even some who accuse him of heresy. Their numbers are relatively small globally speaking but they appear to be well-financed and so they have the instruments for the public dissemination of their ideas. One such instrument is the Napa Institute, founded and financed by Catholic millionaire attorney and businessperson Timothy Busch. Annual gatherings of the Institute regularly feature such speakers as Cardinal Raymond Burke who has been described as "the leader of the conservative resistance to [Pope] Francis inside the church," and George Weigel, a popular conservative Catholic commentator. Reviewing a recent book by Weigel historian James Chappel writes as follows: "Weigel matters because the conservative Catholicism he represents matters. Especially on the Supreme Court, but elsewhere too, this strange Catholic brew brings together gender conservatism and libertarian economics in ways that seem alien to the Gospels but which are perfectly at home on the contemporary right."[35]

---

32. Sedmak, *A Church of the Poor*, 142.

33. Sedmak, *A Church of the Poor*, 178–79.

34. Brown, *Origin*.

35. Chappel, reviewing Weigel, *The Irony of Modern Catholic History*.

On the downside, it is probably fair to say that until a year or so ago (writing in March 2019) Pope Francis did not have a substantive grasp of the sexual-abuse crisis throughout the church. Now, however, he has taken this with the greatest seriousness and is holding the worldwide episcopate accountable over this egregious issue. Cardinal Theodore McCarrick, former archbishop of Washington DC, credibly accused of sexual abuse and of sleeping with seminarians, has been stripped of his clerical state. Cardinal George Pell—one of Francis's inner circle of cardinals and a former archbishop of Sydney—has been jailed in Australia for six years, although he is appealing the sentence and conviction. Pell's appeal was turned down in August 2019. While waiting for the results of the appeal sometime in June 2019, he may not minister in any public way. One could go on with other less headline-grabbing examples of the pope's dealing with the sexual abuse issues.[36]

Francis has shown himself more aware of the role of women in the church. In this regard, he has set up a commission to investigate the ordination of women to the permanent diaconate. It has to be said, at the same time, that he also shows himself less aware of first-world feminist language and sensitivities, and whatever one thinks of these feminist positions, they are not going to go away. The commission on the diaconate for women was unable to reach agreement. Pope Francis in 2020 appointed a second commission to investigate the diaconate for women.

Trip to the Holy Land, 2014

Pope Francis made a trip to the Holy Land in May 2014, a trip that was billed by the Vatican as a purely religious pilgrimage. It was inevitable that the trip would be understood in various quarters as political also. Francis prayed at the Israeli built security barrier in Bethlehem, something that was bound to make a deep impression on the Palestinians. He called for a two-state solution and considered the present situation as simply unacceptable. These gestures can be clearly seen as pro-Palestinian. At the same time, the pope was persuaded by prime minister Benjamin Netanyahu to pray at a cemetery for victims of terrorism on Mount Herzl, and, of course, this was seen as a pro-Israeli gesture, just as was his visit to the Yad Vashem Holocaust Museum. It would be much too cynical to see him playing to both sides of the divide. What he was really doing was listening to both sides, Palestinians and Israelis, and making a prophetic protest in the name of peace and justice. One Israeli-based Rabbi described Francis's position on the Jews as "certainly the most friendly, proactive, accommodating position of any Pope probably in history."[37] More than anything else Pope Francis was trust building in this land torn by centuries of conflict. The same trust building was in evidence when Pope Francis met Patriarch Bartholomew of

36. The Supreme Court of Australia in April 2020 considered Pell's appeal and found in his favor, and he was released that month from prison.

37. Cited in McIntyre, "Trust Where It Is Needed Most," 4

Constantinople at a prayer service in the Church of the Holy Sepulcher in Jerusalem. Perhaps the most memorable and moving photograph of the trip was that taken of Pope Francis at the Western Wall with two friends from Buenos Aires: his Jewish friend Rabbi Abraham Skorka and his Muslim friend Omar Abboud. This snapshot powerfully showed the world even if only for a moment the three Abrahamic traditions in a welcoming embrace. This welcoming embrace was to continue in Pope Francis's invitation to the Palestinian leader Mahmoud Abbas and the Israeli leader Shimon Peres to come to the Vatican to meet and to talk.

World Youth Day, Rio de Janeiro, July 2013

World Youth Day is a biennial event established by Pope John Paul II. In July 2013, it took place in Rio de Janeiro, Brazil, the continent from which Pope Francis came. By all accounts, it was a wonderful success, expressed especially in the final Mass celebrated by the pontiff on Copacabana beach with an estimated congregation of over three million.

Returning to Rome Pope Francis had an open interview with the journalists on his plane. Two things emerged particularly from their questions and his responses. First, in respect of women and their roles in the church, he insisted that they should have greater roles in the church far beyond what is the present situation, but with the position of his predecessor Pope John Paul II, he regarded the ordination of women to the priesthood as impossible, and this teaching as definitive. Second, in respect of homosexuality, the pope insisted that if gay people were searching for God with a good heart, who was he to judge them. As with the former case, he insisted, again with his predecessors, that homosexual acts were immoral, even if homosexual persons could not be judged in that way. What we see in these responses of Francis to the journalists' questions is not a change in *doctrine* so much as a change in *style*. The approach to doctrine and to the principles that lies behind it is more compassionate, more pastoral, and even perhaps more flexible.

Encyclicals

This is a summary of Pope Francis's first encyclical, *The Light of Faith*, 2013. As the pope himself has said, it is the work of four hands—the hands of his predecessor Pope Benedict XVI and his own hands. The encyclical is much more the work of Benedict than it is of Francis.

> The encyclical is in fact a thoroughly Ratzingerian utterance, an eloquent exploration of the biblical concept of faith, rich in allusions from Benedict's wide reading, from St. Augustine and medieval theologians like William of St. Thierry to Nietzsche, Wittgenstein and T. S. Eliot. . . . Though far more

positively expressed, this is unmistakably the voice of the author of *Dominus Jesus*, the CDF's 2000 declaration on the unique salvific value of the Incarnation and the ultimate inadequacy of all other human value systems and religions. Bergoglio no doubt endorsed the encyclical's central theological claims, but his own religious instincts, intuitions and gestures were manifestly more open-ended and inclusive.[38]

The Joy of the Gospel also followed in 2013. This apostolic exhortation published in November of that year is more typically Pope Francis, and has been described as "a magnetic actualizing of Vatican II's account of divine revelation and faith."[39] It brings together in a sort of integrated way many of his themes in interviews and sermons of his first eight months in office and it "was pitched in a consciously personal and informal tone, unlike any previous papal utterance."[40] The tone throughout is positive and upbeat, full of hope and joy without naïve optimism, and emphasizes God's love and mercy. It is wide-ranging in its entirety, but two particular issues seem especially worthy of note. First, he insists that the Eucharist "is not a prize for the perfect, but a powerful medicine and nourishment for the weak."[41] Second, is his incisive critique of free-market economics, too often exclusive of the poor and the needy globally. He writes:

> We can no longer trust in the unseen forces and the invisible hand of the market. Growth in justice requires more than economic growth, while presupposing such growth: it requires decisions, programs, mechanisms and processes specifically geared to a better distribution of income, the creation of sources of employment and an integral promotion of the poor which goes beyond a simple welfare mentality. I am far from proposing an irresponsible populism, but the economy can no longer turn to remedies that are a new poison, such as attempting to increase profits by reducing the work force and thereby adding to the ranks of the excluded.[42]

Throughout this exhortation, he excoriates pessimism and sounds a constant note of joy in the proclamation of and the living out of the gospel. "This manifesto delighted those who felt that under John Paul II and Benedict XVI the church had boxed itself into a sterile confrontation with the modern world: it appalls those who looked

---

38. Duffy, *Saints and Sinners*, 425–26. Theologian, Tina Beattie writes: "*Lumen Fidei* is the first encyclical to be promulgated under the name of Pope Francis, but this is an act of papal ventriloquism. In style and content this is undoubtedly Pope Benedict's last and possibly greatest encyclical—deeply problematic though it is in places." See her comments in *The Tablet*, July 6, 2013, no pagination in the online edition.

39. By Wicks, *Investigating Vatican II*, 2.

40. Duffy, *Saints and Sinners*, 429.

41. Pope Francis, *The Joy of the Gospel*, paragraph 47.

42. Pope Francis, *The Joy of the Gospel*, paragraph 204.

longingly back to the previous two pontificates as a golden age of doctrinal clarity and fidelity to a demanding gospel."[43]

Sociologist Michelle Dillon describes the 2016 encyclical *The Joy of Marriage* as follows: "[This encyclical] underscores the secular accessibility of Francis's discourse. It deploys a mostly straightforward and culturally resonant vocabulary, with several evocative passages on the joys of love building on St. Paul's well-known epistle ('Love is patient and kind . . .')."[44] This is a fine outline-summary of the letter. Paragraphs 8–30 offer biblical meditations on marriage, sexuality, and the family, and paragraphs 31–37 pick-up various insights from the experiences and challenges of families as well as from Francis's own pastoral experience. Rather than decrying all present-day evils, he insists that "What we need is a more responsible and generous effort to present the reasons and motivations for choosing marriage and the family, and in this way to help men and women better to respond to the grace that God offers them" (35). It is a most positive and life-affirming view of marriage and family. The pope goes on to say this in paragraph 36–37:

> We need a healthy dose of self-criticism. Then too, we often present marriage in such a way that its unitive meaning, its call to grow in love and its ideal of mutual assistance are overshadowed by an almost exclusive insistence on the duty of procreation. . . . We also find it hard to make room for the consciences of the faithful, who very often respond as best they can to the gospel amid their limitations, and are capable of carrying out their own discernment in complex situations. We have been called to form consciences, not to replace them.

That last sentence is the nub of the issue—the teaching office of the church, and so of all clergy and those involved in faith formation is to assist in the formation of conscience, and not to become moral dictators. As Pope Francis says himself in paragraph 350, "It is [not] helpful to try to impose rules by sheer authority."

When it comes to couples who are living together or to those who are divorced and remarried without a church annulment of the prior marriage, Francis does not change church teaching as such. Rather, such sisters and brothers in the faith should be encouraged "to participate in the life of the [Christian] community" (paragraph 243). The quality of such ecclesial participation will necessarily vary in relation to the different circumstances of couples, but Francis insists that "it can no longer simply be said that all those in any 'irregular' situation are living in a state of mortal sin and are deprived of sanctifying grace" (paragraph 301). Furthermore, even when people are judged to be in situations of objective sin, they are not necessarily subjectively culpable, and there may be the possibility of the help of the sacraments. One commentator on the contemporary church says that "given the context of Synod

---

43. Duffy, *Saints and Sinners*, 430.

44. Dillon, *Postsecular Catholicism, Relevance and Renewal*, 157.

debate about participation in Communion, it is significant that Francis states here that 'the Eucharist is not a prize for the perfect.'"[45] Needless to point out, the mere mention of such issues is anathema in some Catholic quarters, while being greatly welcomed in others. As Michele Dillon writes, "In many respects [*The Joy of Marriage*] represents a delicate postsecular negotiation of faith and reason, of doctrinal ideas and secular realities."[46]

Continuing along this line, Pope Francis invited Cardinal Walter Kasper to address the cardinals on the issue of admitting divorced and re-married Catholics to receive the Eucharist. Kasper's point of view has had a positive echo throughout many parts of the Catholic and indeed the non-Catholic world. However, not all in the Roman Curia, as well as other parts of the Catholic world, were open to his ideas. Cardinal Raymond Burke, former prefect of the Supreme Tribunal of the Apostolic Segnatura, made a presentation on the EWTN Catholic network in which he stated that not all the cardinals were favorably disposed towards Kasper's point of view. Burke certainly would find himself in disagreement with Kasper, and one assumes at least in some measure with Pope Francis on this point. Burke's critical comments signal a certain degree of curial opposition to Francis and his vision/policies. Cardinal Oscar Rodriguez Maradiaga, coordinator of the Council of Cardinals created by Francis in 2013 to help reformulate policies in respect of the Roman Curia and other things, made the following comments in a talk on April 8 in St. Petersburg, Florida: "We have to be prepared, since this beautiful but strange popularity [of Pope Francis] is beginning to strengthen adherences, but equally to awaken deaf opposition not only in the old Curia, but in some who are sorry to lose privileges in treatment and in comforts. . . . Expressions like 'What can it be that this little Argentine pretends?', or the expression of a well-known Cardinal who let slip the phrase, 'We made a mistake.'" Rodriguez went on to comment that Pope Francis is developing "a new way of being church," that would be characterized, among other things, as follows: "at the service of this world by being faithful to Christ and his Gospel"; "free from all mundane spirituality"; "free from the risk of being concerned about itself, of becoming middle-class, of closing in on self, of being a clerical church"; able to "offer itself as an open space in which all of us can meet and recognize each other because there is space for dialogue, diversity and welcome in it"; a church that pays "just attention and gives importance to women in both society and its own institutions."[47]

---

45. Dillon, *Postsecular Catholicism, Relevance and Renewal*, 159.

46. Dillon, *Postsecular Catholicism, Relevance and Renewal*, 160.

47. Cited in McElwee, "Francis encountering curial opposition, Cardinal says." *National Catholic Reporter,* April 21, 2014, no pagination in the online edition.

The Ecclesiology of Pope Francis

Few theologians have written as skillfully on the ecclesiology of Pope Francis as Boston College theologian Richard Gaillardetz and I am happy to acknowledge my indebtedness to him in offering this resumé of Pope Francis on the church.[48] In the judgment of Gaillardetz, the ecclesiology of Pope Francis "marks the end of a thirty-year hegemony of *communion* as the exclusive theological articulation of council teaching."[49] There are of course different forms of what is referred to as "communion ecclesiology,"[50] but in its "official" forms, Gaillardetz finds it problematic in how it privileges the following:

1. The hierarchical character of the church's communion.

2. The priority of the universal church over the local churches.

3. Eucharist over Baptism.

4. Apostolic succession over the baptismal priesthood.

5. The church's sacramental communion over its mission in the world.

Acknowledging that there is no necessary connection between communion ecclesiology and these five issues, Gaillardetz maintains that Pope Francis's ecclesiological preference seems to be for "the people of God," marked by what has come to be called "synodality."

Following Gaillardetz, one may distinguish between two types of reform. One type relates to controversial subjects such as the possibility of communion for the divorced and remarried; the tackling of child sexual abuse throughout the universal church; the review of Vatican finances; the appointment of bishops; and the question of celibacy. A deeper reform is at stake, however, a reform that gives more emphasis to the mission of Christ in the world, with everything else serving this mission. It is this deeper reform that requires the inauguration of a synodal church. The setting up of a synodal church seeks to decentralize authority and power to the local level, demonstrating in action the principle of subsidiarity. A synodal church is about: fostering a spirit of collegiality at all levels, promoting consultation and embracing the voices of the faithful, and so taking seriously the priesthood of the baptized through listening to the sense of the faithful among the people of God.

Pope Francis distinguishes three different layers of synodality within the church. The first layer is synodality at the local level, involving parishes and dioceses in processes of consultation, listening, and learning. Then comes synodality at the intermediate level, undertaken by different regions of a country or countries and

48. See Gaillardetz, *An Unfinished Council*. Also very helpful is O'Hanlon, SJ, *The Quiet Revolution of Pope Francis*.

49. Gaillardetz, "The 'Francis Moment," 65.

50. See the fine overview offered in Doyle, *Communion Ecclesiology*.

episcopal conferences. Finally, there is synodality at the universal level, involving the Synod of Bishops in Rome. Gerry O'Hanlon, the Irish Jesuit theologian, puts this very clearly. "We need to pursue this [synodal] path more systematically and with greater conviction—and bishops as well as faithful need to come to the point where they see consultation as real and not just token, capable of tackling neuralgic issues, reaching out to the young and disaffected and not just to the already committed who would tend to come from a predominantly middle-aged and older demographic."[51] This is no easy path to follow but it is how Pope Francis sees the way and it appears to be how he acts himself.

Opposition to Pope Francis

It is no secret, as already noted, that some Catholics including bishops and theologians are strongly opposed to various elements in Pope Francis's policies.[52] Nor should this be a surprise. Victor Codina, a Spanish Jesuit theologian, centers in on the importance of historical perspective in this regard. He writes: "It is neither unusual nor surprising to encounter discord and opposition in the Catholic Church. Such disagreement stretches back from the present day to the time of St. Paul, who stood up to Cephas in Antioch (Galatians 2:14)."[53] Codina then goes on to instance examples of opposition within the church throughout the tradition, including some examples that have surfaced in this book. He points out, for example, the discord that followed Pope Pius XII's 1950 encyclical *Humani Generis*, condemnatory of the "new theology" discussed in chapter ten. He goes on to mention the discord that was consequent upon Pope Paul VI's encyclical *Humanae Vitae* in 1968, discussed in chapter twelve. Francis's emphasis on the infinite mercy and love of God, his constant support of the poor, the disadvantaged and immigrants, his concern for the environment, and his careful and nuanced outreach to divorced and remarried Catholics have all drawn the ire of traditionalist Catholics. From his historical viewpoint, Codina concludes as follows: "Viewing the shifting winds over the course of time, we can see that the type and orientation of opposition always reflect the historical moment. There are progressive and prophetic voices in periods when classical Christianity or neo-Christianity dominates, and reactionary, fundamentalist and conservative voices in moments of ecclesial reform and attempts to return to evangelical origins and the style of Jesus."[54] In his September 2019 trip to Madagascar, Mozambique and Mauritius, in the airplane interview that he had with journalists and reporters, the question of opposition to his leadership came up. In response, Francis declared that schism

51. O'Hanlon, *The Quiet Revolution of Pope Francis*, 145.

52. A popular but accurate defense of Pope Francis against his critics may be found in Bacik, *Pope Francis and His Critics*.

53. Codina, "Why do some Catholics oppose Pope Francis?"

54. Codina, "Why do some Catholics oppose Pope Francis?"

was always a possibility, easily verified through two millennia of church history, but that his prayer was that it would not happen. To say the least, an eminently sensible and balanced response to a most provocative issue. Codina continues: "Obviously, the problem is not that [Francis] is not a theologian but rather that his theology is pastoral. Francis passes from dogma to kerygma, from theoretical principles to pastoral discernment and mystagogy. And his theology is not colonialist but from the global South, and this bothers the North."[55]

Conclusion

Francis will probably not have many years left as pope. Undoubtedly, the self-styled "pope-makers" or Vatican pundits are already thinking about Francis's successor. However that may be, the definite pastoral orientation of the papacy, the synodal way, established by Pope Francis seems here to stay. Even given the hostility of the ecclesiastical right-wing to him and his policies, it would be almost impossible to imagine a return to pre-Francis days. There will always be politics in the church, swings this way and that, preferences of one group over another, but Pope Francis has captured positively the imagination of most Catholics and, indeed, it would seem of the world at large.

55. Codina, "Why Do Some Catholics Oppose Pope Francis?"

19

The Church Tomorrow By Way of Conclusion

The temptation is found, in present controversy and in our interpretation of the past, to clarify complexity by dividing the wheat from the cockle, the light from the dark, "us" from "them."

—NICHOLAS LASH[1]

The Roman Catholic Church is not the monolithic entity that her enemies and her most zealous members believe. Beliefs are not held univocally, or with clarity, or across the board.

—FERGUS KERR, OP[2]

No one's crystal ball is cloudless, and it would be a foolish person who was too sure of the shape that the church of the future will take.

—PAUL LAKELAND[3]

ONE CONTEMPORARY AUTHOR, THE Czechoslovakian priest-therapist-theologian Tomas Halik, insists that theology, and so faith, must not only be intelligible to people, but also it must be "infectious." "Christianity [has] ceased to be a common ideal for humankind and [has] become sterile—because it *failed to love the world enough*. Its teaching and spiritual practice [has] been crippled by the old heresies—Manichaean dualism that rejected matter and creation, and Jansenism with its pessimistic attitude to natural human behavior, its pathological asceticism, and its obsession with original sin."[4] Essentially the point Halik is making is that many today do not love Christianity because Christianity seems inordinately suspicious of the good things

1. Lash, "Modernism, Aggiornamento and the Night Battle," 51.
2. Kerr, *Twentieth Century Catholic Theologians*, 203.
3. Lakeland, *Catholicism at the Crossroads*, 97.
4. Halik, *Night of the Confessor: Christian Faith in an Age of Uncertainty*, 37–38.

358

that people love. Christians can give the impression of being *against* things and values that are life-giving to modern people, of being too condemnatory, of being too negative. Halik is saying that the church needs to be more positively infectious, and teach the faith with this positive infectiousness, shaping a way of life that will have its own inherent attractiveness and persuasiveness.

Looking Backwards and Forward

Between the First Vatican Council and the Second Vatican Council, the Catholic Church could be likened to a village with a high wall all around it, keeping at bay the jungle outside. The jungle consisted of post-Enlightenment ideas, while the high-walled village with its system of regulations and taboos kept the villagers safe from the dangers of the jungle. "The Second Vatican Council breached the [village] wall at several points and thus ended the seclusion so carefully fostered by several generations of village rulers."[5] This book has looked in a necessarily selective way at the period, more or less, before and leading up to Vatican I and then after Vatican II—popes, policies, people, and theology. Looking at this enormously complex period, it is possible to see both continuity and difference, "more of the same" and points of development from one pontificate to the others.

What will the future Catholic Church be like? What will future popes, policies, and people be like? No one can answer such questions, of course, with exactitude. But the religious journalist David Gibson, in the introduction to his fine book, *The Coming Catholic Church*, has this to say: "The question at hand is not whether American Catholicism will exist in ten years, or twenty or thirty years, but what it will look like."[6] One might re-phrase Gibson's point *a propos* of the entire Western Catholic Church—one recognizes that the church is more than the West, of course—the question is what will it look like in the future in ten, or twenty, or thirty years, given the changes and developments in the church today. Obviously, there can be no clear answer, "no cloudless crystal ball." Nevertheless, one might speculate a little. What seems immediately obvious is that there has been a definitive development, in the words of one historian the church "has embraced modernity. With few exceptions, Catholic thinkers and leaders take for granted that they are living in a religiously plural world, and that their task is to collaborate with others in the name of the common good."[7]

5. Daly, "Catholicism and Modernity," 777.

6. Gibson, *The Coming Catholic Church*, 12.

7. Chappel, *Catholic Modern: The Challenge of Totalitarianism*, 1. This splendid study is not primarily engaged with theology but plots the development from anti-modernity to modernity in much broader terms, even as it offers remarkably fine insight into the contemporary theological situation in the church. In the final chapter of this book Chappel goes on to say that since at least the 1960s "Even if the official church and its dignitaries were sometimes caught flat-footed, Catholic students and laity were more agile. They responded creatively to the demands of a new era, forging styles of thought and activism that survive to this day" (ibid., 228).

Living in a religiously plural world has brought Catholic leaders, especially the pope with the bishops, into positive relationships with other Christian traditions, and also with other religions. Such developments would have been inconceivable before Vatican II, and seem destined to continue developing. There can be no going back into a narrowly confessional ecclesial world.

The English Catholic novelist, David Lodge, helps us to see something of this embrace of modernity. Commenting on his 1980 novel, *How Far Can You Go?* twenty-eight years later in 2008, and asking the question of his Catholic fictional characters, "How Far Have We Come?" Lodge writes:

> The utopian spirit of radical Catholicism in the 1960s and 1970s faded in the 1980s and 1990s as it did in secular society. Some of my characters would have "lapsed," disillusioned by the return of old-fashioned quietist forms of devotion, and the absence of real structural change in the church. Others might have returned to the fold, feeling the need for some reassurance with which to face aging and mortality. But the church is no longer the tightly governed, watchfully policed citadel it once was; membership is no longer defined by visible signs and sanctions—scrupulously regular attendance at Mass on Sundays and holy days, confession before Communion at least once a year, fasting, abstinence, and all the rest—or by an unquestioning acceptance of the whole package of Catholic Christian doctrine.[8]

In David Lodge's terms, Catholics are defining for themselves often in very practical terms what it means to be Catholic.

Lodge's description does not, because it cannot, apply to all Catholics everywhere in equal measure and degree. There are different groupings within Catholicism, self-described as conservative or neo-conservative, progressive or liberal, post-liberal, or even evangelical Catholic. However, it seems undeniable that Lodge is also describing a very large number of Roman Catholics today when he judges that "the church is no longer the tightly governed, watchfully policed citadel it once was" nor is it marked "by an unquestioning acceptance of the whole package of Catholic Christian doctrine." This seems to me to be a simple statement of fact, however undesirable it may be. It certainly reflects the perspective of many at the popular level, who still wish to belong. All manner of statistical surveys conducted in recent years reinforce this perception. The church is changing and changing fast.

The distinguished American church historian, John W. O'Malley, speaks of a "papalcentric ecclesiology," a phenomenon allied to the "papalization of Catholicism." Looking back over the second millennium of Christianity and attempting to locate significant changes in Catholic life, O'Malley maintains that the biggest change of the millennium has been "the papalization of Catholicism." He provides a host of examples of the fact that for most Catholics the papacy did not loom large in the

8. Lodge, "How Far Have We Come?" 17.

daily living out of their Christian faith. Aquinas, for example, maintains O'Malley, hardly mentions the papacy in his comprehensive *Summa Theologiae*. This stands in strong contrast with our contemporary experience of the papacy, and in contemporary ecclesiological reflection. Continuing with O'Malley, "To be a Catholic today, however, as most Catholics and surely everybody else would say, is 'to believe in the pope.' . . . In their publications theologians know that, quite unlike the situation in St. Thomas's day, it is as important to quote writings of the current pontiff as it is to quote Scripture."[9] One suspects a little hyperbole on O'Malley's part here, but his point is well-taken. There is a centeredness on papal documents and texts and on the person of the pope in our contemporary experience that is largely foreign to the period before Pope Pius IX. Papalcentric ecclesiology and to some extent theology largely began with Pope Pius IX, an ecclesiology that, at least at the popular level, seems to presuppose that the Holy Spirit communicates exclusively with the pope.[10] To move on from this papalcentric ecclesiology, but at the same time maintaining a necessary, firm and clear role for the papacy, will demand an informed historical perspective. Church history has too often been the Cinderella of both theology and catechetical instruction. As Paul Lakeland has it: "The laity and the clergy need to become better educated in the history of the Catholic tradition. . . . The history of the church is the rightful possession of every member of the community, and responsible members of the community will take the trouble to learn about their history. There are many reasons why this is good practice, but the principal one is that it discourages us from paying too much attention to the way things are right now. 'It's always been this way!' is a terrible fallacy."[11] The purpose of this book has in part been to avoid this fallacy through a series of historical and theological snapshots.

Recall some words spoken in 1962: "In the daily exercise of our pastoral office we sometimes have to listen, much to our regret, to voices of persons who, though burning with zeal, are not endowed with too much sense of discretion or measure. In these modern times they can see nothing but prevarication and ruin. They say that our era, in comparison with past eras, is getting worse and they behave as though they had learned nothing from history, which is, nonetheless, the teacher of life." These words come from Pope John XXIII at the opening of the first session of Vatican II.[12] They are as relevant now as they were then. Or recall some words uttered in the nineteenth century:

> This is a world of conflict, and of vicissitude amid the conflict. The church is ever militant; sometimes she gains, sometimes she loses; and more often she is at once gaining and losing in parts of her territory. What is ecclesiastical

9. O'Malley, "The Millennium and the Papalization of Catholicism," 10.

10. O'Malley, SJ, "Truth Be Told, Review: Gary Wills, *Papal Sin*," 24. See also Duffy, *Faith of Our Fathers*, 58–87.

11. Lakeland, *Catholicism at the Crossroads*, 110.

12. Cited from Trevor, *Pope John*, 80.

history but a record of the ever-doubtful fortune of the battle, though its issue
is not doubtful? Scarcely are we singing *Te Deum*, when we have to turn to our
Misereres: scarcely are we in peace, when we are in persecution; scarcely have
we gained a triumph, when we are visited by a scandal. Nay, we make progress
by means of reverses; our griefs are our consolations; we lose Stephen, to gain
Paul, and Matthias replaces the traitor Judas. It is so in every age; it is so in the
nineteenth century; it was so in the fourth.[13]

These words come from John Henry Cardinal Newman, introducing his sketches of
church history. Pastoral challenges are with us always.

The point is to recognize that there is no golden age in the history of the church,
an age free of problems and challenges, an age in which the entire assembly of Christians was active in every possible way in their local communities and held fast to the
integrity of Christian practice and doctrine in every respect. Arguably, this sense of a
golden age which seems to perdure stems and flows from this papalization of Catholicism especially during the nineteenth century. If that papalcenric perspective is less
tight now than it has been, that may be no bad thing. As English Catholic theologian,
Paul D. Murray, reviewing and summing up theology in the decades after Vatican
II, writes: "The instincts of the reactionary conservative, the progressive reformer,
the creative retriever, the cautious consolidator, and the counter-cultural critic exist
as differing yet overlapping parameters of concern. They constitute the diverse keys
within which the music of Catholicism has been and is being variously performed
with the possibility of both harmony and dissonance."[14] It is a fine description of
contemporary Catholic theology.

It would be fair to say that Thomism in the wake of Vatican II and as a result of
the mid-century *nouvelle théologie* became much less central to Catholic theology as
other ways of doing theology opened up. As Catholic students of theology pursued
graduate studies at non-Catholic institutions, it was inevitable that a greater theological pluralism would emerge. At the same time, Thomism did not simply disappear but rather developed in various ways in dialogue with other styles of philosophy
and theology. Paul Murray comments sagely: "While a range of appropriations of the
Thomist tradition, from analytic and personalist to more self-consciously historical
readings, still features as an important part of the contemporary Catholic theological
scene, they now feature precisely as a part—and an internally differentiated part—
rather than as a whole."[15] Perhaps it might be helpful to describe the decades after
the council as "the democratization of theology." This is certainly true of the United
States. Prior to Vatican II probably the majority of graduate students in theology
were priests studying more often than not at the Roman universities, for example,
the Jesuit Gregorian, the Dominican Angelicum, and the Benedictine Sant' Anselmo.

13. Newman, *Historical Sketches*, 1.

14. Murray, "Roman Catholic Theology after Vatican II," 265–86.

15. Murray, "Roman Catholic Theology after Vatican II," 272.

While some laity have studied and continue to study at these schools, many more pursue their studies at other universities such as Harvard, Yale, Duke, Chicago, the Graduate Theological Union, Emory, and so forth, as well as in Catholic schools like Catholic University of America, Fordham, Marquette, Boston College, Duquesne, etc. This has led to the "democratization" of theology, as theological expertise and competence has moved away from being a preserve of the clergy to committed and credentialed lay people. The result is both diversity in theologians and in theological methodologies, and, therefore, ineluctably certain tensions. This leads Paul Murray to conclude as follows: "While this proliferation of methodologies and analytical tools has greatly enriched Catholic theology, it has become increasingly difficult to hold it in gathered, cross-boundary, mutually constructive conversation. It is, consequently, as vital to Catholicism's health to develop and to sustain spaces for richly textured conversation between theologians of varying persuasions and differing expertise as it is to nurture the opportunities for similar conversations between theologians and the hierarchy."[16] This is a major challenge for Catholic theology in the twenty-first century. Theologians and Catholics concerned with a critically reflective and adult understanding of their faith can either let themselves be stretched to understand styles and methods different from their own leading gradually to mutual enrichment all around, including at times some serious disagreements, or they can retreat to their ideological fortresses ignoring, excluding or anathematizing one another, and so becoming less relevant to the peoples of the world.

The meeting of the American bishops at Dallas in 2002 (and other such meetings throughout the universal church) to deal with the sex-abuse scandals in the church signaled to some the end of the monarchical shape of the church, the deconstruction of which arguably began with Vatican II and is being accelerated under Pope Francis. There is a populist demand for transparency and accountability at the highest levels of leadership in the church, and never witnessed before. Accompanying this populist demand, and growing over a much longer period of time, and at least since the late 1960s, is the fact that Catholics are making up their own minds about a broad range of issues in ways that do not always coincide with formal church teaching. This is especially true of younger Catholics. The Catholic theologian, Tom Beaudoin, cited by David Gibson, describes the situation among younger Catholics as follows: "Let's be honest and admit that most young Catholics, even into our thirties, are only semi-practicing or non-practicing. . . . That does not mean that they have abandoned God or been abandoned by God. How many of us know young adults who are waiting for a credible, believable church, a church that addresses real life issues, a church that treats us like adults, that takes our cultures seriously, a church that feeds us spiritually, that asks for our gifts."[17] The church tomorrow, then, will be both like and unlike the

---

16. Murray, "Roman Catholic Theology after Vatican II," 272.

17. Gibson, *The Coming Catholic Church*, 50, 60, 79.

church of today just as the church of today in the years following Vatican II is both like and unlike the church of yesterday.

One of the great characteristics of Catholicism is its ability to make room for everyone, for saints and sinners. This is how David Gibson, the religious journalist puts it:

> Catholicism's genius is that for all its doctrinal certitude, one of its main tenets is that all should come under its catholic embrace. Thus one finds an astounding variety of types who proudly wear their Catholicism like a badge—peaceniks such as the Berrigans, charismatics who pray like Pentecostals, traditionalists who chant in Latin, feminists who celebrate underground women's liturgies, and even those annoying "holy idiots" who sometimes turn out to be saints. It also encompasses miscreants who have abused children—even if they are defrocked, ex-priests remain Catholics— as well as an astonishing number of their victims.[18]

This all-embracing Catholic Church, today and of tomorrow, if it is to be faithful to the vision of Vatican II will be a church in which dialogue between different points of view is the order of the day. It will be a church in which the members will need to recognize that they will find themselves in disagreement with one another from time to time. It will be a church in which they will be able to live with these tensions and disagreements amicably if not always comfortably. It will be a church marked by the synodality/systemic dialogue and decision-making encouraged and practiced by Pope Francis. Theologian Paul Lakeland puts it so well when he believes that a basic, deep, and pervasive love for the church is what is called for, and a love for the church that is enormously challenging: "You have to love the whole sorry mess, all those who are praying with you in praying the prayer of the publican, and even those who are not."[19]

18. Gibson, *The Coming Catholic Church*, 105.

19. Lakeland, *Catholicism at the Crossroads*, 25.

Bibliography

Abbott, SJ, Walter M. *Against Ratzinger*. New York: Seven Stories, 2008.

Abbott, SJ, Walter M., and Joseph Gallagher, eds. *The Documents of Vatican II*. New York: America, 1966.

Alberigo, Giuseppe. *A Brief History of Vatican II*. Maryknoll, NY: Orbis, 2006.

Alberigo, Giuseppe, and Joseph A. Komonchak, eds. *History of Vatican II*. 5 vols. Maryknoll, NY: Orbis, 1995–2006.

Allen, John L. *Pope Benedict XVI*. New York: Crossroad, 2000.

Althann, Robert SJ. "Papal Mediation during the First World War." *Studies* 61 (1972) 219–40.

Atkin, Nicholas, and Frank Tallett. *Priests, Prelates and People: A History of European Catholicism since 1750*. Oxford: Oxford University Press, 2003.

Bacik, James J. *Pope Francis and His Critics*. Mahwah, NJ. Paulist, 2020.

Baldovin, SJ, John F. "Cardinal Ratzinger as Liturgical Critic." In *Studia Liturgica Diversa (Essays in Honor of Paul F. Bradshaw)* edited by Maxwell E. Johnson and L. Edward Phillips, 211–27. Portland, OR: Pastoral, 2004.

Balthasar, Hans Urs von. "Current Trends in Catholic Theology and the Responsibility of the Christian." *Communio* 5 (1978) 77–85.

———. *Martin Buber and Christianity*. New York: Macmillan, 1961.

———. *My Work in Retrospect*. San Francisco: Ignatius, 1993.

———. *Mysterium Paschale*. Edinburgh: T. & T. Clark, 1990.

———. *The Theology of Henri de Lubac*. San Francisco: Ignatius, 1991.

———. *The Theology of Karl Barth, Exposition and Interpretation*. San Francisco: Ignatius, 1992.

Barmann, Lawrence. *Baron Friedrich von Hügel and the Modernist Crisis in England*. Cambridge: Cambridge University Press, 1972.

Barton, John M. T. "The Dominican School in Jerusalem and Old Testament Studies." In *Lagrange and Biblical Renewal*, edited by Richard T. Murphy, OP, 5–46. Chicago: Priory, 1966.

Bédoyère, Michael de la. *The Life of Baron Friedrich von Hügel*. London: Dent, 1951.

Bellitto, Christopher M. *101 Questions and Answers on Popes and the Papacy*. Mahwah, NJ: Paulist, 2008.

———. *The General Councils: A History of the Twenty-one Church Councils from Nicaea to Vatican II*. Mahwah, NJ: Paulist, 2002.

Benedict XVI, with Peter Seewald. *Last Testament*. London: Bloomsbury, 2017.

Bergoglio, Jorge M., and Abraham Skorka. *On Heaven and Earth: Pope Francis on Faith, Family and the Church in the Twenty-First Century*. New York: Image, 2013.

Biechler, James E., ed. *Law for Liberty: The Role of Law in the Church Today*. Baltimore: Helicon, 1967.

Blondel, Maurice. *Action: Essay on a Critique of Life and a Science of Practice*. Translated by Olivia Blanchette. Notre Dame: University of Notre Dame Press, 1984.

———. *The Letter on Apologetics and History and Dogma*. Translated by Alexander Dru and Illtyd Trethowan. London: Harvill Press, 1964.

Bockmuehl, Markus. *Simon Peter in Scripture and Memory*. Grand Rapids: Baker Academic, 2012.

Boersma, Hans. *Nouvelle Théologie and Sacramental Ontology: A Return to Mystery*. Oxford: Oxford University Press, 2009.

Bokenkotter, Thomas. *Church and Revolution*. New York: Doubleday, 1998.

———. *A Concise History of the Catholic Church*. Rev. ed. New York: Doubleday, 2004.

Bouyer, Louis. "Liturgy and Mystery: Dom Casel's Theory Explained and Discussed." In Louis Bouyer, *Liturgical Piety*, 86–98. Notre Dame, IN: University of Notre Dame Press, 1955.

Boyle, Nicholas. "On Earth, as in Heaven." *The Tablet*, July 9, 2005, 12–15.

Brown, Dan. *Origin*. New York: Anchor, 2017.

Brown, R. E., J. A. Fitzmyer, and R. E. Murphy, eds. *The New Jerome Biblical Commentary*. Englewood Cliffs, NJ: Prentice Hall, 1990.

Brown, SS, Raymond E., and Thomas A. Collins, OP. "Church Pronouncements." In *The New Jerome Biblical Commentary*, 1166–74. Englewood Cliffs, NJ: Prentice Hall, 1990.

Browne-Olf, Lillian. *Pius XI, Apostle of Peace*. New York: Macmillan, 1938.

Bunson, Matthew E. *Pope Francis*. Huntington, IN: Our Sunday Visitor, 2013.

Burgess, Anthony. *Earthly Powers*. Harmondsworth, UK: Penguin, 1980.

Butler, Christopher. *The Theology of Vatican II*. Rev ed. London: Darton, Longman and Todd, 1981.

Butler, OSB, Cuthbert. *The Vatican Council, 1869–1870*. 2 vols. Westminster, MD: Newman, 1962.

Buttiglione, Rocco. *Karol Wojtyla: The Thought of the Man Who Became Pope John Paul II*. Grand Rapids: Eerdmans, 1997.

Cahill, Thomas. *Pope John XXIII, A Life*. New York: Penguin, 2002.

Caldecott, Stratford, ed. *Beyond the Prosaic*. Edinburgh: T. & T. Clark, 1998.

Callahan, Annice. *Karl Rahner's Spirituality of the Pierced Heart: A Reinterpretation of Devotion to the Sacred Heart*. Lanham, MD: University Press of America, 1985.

Cardinale, H. E. "Pope Pius XII and the Blessed Virgin Mary." In *Mary's Place in Christian Dialogue*, edited by Alberic Stacpoole, OSB, 232–49. Slough, UK: St. Paul, 1982.

Carlen, IHM, Claudia, ed. *The Papal Encyclicals*. 5 vols. Ann Arbor, MI: Pierian, 1990.

Carroll, James. *Constantine's Sword: The Church and the Jews*. Boston: Houghton Mifflin, 2001.

Cassidy, Richard J. *Four Times Peter*. Collegeville, MN: Liturgical, 2007.

Cavadini, John C., ed. *Explorations in the Theology of Benedict XVI*. Notre Dame, IN: University of Notre Dame Press, 2012.

Chadwick, Henry, and J. E. Oulton, eds. *Alexandrian Christianity*. Philadelphia: Westminster, 1954.

———. *The Early Church*. Rev. ed. Harmondsworth, UK: Penguin, 1993.

———. *Tradition and Exploration: Collected Papers on Theology and the Church*. Norwich, UK: Canterbury, 1994.

Chadwick, Owen. *Britain and the Vatican during the Second World War*. Cambridge: Cambridge University Press, 1986.

———. *From Bossuet to Newman*. 2nd ed. Cambridge: Cambridge University Press, 1987.

———. "The Church of England and the Church of Rome from the Beginning of the Nineteenth Century to the Present Day." In *Anglican Initiatives in Christian Unity: Lectures Delivered in Lambeth Palace Library 1966*, 19–38. London: SPCK, 1967.

———. *Freedom and the Historian: An Inaugural Lecture*. Cambridge: Cambridge University Press, 1969.

———. *A History of Christianity*. London: Weidenfeld and Nicholson, 1995.

———. *A History of the Popes, 1830–1914*. Oxford: Oxford University Press, 1998.

———. *Newman: A Short Introduction*. Oxford: Oxford University Press, 1983.

———. *The Popes and European Revolution*. Oxford: Oxford University Press, 1981.

Chappel, James. *Catholic Modern: The Challenge of Totalitarianism and the Remaking of the Church*. Cambridge, MA: Harvard University Press, 2018.

———. Review of *The Irony of Modern Catholic History* by George Weigel. *Commonweal,,* August 26, 2019.

Chardin, Pierre Teilhard de. *The Phenomenon of Man*. New York: Harper & Row, 1959.

Chiron, Yves. *St. Pius X, Restorer of the Church*. Kansas City, MO: Angelus, 2002.

Clancy, John G. *Apostle for Our Time, Pope Paul VI*. New York: Kenedy, 1963.

Clarke, SJ, W. Norris. "Pope John Paul II: The Complementarity of Faith in the Search for Truth." *Communio* 26 (1999) 557–70.

Codina, Victor. "Why Do Some Catholics Oppose Pope Francis?" *America*, September 12, 2019, 12–14.

Coffey, Thomas M. *Lion by the Tail: The Story of the Italian-Ethiopian War*. New York: Coffey, 1974.

Collins, James. "Leo XIII and the Philosophical Approach to Modernity." In *Leo XIII and the Modern World*, edited by Edward T. Gargan, 181–212. New York: Sheed and Ward, 1961.

Collins, Michael. *The Fisherman's Net: The Influence of the Papacy on History*. Dublin: Columba, 2003.

———. *Pope Benedict XVI: The First Five Years*. Dublin: Columba, 2010.

Collins, Paul. *Absolute Power*. New York: Public, 2018.

———. *God's New Man: The Election of Benedict XVI and the Legacy of John Paul II*. New York: Continuum, 2005.

Congar, OP, Yves. "Church History as a Branch of Theology." In *Church History in Future Perspective*, edited by Roger Aubert, 85–96. New York: Herder, 1970.

Conway, Martin. *Catholic Politics in Europe 1918–1945*. London: Routledge, 1997.

Conway, Michael. "Maurice Blondel and *Ressourcement*." In *Ressourcement, A Movement for Renewal in Twentieth-Century Catholic Theology*, edited by Gabriel Flynn and Paul D. Murray, 65–82. Oxford: Oxford University Press, 2012.

Cooke, Bernard, ed. *The Papacy and the Church in the United States*. Mahwah, NJ: Paulist, 1989.

Copleston, SJ, Frederick C. *Memoirs*. Kansas City, MO: Sheed and Ward, 1993.

Coppa, Frank J. *The Life and Pontificate of Pope Pius XII: Between History and Controversy*. Washington, DC: Catholic University of America Press, 2013.

———. *The Papacy, the Jews, and the Holocaust*. Washington, DC: Catholic University of America Press, 2006.

———. *The Policies and Politics of Pope Pius XII*. New York: Lang, 2011.

———. *Politics and the Papacy in the Modern World*. Westport, CT: Praeger, 2008.

———. *Pope Pius IX*. Boston: Twayne, 1979.

Corkery, SJ, James. *Joseph Ratzinger's Theological Ideas*. Mahwah, NJ: Paulist, 2009.

Cornwell, John. *Newman's Unquiet Grave*. New York: Continuum, 2010.

———. *The Pontiff in Winter*. New York: Doubleday, 2004.

———. *A Thief in the Night*. London: Penguin, 1989.

Cox, Harvey. *The Future of Faith*. New York: HarperCollins, 2009.

Crews, Clyde F. *English Catholic Modernism: Maude Petre's Way of Faith*. Notre Dame, IN: University of Notre Dame Press, 1984.

Cross, F. L., and E. A. Livingstone, eds. *The Oxford Dictionary of the Christian Church*. 2nd ed. Oxford: Oxford University Press, 1974.

Cuenot, Claude. *Teilhard de Chardin: A Biographical Study*, Baltimore: Helicon, 1961.

Cummings, Owen F. "Eucharistic Teachings of the Church I: Pope Pius X to Vatican Council II." In *Eucharistic Soundings*, 52–63. Dublin: Veritas, 1999.

———. *One Body in Christ*. Eugene, OR: Pickwick, 2015.

———. *Prophets, Guardians and Saints, Shapers of Modern Catholic History*. Mahwah, NJ: Paulist, 2007.

———. *Thinking about Prayer*. Eugene, OR: Wipf and Stock, 2009.

Cunningham, Lawrence. "The Man Who's Become Benedict." *Notre Dame Magazine*, Autumn, 2007, 40–43.

Curran, Charles. "Dangers of Certitude." *The Tablet*, July 26, 2008, 23–24.

Dalin, David G. *The Myth of Hitler's Pope*. Washington, DC: Regnery, 2005.

Daly, Cahal. "Faith and Reason: Diatribe of Dialogue? A Reflection on *Fides et Ratio*." In *The Challenge of Truth*, edited by James McEvoy, 219–39. Dublin: Veritas, 2002.

Daly, Gabriel. "Catholicism and Modernity." *Journal of the American Academy of Religion* 53 (1985) 773–96.

———. *Transcendence and Immanence*. Oxford: Clarendon, 1980.

Daniélou, SJ, Jean. *God and Us*. London: Mowbray, 1957.

Davies, Norman. *Rising '44: The Battle for Warsaw*. London: PanMacmillan, 2003.

Davis, Charles. "Dom Odo Casel and the Theology of Mysteries." *Worship* 34 (1960) 428–38.

Delaney, John F. "From Cremona to Edinburgh: Bishop Bonomelli and the World Missionary Conference of 1910." *US Catholic Historian* 20 (2002) 33–49.

Dessain, C. S. *John Henry Newman*. London: Darton, Longman and Todd, 1966.

Dick, John A. "The Malines Conversations, The Unfinished Agenda." In *From Malines to ARCIC: The Malines Conversations Commemorated*, edited by A. Denaux (in collaboration with J. Dick) 75–80. Leuven: Leuven University Press, 1997.

DiNoia, OP, Joseph A. "Karl Rahner." In *The Modern Theologians*, 2nd ed., edited by David F. Ford, 118–33. Oxford: Blackwell, 1997.

Doering, Bernard. "Jacques Maritain (1882–1973): A Beggar for Heaven on the Byways of the World." *Theology Today* 62 (2005) 306–16.

Dolan, Jay P. *In Search of American Catholicism*. Oxford: Oxford University Press, 2002.

Donakowski, Conrad L. "The Age of Revolutions." In *The Oxford History of Christian Worship*, edited by Geoffrey Wainwright and Karen B. Westerfield Tucker, 351–94. Oxford: Oxford University Press, 2006.

Duffy, Eamon. "The Age of Pio Nono: The Age of Paul Cullen." In *Cardinal Paul Cullen and His World*, edited by Dáire Keogh and Albert McDonnell, 15. Dublin: Four Courts, 2011.

———. "Benedict XVI and the Spirit of the Liturgy." *Doctrine and Life* 55 (2005) 30–50.

———. "Doctor Douglass and Mister Berington—An Eighteenth Century Retraction." *The Downside Review* 88 (1970) 246–69.

———. "Ecclesiastical Democracy Deleted." *Recusant History* 10 (1970) 193–209, 309–31; 13 (1973) 123–48.

———. *Faith of Our Fathers: Reflections on Catholic Tradition.* New York: Continuum, 2004.

———. "A Giant among Popes." *The Tablet*, October 18, 2003, 4–5.

———. "A Great Pope Ill Served by His Fans." *The Tablet*, December 6, 2003, 15.

———. "Interview." 2003, with PBS.

———. Review of *God's Choice: Pope Benedict XVI and the Future of the Catholic Church*, by George Weigel. *Commonweal*, January 27, 2006, 18–21.

———. *Saints and Sinners.* Rev. ed. New Haven, CT: Yale University Press, 2001.

———. "The Staying Power of Christianity." *The New York Review of Books*, June 20, 2013, 69–70.

———. *Ten Popes Who Shook the World.* New Haven, CT: Yale University Press, 2011.

———. "Urbi, but Not Orbi . . . the Cardinal, the Church and the World." *New Blackfriars* 66 (1985) 272–78.

———. "Style Is Not Enough." *The Tablet*, March 8, 2014, 6–7.

Dulles, SJ, Avery. "Commentary on Profession of Faith's Concluding Paragraphs." Sidebar in *Origins*, August 28, 1998.

———. "From Ratzinger to Benedict." *First Things*, February, 2006, 24–29.

———. *A History of Apologetics.* New York: Corpus, 1971.

———. "*Humanae Vitae* and the Crisis of Dissent." *Origins* 22 (1993) 774–77.

———. *Models of the Church.* Expanded ed. New York: Doubleday, 1987.

———. *Models of Revelation.* New York: Doubleday, 1983.

———. "The Sacramental Ecclesiology of *Lumen Gentium*." *Gregorianum* 86 (2005) 550–62.

Eagleton, Terry. *The Gatekeeper: A Memoir.* New York: St. Martin's, 2001.

Eckardt, Arthur Roy. *Elder and Younger Brothers: That Encounter of Jews and Christians.* New York: Schocken, 1967.

Eisner, Peter. *The Pope's Last Crusade.* New York: HarperCollins, 2013.

Elie, Paul. *The Life You Save May Be Your Own.* New York: Farrar, Straus and Giroux, 2003.

———. "The Year of the Two Popes." *Atlantic Monthly*, January–February, 2006, 64–92.

Ellingsen, Mark. "Joseph Ratzinger (1927–): How Conservative Is Benedict XVI?" *Theology Today* 62 (2005) 388–98.

Elliott, Lawrence. *I Will Be Called John: A Biography of Pope John XXIII.* New York: Reader's Digest, 1973.

Ellis, John Tracy. *Faith and Learning: A Church Historian's Story.* Lanham, MD: University Press of America, 1989.

Endean, SJ, Philip. "Spirituality and Religious Experience: A Perspective from Rahner." In *Christian Identity in a Postmodern Age*, edited by Declan Marmion, 201–19. Dublin: Veritas, 2005.

Ernst, OP, Cornelius. *Multiple Echo.* London: Darton, Longman and Todd, 1979.

Evans, Robert F. *One and Holy: The Church in Latin Patristic Thought.* London: SPCK, 1972.

Fagan, SM, Sean. "Theology in the Making." In *Theology in the Making*, edited by Gesa E. Theissen and Declan Marmion, 65–73. Dublin: Veritas, 2005.

Fahey, S.J., Michael. "Joseph Ratzinger as Ecclesiologist and Pastor." In *Neo-Conservatism: Social and Religious Phenomenon*, edited by Gregory Baum, 76–83. New York: Seabury, 1981.

Falconi, Carlo. *The Popes in the Twentieth Century.* London: Weidenfeld and Nicholson, 1967.

Faricy, SJ, Robert L. *Teilhard de Chardin's Theology of the Christian in the World.* New York: Sheed and Ward, 1967.

Fattorini, Emma. *Hitler, Mussolini and the Vatican.* Cambridge: Polity, 2011.

Fenton, Joseph C. "Pope Benedict XV and the Rules for Theological Discussion." *American Ecclesiastical Review* 135 (1956) 39–53.

Fiorenza, Francis Schüssler. "From Theologian to Pope: A Personal View Back, Past the Public Portrayals." *Harvard Divinity Bulletin* 33 (2005) 56–62.

———. "The New Theology and Transcendental Thomism." In *Modern Christian Thought,* Vol. II, The Twentieth Century, edited by James C. Livingston et al., 197–232. Upper Saddle River, NJ: Prentice-Hall, 2000.

———. "Vatican II and the Aggiornamento of Roman Catholic Theology." In *Modern Christian Thought,* Vol. II, The Twentieth Century, edited by James C. Livingston et al., 233–71. Upper Saddle River, NJ: Prentice-Hall, 2000.

Fiorenza, Francis Schüssler, and Heinz-Joachim Fischer. *Pope Benedict XVI.* New York: Crossroad, 2005.

Fitzer, Joseph. *Romance and the Rock: Nineteenth Century Catholics on Reason and Faith.* Minneapolis: Augsburg, 1989.

Fleischner, Eva. "The Spirituality of Pius XII." In *Pope Pius XII and the Holocaust,* edited by Carol Rittner and John K. Roth, 123–36. London: Leicester University Press, 2002.

Fogarty, SJ, Gerald P. "The Vatican and the American Church Since World War II." In *The Papacy and the Church in the United States,* edited by Bernard Cooke, 119–40. Mahwah, NJ: Paulist, 1989.

———. *The Vatican and the American Hierarchy from 1870 to 1965.* Wilmington, DE: Glazier, 1985.

Fox, Matthew. *The Pope's War.* New York: Sterling Ethos, 2011.

Franklin, R. W., ed. *Anglican Orders: Essays on the Centenary of Apostolicae Curae, 1896–1996.* Harrisburg, PA: Morehouse, 1996.

Franzen, August, and John P. Dolan. *A History of the Church.* New York: Herder and Herder, 1969.

Frend, William H. C. *From Dogma to History.* London: SCM, 2003.

Gaillardetz, Richard R. "Between Reform and Rupture: The Council according to Benedict XVI." *Commonweal,* October 12, 2007, 16–21.

———. "The 'Francis Moment': A New Kairos for Catholic Ecclesiology." *Catholic Theological Society of America Proceedings* 69 (2014) 63–80.

———. *An Unfinished Council: Vatican II, Pope Francis, and the Renewal of Catholicism.* Collegeville, MN: Liturgical, 2015.

———. "What Can We Learn from Vatican II?" In *The Catholic Church in the 21st Century,* edited by Michael J. Himes, 80–95. Liguori, MO: Liguori, 2004.

Gallagher, SJ, Michael Paul. *Clashing Symbols.* London: Darton, Longman and Todd, 1997.

Gamber, Klaus. *Reform of the Roman Liturgy.* San Juan Capistrano, CA: Una Voce, 1993.

George, Timothy. "The Promise of Benedict XVI." *Christianity Today,* June, 2005, 13–15.

Giblin, Marie J. "Quadragesimo Anno." In *The New Dictionary of Catholic Social Thought,* edited by Judith A. Dwyer, 802–13. Collegeville, MN: Liturgical, 1994.

Gibson, David. *The Coming Catholic Church.* New York: HarperCollins, 2004.

———. *The Rule of Benedict.* New York: HarperSanFrancisco, 2006.

Gilley, Sheridan. "New Light on an Old Scandal: Purcell's Life of Cardinal Manning." In *Opening the Scrolls*, edited by Dominic Aidan Bellenger, 166–98. Bath, UK: Downside Abbey, 1987.

———. "Pope Leo's Legacy." *The Tablet*, December 13, 2003, 10.

Giordani, I. *Pius X: A Country Priest*. Milwaukee, WI: Bruce, 1954.

Goodall, Norman. *The Ecumenical Movement*. Oxford: Oxford University Press, 1961.

Gray, Robert. *Cardinal Manning*. New York: St. Martin's, 1985.

Greeley, Andrew M. *The Making of the Popes 1978*. Kansas City: Andrews and McMeel, 1979.

Griech-Polelle, Beth A. *Bishop von Galen: German Catholicism and National Socialism*. New Haven, CT: Yale University Press, 2002.

Guerriero, Elio. *Benedict XVI, His Life and Thought*. San Francisco: Ignatius, 2018.

Gy, OP, Pierre-Marie. "Is Cardinal Ratzinger's 'Spirit of the Liturgy' Faithful to the Council?" *Doctrine and Life* 52 (2002) 426–32.

———. *The Reception of Vatican II Liturgy Reforms in the Life of the Church*. Milwaukee, WI: Marquette University Press, 2003.

Hales, Edward E. Y. *The Catholic Church in the Modern World*. New York: Doubleday, 1960.

———. *Pio Nono*. New York: Doubleday, 1954.

———. *Pope John and His Revolution*. Garden City, NY: Doubleday, 1965.

Halfmann, Janet, ed. *New Catholic Encyclopedia*. 2nd ed. Detroit: Thomson/Gale in association with the Catholic University of America, 2003.

Halik, Thomas. *Night of the Confessor: Christian Faith in an Age of Uncertainty*. New York: Doubleday, 2012.

Hastings, Adrian, ed. *Bishops and Writers*. Wheathampstead, UK: Anthony Clarke, 1977.

———. "Catholic History from Vatican I to John Paul II." In *Modern Catholicism: Vatican II and After*, edited by Adrian Hastings, 1–13. Oxford: Oxford University Press, 1991.

———. "Papacy." In *The Oxford Companion to Christian Thought*, edited by Adrian Hastings et al., 510–12. Oxford: Oxford University Press, 2000.

———. "The Twentieth Century." In *Christianity, Two Thousand Years*, edited by Richard Harries and Henry Mayr-Harting, 218–36. Oxford: Oxford University Press, 2002.

———. "Vatican II, Council of." In *The Oxford Companion to Christian Thought*, edited by Adrian Hastings et al., 738–39. New York and Oxford: Oxford University Press, 2000.

Hatch, Alden, and Seamus Walshe. *Crown of Glory: The Life of Pope Pius XII*. New York: Hawthorn, 1957.

Hebblethwaite, Peter. *In the Vatican*. Bethesda: Adler and Adler, 1986.

———. *Paul VI: The First Modern Pope*. Mahwah, NJ: Paulist, 1993.

———. *Pope John XXIII*. Garden City, NY: Doubleday, 1985.

———. *The Year of the Three Popes*. New York: Collins, 1979.

Heft, SM, James L. "From the Pope to the Bishops: Episcopal Authority from Vatican I to Vatican II." In *The Papacy and the Church in the United States*, edited by Bernard Cooke, 55–78. Mahwah, NJ: Paulist, 1989.

Heidegger, Martin. *The Metaphysical Foundations of Logic*. Bloomington, IN: Indiana University Press, 1984.

Henn, William. "Yves Congar and *Lumen Gentium*." *Gregorianum* 86 (2005) 563–92.

Hennessey, SJ, James. *The First Council of the Vatican, the American Experience*. New York: Herder and Herder, 1963.

Hill, Roland. *Lord Acton*. New Haven, CT: Yale University Press, 2000.

Himes, Michael J., ed. *The Catholic Church in the 21st Century*. Liguori, MO: Liguori, 2004.

Holmes, J. Derek. *The Papacy in the Modern World*. New York: Crossroad, 1981.

———. *The Triumph of the Holy See*. London: Burns and Oates, 1978.

Hughes, John Jay. *Absolutely Null and Utterly Void: An Account of the Papal Condemnation of Anglican Orders 1896*. London: Sheed and Ward, 1968.

———. *Pontiffs: Popes Who Shaped History*. Huntington, IN: Our Sunday Visitor, 1994.

Hughes, Kevin L. *Church History*. Chicago: Loyola, 2002.

Hughes, Philip. *The Church in Crisis: The Twenty Great Councils*. London: Burns and Oates, 1961.

———. *A Popular History of the Catholic Church*. New York: Macmillan, 1954.

Hurley, SJ, Michael. *Healing and Hope: Memoirs of an Irish Ecumenist*. Dublin: Columba, 2003.

———, ed. *The Irish School of Ecumenics*. Dublin: Columba, 2008.

———. *Theology of Ecumenism*. Notre Dame, IN: Fides, 1969.

Imhoff, Paul, and Hubert Biallowons, eds. *Karl Rahner in Dialogue: Conversations and Interviews, 1965–1982*. New York: Crossroad, 1986.

Jedin, Hubert, and John P. Dolan, eds. *The History of the Church*, Vol. 10. New York: Crossroad, 1979.

Jodock, Darrell, ed. *Catholicism Contends with Modernity*. Cambridge: Cambridge University Press, 2000.

John XXIII, Pope. *Journal of a Soul*. Rev. ed. London: Chapman, 1980.

John Paul II, Pope. *Crossing the Threshold of Hope*. New York: Knopf, 1995.

———. *Theology of the Body*. Boston: Pauline, 1997.

Johnson, Luke Timothy. "After the Big Chill: Intellectual Freedom and Catholic Theologians." *Commonweal*, January 27, 2006, 10–14.

Johnson, Paul. *Pope John XXIII*. Boston: Little, Brown and Co., 1973.

———. *Pope John Paul II and the Catholic Restoration*. Ann Arbor, MI: Servant, 1981.

Kaiser, Robert Blair. *A Church in Search of Itself: Benedict XVI and the Battle for the Future*. New York: Random House, 2006.

Keck, David. *Forgetting Whose We Are: Alzheimer's Disease and the Love of God*. Nashville: Abingdon, 1996.

Kelly, John N. D. *The Oxford Dictionary of the Popes*. Oxford: Oxford University Press, 1986.

Kent, Peter C. *The Lonely Cold War of Pope Pius XII*. Montreal: McGill-Queen's University Press, 2002.

Ker, Ian. *Newman on Vatican II*. Oxford: Oxford University Press, 2014.

Kerlin, Michael. "Reginald Garrigou-Lagrange: Defending the Faith." *U.S. Catholic Historian* 25 (2007) 71–113.

Kerr, OP, Fergus. "Comment: Ratzinger's Thomism." *New Blackfriars* 89 (2008) 367–68.

———. "French Theology: Yves Congar and Henri de Lubac." In *The Modern Theologians*, 2nd ed, edited by David F. Ford, 105–17. Oxford: Blackwell, 1997.

———. *Twentieth-Century Catholic Theologians*. Oxford: Blackwell, 2007.

———. "Yves Congar: From Suspicion to Acclamation." *Louvain Studies* 29 (2004) 273–87.

Kertzer, David I. *The Kidnapping of Edgardo Mortara*. New York: Knopf, 1997.

———. *The Popes against the Jews*. New York: Knopf, 2001.

———. *The Pope and Mussolini*. New York: Random House, 2014.

Kilby, Karen. "Balthasar and Karl Rahner." In *The Cambridge Companion to Hans Urs von Balthasar*, edited by Edward T. Oakes, SJ and David Moss, 256–68. Cambridge: Cambridge University Press, 2004.

———. *Karl Rahner. A Brief Introduction*. New York: Crossroad, 2007.

Kilmartin, S.J., Edward J. *The Eucharist in the West, History and Theology*. Collegeville, MN: Liturgical, 1998.

Knowles, OSB, David. *The Historian and Character*. Cambridge: Cambridge University Press, 1963.

Komonchak, Joseph A. "Many Models, One Church." *Church*, Spring 1993, 12–15.

———. "Remembering Good Pope John." *Commonweal*, August 11, 2000, 1–15.

———. "Vatican II as an 'Event.'" In *Vatican II: Did Anything Happen?* edited by David G. Schultenover, 24–51. New York: Continuum, 2007.

Kress, Robert. "Karl Rahner: A New Father of the Church?" *Emmanuel* 110 (2004) 252–60.

Krieg, Robert A. *Catholic Theologians in Nazi Germany*. New York: Continuum, 2004.

Küng, Hans, *The Catholic Church: A Short History*. New York: The Modern Library, 2001.

———. *Disputed Truth, Memoirs II*. New York: Continuum, 2008.

———. *My Struggle for Freedom, Memoirs I*. Grand Rapids: Eerdmans, 2003.

LaFarge, SJ, John. "The Pope Deals with Nazi Persecution." *Catholic Mind* 35 (1937) 209–12.

Lagrange, R. Garrigou-. *Père Lagrange, Personal Reflections and Memoirs*. Mahwah, NJ: Paulist, 1985.

Lakeland, Paul. *Catholicism at the Crossroads*. New York: Continuum, 2007.

Lalonde, Marc P., ed. *The Promise of Critical Theology: Essays in Honour of Charles Davis*. Montreal: Wilfrid Laurier University Press, 1995.

Lane, Dermot A. "Karl Rahner's Contribution to Interreligious Dialogue." In *Christian Identity in a Postmodern Age*, edited by Declan Marmion, 91–112. Dublin: Veritas, 2005.

Lash, Nicholas. *Easter in Ordinary: Reflections on Human Experience and the Knowledge of God*. Charlottesville, VA: University Press of Virginia, 1988.

———. "Modernism, Aggiornamento and the Night Battle." In *Bishops and Writers*, edited by Adrian Hastings, 51–79. Wheathampstead, UK: Anthony Clarke, 1977.

———. *Newman on Development*. London: Sheet and Ward, 1975.

———. "On Learning to Be Wise." *Priests and People*, October, 2001, 355–59.

Lawler, Justus George. *Popes and Politics: Reform, Resentment and the Holocaust*. New York: Continuum, 2000.

———. *Were the Popes against the Jews: Tracking the Myths, Confronting the Ideologies*. Grand Rapids: Eerdmans, 2012.

Lehner, Ulrich. *The Catholic Enlightenment*. New York: Oxford University Press, 2016.

Leonard, Ellen. *George Tyrrell and the Catholic Tradition*. New York: Paulist, 1982.

———. *Unresting Transformation*. Lanham, MD: University Press of America, 1991.

Levillain, Philippe. "Paul VI." In *The Papacy: An Encyclopedia*, Vol. 2, edited by Philippe Levillain, 1131–45. London: Routledge, 2002.

Lewis, Keith D. *The Catholic Church in History*. New York: Crossroad, 2006.

Little, Andrew G., ed. *Roger Bacon: Essays Contributed by Various Writers on the Occasion of the Commemoration of the Seventh Centenary of His Birth*. Oxford: Clarendon, 1914.

Livingston, James C. *Modern Christian Thought*, Vol. 1, 2nd ed. Minneapolis: Fortress, 2006.

Lodge, David. "How Far Have We Come?" *The Tablet*, July 26, 2008, 16–17.

Losito, Giacomo. "Ernesto Buonaiuti and *Il programa dei modernisti*." *U.S. Catholic Historian* 25 (2007) 71–96.

Lossky, Nicholas, et al., eds. *Dictionary of the Ecumenical Movement*. Geneva: World Council of Churches, 1991.

Lubac, SJ, Henri de. *At the Service of the Church*. San Francisco: Ignatius, 1993.

―――. *Christian Resistance to Anti-Semitism*. San Francisco: Ignatius, 1990.

―――. *Teilhard de Chardin, the Man and His Meaning*. New York: New American Library, 1965.

Luciani, Albino. *Illustrissimi*. Boston: Little Brown, 1978.

Lukas, Mary, and Ellen Lukas. *Teilhard: A Biography*. London: Collins, 1977.

Lyons, OSB, Patrick Fintan. "Healing and Hope: Remembering Michael Hurley." *One in Christ* 45 (2011) 260–79.

MacCulloch, Diarmaid. *A History of Christianity*. London: Allen Lane, 2009.

Macquarrie, John. "Ebb and Flow of Hope: Christian Theology at the End of the Second Millennium." *The Expository Times* 107 (1995–96) 205–10.

―――. *Heidegger and Christianity*. London: SCM, 1994.

―――. *Mary for All Christians*. Grand Rapids: Eerdmans, 1990.

―――. "Mascall and Thomism." *Tufton Review* 2 (1998) 1–13.

―――. *Thinking about God*. London: SCM, 1975.

―――. *Twentieth-Century Religious Thought*. Rev. ed. Harrisburg, PA: Trinity, 2002.

Macy, Gary. *The Theologies of the Eucharist in the Early Scholastic Period*. Oxford: Oxford University Press, 1984.

Madigan, Kevin J. "Pope Benedict, Disaffected Anglicans, and Holocaust-Denying Bishops." *Harvard Divinity Bulletin* 38 (2010) no pagination provided in the online edition.

Marchione, Margherita. *Man of Peace, Pope Pius XII*. Mahwah, NJ: Paulist, 2003.

Marmion, SM, Declan. "Christian Identity in a Postmodern Age: A Perspective from Rahner." In *Christian Identity in a Postmodern Age*, edited by Declan Marmion, 162–79. Dublin: Veritas, 2005.

Massa, SJ, Mark S. *The American Catholic Revolution*. New York: Oxford University Press, 2010.

―――. "A Model Theologian: The Legacy of Avery Dulles." *Commonweal*, August 13, 2010, 12–16.

Massaro, Thomas. "The Social Question in the Papacy of Leo XIII." In *The Papacy Since 1500: From Italian Prince to Universal Pastor*, edited by James Corkery and Thomas Worcester, 143–61. Cambridge: Cambridge University Press, 2010.

McBrien, Richard P. *Lives of the Popes*. New York: HarperCollins, 1997.

McCabe, Herbert. "The Involvement of God." In *God Matters*, 39–51. London: Chapman, 1987.

McCabe, Michael. "The Mystery of the Human: A Perspective from Rahner." In *Christian Identity in a Postmodern Age*, edited by Declan Marmion, 47–62. Dublin: Veritas, 2005.

McCool, SJ, Gerard. *Catholic Theology in the Nineteenth Century*. New York: Seabury, 1977.

McCormick, S.J., Richard A. "*Humanae Vitae* 25 Years Later." *America*, July 17, 1993, 6–12.

McElwee, Joshua J. "Francis Encountering Curial Opposition, Cardinal Says." *National Catholic Reporter*, April 21, 2014, 14–15.

McEvoy, James. "The Singular Shape of Karol Wojtyla's Studies." In *The Challenge of Truth*, edited by James McEvoy, 123–33. Dublin: Veritas, 2002.

McIntosh, Mark. *Mystical Theology*. Oxford: Blackwell, 1998.

McIntyre, James. "Trust Where It Is Needed Most." *The Tablet*, May 31, 2014, 4–5.

McClelland, Vincent. *Cardinal Manning: His Public Life and Influence 1865–1892*. London: Oxford University Press, 1962.

McManners, John. *Church and State in France, 1870–1914*. New York: Harper and Row, 1972.

McPartlan, Paul. *Sacrament of Salvation*. Edinburgh: T. & T. Clark, 1995.

McShane, Philip, ed. *Foundation of Theology: Papers from the Internaional Lonergan Congress 1970*. Notre Dame, IN: University of Notre Dame Press, 1972.

Messori, Vittorio. *Kidnapped by the Vatican? The Unpublished Memoirs of Edgardo Mortara* (San Francisco. Ignatius Press, 2017

Mettepenningen, Jürgen. *Nouvelle Théologie, New Theology*. London: T. & T. Clark, 2010.

Mickens, Robert. "New-found Harmony?" *The Tablet*, October 1, 2005, 5.

Modras, Ronald. *Ignatian Humanism*. Chicago: Loyola, 2004.

Moltmann, Jürgen. *A Broad Place: An Autobiography*. London: SCM, 2007.

Molony, John. "The Making of *Rerum Novarum* April 1890–May 1891." In *The Church Faces the Modern World: Rerum Novarum and Its Impact*, edited by Paul Furlong and David Curtis, 27–40. Peterborough, UK: Earlsgate, 1994

Montagnes, OP, Bernar. *The Story of Father Marie-Joseph Lagrange*. Mahwah, NJ: Paulist, 2006.

Moran, James. "Arms and the Churchman." *The Tablet*, March 11, 2006, 20–21.

Moynihan, James H. *The Life of Archbishop John Ireland*. New York: Harpers, 1953.

Murphy, Francesca Aran. "Papal Ecclesiology." In *Explorations in the Theology of Benedict XVI*, edited by John C. Cavadini, 215–35. Notre Dame, IN: University of Notre Dame Press, 2012.

Murphy, Francis X. *The Papacy Today*. New York: Macmillan, 1981.

Murray, Paul D. "Roman Catholic Theology After Vatican II." In *The Modern Theologians: An Introduction to Christian Theology since 1918 (The Great Theologians)* edited by David F. Ford and Rachel Muers, 265–86. Oxford: Blackwell, 2005.

Murray, SJ, Robert. *Symbols of Church and Kingdom*. Cambridge: Cambridge University Press, 1975.

Neunheuser, O.S.B., Burkhard. "Dom Odo Casel and Latest Research." *The Downside Review* 76 (1958) 266–73.

———. "Masters in Israel: 5. Odo Casel," *The Clergy Review* 55 (1970), 194–212

Neuhaus, Richard J. *Catholic Matters*. New York: Basic, 2006.

Newman, John Henry. *An Essay on the Development of Christian Doctrine*. Edited with an introduction by J. M. Cameron. Harmondsworth, UK: Penguin, 1974.

———. *Historical Sketches*, Vol. 2. London: Dent, 1906.

Nicholas, Marc. *Jean Daniélou's Doxological Humanism*. Eugene, OR: Pickwick, 2012.

Nichols, OP, Aidan. *Catholic Thought Since the Enlightenment: A Survey*. Leominster, UK: Gracewing, 1998.

———. *Engaging Theologians*. Milwaukee, WI: Marquette University Press, 2013.

———. *Figuring Out the Church*. San Francisco: Ignatius, 2013.

———. "Odo Casel Revisited." *Antiphon: A Journal for Liturgical Renewal* 3 (1998) 12–20.

———. *Reason with Piety: Garrigou-Lagrange in the Service of Catholic Thought*. Naples, FL: Sapientia, 2008.

———. *Romance and System: The Theological Synthesis of Matthias Joseph Scheeben*. Greenwood Village, CO: Augustine Institute, 2010.

———. "A Tale of Two Documents: *Sacrosanctum Concilium* and *Mediator Dei*." *Antiphon, A Journal for Liturgical Renewal* 5 (2000) 23–31.

———. *The Thought of Pope Benedict XVI: An Introduction to the Theology of Joseph Ratzinger*. New York: Continuum, 2007.

Nichols, Peter. *The Pope's Divisions: The Roman Catholic Church Today*. New York: Holt, Rinehart and Winston, 1981.

Norman, Edward. *The Roman Catholic Church*. Berkeley, CA: University of California Press, 2007.

Novak, Michael. "John Paul II: Christian Philosopher." *America* 177, October 25, 1997, 12–15.

Oakes, SJ, Edward T. "Hans Urs von Balthasar (1905–1988): The Wave and the Sea." *Theology Today* 62 (2005) 364–75.

Oakley, Francis. *The Conciliarist Tradition*. Oxford: Oxford University Press, 2003.

O'Brien, Conor Cruise. *On the Eve of the Millennium: On the Future of Democracy through an Age of Unreason*. New York: Free Press, 1994.

O'Brien, David J. "Americanism." In *The Encyclopedia of American Catholic History*, edited by Michael Glazier and Thomas Shelley, 97–99. Collegeville, MN: Liturgical, 1997.

———. *Isaac Hecker: An American Catholic*. Mahwah, NJ: Paulist, 1992.

O'Malley, John W. "Vatican II: Did Anything Happen?" In *Vatican II: Did Anything Happen?* edited by David G. Schultenover, 52–91. New York: Continuum, 2007.

Denis O'Callaghan. "The Theory of the 'Mysteriengegenwart' of Dom Odo Casel, A Controversial Subject in Modern Theology." *Irish Ecclesiastical Record* 90 (1958) 246–62.

O'Carroll, Ciaran. "Pius IX: Pastor and Prince." In *The Papacy Since 1500*, edited by James Corkery and Thomas Worcester, 125–42. Cambridge: Cambridge University Press, 2010.

O'Connell, Gerard. *The Election of Pope Francis*. Maryknoll, NY: Orbis, 2019.

O'Connell, Marvin R. *Critics on Trial: An Introduction to the Catholic Modernist Crisis*. Washington, DC: Catholic University of America Press, 1994.

O'Connell, Patrick. "Papal Primacy Then and Now." In *Irish Anglicanism*, edited by Michael Hurley, 193–211. Dublin: Allen Figgis, 1970.

O'Connell, William. *Recollections of Seventy Years*. Boston: Houghton Mifflin, 1934.

Oddie, William, ed. *John Paul the Great: Makes of the Post-Conciliar Church*. London: Catholic Truth Society, 2003.

O'Donnell, O.Carm., Christopher. *Ecclesia: A Theological Encyclopedia of the Church*. Collegeville, MN: Liturgical, 1996.

O'Donovan, SJ, Leo J. "Karl Rahner, SJ (1904–1984): A Theologian for the Twenty-first Century." *Theology Today* 62 (2005) 352–63.

O'Gara, Margaret. *Triumph in Defeat: Infallibility, Vatican I, and the French Minority Bishops*. Washington, DC: Catholic University of America Press, 1988.

O'Grady, D. "The Ratzinger Round." *The Month* 6 (1973) 409–12.

O'Hanlon, SJ, Gerard. "The Legacy of Hans Urs von Balthasar." *Doctrine and Life* 41 (1991) 398–405.

———. *The Quiet Revolution of Pope Francis*. Dublin: Messenger, 2018.

Olsen, Glenn W. *Beginning at Jerusalem: Five Reflections on the History of the Church*. San Francisco: Ignatius, 2004.

O'Malley, SJ, John W. *A History of the Popes*. Lanham, MD: Rowman and Littlefield, 2010.

———. "The Millennium and the Papalization of Catholicism." *America*, April 8, 2000, 8–16.

———. *Tradition and Transition: Historical Perspectives on Vatican II*. Wilmington, DE: Glazier, 1989.

———. "Trent and Vatican II: Two Styles of Church." In *From Trent to Vatican II*, edited by Raymond F. Bulman and Frederick J. Parella, 301–20. Oxford: Oxford University Press, 2006.

———. *Vatican I: The Council and the Making of the Ultramontane Church*. Cambridge: Belknap, 2018.

———. "Vatican II: Did Anything Really Happen?" In *Vatican II: Did Anything Really Happen?* edited by David G. Schultenove, 52–91. New York: Continuum, 2007.

———. *What Happened at Vatican II.* Cambridge: Belknap, 2008.

———. *When Bishops Meet.* Cambridge: Belknap, 2019.

O'Regan, Cyril. "Benedict the Augustinian." In *Explorations in the Theology of Benedict XVI,* edited by John C. Cavadini, 21–60. Notre Dame, IN: University of Notre Dame Press, 2012.

Passelecq Georges, and Bernard Suchecky. *The Hidden Encyclical of Pius XI.* New York: Harcourt, Brace and Co., 1997.

Pawley, Bernard, and Margaret Pawley. *Rome and Canterbury through Four Centuries.* New York: Seabury, 1975.

Peddicord, OP, Richard. *The Sacred Monster of Thomism: An Introduction to the Life and Legacy of Reginald Garrigou-Lagrange, O.P.* South Bend, IN: St. Augustine's, 2005.

Pereiro, James. *Cardinal Manning: An Intellectual Biography.* Oxford: Clarendon, 1998.

Perkins, Pheme. *Peter, Apostle for the Whole Church.* Minneapolis: Fortress, 2000.

Perry, Tim, ed. *The Legacy of John Paul II: An Evangelical Assessment.* Downers Grove, IL: InterVarsity, 2007.

Peters, Walter H. *The Life of Benedict XV.* Milwaukee, WI: Bruce, 1959.

Petre, Maude. *Catholicism and Independence.* London: Longmans Green, 1907.

———. "An Englishwoman's Love Letters." *The Month,* February 1901, 120–24.

———. *Modernism: Its Failure and Its Fruits.* London: T. C. and E. C. Jack, 1918.

———. *My Way of Faith.* London: Dent, 1937.

———. *Reflections of a Non-Combatant.* London: Longmans Green, 1915.

Phayer, Michael. *The Catholic Church and the Holocaust, 1930–1965.* Bloomington, IN: Indiana University Press, 2000.

———. *Pius XII, the Holocaust and the Cold War.* Bloomington, IN: Indiana University Press, 2008.

Pieper, Josef. *No One Could Have Known, An Autobiography: The Early Years, 1904–1945.* San Francisco: Ignatius, 1987.

Pitstick, Alyssa L. *Hans Urs von Balthasar and the Catholic Doctrine of Christ's Descent into Hell.* Grand Rapids: Eerdmans, 2007.

Politi, Marco. *Pope Francis among the Wolves.* New York: Columbia University Press, 2015.

Pollard, John F. *Money and the Rise of the Modern Papacy: Financing the Vatican 1850–1950.* Cambridge: Cambridge University Press, 2005.

———. *The Unknown Pope: Benedict XV and the Pursuit of Peace.* London: Chapman, 1999.

Portier, William L. "Church Unity and National Traditions." In *The Papacy and the Church in the United States,* edited by Bernard Cooke, 25–54. Mahwah, NJ: Paulist, 1989.

———. *Divided Friends: Portraits of the Roman Catholic Modernist Crisis in the United States.* Washington, DC: Catholic University of America Press, 2013.

———. *Isaac Hecker and the First Vatican Council.* Lewiston, NY: Mellen, 1985.

———. "Isaac Hecker and *Testem Benevolentiae*: A Study in Theological Pluralism." In *Hecker Studies,* edited by John Farina, 11–48. New York: Paulist, 1983.

Pottier, Bernard. "Daniélou and the Twentieth-Century Patristic Renewal." In *Ressourcement: A Movement for Renewal in Twentieth-Century Catholic Theology,* edited by Gabriel Flynn and Paul D. Murray, 250–62. Oxford: Oxford University Press, 2012.

Pottmeyer, Hermann J. "A New Phase in the Reception of Vatican II: Twenty Years of Interpretation of the Council." In *The Reception of Vatican II*, edited by Giuseppe Alberigo et al., 27–43. Washington, DC: The Catholic University Press of America, 1987.

Purdy, William A. *The Church on the Move*. New York: John Day, 1966.

Quitslund, Sonya A. *Beauduin: A Prophetic Witness*. New York: Newman, 1973.

Radcliffe, OP, Timothy. *I Call You Friends*. New York: Continuum, 2001.

———. *What Is the Point of Being a Christian?* New York: Continuum, 2005.

Rafferty, SJ, Oliver, ed. *George Tyrrell and Catholic Modernism*. Dublin: Four Courts, 2010.

———, ed. *Reconciliation*. Dublin: Columba, 1993.

Rahner, SJ, Karl. "Devotion to the Sacred Heart Today." In *Theological Investigations*, Vol. 23. New York: Crossroad, 1992.

———. *Foundations of Christian Faith*. New York: Crossroad, 1982.

———. *I Remember, An Autobiographical Interview with Meinold Krauss*. New York: Crossroad, 1985.

———. "The Need for a Short Formula of Christian Faith." In *Theological Investigations*, Vol. 9. New York: Crossroad, 1973.

———. *Spirit in the World*. New York: Herder and Herder, 1968.

Ratzinger, Joseph. *Called to Communion*. San Francisco: Ignatius, 1996.

———. *Dogma and Preaching*. Chicago: Franciscan Herald, 1984.

———. *Feast of Faith*. San Francisco: Ignatius, 1986.

———. *God Is Near Us*. San Francisco: Ignatius, 2003.

———. *God and the World*. San Francisco: Ignatius, 2002.

———. *Images of Hope: Meditations on Major Feasts*. San Francisco: Ignatius, 2006.

———. *Introduction to Christianity*. London: Burns and Oates, 1969.

———. *Milestones*. San Francisco: Ignatius, 1998.

———. *A New Song for the Lord*. San Francisco: Ignatius, 1996.

———. *Salt of the Earth, An Interview with Peter Seewald*. San Francisco: Ignatius, 1997.

———. *The Spirit of the Liturgy*. San Francisco: Ignatius, 2000.

———. "The Spirit of the Liturgy, or Fidelity to the Council: A Reply to Pierre-Marie Gy, OP." *Doctrine and Life* 52 (2002) 550–55.

———. *Theological Highlights of Vatican II*. New York: Paulist, 1966.

Rausch, SJ, Thomas P. *Pope Benedict XVI: An Introduction to his Theological Vision*. Mahwah: Paulist Press, 2009.

Reardon, Bernard M. G. *Roman Catholic Modernism*. London: A. & C. Black, 1970.

Reher, Margaret M. "Leo XIII and Americanism." *Theological Studies* 34 (1973) 679–89.

Rhodes, Anthony. *The Vatican in the Age of Dictators, 1922–1945*. New York: Holt, Rinehart and Winston, 1973.

Richards, Hubert J. "Charles Davis, an Obituary." *The Tablet* 6, February, 1999, 190.

Riches, John K., and Ben Quash. "Hans Urs von Balthasar." In *The Modern Theologians*, 2nd. ed., edited by David F. Ford, 134–51. Oxford: Blackwell, 1997.

Rittner, Carol, and John K. Roth, ed. *Pope Pius XII and the Holocaust*. New York: Continuum, 2002.

Rope, Henry E. G. *Benedict XV: The Pope of Peace*. London: Catholic Book Club, 1940.

Rowland, Tracey. *Ratzinger's Faith: The Theology of Pope Benedict XVI*. Oxford: Oxford University Press, 2008.

Rubenstein, William D. "Case for the Prosecution." *First Things* 120 (2002) 54–58.

Safranski, Rüdiger. *Martin Heidegger between Good and Evil*. Cambridge: Harvard University Press, 1998.

Sagovsky, Nicholas. *"On God's Side": A Life of George Tyrrell*. Oxford: Clarendon, 1990.

Sanchez, José M. *Pius XII and the Holocaust*. Washington, DC: The Catholic University of America Press, 2002.

Schall, SJ, James V. *The Regensburg Lecture*. South Bend, IN: St. Augustine's, 2007.

Schelkens, Karim, John A. Dick, and Jürgen Mettepenningen. *Aggiornamento? Catholicism from Gregory XVI to Benedict XVI*. Leiden: Brill, 2013.

Schloesser, SJ, Stephen. *Jazz Age Catholicism*. Toronto: University of Toronto Press, 2005.

———. "Against Forgetting: Memory, History, Vatican II." In *Vatican II: Did Anything Happen?* edited by David G. Schultenover, 92–152. New York: Continuum, 2007.

Schmandt, Raymond H. "The Life and Work of Leo XIII." In *Leo XIII and the Modern World*, edited by Edward T. Gargan, 15–50. New York: Sheed and Ward, 1961.

Schoof, Mark. *Breakthrough: Beginnings of the New Catholic Theology*. Dublin: Gill and Macmillan, 1970.

Schultenover, David G., ed. *Vatican II: Did Anything Happen?* New York: Continuum, 2007.

———. *A View from Rome*. New York: Fordham University Press, 1993.

Schumacher, Michele M. "Ecclesial Existence: Person and Community in the Trinitarian Theology of Adrienne von Speyr." *Modern Theology* 24 (2008) 359–85.

Scruton, Roger. *The Philosopher on Dover Beach*. Manchester: Carcanet, 1990.

Seabeck, Raymond, and Lauretta Seabeck. *The Smiling Pope: The Life and Teaching of John Paul I*. Huntington, IN: Our Sunday Visitor, 2004.

Sedmak, Clemens. *A Church of the Poor: Pope Francis and the Transformation of Orthodoxy*. Maryknoll, NY: Orbis, 2016.

Seewald, Peter, ed. *Pope Benedict XVI, Servant of the Truth*. San Francisco: Ignatius, 2005.

Shortt, Rupert. *Benedict XVI*. London: Hodder and Stoughton, 2005.

———. "A Layman's Guide to the Pope: Help and Hindrance to Understanding Benedict XVI on His Visit to Britain." *The Times Literary Supplement*, September 8, 2010.

Smith, Janet. "Pope Paul as Prophet." *The Catholic World Report*, July, 1993, 52–57.

Smulders, SJ, Piet. *The Design of Teilhard de Chardin*. Westminster, MD: Newman, 1967.

Strange, Roderick. *Newman 101*. Notre Dame, IN: Ave Maria, 2008.

Suenens, Léon-Joseph. *Memories and Hopes*. Dublin: Veritas, 1992.

———. "A Plan for the Whole Council." In *Vatican II by Those Who Were There*, edited by Alberic Stacpoole, OSB, 86–102. London: Chapman, 1985.

Sullivan, SJ., Francis A. "Guideposts from the Catholic Tradition." *America* 173.19 (1995) 6.

———. "Recent Theological Observations on Magisterial Documents and Public Dissent." *Theological Studies* 58 (1997) 509–15.

Sullivan, OP, Maureen. *The Road to Vatican II*. Mahwah, NJ: Paulist, 2007.

Sweeney, Garrett. "The Forgotten Council." In *Bishops and Writers*, edited by Adrian Hastings, 163. Wheathampstead, UK: Anthony Clark, 1977.

Sykes, Stephen. *The Identity of Christianity*. Philadelphia: Fortress, 1984.

Talar, C. J. T. Review of *Were the Popes against the Jews*, by Justus George Lawler. US Catholic Historian 29 (2011) 87–94.

Tanner, SJ, Norman P., ed. *Documents of the Ecumenical Councils*, Vol. I–II. New York: Georgetown University Press, 1990.

Tavard, George. *Two Centuries of Ecumenism*. Notre Dame, IN: Fides, 1960.

Taylor, A. J. P. *English History 1914–1945*. Oxford: Oxford University Press, 1965.

Thompson, Mel. *Through Mud and Barbed Wire: Paul Tillich, Teilhard de Chardin and God after the First World War.* London: Create Space, 2017.

Tillard, OP, Jean M. R. *I Believe Despite Everything: Reflections of an Ecumenist.* Collegeville, MN: Liturgical, 2003.

Tracy, David. *Blessed Rage for Order.* With a new introduction. Chicago: University of Chicago Press, 1996.

Trevor, Meriol. *Newman's Journey.* Glasgow: Collins, 1974.

———. *Pope John.* Garden City, NY: Doubleday, 1968.

———. *Prophets and Guardians: Renewal and Tradition in the Church.* London: Hollis and Carter, 1969.

Turner, Frank M. *John Henry Newman: The Challenge to Evangelical Religion.* New Haven, CT: Yale University Press, 2002.

Twomey, D. Vincent. *Pope Benedict XVI.* San Francisco: Ignatius, 2007.

Tyrrell, George. *Mediaevalism.* London: Longmans, 1908.

Vallely, Paul. *Pope Francis: Untying the Knots.* London: Bloomsbury, 2013.

Ventresca, Robert A. *Soldier of Christ: The Life of Pope Pius XII.* Cambridge: Belknap, 2013.

Vermes, Geza. *Providential Accidents: An Autobiography.* London: SCM, 1998.

Vidler, Alec R. *The Church in an Age of Revolution.* Rev. ed. Harmondsworth, UK: Penguin, 1974.

———. *Twentieth-Century Defenders of the Faith.* London: SCM, 1965.

———. *Scenes from a Clerical Life, An Autobiography.* London: Collins, 1977.

von Hügel, Friedrich. *The Reality of God and Religion and Agnosticism.* London: Dent, 1931.

Vorgrimler, Herbert, ed. *Commentary on the Documents of Vatican II*, Vol. V. New York: Herder and Herder, 1969.

———. *Understanding Karl Rahner.* London: SCM, 1986.

Weigel, George, *God's Choice.* New York: HarperCollins, 2005.

———. *Witness to Hope: The Biography of Pope John Paul II.* New York: HarperCollins, 1999.

Weigel, Gustave. "Leo XIII and Contemporary Theology." In *Leo XIII and the Modern World*, edited by Edward T. Gargan, 213–26. New York: Sheed and Ward, 1961.

Wicks, SJ, Jared. "Six Texts by Professor Joseph Ratzinger." *Gregorianum* 89 (2008) 233–311.

Wilcox, Graham James. "Freedom and Authority in Church and Society: Maude Dominica Petre, 1863–1942." PhD diss., University of Birmingham, UK, 2009.

Williams, Anna N. "The Traditionalist *malgré lui*: de Chardin and *Ressourcement*." In *Ressourcement: A Movement for Renewal in Twentieth-Century Catholic Theology*, edited by Gabriel Flynn and Paul D. Murray, 111–24. Oxford: Oxford University Press, 2012.

Williams, Rowan D. "Archbishop's Presidential Address, 13th Meeting of the Anglican Consultative Council, Nottingham, 18–25 June, 2005." On the Archbishop of Canterbury's website.

———. "Balthasar and Rahner." In *The Analogy of Beauty: The Theology of Hans Urs von Balthasar*, edited by John Riches, 11–34. Edinburgh: T. & T. Clark, 1986.

Wojtyla, Karol. *Faith according to St. John of the Cross.* San Francisco: Ignatius, 1981.

Wolf, Hubert. *Pope and Devil: The Vatican's Archives and the Third Reich.* Cambridge: The Belknap, 2010.

Wood, SCL, Susan K. "Henri de Lubac, SJ (1896–1991): Theologian of the Church." *Theology Today* 62 (2005) 318–29.